Joan Haslip is the daughter of the late George Ernest Haslip, MD, the original planner of the Health Service. From 1940–44, she was editor in the Italian Section of the European Service of the BBC. She is the author of several biographies including *Parnell, Lady Hester Stanhope, Lucrezia Borgia, The Sultan: The life of Abdul Hamid II,* and *The Lonely Empress: a biography of Elizabeth of Austria*

IMPERIAL ADVENTURER

Emperor Maximilian of Mexico

Joan Haslip

CARDINAL edition published in 1974
by Sphere Books Ltd
30/32 Gray's Inn Road, London WC1X 8JL

First published in Great Britain by
Weidenfeld & Nicolson Ltd 1971
Copyright © Joan Haslip 1971

Set in Lectura

Printed in Great Britain by
Hazell Watson & Viney Ltd
Aylesbury, Bucks
ISBN 0 351 16634 3

For Lallie

CONTENTS

ILLUSTRATIONS

ACKNOWLEDGMENTS

Among the many who helped me in the writing of this book and to whom I wish to express my gratitude are the Director of the Archives of the Ministry of Foreign Affairs, Paris, who allowed me to make use of the despatches of the French Ministers in Mexico; the Directors and Curators of the *Haus-Hof und Stadts Archives* in Vienna, and the Congress Library in Washington, for giving me access to the *Mexikanische Archiv*, both in the original form in Vienna and in photostat copies in Washington. I wish also to thank the Directors of the Ministry of Foreign Affaris, Brussels, and of the Rice Institute, Texas, for allowing me to reproduce some of the hitherto unpublished Eloin papers. My thanks are due to the Director and staff of the Public Records Office London, the Press Department of the US Embassy in Paris and the Curator of the castle of Miramar, Trieste.

In Mexico, I would like to thank Senor Ignazio Condé, Madame Norma Hueffer de Redo and Senor Pedro Aspé for granting me access to their rare collection of 'Maximiliana', and to the latter for allowing me to reproduce a hitherto unpublished portrait of the Empress Charlotte. In Brussels I was given valuable assistance by Monsieur Albert Duchesne, Curator of the Royal Army Museum; the late Monsieur Sabbé, Director of the Archives du Royaume; Le Chevalier Albert de Selliers Moranville, Curator of the Musée de la Dynastie; His Excellency Monsieur Wéry who was Belgian Ambassador at the time of my visit to Mexico; Count Guillaume de Grünne and Baron Bassompierre who kindly put at my disposal the unpublished correspondence of his great-aunt, who acted as lady-in-waiting to the Empress Charlotte after her return to Belgium in 1867.

My gratitude goes to Mr Henry Clifford, whose knowledge of Mexico was of enormous help to me when I was in the country, and who was kind enough to check my manuscript for Mexican spelling; to Mr

11

Handasyde Buchanan who also found time to read the MS; to Mr Kenneth Rose who took the trouble to correct my proofs; to Mr Frederick Koch and to Mrs Jean Guépin who travelled with me in Mexico and drove me all over the country.

I would also like to thank Mrs Kuni Parr and Annemarie Selinko, the well-known author of *Désirée*, for their help in deciphering some of the German correspondence.

And lastly I wish to thank Miss Gila Curtis who was so helpful in editing this book.

I

The family

'I have a terrible presentiment that Reichstadt will die during my confinement.' In a bleak, pathetic letter to her mother, dated from Schönbrunn 21 May 1832, the Archduchess Sophia admitted for the first time what she had been dreading for the past months. The tender friendship which linked her to Napoleon's son was no secret at the Austrian Court. He had been her constant companion ever since her arrival in Vienna eight years ago, when he was a lonely fourteen-year-old boy, a child in the eyes of the nineteen-year-old Sophia, but a child who was already mentally far more awake and intelligent than the majority of her husband's relatives. And the brilliant Bavarian Princess whose father's dynastic ambitions had sacrificed her in marriage to the Hapsburg Emperor's second son, the mediocre, physically uninspiring Archduke Franz Karl, had befriended the young Napoleon, whose company had helped to alleviate the disillusions of the first years of marriage.

Coming from the stimulating atmosphere of Munich, she had found life in Vienna intolerably tedious. The glitter of the Congress days had faded to a twilight gloom. The Emperor Franz was a tired, disappointed man, disappointed even in his private life, for his four marriages had given him only two sons, of whom the eldest, Ferdinand, was an epileptic and the younger Franz Karl, Sophia's husband, no more than an amiable nonentity. Of all his family, the one he loved the most was his grandson Franz Reichstadt, child of Napoleon and his second wife, the Hapsburg Princess Marie Louise. It was a love he did not dare to show too much in public, for fear of offending the all-powerful Chancellor, Prince Metternich who persisted in treating Napoleon's son as a dangerous hostage in the game of power politics. Small wonder if the boy who found himself in the anomalous position of being at once Metternich's prisoner and the petted darling at Court, spied on by his servants, yet adored by his tutors of whom he was at once the pride and the despair, grew up diffident and suspicious, unable to confide even in his closest friends. And it was only with the arrival of the Archduchess Sophia that he found someone whom he could love and trust.

For Sophia, the first years of marriage to a man she barely tolerated – a marriage as yet unblessed by children (for the poor Archduchess had one miscarriage after another) – would have been hard to bear had it not been for the comforting presence of 'Franzi' Reichstadt. He was always at hand, ready to act as the most charming and devoted of *cisisbeos*, accompanying her to the opera and the *Brug Theater*, sending her the latest French novels and reading with her in secret the liberal German newspapers frowned on by Metternich's police.

Then in the sixth year of Sophia's marriage came at last the long prayed for, hoped for, son, and the old Emperor's joy and the jubilating crowds in the Vienna streets compensated Sophia for all that had gone before. She was now the mother not only of a son, but of a future Emperor. For in view of his brother's infirmity Franz Karl was generally considered to be his father's heir. No one was more ready to share in her happiness than Franz Reichstadt, who showed the most charming and unselfish side of his character in his love for his little cousin, whose brilliant future was such a contrast to his own.

In the intervening years the relationship between the Duke of Reichstadt and the Archduchess Sophia had undergone a subtle change. The moody, capricious boy had grown into a fascinating young man, the high-spirited girl had matured into a beautiful and sophisticated woman. Though the Archduchess's letters to her mother continued to stress her maternal feelings for her 'nephew', making fun of his little affectations, his inordinate interest in clothes, his love of pretty women, the references to his beauty and his charm were all too frequent and Queen Caroline was becoming aware that the maternal relationship was gradually drifting into the dangerous sphere of an *amitié amoureuse*.

It was the year of 1830. The year when Europe revolted for the first time against the rigid principles of legitimacy upheld at the Congress of Vienna and, in the Hofburg, the Archduke Johann, the most intelligent and liberal-minded of the Emperor's brothers, advocated Reichstadt's return to France. But though at heart the Emperor would have liked to see his grandson on a throne, he did not have the courage to say so openly and the only one to support the Archduke was Sophia.

She was soon to regret her temerity. Prince Metternich distrusted

14

clever Archduchesses who played at politics and quickly took his revenge. In November 1830 a Court Circular announced that his doctors had declared the Crown Prince Ferdinand to be fit to marry and that his Royal Highness had chosen the Princess Maria Anna of Savoy for a bride. The news was received in Vienna with incredulity and horror, a horror which was followed by ribald laughter. Only Sophia was in no mind for laughter for all her plans and ambitions for the future were menaced by the fear that, in spite of his infirmities, Ferdinand might yet produce an heir. The Court doctor assured her that this was extremely unlikely and that 'it would probably never occur to the poor Crown Prince to make any attempt to assert his marital rights'. But the next few years were constantly shadowed by this threat.

In the Hofburg, the royal marriage provided an endless subject of conversation for bored and malicious courtiers. The Archdukes were among the first to make fun of their unfortunate relative. Only Reichstadt appears to have been more tolerant in his judgement of his Uncle Ferdinand, whom he looked upon as a 'pathetic child, feeble-minded but fundamentally good at heart'. The Archduchess, however, found it hard to accept the fact that Metternich intended to make 'this feeble-minded child' into an Emperor and she wrote on a note of anguish, 'One dreads to think what will happen to this poor country once our beloved Emperor is gone.' Nevertheless, she had learnt her lesson and from now on her letters to her mother were written with an eye to the censorship of Metternich's police.

When the Great Powers forgathered to readjust the frontiers of Europe, the Duke of Reichstadt's name was occasionally mentioned as a likely candidate for the vacant thrones of Belgium and Greece. But the moment had not come for the Allies to accept a second Napoleon on a throne. And by the autumn of 1831 the young Duke was in such a bad state of health that, even if there had been a throne at his disposal, he would have been in no position to accept it.

The doctors of the day appear to have been curiously ignorant of the causes and treatment of tuberculosis. And in Reichstadt's case their task was further complicated by their patient, who was always trying to dissimulate his illness. He wanted desperately to be robust, a worthy son to a great father. He was so proud when his grandfather gave him the command of a regiment that he overtaxed his strength in carrying out his duties, drilling his troops in a biting autumn wind, getting up after a bout of fever to appear on parade when snow was already on the ground. His presence on the parade ground always drew large crowds of sightseers attracted by his romantic appearance and legendary name.

In his longing to resemble Napoleon, Reichstadt went to the length of pretending to himself that he was not consumptive, but was suffering from the cancer of the stomach which had killed his father. The doctors found him a difficult patient, but not one of them prescribed the obvious remedy, which was to winter in a milder climate than Vienna. When Queen Caroline suggested this to her daughter, Sophia replied that she had spoken about it to the Emperor, but the doctors did not seem to think a change of climate necessary: 'Though he suffers so terribly from the cold and his rooms are kept at such a hot-house temperature that in my present condition they make me feel quite faint.' For by the late autumn of 1831 Sophia was again with child. This time her joy was overshadowed by anxiety over Reichstadt's illness and she writes 'It is tragic to see someone so young and beautiful slowly wasting away, so that at times he looks like an old man.'

The Archduchess's letters during these winter months show all too clearly that she had fallen in love with her husband's nephew. Whether he reciprocated her feelings is open to doubt. He loved and admired her, but one wonders whether he was ever really in love. His friend, Prokesch von Osten, emphatically denies it and in his memoirs maintains that the Duke died a virgin. But Reichstadt was by nature evasive and suspicious, and though Prokesch was his closest friend he would never have confided the secrets of his private life to a diplomat in the service of Prince Metternich.

The Archduchess Sophia has come down in history as an uncompromising reactionary in politics and a model of moral rectitude in her private life; hardly a picture which suggests an illicit love affair with her husband's nephew. But in recent years some of her private letters and journals have been made public, and from these she appears to have been far more lovable and human than history would have us believe. There is no documentary evidence to suggest that she and the Duke of Reichstadt were ever lovers, but the son she conceived in the late autumn of 1831 and who was born a fortnight before the Duke's death, was always associated in her mind with the sad and tender memories of these last months, and on the day after her confinement when the state of her health was beginning to give cause for concern, Reichstadt was writing to his mother in Italian, 'She must live on account of the child she carries at her breast.'

Throughout the winter the Archduchess kept saying 'Reichstadt will be better in the spring when the Court moves to Schönbrunn.' She was even ready to give up some of her own beautiful rooms looking out over the gardens, so that he could sleep in the bed Napoleon had occupied on his historic visit to Vienna. It seems extraordinary that a doting mother like Sophia should have had her babies' nursery practically adjacent to Reichstadt's sickroom, particularly as she was under no illusion as to the gravity of his disease.

The first weeks at Schönbrunn saw a slight improvement in his health. But no sooner was he better than the old recklessness returned and he defied his doctors by overtaxing his strength and going out for long drives into the country. One afternoon in June, on returning from Laxenburg, he was caught in a storm and came home shivering and wet with a high temperature. The storm lasted throughout the night, at one moment becoming so violent that a golden eagle above the castle clock was struck by lightning. The Archduchess, who was in her eighth month of pregnancy, was so frightened by the lightning, so full of uneasy premonitions, that she jumped out of bed and ran into the room of her peacefully sleeping child to snatch him out of his iron cot. And she had barely gone to sleep when her husband woke her early in the morning with the news that the Duke of Reichstadt had had a bad attack in the night and the doctors took such a grave view of his condition that there was talk of administering the Last Sacraments.

Nevertheless, he survived those critical days in June. But from now on he rarely left his bedroom, except to be carried out on to the balcony or into the gardens where he lay surrounded by screens to protect him from prying eyes. Every day the crowds besieged Schönbrunn to get the latest bulletins on his state of health. The public interest in him was such that his pictures were sold out in the shops, and even Prince Metternich, who until now had made light of his illness, had finally to inform the Emperor, who was in Italy at the time, that his grandson was seriously ill and that the people were beginning to ask why the Duchess of Parma was not at her son's sick-bed.

Meanwhile the Archduchess Sophia continued to take his mother's place. The weather was abnormally hot which added to the invalid's discomfort and he had difficulty in breathing. The Archduchess also suffered from the heat and at times when she sat reading to him in the garden she felt too sick and inert to continue. On one occasion she brought little Franz Josef to visit his cousin, excusing herself to her mother, who obviously disapproved of these sickroom visits by writing, 'He wanted so desperately to see him as he is so alone.' And she adds: 'I am glad you are coming here for my confinement, so that you will be able to keep him company in my absence.' All her thoughts were of Reichstadt rather than of herself and she had few good words for Marie Louise who, detained first by what she considered her duties as Duchess of Parma and then by illness, only arrived in Vienna at the end of June.

The Archduchess saw the Duke of Reichstadt for the last time on the morning of 4 July. Two days later on 6 July 1832, she gave birth to a second son. Once more the bells of the Vienna churches rang out in jubilation, the guns thundered, the flags waved and cheering crowds gathered outside the Castle of Schönbrunn. But in spite of an easy and comparatively painless birth, the young mother was afterwards so physically and mentally exhausted that she spent her days in tears. The baby was given the names of Ferdinand Maximilian, Ferdinand after his godfather the Crown Prince and Maximilian in memory of Sophia's father. The Bishop of Eylau who officiated at the christening, relates that when he visited the Archduchess after the ceremony, she never spoke to him of herself, her husband or her child but only of the Duke of Reichstadt, begging the Bishop to visit him and to help him with his prayers.

Franz Reichstadt was seen to smile for the last time when he was given the news of Ferdinand Maximilian's birth. The will to live, which till now had enabled him to fight his disease, had finally deserted him. In June he was still talking of convalescing in the sun of Naples, but by the middle of July he was resigned to die. It was as well for Sophia that she was spared those last tragic days, that she did not have to hear that terrible, tearing cough which left him without the strength to speak. She was still confined to her room when the end came on the 22 July and only his mother Marie Louise and the Archduke Franz Karl were present at his deathbed. The latter had the unenviable task of announcing Reichstadt's death first to his wife, then to the Emperor, who in a heartbroken letter to Prince Metternich wrote, 'My grandson's sufferings were such that death came as a welcome release. It may also have been a blessing for my children and for the peace of the world. But for my part I shall always miss him.'

The Emperor Franz was an old man with very few years to live, but the Archduchess Sophia was a young woman who had buried her youth in the Duke of Reichstadt's grave.

When she reappeared at Court everyone noted how much she had changed. At twenty-seven she gave the impression of being middle-aged as if she had lost both the will and wish to attract. She rarely spoke of Reichstadt or of herself. From now on all her thoughts and energies appeared to be concentrated on her children. In 1833 she gave birth to a third son, christened Karl Ludwig, and the Emperor's joy and her husband's pride compensated for the strain of these continual pregnancies. 'I have certainly done my duty,' she wrote. 'Three sons and seven pregnancies in nine years of marriage.' But what else was there to look forward to, other than a crowded nursery? It is to her credit that in a dull and hidebound Court, where even Reichstadt's tutor had complained of the low level of conversation at the Imperial table, Sophia managed with intelligence and imagination to give her sons a rich and varied childhood.

In March 1835, her father-in-law's death deprived her of her best friend, and such was her veneration for the Emperor Franz, that she did not allow herself a word of criticism of the will dictated by Metternich, in which he bequeathed his Empire to the feeble-minded Ferdinand. Loyalty to the dead Emperor and Prince Metternich's almost mythical prestige enabled the succession to pass unquestioned. For one of the most remarkable traits of the prosaic, narrow-minded Emperor Franz was his capacity to inspire love not only in his family, but also in his people.

Yet there has rarely been a monarch weaker and more supine than Franz, who for the past thirty years had allowed himself to be entirely dominated by Prince Clemens Metternich. His two brilliant brothers, the Archdukes Karl and Johann, who on occasion had dared to oppose the Chancellor, were systematically kept away from Court. And it was Metternich who dictated the Emperor's will, nominating the Archduke Ludwig, the least distinguished of the brothers, to preside over the 'Council of State', the thinly veiled regency which was to govern in the name of the Emperor Ferdinand. No choice could have been more disastrous, for the kindly, self-indulgent Ludwig, who had never done a day's work in his life, was so afraid of offending one or other of his Ministers that he could rarely be persuaded to put his name to a decree. Years later, when the revolutionary tide of 1848 had swept him into exile, Prince Metternich admitted that the evil had been in 'not governing'. For thirteen years, from the old Emperor's death to the March days of '48, the Austrian Empire was administered rather than governed.

It was hard for Sophia to remain a passive witness to the disintegration of the Empire and to see her husband, though officially the heir apparent, excluded from the 'Council of State'. She had arrived in Austria in time to capture the afterglow of the fireworks of the Vienna Congress. But the last flicker of light had faded at the old Emperor's funeral. Prince Metternich had lost his touch and the horses of the coach of state, which for over twenty years he had driven with such consummate skill, were growing restless. He could dress his puppet monarch in the trappings of an Emperor and drag him on State visits from the Diet of Pressburg to the Cathedral of Milan, but the beauty-loving Hungarians looked away in disgust from their poor, misshapen little King, while the more compassionate Italians murmured, '*poveretto*' as he drove through the streets.

All that Sophia could do was to watch and wait for her eldest son to grow to manhood. Meanwhile she tried to give her children the illusion that the Vienna of the Hapsburgs was still the centre of the civilized world. It was not an easy task when from their earliest childhood they had to assist at the Imperial dinner table and watch the antics of their unfortunate uncle, whose face was so distorted from his constant attacks that Sophia admitted to her mother that 'looking at the Emperor sometimes makes me feel physically ill.'

There were worse sights than the Emperor Ferdinand to be encountered at Schönbrunn. It sounds incredible that in a palace of fourteen hundred rooms, the Archduchess should be complaining of 'her cramped quarters' and of how her children's rooms overlooked the part of the gardens where a mad old aunt took her daily exercise. The Archduchess Marie was perfectly harmless, but repellant to look at, and was said to have been afflicted in this manner because her mother had been chased during her pregnancy by an orang-outang, escaped from the Schönbrunn zoo. But no one gave much credence to this tale, for both Ferdinand and his sister were known to be victims of heredity, the result of centuries of interbreeding between Spanish and Austrian Hapsburgs, Neapolitan Bourbons and Bavarian Wittelsbachs.

Sophia was conscious of the family skeletons and feared for her children. Her three sons were all perfectly normal and healthy, but the baby girl, who to her joy was born in the summer of 1835 and christened Anna, was delicate from birth. And though the doctors did their best to reassure her, Sophia was the first to recognize the symptoms of inherited epilepsy. Little Anna died before she was five, leaving her mother desolate and frightened of having another child. Nevertheless, two years later, at the age of thirty-seven, she gave birth to her fourth son, a puny, sickly baby called Ludwig Viktor, known as 'Bubi' in the family.

When it came to the children's education, Sophia had only herself to rely on. Her husband might be a delightful father in the nursery, but he cut a poor figure in the schoolroom. Having no one in the family to advise her, she turned to her old enemy Prince Metternich. 'It's a pleasure to talk to someone who has such a wealth of experience, such a consummate knowledge of the world and at the same time is such an agreeable companion, such a delightful conversationalist.' Prince Metternich was also beginning to court the Archduchess who in all probability was the wife, and most certainly the mother, of a future Emperor. As a result of this courtship, the Archduke Franz Karl became a member of the 'Council of State' while two of Prince Metternich's closest friends, Count Henry Bombelles and Count Coronini-Hochberg, were appointed as governors to the little Archdukes. The Chancellor's children and grand-children by his various marriages were constant visitors to the Hofburg nursery. But though Sophia's letters are full of praise for 'the kind understanding Chancellor', she resented the overbearing pride of the Princess Melanie, who gave herself the airs of royalty, as much as she resented the political domination of her husband. None of her children's tutors was ever allowed to attain too great an influence over their charges, and one of the first lessons she taught her sons was that no Minister or servant was ever indispensable. She was a wise but also an indulgent mother and the tutors complained of too many distractions, such as visits to the theatre and circus, which upset the curriculum of studies. But it was not just the pride of a doting mother that made the Archduchess show off her sons in public. She realized the necessity of reassuring the Viennese, saddened by the spectacle of their poor little Emperor, that the Hapsburgs were still a strong and virile race.

The revolutionary currents which had spread from France to Germany, causing panic among the princes and margraves, had not yet infiltrated into Austria, and warm demonstrations of affection greeted the Imperial family wherever they went. All was outwardly serene in the Vienna of the 1830s before the 'hungry forties' had claimed their victims from among the unemployed. A rigid censorship kept all unpleasant news out of the papers which, being unable to indulge in political criticism, devoted whole columns to theatrical and musical reviews. And in the coffee-houses the waltzes of Lanner and the elder Strauss drowned the complaints of disgruntled politicians.

The Archduchess was a generous patron of the arts. Famous actors and singers visiting Vienna were always invited to perform at the Hofburg and rewarded with some jewelled token of her appreciation. A few like Jenny Lind were even admitted to her friendship. During a visit to Vienna, Hans Christian Andersen was invited to the Hofburg to read some of his stories to her sons. But apart from a certain talent for drawing, Franz Josef appears to have had little interest in the arts and his mother had to console herself with 'Maxl' who already as a small boy showed a sensitive appreciation of all that was beautiful and exotic.

The first time Maximilian emerges with an identity of his own is in a description given by the Archduchess, when he was three years old. 'In his long white trousers and loose white shirt, Maxl flutters round me like a great white butterfly' – a description which could never have applied to the sturdy, sensible Franz Josef who already as a child showed the self-discipline which in later years was to make him the most dedicated, if not the most brilliant, of monarchs.

At the age of five Ferdinand Maximilian was already a romantic. We hear of him one evening at Schönbrunn asking his mother for permission to accompany his uncle Ludwig 'to the land where the orange flowers bloom.' It took the Archduchess several minutes to grasp that he wanted to go out on to the balcony, where some orange trees were growing in tubs. Nothing for him was ever ordinary and dull. The first time he was invited to dine at the Emperor's table, an invitation calculated to damp the most cheerful spirits, he was in such a state of excitement that he talked incessantly throughout the meal and burst into song. His mother had not the heart to punish him when she saw that even the sad young Empress was moved to laughter.

But Max was not only the most charming, he was also the naughtiest and most undisciplined of her children, one moment radiantly happy, the next moment cross and bad-tempered. 'You have no idea,' wrote Sophia, 'how his face changes when he is in one of his tantrums. His underlip and jaw stick out and his eyes narrow in rage, so that he really looks quite terrifying and you wouldn't believe it's the same dear little face we know.' Nevertheless Sophia adored her *enfant terrible* whose fantasy and humour made him into a universal favourite. Franz Josef was her strength, her stake in the future, but Max was her weakness and her delight. Unkind tongues asserted that at times he bore an uncanny resemblance to the Duke of Reichstadt and in a curious letter to her mother the Archduchess unwittingly gave substance to these rumours by dwelling on the difference between Max and his brothers.

'Max is so good and full of heart, but his carelessness and laziness make me worry for the future, and one wonders what will become of him. Bombelles is optimistic, but Coronini is sometimes in despair, for on occasion he behaves just like a *"lazzarone"* or a Parisian guttersnipe. The French blood of the Lorraines and the Italian blood of the Neapolitan Bourbons have in him the upper hand over our German blood. He has all the exuberance and imagination of the Southerner.' One is tempted to say *Qui s'excuse s'accuse*, but the Archduchess spent forty years of her life in creating an image which completely obliterated the memory of the passionate young woman who had been in love with Napoleon's son and hated his enemy Prince Metternich. So well did she succeed that it is difficult to believe that she could ever have transgressed from the high moral principles she professed in later life. Yet the rumour persisted with the years and is even said to have caused the later estrangement between the two brothers, who were so devoted in the schoolroom.

Few children can have had a happier childhood. The spring and autumn months were spent at Schönbrunn and Laxenburg, both within easy distance of Vienna. Franz Josef's favourite home was Laxenberg, where he went out shooting with his father on lakes teeming with wild duck, but Max preferred Schönbrunn with its zoo full of strange animals and the conservatories with their heavily scented tropical plants, where he, who was always cold, could take refuge on blustering autumn days. At Schönbrunn the children had their own playground, by the old bowling green, a place which must have had sad memories for their mother, for it had been Reichstadt's playground in his youth and it was where he liked to come and sit in that last tragic spring.

In August, the family migrated to Ischl, the little mountain resort in the Salzkammergut whose health-giving waters, according to the Archduchess, had helped her to produce a family after years of miscarriages. At Ischl they lived a simple life in a rented villa by the river Traun. The children wore *lederhosen*, Franz Karl drank beer and Sophia ordered the local dishes which were never served at the Imperial table.

But every season had its pleasures. Even winter in the gloomy Hofburg was brightened by sleigh rides in the Prater woods and visits to the theatre and to the opera. There were the delights of Carnival with mimes and masquerades and a succession of children's parties held in one or other of the great palaces, whose families had the '*entrée*' at Court. And sometimes as a special treat the children would be allowed to sit up in the gallery of the *Marmor* or the *Redouten Saal* and watch their mother, a glittering unfamiliar figure, deputizing for the Empress at one of the Court balls.

At Christmas and on birthdays they were overwhelmed with presents. There were model forts and regiments of tin soldiers for Franz, while Max who shared none of his brother's enthusiasm for the Army, collected pet animals and birds, the stranger and more exotic the better. Writing to her mother, the Archduchess describes Max's delight with the aviary which she had had built in her private garden at Schönbrunn, and which he found waiting for him on the morning of his eighth birthday. The head gardener, who was one of his special friends, had planted out a small grove of palms and tropical plants where a couple of parrots swung on a perch and some squirrels chattered in a cage camouflaged with twigs. In the midst of this grove Max found a native hut decorated with spears and painted shields, where a wooden idol sat enthroned.

'The effect is really enchanting,' wrote the Archduchess. 'And Maxl is delirious with joy. He has taken immediate possession of his jungle kingdom, arranging his hut with the utmost fantasy, calling himself King Babanini and inviting all and sundry to visit his realm. Franz is equally enthusiastic, but his reaction is already that of an adult, worrying as to how much it must have cost, whereas Maxl has no such worry. He merely sidled up to me like a young cat, stroking my face, whispering in my ear, "To think you have done all this for me." He is so loving with me,' adds Sophia. 'So are they all, but Maxl has the softest heart.'

Nevertheless he was more superficial than Franz Josef. When their little sister died, the older brother shared in his mother's grief with an understanding beyond his years, while Max when confronted for the first time with his mother's tears was at a loss as to how to console her and went and spent his entire month's pocket money on buying her a pet monkey, saying 'I cannot buy you another little girl but at least I can buy you a monkey.'

Gradually the children were beginning to learn that life was not all holidays and treats and the curriculum of studies grew longer every year. At twelve years old, Franz Josef, who was not a particularly brilliant child, had a fifty-hour week of study, and it was taken for granted that he and his brothers had to speak half a dozen languages and be as familiar with Shakespeare as with Goethe. The Archduchess continued to complain of Max's 'idleness and lack of application', but he was by far the most talented of her children, with a natural gift for expressing himself and a passion for literature and history, particularly family history. He was only seven when he announced that he wanted to have a family portrait gallery to which his Bavarian grandmother immediately responded by sending him an enormous oil painting of his grandfather, King Maximilian Josef.

His masters found him difficult to teach. Whereas Franz Josef respected authority and was hard working and conscientious, Max on the contrary seemed to take a mischievous delight in detecting his tutors' weaknesses and foibles. A snobbish and unctuous professor, who was forever dwelling on their titles, was referred to as 'His Royal and Imperial Highness the Professor of Geography.' An affected and mincing Frenchman was nicknamed 'Monsieur Foppabile'. But the teacher who knew how to stir his imagination found him an intelligent and rewarding pupil. His favourite professor for a time was a half-brother to Mary Shelley, Charles Gaulis Clairmont, who occupied the chair of English Literature at Vienna University. The Archduke was so devoted to this middle-aged Englishman that he insisted on having him once a week to dinner, thereby making excellent progress in his English and learning to recite long passages of Shelley, whose work, had it been known to the Vienna censorship, would undoubtedly have been banned.

Max's ebullience and gift of mimicry introduced an element of gaiety into the most solemn gathering. His jokes were not always in the best of taste, as when he dined at the Emperor's table and pretended to take snuff and to sneeze, just for the pleasure of hearing the simple-minded Ferdinand saying 'God bless you' after every sneeze. Another time he dressed up in women's clothes and with the connivance of Franz Josef had himself introduced at Court as a Princess of Modena. The Empress was enchanted with her young cousin, wondering why she had not met her before, till the so-called Princess let out a very unladylike and this time genuine sneeze. But Max could also laugh at his own expense. When confined to bed after a bad fall, with leeches applied to a sore back, feeling particularly miserable on account of missing a children's ball given by the Empress, he still had the courage to joke that Franz would be dancing at the party while these 'nauseating leeches are dancing on my back.'

He despised any form of cowardice and would never let anyone accompany him to the dentist, in case they might see him weaken, while his recklessness on horseback was the despair of his riding master. He was incapable of riding slowly. 'For the most wonderful sensation in the world was a fast gallop.' Franz Josef on the contrary disliked riding as a child and only years of practice and perseverance made him into one of the best horsemen in his Empire.

In spite of leading a healthy outdoor life, for the Archduchess insisted that the daily curriculum should include plenty of sport and exercise, Max remained delicate throughout his childhood, catching one illness after another and at times looking so wretched that his mother was painfully reminded of 'poor Reichstadt'. When he was eight years old an attack of scarlet fever kept him isolated for over ten weeks, during which time Franz Josef wrote him daily letters telling him how much he was missing him, giving him all the family news and amusing him with a series of comic drawings, depicting the adventures of 'Monsieur Maigrelaid', their mother's nickname for her poor little invalid.

No sooner was he out of quarantine than he was sent to recuperate with his grandmother on the Tegernsee in the Bavarian Alps. Here he broke all hearts, charming not only Queen Caroline but all his other Wittelsbach relatives. This family of brilliant self-willed individualists, who had ruled Bavaria for seven hundred years and over the centuries had provided generations of Hapsburg brides, had always had a certain jealousy and contempt of their Austrian cousins, who without the element of greatness or any spectacular feat of arms, had nevertheless succeeded by a series of successful marriages and alliances in making the Imperial Crown hereditary to the Hapsburg family.

What delighted the Wittelsbachs was that Max had so little of the Hapsburgs, so much of themselves. Their only criticism was that he looked rather 'Austrian', by which they meant Hapsburg, with his 'long face and heavy lip' and that 'he talked rather loud in the way all Austrians do.' As for Ferdinand Maximilian, he was enchanted with them all, from his grandmother Queen Caroline, who shared his love of animals and birds, to his uncle King Ludwig, who with his dreamer's eyes and threadbare coat, would appear at Tegernsee, his pockets bulging with projects and designs for Renaissance palaces and Greek temples, and who, while lecturing his stepmother on the extravagances of her table, would present his little nephew with an exquisite jewel or a rare Byzantine coin. Queen Caroline grumbled that Munich was not fit to live in any more with the dust and constant hammering of the stonemasons, but the boy who visited Munich for the first time and who had the Wittelsbach passion for building in his veins saw it as the most exciting and enchanting of cities.

'Maxl fait ici la pluie et le beau temps,' wrote his mother when she arrived with Franz Josef to take him back to Vienna. And Sophia noted as she had so often noted before that, in spite of his attractive appearance and beautiful manners, Franz could not compete in popularity with his younger brother. The Wittelsbachs made no secret of their preference, and it was the same at the Austrian Court and among her own ladies. Max was always the favourite. Franz himself was becoming aware of it and all unconsciously showed the first signs of jealousy.

As the children grew older the Archduchess made a point of bringing her elder son to the fore. Even his birthday took on an official character as that of the eventual heir to the throne. At the amateur theatricals and *tableaux vivants* which were such a feature of Court life, she always insisted on Franz Josef playing the leading role, in spite of the fact that he was extremely untalented, whereas Max was a born actor. Both suffered from this decision, the elder because he hated acting, the younger because he resented being relegated to second place. Every year was making Ferdinand Maximilian increasingly aware of the enormous gulf which separated a mere Archduke from an Heir Presumptive. The knowledge rankled, driving a gay, carefree boy to become ambitious, to strike out in fields where he could outshine his brother, while outwardly disclaiming any interest in the responsibilities of power. 'The last thing I want is to be an Emperor. All that I ask from life is a beautiful castle with a large garden on the seashore.' The day would come when he would have his dream castle, but it would still find him longing for an Empire.

2

The Revolution of 1848

From his earliest childhood, Maximilian had been fascinated by Italy. Delicate and always suffering from the cold, he longed for the South, for orange groves and sunlit seas. And at thirteen he realized his wish when, in the spring of 1845, the three young Archdukes made their first official tour of Austria's Italian provinces.

The Austrians were not loved in Italy. The ideals of nationalism released in Napoleon's time had generated hostility to the foreign yoke. Secret societies of Italian patriots sprang up all over the peninsula, bent on throwing off Austrian rule with its army of police, spies and informers.

But at the veteran Marshal Radetzky's headquarters in Verona the young Archdukes saw only the cheering crowds, carefully selected from among the reliable elements of the population and duly rewarded for their cheers at a few lire a head – the hand-picked troops, the pretty girls throwing flowers from the balconies of Verona's rust-brick palaces. Radetzky was running no risks and the whole town was honeycombed with spies, though it is doubtful whether even the most hardened of Mazzinian republicans would have had the heart to throw a bomb at those charming adolescents with their friendly open faces, even if their white uniforms represented the detested Austrian rule, and they themselves the hated Hapsburg dynasty.

The old Marshal laid himself out to please his young guests with carousels, reviews and fireworks culminating in an aerial display in the old Roman arena, where a balloon used for military reconnaissance was sent up into the sky. Count Bombelles, who accompanied the young Archdukes on their tour, was surprised to find that on this occasion Ferdinand Maximilian, who until now had not shown the slightest interest in any military matters, suddenly became wildly enthusiastic, watching the display with shining eyes and remarking 'If ever flying becomes practical in my lifetime I will certainly take to the air, for I can image no greater happiness than to fly higher than the birds.'

This was no childish fantasy or momentary impulse. Throughout his life Maximilian remained interested in the future of aeronautics, a subject he would often discuss with the scientists and scholars with whom he surrounded himself at Miramar. During the last years in Mexico he was still toying with the idea of staging an aerial display to impress his Indian subjects.

Maximilian's lack of interest in military affairs labelled him as 'effeminate' in the eyes of Radetzky's stiff-necked aides-de-camp. While Franz Josef hero-worshipped the old Marshal and hung on his words, only too proud to be initiated into the secrets of the Quadrilateral, the four fortified cities on which Austria based her military strength in Italy, Maximilian was always lagging behind, wandering off on his own and lingering in churches and museums.

The three brothers had little in common. The youngest, Karl Ludwig, a dull, solid boy of mediocre intelligence, resembling his father rather than his mother, remained in the background, silently adoring the gay and volatile Max who teased him unmercifully for his laziness and greed, but was always ready to protect him from the scoldings of their tutors. Poor 'Karly' was quite incapable of appreciating Max's love for Italy. All he wanted was to be at home, shooting rabbits in the woods of Laxenburg. But even the dullest and most phlegmatic of little boys cannot fail to have been infected by his brother's excitement at seeing Venice for the first time. It was late in the evening when they crossed the lagoons and saw Venice, white and shining in the moonlight, with the bells of a hundred churches ringing out in welcome. A fleet of gondolas escorted them up the Grand Canal, past torchlit palaces decorated with tapestries and banners, to land by the Square of St Mark which that night was illuminated by gas for the first time. So great were the crowds that the Austrian authorities reported with complacency of the thousands of Venetians who had come to cheer Their Imperial Highnesses. They omitted to mention that the majority had come to see the new gas lighting rather than the Archdukes. Even the prosaic Franz Josef appears to have been moved by the beauty of Venice, and he was thrilled to see that the famous bronze horses of St Mark's, which had been stolen by Napoleon, were now 'back in their rightful place.'

We know little of Maximilian's reactions to Venice. The carefully

annotated diary kept for the Archduchess's benefit and illustrated by Franz Josef, which in all probability was inspired and corrected by their tutors, gives little idea of what Venice must have meant to a romantic thirteen-year-old boy who on this first visit conceived a passion for the sea and, when travelling by warship along the Istrian coast, suddenly announced to his companions that he was going to be a sailor. This youthful ambition was later to be deliberately encouraged at Court, giving the Emperor Franz Josef an excellent opportunity of providing a too popular younger brother with suitable employment at a safe distance from the capital.

Till now Austria had done little to exploit the naval power Napoleon had cynically handed over at Campo Formio, when he presented his defeated enemy with the territories of the decaying Venetian Republic in exchange for Belgium, the Rhine frontier and Lombardy. After Napoleon's fall, Austria had extended her hegemony over practically the whole of the Italian peninsula. Hapsburg Archdukes were restored in Modena and Tuscany; a Hapsburg Queen returned to Naples; a Hapsburg Archduchess reigned in Parma. For over thirty years the Austrian flag had flown in every Adriatic port from Venice to the Bocca di Cattaro on the Turkish frontier, but in 1845 the Austrian navy was still almost entirely manned by Italians and no one in Vienna appeared to have any interest in the navy. The days when an Austrian prince made the whole world ring with the fame of his naval exploits belonged to an almost mythical past, and only an imaginative boy of thirteen with a passion for family history, saw himself as another Don John of Austria winning new and more glorious victories.

Some of the dreams and ambitions confided to his Italian teacher on this journey came to flower a few years later, when for a brief period, the happiest in his life, Maximilian was the ruler of Venice. Gian-Battista Bolza, the young Italian professor whose nationalist principles appear to have escaped the notice of the Archduke's entourage, had a determining influence on Maximilian's career, planting the seeds of liberalism in a mind already indoctrinated in the divine right of kings, and in particular the divine right of the Hapsburgs to rule the world. From now on, the liberal was constantly in conflict with the autocrat, making him unduly susceptible to outside influences, and causing him to vacillate continually in his judgements. Bolza may also have tried to influence Franz Josef but the young Prince had already taken on the prejudices of Metternich and Radetzky and while attending his Italian lessons as a duty, remained profoundly inimical to the Italians themselves. Ferdinand Maximilian on the contrary was ready to love both the country and the people – and Bolza opened his eyes to some of the injustices committed under Austrian rule: the overbearing arrogance of the army of occupation, the unnecessary humiliation inflicted on a proud and ancient race. When asked as to whether it was possible 'to gain the affection of the Italians', Bolza gave the example of Napoleon's stepson Eugéne de Beauharnais, who as Viceroy of Milan had succeeded in making himself both loved and respected. There was nothing the Italians admired so much as *grandezza*, nothing they despised so much as pettiness and parsimony. Used to the munificence of Napoleon's Viceroy, the Milanese resented the avarice of the Archduke Rainier, the Austrian Viceroy of Venetia-Lombardy, who collected his revenues and did so little in return. On their return to Vienna, the Archduchess Sophia was amused to find that 'Maxl had completely lost his heart to Italy and the Italians'. But he was still too irresponsible, too much of a 'madcap' to be taken seriously. At present her hopes and ambitions were centred on Franz Josef, who in his sixteenth year was already being prepared for public life.

It is strange to find the Archduchess, who in the past had been so bitterly opposed to Metternich, now begging him to spare some of his valuable time to instruct her son in the art of statecraft. But in spite of her admiration for Prince Metternich's talents, Sophia appears to have been fully aware of his limitations, his refusal to recognize the existence of those nationalist forces which were threatening to disrupt the old feudal order in Europe. And in order to prepare Franz Josef for the future, she deliberately encouraged him to read the German newspapers censored by Metternich's police. Her son must learn to know his enemies and to appreciate the difficulties with which he would have to contend should he ever come to the throne.

In spite of the clouds on the horizon, the seditious speeches in the Frankfurt Diet, the political unrest in Italy and Hungary; in spite of Austria having to reinforce her garrisons in all four corners of the Empire, the Vienna season of 1846 had never been more brilliant, with some of the greatest artists of the world gathered in the Austrian capital. The concerts of Franz Liszt were attracting such enormous crowds that the police had to intervene to protect him from the hysterical ardour of his fans. First among his admirers was the Archduchess Sophia, who paid him the unprecedented honour of inviting him to a family dinner. The exquisite Fanny Ellsler was back in her native town after a triumphal tour of America. 'No one can equal her in dancing or in mime,' wrote Sophia in her diary, after taking her elder sons to see her dance in *Esmerelda*. The presence of Fanny Ellsler recalled poignant memories of Franz Reichstadt and his passionate admiration for 'that fairy child'. Now her own *Franzi* was incurring his first bills at the florist to send the dancer bouquets of roses.

Jenny Lind, 'the Swedish Nightingale', was enrapturing her audiences in Bellini's *Sonnambula* and the Archduke Franz Karl and his family headed the list of patrons at her benefit performance. But Sophia had to admit that none of her sons was really musical. Franz Josef enjoyed nothing so much as a military march while Max, of whom she might have had some hopes, was almost tone deaf. Instead of being moved by the beauty of Jenny Lind's singing, he was struck only by the absurdity of the plot. The night after the performance, the soldiers on guard at Schönbrunn saw a strange white figure carrying a lighted candle, moving across the roof. For a moment they were paralysed with fear that this might be the ghost of the legendary white lady of the Hapsburgs. Then one of them shouted: 'It's the Archduke Max!' and forgetting all discipline burst into loud laughter. The laughter roused the officer on duty, but he also broke down at the sight of Max disguised in a woman's nightdress, miming the *Sonnambula* on the roof of Schönbrunn.

The Archduchess sometimes wondered whether Maxl would ever grow up or whether he would always continue to act the clown. We hear of him at a teenage *Backfisch Balle* given for Franz Josef at which the latter appeared very proud and self-conscious, wearing tails for the first time. Max, who was not so accomplished a dancer as his brother, delighted on this occasion in mimicking the poses and affectations of the dancers, seizing hold of his brother's tails, galloping with him round the room and, as usual, succeeding in attracting most of the attention. He was a firm favourite both with his Uncle Ferdinand and with the Empress, whose miserable married life made her pathetically homesick for her native country. With Max she could talk about Italy, warmed and flattered by his enthusiasm. And Sophia was well aware that the Empress surreptitiously paid up Max's debts when he found himself without a *kreuzer*, having dissipated his whole month's allowance in the first week.

While Franz Josef kept an account book with every item carefully noted even to the few *kreuzers* for a piece of soap, Max was always acquiring books and paintings whose prices far exceeded his allowance. The first to note his extravagance had been his old nurse, Baroness Sturmfeder, who, when he was six years old, took him one day to a picture exhibition. Here he was so impressed by a painting by Daffinger that he insisted on buying it, though it cost far more than the sum he had collected in his savings bank. His mother was apt to indulge him in his extravagance. As a Wittelsbach she sympathized with his love of beautiful things and was probably the first to tell him: 'Avarice in princes is a cardinal crime', a maxim he was fond of quoting in later years, when he insisted that 'princes must be generous, for the ordinary people know we get our money from their toil, so we are only good to make it circulate.'

But the time was approaching when the ordinary people were beginning to question the extravagance of their princes, and politics were beginning to intrude into the Hofburg schoolroom, where Max's ill-defined liberalism led to sharp arguments with Franz Josef. His opinions were not very consistent. Gian-Battista Bolza's descriptions of the sufferings of the Italian prisoners in the Spielberg moved him to indignant tears at the inhumanity of the Austrian jailers, but he was the first to disapprove of his cousin the Duke of Parma for having allowed himself to be coerced by the mob into granting humiliating concessions. When the Duke arrived in Vienna to explain his conduct and to excuse himself to the family, Max, much to his mother's amusement, made a point of snubbing his cousin – addressing him as *Sie* instead of the familiar *Du*. On a visit to Bohemia with his elder brother, staying at the castles of some of the richest landowners of the Empire, we find Max writing to his mother: 'Thank God everyone here is loyal to the core.' But the summer of 1847 saw fighting in the streets of Milan and the burning of the German theatre in Budapest by a mob of Magyar Nationalists, and by the end of the year Sophia was writing in her diary: 'God knows what the future holds for our poor country.'

The beacon fire which gave the signal for the general conflagration was lit in Paris, where a monarchy born from revolution was the first to fall. 'France is bored,' wrote Lamartine, and the answer to boredom was violence with rioting and fighting in the streets. Louis Philippe, 'The Citizen King', was forced to take the familiar road of exile leading to the Channel ports and for a few weeks it seemed as if Paris was to experience again the excesses of 1789. 'Those poor Orleans, my heart bleeds for them,' wrote the Archduchess Sophia, who till now had always detested the family of Philippe Egalité.

The flames of revolution spread through Germany where princes and margraves toppled off their cardboard thrones and abjectly signed away their rights and privileges. Barricades appeared in the streets of Berlin and the mercurial King Frederick William IV of Prussia became overnight the champion of liberty. But when on 13 March, a mob of students invaded the Austrian Hofburg and hammered on the doors of the Ball-platz demanding Prince Metternich's resignation, both the Government and the Imperial family appear to have been taken completely unawares.

It was a day neither Sophia nor her sons were ever to forget, when in frozen inactivity they had to witness the whole edifice of Hapsburg power crumbling before the threats of a mob of students. And what was even more incredible was that the loyal, peace-loving citizens of Vienna were backing up the students, echoing their slogans, shouting for a 'free constitution' and 'liberty of the press'. Then everything seemed to disintegrate at once and the news flashed round the town that Prince Metternich had fled. The man who had driven the coach of state for forty years had gone, and the coach – lumbering, rusting and out-of-date – remained behind with no-one on the box. Prince Metternich must now have regretted that he had surrounded himself with puppets rather than with men. Neither the poor little Emperor, who was only too anxious to placate the 'good people of Vienna', nor the weak and indolent Archduke Ludwig appear to have made a move to save him. As for the Archduchess Sophia, this may have been the moment for which she had waited twenty years, though mob rule was a heavy price to pay for Prince Metternich's fall. After persuading her husband to resign from the Council of State, she deliberately disassociated her family from the humiliating compromises of a Government too weak to resist the demands of the insurgents. The army was still loyal, but the best troops were immobilized on the other side of the Alps where the King of Piedmont had declared war in the name of a united Italy. And in the spring of 1848 the Archduchess identified herself with the army by sending the seventeen-year-old Franz Josef to serve under Radetzky on the Italian front.

The situation was rapidly deteriorating. All the disaffected elements of the hydra-headed Empire, from the banks of the Po to the forests of Transylvania, were in revolt. In Vienna, German Democrats clashed with Slavs; radical Nationalists with Constitutional Liberals, while in Hungary the extremists led by Lajos Kossuth had gained the upper hand over the more moderate elements, and the popular young Palatine, the Archduke Stephen, who had been among the first to advocate the necessity for reforms, had now to flee the country.

With the coming of spring, the political demonstrators followed the Court from the Hofburg to Schönbrunn, where panic-stricken courtiers hardly dared to venture out-of-doors, till the day came when the Viennese learnt that their Emperor had left for Innsbruck supposedly 'for the benefit of his health' and that accompanying the Emperor was the whole of the Imperial family. No one resented this decision more bitterly than the Archduchess Sophia who was heard to say openly in front of her children that she would rather have seen one of them die than suffer the ignominy of submitting to a mob of students and that when history came to be written the shame of 1848 would seem to be incredible.

Franz Josef was in Italy when the Court left for Innsbruck, and it was Ferdinand Maximilian who rode beside his parents' carriage as they drove out of Vienna on a lovely summer morning; his father silent and embarrassed, his mother smiling through her tears at the 'good people' in the suburbs who were still sufficiently loyal to cheer them on their way. He was barely sixteen at the time, but old enough to know that this so-called pleasure trip was in reality a flight.

On 2 December 1848 Maximilian assisted at the abdication of his uncle and the crowning of his brother Franz Josef as Emperor of Austria. The secret had been jealously guarded up to the last moment, and the plans which had taken months to mature had been confided to only a few. The coronation took place, not in the historic Hofburg, but in the Summer Palace of the Prince-Archbishop of Olmütz, the Moravian fortress town where the Imperial family had taken refuge after fleeing for the second time from the threat of mob rule.

When the Imperial family fled for the second time, the situation appeared more desperate than in the spring, but the counter-revolution was already under way and the Empire had found its paladins. Radetzky's victories in Italy had set free an army exalted by success, devoted to its officers and to the ruling House; Field Marshal Prince Windischgrätz had crushed an insurrection in Prague and was marching on Vienna; General Jellacic, Governor of Croatia, had proclaimed his loyalty to the Crown and crossed over into Hungary to fight against the rebels. The country was in a state of civil war, but the loyalists had gone over to the attack.

Behind the counter-revolution was the Archduchess Sophia, whose pride had suffered a mortal blow from the humiliating flight to Innsbruck, and who during the months of exile had been working to rally the loyal elements round the Crown. In sending her son to fight on the Italian front, she had won the respect of the army, to whom she was known as 'the only man in the Hofburg'. That summer the Archduchess lived up to her proud reputation in making what must have been the most difficult decision of her life. For over twenty years she had lived for the day when she would be crowned Empress of Austria. But now she had come sadly to the conclusion that her husband, who in ordinary times would have occupied the throne as adequately as many of his ancestors, would in the present situation be incapable of standing up to the revolutionary forces. In exile he had shown himself a man of straw, grumbling, querulous and indecisive. If the army was to save the Empire, it needed a leader more inspiring than either Franz Karl or the pathetic little Ferdinand, someone who was young and strong and uncommitted and who could not be blamed for the mistakes and weaknesses of the past.

At eighteen, Franz Josef was already enormously popular with the army. He had received his baptism of fire on the Italian front, where he had displayed the cool courage which was to distinguish him throughout his life. Sophia could be proud of her son, who was sensible beyond his years and at the same time modest, ready to be guided by men like Field Marshal Windischgrätz and Prince Felix Schwarzenberg, the forty-eight-year-old diplomat who had resigned his post as Minister in Turin to fight in Radetzky's armies and who now emerged as the brain behind the counter-revolution.

From November 1848, the direction of the counter-revolution passed into Schwarzenberg's hands, while Windischgrätz took command in the field. Recognized as one of the most fascinating men of his time, whose amatory adventures had been the scandal of Europe, Schwarzenberg at forty-eight was a cold, disillusioned cynic who had exhausted all his emotions other than ambition – an ambition not for himself but for his country. And it was the bright flame of his patriotism, his passionate belief in the undying greatness of Austria, which inspired the eighteen-year-old Franz Josef to accept unquestioningly and without fear the heavy burden of a crown.

The secret of the abdication was so jealously guarded that even Franz Josef's brothers were kept in ignorance up to the last moment. Max had suspected that something was in the air and had come to the conclusion that 'Franzi was to be made Governor of Bohemia'. One of the Archduchess's hardest tasks in the past months had been to maintain a sense of discipline and order in her younger children. Max had been the most difficult and restless, resentful of the fact that Franz lived already in a world of men, while he was virtually still in the schoolroom. The hardest task of all for the Archduchess, who had brought up her children to love and respect their father, was having to explain why 'darling Papa' had renounced the succession. Max, as always, wanted to know the whys and wherefores of everything and, being so close to her, was the first to regret that 'now she can never become an Empress.'

But she seemed very much an Empress on the morning of 2 December 1848, when the Court assembled in the banqueting hall of the Archbishop's Summer Palace to hear the Emperor Ferdinand hand over an Empire of thirty-eight million people to her eighteen-year-old son. Wearing a gown of white brocade, a diadem of pearls and diamonds, Sophia completely outshone the modest little Empress, whose eyes were focused on her husband, praying he would carry out with dignity the last official act of his reign.

Even the most cynical were moved to tears at the sight of the young Franz Josef, so boyishly slim and straight in his white uniform, kneeling before his uncle asking for his blessing, to which, in his simple faltering fashion, the old Emperor replied: 'Bear yourself bravely, everything will be all right.' Standing first among the Archdukes was Ferdinand Maximilian, proudly conscious of his position as next in succession to the throne, feeling no envy of his brother, only an immense awe and admiration at the natural manner in which Franz was receiving the homage of his ministers and generals. Did Max realize that from now on those ministers and generals would form a living wall between them; that from today, he would never be able to walk into his brother's room without first asking for an audience; that any form of argument or criticism would be taboo and independence of action rendered suspect?

Franz Josef appears to have been the first to chafe against these new restraints. And an incident recorded in his mother's diary is more significant than the apocryphal phrase, 'Farewell my youth,' which history records him as having said immediately after his coronation. It was in the late afternoon, when the speeches were over and the courtiers were dispersed, and Sophia's younger sons were giving free reign to their spirits in a wild romp in the Archbishop's audience chamber. A ball thrown by the six-year-old Bubi had crashed into a mirrored door just as Franz Josef and his mother came into the room. The little boy was already in tears expecting a scolding when, to Sophia's intense surprise, Franz Josef turned to her saying, 'Darling Mama, will you give us permission to smash that door?' And, with shouts of delight, the four brothers banged and smashed in a holocaust of splintered gilding and broken glass. Between tears and laughter the Archduchess cried: 'What will the poor Archbishop think of these vandals who are my sons?'

But this was the last recorded gesture of Franz Josef's childhood. Under Prince Schwarzenberg's tuition he was to grow up all too soon. An eye-witness recalls one winter's morning, only a few weeks later, when the Emperor, accompanied by the Archduke Ferdinand Maximilian and two of their cousins, was returning from a military inspection. It was a fine sunny day and the Archbishop's garden glittered under a pall of snow. The weather was exhilarating and the young princes, led by Max, began to pelt one another with snowballs. Only Franz Josef stood apart, laughing as gaily as the rest but making no attempt to join in the game.

There was little time for play during that first year, with one third of the Empire still in revolt. War had broken out again in Italy and Charles Albert of Savoy had marched into Lombardy. This time the campaign was disastrous to his cause and Radetzky's resounding victory at Novara re-established Austrian rule in Venetia-Lombardy and heralded Franz Josef's return to his capital. By the end of May 1849 the Court was back at Schönbrunn and the Viennese were giving a hero's welcome to the young Emperor.

But rebellion was still rife in Hungary, where the Imperial troops were making little headway and where the nationalist leaders refused to acknowledge as their King an eighteen-year-old boy, still tied to his mother's apron strings – a boy who, moreover, had no right to call himself their King before he had been anointed and crowned with the legendary crown of St Stephen. Both Schwarzenberg and the Emperor had been averse to accepting the military aid offered by the Czar. But by the summer of '49 the situation was so desperate that Russian help had to be gratefully accepted. It was a humiliating blow to Franz Josef's pride, and in order to assert his position as supreme head of the army, he insisted, against the advice of his ministers, on visiting the Hungarian front. Ferdinand Maximilian accompanied his brother and one can picture the fears and anxieties of the poor Archduchess at having her two sons in the front line. Max's vivid letters from the front did little to reassure her. While making allowances for his poetic licence and sense of the dramatic, she nevertheless trembled to read of 'bullets whistling above our heads and rebels shooting at us out of burning houses'. His description of the victory of Raab was particularly dramatic, and what touched his mother most of all was his admiration for his elder brother.

He wrote: 'The Emperor was magnificent, always in the front line of the battle. You can picture the enthusiasm of the troops at seeing him share their dangers and fatigues. The advance guard had barely reached the outskirts of Raab when the Emperor was already spurring on his horse to cross over the bridge which was half in flames. . . . You should have heard the "vivas" and "hurrahs" from the soldiers on both banks of the river. . . . It was the most wonderful sight I have ever seen . . . an indescribable enthusiasm such as one only finds in the army.'

But it was one thing to be brave, another to be foolhardy, and the ministers and generals complained that the Emperor was running far too many risks. Max wrote to his mother that Felix Schwarzenberg was fussing round his brother 'like an old hen with her prize chick' – not a very flattering description of Europe's most fascinating statesman. But thanks to Schwarzenberg, Sophia had her sons home within a few weeks. They arrived back at Schönbrunn on the eve of Ferdinand Maximilian's seventeenth birthday 'both well and sunburnt', particularly Max, who with his fair complexion looked as if he were wearing 'a golden mask'. They had so much to tell their mother that they spent most of the night chatting in her bedroom, with Max doing most of the talking and Franz Josef occasionally intervening to correct an over-dramatized incident.

The two brothers appear to have been devoted during this first year, with the elder relying on the younger to supply a little fun and relaxation whenever it was possible to escape from the unending round of audiences and conferences. Max at seventeen was free from the tutelage of the schoolroom and, with a large allowance from the civil list, was able to indulge his most extravagant whims. There is still today a

'Maxing Strasse' in Hietzing, the suburb which adjoins Schönbrunn, where the name recalls the Archduke's favourite folly, a casino built to his own design.

Sophia describes in a letter a house-warming party at the Maxing 'to which the whole family was invited' and where the young host received them in oriental fashion, his hands crossed on his breast, while a servant handed round the traditional bread and salt. Everyone had to sign their names in a beautifully-bound leather book, then they sat down to a superb breakfast at the end of which 'Maxl' recited a speech in verse of his own composition and an enormous goblet of champagne was handed round from which everyone had to drink, beginning with the Emperor and ending with the cook. But the sensation of the party came when the breakfast table was pushed aside, revealing an opening in the floor through which a winding stair led underground through a tunnelled passage out into the 'Tyroler Garten'. The Archduchess writes: 'For years this tunnelled passage has been one of Max's idées fixes, though in my opinion the whole establishment is a ridiculous waste of money. But my dear Max can only learn by experience so I never attempt to interfere.'

She may also have had a certain indulgence for faults which were in the best Wittelsbach tradition. As Max grew up, he was becoming more and more like her family, with his mania for building and inventing curious devices, his delight in composing verses on any and every occasion. We hear of him congratulating Grillparzer on his birthday by sending him a laudatory ode attached to a laurel wreath. And the aging poet, who had been such a bitter opponent of the Metternich régime, was touched at receiving a tribute from a Hapsburg.

The Viennese found in Max the most charming and amiable of Archdukes, and before long he had become a popular figure among all classes of society. The lanky boy with the long, pale face had grown into an elegant young man who, if not strictly handsome with his receding chin and prominent lip, was nevertheless generally considered to be irresistible. The face was gay and alive, the blue eyes narrowed and crinkled when he laughed, and he laughed loud and often, from the heart. But there were times when the eyes were pensive, almost sad. And only those who knew him as well as his old tutor, Count Bombelles, recognized the change that had come over him since his brother's accession; he longed to play a prominent part in public life, to be more than an ornamental Archduke whose duties were confined to opening exhibitions and meeting foreign potentates.

Preserved in the Vienna State Archives is a little box containing some frayed, well-fingered notes in which the Archduke listed the twenty-seven precepts he considered to be the guiding rules of life. 'Be amiable with everyone.' 'Judge fairly and be fair to all.' 'Consider your own faults before condemning others.' 'Above all never complain.' All were admirable principles from which Ferdinand Maximilian never deviated. But there were others which, unfortunately, were alien to his open, impulsive character. 'Never let yourself be carried away by your first impressions.' 'Reflect before you speak so as not to fall into a trap.' 'Never make a decision before weighing the consequences.' If Ferdinand Maximilian had kept to these principles, his life might have run on a different course, but he gave his friendship too readily and voiced his opinions too openly. He had not celebrated his eighteenth birthday before his liberal ideas had made him suspect at Court. The one who disapproved of him most was his brother's chief adjutant, Count Grünne, a cold, worldly cynic who had learnt nothing from the lessons of 1848 but who was a great favourite of the Archduchess because of the attitude that he had taken over Hungary, resigning his position as aide-de-camp to the Archduke Stephen when the young Palatine made concessions to the rebels. Max, on the contrary, was a fervent admirer of his cousin Stephen, who was handsome, idealistic and genuinely devoted to the Hungarian people. Both of them were shocked and disgusted by the reprisals taken by Austria in the late summer of 1849 when the rebellion finally broke under the combined weight of Russian and Austrian arms.

The last desperate stand had failed, but the Hungarians had succeeded in humiliating the Austrians, even in defeat, by surrendering to the Russian Czar rather than to the Hapsburg Emperor. It was a humiliation Franz Josef never forgave and he resented the avuncular tone of the letter in which Nicholas of Russia advocated mercy. Wounded in his self-esteem, he allowed men like Schwarzenberg and Grünne to have their way. 'Mercy,' said Schwarzenberg, 'is a good idea, but we must have some hanging first.' This cold-blooded cynicism permitted the excesses committed by the Austrian commander, the sadistic half-crazy General Haynau, excesses for which the young Emperor stood condemned in the eyes of the civilized world.

It was hard for someone as impressionable and warm-hearted as

Max to accept his brother's policy in silence and to remember that it was not for him to question the orders of 'the All Highest'. It was still harder to find that the mother he adored was as uncompromising as the Emperor on the subject of Hungary. For the Archduchess found it impossible to forgive those who refused to acknowledge her son. There were bitter arguments and quarrels, occasions when Max lost control of his temper and said things which in public would have been considered treason. The senseless brutality of the reprisals, the hangings and the floggings of men whose only fault was to defend their freedom, disgusted him. He was thinking of Hungary when, a few years later, he noted in his journal: 'We call our age the Age of Enlightenment, but there are cities in Europe where in the future men will look back in horror and amazement at the injustice of tribunals, which in a spirit of vengeance condemned to death those whose only crime lay in wanting something different to the arbitrary rule of governments which placed themselves above the law.'

Unfortunately, Ferdinand Maximilian did not keep his opinions to himself. The Emperor was particularly sensitive to criticism on Hungary and he resented the disapproval of a younger brother being noted in the files of the secret police. He was devoted to Max and stimulated by his company, but there were too many disaffected elements in Vienna ready to rally round a liberal Prince. His Ministers hinted it would be as well for His Imperial Highness to find employment at a certain distance from the capital. And, in view of the Archduke's enthusiasm for the sea, it was decided that he should join the navy and make his headquarters in Trieste. But before taking up his duties, the Archduchess Sophia, who had seen the rift between her two sons with a growing apprehension, suggested that both Max and his younger brother Karl would benefit by a classical tour of Greece. Travelling in a corvette of the Imperial Navy, Max would both complete his education and have his first apprenticeship at sea. And in September 1850 we find him writing from Trieste: 'At last I am about to realize my dearest wish and am embarking on a long sea voyage.'

3

The younger brother

For the next few years, Ferdinand Maximilian made his headquarters in Trieste, and paid only brief visits to Vienna. He spent most of his time sailing the Adriatic and the Mediterranean, gaining experience at sea and gradually growing up. The adolescent was slow to become a man and the diary kept on his first journey to Greece is a mixture of sophistication and naïveté, of precocious wisdom and childish innocence. Freed from the restrictions of Court life, no longer overshadowed by his older brother, he warmed and sparkled in the sunlight of Greece. Everything was new and exciting, even the noisy, jostling, gesticulating crowds at Patras, who appeared to be quite indifferent to the arrival of the Hapsburg Princes.

'The sight of a people among whom there is no division of classes is interesting,' he writes. 'They are all brothers of one race, who having formerly languished under the same yoke have now shaken it off together. . . . Those families whose fathers have fought in the war of freedom alone have a higher rank.'

For seventeen years a Wittelsbach cousin had sat on the throne of Greece, but there was no Court Chamberlain to receive them at Patras, no guard of honour waiting at the port – no one except a rather shabby Austrian Consul, an Italian by birth, who greeted them in 'negligé' and produced some pathetically emaciated horses to transport them the one-hundred-and-twenty miles to Nauplia – but Ferdinand Maximilian and Karl Ludwig and their two gentlemen-in-waiting, a Prince Jablononsky and a Count Coudenhove, were all young and gay, ready to ride their sorry nags with as much panache as if they had been thoroughbreds from the stables of Schönbrunn. The party was made up of the usual appendages of the Grand Tour: a classical scholar, an artist and a doctor. And to the Greeks, they must have looked like any of those young milords who for the past fifty years had been landing on their

43

shores, riding across the country distributing largesse and then sailing away with pieces of broken marble as ballast for their yachts. Sporting a large Chinese parasol which he had acquired in Trieste, Ferdinand Maximilian struck the right note of eccentricity which, ever since the days of Byron, had been associated with the rich *milord*. And the presence of two stalwart Bavarian gendarmes, enlisted by the consul to protect his precious charges, impressed the natives far more than the fact that they were brothers to the Austrian Emperor.

In Athens they were welcomed by the Queen who, acting as Regent in her husband's absence, invited the Austrian Princes to stay at the royal palace. It was a palace which in Maximilian's eyes 'was much too large for a little town and a little country', while the vast frescoed ballroom and innumerable statues were 'all a reflection of Munich taste'. He meant the taste of King Ludwig, who, when his second son Otto was made King of Greece, had not been able to resist giving free rein to his creative impulse and designing a whole series of marble palaces and triumphal arches for a town which, when it became King Otto's capital, consisted of no more than one hundred and sixty houses rising from a heap of ruins.

Living in an age when the Great Powers disposed of countries at their will and sent foreign princes to reign in places where they could not even speak the language, Ferdinand Maximilian saw nothing incongruous in a Wittelsbach ruling with the help of Bavarian ministers over a race of Balkan warriors who, in their centuries-long struggle against the Turks, had lost most of the civilizing graces of ancient Greece. He belonged to a generation who, following in the steps of Byron, still talked of 'Hellas' rather than of Greece, and we hear of a visit to the Parthenon celebrated in a romantic and somewhat Teutonic fashion with Ferdinand Maximilian and his companions drinking a toast to the fatherland in Austrian wine, while the scholar of the party delivered an impromptu oration in classical Greek. 'I offered a libation to the mythological gods,' writes Maximilian. 'We drank, then dashed the flask on to the marble. The Greek officers in attendance looked on at this scene with astonishment.'

He was an inveterate sightseer. Karl Ludwig, whose enthusiasm for temples was limited, remained behind while his brother and their hostess spent hours in each other's company. Queen Amalia was both a beautiful woman and a superb rider and Maximilian was full of admiration for her beauty and her courage. She was the first mature, sophisticated woman, other than his mother's ladies-in-waiting, with whom he had come into close contact, and by the end of a week he was willing to believe 'that the newly-established throne was supported by the Queen's personal influence and the affections of her people'. He ignored the fact that, only seven days ago, the young sovereigns had been forced to grant a constitution, under the threat of revolution; that the very energy and driving force he admired in Amalia had caused more dissension among her Greek subjects than the weakness and indecision of her husband.

He was in Athens for the celebration of the Feast of the Constitution, when the Queen, much against her will, was forced to attend the service of thanksgiving. And Maximilian was sufficiently infatuated to forget his liberal principles and to write full of sympathy for the poor Queen 'who, pale and tight-lipped, was expected to pray for the preservation of institutions she disliked. . . . There was an expression almost of displeasure on her usually amiable features and I noticed she did not pray.'

If only Maximilian had been a few years older, he might have learnt a valuable lesson for the future. He might have realized that not even the most capable of ministers, or the best-intentioned of monarchs, can hold the affections of an alien people. The only criticism he allowed himself to make on this visit to the Greek Court was to wonder whether 'the way of life, the magnificence of the festivities given by the Crown, was constant with the customs and revenues of the country'. He did not presume to judge, but he realized that something was wrong, that the Court was not in touch with the people. He was shocked to find Greek and Bavarian officials having to speak to one another through interpreters 'for one is always taken in by this kind of conversation and cannot tell how the spirit of the words is rendered in the other language.'

He never imagined that the proud young Queen, whom he saw cheered in the streets of Athens, would in twelve years' time be fleeing from the country under the threat of assassination and that, at the instigation of England, the Great Powers would offer him his cousin's vacant throne, an offer indignantly refused as being 'in the worst of taste and typical of English tactlessness'.

There was a last moonlight visit to the Acropolis, followed by sad, sentimental adieux. One suspects the Queen to have been the sadder of the two, regretting the departure of the dashing young Archduke whose romantic idealism recalled her youth. Maximilian had fresh prospects, new adventures to look forward to, for the *Vulcan* was now bound for Smyrna, which was to be his first encounter with the East.

In Smyrna, in place of a beautiful Queen there was a fat, amiable Pasha with orders from Constantinople to do all in his power to entertain the Austrian Princes. Menaced by the growing pretensions of Russia, the Sultan was eager to secure the friendship or at least the neutrality of Austria. Turkey, who in the days before the Crimean War brought red-kneed highlanders to the streets of Pera and unveiled women to the hospitals of Scutari, was still untouched by Western influence. Smyrna was still an Eastern city, sufficiently exotic to appeal to Maximilian's imagination. He envisaged a mysterious drama enacted behind every latticed window and saw a beauty in every veiled figure hurrying through the streets.

With his natural good manners and effortless charm, no prince could have been a better ambassador for his country. Maximilian pleased and flattered his hosts by his readiness to admire the customs of countries other than his own. In spite of being a devout Catholic, he was impressed by the spirit of calm and contemplation in the mosques, and the peace of Turkish graveyards 'which have a greater purity and simplicity than ours'. Bazaars, mosques and Turkish baths were all visited in turn, but their guides showed a certain reluctance when Maximilian suggested visiting the slave market. He thought this was because the Turks were ashamed to admit to the Christians that they still indulged in the barbarous sale of human beings, but it was more likely that the Consul did not feel it to be a very edifying spectacle to show the Emperor's brothers. Maximilian was, however, so insistent that he got his own way, only to be sadly disillusioned. Here were none of the rounded odalisques immortalized by Ingres and Delacroix, only hideous greyskinned negresses clutching a few rags to their shrivelled bodies. One with elephantiasis in the legs was so utterly repellant that Maximilian turned away almost sick with disgust. The only good-looking woman he saw was fully clothed and turned out to be a Jewish overseer.

This visit may momentarily have cured him of his passion for the exotic. He was now eager to get back to Trieste, to take up his duties as a lieutenant in his brother's navy. Admiral Dahlerup, the blunt and honest Dane who, since 1848, had commanded the Austrian fleet, had not welcomed the idea of having the charge of a pampered Archduke who would be the constant object of Court intrigue. He was surprised to find that, contrary to his expectations, Ferdinand Maximilian showed both energy and initiative and was ready to work as hard as, if not harder than, any other subaltern. 'I gather that Max is flourishing, strong as a bear and as gay as ever, always to be found on board ship. And apart from all this, he seems to be working hard,' wrote Franz Josef to his mother. Admittedly, his duties were not very onerous. One of the most luxurious villas in Trieste, belonging to a rich Levantine merchant, was placed at his disposal, where he maintained what the Archduchess described as 'a suitable bachelor establishment.' A naval instructor was attached to his service during the first months, but he gradually made his own friends among a group of ensigns and lieutenants who, being keen and full of zeal for their profession, resented the fact that in the great commercial city of Trieste, the merchant ships of the Austrian Lloyd had priority over the corvettes and frigates of the Imperial Navy. The navy, they complained, was the step-sister of the services and it was scandalous for Austrian officers to have to give their orders in Italian. Nor was it surprising that morale was low among the crews when they were almost entirely recruited from the disaffected provinces of Venetia-Lombardy and continually subjected to Italian nationalist propaganda.

When Ferdinand Maximilian returned to Vienna at Christmas he was already the navy's champion, determined to open his brother's eyes to the intrigues of ministers who undermined Admiral Dahlerup's position by keeping him short of money and supplies and ignoring his demands for reform. Most of these facts had been supplied to him by one of his new friends, a brilliant young ensign called Wilhelm von Tegetthoff who later became Austria's greatest admiral. But the harassed, overworked young Emperor had more urgent problems to attend to. The Eastern Question was occupying the Chancelleries of Europe and in particular the Ball-platz, where the Czar was making it embarrassingly clear that he expected Franz Josef to repay the debt of gratitude he owed him for the help he had given him in Hungary by supporting him in an eventual war with Turkey. But neither Franz Josef nor his ministers showed any inclination for Eastern adventures and, in the words of Prince Schwarzenberg, 'Austria was ready to astonish the world by her ingratitude.' Russian ambitions were not the only problem to contend with. On Austria's western frontier, a powerful and aggressive Prussia was bidding for the leadership of the Germanic Federation while, within the empire, Hungary and the Italian provinces were still ruled by martial law. In these circumstances, one can hardly blame the Emperor for having little interest in a navy which, given Austria's geographical position, could be of little use except in battle against the Turks.

But Ferdinand Maximilian's visit to Vienna was not entirely fruitless. One of his complaints had been that the Austrian navy rarely ventured out of the Adriatic, and he now found himself in the role of a roving ambassador, showing the flag in the various Mediterranean ports. In rank he was no more than a lieutenant who took his turn at night watches, but at the same time he occupied the best cabin on board and was received with royal honours wherever he went. Illness prevented him from taking part in the longest and most ambitious journey ever undertaken by the Austrian navy when the battleship *Novara*, fitted out with special scientific instruments, sailed to America and the Caribbean in the early spring of 1851. Ferdinand Maximilian had always longed to explore the New World. In his library at Miramar one finds numerous volumes of American history and anthropology, rare prints and drawings of the birds and fauna of the Andes and the Amazon, books he had acquired long before there was any question of the Mexican throne. Now, on the eve of leaving for a journey he had inspired and helped to bring about, he was suddenly taken ill with a particularly virulent form of typhus fever. For the first few days his life was in danger and the Archduchess Sophia was summoned from Schönbrunn. She arrived to find him looking so ill and emaciated that she remained with him throughout his convalescence rather than leave him in the care of strangers. However much she might love and admire Franz Josef who was now the centre of her world, Max was still her beloved *enfant terrible*, whose indiscretions were always getting him into trouble and whose restless ambition she had been the first to recognize and fear. When she sat reading to him in the garden overlooking the sea, she must have been reminded of the times when, in the gardens of Schönbrunn, she sat reading to another invalid as young, as ambitious and as impatient as Max.

He took a long time to recover and he was still on official sick-leave when the *Novara* returned to Trieste and a crowd of gay, sunburnt officers invaded the Villa Lazarovic with their albums of watercolours and their stock of travellers' tales, delighting the bored young invalid with descriptions of the Caribbean, their adventures in New Orleans and accounts of expeditions to the frontier towns of Texas. But it was already midsummer before Maximilian was sufficiently recovered to embark on the *Novara* for a Mediterranean cruise, where he experienced his first watch at sea in the middle of a violent storm.

Once more we follow his life through his journal, which takes us from Trieste to Naples, from Naples up to Leghorn and across the Mediterranean to Valencia and Cadiz. His writing is more mature and less spontaneous than in the Greek diaries and the descriptions of places, particularly of Florence and of Naples, could have been written by any cultured young man who fancied himself as an art critic and a littérateur. But amid the aphorisms and truisms are certain passages which throw light on his character. Underlying the elegant dilettante was a man who was enormously proud of his birth, conscious of his duties and his responsibilities. His exaggerated admiration for Van Dyck, whose painting of King Charles of England and of Queen Henrietta he regarded as one of the greatest treasures of the Medici collections, was very characteristic and there was a strangely prophetic note in his description of the picture: 'On Charles' serious features the tragic future has already settled like a mourning veil. He is a victim of the noblest kind, who submitted to fate too passively and too unresistingly. He failed through weakness but had the opportunity, if not to live well, at least to die well.' Maximilian believed in the mystique of royalty. He despised those who, like the King of Naples, asserted their right to live as they pleased and had bourgeois tastes of the meanest kind. He found it hard to forgive King Ferdinand who, since the revolution of 1848, preferred to live in the security of the fortress of Gaeta, rather than in one of his many beautiful palaces. In Maximilian's opinion, it would have been better to abdicate rather than to change Caserta for an ugly house surrounded by battlements, where the rooms were so plainly furnished that they might have belonged to an army captain rather than to a King and where the food was so mediocre that the 'inevitable Neapolitan spaghetti alone gave brightness to the table'. He was horrified to see the King ordering cigars after dinner and compelling him against his will to smoke in front of the Queen, who was both his aunt and an Austrian Archduchess.

All his love of the magnificent found expression in the baroque palace of Caserta, built by his Neapolitan ancestor, King Charles III. 'When one sees the four colossal courtyards,' he writes; 'the gigantic halls which, beautifully arched, support the lofty domes of the massive palace, the staircase which seems to be created for the steps of gods,

49

the gardens with the gigantic cascades, then one feels that Caserta is not a royal folly but a work of genius which could only have been conceived by someone as great and as courageous as Charles III.' Giving free rein to his fantasy, he describes the staircase, 'planned in such a way that the man standing at the head seems to make the world climb up to him, while the gardens with the fountains and cascades, the statues and close-clipped laurel hedges running in parallel avenues, are all trained and dressed so carefully that even nature may not come in the way of the ceremonious walk, the measured step of a Court surrounded by the nimbus of royalty.' The last sentence holds the key to Maximilian's character. For all his simple tastes, his democratic manner and liberal principles, he was obsessed by the nimbus of royalty.

At a *corrida* in Seville, when the *coup de grâce* to the dying bull was given in his honour, he wrote: 'A strange feeling came over me for the eyes of the whole arena were turned towards me and a tremor ran through the crowd. I cannot deny that I felt flattered by this national homage. For a moment I fancied myself back in the days when the Hapsburgs ruled over this noble race.' His ancestors haunted him throughout the Spanish tour. In the cathedral of Granada he visited the royal chapel and prayed at the tombs of Ferdinand and Isabella. 'My ancestors were great men who made history in their day, who accomplished something on this earth and begot a mighty far-ruling race, and now they rest alone in a solitary chapel. . . . Here in Spain, I was the nearest legitimate relation to those poor dead; nearer than the present ruler and princes of the country . . . and I was filled with a melancholy regret to see them thus forsaken and not thought of by the new dynasty.'

Even in British Gibraltar he passed through a gate 'where a forlorn Imperial eagle bore witness to the days when the Hapsburgs ruled the world.' But, in Gibraltar, Maximilian was ready to enjoy himself and forget his ancestors in his wholehearted admiration of English organization and efficiency. He was impressed by the scrupulously clean barracks, 'the comfort which extends even to the inferior ranks and shows the richness of this nation and its thorough knowledge of how to live.' 'The British sergeant,' he wrote, 'has his dining hall, his cleanly laid-out table, his elegant and tasteful plate in English metal as the officer has with us . . . and whatever the private has, the officer has in a greater degree.' The colonels of the various regiments stationed on the Rock, headed by the Governor, Sir Robert Gardiner, made a splendid show of hospitality and Maximilian was both flattered and amused by the strange customs of the English: 'the informal lunches which require a guest to ask for everything and help oneself, the lavish regimental dinners where the noblest wines, the best dishes and the finest silver, show the wealth of the English army, and every guest has his bottle of sherry and his decanter of water in front of him; the endless toasts after which the ladies leave the table to await the arrival of the gentlemen in the drawing room.' 'Many blame this habit as barbarous,' he wrote. 'I like it. The ladies should learn that they have to obey the men.'

But what touched him most of all was the kindness and the warmth of the welcome given him both by the Governor and his wife. 'Dear Sir Robert, whom I learned to love and appreciate so much.' There appears to have been a real affinity between the nineteen-year-old Prince and the gouty old general in his felt slippers who, at a gala dinner, drank a toast to the Austrian Emperor in German, 'which, even if not grammatically correct, went straight to our hearts.' In a strange way, Sir Robert and his wife appear to have been far closer to Ferdinand Maximilian than any of his Neapolitan or Tuscan relatives, and it was with real regret that he said goodbye to 'dear Gibraltar'.

The wise old Governor seems to have realized that, beneath the brilliant exterior, the impeccable manners, was a lonely, rather homesick, adolescent, who at moments felt himself an exile and, on his brother's birthday celebrated at sea, confided in his diary: 'I felt very sad during the service, for it was the first time that I had not been with my brother on this happy day. I was alone, quite alone, in strange seas under another sky; I also thought long and deeply of a beloved one at home.'

4

Romantic interlude

Among the group of young girls in Vienna known as 'the Emperor's little countesses' (*die kleine Contessen*) was seventeen-year-old Paola von Linden, daughter of the Minister of Wurtemberg. Her father, who had been accredited in Vienna since 1842, was now the doyen of the diplomatic corps, a position which entitled his daughter to the *entrée* into that small, exclusive world which revolved around the young Emperor. She had known the Imperial Family since her childhood. Pauline Metternich, the Chancellor's grand-daughter, was her closest friend and they had together graduated from the children's parties at the Hofburg to the teenage balls (*Backfisch Bälle*) and were now among the most popular of the young girls whom the Archduchess Sophia invited to the intimate '*Kammer Bälle*' she gave in honour of her sons.

Franz Josef was passionately fond of dancing and, for a few short weeks during the winter season, he would forget the cares of state and throw himself wholeheartedly into the delights of the Vienna Carnival, when the waltz-king Strauss took possession of the city and no one dared to give a ball for the Emperor without having Strauss to conduct the band. It was at one of these balls during a brief visit to Vienna in the winter of 1851 that Ferdinand Maximilian met Paola von Linden and found her transformed from a round-cheeked, shy little girl into the prettiest and gayest of debutantes. With her large blue eyes, her delicate features and heart-shaped face, dressed in the traditional white ball dress of muslin or of tarlatan, Paola must have appeared the very quintessence of innocence, a refreshing contrast to the Italian actresses and dancers to whom the Archduke's brother officers had introduced him in Trieste, and with whom he had had his first amatory experiences. His sentimental friendship with the Queen of Greece had aroused dormant emotions which found little satisfaction in the brothels and dance-halls of Trieste. And now he was ready to invest what was never more than an innocent flirtation with all the trappings of a romantic love affair.

It was so easy to imagine oneself in love in the Vienna Carnival, where the dances lasted till dawn and day was only a continuation of the night, with waltzing couples on the ice locked in each others' arms while the confetti mingled with the snow and paper ribbons hung in garlands from the winter trees. In her memoirs Paola von Linden evoked the frenzy of dancing which took hold of Vienna during the weeks of Carnival, and told how 'one night during a ball at the Lichtenstein Palace, there was such a terrible snowstorm that the windows burst open and snowflakes blew into the room but no one dreamt of stopping the dance. Mattresses were laid against the windows and servants held them in place.' Our hearts go out to the poor chaperones sitting in 'a howling draught', so tired that they sometimes fell asleep and toppled off their hard gilt chairs. They were even more to be pitied than the coachmen who had to wait up till dawn, for at least the latter could keep themselves warm and merry with *glühwein* and beer.

Paola describes the Archduke Ferdinand Maximilian as 'an enchant- ing personality'. 'We were always laughing and chatting together,' she writes, 'and at every ball he partnered me for a waltz and a cotillon. He was not such an accomplished dancer as the Emperor but so much better company.'

The short winter season appears to have been the only time of the year when the Imperial Family went out into society. 'Once the Carnival was over,' writes Paola, 'the Court lived apart. The only opportunity to meet was at the summer promenades in Schönbrunn, when on cer- tain days there was a military band on the parterre in front of the castle and all Vienna congregated there.' It does not sound as if these meetings provided much opportunity for an intimate talk, still less for a flirtation. Paola and Maximilian did not see one another for a year, but one suspects that they corresponded, a detail carefully omitted from her memoirs published many years later when Paola von Linden was the widowed and still beautiful Countess von Bülow. In Maxi- milian's imagination the romance grew in proportion to his loneliness. He had so much time in which to think of Paola, both during his illness and the long months at sea. In the galleries of Florence and the gardens of the Alcazar he would picture himself with Paola at his side. This explains the depression and homesickness he felt on his brother's birthday when he wrote: 'I thought so long and deeply of one of my loved ones that I was in that forlorn state of mind when one feels a sort of sweet despair.' But the budding romance was already doomed. At the time of Maximilian's illness, when his mother was staying with him in Trieste, she appears to have come across a series of love poems written in his hand, and in the following winter had little difficulty in identifying the object of his affections.

It was February 1852, and Ferdinand Maximilian was once more on leave in Vienna. The round of Carnival balls was in full swing, and little Paola von Linden found her Archduke 'even better looking and more fascinating than before'. He had become more serious, talking to her not only of his travels but of his own personal problems, criticizing an antiquated system of government and advocating the introduction of new blood into the administration. Paola was immensely flattered by his confidences, even if he sometimes talked of matters she did not understand. At every ball she received his cotillon favours, but it was only on the last day of the Carnival that he dared to send her flowers to her own home.

'On Shrove Tuesday,' she wrote, 'we danced all day, beginning with a *déjeuner dansant* given by Prince Auersberg which lasted from twelve to six and returning home just in time to change for a ball at the Archduchess Sophia's, which ended at the stroke of midnight.' She added that, at Prince Auersberg's *déjeuner*, she wore a white dress with a wreath of cornflowers in her hair and that, just before she left the house, a beautiful bouquet arrived without a name. Her father refused to let her wear it without knowing from whom it came, so she told him it must have been sent by an old Countess of their acquaintance.

One feels that Paola was not quite so ingenuous as she would have us believe in her memoirs. She tells us that the Archduke Ferdinand Maximilian was representing the Emperor at Prince Auersberg's party and had therefore to dance the first waltz with his hostess. But no sooner had the cotillon begun than he was at her side, whispering in the middle of the dance that he had sent her the flowers. That evening, as she was dressing for the Archduchess's ball, a second bouquet arrived, even more beautiful than the first. When she confessed to her father from whom it came, he told her quite bluntly, 'Do not have any illusions. The very position of your admirer precludes any danger.' Flushed and flattered by all the attention, Paola danced what she little thought to be her last cotillon with her Archduke. His brother, Karl Ludwig, appears to have been in the secret for he gave her a laughing look and pointed to the bouquet. Even the Emperor smiled indulgently. But the Archduchess Sophia, who was usually so charming to the young girls whom she invited to amuse her sons, raised her gold lorgnette with a critical look.

The rest of Paola von Linden's memoirs gave way to fantasy. She writes that Ferdinand Maximilian was sent off the following day to join the navy, whereas in 1852 he had been in the navy for over a year. Nor was Franz Josef 'so lonely without him that he recalled him to Vienna for a few days in the middle of Lent'. For by now the Emperor had learnt to live quite well without the brother who was always causing trouble with his entourage. Ferdinand Maximilian did return to Vienna in the middle of May, but it was in order to visit his father, who had been ill. Immediately on his arrival Paola received a magnificent bouquet of pansies and of orange blossom fresh from his greenhouses in Trieste.

That same evening, she accompanied her mother to a guest performance at the *Burg Theater* and they sat immediately opposite the Royal Box occupied by Max and his mother. The Archduchess cannot fail to have noticed what Paola describes as 'the silent pantomime, directed and composed by Max', which was taking place between her son and the young girl with the outsize bouquet who was sitting directly opposite. Neither appears to have had any interest in what was going on on the stage and Paola writes, 'Throughout the evening Max kept looking at me through his opera glasses, and I pressed my face in his flowers and then looked back at him.'

One would like to think they had some other opportunity of meeting, but there is no mention of it in her memoirs. Shortly afterwards, the Archduchess took action, and it was tactfully suggested to the Court of Wurtemburg that Count von Linden had been so many years in Vienna that he was due for a change of post. Max was despatched on another Mediterranean cruise, officially to visit certain units of the British fleet off Minorca, though his mother had also made plans for him to visit the Spanish and Portuguese Courts, in the hopes that he might find a suitable Catholic princess for a bride.

Von Linden was accredited to Berlin and Paola's romance with the Archduke had a sad little epilogue which, like any other pretty woman, she tried to interpret in the manner least hurtful to her vanity. It was in the New Year of 1853, when the Emperor accompanied by the Archduke Maximilian paid a state visit to Berlin, a visit which, in view of the strained relations between Austria and Prussia, might have been very stiff and formal had it not been that King Frederick IV was married to their Aunt Elise. A few months earlier, on a visit to the fleet in Venice, both the Emperor and the Archduke had narrowly escaped being drowned in an Adriatic storm. Since then, their mother had been obsessed with the idea of marrying off her sons and securing the succession. In Berlin, the Wittelsbach sister had secretly planned an engagement between Franz Josef and a Prussian princess – a plan which was to founder partly on the religious question, partly on account of the opposition of the *Junker* Party led by the Prussian Ambassador in Vienna, Count Otto von Bismarck.

Meanwhile, no effort was spared to give the young Emperor a brilliant reception, and the von Lindens were among the diplomats invited to the Court ball held in his honour. One can picture the excited anticipation with which Paola dressed for the party. But this time there were no flowers, no secret message from the Archduke. On arrival at the Palace, she saw him in the distance, hemmed in by a circle of royalty. The Emperor, who had a gracious word for everyone presented to him, made a special effort to single out the von Lindens, whom he greeted as old friends. But Max did not cross the room to speak a word with Paola. When she looked at him reproachfully, he merely appeared embarrassed, and he did not dance at all throughout the evening. The very graciousness of the Emperor only made his conduct more wounding, and the more difficult to understand. A few weeks later Paola heard from a friend in Vienna that, before leaving for Berlin, Max had been ordered by his mother not to speak or to hold any form of communication either with her or her parents. It was an explanation which, even if it did little to comfort her feelings, at least served to spare her pride. The truth would have been much more humiliating. There had been no need for the Archduchess to give orders to her son for, by January 1853, Max had lost all interest in Paola and was half-engaged to a young Braganza princess with whom he had fallen in love when on a visit to Portugal. He may well have felt embarrassed when faced with Paola's reproachful looks, avoiding, like any other man in the same position, what he feared would be a painful and awkward scene.

He had set out on a Mediterranean cruise in that summer of 1852 with none of the pleasant sense of anticipation of the previous years. He was depressed not only by his frustrated love affair with Paola but by recent events in the navy. His old friend Admiral Dahlerup had been made the scapegoat for having allowed the Emperor to risk his life at sea in a storm which had cost the Austrian navy one of its newest battleships. Dismissed from his post as commander-in-chief, he had been succeeded by an incompetent army general who had never won a victory in his life, who knew nothing of naval affairs and who owed his appointment entirely to his friendship with the Emperor's adjutant, Count Grünne. In the whole of this affair, the Emperor had persistently ignored his brother's advice, and some of Ferdinand Maximilian's bitterness and frustration was reflected in his travel journals of 1852. Wandering along the quays of Messina, where a statue of Don John of Austria commemorates the victory of Lepanto, he wrote with sympathy and understanding of the bastard son of the Emperor Charles v as one 'who, by birth though not by law, the brother of a King, found the free unchequered course of his genius closed to him by the cold suspicion of a Court which feared he might appropriate by force what was denied him by law.' Was Maximilian half-unconsciously thinking of himself and of how the Palace *camarilla* always kept him separated from his brother?

Yet, only two months later, when celebrating his twentieth birthday on the island of Madeira, we find him in the happiest and most euphoric of moods: 'If there be any prophetic meaning in the manner in which one's birthday is spent, then the year to come will indeed be bright and happy, for never have I spent a gayer and more enchanting anniversary.' It was Ferdinand Maximilian's own mood which invested everything in Madeira with a magical quality. An excursion up the mountain with some of his brother officers to lunch in a villa 'furnished in the English style, where our kind host provided us with an excellent English dinner', was probably extremely enjoyable but hardly sufficient to warrant such exaggerated enthusiasm. But Madeira was the first port of call after Lisbon – and in Lisbon he had fallen passionately in love for the first, and probably the only, time in his life.

'I remained in Lisbon for a fortnight, devoting most of my time to my friends and relatives.' Maria de Gloria, Queen of Portugal, was Maximilian's cousin. Her mother had been his aunt Leopoldine, one of those blue-eyed, long-chinned daughters of the Emperor Franz, whose dynastic marriages were intended to ensure Hapsburg hegemony throughout the world. Maria de Gloria's father had been the turbulent Pedro i, Emperor of Brazil, who on his own father's death had renounced his claim to Portugal in favour of his seven-year-old daughter, only to find her inheritance usurped by his brother Miguel. When a revolution in Brazil forced Pedro to abdicate, he returned to Europe and, putting himself at the head of the Liberal Party in Portugal, had reconquered his kingdom for his daughter. But he was too forceful and dynamic a character to be tolerated by a Court of ambitious place-seekers. And at the age of thirty-five he retired from public life, to die of consumption only a few months later.

Before leaving Brazil, Pedro had married for the second time, yet another of Ferdinand Maximilian's relatives, the beautiful and talented Amalia of Leuchtenberg, daughter of that Wittelsbach princess whom the King of Bavaria had married to Napoleon's stepson Eugéne de Beauharnais. What at the time had been considered a *mésalliance* had turned into the happiest of marriages and their daughter, Amalia, had inherited all her parents' intelligence and charm. Sent across the world at the age of seventeen to become Empress of Brazil and the wife of a man of violent character and dissolute morals, she had succeeded with patience and tact in ousting the reigning mistress from the Palace and winning her husband's love. After accompanying the Emperor into exile, she had given birth to a daughter in Paris, and it was Maria Amalia with whom Ferdinand Maximilian fell in love at first sight.

From all accounts Maria Amalia must have been exquisitely lovely with that fair, transparent skin which is all too often the sign of a consumptive. 'A perfect princess, such as one rarely meets,' wrote Maximilian, for she had all the qualities most likely to appeal to his imagination. The memory of Paola von Linden vanished overnight. How could a little German debutante compete with this fairy-tale Princess, who combined the romance of the Braganzas and the poetry of the Wittelsbachs with the grace and elegance the Beauharnais had inherited from their Creole ancestress, the Empress Josephine? Maximilian had always been fascinated by the New World. When visiting the home of the widowed Empress of Brazil, he found many relics of her former Empire, negro servants in fading imperial liveries, conservatories full of tropical flowers and brightly plumaged birds. Maria Amalia's delicate beauty was enhanced by her exotic background.

Their courtship flowered under the summer moon in tropical gardens overlooking the Tagus. They formed the most romantic of couples at the balls and fêtes given in the Archduke's honour, and it was at the most beautiful of all these fêtes, held by the Duke of Palmella in the Gardens of Lumiera, that Ferdinand Maximilian first spoke of marriage.

'On this evening,' he writes, 'the mysterious shadows of the rich green foliage appeared to be doubly enchanting, the many coloured flowers more scented than before.' Maria Amalia was ardent and responsive and her mother was only too ready to give her blessing, delighted to secure a Hapsburg Archduke for a prospective son-in-law. But nothing could be settled until Ferdinand Maximilian returned to Vienna to obtain the Emperor's consent, and he had still to complete another six weeks' cruise in the Mediterranean. He left Lisbon on a wave of euphoria. Madeira and Algiers were seen through rose-coloured spectacles and Maria Amalia received letters and poems from every port of call.

In Vienna there was no great enthusiasm at his news. The Emperor, his father and the old uncles all disliked the Beauharnais connection and did not consider the daughter of the deposed Emperor of Brazil to be a good enough match for a Hapsburg. His mother, on the other hand, was ready to accept his choice. Maria Amalia was her sister's granddaughter and Sophia remembered the respect and the affection with which Eugéne de Beauharnais had been treated at her father's Court. The Emperor gave in to his mother and it was decided that Max 'should wait for a year and announce his engagement on attaining his majority'.

That winter, the Archduchess noted with satisfaction that her two sons were again on the best of terms, and she was delighted when the Emperor invited Max to accompany him on a state visit to Berlin. There was no need for her to worry about little Paola von Linden or even to give her a thought. Ferdinand Maximilian himself had probably forgotten all about her till he suddenly found himself face to face with her at the Court ball – an awkward situation but nothing more for a young man completely obsessed by another face and another voice. If Paola von Linden had wished for revenge, which was hardly in her nature, she could not have expected it to come so cruelly and so swiftly. Ferdinand Maximilian had barely returned to Trieste before he received the news of his fiancée's death. He must have known from the beginning that Maria Amalia was delicate. While he was in Portugal her mother had made no secret of the fact that she was taking her to Madeira for the winter to get her away from the fogs of Lisbon. The mild climate of Madeira from which the girl's mother had hoped so much had proved detrimental to her health. Galloping consumption had set in and Maria Amalia was dead within a few weeks of her arrival.

Her young lover was heartbroken. In some strange fashion, this twenty-year-old girl he had known for little more than a week was to haunt him all his life. Fragile and unattainable, she remained present in his dreams. Seven years later, when revisiting Madeira with a young and pretty wife, we find Maximilian paying a solitary visit to Maria Amalia's grave, 'lingering in grief and sadness by the house from which this lovely angel winged her flight to Heaven'.

5

Admiral of the Fleet

The year 1853, which promised so much when Ferdinand Maximilian celebrated his twentieth birthday on the island of Madeira, had opened on a note of tragedy. Maria Amalia's death had left him stunned and shocked, with no one at hand to talk to or to confide in. Her mother's letters took many weeks to reach him and the condolences of his family made it all too plain that, however much they might sympathize with his grief, it must on no account be allowed to affect his future life.

He sought refuge from his unhappiness in his work and was glad when his duties took him to the Bocche di Gattaro on the Turkish frontier. Maximilian loved the Dalmatian coast, the crumbling Venetian towns, the sleepy ports with their orange-sailed caiques, the islands overgrown with myrtle and thyme. Already he felt the Adriatic to be his home and was settling down to the even rhythm of life at sea, when the news of an attempt to assassinate the Emperor summoned him to Vienna. The full details reached him at Trieste. The would-be assassin Libenyi was a Hungarian revolutionary, a tailor's assistant by trade, who had been lying in wait for the Emperor on the ramparts and struck at him with a knife before the adjutant on duty, a young officer of Irish extraction called O'Donnell, managed with great bravery and presence of mind to fling himself on the man and disarm him before the police arrived on the scene.

A letter from his mother told Ferdinand Maximilian of how his brother had behaved with superhuman courage, even going so far as to intervene in preventing the police from maltreating his assailant. But now the reaction had set in. The loss of blood from his wound had been considerable and the shock greater than Franz Josef would admit. He was in bed with a high fever and the doctors feared that his sight might be affected. In an almost hysterical postscript, the Archduchess begged Max to come to Vienna without delay. She apparently did not know that this was the last thing that Franz Josef wanted him to do and that, when in the first moment of panic Count Grünne had suggested sending for the Archduke, the Emperor had forbidden him to do so.

Red-eyed from lack of sleep, his heart overflowing with love and affection, Ferdinand Maximilian arrived at his brother's sick-bed, only to be asked in a cold, almost hostile tone why he had left his post without permission. Nothing could have been more wounding for someone as proud and sensitive as Max, and the Emperor's only excuse for his behaviour was that he was ill and frightened of going blind, and already saw his brother aspiring to the succession.

So much had been expected of Franz Josef in the past year. Felix Schwarzenberg had lived just long enough to place him firmly on the throne and to see Austria established as a strong unitary monarchy. But the minister's death in 1852 had left him terribly alone, and although Prince Metternich was back in Vienna asking nothing better than to be recalled to power, Franz Josef made no attempt to reinstate him at the Ball-platz, relegating him to the position of an old and valued friend who could occasionally be called on for advice. There were many, including Metternich's wife, who held the Archduchess Sophia responsible for keeping the ex-Chancellor out of office, but it was Franz Josef himself who, at the age of twenty-three, was determined to be self-reliant and to make his own decisions, refusing the help and co-operation even of those who, like his brother, really loved him.

Libenyi's knife might have changed the course of history. So many pages might never have been written, so many tragedies might have been averted. But although Ferdinand Maximilian was hurt and angry at his brother's behaviour, he seems never to have let his own ambitions interfere in his loyalty to his Emperor or his prayers for his recovery.

Franz Josef not only recovered but gained enormously in popularity. Till now he had been respected rather than loved, for he lacked the gift of endearing himself to the masses, to whom he appeared as a stiff, unbending figure, always in uniform, always surrounded by a military entourage. But this dastardly attempt at murder had aroused a wave of indignation throughout the country. The heart of every woman went out to the brave young Emperor and enthusiastic crowds mobbed his carriage when he appeared in public for the first time, driving a four-in-hand in the Prater without any escort of police.

The Emperor must have been touched and perhaps ashamed on hearing that his brother had launched an appeal for funds to build a church in thanksgiving. The appeal was over-subscribed and in a letter to Prince Metternich thanking him for his contribution, the Archduke wrote: 'We live in such a materialistic age that I feel that the best way in which we can express our gratitude to our Saviour in protecting our dearly beloved sovereign is to combine art with religion in building a house of God.' Ferdinand Maximilian might have called it a bigoted as well as a materialistic age, for this was the year in which the directors of the *Theater an der Wien* were prevented from staging Richard Wagner's *Tannhäuser*, on the grounds that it was 'a godless and immoral work'. Ferdinand Maximilian was destined never to see the handsome neo-Gothic *Votiv Kirche* which stands on what is now the Schotten Ring. A stained-glass window decorates the nave, a tribute from the Emperor Franz Josef to the memory of his brother, the Emperor of Mexico – a tribute perhaps of love and certainly of remorse.

In that summer of 1853 Ferdinand Maximilian received his first diplomatic mission, to enquire into the alleged ill-treatment of Catholic priests in Turkish Albania. It was not an important mission, but it required a certain amount of delicacy and tact, as Austria wished to assert her position as a protecting power without running any risk of offending the susceptible Turk. The young Archduke was delighted to go. Only a year had elapsed since he had proposed marriage to Maria Amalia in the gardens of Lumiera, and only a few months since he had heard of her death. His lack of interest in other women, his reluctance at present to take part either in social or in family life, made him all the more eager for a life of adventure.

The Emperor's advisers were aware of Maximilian's youthful vanity, the pleasure he took in impressing foreign countries with the power and prestige of Austria. But even Franz Josef admitted that there was no one more qualified than Max to deal with foreigners, whether they were Bourbon princes or Balkan ruffians, 'for he was so good-hearted that he saw good in everyone else'. But there was little opportunity of impressing the native population in the dilapidated Albanian ports where the Austrian Consul was usually one of the local merchants with little wish to antagonize the Turkish authorities by showing too great a zeal for the lot of his fellow Christians. As for the Christians themselves, they had long since learnt that the best way of living with the Turks was to make themselves as inconspicuous as possible and to pay whatever was demanded of them by the local Aga. What is known as 'showing the flag' had not much effect when half the population were so ignorant that they did not even recognize the Austrian flag. But Ferdinand Maximilian succeeded in impressing the Turks by a combination of haughtiness and affability, of eccentricity and elegance. Rumours of an armed warship anchored off their shores, of foreign sailors bathing from their beaches and hunting in the forests, reached the Pashas and Agas in the interior. Some came in curiosity, others in alarm, but all were equally impressed by the tall, fair young prince, who on a scorching summer day would receive them sitting cross-legged on the grass, wearing an Algerian *burnous* for comfort and fanning himself with a Chinese fan; but on the next occasion would welcome them on board his ship to the salute of gunfire, surrounded by his officers all wearing full uniform and entertaining them to melons and cooled champagne, which even the most orthodox of Moslems was unable to resist.

In his diary, Maximilian confesses that he secretly longed for the opportunity to assert his authority, but the Turks persisted in being amenable and in acceding to his requests. What he first took to be a threatening message from the Pasha of Tirana turned out to be dictated by nothing more than curiosity to be shown over the *Minerva*. News that the Catholic Archbishop of Durazzo was being held in duress by a powerful Turkish Bey led him to send an armed expedition demanding his release, which took place in less than twenty-four hours. And the Emperor's birthday was celebrated on board with the rescued Archbishop serving Mass. It must have been an extraordinary experience for a priest who had known years of hardship and frustration to find himself the central figure in an elaborate ceremony designed by Ferdinand Maximilian for the benefit of the Christian population of Durazzo, who one and all had accepted his invitation.

On the very day when Ferdinand Maximilian was celebrating the Emperor's birthday on board the *Minerva*, Franz Josef, who was on holiday in the mountain resort of Ischl, had become officially engaged. In a sense, it had all been planned by his mother, who ever since his escape from drowning had been obsessed by the necessity of getting him married. His admiration for a young Prussian princess had held hopes of a brilliant political alliance. But with the failure of these hopes, the Archduchess had reverted to her own family. The Wittelsbachs were still the most powerful Catholic reigning family in Germany, and throughout the years they had produced successive generations of

Hapsburg brides. In her immediate family circle was her younger sister Ludovica, the only one of King Maximilian Josef's seven daughters for whom he had failed to make a political marriage and who had had to content herself with a cousin, a mere Duke in Bavaria belonging to the collateral and not the reigning branch. Ludovica had five daughters, of whom the eldest, Helen, was already of marriageable age, a girl on whom the Archduchess had kept a watchful eye during the past years and who, according to the Austrian Minister in Munich, had all the qualities desirable in a young princess.

This summer the Archduchess had invited her sister to bring the nineteen-year-old Helen to Ischl at a time when the Emperor would be there on holiday. What Sophia had not reckoned with was that Ludovica, who was a devoted mother, would bring not only Helen but the fifteen-year-old Elisabeth, or 'Sisi', and that from the moment Franz Josef laid eyes on her lovely face, framed in a mass of auburn curls, he would fall utterly and irrevocably in love. No motherly warning, no gently-worded advice, could put a curb to his infatuation. The Archduchess had to accept the inevitable and give in with a smiling acquiescence.

At heart, she knew it was midsummer madness for her son to become engaged to a girl of fifteen – a child who was still as shy and frightened as a wild deer and, unlike her elder sister who, owing to an understanding between mother and aunt, had had some kind of training for the role of Empress, had been allowed to run wild in the country with no form of education. Their father, Duke Max, was the most eccentric member of an eccentric family, preferring the company of poets and journalists to that of his own class, and his only idea of educating his children had been to teach them to play the zither and to ride bareback like circus riders. Elisabeth had been an apt pupil, the only one of his daughters in whom he took the slightest interest, and Sophia, who detested her brother-in-law, feared that she might also have inherited some of her father's characteristics. But life had taught the Archduchess never to try to swim against the tide. Her son had fallen in love with the wrong niece, but she was still a member of her family, whose very youth and inexperience might make her easier to train and more amenable to advice. It was not long before she was to realize that the sweet, shy little girl had a determined will of her own and a marked disinclination to listen to her mother-in-law's advice. But for the moment Sophia allowed herself to be caught up in the general atmosphere of rejoicing, and not a word of criticism transpired in her letters to Ferdinand Maximilian. Her only regret was that he was not with them to share in this joyful occasion. But the extraordinary transformation was in Franz Josef himself. Max could hardly believe that these long, poetical effusions on 'Sisi's grace and beauty' were written by his brother, who was usually so terse and matter-of-fact. His happiness made him much more human and affectionate, and he wrote that he was longing for Max's company, for the marriage was not to take place until the following spring when the bride would be sixteen. The political situation, which made no allowances for lovers, did not permit the poor, overworked Emperor to take more than a few days holiday during the winter months.

The Eastern Question was about to explode into war, with France and Britain aligned with Turkey against an aggressive Russia threatening the Dardanelles. Society in Vienna was divided between the pro-Russian army generals, who maintained that the moment had come when Austria had to pay her debts, and the Foreign Office represented by Count Buol, who advocated an alliance with the Western Powers. Caught in the tide between Scylla and Charybdis, with only one wish, to remain safely on the shore, the young Emperor kept to a policy of armed neutrality, saying that he was 'first and foremost an Austrian, only interested in safeguarding Austria's interests'.

With his liberal principles, Ferdinand Maximilian favoured the Western Powers. As a sailor, he was full of admiration for Britain and the British navy, and nothing would have given him more pleasure than to take part as Britain's ally in a naval battle with the Russians. He felt no gratitude towards the Czar, only shame and disgust at the manner in which Hungarian freedom had been crushed under the combined weight of Austro-Russian arms. But the Eastern Question was not the only problem over which Maximilian differed from his brother. His naval duties, which centred on Venice and Trieste, gave him an insight into the political situation of Venetia-Lombardy, where Radetzky's repressive policy only served to encourage subversive propaganda which inflamed the hatred against Austrian rule. The Marshal was too old for the job, too ready to listen to spies and informers. But Franz Josef was still so dazzled by Radetzky's reputation and so much under the influence of his military advisers that he made no attempt to interfere with a régime which was driving the Italians towards another revolution.

There were times when Maximilian was very lonely in Trieste and his brother's happiness only served to accentuate his loneliness. It was not that he grudged it to him, but he must have felt a certain bitterness at the cruel stroke of fate which had robbed him of his own twenty-year-old bride, whose radiant beauty would have matched that of the loveliest of Wittelsbach princesses. Trieste society had little to offer him, other than the company of his brother officers. It was a rich commercial society of merchants and shipowners, where the wives rivalled with one another in getting the Archduke to patronize their charity balls and fêtes. He was spoilt and adulated and able to indulge in all his extravagances, thanks to the unlimited credit of complaisant bankers. And there is little doubt that these early years in Trieste, when he was still an adolescent, had a detrimental effect on his character, accentuating his natural arrogance and self-esteem.

He might have found a more congenial society in Venice, but Radetzky's policy of repression had closed the doors of the Venetian aristocracy to anything which savoured of Austrian rule. Deprived of sympathetic female companionship, he depended on an almost entirely masculine society, sharing the habits of his brother officers and, in spite of an initial repulsion, gradually becoming an habitué of the brothels and music halls of Trieste, where the proprietors were only too ready to cater to his taste for the exotic. But for all his youth and immaturity, Ferdinand Maximilian had the perception to realize that Wilhelm von Tegetthoff was the one outstanding figure among his friends. And Tegetthoff was the first to receive promotion when, in September 1854, the month of the Anglo-French landings in the Crimea, the Emperor, acting contrary to the advice of his military advisers, dismissed Baron Wympfen from his post as naval Commander-in-Chief and replaced him by his twenty-two-year-old brother, whom he raised at the same time to the rank of Rear-Admiral.

The appointment was bitterly criticized in Court circles where stress was laid on the Archduke's youth and inexperience. Baron Wympfen's friends did not hesitate to say that it was the Archduchess Sophia who had insisted upon the post being given to her beloved Max, and that to placate his mother, who was already on bad terms with her daughter-in-law, the Emperor had ended by giving way. But naval circles in Trieste and Venice were enthusiastic over the appointment. 'At last something will be done,' wrote Tegetthoff in his diary, 'the Archduke may be young and inexperienced, but he has the interests of the navy really at heart.'

Ferdinand Maximilian received the news with gratitude and joy, and he was determined to prove himself worthy of his brother's trust, though he foresaw that there would be many battles 'with the rusty old men at the War Office'. Only a week after his appointment, Tegetthoff was writing, 'The Archduke has set to work with energy and zeal. He goes into every detail and I feel he will at last bring about a thorough re-organization of the service which Dahlerup and Wympfen merely bungled with their superficial policy.'

Max had learnt a lot on his Mediterranean cruises. At Gibraltar he had been impressed by the high standard of patriotism and self-respect which prevailed even among the simplest ratings, and by the way every little midshipman was taught to assume responsibility from the earliest age. Profiting from these examples he set out to infect a spirit of patriotism in Venetian and Dalmatian crews which now for the first time became proud of belonging to the Imperial Austrian Navy and were ready to accept their orders in German.

The antiquated fleet, the Cinderella of the fighting services, was entirely remodelled on British lines. It all cost a lot of money, and there was grumbling and opposition in the Imperial entourage. But the Archduke's enthusiasm was contagious and for once Franz Josef refused to listen to the hitherto omnipotent Count Grünne and let his brother have his way. In the first years from 1854 to 1859 Ferdinand Max may be said to have laid the foundations of the modern Austrian navy. His visits to Mediterranean ports and dockyards had familiarized him with the newest steam frigate and made him aware of the revolutionary changes in naval design in which England was at the time leading the world. He saw how in English dockyards, the ironclad was replacing the old wooden fighting ship and steam was being used instead of sail. For the first time in its history, the Austrian navy placed orders with English shipyards and in 1856, launched its own giant ironclad, the *Radetzky*, manned with ninety-one guns and the biggest battleship ever to have been built in an Austrian dockyard.

But his most formidable and successful enterprise, and also the most bitterly opposed, was the building and fortifying of the new naval dockyard and arsenal at Pola. His opponents stated that for Austria to have a large fleet was merely a waste of money, and that the vainglorious young Archduke was only interested in building up his own ego and in financing expensive expeditions which would rebound to his own credit. But Max was genuinely interested in his job and fascinated by every branch of naval science. He founded a maritime museum and hydrographical institute, interesting himself in oceanography and corresponding on that subject with the director of the naval observatory in Washington, a southerner whom the fortunes of war were later to bring to Mexico. However much Max may have been criticized by the old 'die-hards' of the Admiralty, one still to this day comes across retired naval officers, living in Vienna or Trieste, who in their early youth had served in the Imperial Austrian Navy, and whose faces light up with enthusiasm when the name of the Archduke Max comes up in conversation. For them he is not the misguided and ill-fated Emperor of Mexico, but the brilliant Commander-in-Chief who created the modern Austrian navy.

6

At the Tuileries

The Crimean War had been fought and won and Austria, who had kept to her policy of armed neutrality, now claimed the right to negotiate the peace, only to find that the former enemies were united against the peacemonger. Nicholas of Russia had died during the war, and the new Czar, Alexander II, was unable to forgive Franz Josef for 'the monstrous ingratitude' which had hastened his father's death. Neither England nor France could bring themselves to trust an ally who, after signing a pact of friendship, remained sitting on the fence and, without having sent a single soldier to fight in the Crimea, felt himself in a position to impose the peace terms.

With the supreme self-confidence of youth, Franz Josef prided himself on acting in the best interests of his country. But his equivocal attitude to Russia had weakened his position as leader of the German Federation, most of whose members were bound to the Czar either by sentiment or interest, and his uncles, the Kings of Prussia and Saxony, were the first to criticize his loyalty to an old and valued friend. He had meant so well, but his policy of armed neutrality had been almost as expensive as a war and, in the end, it had left Austria friendless and isolated between a Russia still licking her wounds, only waiting the moment for revenge, and a Prussia only waiting for the moment to take over the leadership of Germany. Meanwhile, there were others who had profited by his overcautious policy. In Turin Count Camillo Cavour, Foreign Minister of Piedmont-Sardinia, had succeeded in persuading King Victor Emmanuel to send a contingent of troops to support the hard-pressed Anglo-French armies in the Crimea. It was a gesture which was to reap enormous dividends. And when the peace conference opened in the last days of February 1856, the Austrian delegates were unpleasantly surprised to find Count Cavour seated among their colleagues. Moreover, he was there at the express invitation of the

Emperor Napoleon III, who, in conversation with the Austrian Ambassador, Count Hübner, suggested that this might be the right moment to settle not only the Eastern Question but other outstanding problems which threatened the peace of Europe, of which Italy was one.

By character and instinct, Franz Josef was profoundly antagonistic to Louis Napoleon, the man who, on the Duke of Reichstadt's death, had become heir to his uncle's glory. In Austrian eyes he was an adventurer, an upstart, and ex-revolutionary who had been expelled from Italy on Metternich's orders and who would not hesitate to intrigue with his former friends among the *Carbonari* to ferment trouble in Venetia-Lombardy. When the Paris coup d'etat of 1852 gave Louis Napoleon the Imperial crown, Franz Josef would willingly have followed the example of the Czar and refused to honour him with the title *'Monsieur mon Frère'*. But Felix Schwarzenberg had warned him that 'the days of principles are gone' and that by treating Louis Napoleon as an equal, he would make him forget his revolutionary past and leave the Italians to sort out their own affairs.

Unfortunately, Schwarzenberg died too soon and Franz Josef allowed himself the luxury of showing his dislike by offending the new Emperor in countless little ways. No Austrian officer was allowed to wear the Order of the Legion of Honour stamped with the effigy of Napoleon I. When Louis Napoleon, in search of a bride, asked for the hand of the young Princess of Wasa, daughter of the last surviving descendant of the old Swedish Kings, who was now living under the protection of the Hapsburgs, Franz Josef, this time influenced by his mother, deliberately vetoed the marriage. And the French Emperor's so-called love match with the beautiful Eugénie de Montijo was the deliberate defiance of a parvenu who felt himself slighted by the Courts of Europe.

But times had changed. By the spring of 1856 Louis Napoleon's star was in the ascendent. He was the friend and ally of England, and even the formidable Victoria had allowed herself to fall under his charm. His colonial empire was expanding in Africa, where the Napoleonic eagles were blazing new trails of glory, and throughout the Middle East and the Levant where the Catholics looked to France rather than to Austria for protection. Franz Josef had finally to listen to the advice of his wise and experienced ambassador in Paris who for years had been telling him that a France allied to Austria would be a conservative power, and that hostile, she would be a revolutionary force. It was the same advice which Schwarzenberg had given him in the past but he had ignored it for too long, with the result that Cavour was now in Paris and with Cavour was his cousin, the beautiful Countess of Castiglione, with whom the impressionable Napoleon had fallen passionately in love, regardless of the fact that his wife was in the last stages of pregnancy.

Austria may have dictated the peace terms and assured the freedom of her Danube shipping, but her Foreign Minister, Count Buol, was the most-hated delegate of the peace conference, while the handsome and elegant Prince Orloff, representing a vanquished enemy, was the fêted lion of the Parisian drawing rooms. And the moderation of the French demands to Russia made it all too clear that Napoleon was already envisaging the Czar as a future ally.

The Austrian Ambassador suggested that the only way to retrieve the situation was to send an Archduke to Paris. This would flatter the vanity of an upstart Court and pave the way towards a better understanding. The birth of an heir to the French Crown provided an excellent opportunity for the Emperor Franz Josef to send a personal message of congratulation. And who more suitable for such a mission than the Archduke Ferdinand Maximilian, who happened to be in Vienna at the time for the laying of the foundation stone of the new *Votiv Kirche*?

Vienna had seen little of him during the past two years, partly because his naval duties claimed him in Trieste, partly because the palace *camarilla* made every effort to keep the two brothers apart. Malicious tongues were even ready to misinterpret the spontaneous sympathy which the young Empress felt for a brother-in-law who was so much more of a Wittelsbach than a Hapsburg. Bored and depressed by the rigid etiquette of the Vienna Court, unable to understand why the husband who said he loved her could spare her so little time, Elisabeth was grateful to anyone who would alleviate the tedium of her days. She was fascinated by Max's conversation, the originality of his ideas, the descriptions of his travels. And there may well have been moments when Franz Josef, possessively in love with his enchanting little wife, felt a certain jealousy of the brother who could speak with such fluency and ease of people and places of which he had only the most superficial knowledge. In May 1856 he acted on Count Hubner's suggestion and entrusted the twenty-four-year-old Archduke with his first important diplomatic mission.

Maximilian's letters from Paris which are preserved in the Vienna State Archives, start off by being heavily biased against what he considered to be a court of parvenus. But in less than a week, he had fallen under the spell of Napoleon's kaleidoscopic personality. He became completely fascinated by the man who at first sight he described as 'not so much an Emperor with a sceptre as a circus master with a riding crop', whose unimposing physique, 'with the bow legs and sidling walk, the furtive look out of half-closed eyes' he had sneered at as being 'lacking in all nobility and breeding'. The mission in itself was a success, but it was a visit which was later to have fateful consequences. If those two ambitious dreamers, Ferdinand Maximilian and Louis Napoleon, had never met and been mutually attracted to each other, the former might never have become involved in the ill-starred Mexican adventure.

A visit which began with suspicion and prejudice ended with Ferdinand Maximilian falling in love with Paris and succumbing to the charm of its Emperor. He arrived in May, the month when Paris is at its loveliest, with the chestnuts in flower in the Champs-Elysées and the lilac out in the Bois; when the freshly-painted cafés on Baron Haussmann's new boulevards were putting out their striped umbrellas and spilling their tables out on to the pavement; when the paddleboats on the Seine had inaugurated their summer season and the Court was in residence at St Cloud.

Gradually he forgot the inhibitions of his upbringing in what must have been the most delightful of Courts – a Court of beautiful women and of brilliant men, where royal bastards like the Foreign Minister, Count Walewski, son of the first Napoleon by his Polish mistress, and the Emperor's half-brother, the handsome Duke de Morny, son of Queen Hortense by the Count de Flahaut (himself a natural son of Talleyrand), took the lead both in politics and society. It was a Court where wealth counted more than quarterings, where rich Jews and clever adventurers could buy their way into the most exclusive drawing rooms – men who would never have passed the threshhold of the Hofburg or Schönbrunn – and where the most fêted and flattered of all the beautiful women was the Italian Virginia di Castiglione, already recognized as the Emperor's 'maîtresse en titre'.

One suspects that Ferdinand Maximilian may have been more fascinated than he admits and that the priggish tone he adopts in describing the Countess was largely for his mother's benefit. 'She is very beautiful,' he writes, 'but her behaviour is so uninhibited and she exposes her charms so freely that, both in manner and in dress, she is more like a

73

dancer out of the French Regency period than the wife of a diplomat. ... Some of the ladies profess great indignation at the way in which this person deliberately chose the time of the Empress's pregnancy in order to seduce her husband.' And he adds, 'Napoleon's habit of running after every pretty woman makes a rather disagreeable impression and detracts from his Imperial dignity.' Yet, for all his shortcomings, Napoleon ended by winning his sympathy and admiration. No one was more versed in the art of combining simplicity and cunning, frankness and duplicity, confiding in those he wanted to flatter with his confidences; capable of being all things to all men, yet lovable in a way, for his very weaknesses and faults only made him the more human.

The shyness which Maximilian noted at their first meeting was probably genuine. The Second Empire was still in its first decade and the scions of ruling houses were still rare visitors at the French Court. Napoleon, and more particularly Eugénie, who was Spanish but not of royal blood, may have been intimidated by the Hapsburg Prince who, in spite of his youth and modesty was so totally at ease, so confident of his divine right to rule. Napoleon must have been familiar with the rumours which had circulated round the Vienna Court at the time of Ferdinand Maximilian's birth and may well have felt a certain nervous embarrassment in front of one who perhaps was the Duke of Reichstadt's son and the rightful heir to all the glory he had usurped. But this tall, elegant Archduke, with his long, pale face, his weak chin and pouting lip, was so obviously a Hapsburg. The blue eyes were so very Austrian, as was the loud laughter, the fluent but guttural French. It was a face which aroused enthusiasm in Eugénie, who professed a cult for Marie Antoinette and was enchanted to have her great-grandnephew as her guest.

'I breakfast every day with the Emperor and Empress,' writes Maximilian. 'Napoleon is one of these men whose personality does not attract at first but who gains on knowing through his quiet charm and great simplicity of manner. . . . Once he has got over his shyness, he becomes very expansive and the more I get to know him, the more I feel he trusts me.' It was flattering for a young man of twenty-four to be taken into the Emperor's confidence and to discuss with him the intricacies of world politics. Napoleon was full of praises for Franz Josef, 'who, in spite of his youth, has already accomplished so much'. And whatever faults Austria had committed in recent years were all blamed on her unfortunate Foreign Minister — 'but perhaps also the allies had been at fault'. With a disarming frankness Napoleon said, 'It might have been better to have carved up the Turkish Empire, instead of trying to save it.' Half laughing, he added that 'it was a sorry business, having to bolster up the Turks, who were the stupidest people on earth', whereupon Maximilian ventured to say that, in the recent campaign, the Turks had shown themselves to be neither so stupid nor so decadent as their friends seemed to think.

It was all too easy for a subtle, experienced diplomat like Napoleon to encourage an ingenuous and rather vain young man in the belief that Austria and France between them could settle the peace of Europe. Only in parentheses he added that an alliance with England was necessary to them both but it was unfortunate that England had such perverted principles. Maximilian writes, 'The Emperor appears to be delighted with the humiliation of Russia.' One wonders whether he was aware that Napoleon's half-brother, the Duke of Morny, was about to leave for St Petersburg, where he was to represent the Emperor at the coronation of the Czar and lay the foundations for a Franco-Russian alliance.

Time and again, the Archduke tried to bring the conversation round to the subject of Italy but the Emperor refused to commit himself beyond saying that the allies owed a debt of gratitude to Piedmont-Sardinia for their gallant behaviour in the recent war, and that there could be no durable peace till the great powers got together and re-made the map of Europe. On the evening before departure, during a party at St Cloud where the 'great Houdini' was entertaining the guests with his conjuring tricks, the Emperor took Maximilian aside for a last confidential talk. The Archduke seized the opportunity to ask him point blank whether he was prepared to co-operate with Austria in the settling of the Italian Question, whereupon Napoleon replied that he had every intention of working hand in hand with Austria and that, in spite of his regard for Piedmont-Sardinia, he would never allow the Italians to come between them. Cavour would have liked him to renounce the Austrian alliance, he said, but that was something he would never consent to.

The words and tone were so convincing that it would have needed someone far older and more sceptical than Maximilian to doubt Napoleon's good intentions, intentions which for the moment he may have even believed himself. For the sympathy and admiration were mutual. At those intimate breakfast parties at St Cloud, where hosts and guest relaxed and chatted gaily and without reserve, Napoleon and Eugénie were as much impressed by Ferdinand Maximilian's culture and versatility as he was charmed by Eugénie's vivacity and Napoleon's kindly humour.

His visit coincided with that of another royal prince, the Crown Prince Oscar of Sweden, who he feared at first might cut him out. He soon saw that there was no cause for jealousy and noted with pleasure that he more than held his own at the great military review given in their honour and that, in spite of being a sailor, 'I did not appear at a disadvantage riding my fiery Andalusian, and was grateful for the riding lessons that we had in our youth.' The Austrian Ambassador wrote home in his dispatches: 'Prince Oscar of Sweden, who is staying here at the moment, is completely eclipsed by the Austrian Prince, by whom everyone is enchanted.' How could a Bernadotte, descended from one of the first Napoleon's marshals, compete with a Hapsburg in the eyes of the tradition-loving Eugénie, particularly when the Hapsburg was as charming and as fascinating as Ferdinand Maximilian? In conversation with one of her ladies, the Empress was heard to say that he was one of the only Austrians she had ever met with whom it was possible to hold an intelligent conversation and, writing to Franz Josef, Maximilian commented, 'Everyone says that the Emperor Napoleon has treated me with a greater regard than he shows towards certain reigning sovereigns, among them the King of Piedmont.' It was a letter which must have given immense satisfaction to his brother, who wrote in reply congratulating him on having 'managed the French Emperor with great cleverness and tact and thereby improving Austria's position in Europe'.

On leaving Paris, every member of the Archduke's suite was personally decorated by Napoleon. The Imperial yacht *Queen Hortense* was placed at his disposal to take him from Havre to Antwerp and, on saying goodbye, both Emperor and Empress pressed him to return to Paris, with Napoleon adding, 'We are now quite like old friends.' Yet still we find Ferdinand Maximilian writing to Schönbrunn that, in spite of being touched with all the kindness and civility he had been shown, he had no regrets on leaving Paris. 'In fact, I bless the day when I can turn my back on this centre of civilization.' Again, one suspects that this letter was written largely to please his mother who, without ever having visited France, was bitterly anti-French and considered that all the trouble in Europe had originated in Paris. Ferdinand Maximilian was far more impressed by his visit than he would ever have admitted in Vienna, and his aunt, the Queen of Prussia, with whom he stayed on his way home, was shocked to find that 'he was quite won over by Napoleon'.

Nevertheless, the mission had been a success and, with his family's blessing, he now proceeded to Belgium, ostensibly to pay a courtesy visit to the sixty-five-year-old King Leopold who, by a combination of astuteness and diplomacy, had during his twenty-five-year reign succeeded in raising his little country to the rank of a European power, and the obscure family of Saxe-Coburg to that of princes of the blood royal, related to half the ruling families in the world. So important had they become that the proud Archduchess Sophia, in search of a marriageable Catholic princess for her son, was ready to contemplate the prospect of a Coburg daughter-in-law. King Leopold was reputed to have a pretty and intelligent sixteen-year-old daughter, and Max, who since Maria Amalia's death had shown little inclination for marriage, might be more ready to fall in love with a clever little Belgian princess than with one of those eminently suitable Spanish or Neapolitan Bourbons whom he so persistently avoided on his travels.

7

The Princess Charlotte

Charlotte of Belgium was only ten years old when she lost her mother, the gentle and loving Louise of Orléans, who in 1832 became King Leopold's second wife. Love at first had played little part in what was essentially a political alliance. Even King Louis Philippe is said to have wept at having to sacrifice his favourite daughter to a middle-aged widower, twenty-two years her senior, a man whose youthful ardour and romanticism were long since buried in a grave at Windsor, and whose every action was now dominated by a calculating ambition. It was not an inviting prospect for a gay, affectionate young girl, who had grown up in the midst of a large and united family. But she ended by falling in love with her cold, pedantic husband, who lectured rather than talked, and treated her much in the same way as he treated his niece Victoria, the young Queen of England.

Leopold was grateful for his wife's affection and impressed by her 'moral qualities and cultivated mind'. But having loved the voluptuous and magnificent Charlotte of Wales – a Rubens painted by Lawrence – he was hardly likely to be physically attracted by his delicate little Queen, with her long, pale face and thin Bourbon nose, a woman who, after giving him four children, the eldest of whom died in infancy, was so physically exhausted that she was incapable of satisfying his strong Coburg appetites. Outwardly, their marriage presented to the Belgian people a model of domestic bliss, and it was characteristic of the sweet, unselfish Louise that, when a baby daughter was born in 1840, she suggested calling her Charlotte in memory of the blue-eyed English Princess, whose portrait still hung on the walls at Laeken.

If the King kept mistresses, they were discreetly hidden in the background – till the day when he met Arcadie Clairet de Viescourt, an opulent Flemish beauty with all the qualities most likely to attract the bored and aging Leopold. Her father, who was a highly respected officer, disapproved of these royal attentions, whereupon the King had her cynically married off to a member of his household, a certain Monsieur Meyer von Eppinghoven, who was promptly dispatched to Germany, while the young bride became the King's *maîtresse en titre*. But Madame Meyer, who was as ambitious as her lover, was not content to hide her charms in a discreet villa in the Forêt de Cambres. With blatant effrontery she insisted on a mansion in the Rue Royale, a carriage with postillions and outriders. And her tactlessness earned her the hatred of the Belgian people, who revered their 'good little Queen'.

The King's infatuation was particularly hard on his wife, as it came at a time when the Revolution of 1848 had driven her father into exile. Conscious that her relatives were no longer of political importance to her husband's dynastic ambitions, that he regretted having married a Coburg nephew and niece into the Orléans family, Louise was more than ever aware of her own physical shortcomings. And her extraordinary selflessness and humility transpire in a letter to her husband, written towards the end of 1849: 'What more could I ask on earth than to be your friend, your only friend? I owe all my happiness to you and what is lacking from my happiness is my fault alone. I blame only myself for all that troubles me. If I am no longer young ... if I have been unable to bring any pleasure to your life, I can only attribute it to my ill-fortune. And though I cannot but regret, I only regret what I cannot do for you.'

Surely Leopold must have felt a certain compunction on receiving such a letter from a wife to whom he was devoted if not in love. But it did not make him forgo his daily visits to Madame Meyer, thereby embittering his relations with his sons, in particular with the Duke of Brabant who, having a critical mind and a sarcastic tongue, refused to place his father on a pedestal. Charlotte was only nine at the time, too young to become involved. Louise had never allowed her to see the tears brought on by her husband's infidelity and she brought up her daughter to regard her father as a hero and an oracle of wisdom. While adoring her mother, Charlotte worshipped her father, whom she resembled in so many ways that Louise described her as his 'living miniature'. It was characteristic of Leopold not to have wanted a daughter, for a third son would have assured his dynasty. But by the time of the little girl's fourth birthday, Louise was writing to her mother: 'Charlotte, as you predicted, has become her father's pet.

Today being her birthday, she dines with us, surrounded by her presents and crowned with a wreath of roses.'

No one could have been a more loving mother than Louise, doting on her 'little elf' who was sweet and affectionate and so extraordinarily intelligent that she wanted to read before she was three. Like Leopold, she was interested in the most varied subjects, 'talking just like a grown-up and using the most complicated words'. At five years old, we hear of her attending a *Te Deum* at St Gudule, 'studying the prayer book with the utmost attention and looking just like a little angel'. But the fond mother was not blind to her daughter's faults and was the first to recognize that Charlotte was 'as proud and self-willed as her father', though these faults were largely redeemed by her own efforts at self-discipline. At eight, she was old enough to share in her mother's grief when her grandparents had to flee from Paris. And the sad, bitter letter of a disillusioned King who throughout his reign had worked for the good of his people, was read aloud over the breakfast table at Laeken. 'What more could I do but abdicate,' wrote Louis Philippe, 'when not a hand out of all those who had asked for favours in the past, was raised in my defence; when all my ministers had resigned and all my supporters had deserted me; when the National Guard had laid down its arms and even the voice of the public conscience was stilled.'

It was a letter his little granddaughter was never to forget. Instinctively, she resented and rebelled against her grandfather's decision. Neither she nor her father were of the kind to abdicate. Leopold's first lessons to his daughter were of the burdens and responsibilities of power, the danger of neglecting one's duties. When King Louis Philippe died in England in the summer of 1850, Charlotte was convinced he had died because no king could survive the humiliation of exile. Queen Louise never recovered from her father's death. Her fragile constitution could not stand up to this series of family tragedies allied to the unhappiness of her private life. Her lungs had always been delicate and she gradually sank into decline. By the end of September 1850, Leopold was writing to his niece, Victoria, that there was no longer any hope. By 10 October she was dead, selfless and resigned to the very end, thinking only of her husband who had done so little to deserve her, and of her children, in particular her daughter, who was now left so frighteningly alone.

There are several portraits of Charlotte as a child. We see her serious little face with the large dark eyes, looking out from under flowered Leghorn hats, painted in a family group with her two brothers or playing with a pet cat. Winterhalter paid several visits to Brussels to paint the royal children, and his two portraits of Charlotte between the ages of six and ten form a tragic contrast. In the one, she is a petted, demure little girl dressed up in her party silks, a child for whom the world is still a secure and happy place; in the other, she is in mourning, a sad, lost figure in her grey dress and black mantilla, which banishes the look of childhood from her face, a face grown old with tears. Winterhalter, the Court painter *par excellence*, who made every king a hero and every queen a beauty, succeeds in transferring on to canvas the bleakness of a child's despair. We can envisage the little girl who, only a week after her mother's funeral, when her grandmother had returned to England, wrote: 'We were grateful you were with us to share in our grief. But Laeken is a very lonely place now that you have gone. It has been a terrible blow to you, but I will try to be very good to make up to you as far as I can for all that you have lost.'

There was not only her grandmother to console, there was also her father, for Leopold's grief was as genuine as his remorse and Madame Meyer von Eppinghoven was sent on a long journey. The King, who had never been close to his sons, found his only consolation in his daughter's company, and Charlotte made superhuman efforts to take her mother's place. But it was too much of a strain for her and her character suffered in consequence. The gay, affectionate child changed almost overnight into a serious, introspective schoolgirl, as hard on herself as she was critical of others. Her mother's gentle, feminine influence had helped to restrain the arrogance and self-will of the Coburgs, but from now on she was either in the company of an aging father who found it quite natural for a child of eleven to enjoy reading Plutarch's *Lives*, or of her pious, middle-aged governesses under the supervision of her mother's oldest friend, a Countess d'Hulst who, for all her excellent qualities, was too inclined to moralize and to encourage her pupil in the reading of religious tracts far too heavy for her years.

Whatever comradeship might have existed between Charlotte and her brothers was spoilt by King Leopold, who always praised his daughter at the expense of his sons. Writing to the Vicomte de Conway in 1851, he notes: 'Charlotte is so much more attentive than her brothers. It is a tragedy she is not a little boy.' And a few years later, in a letter to one of his English friends, Lady Westmorland, we read:

'Charlotte is more intelligent than her brothers.' For once the King seems to have been lacking in his usual perspicacity, for the future Leopold II was as clever, if not cleverer, than his father. But they were profoundly inimical to one another and would remain for weeks under the same roof without exchanging a word.

As a boy the younger Leopold was delicate and narrowchested, suffering from occasional bouts of depression when he hated the whole world and was even cruel and sarcastic with his little sister, whose precocious brilliance he resented in the same way as he resented his younger brother's superb health and vitality. No two brothers could have been more unalike. Philippe, Count of Flanders, was a gay, lovable extrovert with no intellectual pretensions but a lot of charm, which made him into a universal favourite. Charlotte always preferred him to Leopold, with whom she was never at her ease, whereas her 'dear fat Philippe' was always sweet and kind to her.

She does not emerge in her letters as a very lovable character. She is too preoccupied with herself, to inclined to analyse her own re-actions. We may admire the spirit which forced her to dominate her pride and temper. But there is nothing very endearing about the girl who went riding and swimming not so much for pleasure of the exer-cise, but because it was 'so good for the health and figure', and who wrote detailed reports of her physical and moral progress. At the same time there is something rather pathetic in her efforts to reflect her mother's image and her consciousness of her own defects. We find her writing in a moment of discouragement: 'I am apathetic. I have no desire to pray. I am not sufficiently keen on my studies. When I try to reason with myself, it makes no sense. I feel it is very wicked of me to be so little grateful towards God for all the spiritual and material blessings He has given me. The only thing I want is what I cannot have, which proves that I must have a very twisted mind. I cannot conquer my laziness and I fall so easily, making resolutions which I cannot keep. ... Whatever efforts I make, I never seem to improve and the effort itself is so fatiguing ... it is terrible to be so easily discouraged.'

She had none of her mother's gaiety and humour and was censorious of anything which savoured of the frivolous. When, in 1853, her father arranged a marriage between her brother Leopold and an Austrian Archduchess, a marriage for which neither the eighteen-year-old bride-groom nor the bride had the slightest inclination, we find Charlotte criticizing her new sister-in-law with the severity of an embittered spinster. The plump, jolly little Archduchess, daughter of the former Palatine of Hungary and the youngest of a large and happy family, had grown up in the Hungarian countryside and was interested in little else but riding and music. Both in character and upbringing she was totally unfitted to become the wife of a delicate, highly-strung and extremely cultivated young man to whom she ruefully admitted she would be nothing but a nurse. Physically, she was far more of a type to appeal to the father than the son, and both King Leopold and the Belgian people were enthusiastic over the young Crown Princess. At first, Charlotte echoed this enthusiasm for the sister-in-law 'who is as good as she is pretty, and if Leopold is not happy with Marie, then it is his own fault for she is in every way worthy of his affection'. But two years later she was of a very different opinion. Marie got on her nerves and she admitted that she could not stop saying unpleasant things about both Leopold and his wife, 'who has a good heart but is so utterly frivolous, spending all her time in arranging concerts. Every few weeks she gets hold of some opera singer to perform. It is all so utterly trivial. All day we hear of nothing but as to whether Madame Sforlaconi is writing or whether she's coming. Everything revolves round Madame Sforlaconi and her concert. It bores me to death, and it seems absurd to have nothing but music in one's head.'

But the fifteen-year-old girl who was so sharp in her judgments, was soon to mellow under the influence of a love which swept her off her feet, making her blind to faults which in normal times she would have been the first to criticize, so that a charming but rather superficial young man appeared to her eyes like a knight of the Holy Grail. The Archduke Ferdinand Maximilian was not the only prince to arrive in Belgium with a view to matrimony. Before Charlotte was sixteen, two suitors had already asked for her hand. One of them was her cousin, King Pedro of Portugal, whose mother, Maria de Gloria, had died in the previous year. The other was the twenty-four-year-old Prince George of Saxony, younger brother to the new King. Pedro had the advantage of being not only a ruling monarch but the candidate put forward by Queen Victoria, who considered him 'out ond out the most distinguished young Prince there is, and besides that, good, excellent and steady according to one's heart's desire – all one could wish for an only and beloved daughter. . . . I would give any of my daughters to him were he not a Catholic.' But Charlotte appears to have remained indifferent to his charms, largely through the influence of the Countess d'Hulst, who had some strange notions about the Portuguese, considering them to be 'little better than orang-outangs; people with no resources and not even a priest capable of understanding you'. Lisbon seemed very remote from Charlotte's world — a world made up of holidays spent by the sea at Ostend or in the forest of the Ardennes, or visiting her grandmother and Orléans cousins in England, where the exiled family had installed themselves at Twickenham and Claremont, the same house where King Leopold had lived the brief idyll of his first marriage.

If Lisbon seemed too remote, Dresden seemed too provincial to satisfy Coburg's ambitions, and Charlotte's suitors were still waiting in the wings when Ferdinand Maximilian arrived in Brussels in the last days of May.

Travelling from Antwerp to Brussels he was touched by the warm welcome he received in towns which had once formed part of the Austrian Netherlands, and where so many monuments and palaces recalled the days of Hapsburg domination. 'Belgium,' he writes, 'is in every way the model country which it claims to be. . . . I have never seen a greater prosperity anywhere and one cannot help but be impressed by the cleanliness and order which prevails in the smallest villages and the most crowded factory towns. There is no doubt that it owes much of its prosperity to the wise and prudent government of the King.' At Laeken he felt more at home than at St Cloud. The Saxe-Coburgs might be a new dynasty but Leopold had lived in too many Courts not to know how to conduct his own, and the difference between France and Belgium was that in Brussels Maximilian felt to be among his equals. The King, who had spent so many years in England, had acquired the art of English hospitality and did not overburden his guests with tiresome official ceremonies, while Laeken, which was only a few miles out of Brussels, was a delightful place to stay in. In his letters to his brother, the Archduke appears to have been in two minds about King Leopold. He admired his shrewdness and political acumen, but was irritated by his pedantic manner, his interminable lectures on the concert of Europe. On the very first evening, he was taken aside after dinner and treated to a monologue on the balance of power, in which Leopold referred to himself as the 'Nestor of Monarchs, from whose fund of experience everyone could learn'.

There can have been little affinity between the idealistic, impulsive young Archduke and the wise and cynical old King, whose tired eyes in a raddled face under the shiny black wig gave nothing away. Maximilian distrusted him instinctively: 'In everything he says and does, the old fox keeps showing through.' He did not appreciate King Leopold's morning visits when he appeared in his rooms just before breakfast, which had to be put off for an hour, while he pontificated on world affairs with considerable judgment and intelligence, but at such length 'that it was like listening to an article being read out of *Debats* or *L'Independance*'. And the Archduke, who was longing for his breakfast, had difficulty in suppressing his yawns. King Leopold was a bore, but his daughter was charming, with her magnolia skin, her dark luminous eyes which reflected green in the sunlight, and which gazed at him with such an undisguised admiration. For if Maximilian was attracted by Charlotte, she for her part had fallen in love almost at first sight with the handsome young Archduke, who was 'so chivalrous in his manners, so estimable in his sentiments'.

Maximilian must have realized instinctively that the gay, frivolous side of his nature, which was so essentially Viennese, would meet with little response from this quiet, serious girl, who preferred the music of Bach to that of Strauss and read history and philosophy for pleasure. Conversation with Charlotte had to be on the highest plane, and Maximilian, who was never short of a topic, entranced his listener with descriptions of his travels in the Eastern Mediterranean and his visits to the sacred shrines of Jerusalem. 'What delights me most in Max,' wrote Charlotte, 'is that he is so profoundly religious. There is nothing dry and narrow about his religion, it is a part of himself, of his true nobility of spirit. He is innately chivalrous and only thinks of doing good.' She saw in him the humanity and warmth which both the older and the younger Leopold lacked, and the lonely young girl who had been so starved of affection fastened all her romantic aspirations on a stranger who would have been the first to take fright had he realized how much she expected of him.

King Leopold saw with pleasure the mutual attraction between the young couple and played his part in flattering his guest while extolling the virtues of his daughter who, in his opinion, 'promised to be the most wonderful Princess in Europe'. Maximilian left Brussels without actually declaring himself, but matters were sufficiently advanced for King Leopold to entrust Count Mensdorff, a nephew resident in Vienna, with the task of conducting the preliminary negotiations. Though still haunted by the memory of Maria Amalia and the romance of their summer idyll, Maximilian was now in the mood to settle down. He was tired of his bachelor life in Trieste and his mind was finally made up when he returned to Austria to find his younger brother, Karl Ludwig, engaged to a Princess of Saxony. His first reference to Charlotte is in a letter to this same brother: 'She is small, I am tall, which is as it should be. She is brunette and I am fair, which is also good. She is very clever, which is a bit worrying, but no doubt I will get over that.' There is nothing very poetical or inspired in his description, written at a time when poetical effusions were the fashion. He appears to have felt a certain hesitation at becoming involved with the Coburgs, who were altogether too clever and too ambitious for his taste, and he was reluctant to become a pawn in King Leopold's dynastic schemes. On the other hand, it was flattering for him to feel that Charlotte so obviously preferred him to her other suitors, and that while he hesitated the King of Portugal was still waiting in the wings with Queen Victoria advocating his cause.

Victoria disapproved of the Austrian alliance, and it was now her turn to advise the uncle whose advice her ministers had so often resented in the past. In a letter from Balmoral we read: 'I hope by your letter that Charlotte has not finally made up her mind, as we both feel so strongly convinced of the immense superiority of Pedro over any other young prince ... besides which, the position is so infinitely preferable. The Austrian society is scandal-mongering, profligate and worthless and the Italian possessions very shaky. Pedro is full of resources, fond of music, fond of drawing, of languages, of natural history and literature, in all of which Charlotte would suit him and would be a real benefit to his country ... if Charlotte consulted her friend Vicky [the Queen's eldest daughter], I know what her answer would be, as she is very fond of Pedro.'

But Charlotte did not think of consulting Vicky, for her heart was irrevocably set on her romantic Archduke. And her father was set on strengthening his ties with Austria to secure an ally against possible French aggression. Louis Napoleon was an uncomfortable neighbour who might at any time be inspired to follow in his uncle's footsteps and incorporate Belgium in his empire. In Vienna, the prospect of a Coburg alliance was favourably received, chiefly as a means of improving relations with England. But Maximilian was back in Trieste, apparently more concerned in supervising the plans for the castle he was building on the Istrian coast than in any thoughts of marriage. And it was not until the month of October that he finally proposed. The King, who had noted a certain hesitation in the Archduke's courtship and had had certain indiscreet remarks repeated to him, adopted a half-chiding, half-teasing tone in his reply: 'My dear and honoured friend appears to regard me as a wily diplomat, whose every move is dictated by politics. I assure you this is not the case. As long ago as last May, you succeeded in winning my confidence and esteem, irrespective of any other consideration. I soon noticed that my daughter was of the same opinion. But it is always better not to rush these matters and now I am delighted to inform you that my daughter has made her choice and prefers you to all her other suitors, and that I am only too pleased to give my consent.'

But Coburg ambitions were still unsatisfied. Leopold was delighted at having secured a Hapsburg son-in-law, but life in Trieste did not afford sufficient scope for Charlotte's talents. A fond father envisaged her as Vicereine of Venetia-Lombardy. In a letter to Queen Victoria, gently breaking to her the news of Charlotte's prospective marriage, he added, 'If it takes place, the Emperor ought to put him at the head of Venice.'

8

New responsibilities

King Leopold's wish was realized sooner than he had hoped. Conditions in Austria's Italian provinces were so rapidly deteriorating that even the Emperor's advisers were beginning to realize that the oppressive military régime had been a failure and that more conciliatory methods would have to be adopted to prevent another revolution. The Minister of the Interior, Alexander Bach, suggested that a state visit to Italy might help to improve the situation, for recent visits to Styria and Bohemia had shown that the Emperor's greatest asset was his wife. Bach believed that the Empress's charm might succeed where Radetzky's bayonets had failed and, braving the disapproval of the Archduchess Sophia, he proposed not just a passing visit, but a prolonged stay of several months, with the Imperial couple holding Court in Venice and Milan in an attempt to win over the hitherto intransigent aristocracy.

The suggestion was eagerly seconded by Elisabeth, who was delighted at the prospect of escaping from Vienna for the winter and avoiding the supervision of a mother-in-law she was rapidly growing to dislike. Also Franz Josef welcomed the idea of getting away from the strained atmosphere of the Hofburg and the continual bickering between mother and wife. Only the Archduchess was bitterly opposed to his ministers exposing her beloved son to the dangers of assassination in order to please a few treacherous Italians, whose own sons were openly enlisting in the Piedmontese armies. She was still more outraged when Elisabeth insisted on taking her eldest child, a pale, delicate little girl who, according to the doctors, would have been far better left at home. But the Emperor was still so much in love that he always ended in giving way to his wife.

Preparations for the journey proceeded without the Archduchess being consulted. The royal palaces in Venice and Milan were swept and garnished, reinforcements of police were drafted to round up all likely suspects, and loyal shopkeepers, hoping for profit, produced portraits and photographs of the Imperial couple in their windows. In Trieste, Maximilian worked day and night to prepare for the royal visit, which was to include an inspection of the fleet in Venice and the laying of the foundation stone of the new naval arsenal at Pola. He was looking forward to showing his brother all he had accomplished in the past two years, and he had little time to think of Charlotte and their engagement, which was only to be publicly announced when he returned to Brussels in December.

Fortunately, Charlotte was only too ready to forgive him for his short and perfunctory notes, seeing herself as a noble sacrifice to his 'dedicated sense of duty'. Describing a man she had known for little more than a week, she writes, 'Happily we are never short of a topic for conversation. I see with joy that we really understand one another and have the same point of view on so many different things, which is the basis of a successful marriage. . . . I know it is dangerous to have too many illusions and to imagine that everything is perfect on this earth, but it would be hard to find a happier combination of talents and virtues than are to be found in Max and his family.'

While Charlotte was weaving her daydreams for the future, dramatic changes were taking place in Austria's Italian policy, which were directly to affect her married life. Contrary to the forebodings of the Archduchess Sophia, the Italian visit was sufficiently successful to cause uneasiness to Austria's enemies, and in particular to Count Cavour. The beauty-loving Italians found it hard to resist the fascinating Empress. Even those who abstained from cheering were too curious to stay away. The Venetian aristocracy might refuse to attend the gala performance at the Fenice Theatre, but in the *calles* and *piazzas* the people murmured, '*Com' è bella*' when Elisabeth went by. A witness recalls seeing her dressed in a blue velvet dress trimmed with sable, walking across the square with such an air of *grandezza* that even the most fervent of patriots involuntarily cheered. The cheering increased in volume when it became known that the Empress sympathized with the Italian nationalists, and was doing all in her power to influence her husband to grant free pardons to political rebels and to lift the ban on sequestered properties.

How could Maximilian fail to fall under the spell of a sister-in-law who subjugated the most hostile stranger to her charm? Though already the mother of two children, she was still only nineteen and in the first bloom of her radiant beauty, that mysterious, elusive beauty which fascinated and disarmed. Max was warmed by her enthusiasm for Venice, her understanding and sympathy for the Italian people and, accompanying her through the streets and canals of Venice, he appeared to have forgotten the young girl waiting for him in Brussels. That he had very little knowledge of women is apparent from the fact that when he finally joined his fiancée, just before Christmas, among his presents for Charlotte was a full-length portrait in oils of the Empress Elisabeth.

Max was in high favour with his brother, who was full of praises for the good work he had done in Venice and Trieste. In reward for his services the Archduke was promoted to the rank of Vice-Admiral, but heavier responsibilities were soon to fall on his shoulders. It had not taken the Emperor long to realize that a new brush was needed to sweep clean the Augean stables of Austrian misgovernment. What Prince Metternich referred to contemptuously as 'the Verona boutique' had outlived its purpose, and the time had come for Marshal Radetzky to be placed in honourable retirement. Franz Josef had been shocked to find how the hero of his childhood had degenerated into a pathetic and senile dodderer. But careful handling was required so as not to offend the susceptibilities of the army, who worshipped their old leader. And in an attempt to compromise, the Emperor decided to appoint his brother Max as the new Governor of Venetia-Lombardy, minus the military command, which was to be given to General Count Gyulai, the senior military officer in Italy. It was a dangerous compromise, the success of which depended on a perfect understanding and co-operation between the young Archduke and the General. And, given their opposite temperaments, this was hardly likely to succeed. In spite of his Hungarian blood, Gyulai was as reactionary and unsympathetic to nationalist aspirations as his friend and protector, Count Grünne, to whom he owed his rapid advancement in the army. He had hoped to step into Radetzky's shoes and to live in Vice-regal splendour at Monza, and his bitterness and jealousy were destined to complicate Maximilian's already difficult position.

In spite of his ambition, Maximilian appears to have shown a certain reluctance in accepting the post. Perhaps he had hoped for the full powers of Viceroy and was disappointed to be offered no more than an emasculated governorship, stripped of the military command. He also appears to have understood what later he was to forget in his enthusiasm for his task: that his brother never intended him to be more than a decorative figurehead in a country where, according to the Emperor, 'It was all-important to have a well-run Court, setting proper standards on an unruly race.' When Maximilian pleaded his youth and inexperience, Franz Josef reminded him that their younger brother, Karl Ludwig, was already Governor of the Tyrol. But Italy was not the Tyrol. It was a country which for the past ten years had been virtually an armed camp, where the Austrian garrisons were still maintained at full strength. The fact that he loved both Italy and the Italians made his task only the more difficult. Even the Archduchess Sophia appears to have had doubts as to whether Max was suited for the job. But the Emperor hastened to assure her that there was no need to worry: 'I have not the slightest doubt of his success. I consider him eminently suited to deal courteously but firmly with a people who still need a lot of schooling. He will not only educate them, but also teach them to treat the Court with proper respect. . . . Here in Venice, it should be comparatively easy, as the situation has greatly improved during our short visit. But he will have a difficult task in Milan. The fact that Max is a little afraid of it is a good sign. It shows he is conscious of the importance of his post and the seriousness of the situation.'

The Emperor was aware of the risk he was taking in separating the governorship from the military command, for the lack of understanding between the then Viceroy, the Archduke Rainier, and Field Marshal Radetzky had been largely responsible for the disasters of 1848. He writes, 'I have impressed on Max very seriously the necessity of maintaining good relations with Gyulai, and I shall repeat it a hundred times.' But neither Max nor Gyulai appears to have taken much notice of his advice.

All Maximilian's doubts and hesitations were dispelled the moment he arrived in Brussels, where the news of his appointment was received with enthusiasm both by King Leopold and his daughter. Charlotte had no doubts whatever as to her ability to play the role of Vicereine. 'I confess the prospect pleases me,' she writes. 'It will be a difficult mission, but a very rewarding one. Already I feel the thorns, but at the same time there will be an immense satisfaction in the knowledge that one is doing some good.'

The Archduke arrived in Brussels a few days before Christmas to find the whole town *en fête* for his visit. Glowing with love and pride, Charlotte produced her fiancé to the Belgian people. His new Vice-

Admiral's uniform was 'highly becoming' and she found him even better looking than before, 'while morally and spiritually he is everything I could wish'. She had been nervous that her brother Leopold might take one of his unreasoning dislikes and be rude, but she was pleasantly surprised to find that Leopold shared her enthusiasm for Max, telling her that 'if he had found anything to say against him, he would not have hesitated to do so, but he was an exceptional person from every point of view'. She had never expected they would get on so well together, 'which showed that Leopold could be agreeable when he chose'. Charlotte was too young and self-centred to grasp that Leopold too might be starved of affection, and that the delicate, sensitive young man who throughout his youth had been bullied by his father and while still an adolescent married off to a girl to whom he was not even attracted, might have found in his future brother-in-law for the first time in his life a warm and sympathetic human being.

There is something rather pathetic about Charlotte's letters, the letters of a young girl who had known so little happiness that she could not yet believe in her good fortune, while the austerity of her upbringing made her doubly appreciative of the compliments and attentions which were second nature to a Viennese. 'The Archduke is charming in every way, and you can imagine how happy I am to have him here for a week. He comes to breakfast every morning and we spend most of the day together, chatting happily till three or four in the afternoon. Naturally most of the talk revolves round our future plans. He has brought me a drawing of the castle he is building in the neighbourhood of Trieste, together with a plan of our apartments. There is to be a terrace with a fountain, a Moorish pavilion furnished in oriental style and a winter garden with various species of tropical birds.' Writing to the pious Countess d'Hulst, Charlotte adds, 'Max has promised that Mass will be said every day at Miramar.'

The Countess was bombarded with letters describing that 'paragon of Max', who dined with them every evening and, at Christmas, showered Charlotte with presents: 'a diamond brooch and earrings, a bracelet containing his hair', and the gift which was probably less appreciated but which Charlotte loyally described as 'a lovely portrait of the Empress'. Her happiness knew no bounds. She was sixteen and in love with all the ardour of a strong, passionate nature. Max, for his part, was touched by her affection and daily growing more fond of his 'clever, pretty little Charlotte', but she never inspired the romantic, chivalrous devotion he had felt for Maria Amalia. There is a small picture, painted by Marbonne at the time of their engagement, which is curiously revealing of their different characters. It shows the young couple in the gardens of Laeken, with Charlotte holding the traditional engagement bouquet, sitting very stiff and upright on a garden seat, while Maximilian leans against a tree, graceful, nonchalant and completely at his ease.

In Brussels he charmed the Belgian people as easily as he had charmed their Princess. 'Everyone sings his praises,' wrote an old friend to Charlotte's grandmother in England. But Maximilian's letters to his family made it all too clear that he was not in love. He was bored by the official ceremonies in which Charlotte delighted, and he made fun of the tedious receptions where the King presided, 'making soft and honeyed speeches which were so incredibly dreary that one had difficulty in stifling one's yawns'. His visit coincided with the twenty-fifth anniversary of Belgian independence, which gave Leopold and his ministers endless opportunities to indulge in long-winded, pompous speeches, 'glorifying the country's wonderful constitution and the King's wise administration'. Writing to Franz Josef on New Year's Day, Max described how for nearly five hours he had to 'swallow all the platitudes which were churned out by a constitutional monarch and the various local authorities'. And the Prince who prided himself on being a liberal added, 'It was an ordeal sufficient to inspire an unprejudiced observer with a profound revulsion for constitutional shams.'

There is the same note of sarcasm in his description of a constitutional Court ball, 'where the aristocracy rubs shoulders with its tailors and its cobblers, and every English shopkeeper who has retired to Brussels for reasons of economy can secure an invitation for himself and his family. All this because the Belgian régime prides itself on being democratic and does not establish a hard-and-fast rule for presentations at Court.' At this ball he appeared for the first time as officially engaged and therefore allowed to waltz in public with his fiancée, who looked exquisitely pretty in white muslin trimmed with green ribbons and garlands of flowers. It was an occasion when one would have thought he might have been too carried away by his emotions to notice the shortcomings of his fellow guests.

When it came to the question of a dowry, he behaved like a hardheaded businessman rather than a lover. He was already deeply in debt at the time and neither his large private income nor the allowance he received from the Civil List was sufficient to meet the enormous expenditure incurred in the building of the Castle of Miramar, where the granite for the terraces had to be brought from the Tyrol and even the garden soil had to be imported. He appears to have taken the attitude that, if Leopold of Saxe-Coburg wanted a Hapsburg for a son-in-law, he must expect to pay for the privilege, and within a week of his engagement he was already bringing up the question of marriage settlements and the heavy expense of maintaining a 'princely household'. But the old King was a past master at evasive replies and Maximilian left Brussels with the matter of Charlotte's dowry still unsettled.

A member of his household, a certain Baron Gagern, was entrusted with the delicate mission of bargaining with the King who assured him that he fully appreciated the situation and only hoped the Archduke would never have the unpleasant experiences he had had as a son-in-law of two of the most powerful kings in Europe. 'On the first occasion,' he said, 'my amiable father-in-law [the future George IV of England] handed me as my marriage portion the privilege of paying off the Princess Charlotte's debts, going back over several years. He seemed to think that this would make a good impression on the Princess, but I can assure you that it made a very poor impression upon me. Even now I have not forgotten it. My other father-in-law, King Louis Philippe of France, granted me what amounted to a prospective dowry, which was not paid out in full till several years later.'

But after weeks of hard bargaining, Maximilian was able to report in triumph to his brother: 'I have at last succeeded in getting the old miser to part with some of the gold on which he sets so much store.' He had every reason to be pleased, for apart from her mother's inheritance to which her father now renounced the income, the Belgian Parliament voted Princess Charlotte a dowry of one hundred thousand gulden, the same sum being contributed by the Emperor Franz Josef, who added a personal wedding gift of another thirty thousand gulden. King Leopold's own contribution was a yearly allowance of twenty-five thousand gulden, apart from the trousseau, which included some magnificent jewellery and a fine collection of gold and silver plate, the whole valued at no less than half a million gold francs. If Charlotte was aware of the haggling which went on behind the scenes, no trace of it appears in her ecstatic letters: 'Max's visit only served to confirm my good impression of his character . . . he was so kind and considerate towards me, so full of tenderness and affection.' And from Monza, the summer palace of the Italian Viceroys, the Archduke wrote to his fiancée: 'This is an enchanted domain, which only waits for its fairy Princess.'

He had rejoined his brother and sister-in-law on the last lap of their Italian tour. In Venice, the Empress's charm and affability had succeeded in dispelling the atmosphere of hostility and, during the last weeks of their visit, the Imperial couple were cheered wherever they went. But it was another matter in Milan, where all the revolutionary propaganda had been concentrated and where secret lists were carried from house to house, pledging the owners to boycott the Imperial visit. 'It is almost inconceivable how the Piedmontese are doing all in their power to sabotage our reception in Milan,' wrote Franz Josef to his mother, 'and for all these machinations, Cavour alone is responsible.' Nevertheless, the Emperor still hoped that a change of government would bring about a change of heart, and a few members of the aristocracy began to relent after the first lists of amnesties were published in *Gazzetta di Milano*. On 1 March 1857, the Emperor announced the changes he had been negotiating in the past months: the retirement of Field Marshal Radetzky and the appointment of his brother, the Archduke Ferdinand Maximilian, as Governor-General of Venetia-Lombardy. In a letter to his mother, written that same evening, we read: 'Everything here is very uncertain and the terrain could not be more difficult. Only God can help us and let us hope that Max's tact can do some good.'

From the beginning, it was clear that Maximilian had a conception of his duties very different from what had been planned in Vienna at the ministerial council, to which he had not even been invited. On the grounds of having to settle his affairs in Trieste, he deliberately abstained from making his state entry into Venice till nearly a month after the Emperor's departure when, escorted by destroyers and a fleet of merchant ships of the Austrian Lloyd, he sailed down the Adriatic from Trieste. But his arrival was ill-timed, for 22 March was the anniversary of the rising of 1848, and the Venetians woke to find the red, white and green flag of Italian nationalism fluttering from a standard in the square of St Mark. No one ever discovered who had succeeded during the night in running up the banner under the eyes of the Austrian sentries in the gas-illuminated square, and there was a further unaccountable delay in hauling it down. The offending flag was only removed a few hours before the Archduke's arrival, and the reinforcements of army and police, hastily mobilized by the frightened Podesta, cast a chilling gloom over what might have otherwise been a favourable reception.

Disappointed in his welcome, Maximilian postponed his visit to Milan and settled down to grapple with the urgent problems which confronted him. First and foremost he had to abolish the abuses and petty tyrannies which dishonoured the name of Austria, to show that he had come to Italy to protect the people rather than to exploit them. In his first speech, spoken in fluent Italian, he referred with pride to 'the Italian blood in my veins, which makes me as sympathetic to your problems as my great ancestor, Leopold II, who as Grand Duke of Tuscany succeeded in winning the love of his subjects.'

Following the demonstration in Venice, Franz Josef wrote to his brother to exert severity with justice and to see that the perpetrators of outrages were firmly punished. But Maximilian was more anxious to placate than to punish. In his enthusiasm for his task he was beginning to forget the limitations of his mission and to see himself in the role of a reigning prince. We hear of him writing to Charlotte of his plans for a Court which would rival in brilliance the great Courts of the Renaissance; envisaging a congress of Italian princes to be held at Monza where, in the intervals between shooting parties, operas and masquerades, he would discuss with his cousins of Modena and Tuscany and Naples the possibility of a customs union and a railway linking their dominion. His imagination took flight and he already saw himself at the head of the federated states of Italy.

But for the time being all plans were subordinated to his approaching marriage. On 30 May he set sail from Venice for England, where Queen Victoria, who had been so opposed to her cousin Charlotte marrying 'one of those worthless Archdukes', had relented sufficiently to invite him to stay. A visit from Charlotte a few weeks earlier had done more to mollify the sentimental Queen than all her uncle's arguments. Both she and Prince Albert had been struck by the miraculous change in the shy, introspective young girl. 'Charlotte's whole being seems to be warmed and unfolded by the love that is kindled in her heart. I have never seen so rapid a development in the space of one year,' wrote Prince Albert in a letter to Maximilian; and by 14 June, when the Austrian steam frigate *Elisabeth* was sighted off Spithead, the English Court was prepared to welcome the Hapsburg Prince into their closely-knit family circle.

On his way to England Maximilian paid a number of courtesy visits. The first was to His Holiness Pope Pius IX, who was touring the Papal states and was in residence at the Adriatic town of Pesaro. Pius IX had long since recanted his patriotic fervour of 1848, and was now living surrounded by Jesuits, in continual fear of revolution. The neglect and mismanagement which prevailed throughout his dominions were reflected in the running of the Court at Pesaro, where Maximilian accompanied His Holiness to High Mass in the Duomo, 'driving in a rickety old carriage with patched-up harness and outriders in faded liveries', after which 'the dinner served at the Papal table was more fit for a parish priest than the Head of the Roman Church. Monsignori acted as footmen and the poor quality of the meal was only partly relieved by the excellent company of the four attendant Cardinals.' His Holiness appeared to be in the best of spirits, cheered by the reception he had received in the provinces, though Maximilian himself saw little sign of enthusiasm in the apathetic crowds who lined the road on the way to the Duomo.

He writes that, by the end of the day, he was half dead with fatigue, having been in full uniform from seven in the morning to four in the afternoon, but he could pride himself on the visit having been a success. His Holiness had presented him with one of his highest Orders and condescended to the lengths of serving him with coffee and ices with his own hands. But relations with Pope Pius IX were not destined to be always of such a cordial nature, and the Emperor of Mexico was to find little sympathy and understanding from the former liberal Pope when he refused to hand back to the Mexican bishops one third of the revenues of the country.

From Pesaro, Maximilian went on to Florence, where he spent a few days as the guest of his cousin, the Grand Duke of Tuscany, before re-embarking at Leghorn en route for Lisbon, where he stayed not at the Royal Palace but at the *quinta* of the widowed Empress of Brazil. It is strange that, at a time when he should have been thinking of the future, Maximilian should have deliberately evoked the past, reviving nostalgic memories and reopening wounds which were only partially healed. His friendship with Maria Amalia's mother was to last to the end of his life and he left her in his will the holy medal he was wearing when he died.

On Sunday 15 June the S.S. *Elisabeth*, escorted up the Channel by a fleet of destroyers and greeted with a salute of twenty-one guns by the battleship *Cumberland*, arrived at Portsmouth, where the Austrian Ambassador, Count Apponyi, and the Queen's Equerry, Lord Charles Fitzroy, came on board to welcome the Archduke. From Portsmouth, a special train conveyed him to Windsor, where he was straightaway plunged into the intimate family circle of the most united of royal couples. It must have been an unnerving experience for a stranger to arrive at a time when the whole family were gathered together for the christening of the Queen's youngest child. But Maximilian appears to have felt completely at home in an atmosphere which was at once bourgeois and grandiose, where the spartan routine of life at Windsor contrasted with the traditional splendour of the Court at Buckingham Palace. His visits to units of the British Mediterranean Fleet had filled him with admiration for 'the comfort and the elegance' of the British way of life. 'England,' he wrote, 'is the only northern country in which I could forget the South.' He found in the dowdy little Queen, who somehow managed to combine cosiness with stateliness, the same qualities he had found so endearing in the Governor of Gibraltar and his wife – the unaffected friendliness and innate simplicity of people who are completely sure of themselves.

Victoria, for her part, reacted just as her uncle had foreseen, and she enthused to King Leopold, 'I cannot tell you how much we like the Archduke. He is charming, so clever, natural, kind and amiable, so *English* in his feelings and likings, and so anxious for the best understanding between Austria and England. With the exception of his mouth and chin, he is good-looking, but I think one does not in the least bother about that, as he is so very kind, clever and pleasant. I wish you really joy, dearest Uncle, at having got such a husband for dear Charlotte, and I am sure he is quite worthy of her. He may and will do a great deal for Italy.' King Leopold must have smiled at this rapturous description of a young man who, only a few weeks before, had been dismissed as 'one of those worthless Archdukes'.

The Prince Consort was at once attracted to Maximilian, discovering in him tastes similar to his own. Two days after his arrival, he was already noting in his diary, 'We have grown quite attached to the Archduke,' and in a letter to Baron Stockmar, he describes Charlotte's fiancé as 'a very remarkable young man, very *anglomâne*, with nothing of the bigot about him'. The same note of praise is echoed when writing to his brother, the Duke of Saxe-Coburg Gotha: 'The Archduke has been with us since the fourteenth. We have learnt to appreciate him as a very distinguished and promising young man whom we are pleased to welcome into our family. His liberal-minded political views give hope of a happier prospect for the Italians.'

Maximilian's popularity in England extended beyond the family circle. Queen Victoria's Whig ministers, who were usually so suspicious of her Continental relatives and particularly prejudiced against everyone with the name of Hapsburg, were won over by his tolerance and frankness, his willingness to discuss not only Italian politics but such controversial subjects as the Hungarian situation, on which the Archduke expressed far more liberal opinions than were voiced by the Austrian Ambassador. London hostesses, so avid for celebrities, were ready to lionize the Hapsburg Prince in the same way as they had lionized the revolutionary Kossuth. But Maximilian had little time to spare for the routs and balls of the London season. This was strictly a family visit and when he was not accompanying the Royal Family to one of Handel's oratorios at the Crystal Palace or the Italian Opera at the Haymarket, he was visiting Charlotte's grandmother, the widowed Queen of France, at Claremont, or his Orléans cousins at Twickenham. His success in England was viewed with a jaundiced eye both in Paris and Turin. This flirtation between Austria and England did not suit the plans of Napoleon III, while Cavour feared that a liberal-minded Archduke on friendly terms with England might prove a far more formidable opponent to Italian aspirations than all Radetzky's bayonets. But the success of Maximilian's visit aroused just as many suspicions in Vienna as in Paris or Turin. Neither Franz Josef nor his ministers approved of his brother discussing politics with Queen Victoria, nor was it appreciated when Lord John Russell suggested to the Austrian Ambassador that the best solution to the Hungarian problem would be to make it into a separate kingdom with the Archduke Ferdinand Maximilian as King.

Meanwhile, Brussels was preparing for the royal wedding. The old aristocracy, the princes and counts of the former Holy Roman Empire like the de Lignes, the Merodes and the de Grünnes, were opening out their palaces and hanging out their finest tapestries to receive the influx of royal guests. First to arrive was the Milanese nobleman, Count Archinto, who in reward for his Austrian sympathies had been nominated by the Emperor as Ambassador Extraordinary to the Court of Brussels. The Count, who was noted for his wealth and love of ostentation, had served in his youth as chamberlain to the first Napoleon, and now paraded with an equal enthusiasm his devotion to the Austrian Emperor. To this day, the Archinto family lament the folly and extravagance of their ancestor who, on this mission to Brussels, travelled at his own expense in a gala carriage with postillions and outriders, renting and at times actually buying the villas and castles he stayed in on the way, saying it was not fit for an Ambassador of His Imperial and Apostolic Majesty to put up at wayside inns.

The Hapsburgs were represented by Maximilian's younger brother, Karl Ludwig, and his bride, Margaret of Saxony. The Coburgs and Orléans were there in strength, from the reigning Duke of Saxe-Coburg Gotha to the ex-Queen Marie Amélie of France who, supported by four sons, had crossed the Channel to assist at the marriage of her favourite granddaughter. Among the most honoured of the guests was the Prince Consort of England, whose presence was a proof of Queen Victoria's attachment to her uncle. She herself admitted to being the most possessive of wives, who could not bear to be separated from her husband for a day, and in a letter to King Leopold she writes, 'I cannot give you a greater proof of my love for you all and of my anxiety to give you and dearest Charlotte pleasure, than in urging dearest Albert to go over. Your cannot think how much this costs me, or how completely forlorn I am and feel when he is away, or how I count the hours until he returns.'

The most enthusiastic of the wedding guests, outnumbering the Imperial, Royal and Serene Highnesses, were the rich burghers of Brussels, who were devoted to their pretty little Princess, to whose dowry they had all contributed and whose wedding dress of white and silver brocade had been woven in the looms of Ghent, while her veil, a work of art of the lace-makers of Brussels, had been presented to her by the town.

The Archduke arrived at Laeken on 24 July, only three days before the wedding, to find Charlotte in an emotional and somewhat tearful state at the prospect of leaving her father and her old home. Even the cold, self-contained Leopold was showing signs of stress and Prince Albert reported back to Victoria that he had 'never seen Uncle so moved'. But Charlotte was a radiant bride on the morning of 27 July, and Maximilian, dressed in the full dress uniform of an Austrian Admiral, with the collar of the Order of the Golden Fleece round his neck, was as handsome a bridegroom as any young girl could have wished. The general comment of the guests assembled in the Royal

Chapel was that the young couple seemed very much in love. But the Prince of Saxe-Weimar struck a discordant note when he wrote: 'The young Princess has an elegant disposition and an excellent figure but she has a rather strange look and is totally lacking in charm and grace.'

The following days were so taken up with social functions, culminating in a great ball given by the town of Brussels, that bride and bridegroom had not a moment to themselves before they left Laeken on 30 July, by which time Charlotte was showing signs of strain and Maximilian was longing for the peace of his garden in Trieste. *L'Independence Belge* reports a curious scene which took place on the morning of their departure, when Charlotte paid a last visit to her mother's grave. The Archduke, who accompanied her to the church, was kept waiting for over an hour while Charlotte, with tears pouring down her face, remained deep in prayer kneeling by the tomb. In the end, he had almost to carry her away in an exhausted, half-fainting condition. Faced with such religious fervour, a filial piety bordering on hysteria, Maximilian may have realized for the first time how little he knew his wife. But the tired, overwrought girl was infinitely more touching than the brilliant, self-assured young woman who had danced till dawn the night before. And this new, vulnerable Charlotte aroused all that was best and most chivalrous in his nature, so that by the time they had crossed the Belgian frontier into Germany, Charlotte had dried her tears and Maximilian had fallen in love.

At Bonn they embarked on a river steamer and travelled up the Rhine to Mainz. From Mainz to Nuremberg and on to Ratisbon, where a flower-decked boat was waiting to take them down the Danube to Vienna. All that we know of the first days of their married life is from Charlotte's ecstatic letters. 'I could not be happier than I am,' she writes. 'Max is perfection in every way.' These words give the lie to the many rumours of Max's reputed deficiencies as a husband. Few men have been so slandered in their private life as he was, first by the Emperor's military clique, the Gyulais and the de Grünnes, who, unable to understand or sympathize with his poetic sensibility and artistic enthusiasms, did not hesitate to label him effeminate and impotent. In later years in Mexico, the rumours were of another nature. First the clergy in their rage against the liberal Emperor, then the Republicans in their efforts to destroy him, denounced him as a libertine, a womanizer, a corrupter of public morals. Only the Italians came near to understanding his strange, complex character, that mixture of idealism and vanity, of weakness and of bravery, of modesty and pride. And it is to their credit that not even his political opponents, not even the Mazzinis and Cavours, ever cast a single aspersion on his private life. The rumour of Maximilian's alleged impotence was entirely confined to what Queen Victoria called 'the *médisante* society of Vienna'. In spite of her piety and the austerity of her upbringing, Charlotte was very much her father's daughter, with the strong sexual appetites of the Coburgs, and for all her inexperience, Maximilian must have been a satisfactory lover to rank as 'perfection' in her eyes.

The Archduchess Sophia who had travelled from Vienna to meet the young couple at the Danube port of Linz, was enchanted to see them looking 'so blissfully happy'. She had left the Vienna Court in mourning, with the Emperor and Empress suffering the first tragedy of their married life. Their eldest child, Sophie, who had been delicate since birth, had died during a state visit to Hungary and Elisabeth felt herself to be directly responsible for her death. Again she had openly defied her mother-in-law by taking both her children with her. A slight attack of measles, from which the baby Gisela had recovered in a week, proved fatal to the already ailing Sophie. And a visit which began in triumph, with the beautiful Empress making an even greater impact than in Italy, ended in disaster. Miserable and contrite, blaming herself both as a wife and mother, Elisabeth shut herself away from the world, refusing to see her mother-in-law for fear of her reproaches. And the Archduchess, who adored her grandchildren and was just as unhappy although more controlled than her daughter-in-law, had come to Linz to warn Max that in the circumstances he would have to curtail his visit to Vienna, for no one was in the mood for the festivities which a young bride had the right to expect on her first meeting with her husband's family.

In private, the Archduchess may also have confided to Max that life at Schönbrunn during the past year had been completely disrupted by the whims and moods of the young Empress, who from a shy and wayward girl had grown into a spoiled and capricious young woman who made no attempt to carry out her obligations and was obsessed by her own beauty. Sophia looked with approval at the radiantly healthy Charlotte, whose somewhat stocky figure seemed ideal for child-bearing and who would surely produce the sons which Elisabeth had so far failed to have. 'She was so pretty, so clever and fascinating as well.' The Archduchess was loud in praise and Max was delighted to see that his wife and mother were instinctively drawn to one another. 'The dear Archduchess already treats me as a daughter,' wrote Charlotte to her beloved Countess d'Hulst.

But the atmosphere was less congenial in Vienna, in spite of the Emperor having given orders for the Court to come out of mourning for a gala reception in honour of the new Archduchess. Franz Josef had learnt early in life to put his public duties before his personal feelings. The sorrowing father was first and foremost an Emperor, welcoming Charlotte into the family with an exquisite courtesy, treating Max with a brotherly affection, while making it quite clear that he expected them to leave for Italy the following day. But Elisabeth, who was neither as restrained nor as disciplined as her husband, bitterly resented having to come out of her retirement at Laxenburg in order to receive a sister-in-law in whom she had not the slightest interest and who was already rendered unsympathetic by her mother-in-law's praises. Max as a bachelor had been a gay and charming companion, sharing her love of poetry and of nature. There would never be the same happy relationship now that he was married to a tiresomely clever wife. Nor were matters improved when Elisabeth's enemies at Court, the princesses who had been denied the right of *entrée* to her apartments, the ladies-in-waiting who had been dismissed, echoed the Archduchess's praise of the Belgian Princess, daughter and granddaughter of kings, whose manner and bearing proclaimed her Bourbon blood. 'Such a contrast,' they whispered, 'to the wilful young Empress who had never received any education and had been allowed to run wild on the farm at Possenhofen.'

Elisabeth appeared at the gala reception at Schönbrunn dressed in white, looking spectacularly beautiful and pathetically sad, making no attempt to put her young sister-in-law at her ease and barely opening her mouth throughout the evening. It was a glittering reception, with all the traditional formality of the Austrian Court. The highest dignitaries of the Empire were present: Archdukes and Princes, Knights of the Golden Fleece, Archduchesses weighed down by their tiaras, Hungarian Magnats ablaze with gold-embroidered cloaks and jewel-encrusted swords, and paladins of the army in white uniforms, with the diamond cross of the Maria Theresa Order – the most aristocratic Court of Europe parading its archaic splendour in honour of the little Belgian Princess, who found it all very different from the 'constitutional' balls of Brussels.

Glowing with pride, she wrote: 'Already, I feel myself heart and soul an Archduchess. I am so fond of my new family and from the first day, feel completely at home with them.' She left Vienna before she had time to be disillusioned, for after twenty-four hours she and Max were already on their way to Italy. But if Charlotte was too young and impressed to note the underlying tensions, or to wonder why they had made the long journey down the Danube in order to spend only one day in Vienna, Max was acutely aware of the strained relations in the family circle, the growing estrangement between his mother and the Empress, the difficulties of the Emperor in dealing with a wife he adored but failed to understand. He was hurt that Franz Josef no longer confided in him, treating him in public as a brother but in private as a stranger. And he resented the elaborate preparations, the festivities laid on in Trieste, the royal progress to the Italian frontier, all planned in such a way as to ensure that they would not extend their stay at Schönbrunn by as much as another day.

The disagreeable impressions of Vienna faded the moment they reached Trieste – a white city, glittering in the August sunlight, decked out with flowers and banners to welcome the beloved Archduke and his bride. The strains of the *Brabançonne* mingled with the Austrian *Gott Erhalte Unser Kaiser*; gunfire re-echoed across the water from the battleships anchored in the harbour, and amidst scenes of tumultuous rejoicing the Archducal couple drove to the municipal palace where Charlotte made her first speech in Italian, thanking the mayor and council for their welcome, delighting them by saying that her husband had spoken to her so often of Trieste and his affection for the Triestini, that she had grown to love the city before she had even seen it, 'and now, after the warmth of my welcome, I love it even more'.

Italy was a revelation to a girl born under the pale, washed skies of Flanders, who till now had only known the cold North Sea breaking against the beaches of Ostende and Zoute. Flowers she had never seen growing outside the conservatories of Laeken bloomed in a riot of colour in the gardens of the Villa Lazarovic – 'a gem of a house, set in this marvellous southern climate, overlooking one of the most beautiful gulfs on earth. In the North, one cannot imagine that a sea can be so intensely blue. I was beside myself with excitement when I saw it for the first time.' What Charlotte described as 'a wonderful week in Trieste' culminated with a state visit to Venice, and not even a rough crossing could damp her enthusiasm when, entering into the lagoons, she had her first vision of the city whose magical beauty surpassed all she had imagined. 'Venice,' she wrote, 'has something that attracts, seduces, fascinates to a point that one feels one has always lived there and longs to live there forever. It has an enchantment that enslaves the soul.' If Venice enchanted Charlotte, she in turn enchanted her husband by her interest and knowledge of history and of art. A few months before, he might have labelled her as a blue-stocking, but that was a time when he was still under the spell of Elisabeth, who in Venice had only her poetic intuition to guide her and preferred fairly tales to fact. Charlotte, on the contrary, was eager to learn, sharing his passion for sightseeing, spending every free moment in visiting churches and museums. And what pleased him even more was to find that she thoroughly enjoyed the civic banquets and receptions which he looked upon as unavoidable and often tiresome duties. In a letter to her old governess, we find Charlotte admitting to being still of an age when everything has the charm of novelty: 'I confess that I really enjoy myself at all these receptions and dinners and am not in the least exhausted by them. Perhaps later, when I am older, I will begin to be bored.'

The atmosphere in Venice was rather more friendly than on Maximilian's first arrival. His reforms were beginning to take effect. Acting against the advice both of the bureaucrats and of the military authorities, he had allowed free municipal elections for the first time in many years. His faith was justified, for there were no political disturbances during the election, at which Count Marcello, a Venetian nobleman who had spent many years in England, was elected mayor. Marcello was one of the few patriotic Italians who, without ever having been an *Austriazzanti*, genuinely believed that his people had more to gain under the rule of a mild and liberal Archduke than by linking up with the nationalists of Turin and relying on the eventual support of France.

In his youthful optimism, Maximilian counted on overcoming the opposition of Milan, and the long-heralded state visit took place on 6 September. It was an occasion for all the pageantry and pomp in which Maximilian and the Italians delighted. Gala carriages, mouldering in museums since the days of the Spanish Viceroys, were upholstered and regilded, powdered wigs and eighteenth-century liveries were taken out of store. The Archducal couple, arriving from Monza, mounted the state coach two miles outside the city, Maximilian wearing his Admiral's uniform and the seventeen-year-old Charlotte looking very regal and mature in a red velvet crinoline trimmed with heavy lace, and a diamond crown entwined with roses. The civic and military authorities were waiting to receive them in a pavilion erected at the Porto Venezia, from where the procession moved slowly down the Corso to the Royal Palace. There were more presentations, more flattering addresses, and a crowd of notables filled the state apartments. But the great names of the Milanese aristocracy could be counted on one hand. Viscontis and Borromeos, Addas and Maffeis were conspicuously absent. Those who were there had come largely out of curiosity to see the young Archduchess, whose father King Leopold was admired and respected as the liberal ruler of a model kingdom. But, having come, they were one and all charmed by Charlotte's perfect Italian and Maximilian's affability. It was impossible to dislike this good-looking young couple who were so anxious to please, so full of good intentions. But the nationalists of Turin were determined these good intentions should come to nothing, and we read in the memoirs of Giovanni Visconti-Venosta: 'Up till now, Milanese society had ignored the Austrian Governor-Generals and their Courts. We made a point of never referring to them in conversation. But Maximilian had only been here two months, and already everyone was speaking about him, something which had never happened before to any Austrian Prince or Governor. He liked to be in the public eye and to attract attention, and because we could no longer ignore either him or his mission, we had to fight him by every means in our power and make it impossible for him to carry out his plans.'

9

The end of Venetia-Lombardy

Preserved in the files of the Vienna State Archives is a pile of documents which includes an incomplete manuscript entitled, 'The Story of the Government of Venetia-Lombardy, 1857–1859'. These papers, giving Maximilian's own account of his two years' rule as Italian Viceroy, were entrusted by him to a Professor Wildauer of the University of Graz, with a view to eventual publication. The most interesting part, a preface written in French by Charlotte, reads as a passionate indictment of the Imperial government in Vienna who, by its crass stupidity, ended in destroying all her husband's hopes of reconciling the Italians to Austrian rule.

No wife could have been more dedicated than this little Belgian Princess, who distributed large sums out of her private income to Italian hospitals and schools, absorbed every aspect of Italian culture – patronizing the local artists, studying Tasso with her gentlemen-in-waiting – and only regretting that she could do so little to help her husband who had 'so much on his hands'. 'Every day,' she writes, 'I grow to appreciate and love him more, for he does everything to please me and is, at the same time, so utterly selfless, only wanting to do good and to succeed in his difficult task.'

In the first year, it seemed as if Maximilian might yet achieve a miracle. He was tireless in his efforts to woo all sections of the population and to eradicate the causes of their discontent. Gian-Battista Bolza, who had taught him Italian as a boy, was summoned to Monza to put him in touch with the deans and rectors of the various universities. Italian jurists and economists were invited to take part in the reorganization of the provinces, which years of military government had reduced to a state of economic depression. The silk industry, which in those days provided Lombardy with its chief means of livelihood, had been allowed to fall into decline; bad harvests had brought famine to the Valtellina;

irrigation and drainage schemes had been suspended and large areas of the Po and Ticino valleys were still uncultivated wasteland. To meet the needs of the military government, exorbitant taxes had been levied in some of the poorest districts, while the educational system in a country which, to quote Maximilian, boasted 'a Galileo, a Dante and a Volta', was subjected to an alien culture, with German as the compulsory language in schools. The Archduke's greatest triumph was when the celebrated historian, Cesare Cantú, accepted the task of collaborating in the projected educational reforms. The intransigent nationalists of Turin never forgave Cantú for his friendship with a Hapsburg and he was never made either a Senator or the Chancellor of a university. The economist Jacini suffered the same fate in being penalized and ostracized by his friends for acts of disinterested service to Maximilian's government. But only a small minority collaborated. Most of the intellectuals followed Manzoni's example in refusing invitations to the Court of Monza. When Milan's most celebrated citizen fell ill in the autumn of 1857, Maximilian ordered daily bulletins to be published in the press and carried condescension to the lengths of calling in person at Manzoni's house to enquire after his health. But when he wished to present him with a decoration or a pension, Manzoni answered that, having refused the decorations both of the King of Prussia and the Grand Duke of Tuscany, he could 'hardly make an exception for the Emperor of Austria', thereby underlining the fact that, in the eyes of the author of *I Promessi Sposi*, Franz Josef was no more than a foreign monarch.

Nevertheless, Maximilian's open-handed generosity began to make an impact on the masses. He was the first to inaugurate a public lottery in aid of the distressed areas of the Valtellina; the first to arrive on the scene of disaster when floods devastated whole districts of the Po valley, leaving thousands of people homeless. Every case of hardship brought to his notice was helped out of his privy purse, and he did everything in his power to expedite the repatriation of political exiles, obstructed in almost every case by the military authorities and the dreaded *Geheim Polizei* who, in spite of his protests, were still directed from Vienna. Maximilian's enemies maintained that all these generous actions were dictated by personal ambition. And if he made a mistake, it was in encouraging the illusion that he was possessed of greater powers than in reality he had. But given his Utopian character, he was probably the first victim of his own illusions, seeing himself as another Eugéne de Beauharnais, hoping to revive in Italy the glories of Napoleon's Viceroy. Times had changed and some of his most loyal advisers, Cantú among them, tried to tell him that all this luxury was out of place. But he was too much of a Wittelsbach to resist the temptation to restore the splendours of the past in palaces where, for so many years, the frescoes had been allowed to moulder and the tapestries to fade. The Emperor had ordered him to conciliate the aristocracy by holding a brilliant Court and he carried out his orders to the letter. In Charlotte, he had a beautiful and clever wife who, in spite of her youth, was already the most accomplished of Vicereines, never so happy as when she had the opportunity of wearing full regalia, receiving homage in the Reggio of Milan.

Some of the loveliest palaces of Italy were at their disposal: the old palace of the Doges of Venice where they delighted in reviving the ancient ceremonies of the Republic; the former home of the Gonzagos in Mantua; Stra, with its hundred statues mirrored in the Brenta, and Archduke Rainier's cypress-shadowed villa on Lake Como. But it was at Monza that they made their home in the yellow eighteenth-century villa, eight miles outside Milan, 'where even in November', wrote Charlotte, 'the magnolias and ilexes still give one the illusion of summer', though she had to confess that at the moment of writing, 'there is a fog that is worthy of London'. At times she must have wondered what those austere Belgian countesses, Mesdames de Grünne and d'Hülst, would have made of their Court, where Max indulged to the full his taste for the exotic, and Dalmatians in their national costume, with jewelled *yataghans* and a whole arsenal of other weapons, stood guard at the doors. Twenty to thirty people were invited every day to dine, entertained to a first-class orchestra and served by footmen in eighteenth-century liveries, with buttonholes of fresh roses, while little negro pages, living replicas of the sculptured blackamoors in Venetian palaces, served the coffee and handed round the ices.

Maximilian was always trying to attract new elements to Monza. Once it was a congress of scientists, another time of poets. He was at his happiest in the role of a Maecenas and he obtained large sums from the Imperial Treasury for the restoration of artistic monuments neglected by the military régime. Artists and architects were favoured guests at Monza, and Milan in particular owes much to Maximilian's interest in the arts. It was he who inspired the vast monumental square in front of the Duomo and the opening out of the Piazza della Scala, where the statue of Leonardo still stands. The famous Ambrosiana Library was restored under his direction and he gave the city its public gardens. St Mark's in Venice and St Antony's in Padua were both restored out of government funds. But there were times when his Italian advisers had to put a curb to the unrestrained romanticism of his German blood, and he was fortunately dissuaded from placing orange trees in the Square of St Mark, and using the Campanile as a lighthouse.

The greater part of the aristocracy stayed away from Monza with the exception of the hard core of the *Austriazzanti*, who throughout the centuries had served foreign powers and who, according to Maximilian, 'were on the whole a lot of frivolous and servile place-seekers'. But now and then one of the old families, a Bembo from Venice, a Valmarano from Vicenza, a Cicogna from Milan, succumbed to his blandishments and, with characteristic optimism, he recounted that he was 'gaining adherents every day'. The Archduchess Sophia, who visited the young couple in the late autumn of 1857 and found in the serenity of Monza a happy escape from the nervous tensions of Schönbrunn, wrote home to the Emperor of 'the wonderful work dear Max is accomplishing in Italy'. Others, more impartial than the Archduchess, echoed her praise.

Maximilian's dream of autonomous government for Venetia-Lombardy, with a Ministry of Italian Affairs in Vienna, was anathema both to the nationalists of Turin and to the military die-hards of Verona. 'We must do something to bring back martial law in Lombardy,' was Cavour's exasperated comment on Maximilian's growing prestige. In the memoirs of Prince Alexander of Hesse, who was serving with the Austrian army in Italy, we read of 'the bitterness of Austrian officers who found themselves excluded from the balls at Monza, for fear that the sight of their uniform might offend the delicate susceptibilities of the Italian ladies'. Officers who had worshipped Radetzky had little use for the artistic, pro-Italian Archduke, who was always writing to Vienna to try to get some political offender pardoned, some military sentence rescinded.

At the beginning of 1858, Maximilian's star was still in the ascendant. But on 15 January a bomb thrown outside the Paris Opera House attracted world attention to the Italian Question. Orsini's attempt to assassinate the French Emperor, who had betrayed his *Carbonari* past and broken the promises he had made to the cause of Italian freedom, shattered the glittering façade of the Second Empire. The most brilliant lawyer in Paris undertook Orsini's defence, drawing the attention of Europe to the 'oppressed provinces of Italy, groaning under the foreign yoke'. The publication of the famous letter of accusation against Napoleon made the assassin into a hero, the victim conscious of his guilt. While Maximilian pressed forward with his reforms which, in Vienna, were dismissed as 'so much youthful and undigested nonsense', printed copies of Orsini's letter were being smuggled into Venetia-Lombardy and circulated through all classes of the population. The revolutionary fanatic, who had devoted his life to free his country from oppression, became almost overnight the idol of the students of Padua and Pavia.

Orsini's trial, where not even the eloquence of Jules Favre could save him from the death penalty, coincided with the tenth anniversary of the 1848 revolution. Maximilian did his best to minimize the demonstrations which took place both in Venice and Milan, making a point of walking with Charlotte through the most crowded streets, past cafés frequented by the revolutionaries, and feigning not to notice when patriotic ladies appeared at the Scala and Fenice Theatre wearing mourning in sympathy for Orsini. But the anniversary put the military authorities into a panic and he was unable to prevent them from reporting to Vienna the most trivial of student demonstrations. There was a renewal of perquisitions and arrests. Harmless family gatherings, such as the funeral of a member of the opposition, or a race meeting held on a private estate, were broken up by the police and all Maximilian's protests fell on unheeding ears.

Meanwhile, the European Chancelleries were discussing the possibilities of a congress devoted to Italian affairs. The evacuation of foreign troops from Papal Rome was to be the focal point of discussion, but conditions in Venetia-Lombardy were also to come under review, a decision bitterly resented by the Austrian Emperor. In May 1858, Maximilian travelled to Vienna to urge that his plans for local government should come into effect before the opening of the conference, but he found his brother completely under the influence of his ministers and entirely committed to the old unilateral system. Franz Josef declared: 'Neither now nor ever can there be any question of the Italian provinces being governed independently of Vienna. Such a thing might have been possible a hundred years ago, but now it would only weaken the monarchy and encourage revolution. Our interests in Italy cannot be judged purely from the Italian point of view. They depend far more on the solidarity of the Empire as a whole.' To stress this 'solidarity' his Finance Minister, Baron Bruck, was contemplating a measure which was to sound the death-knell of all Maximilian's hopes: the old Italian coinage was to be replaced by the Austrian florin and depreciated by three per cent to bring it into line with the rest of the Empire.

Mutual resentment and distrust was growing between the two brothers. Franz Josef suspected Maximilian of confiding in King Leopold and of acting on his advice. The Belgian King owned the Villa d'Este on Lake Como, which he had inherited from his first wife, and he had been staying there for several weeks, in constant touch with his son-in-law and daughter, whose villa on the lake adjoined his own. Confidences made to King Leopold found their way to England and Lord John Russell, one of the leading spirits behind the European Conference, openly advocated that Venetia-Lombardy should become an autonomous province under the Archduke's rule.

Maximilian, on his side, regarded the attitude of his brother's ministers as slighting and offensive. Disillusioned but not wanting to return with empty hands to those who still believed in him, he deliberately absented himself from his dominions for nearly three months, thereby showing for the first time that intrinsic weakness in his character which was so often to betray him in later life, when periods of restless activity and almost dynamic energy gave way to disillusion and inertia. He returned with Charlotte to their villa in Trieste, seeking escape from the disappointments of public life in superintending the works at Miramar, the white limestone castle with the terraced gardens he had conjured from the bare rocks of the Karso. A fortune had been spent in the realization of a dream cherished from his earliest childhood, when he had said that all he wanted in life was 'a castle with a garden by the sea'. Charlotte was still sufficiently young and sufficiently in love not to question his decisions. But she was a fighter by nature and would have been happier to have stayed in Venice or Milan, putting up a brave front to the opposition rather than to have retired to the rose gardens of Miramar. But life with Max was still full of enchantment and the girl who wrote home, 'I am as happy in my private life as it is possible to be', had not yet learnt to criticize her husband. They celebrated their first wedding anniversary by taking an Adriatic cruise, travelling *incognito* as the Marchesa di Miramar, and visiting the shrine of the Madonna of Loreto, where Charlotte prayed for what she had most at heart — to have a child by her beloved Max.

Only a few weeks later came the birth of a Hapsburg heir. Elisabeth had at last produced the long-awaited son and *Te Deums* were celebrated throughout the Empire. Maximilian, who was no longer the Heir Apparent, returned to Milan to stage a whole series of festivities in a town where even some of his former friends no longer dared to be seen in his company for fear of being insulted in the streets. The proud young Archduke, who had mocked at the parvenu society of Paris and the constitutional balls of Brussels, now opened his doors to bankers, Jews and tradespeople to fill the gaps left by the absent members of the aristocracy, while a few minor reforms grudgingly conceded by Vienna were publicly announced as being the forerunners of a whole series of concessions. But no one was any longer under the delusion that these concessions would be granted.

News of a secret meeting in the Vosges Mountains between Napoleon and Cavour had filtered through to the Ball-platz, but little was known of what had taken place at the meeting, and we find Maximilian writing to his brother: 'Cavour's recent visit to Plombières, where he went without being invited, is causing me considerable anxiety and strikes me as having been a very able move on his part.' He himself had tried to play the diplomat, with one of those well-intentioned gestures which only served to irritate Franz Josef, sending a special envoy to Paris to present the French Emperor with a small bronze medal of Canova's statue of Napoleon. Apart from the usual exchange of complimentary letters, very little was achieved by this, for the French Emperor was already definitely committed. Haunted by the ghost of Orsini and dreams of Imperial grandeur, Napoleon had allowed himself to be seduced by Cavour, and the offer of Nice and Savoy as the price of his alliance in a war with Austria. It was a war in which he insisted that neither France or Piedmont-Sardinia must appear as the aggressor, so long as the English still cherished the hope that the Italian Question could be settled round a conference table.

Encouraged by French support, the nationalists of Venetia-Lombardy redoubled their activities. Dreams of an independent Mazzinian republic were vanishing as more and more patriots gave their allegiance to Piedmont, and the cross of Savoy became the symbol of Italian unity. In retaliation, the Austrian government reverted to its old policy of coercion and repression. The promised concessions remained a dead letter; a congress of educational reform convoked by Maximilian was abruptly suspended by order of the Vienna Minister of Education; the introduction of the Austrian florin and the subsequent depreciation of the currency enraged the bankers and the merchants, who till now had been the classes most favourable to Austria; extra levies were conscripted for the army, from which only-sons and the fathers of young families were no longer exempt, and a new proviso was enforced by which no man could marry under the age of twenty-three, before he had completed his military service. These laws were of such an appalling stupidity that Count Cavour was tempted to believe that Vienna had introduced them on purpose, so as to stir up opposition and give the authorities the excuse to reintroduce martial law. But, on second thoughts, he realized he was giving the Austrians 'credit for an intelligence they did not possess'.

It was tragic for Maximilian to see everything he had worked so hard to achieve destroyed almost overnight. General Gyulai was triumphant and the secret police were in full control. On 12 September 1858 the Archduke addressed a formal letter to the Emperor asking to be relieved of his duties as Governor-General and to return to his post in the navy, only to be told that his resignation then would have a deplorable effect and that, in loyalty to his country, he would have to remain. Family mourning now added to the political gloom: while on a visit to Monza, Karl Ludwig's young wife died from an attack of fever. Maximilian was able to note how the Italians deliberately separated their personal feelings from their political opinions. Those who still liked and respected him as a private individual offered their condolences in a family tragedy, while openly supporting the House of Savoy. In an embittered letter to his mother, he wrote: 'If I did not feel it was my sacred duty to remain here, I would have long since left this unhappy country where every day I feel more and more humiliated at having to represent a supine government totally devoid of common sense. Today, when I came to Milan, I was profoundly ashamed to see how the very people who are willing to show me respect as a private individual, completely disassociate me from the government I represent. Nothing is more calculated to show me how powerless I am. Today the whole country speaks with one voice, expressing indignation and disapproval. I am not afraid, for the Hapsburgs were not born to be afraid, but I am humiliated and silenced. If the situation gets worse, I plan to send Charlotte to her father in

Brussels, because I do not see why she should be sacrificed, and in times of danger this is no place for a young and inexperienced woman. At present everything is in complete chaos. Everyone around me seems to have lost their head and their courage and I ask myself for how long will my conscience allow me to follow blindly the orders of Vienna.'

Unfortunately, the Archduchess Sophia was not the only one to hear his complaints. He was always too ready to confide, too impulsive in his speech and Charlotte was still more outspoken in criticizing the Austrian authorities in front of her Italian ladies-in-waiting. The foreign press delighted in reporting that the liberal-minded Archduke was in opposition to Vienna, and it is not surprising if Franz Josef ended in resenting what he regarded as his brother's disloyalty. We find him writing in his coldest and most formal manner: 'I cannot expect you always to agree with my decisions, but I have got to be sure that what I have decided upon will be promptly carried out and that the opposition will not be encouraged in the idea that you are on their side. This, naturally, does not deny you the right to your own opinions. What I object to is having your actions and remarks reported in the foreign press, in particular the *Algemeine Zeitung*, who publish your plans for local government and your criticism of the new conscription laws in such a way that all the odium and unpopularity falls on my shoulders. Above all, I must insist that the present disturbances are not blamed on Vienna but rather on the bad faith and innate antagonism of the Italian people as a whole, and the subversive activities of Turin and Paris, who are doing whatever they can to ferment trouble. This situation cannot last for long. Either it will come to war, from which with the help of God we will emerge victorious, but which it is our duty if possible to prevent, or things will settle down and better times will come again.'

From this letter, it appears that Franz Josef suspected his brother of sympathizing with the opposition. And the last appeal from Maximilian, to dismiss the incompetent Gyulai and put him in sole control in case of a general uprising, was abruptly refused. Gyulai retained the confidence both of the Emperor and of his ministers and the Archduke was exhorted to abide by his decisions. By the beginning of 1859, the Italian situation was verging on a crisis. The Austrian Ambassador was coldly received at the New Year reception at the Tuileries, at which the Emperor Napoleon regretted that relations between their two countries were not as friendly as in the past. And the announcement of the engagement between King Victor Emmanuel's eighteen-year-old daughter and the French Emperor's cousin, the forty-year-old Prince Napoleon, put the official seal to the Franco-Piedmontese alliance. At the eleventh hour, the European Chancelleries decided that the congress should open in March. But in Piedmont, the troops were already mobilizing, volunteers were streaming in from Lombardy and in Austria all military leave had been suspended.

Charlotte, who had insisted on remaining with her husband, appearing with him in public unescorted by police and being treated with respect even by their opponents, was now for the first time hissed in the streets of Venice. The following day, Maximilian sent his wife to Trieste, while he remained 'solitary as a hermit' in the vast Reggio of Milan. Writing to his mother at the height of Carnival, he describes the noise and dancing in the streets outside while 'Here in the palace, it is as gloomy as Ash Wednesday. I am the derided prophet, the one who now has to swallow everything I preached to deaf, unheeding ears – now they want to make me responsible for all that has happened, blaming me for having been conciliatory and weak. But in spite of their mockery and calumnies, I remain firmly at my post, trying to restrain unnecessary excesses dictated in a moment of panic.'

There was a slight improvement in the situation when the congress opened in March, and Charlotte was able to return to her husband. But the truce was short-lived. Austria demanded the disarmament of Piedmont as the price of its attendance and Piedmont persisted in ignoring these demands. By the end of the month, Charlotte was back in Trieste, taking with her large trunks of valuables and silver. On 19 April, Maximilian received a formal letter of dismissal. The powers he had asked for himself were to be entrusted to Gyulai, and although the Emperor formally thanked him for his loyal and devoted services, it was made quite clear that he no longer had his trust. There was no need for Maximilian to defend his policy or to vindicate himself in print. The reaction in Turin to the news of his dismissal was a sufficient proof of his good faith.

'At last we can breathe again,' wrote Count Cavour. 'The man who was our worst enemy in Lombardy, whom we feared the most, and of whom every day we watched the progress, has been dismissed. Already his perseverance, his fair and liberal spirit, had won him many of our supporters. Lombardy had never been so prosperous, so well administered. Then, thank God, the dear Viennese government intervenes, and in its usual way manages to make a mess of everything and to ruin its chances by recalling the Emperor's brother, because his wise reforms had displeased the old die-hards in Vienna. . . . Nothing was lost and Lombardy was ours for the asking.'

Two days after Maximilian's dismissal, Austria and Piedmont-Sardinia were at war. Spurred on by his Foreign Minister, Count Buol, overconfident in the strength of his armies, Franz Josef dictated the fatal ultimatum, calling on Piedmont-Sardinia to disarm within three days, thereby playing into the hands of Cavour and branding Austria as the aggressor. 'Above all, no ultimatum,' had been Prince Metternich's sound advice when the young Emperor called at his palace on the Rennweg to consult the old statesman who had kept Europe at peace for over thirty years. But the ultimatum had already been sent off the day before, in terms which left no room for compromise. The abortive European Congress vanished into smoke, and Napoleon had no choice but to mobilize his armies and to honour his commitments. But there would still have been time for the Austrian troops, who outnumbered the Piedmontese by almost two to one, to cross the Ticino and secure a quick victory before the French arrived in Italy. Unfortunately, Franz Josef's diplomats were in more of a hurry than his generals, and precious weeks were wasted in marches and countermarches.

While Vienna waited in suspense for the news of another victory like Novara, the French armies had crossed the Alps at Mont Cenis, linked up with the Italians and gone over to the offensive. The first battle took place, not in Piedmont on the outskirts of Turin, but at Magenta, in the heart of Lombardy, only sixteen miles west of Milan. It was a battle irrevocably lost by the Austrians, not so much on account of a military defeat as because of the ignominious retreat which followed. The pusillanimous Count Gyulai, newly appointed to the rank of Marshal, lost his head and in a moment of panic ordered a completely unnecessary withdrawal across the Mincio, leaving the whole of Lombardy to the enemy. Second in command to Gyulai was General Wympfen, yet another of Count Grünne's elegant protégés, who had preceded Maximilian as Commander-in-Chief of the navy and was known in military circles as 'the General who had never won a battle'.

'Both Gyulai and Wympfen deserve to be shot for cowardice,' was

Maximilian's outraged comment on hearing of the loss of Lombardy. Two days after his dismissal, the Archduke left Milan for Venice to prepare the defences of the arsenal and harbour against incursions by the French fleet. But again he had to suffer endless vexations and disappointments at finding himself entirely subordinated to the military command under an officer junior to him in rank. 'Even here in the navy, the thing I have most at heart, I find myself humiliated and obstructed at every turn. Those to whom I have shown preferment are set aside, those I have dismissed are immediately reinstated. At least I should be entitled to the respect due to an Archduke.'

A few days after Magenta, units of the French fleet appeared in the Adriatic, anchoring off the Lido, blockading Venice and bottling up the Austrian ships in the harbour. Maximilian's instinctive reaction was to force the blockade and engage the French in naval battle, but prudence won the day. Advised by Wilhelm von Tegetthoff, he desisted from being heroic, knowing that in the present circumstances the Ministry of Finance would never sanction the replacement of the ships if they were lost. The fleet created by Maximilian had to wait a further seven years to win its laurels at sea, when Tegetthoff defeated the Italians in the great naval battle of Lissa – a battle he was generous enough to call 'the victory of the absent Archduke'.

But in the present war, there were no victories to be gained either by Maximilian or by Franz Josef. Hapsburg pride had to endure the humiliation of Napoleon and Victor Emmanuel riding victorious through the streets of Milan, hailed as liberators by the cheering crowds, surrounded by the sons of the Milanese aristocracy who had fought in their armies. The defeat of Magenta resulted in the dismissal of Marshal Gyulai and the Emperor taking direct command of his armies. But Franz Josef had still to realize that personal courage was not sufficient to win battles. We hear of Maximilian joining his brother at his headquarters at Vallegio, from where he wrote: 'The army is on the march. Let us hope we will not have to pay for the mistakes we have made in the past.' But the confusion which prevailed at headquarters in Verona, the jealousies and dissensions of the General Staff and the breakdown in supplies, all contributed to defeat. On 24 June, on the hills above Lake Garda, the Austrians went over to the offensive and, at Solferino, fought the battle which decided the course of the war. Both Franz Josef and Napoleon were in command of their troops but the Italian King Victor Emmanuel proved himself a better soldier than either of the Emperors, both of whom were ready to expose themselves to danger, but both of whom were sickened by the carnage of battle, the unnecessary waste of human life. 'War is a risky game in which luck plays too great a part,' was Napoleon's comment after the battle was won, not because his troops fought better than the Austrians, many of whom performed miracles of valour, but because of the lack of co-ordination in the Austrian high command for which the young Emperor was himself partly to blame. At a moment when the fate of the battle was still uncertain, Franz Josef, seeing that the French had penetrated the left flank of his armies and thinking all was lost, gave the order to retreat – a retreat which turned into a rout. On the following day, Maximilian wrote to Charlotte from Verona: 'Exhausted and broken in spirit, I am sending you these few lines to tell you we have lost the battle which yesterday raged throughout the whole hot summer's day, from four in the morning until twilight. The losses on both sides must have been very heavy. Our army has had to retreat. Last night we spent at Villafranca, and this morning we accompanied the Emperor to Verona. ... I had never much hope of the outcome, but I did not imagine it would come so swiftly and would be quite so overwhelming. The retreat in the evening presented a scene of desolation I will never forget. The sight of all the wounded was terrible. How many people have been made unhappy? ... What happens in the next few days remains to be seen.' Two days later, still from Verona, he wrote: 'The army continues to retreat. We have already crossed the Mincio and are now retreating behind the Adige. We have not got a single good General, and the troops are not well looked after. They have been used to parades rather than war. They are completely demoralized, and in the aftermath of defeat, are all asking, "Where will it end?".'

After Solferino the Italians had every right to believe that their victorious armies would now march on to Verona and push the Austrians back into the mountains. But they were reckoning without Napoleon, that strange, complex character who in the hour of victory had lost his enthusiasm for war, and was beginning to wonder whether the cause of Italian nationalism and the ambitions of Count Cavour justified the thousands of French dead left to be buried on the hills of Garda. While Franz Josef was reorganizing his armies behind the Adige and reinforcements were being rushed across the Brenner Pass, he suddenly received the astonishing news that Napoleon was asking for an armistice and was willing to leave Venetia in Austrian hands. Was it because he feared the consequences of a prolonged war, which might bring the hitherto neutral Prussia in on Austria's side? Or was it because he was sickened by the senseless futility of it all? Solferino had been fought in conditions of tropical heat. Napoleon was suffering from his gall-bladder, and Cavour may have been right when he accused the French Emperor of sacrificing the Venetians 'because he was tired, hot and bored, and longing for the sea breezes of Biarritz'. Napoleon was completely ignorant of the country of which he professed to be a champion and he even went so far as to admit to the British Ambassador in Paris that when he met Franz Josef at Villafranca to discuss the first preliminaries of peace, he had no idea 'who ruled what in the various Italian Duchies'.

It was at Villafranca that Franz Josef's jealousy and distrust of Maximilian came out into the open. Napoleon's proposal to make Venice into an independent state under the Archduke's rule met with the cold reply: 'Rather than have this happen, Austria will continue the war.' The same intransigence was shown at the peace conference, when King Leopold tried to intervene to obtain the Governorship of Venice for his son-in-law, only to be told that the administration of an Austrian province was a matter of internal policy. Franz Josef's treatment of his brother was in marked contrast to the loyalty with which he fought for the right of his Hapsburg cousins in Modena and Tuscany, both of whose states now became part of the new united Italy. In these circumstances, it is not surprising to read in a letter to King Leopold of Maximilian's open opposition to Vienna. 'It is depressing,' he wrote, 'to see our great and once-powerful monarchy slowly sinking into decline through incompetence and muddle-headedness for which there is neither excuse nor explanation.'

IO

New horizons

Maximilian was now back in Trieste and reunited with Charlotte, who for the past months had been living in constant fear for the man to whom she felt she belonged 'heart and soul'. For the first time in their married life they were living as private citizens with no Court other than their ladies and gentlemen in attendance, no occupation other than his now largely nominal duties as Admiral of the Fleet, and her various local charities. It was almost harder for Charlotte than for Maximilian, who could always find escape in the gardens of Miramar, planting yet another terrace of oranges or magnolias, designing aviaries and glasshouses for his tropical birds and plants. But Charlotte, who still believed that her husband possessed every quality of leadership and had all her nascent ambition fed by the adulation of a Court, could not resign herself to live without a throne. From her earliest childhood she had felt herself called upon to rule, and she listened all too willingly to the reports from Vienna of how the Emperor had been hissed in the streets on his return from Italy, and had shut himself up at Laxenburg to avoid the hostile demonstrations at which voices in the crowd called on him to abdicate and others shouted, 'Long live the Archduke Max!' The whole of what was known as the *Zweite Gesselschaft,* the intellectuals, the bankers and the heads of industry, were in opposition to the aristocratic military caste whose arrogant complacency had lost the war. Even the Emperor was not spared and it was openly said that the troops at Solferino had been sacrificed to the ineptitude of the high command.

All the gossip and rumours reached Trieste, where they encouraged Charlotte's daydreams of her Max, if not as Emperor, at least as Regent, with only a sickly baby standing between him and the throne. But already the heads were falling in Vienna. Franz Josef was saving his throne by sacrificing his Ministers. The incompetent Foreign Minister,

Count Buol, whose policy had succeeded in alienating every one of Austria's neighbours, was the first to go, followed by Alexander Bach, whose policy of centralization was so dear to the Emperor's heart. But the greatest sensation of all was that of the fall of Grünne, the man who had hitherto been the Emperor's closest confidant and who was now removed from the post of Adjutant-General to the comparatively unimportant position of Master of the Horse.

It was a sad summer and the Archduchess Sophia made a pathetic attempt to reunite the family by inviting Charlotte and Max to visit her in Ischl at the same time as the Emperor and Empress. To please their mother, the two brothers attempted to revive the intimacy of their childhood, eschewing politics and keeping to family topics. As usual, Franz Josef ended by falling under Max's charm, while Max forgot his grievances and, with his innate goodness of heart, put himself out to cheer the brother who, for the first time, had lost confidence in himself. If the visit was a failure, it was largely owing to their wives. The Empress, who was in a very neurotic state, blaming her mother-in-law and her protégé, Count Grünne, for the disaster of the war, had been with difficulty persuaded to come to Ischl, and having come, spent most of the day in her room. The Archduchess's fondness for Charlotte was sufficient to make Elisabeth dislike 'that pretentious little Coburg, who was always showing off her knowledge and was so boringly possessive with Max'. Charlotte, on her side, was not prepared to be ignored. Conscious of her royal birth, she resented the attitude of a sister-in-law who came of a princely but not of a ruling family and only owed her position to her beauty. Jealousy may also have played a part, for Max was still under Elisabeth's spell: Charlotte, who in Italy had basked in the admiration of poets and artists patronized by Max, was just a pretty little Archduchess at the Imperial Court, where everything revolved round Elisabeth's whims and moods.

Contemporary evidence is contradictory on the subject of Charlotte's looks. But even the most enthusiastic descriptions do not appear to justify a doting father calling her 'the loveliest Princess in Europe'. A portrait of her as a young married woman hangs at Miramar. Painted by the Belgian artist, Portaels, it depicts her in the national costume of the Brianza, the red dress with the laced-up bodice and gold ornaments, which sets off her dark, Italian type of beauty. Though painted at a time when she was still a young and adoring bride, the eyes have kept the look of melancholy which characterized them as a child; the small head rises proud and arrogant from a long slender neck, the supercilious mouth has a downward turn. It is a face at once passionate and cold, beautiful but lacking appeal. Looking at her portrait, one can understand why Charlotte commanded admiration rather than affection and why Maximilian, in speaking of her, rarely referred to her in more loving terms than as 'my clever, energetic wife'.

After all the attempts at a reconciliation, Charlotte and Maximilian left Ischl as empty-handed as they came. There was no new and important job in the offing, not even the Governorship of an Austrian province, and it was all too clear that not only the Emperor's ministers but Franz Josef himself fundamentally distrusted Maximilian and held his liberal policy in Italy partly responsible for the loss of Lombardy. There are those who maintain that when Prince Metternich returned from exile he confided to the young Emperor certain family secrets regarding Maximilian's birth, secrets which in loyalty to his mother Franz Josef may have preferred to ignore, but which must have been at the back of his mind, adding to a growing distrust of a more popular younger brother and even making him suspicious of his charm.

Maximilian now concentrated his energies on the building of Miramar, and in the late summer of 1859, we find Charlotte writing to her old governess 'Now that he has so little to do, the Archduke spends most of his time in putting the last touches to what is entirely his own creation. Both the house and gardens are of outstanding beauty and the situation is unique. As for me, I do a certain amount of painting, and am at present correcting the diary I kept on our recent travels. We have the intention of taking some more yachting trips along the Istrian coast, for we must make the most of our present leisure. Who knows what the future holds?'

Tastes have changed and the limestone towers of Miramar, with its granite terraces and marble steps leading to a landing stage, guarded by Egyptian sphinxes, no longer appeal to the aesthetic standards of today. But the situation remains unique. Built on a rocky promontory above the Adriatic, Miramar has still a romantic fascination, and thousands of tourists come from all over the world to visit the castle, where the people of Trieste have lovingly preserved the memory of the Hapsburg Prince. Maximilian's statue dominates the gardens. One still sees a replica of his cabin aboard the frigate *Novara*; in his library, reflecting his varied and somewhat eclectic tastes, British naval histories and horticultural manuals alternate with rare editions of the birds and fauna of the Andes and the Amazon, and volumes of romantic poetry in half a dozen languages are ranged next to Froissart's *Chronicles* and Plutarch's *Lives*. Here at Miramar is Charlotte's writing desk, which once belonged to Marie Antoinette, and the sad and empty throne room, where the young Archduke grasped at the illusion of an Imperial Crown. Ill-fated Miramar, where no one was ever destined to live in happiness – a childhood wish evoked too late to satisfy an adult's dream.

In his journals, Maximilian sees himself as another Diocletian, 'renouncing the vanities of the world, to live far removed from the deceit, the weariness and the fraud we have experienced in the last years, content to retire to a serene and sunny climate, studying the arts and sciences and cultivating my garden'. But these fine phrases had little bearing on reality. He was young, restless and dissatisfied both in his public and his private life. For a few brief months he had imagined himself to be in love with Charlotte. She had been the perfect Vicereine in Italy and her personal popularity with the Italians had considerably facilitated his task. There were many occasions when he deferred to her judgment and took her advice. But however much he admired her mind, she no longer attracted him as a woman. She was too possessive, too demanding and maybe too passionate for a nature as volatile and inconstant as his. When he was a child, his mother had noted: 'Though Max has the warmer heart, Franz Josef is capable of far deeper feelings.' There was a certain superficiality in Max allied to a strong feminine streak, which made him both irresistible to women and curiously indifferent to them. Used to moving from palace to palace, he was irked by the domestic proximity of life at the Villa Lazarovic, the even closer proximity of life on board their yacht, the *Fantaisie*. In Charlotte's diary, one sees that for her a journey along the Istrian coast was still a romantic honeymoon, whereas for Max it was merely a means of passing the time.

Miramar was not finished before he was in search of new diversions, planning to rebuild a deserted monastery on the island of Lacroma, only a short distance from Ragusa. He and Charlotte had discovered it in the autumn of 1859, when they were cruising off the Dalmatian coast, and stopped to picnic on the island in a pine wood by a lake. Built on the spot where Richard Coeur de Lion had been shipwrecked on his way home from the Crusades, the monastery was now little more than a ruin half-smothered in myrtle and oleander. But Maximilian had no sooner seen it than he envisaged it as a summer home, planning terraces and loggias with vistas opening out to the sea. He was still so full of debts from Miramar, some of which his old godfather, the ex-Emperor Ferdinand, had been prevailed upon to pay, that even he hesitated to acquire another house. It was Charlotte, always so ready to share his enthusiasms, so anxious to please, who purchased the island in his name – a poetic extravagance which would hardly have met with the approval of the rich burghers of Flanders who had contributed to her dowry.

Seventy years later, when cruising off Dalmatia, Lady Diana Cooper came across an old gentleman who remembered the handsome young Archduke and his pretty wife on their visit to Ragusa, when through the eyes of a little boy, they seemed so happy, so very much in love, carving their names upon a tree like any bourgeois couple. Across the gulf of years, the old man could still hear Charlotte's clear young voice calling out in French, 'Oh Max, if only we could always be as happy as today!'

Yet it was only a few months later that Charlotte was abandoned for the whole winter on the island of Madeira, while her husband satisfied his wanderlust in exploring the New World. The first report of their journey said that the Archducal couple were going round the world. This was followed by the official announcement of a state visit to their cousin, the Emperor Pedro II of Brazil, and at the end of November the S.S. *Elisabeth*, with Charlotte and Maximilian on board and Wilhelm von Tegetthoff serving as flag captain, set sail from Trieste. Charlotte had originally intended to cross the Atlantic with her husband, but she and her ladies suffered acute discomfort on a frigate which was not designed for an ocean crossing in the winter. After two days of pitching and rolling in a violent storm between the Canaries and the Cape Verde Islands she was persuaded to return to Madeira, where she finally woke to the fact that marriage was not always a romantic idyll.

Their first differences appear to have dated from this journey, with Charlotte ill and complaining and Maximilian irritated and unsympathetic, remaining all day on the bridge with Tegetthoff. But there was another, more serious rift in their relationship, for Maximilian now took the opportunity of sleeping in his own quarters and according to the gossip of his valet, it was the first step towards a break in their conjugal life.

There are many interpretations, mostly of a slanderous nature, as to

125

why this good-looking, healthy young couple, who in public seemed so devoted, rarely shared a bed after the first years of marriage. One of the most popular versions, circulated by Maximilian's enemies, was that the Archduke had contracted a contagious illness from a prostitute, which he then transmitted to his wife. More or less the same story has been told of the Emperor Franz Josef, though in his case there appears to have been a greater foundation of truth. The very fact that Charlotte continued to love her husband and suffered from his neglect gives a lie to this story. A far simpler, more likely explanation is that Maximilian, who was neither very virile nor highly sexed and who was only attracted by the novel and the exotic, found that with Charlotte he could no longer function as a man, while Charlotte was both too proud and too inexperienced to consult her doctor or ask the advice of one of her older ladies-in-waiting.

Both kept diaries on the journey and neither made any reference to their personal relations. Each seems to have deliberately avoided mentioning the other. Charlotte's journals are factual, well-written essays, describing the artistic beauties of the places they visited. Maximilian's are as always varied and discursive, with a fondness for purple passages and a tendency to philosophize in a somewhat immature fashion. But, in contrast to those of his wife, they are intensely personal and spontaneous and are at their best when he is being humorous and light-hearted – describing Gibraltar 'so bristling with cannon that one should offer a reward to whoever finds a spot on Gibraltar on which to place an additional gun'. He gives an account of a pompous tea party at Lady Codrington's, whose husband was now Governor of the Rock: 'We all sat round sipping tea in a semicircle, like Roman senators receiving the Gauls.' But for all his mockery, he was a great admirer of the English way of life, and stores of groceries from Saccone and Speed were loaded on to the *Elisabeth*. No one, in his opinion, 'equalled the Anglo-Saxon in producing culinary delicacies, delicious jams and pungent sauces and excellent Scotch salmon, in tins which transformed the everyday breakfast into a gastronomic feast, so that once tasted one cannot understand how one could ever have done without them.'

Gibraltar was teeming with activity, for across the Straits Spaniards and Moors were engaged in a frontier dispute, and though the 'supercilious' English officers ridiculed the fighting as a 'farcical little war', Maximilian noted that England had taken the precaution of controlling the 'farce' by having the greater part of her Mediterranean fleet anchored off the Rock. The French too had brought their men-of-war into the Straits to keep a watchful eye on Spanish ambitions in Morocco and among them were the very ships that, only a few months before, had blockaded Venice.

From Gibraltar, the *Elisabeth* proceeded to Madeira and Maximilian had no sooner sighted the island than he realized it was a mistake to revisit a place where he had been so happy in the past. 'It was with a feeling of sadness that I again beheld the valley of Machico and lovely Santa Cruz, where we spent such happy hours seven years ago. On board our large ship, so filled with people, I was the solitary pilgrim of former days. . . . Since those times, seven years full of pain and joy, full of fortune's storms with a few of its blessings, have passed over my head, and a sadness comes over me when I compare that time with the present.'

Where was Charlotte when he wrote those lines? Where was Charlotte when he went off with his physician to visit the hospital built by the widowed Empress of Brazil? A slab of black marble, inscribed in gold lettering, recorded that the hospital was dedicated to the memory of the Empress's only daughter, Maria Amalia, who had died of consumption on the island. Maria Amalia spent the last months of her life in the house next door, where Maximilian now went in pilgrimage, 'to linger in grief and sadness in the shade of an Indian fig tree and pick a bunch of flowers to place on her grave.' A loving and devoted wife, in all the bloom of her nineteen years, had not succeeded in making him forget the blonde and fragile Braganza Princess he had courted under a summer moon seven years before.

In 1860 the vast and half-unexplored Empire of Brazil had been ruled for twenty years by Pedro II, son of the Austrian Archduchess Leopoldine, whose only claim to immortality was to have given her name to the first railway in Brazil. Thirty years after her death, the railway hardly extended beyond the fringe of the great forests and impenetrable jungle over which her son ruled only in name, and where any enterprising and hard-working colonist could, with the help of slave labour, clear thousands of square miles of fertile territory from the swamps and forests and establish himself as a *fazendero*, owing allegiance to no one but himself. The enormous distances between Rio de Janeiro and the northern provinces, the lack of communications and economical and financial difficulties prevented the Emperor Pedro from paying more than an occasional visit to the old capital of San Salvador di Bahia, while in the interior of the country, in the provinces of São Paulo and Las Minas and only a day's distance from the coast, the name of Braganza was as little known as that of Hapsburg or Saxe-Coburg.

Early on 11 January, the S.S. *Elisabeth* cast anchor in the Bay of All Saints, and Maximilian had his first sight of the coast of the New World. He wrote that the whole vessel was in a state of feverish excitement, waiting for the health officers to come on board. 'Here we were standing at the Gates of Paradise, with an indescribable, almost childish, impatience, for this was the day on which that dream of years, the landing on the tropical coast of America, was to become reality.'

Everything surpassed his expectations from the moment his launch grounded on the shingle of a lonely, palm-fronded beach to the north of Bahia, thereby avoiding the mayor and other notables who, having heard of the arrival of a foreign prince, were waiting to receive him on the pier. For once, he had refused to be hampered by protocol. Nothing must be allowed to disturb his first impressions of the New World. 'All around breathed life and beauty. It was necessary to strain every nerve so as to leave nothing unseen, nothing unappreciated among the wonders presented by nature. It was a moment when all we have read in books becomes imbued with life, when the rare insects and butterflies contained in our limited and laboriously formed collections suddenly take wing, when the pygmy growth of our confined glasshouses expand into giant plants and forests, and the animals with which we are only acquainted through the forlorn specimens in our zoological gardens, or as stuffed objects in our museums, surround us in joyous freedom – the moment in which the book gains life – the dream reality.'

A month ago, he had been describing himself as 'a melancholy pilgrim', weighed down by the burdens of the past, and one can hardly believe that the almost lyrical note of happiness of his first impressions of Brazil are written by the same person. All that was best in Maximilian, his passionate love of nature and of every form of wild life, responded to the physical, sensuous beauty of Brazil. As a little boy, shivering in the cold of a northern winter, he had found comfort in the conservatories of Schönbrunn, and with a feeling akin to ecstasy, he now saw orchids hanging from the trees, a humming bird alighting on a bignonia bush. A primitive slave cabin, fashioned from bamboo, was almost the exact replica of the hut on the '*bolingrin*' of Schönbrunn which his mother had prepared for him as a surprise on his eighth birthday, when for the first time in his life, he saw a real parrot swinging from a perch — a birthday present from the ex-Empress Marie Louis. There were hundreds of parrots for sale on the quays of Bahia, red and blue and emerald-winged, chatting in raucous Portuguese, and the negresses walking along the shore, bearing great baskets of tropical fruits on their heads, wore clothes the colours of the parrots' wings. But never in all his rapturous descriptions is there a single mention of Charlotte. Never once does he express regret that she is not there to share in these delights. His gentleman-in-waiting, Count Zichy, and his secretary, Baron du Pont, had remained behind in Madeira to look after the Archduchess's household, but he was perfectly happy in the company of Tegetthoff and the other officers of the *Elisabeth*, touring the old Portuguese mission churches with his doctor or sharing in the excitement of his botanist at discovering rare and fragile blooms growing like weeds among the undergrowth.

Maximilian's Brazilian diaries have all the spontaneous enthusiasm of his Greek journals. He is once more an adolescent, gaily playing truant from the authorities, exploring *incognito* the amenities of Bahia and being finally tracked down by a hot and flustered consul who had been chasing him around the town, only to find him having a delicious meal in a simple French hotel which he had discovered by chance. The consul turned out to be a charming young German from Hamburg who, once having got over the shock of finding his Prince sitting in the smoke-laden atmosphere of a communal dining-room, was sufficiently tactful to respect his *incognito*.

A mule-driven carriage was provided to drive Maximilian and his friends through the European quarter of Vittorio to a beautiful lake on the outskirts of the forest, where 'the landscape was so idyllic, the trees so perfectly grouped, the grass so soft and green that it might have been an English park laid in a tropical setting.' Here the botanist secured specimens of the rarest plants, while enormous butterflies brushed against their faces and the courageous Tegetthoff won the admiration of his companions by killing a venomous snake just as it was about to strike. Later that night, when Maximilian was back aboard the *Elisabeth* lying on his bunk, thousands of miles from home, he noted in his diary: 'Today, I have spent one of the happiest days of my life.'

It was the first of a series of blissful days in which the consul and the leading members of the foreign colony of Bahia laid themselves out to gratify the tastes of the adventurous young Prince, whose greatest wish was to explore the Matto Grosso (the Virgin Forest), and who was so easily pleased, whether with some seeds and cuttings from their gardens or the gift of a yellow-billed toucan for the aviaries of Schönbrunn. One day was spent on a botanical expedition to the little island of Itaparica, followed by a trip up the Paraguasa river to visit one of the largest sugar plantations in the district. Here, Maximilian had his first experience of life on a great *fazenda*, entertained by a rich Brazilian, the owner of hundreds of slaves. But all the Brazilian's affability could not condone the jesting manner in which he referred to the *chicoto* – the double-pronged oxhide slave whip which was left openly on view on the hall table, 'just as a dog whip would be left in Europe'. All Maximilian's liberal and humanitarian instincts revolted against the practice of slavery and he condemned both the government and the clergy who tolerated this barbarous practice. 'They who degrade their fellow men call themselves the citizens of a free country which is said to prosper from such institutions. They never sense the disgrace, the shame that lies in these words. . . . How can a conscience exist . . . when there are men beyond the pale of law, when beings who have souls depend exclusively on the arbitrary power and caprice of a few of their fellow creatures? . . . Is not religion a mockery when a white man arrogates the right to treat men who, like himself, are born in the image of the Creator, as if they were beasts of burden, or bales of goods?'

What Maximilian resented most was the attitude of the Catholic Church; he could not understand how a priest had the courage to preach the Gospel in Brazil. He understood it even less after visiting what was supposed to be a great religious ceremony, but which seemed 'more like a witches' Saturnalia with hundreds of negresses chatting and laughing in what was meant to be a church but had all the appearance of a dance-hall, with hucksters peddling their wares, both amulets and eatables in the precincts of the high altar'. It was only later that 'it dawned on me that a priest was actually serving Mass, and that all these chattering negresses had come here in pilgrimage and were baptized Christians'. It was Maximilian's first experience of a Latin American fiesta, with all the gaiety and colour which the priests maintained to be the only way of attracting a primitive people to church. But his own innate piety allied to the strictness of his religious upbringing could never reconcile him to the sophistry of the Latin American clergy who, by adapting pagan rituals to Christian ceremonies, exploited the superstitious and childish faith of an ignorant people.

But in spite of his horror of slavery, his disapproval both of the government and the clergy, Brazil continued to open out enchanted vistas of a freer life in the New World. He was fascinated by the strange characters he met in the most unlikely places. In the heart of the Matto Grosso, on the shores of a river which was only navigable by canoe, he came across an Italian nobleman dressed in the height of fashion, living with an elegant French wife, in a house where the antique furniture and ancestral paintings made a strange contrast to the floors and ceilings of battened earth. An aura of mystery surrounded this sophisticated couple who had adapted themselves so little to the settlers' life and whose name evoked memories of Maximilian's 'beloved Lombardy'. 'But one of the charms of America,' he noted, 'is that no one asks the newcomer from whence or wherefore he has come, for the ocean is so wide it is like a lake of oblivion, and America is the perfect asylum for those who, in Europe, want to break with the stormy past and to work their way to a brighter future.'

Maximilian had insisted on visiting the Matto, much to the discomfort of the poor Consul, who had to endure a rough trip on the *Elisabeth* one hundred and twenty miles down the coast to the mouth of the Cacheroia, and from there up the river by canoe to a settlement hewn out of the forest by a wealthy German coffee planter. A night camping out in the Matto, against the advice both of the Consul and their host, who had planned short expeditions from the *fazenda*, was sufficient to cure Maximilian and his companions of a taste for primitive life. They came back in a sorry condition, covered in insect bites and half-starved, as most of the ample provisions with which they had been provided had been gobbled up at the first meal by the hungry young officers. Maximilian admitted afterwards: 'We took with us everything we needed, except experience.' The hardy colonists must have suppressed their smiles at the Archduke's bizarre appearance as he sallied out into the jungle in a white merino suit and enormous hat with a green veil, followed by a servant carrying an elegant dressing case, a large cutlass and a butterfly net. Overhanging creepers made short work of both the hat and veil, while the butterfly net remained impaled upon a tree. But they were all in the best of spirits after they had been fed and revived with invigorating draughts of 'Lisbon wine', and it was with real regret that Maximilian parted from his hospitable host and his charming Brazilian wife. The days of freedom were coming to an end; he had now to put on his uniform and decorations for the official visit to his cousin, Pedro of Brazil.

In spite of its natural beauties, the visit to Rio de Janeiro was an anticlimax. The Emperor Pedro, who was staying in his summer palace at Petropolis, was a dull, scholarly man with a lame and ugly wife and two rather unattractive little girls. The so-called 'palace' was no more than a suburban villa, and the Imperial Family's chief amusement was to attend the weekly dance at the local hotel. In Maximilian's eyes, neither Pedro nor his surroundings lived up to the exotic title of Emperor of Brazil. It was a title he envied, for nothing would have pleased him more than to dedicate his life to exploring the vast and unknown resources of the Brazilian Empire. Pedro had no male heirs, and Maximilian saw in the fourteen-year-old Isabelle a suitable wife for his youngest brother. The fact that Ludwig Viktor was weak and effeminate and totally devoid of ambition made no difference to his plans. On the contrary, it was a chance of making a man of him by getting him away from the bad company he was keeping and the useless existence he was leading in Vienna. But though Pedro was only too ready to fall in with his plans, there was little response in Vienna either from his mother or Franz Josef, both of whom dismissed it as yet another of 'Max's ridiculous ideas', while the prospective bridegroom was against the very idea of marriage and in particular to a marriage which would take him far away from the cafés of Vienna. But the idea of a Hapsburg Prince in the New World had taken hold of Maximilian's imagination and he returned to Europe haunted by memories of tropical skies, the scent of tropical flowers and raucous jungle cries. Everything in Europe seemed pale and muted by comparison with the intensity of life in the Americas, and the existence which awaited him at Miramar seemed painfully narrow and constricted.

By the end of April, Charlotte and Maximilian were back in Trieste, living in the garden pavilion of Miramar, waiting to move into the castle by the end of the year. 'We are leading at present a very peaceful existence and trying to make people forget us,' wrote Charlotte to the Countess d'Hulst. 'Miramar will be our town house and Lacroma our country place, thus our modest life arranges itself in a very pleasant pattern. Past splendours are forgotten and we are quietly enjoying what the present has to offer. Providence has given us so much, that even if some of its gifts are now taken away, we have still got enough to make us happy, even if it is in quite a different way.' It is a curious letter, coming from a young woman who had still everything to expect from life. Three weeks later, she was writing again on the same theme: 'Even though the life which we live at present is not what I imagined, I can assure you that there are times when I thank God for it, for conditions being as they are at present, it is better to live out of the world, for when one possesses less, one has less to lose. I do not know what will happen in the future, but should the situation return to normal, then I believe the day will come, and I am not being just deluded by ambition, when the Archduke will again play a leading role in world affairs, for he is made to rule, being endowed with all the qualities to make people happy. It seems to me impossible that all these gifts should be wasted, after being so brilliantly employed for less than three years.'

Charlotte wrote only of her husband, but she must also have been thinking of herself and of her own wasted talents. She craved for an active life, if only to console her for the disappointment of not having a child. But she was too proud and too reserved to confide even in her governess. The letters give no hint of any rift in her domestic happiness, no mention of those lonely months in Madeira, or of being left behind in Trieste while Max went off on a visit to Vienna, a visit in which she was not included as the Empress was suffering from a nervous break-down and refused to appear in public.

Max returned from his visit extremely depressed and more than ever convinced that he had no future in Austria. The cheers which greeted him in the streets of Vienna and the tributes of the foreign press had closed the doors to all further promotion, and the situation generally was so gloomy that he was seriously considering moving some of his assets out of the country. The aftermath of defeat had revealed scandals and corruption in every branch of public life. The Quartermaster-General in charge of military supplies had been found guilty of embezzlement; the Minister of Finance had committed suicide; Hungary, where the Archduke had invested the greater part of his private fortune, was again on the verge of revolt. Economically and politically, the Empire was facing bankruptcy. We find Maximilian writing to his father-in-law: 'I find conditions in the country very depressing and confused, corruption on the one hand and a rising indignation on the other, just as it was in France at the time of Louis XVI. In government circles, there is nothing but inactivity allied to perplexity. They do not understand and, what is more, they do not want to understand the situation, and all one sees and hears only makes one more indignant. Maybe I am too much of a pessimist, but I am trying to put my affairs in order in the event of a crisis.'

Shortly afterwards, King Leopold received a secret visit from the Archduke's secretary, who asked him to make a fictitious acquisition of both Miramar and Lacroma so that they could be considered neutral property in case the Italians made a sudden attack on the Adriatic coast. The wise old King, who had seen so many crises in his day, made haste to reassure his son-in-law that there was no need to worry over Miramar, as Trieste was part of the German confederation which would never tolerate a violation of their territory, nor was there any reason to sell his Hungarian bonds, which would be honoured by whatever government was in power. With regard to Lacroma, he was willing to have it placed in his name, for no other reason than to put their minds at rest.

Reassured as to the financial future, Maximilian went on spending money as recklessly as before. By Christmas Charlotte and he were installed in the castle at Miramar, entertaining a hundred poor children of Trieste to a magnificent party with four illuminated Christmas trees laden with presents. As a private individual he still entertained on the scale of an Emperor's Viceroy and old friends from Venice and Milan were given a royal welcome, though it irked his pride to note that many kept their visits secret, so as not to risk their position with the new Italian government. He made every effort to keep in the public eye, and with the coming of spring, the gardens of Miramar were thrown open every Sunday, with a naval band playing on the *parterre* in front of the castle, in imitation of Schönbrunn. 'Everyone who comes,' wrote Charlotte, 'and there are many foreigners among them, is full of admiration for what the Archduke has been able to create out of the barren rock; on the days when the gardens are open to the public, we dine out on the terrace, where we can watch the crowds and also be seen by them.' A pathetic consolation for the days when she sat enthroned in the Reggio of Milan. But in government circles in Vienna they even grudged them their popularity in Trieste.

Maximilian was also accused of having influenced the Empress Elisabeth's journey to Madeira, a journey undertaken in a mood of neurotic despair, against the advice both of the Hapsburgs and of her own family. The Emperor had to submit to having his private life discussed, both in the drawing rooms of his capital and the Chancelleries of

Europe, with the ambassadors accredited to Vienna giving their various interpretations on the young Empress's breakdown in health and the rift in her relations with her husband. There would have been none of this publicity had Elisabeth consented to winter in Meran or Abbazia, where loyal subjects would have been ready to put their villas and castles at her disposal. But her insistence on travelling to a remote island in the middle of the Atlantic, of which she would hardly have heard had it not been for Max's lyrical descriptions, had turned what would have been a journey of convalescence into a premeditated flight. None of the available Austrian ships being suitable for an Atlantic crossing, the Empress accepted Queen Victoria's offer of the largest and most comfortable of the English royal yachts, a fact which only added to the Emperor's humiliation.

Elisabeth remained for five months on the island, but by spring she was sufficiently bored to announce her recovery, and in May 1861 the *Victoria and Albert* sailed into the Gulf of Trieste, bringing the Empress home. Franz Josef and Maximilian had gone by yacht to meet her at Lacroma, and there was a family reunion at Miramar, which Maximilian's court artist, Cesare d'Acqua, recorded in a painting still preserved in the castle. It shows us Charlotte in a white dress, advancing to embrace Elisabeth as she steps from the launch of the *Victoria and Albert*, while Franz Josef and Maximilian stand rigidly to attention, saluting the British flag. This visit, which had all the appearance of a reconciliation between the two brothers, was spoilt by the Empress's treatment of the Archduchess. No sooner had their husbands left to fulfil public engagements in Trieste than she would retire to her rooms and stay there till their return. The crowning insult was when one of the big English sheepdogs she had brought back from Madeira and which she refused to keep shut up in the kennels, attacked and killed the little lapdog Charlotte had been given by Queen Victoria. The Archduchess's grief made little impression on Elisabeth, who merely expressed her dislike for all small dogs. But Charlotte was to suffer an even greater insult a fortnight after the Empress's return to Vienna. For the first few days she appeared to be in the best of health, but she fell again into a mysterious decline and the unfortunate Emperor, who despite all the vicissitudes of their married life was still very much in love with his wife, turned in despair to Maximilian, asking him to accompany Elisabeth to Corfu and to see her comfortably settled. One sympathizes with Charlotte's indignation, not only at finding herself completely ignored, but having her 'wonderful and brilliant Max', whom jealousy had excluded from all the positions worthy of his talents, now treated as if he were a mere gentleman-in-waiting, to be called on at a moment's notice to look after a neurotic sister-in-law. All her Coburg pride was up in arms and, being a far stronger character than Max, she made him resent what on his own he would have accepted. One finds a new note of sarcasm in his comments on the Empress. Seen through the eyes of his wife, Elisabeth was no longer the fairy child, the beautiful Undine, but a spoilt and tiresome woman who had failed in her obligations to her husband and her country. He was quick to discover that the 'mortal illness' she was supposed to be suffering from was largely nerves and they had not reached Corfu before he was writing home that 'her recovery is little short of miraculous'.

Boredom, frustration, and the unconscious nagging of an ambitious wife, were combining to warp his character. Living in daily contact with the young couple was the mistress of their household, Countess Lutzoff, who, after presiding over the Court at Monza, had followed them to Miramar, where she had witnessed the disappointments and disillusions of the past year. It was this charming old lady who, with the kindest and best of intentions, sent out the first feelers which led to the ill-fated Mexican adventure: in the spring of 1861 she wrote to her Mexican son-in-law in Rome that, should his dream of an Empire ever materialize, the Archduke Ferdinand Maximilian would be a likely candidate for the throne.

I I

The Mexican Throne

José Maria Gutierrez d'Estrada, who was Countess Lutzoff's son-in-law, was a man with a mission. Throughout his life he had dreamt of establishing a monarchy in a country with no monarchist tradition other than the vague image of a Spanish king who for three hundred years had ruled through Viceroys over the vast heterogenous territory of Mexico, which stretched for over three million square miles from the plains of Texas and the deserts of Arizona to the jungles of Guatemala. Before the coming of the Spaniards in 1519, Mexico had been a flourishing Empire, ruled by the Aztec Emperor Montezuma whose capital Tenochtlican was one of the wonders of the Western world. The Aztecs were on the one hand warlike and ferocious, appeasing the war god Huitzilopochtli with human sacrifices, and on the other hand gentle and civilized in everyday life, cultivating the arts and sciences, with a love of flowers one still sees among their descendants. On the ruins of the civilization they destroyed, the Spaniards built New Spain. Before the Catholic Church triumphant, the old Aztec Gods retreated into the remote jungles and primeval forests.

Cortés encouraged colonization by distributing large tracts of land among his followers. The Spanish viceroys, who followed after him, never staying for more than ten years, attracted their friends and relatives to Mexico by offering them lucrative appointments and rich rewards. The government was entirely in the hands of the Spanish settlers, the so-called *Gachupines*, as opposed to the Creoles, the white man born in Mexico, who was not given any position of responsibility, or the *Mestizo*, the half-castes who by the end of the eighteenth century numbered over a third of the eight million inhabitants of Mexico. This exclusion of the greater part of the population from the running of the country gradually fomented discontent among the more educated classes.

The civilization of New Spain was the work of the Dominican and Franciscan Fathers, who converted and at the same time protected the Indians from the brutality of their overlords, learning their language, founding their schools, and encouraging their natural fantasy and talent to flower in the marvellous churrigueresque art, so typical of Mexico. But power breeds corruption and there was little connection between those early monks and the Mexican clergy of the end of the eighteenth century. The friars whom Charles v called 'the twelve apostles' and who walked bare foot from Vera Cruz to Mexico City where the Indians were astounded to see Cortés, the great conqueror, go on his knees before those ragged men with bleeding feet, would have been horrified to hear of their eighteenth century successors demanding high fees for administering the sacraments.

The rule of the viceroys rested on the mystique of royalty. First the American revolution and then the French fanned a spirit of discontent among the unemployed Creoles. The tramp of Napoleon's victorious armies which swept the dynasties of Europe off their thrones, re-echoed across the Atlantic. The imprisonment of the Spanish King Ferdinand vii gave the Mexicans the chance to assert their independence under the inspired leadership of a young Creole officer, Miguel Allende and a heroic priest, Hidalgo. The millions who till now had had no say in the running of their country raised the standard of revolt against the hated Spaniard. And on 16 September 1810 the bells of the parish church of the little village of Dolores summoned the people to battle, to the cry of 'Mexico for the Mexicans'. But the country was not yet ripe for revolution and Hidalgo and Allende were the first martyrs of the Mexican revolution.

It was only after ten years of bitter fighting, by which time Gutierrez d'Estrada was already a young man of twenty-one, that Agustín Iturbide, a brilliant and ambitious young officer trained in the armies of Spain, established the country's independence; proclaiming it not as a republic but as a monarchy and himself assuming the Imperial crown.

But the Empire was shortlived. Within two years, Iturbide was condemned to death and shot by his own people, and now, forty years later, Mexico was still convulsed by civil war, with Centralists and Federalists, *Moderados* and *Puros*, Liberals who paid lip service to democracy and Conservatives supported by the Church, engaged in a continual struggle for power. It was the era of the *pronunciamento* and the barrack revolt, when any general with sufficient funds at his disposal could pronounce against the existing government, condemning with a wealth of patriotic rhetoric, promising a whole series of reforms and offering generous rewards to anyone who joined his party. There were thirty Presidents in thirty years, each of whom lasted as long as there was money in the Treasury to pay the army and provide jobs for the vast horde of bureaucrats and place-seekers, always ready to trim their sails to the prevailing wind.

In this struggle for survival, there was little room for idealism or patriotism, and Gutierrez d'Estrada soon found he was better equipped to serve his country abroad, by representing her in various European capitals, than in preaching the blessings of absolute monarchy in a land where every politician saw himself as a future President, and where one and all were united in their dislike of foreigners. This xenophobia was partially justified, for foreign conquest and exploitation had done little for the Mexicans. The four million Indians, who in 1860 made up half the total population of Mexico, still lived in the same primitive conditions as their ancestors had lived in under the Conquistadores.

England had been among the first to recognize Mexico's independence, hoping to find in the former colonies of Spain new markets for her ever-expanding economy. Two loans were floated on the London Stock Exchange, but the bankers demanded such a heavy rate of interest that not more than half the money ever reached the Mexican government. Others followed in England's wake, with France obtaining a substantial share of Mexican commerce. The most feared and hated of the foreign powers, however, was Mexico's North American neighbour, who, between 1837 and 1849, partly through war and partly through acquisition, absorbed over a million and a half square miles of Mexican territory, including the whole of Texas, New Mexico and Southern California.

Gutierrez d'Estrada had spent the greater part of his life in Europe, first as minister to Vienna and then in Rome, returning to Mexico in 1840 to serve as Foreign Minister during a comparatively peaceful spell in his country's chequered history. But the missionary in him was stronger than the politician, and a pamphlet published when he was still in office, advocating a monarchy with a European prince as the only means of ensuring a prosperous and stable government, roused the fury of all political parties and exposed him to the danger of losing his property and his life.

Disillusioned by his countrymen, he retired from politics and returned to Europe, taking with him the greater part of his fortune and settling down to live in splendour in a Roman palace. Here he married a daughter by a former husband of the Countess Lutzoff, wife of the then Austrian Ambassador to Rome. The smallness of her dowry and his own lack of quarterings were more than compensated by the vast wealth he derived from his Henneguen plantations in Yucatan. A zealous Catholic and a confirmed snob, he was very much at home in Vatican circles and, as the years went by, he got more and more out of touch with his country, believing in the promises of Antonio López di Santa Anna, one of the most dishonest and unscrupulous of all the political adventurers who exploited Mexico in her first forty years of independence.

A master in the art of the *pronunciamento*, Santa Anna succeeded in getting himself elected as President no less than six times and in emerging victorious in wars both against the Spanish and the French. Wars which began as punitive raids on the coast to assert the rights of foreign nationals, were dramatized into glorious victories, making him into a national hero. His disastrous leadership against the United States during the Texan war showed the Mexicans that their idol had feet of clay. Yet still he managed to survive a defeat which cost the country one third of its territory, mainly by playing up one party against the other and by making a financial deal with Washington, by which the Americans acquired one half of Arizona, a percentage of the ten million dollar sale going to pay Santa Anna's private army. The repercussions of this deal brought about the downfall of his government. But after three years of retirement in his magnificent *hacienda* of Magna Clavo, Santa Anna was back in office with almost unlimited powers, supported by the Church and the rich landowners, who saw in him their only defence against anarchy.

But the Santa Anna of 1853 was no longer the dashing figure, the self-styled 'Napoleon of the West' who, thirty years before, had overthrown Iturbide's Empire and whose leg, blown off in battle, was reverently embalmed and preserved in the Cathedral of Mexico City. Though he still travelled round the country with cages full of fighting cocks and a retinue of women, all reputed to be his mistresses, he himself was beginning to be conscious of his shortcomings. The people had grown tired of his posturings, tired of seeing his features on every hoarding. A European prince with an historic name, an elegant puppet figure whom he could still manipulate, would provide a new image for a fickle public. It was now that he remembered his old friend Gutierrez, who was forever tilting his lance in the monarchist cause, and in 1854 Gutierrez received secret instructions to sound the various Courts as to whether some archduke or prince might be sufficiently adventurous to seek a crown in the New World. Gutierrez was in no need of instructions. For thirty years he had been trying to interest European statesmen in Mexican affairs, and already at twenty-one had been one of the delegates sent to offer the Hapsburg Archduke Charles, brother to the Emperor Franz, the throne of Mexico before it fell into the hands of Iturbide. The offer had been declined, and in 1846 Gutierrez was still hanging around the corridors of the Ball-platz bombarding Prince Metternich with *aide-memoires*, running into thousands of words, for he was incapable of writing a letter of less than thirty pages. But in spite of the ornate and flowery language, his writings were not devoid of common sense. At the outbreak of the Mexican War, we read in one of his pamphlets: 'If the European Powers persist in ignoring America's aggressive policy towards her neighbours and allow it to go unchecked, still regarding this growing giant as a child, how will they be able to defend themselves in the future against America's encroachment in the field of industry and commerce? The triumph of America is only possible at the expense of Europe, who will have to pay dearly for her indifference and lack of foresight.'

But in 1846 Prince Metternich was more concerned with the revolutionary movement in Germany than in America. In his eyes, the Mexicans were now paying the price of their rebellion against the legitimate government of Spain. If Gutierrez d'Estrada was received with politeness at the Ball-platz, it was as Countess Lutzoff's son-in-law rather than as a Mexican diplomat, and his letters and pamphlets were barely read before they were committed to the vaults of the Ministry for Foreign Affairs, or dropped into a Chancellery waste-paper basket.

Eight years later, Gutierrez was to find European statesmen even less welcoming than Prince Metternich. In England, Lord Palmerston scarcely troubled to be polite to this verbose and elderly Mexican who had consorted so much with Jesuits that he practically smelt of incense; while the exiled King Louis Philippe showed no enthusiasm at the thought of exposing an Orléans prince to the vicissitudes of a Mexican throne. Nor was the moment propitious. With Europe on the eve of the Crimean War, all eyes were focused on the East. But Gutierrez refused to despair, concentrating his activities on Spain, which had never become reconciled to the loss of her colonies in the New World. In Madrid, he had an ally in a young Mexican diplomat who had served in London as second secretary to the legation before being posted to Spain, where his attractive appearance and charming manner gained him the entry into Madrid society.

José Hidalgo was the son of a Spanish officer who had declared for Iturbide during the Wars of Mexican Independence, and acquired large estates in Mexico. José himself had spent most of his youth in Spain, only returning to Mexico for a few years before he was posted back to Europe as a diplomat. In politics a Conservative, not so much out of conviction as from the desire to preserve his father's estates, Hidalgo, like Gutierrez, belonged to the class of patriot who, while professing to love his country, is happiest living out of it. Together they intrigued in the monarchist cause, keeping their instructions secret from the Mexican Ambassador, and were on the point of persuading a Spanish Bourbon prince to become a candidate for the Mexican throne when, in 1854, two revolutions, one in Spain and the other in Mexico, combined to wreck their plans. Gutierrez had to go back to his Roman palace and Hidalgo moved on to Paris, where his connections were even more dazzling than in Madrid. For among the friends of his youth was a certain Countess of Montijo, who had two lovely daughters, one of whom was now Empress of the French.

Meanwhile, the Liberals had come into power in Mexico, and Santa Anna had been forced to flee the country and seek refuge on a Caribbean island. The new government was composed of stern, uncompromising men, who represented for the first time the three million *Mestizos*, or half-castes, who till now had allowed themselves to be dominated by one million Creoles. The coldest and most incorruptible of these lawyers, doctors and philosophers who planned to rid their country of feudalism and to make her into a modern nineteenth-century state, was a pure-blooded Zapotec Indian from the mountains above Oaxaca, by the name of Benito Juarez. Neither Juarez nor his colleagues had any of the glittering panache of Santa Anna, but they were far more formidable than any of their predecessors. This time, the old Dictator had not dared to retire to his *hacienda* of Magna Clavo to cultivate his orchids and await the turn of events. Sensing the danger of the situation, he made provision for the future, transferring large sums of money to Cuba, which was still a Spanish colony, and acquiring a plantation on the island of St Thomas, at a safe distance and yet not too far from

Mexico. What neither Santa Anna nor exiles like Gutierrez and Hidalgo realized as yet was that he would never be called on again to launch one of his famous *pronunciamentos* – that from now on it was to be a battle not of personalities but of ideologies, of Liberals versus Conservatives, anti-clericals versus clericals, *mestizos* versus Creoles. It was to be a grim, bitter struggle, draining the life-blood of the country and destroying the economy.

The foreign concession-owners of the silver mines, which produced one-third of the silver in circulation throughout the world, protested when one of the 'silver trains' to the coast was attacked and robbed by a Liberal general, short of funds with which to pay his army. European merchants and businessmen resident in Mexico demanded compensation when their property was damaged by guerrilla bands and they themselves subjected to violence. British bondholders were indignant when the Liberals took over the custom houses at Vera Cruz and expropriated the excise duties, of which a third was already mortgaged in payment of interest on their bonds. European investors in general took alarm when they saw that the new government, going against the traditional policy of Mexico, was more inclined to favour the United States than Europe. From their island bases in the Caribbean, England, Spain and France saw with jealous eyes the new trade agreements between America and Mexico. For all his reputed incorruptibility, the new Liberal leader, Benito Juarez, was just as ready as Santa Anna to sacrifice national sovereignty for the sake of a few million dollars. Reports of a treaty giving the Americans the perpetual right of transit across the fifty-mile-wide isthmus of Tehuantepec, the shortest land route linking the Atlantic and the Pacific Oceans, coupled with the right of bringing in troops to protect their property and enforce order, aroused bitter and justifiable indignation, not only among the Conservative opposition but among some of the Liberals as well. By a strange irony this treaty, so favourable to the Americans, always in search of new trade routes between the Atlantic seaboard and California, was rejected in Congress by a group of Senators from the Eastern states, on grounds that it favoured the South. Two years before the outbreak of the Civil War, the feelings between the puritan democracy of the North and the slave-owning oligarchy of the South was already sufficiently bitter to confuse a national issue.

Right up to the spring of 1861, the Liberal Party of Mexico was supplied with money and arms by the United States, and it was American aid which, in the last months of 1860, finally gave the victory to Benito Juarez. Till then, the political situation had been in a continual state of flux. In 1857 the Liberals had been driven from the capital by the Conservatives and in 1858 there were two Conservative Presidents, Zuloago and Miramon, rivals for power in the central provinces, while Juarez kept control of Vera Cruz, the port which served as the lifeline to Europe. So desperate was the situation that Zuloago approached the French Minister to Mexico with the suggestion that French troops should be sent in to restore order in a country which was incapable of governing itself. But at the time Napoleon III was too absorbed in the cause of Italian nationalism to be interested in adventures overseas, and by the summer of 1859, Zuloago had been supplanted by Miguel di Miramon, the young Creole aristocrat who was the chosen champion and paladin of the Church.

The clergy was in the forefront of the battle. When the Liberals came into power in 1855, they made it illegal for the Church, who had been the biggest landowners in the country, owning nearly one third of the land, to possess land. In its original form the 'Ley Lerdo', named after the minister who had drafted the act, offered monetary compensation for the land. But the bishops had refused to make any concessions and preferred to plunge the country once again into civil war rather than give up their properties or renounce the tithes and dues they exacted from even the poorest of their Indian parishioners. Militant friars refused to abandon their *haciendas* and inside the great Franciscan and Dominican monasteries, reactionary leaders plotted conspiracies and collected the munitions of war, while the gold and silver ornaments of the sacristies were melted down to finance the armies of Miguel di Miramon, who at twenty-seven had the reputation of being the ablest general in the country. But Miramon was better at winning battles than at administering his finances. Juarez was still in receipt of the custom dues of Vera Cruz where two Conservative attacks had been repulsed, not so much through the valour of the defenders as through the dreaded *Vomito Negro* – the yellow fever prevalent in those areas, which decimated the ranks of the armies coming down from the High Plateau.

While the Americans continued to recognize the government of Benito Juarez, the European Powers accredited envoys to Miramon. In Paris, José Hidalgo was reinstated in his position as first secretary and in Rome, Gutierrez d'Estrada found many new adherents, now that Mexican bishops, banished from the towns under Liberal jurisdiction, were arriving at the Vatican with tales of the desecration of the churches. In Vera Cruz, Juarez passed a new decree by which all ecclesiastical property was to be confiscated without compensation, all cemeteries were to become national property and marriage a civil contract, so that there would be no obligation to pay the clergy either funeral or marriage fees. In Mexico City, the pro-clerical Miramon was beginning to realize that his funds were not inexhaustible. Without pay, his soldiers began to desert in the usual Mexican fashion and in desperation he turned to the Swiss banking house of Jecker, contracting at exorbitant rates a long-term loan: in return for three-quarters of a million Mexican dollars in cash, Jecker received government bonds at the face value of fifteen million dollars. He can hardly have expected future governments to honour a debt on such usurous terms, but he had powerful friends at the French Court and the claim of a Swiss banker who was later naturalized a Frenchman was added to the staggering total of Mexico's debt to France.

In the summer of 1860, Miramon was defeated for the first time by a Liberal army which outnumbered his troops by two to one. The Liberals, advancing from the Tierra Caliente towards the temperate zone of the central plateau, stripped and gutted the churches in every town and village they passed, making a bonfire out of the sacred images in every public square. The superstitious Indians saw their holy relics burnt by order of a man of their own blood, but the heavens did not open to destroy him, nor were his generals stricken down by the threat of excommunication. Miramon had meanwhile resorted to the methods of a guerrilla chieftain. In despair, the Creole aristocrat degenerated into a bandit, raiding the buildings of the British Legation in Mexico City and seizing the seven hundred thousand dollars on deposit for British bondholders. But this sum was not sufficient to feed his troops and, by the end of 1860, European ambassadors in Washington were reporting news from Mexico of the complete defeat of the Conservative Party and the victory of Benito Juarez.

Miramon fled the country, but he left behind him two of his lieutenants to carry on a guerrilla warfare in the mountains. One was the hard and merciless Leonardo Marquez, a man who gave no quarter to his prisoners and was considered savage even by Mexican standards. The other was a gentle and compassionate Indian, Tomas Mejía, who defended the clerical cause with a chivalry all too often lacking in the clergy themselves. The Liberals could not consider themselves secure so long as these two men were still at large and, on the very eve of victory, the Liberal commander-in-chief, Santos Degollado, was so depressed at the general situation that he believed foreign mediation to be the only means of pacifying the country. Juarez's reply to this suggestion was to dismiss him from his command, and the General, who more than anyone else was responsible for the Liberal victory, watched the triumphal entry of his army from a hotel balcony.

On 1 January 1861, the entire population of Mexico City, even to the Conservatives, were out cheering in the streets, for everyone was happy to see the end to a cruel, bitter war. The handsome young officers riding at the head of their troops, who marched to the sound of music, waving their regional banners and singing patriotic songs, provided the kind of spectacle in which the Mexicans delighted. But there was no music and little cheering when, ten days later, the plain black carriage of Benito Juarez drove into the capital. Creoles and even *Mestizos* looked with suspicion and dislike at the little Indian lawyer, dressed in a dark civilian suit, presenting a strange, incongruous figure against the vivid Mexican background of hot blue skies and churrigueresque buildings, of glittering uniforms and striped *serapes*. The flat Indian face with the dark, unblinking eyes was cold and austere – the face of a man who believed in the democratic ideal and was determined to govern legally and abide by the constitution, hoping to transform this rich, priest-ridden city into the capital of a nation of small peasant-proprietors. But he was soon to discover that, behind the opulent baroque façade, lay an empty treasury and a country in ruins, with European creditors pressing for payment, while the powerful American neighbour on whom he had counted for support was on the verge of a long and exhausting civil war.

12

French intervention in Mexico

In October 1861 Count Rechberg-Rotheulöwen, the Austrian Minister of Foreign Affairs, received a confidential letter from the Ambassador in Paris, Prince Richard Metternich. It informed him that a former Mexican diplomat, a certain Señor Gutierrez d'Estrada, an old acquaintance of Prince Metternich's father, had approached the Embassy with a view to ascertaining the reactions of Vienna to the Archduke Ferdinand Maximilian being offered the Mexican throne. D'Estrada assured the Prince there was a strong monarchist movement in Mexico, that the people were beginning to realize that the only salvation lay in foreign intervention.

Metternich, who was a prudent and experienced diplomat nurtured on statecraft, would have paid little attention to a man who for the past forty years had been hammering on the same theme, had he not been approached by another Mexican diplomat, a former ambassador in Paris called Juan Almonte, who was also of the opinion that his country would welcome a different system of government and even a foreign monarch. Metternich admitted that the idea of placing an Austrian Archduke on the throne of Montezuma appealed to his sense of the 'grandiose', but he was discouraged by the way in which the matter was being handled. In his reply, Count Rechberg agreed that 'the idea itself was tempting but could not come under any serious consideration without proper guarantees from France and England, the two great maritime powers, neither of whom would be willing to give active support to the establishment of a monarchy overseas'. Nevertheless, he did not want to turn the offer down completely, or to rebuff the Mexican advances, but merely to point out that the general situation, and Austria's position in particular, did not permit her to think in terms of adventures across the ocean.

Neither Count Rechberg nor Prince Metternich appears to have been surprised at the choice of the Archduke Ferdinand Maximilian. Spanish Bourbons and Austrian Hapsburgs were the natural choice of Latin American republics in search of a monarch. But they would have been astonished to hear that the whole idea had originated in the head of that charming old Countess Lutzoff, whom the Emperor's mother had appointed mistress to the household of the Archduchess Charlotte. Prince Metternich would probably not have given the idea another thought had he not noticed that the Emperor Napoleon, and even more so the Empress Eugénie, were taking an increasing interest in Mexican affairs and that Hidalgo, the handsome Mexican whom he met at the shooting parties at Compiègne, was becoming more and more popular at Court.

With the Liberals in power, Hidalgo was again out of a job, but he had sufficient means to keep up an elegant bachelor establishment in Paris, where his ex-chief, Almonte, had also taken up his headquarters. One of Eugénie's most charming traits was her loyalty to her old friends, and the young Mexican diplomat who had frequented her mother's drawing room in Madrid was equally welcome at St Cloud and at Compiègne, and even in the intimacy of Biarritz, where the Imperial couple spent their summer holidays in a villa by the sea which they referred to as 'our nest' (though no one was under any illusions as to the Emperor's periodic flights from 'our nest', nor how much the proud, high-spirited Empress suffered from her husband's infidelities).

It was during the Emperor's long and tempestuous affair with Virginia di Castiglione that Eugénie had again come across her old friend Hidalgo, when he was passing through Biarritz on the way to take up his post in Paris. She was lonely and unhappy at the time and found comfort in reviving childhood memories with someone who spoke her own language, forgetting that she was now the Empress of France and Hidalgo no more than the secretary of a second-class legation. For the next four years, Hidalgo was a member of that charmed circle which gravitated round the Empress with invitations to the boating parties at St Cloud and the shooting parties at Compiègne. With his gentle, insinuating ways he was able to make the most of his opportunities, profiting by his privileged position to advance the monarchist cause even at a time when he was ostensibly serving under Miramon and representing a republican government. It did not take him long to arouse the Empress's interest in a country which was a former colony of Spain, from where the Conquistadores had brought back to Europe the first gold and silver of the New World. Being a passionate royalist at heart, she disliked all forms of republicanism and bitterly resented the idea of a great Latin-American Empire falling under the domination of the Yankees. She was fond of airing her political opinions, and with no more than the most superficial knowledge of her subject, was heard to say as early as 1853 that 'the day will come when the French will find themselves fighting the Americans', whereupon her husband, who having spent several years in the States had probably a greater knowledge of the people than the majority of his subjects, interposed with an ironic smile that 'war was no longer possible in France, for all its energies were now absorbed in commercial and material interests'. This remark was made on the eve of the Crimean War, on which the Emperor was about to embark not for any material gain but because he was inspired by the Napoleonic passion for 'La Gloire'.

In his quieter and less impulsive manner, the French Emperor was just as much interested in Mexico as his wife. He had always been attracted by the New World. At the lowest ebb of his fortunes, when he was a prisoner in the Fortress of Ham, there was a moment when he even considered accepting an offer to become President of Ecuador. Long before Juarez had given the Americans the opportunity of cutting a canal across the isthmus of Tehuantepec, Louis Napoleon in his prison cell was studying the possibility of constructing a canal through Nicaragua and was the author of a brochure published in London, with a view to raising capital for the building of a 'Canal Napoleon'. But however thoroughly he may have studied the geography of Nicaragua, his knowledge of Mexico was as superficial as that of his wife. He relied almost entirely on the tales of a few émigrés and the highly-biased reports of his new Minister in Mexico, Dubois de Saligny, a diplomat who had already been placed on the retired list and owed his reinstatement to the protection of the Emperor's half-brother, the Duke de Morny.

Among the brilliant figures in the limelight of the Second Empire, none was more brilliant or more talented than Charles Auguste de Morny, son of Queen Hortense by the Count de Flahaut, whom Maximilian had met on his visit to Paris in 1856. The finest horses, the most beautiful women and the most exquisite *objets d'art* in Paris came within range of his acquisitive tastes, but the dominating passion of his life was gambling and even the enormous income of his Russian wife could not satisfy his needs. These were the occasions when the President of the Legislative Assembly degenerated into a company promoter and a Queen's son indulged in friendships with shady financiers. When Juarez refused to honour his claims and the Swiss Mexican banker, Jecker, found himself on the verge of bankruptcy, he approached the Duke de Morny, offering him in return for his political support thirty per cent of his Mexican bonds. The result was that Herr Jecker became a naturalized Frenchman and the claims of a Swiss banker became the concern of France. The Mexican émigrés, who had relied on a light-weight society diplomat as their chief contact at the French Court, could now count on the goodwill of the powerful Duke de Morny and his protégé, Dubois de Saligny, whose highly critical reports on Juarez and his government favoured the restoration of the monarchy. There was no direct telegraphic communication between France and Mexico (telegrams via Washington took nearly fifteen days and letters had to wait for the monthly packet boat which, when the Norte was blowing off Vera Cruz, was very often delayed) so the foreign envoys were left comparatively free to interpret their country's policy as they pleased.

Only the Emperor was still inclined to be cautious, listening with interest to news from Mexico but refusing to commit himself. The Empress would arrange intimate dinners with Hidalgo, at which the young diplomat would expatiate on the sad condition of his country and implore the Emperor to come to its rescue. But Napoleon inevitably replied: 'I would like to, but it is just not possible.' His reasoned opinion, before he allowed himself to be carried away by the Empress and de Morny and his own visionary dreams, was that no foreign intervention in Mexico was possible without the co-operation of England. He had once discussed the possibility with Lord Palmerston, but the English statesman had maintained that to intervene in Mexico would require 'millions in money, a vast army and a complaisant prince', and that England was not prepared to provide any of the three.

But by 1861 the situation had radically changed. America, who was strongly opposed to any form of European intervention in the Western Hemisphere, was now fully occupied with her own troubles. Two months after Juarez had entered Mexico City, the first guns had sounded at Fort Sumter, and the ally on whom he relied for his chief financial support was immersed in the grim struggle of a civil war. He had promised to honour the claims of the European bondholders, but the money brought in by the confiscation of Church property had gone to pay the army, and the finances of the country were in such a state of chaos that one secretary of the treasury after another resigned in despair. Realizing that for the time being he would be getting no more help from Washington, Juarez had no alternative but to declare a two-year moratorium, suspending all payments of foreign debts.

The envoys of France and England received the notice on 17 July 1861, and as neither Juarez nor his ministers were diplomats, no attempt was made to sugar the pill. Both Sir Charles Wyke, the British minister in Mexico and the Count de Saligny reacted violently to what Wyke defined as 'barefaced robbery'. Presenting a united front in spite of their mutual dislike, they broke off diplomatic relations with Mexico and threatened armed intervention, making no allowances for the difficulties the new government had to contend with in a country where guerrilla forces were still fighting in the mountains and the Church was silently sabotaging all efforts at progress. Without waiting for instructions, they immediately advised their naval bases in the Caribbean to prepare for an attack on Tampico and Vera Cruz. Meanwhile Spain, who was not in a position to break off diplomatic relations, her ambassador having already been expelled, threatened the landing of troops already fully mobilized in Cuba.

So bad were the communications between France and Mexico that José Hidalgo would have us believe that he was the first to inform the French Court of these stirring events nearly seven weeks later, when he was dining with the Emperor and Empress at Biarritz at the beginning of September. But by that time, Napoleon must have already been informed of Saligny's dispatch, which had arrived at the Quay d'Orsay on 30 August, though in view of Eugénie's impulsive temperament and not wishing to be rushed into a hasty decision, he may well have kept the news to himself.

Hidalgo writes of how, after dinner, Napoleon retired to his study while Eugénie and her ladies gathered round a table with their needlework. On the pretext of helping the Empress to sort some skeins of silk, he was able to whisper into her ear that he had received some very interesting letters from Mexico 'where events had occurred which might finally bring about the realization of their hopes', whereupon Eugénie left the room, returning a few minutes later to summon him to the Emperor's study. What Hidalgo regarded as being of the utmost importance was that now, for the first time, both England and Spain were prepared to intervene. Napoleon did not dare to admit in front of his wife that he knew all this already. He merely evaded the issue by saying that he 'had not yet received his minister's latest dispatches'. By his comments, it was clear that he had already given the matter considerable thought. 'If England and Spain are ready to take action,' he said, 'then France will follow suit so long as it is in our interest to do so. I am prepared to send a naval squadron to Vera Cruz but no landing troops.' According to Hidalgo he added: 'Should the people of Mexico wish to re-organize their country with the support of the European Powers, then France will be willing to lend a helping hand, for owing to the present situation in America, the moment is highly propitious.'

One doubts whether the French Emperor would have committed himself to this extent in front of a young Mexican whom he knew only as one of his wife's protégés, charming and entertaining at the dinner table but hardly to be taken seriously. He would have been far more likely to discuss the Mexican question with Hidalgo's old chief, General Almonte, who as Miramon's Ambassador in Paris and a former lieutenant of Santa Anna, had far more political experience and knowledge of the country. There was even a time when Almonte, who was reputed to be the natural son of the priest Morelos, one of the founder members of Mexican independence, had himself aspired to be President. But he was more of an intriguer than a leader, and now he was ready to advocate a monarchy, hoping, as Santa Anna had hoped in the past, to find a puppet prince whom he could control.

None of the Mexican exiles trusted the other, and Hidalgo owed his position in their ranks entirely to his friendship with Eugénie. In his highly-romanticized account, we hear of him discussing with the Emperor and Empress which Prince or Archduke would be prepared to accept the Mexican throne. When the name of the Archduke Ferdinand Maximilian came up, both Napoleon and Eugénie were of the opinion that he would never accept the offer, till suddenly the Empress appeared to have an inspiration and, striking her breast with her fan, cried out, 'Something tells me that he will accept!' Hidalgo would have us believe that this somewhat operatic scene was entirely unrehearsed, and that it was the first time the Archduke Ferdinand Maximilian's name was ever mentioned in connection with Mexico, and that it was entirely on his suggestion that Gutierrez was instructed to send out feelers in Vienna.

But what of Prince Metternich's letter to Count Rechberg, written as early as 5 July, by which time the Ambassador had already received a communication from Gutierrez and had held a conversation with Almonte, who would certainly have brought up the question of the

Archduke's candidature? Hidalgo appears to have had no knowledge of a conversation the Empress had with Prince Metternich on the evening of 17 July, at a party held by Count Walewski at his Château d'Etoiles. On this occasion, Eugénie spoke of nothing but Mexico, expressing the hope of establishing a monarchy and of bringing the country back to Christianity. The Archduke Ferdinand Maximilian's name may not have been directly mentioned, but Metternich, who had already been approached by Gutierrez and Almonte, had no doubt of the candidate she had in mind. Eugénie was never famous for her discretion. Richard Metternich was one of her closest friends, and the relaxed atmosphere of a summer fête, the absence of the Emperor, who was taking his annual cure at Vichy, combined to give free rein to her tongue. The Ambassador on the contrary was guarded and reserved, but the Empress's confidence showed him that her love of playing at politics was developing into an obsession, and that she was determined to push the Mexican question to the forefront.

Two months later, Metternich, who was on leave in Austria, received a highly-confidential letter from Count Walewski, in which the former French Foreign Minister informed him that 'government circles in Paris favoured the establishment of a monarchy in Mexico and were prepared to give *moral* support to the nomination of the Archduke Ferdinand Maximilian.' Walewski pressed for an early reply as to whether Vienna was in favour of the idea. Should this be the case, France was willing to take the initiative in gaining the support of London and Madrid. The Prince's reply would be communicated to the Empress, who was taking a personal interest in the matter. This letter, which was addressed from Biarritz and must have been written at the Empress's dictation, gave the Ambassador considerable food for thought.

Writing to his Chargé d'affaires in Paris, he noted, 'This insistence is very curious. You may mark my words, that if it is a question of the Empress, then the Emperor is also involved.' The Archduke's candidature was no longer just the wishful dream of a few Mexican exiles. Walewski's letter may have been dictated by Eugénie, but he would never have dared to send it without approval by the Emperor, who, though he may not yet have pronounced himself, already appeared to be as committed as his wife, though for somewhat different reasons. Eugénie saw herself as the champion of the Catholic Church, restoring a former colony of Spain to a descendant of Charles v; Napoleon took the broader view, envisaging France as the great civilizing influence of the Western Hemisphere with French commerce obtaining the lion's share of the South American markets. Behind them were others with less laudable motives, among them the Duke de Morny with his thirty per cent of Herr Jecker's bonds — bonds which would be valueless if Juarez remained in power.

Count Rechberg handed on Metternich's report to the Emperor Franz Josef, though neither Minister nor Ambassador ever contemplated the possibility of the Emperor's taking it into consideration. But neither of them realized the extent to which Maximilian had antagonized his brother during the past year, nor how infinitely attractive appeared a prospect which would take him to the other side of the world. Hardly a month went by without the secret police in Trieste reporting some injudicious remark or criticism of the government made by the Archduke Ferdinand Maximilian. Even visitors to Miramar were suspect, for among them was always some discontented Venetian nationalist, some liberal politician or a representative of the foreign press. Franz Josef had not forgotten the shouts of 'Abdicate!' and 'Long live the Archduke Max!' which had greeted him on his return from Solferino. Nor could he help resenting the spontaneous welcome the populace always gave Max on his rare visits to Vienna; the laudatory articles of the foreign press; the impertinent suggestion put forward by the British Foreign Minister that Hungary should be given back her independence with Ferdinand Maximilian as King. These were the continual stabs piercing his armour of arrogance and pride, and the most wounding of all was the knowledge that his mother secretly favoured Max, and was forever bringing up the subject of a suitable job for the son who, according to her, was wasting his talents in the navy.

Then out of the blue came the offer of the Mexican throne. Unfortunately, it was sponsored by the very man Franz Josef disliked and distrusted the most. In ordinary times, he would have sent a negative and proud reply, reminding the presumptuous Bonaparte that Hapsburgs had been offered and had refused the throne of Mexico at various times during the past forty years, and that therefore they had no need for the sponsorship of France. But in his present mood the thought of pleasing his brother's vanity and of getting rid of him at the same time was too tempting to be ignored. While treating the matter with his customary reserve, the Emperor instructed Count Rechberg to proceed to Miramar to discuss the project with the Archduke.

Ferdinand Maximilian was no stranger to the project. For the past month he and Charlotte had been thinking and talking of nothing else. He could hardly have ignored it with Gutierrez's mother-in-law living in the house, and King Leopold priding himself that Brussels was the best listening-post in Europe. What probably surprised him even more than the offer was the fact that his brother should have given it sufficient consideration to send his Foreign Minister to Miramar, and that Charlotte should have welcomed the prospect of the Mexican throne with such wholehearted enthusiasm. If Maximilian had his moments of boredom and dissatisfaction, they were always carefully hidden from his wife, and it was part of Charlotte's loyalty to her husband to pretend in public that nothing was more delightful than their present life spent between Lacroma and Miramar.

That this was far from being the case only becomes apparent in her later letters from Mexico, where, in the midst of her struggles and disappointments, she writes home to her former governess: 'Put yourself in my place and ask yourself, whether life at Miramar was preferable to our life here – no, no, a hundred times no. For my part I prefer a full active life, with duties and responsibilities – and even difficulties if you will – to an idle existence spent in contemplating the sea from the top of a rock until the age of seventy. That is what I have left behind, this is what I have gained. Balance one against the other, and you will no longer be surprised to hear that I am happier in Mexico.'

The measure of Charlotte's unhappiness at Miramar can be judged by this letter, and explains the eagerness, one might almost say the avidity, with which she grasped at the chance of a wider and more varied life. It was Max who hesitated, attracted on the one hand by the lure of the New World, but loath to tear himself away from the navy he had created, from his beloved Italy, and above all from Miramar, where he had watched and nursed every plant and tree. It was characteristic of him to put his doubts and hesitances on paper, to weigh the pros and cons in the form of a memorandum which he circulated among his friends. Unfortunately, the majority of his friends were not qualified to give him advice, for in spite of his intelligence he showed a curious lack of judgment in his choice of the people with whom he surrounded himself. His closest companion was Charles de Bombelles, who as his governor's son had shared his studies at Schönbrunn and followed him into the navy. Bombelles was a light-hearted spendthrift and libertine who encouraged the Archduke in his extravagances and earned the dislike of Charlotte by acting as a go-between in certain amorous adventures. But his influence was comparatively harmless compared to that of Sebastian Schertzenlechner, a valet at Schönbrunn, who had accompanied Maximilian on his travels and, by his resourcefulness and wit, had succeeded in ingratiating himself into his confidence. At Miramar, the ex-valet was elevated to the position of private secretary, where he was entrusted not only with official documents but with all Maximilian's personal papers and journals, which later provided him with endless opportunities for blackmail, the Archduke being sufficiently unwise to express his opinions on paper.

So strange was the relationship between the Archduke and the ex-valet that one would be inclined to give it a homosexual interpretation, had Schertzenlechner not had the reputation of being a womanizer who paraded his conquests in the most brazen manner, even going so far as to flaunt them in his master's presence. For all his feminine vanities, his love of the picturesque and the exotic, Maximilian was so little of a pervert that he was the only member of the Imperial family openly to condemn the homosexual tendencies of his younger brother, Ludwig Viktor, urging marriage as the only means of getting him away from his dissolute companions. There have been many examples of royal princes who found it easier to trust men in the lowest ranks of society. Even Franz Josef, who was so proud and correct, was more likely to unbend in the company of mountain guides than with his own courtiers. Where Maximilian erred was in the nature of the missions with which he entrusted Schertzenlechner, of which the first was to Paris to get in touch with the Mexican exiles, the second to Rome to seek the advice of the Holy Father. The ex-valet does not appear to have been appreciated, either by Creole aristocrats or by Cardinal Antonelli. It was particularly unfortunate that the Mexican offer should have come at a time when Wilhelm von Tegetthoff, the only good influence in Maximilian's entourage, was away at sea, and that both Bombelles and Schertzenlechner, neither of whom had any knowledge of Mexico or its people, were in favour of his accepting, the one from the love of adventure, the other because he hoped to acquire a more important position in a country where he would not always be reminded of his humble origin.

The memorandum, in which Maximilian declared that he would 'always and in every circumstance be found ready to make sacrifices, however hard, for the sake of Austria and the Hapsburgs', was couched in high-flown and idealistic language. He talked of reviving the ancient lustre of his house, dimmed in recent years by the loss of two sovereignties,* and stressed the advantage it would bring to Austria to have him on the throne of Mexico. That the sacrifice was not so great transpires in the pages of a private journal, written after one of his bitter quarrels with the Emperor: 'Neither my personality nor my individuality are in agreement with my elder brother, as he has made me understand in the most blatant manner. My liberal ideas scandalize him. He fears my outspoken ways and my impulsive nature. The experiences I have accumulated on my travels arouse his jealousy, but he is the sovereign who has the power, as I am the first to recognize, and in the circumstances all I can do is to retreat completely into the background. This I have done, retiring to the peace of Miramar, the silence of Lacroma. Now, out of the blue comes the offer of the Mexican throne, which gives me the chance to free myself once and for all from the pitfalls and oppressions of a life devoid of action. Who, in my position, in youth and health, with a devoted and energetic wife spurring me on, would do other than accept the offer?'

Here recorded in his journal is the fact that, from the very first, it was Charlotte who spurred him on, encouraged by King Leopold who, usually so wise and prudent, for once allowed himself to be carried away by his ambition for his daughter and the prospect of extending Coburg influence in the Western Hemisphere. But both King Leopold and the Emperor Franz Josef advised acceptance only on the condition that both France and England, the two maritime powers, guaranteed their military and financial support.

On 7 October 1861, Prince Metternich, who was still on leave in Austria, sent a secret dispatch to his Chargé d'affaires in Paris, telling him to inform Gutierrez in the strictest confidence that his Imperial Majesty, the Emperor Franz Josef, would not reject the proposals if they were deemed to be compatible with the dignity of an Austrian Archduke, and that, given certain guarantees, the Archduke Ferdinand Maximilan would be 'ready to respond to the wishes of the Mexican nation, should they call him to the throne'.

Prince Metternich, who had never for one moment considered the possibility of his master accepting a favour from France, was appalled at the speed in which events were taking shape and shocked by the way in which the French Emperor was allowing himself to be dominated by his wife and a handful of self-interested Mexican émigrés. The Ambassador

* The incorporation of Modena and Tuscany in the Kingdom of Italy was accounted a bitter blow to Austrian prestige.

had a great admiration and affection for Eugénie but he had very little opinion of her political acumen. What worried him most of all was that he did not think the young Archduke had any idea as to what he was letting himself in for. In a gloomy mood, he reflected, 'How many cannon shots will be needed to put him on the throne, and how many more to keep him there?' But the die was cast and with tears of joy, Gutierrez heard that, after nearly half a century of bombarding the Chancelleries of Europe with pamphlets and petitions, an Austrian Archduke had finally been persuaded to become candidate for the Mexican throne.

Never was a political venture launched with more publicized secrecy or more deliberate indiscretions. The fact that it was Gutierrez rather than the Quai d'Orsay who received the first intimation of the Austrian acceptance, shows that Franz Josef still hesitated to involve himself directly with France. Nor had Napoleon openly pronounced himself on the Mexican question, and it was only after being told of Austria's favourable reply that he composed his famous letter to his Ambassador in London, the Count de Flahaut, who as one of his mother's lovers and Morny's natural father, belonged to the closely-knit hierarchy of the Imperial Court. In this letter, Flahaut was instructed to sound the British government as to how far it would be prepared to go in the matter of armed intervention in Mexico, and to stress the benefits which Europe and the world at large would derive from a firm and stable régime in this vital area of Central America. Napoleon wrote that he had 'always been interested in Mexico, which, if properly governed, would serve as a powerful bulwark against the encroachment of the United States as well as providing new markets for European commerce. It is in the common interest of the maritime powers to come to the rescue of a country disintegrating through anarchy and misrule. Britain may have hesitated in the past for fear of endangering her relations with America, but now is the moment for action, when the war of secession renders it impossible for America to interfere, while Mexico's ill-treatment of foreign nationals and her suspension of payments justifies intervention on the part of the three naval powers, England, France and Spain.'

If the Ambassador felt a certain scepticism on getting this letter, it was nothing compared to the scepticism and even the embarrassment with which the contents were received by the British government. Though Lord Palmerston openly favoured the Confederates in the American Civil War and would have welcomed a Southern victory, he had too much common sense not to realize that, given their preponderance in both wealth and manpower, the Unionists in the end were bound to win, and once they were at peace, would never tolerate a European intervention in Mexico. The English were also far better informed than the French on conditions in Central America. Their minister in Mexico City had provided the Foreign Office with a long and impartial report in which he stated: 'So long as the present dishonest and incapable administration remains in power, things will go from bad to worse. But with a government formed of respectable men, the resources of the country are so great that it might easily fulfil its engagements and increase threefold the amounts of its exports. ... Unfortunately, the wealthy men of the Moderate Party are devoid of moral courage and afraid to move unless they have material support from abroad, and though there is no doubt that a constitutional monarchy would be the most likely to have sufficient power to consolidate the nation, the question is not 'What is the best for Mexico?' but 'What are the wishes of the Mexican people themselves?', and I feel the answer must be that the more intelligent people in this country favour Republican institutions.'

Such reports did not encourage the British government to waste men and money in placing an Austrian Archduke on the Mexican throne. The French Emperor's letter to his ambassador was completely ignored and both Lord Palmerston and his Foreign Secretary, Lord Russell, committed themselves only as far as to join in the action already recommended by the diplomatic representatives in Mexico. On 30 October a convention was signed in London by which the three naval powers, England, France and Spain, agreed on the joint occupation of Vera Cruz. England, who by now already suspected her allies of ulterior motives, insisted on inserting a clause in the convention to the effect that none of the powers was to aim at any territorial or other advantage for itself or make any attempt to interfere in the internal matters of Mexico. But the wording was so vague that neither France nor Spain had any difficulty in interpreting the convention to suit themselves, and the ink on the signatures was hardly dry before the powers had begun to quarrel.

The intentions of Spain became clear when, without waiting for her allies, she landed at Vera Cruz the six thousand troops she had already mobilized in Cuba. The commander-in-chief of the expedition was General Juan Prim, one of the most important and ambitious men in Spain, who would never have accepted the command had he not hoped to gain glory both for himself and for his country. The news of his appointment gave rise to fury and despair among the Mexican émigrés of Paris, for Prim was known for his democratic principles and had a rich Mexican wife related to one of Juarez's ministers. He was the kind of man who, once the honour of his country was satisfied, would have no hesitation in coming to terms with a Liberal government.

'The Empress is hopping mad [*fuchsteufelswild*] with the Spaniards,' reported Prince Metternich, who was now back in Paris and more than ever concerned at the way in which a foolish and impulsive woman was involving her husband and her country in a war. But Napoleon was already more involved than the Ambassador suspected. Unknown to his wife or to his ministers, he had met General Prim earlier in the year at Vichy, and together they had discussed the Mexican situation and the plans for a joint intervention. The French Foreign Office viewed with a jaundiced eye these '*villes d'eaux*' conspiracies where Napoleon, still tainted by his *Carbonari* past, conspired behind the backs of his ministers. But this year, the family holiday at Biarritz was to have more disastrous consequences than the secret meetings of Vichy, for by the autumn the Emperor was definitely committed to the creation of a Mexican Empire.

At first, he limited his expeditionary force to two thousand marines under the command of a Vice-Admiral, but both Hidalgo and the Empress begged him to send 'a few red trousers as well' and five hundred *Zouaves* and a field battery were added to the contingent. As soon as she heard of the Spanish landings, Eugénie began to press for further reinforcements, and two thousand five hundred troops under the command of a senior general set sail from St Nazaire on 9 January, the same day that the allied ships cast anchor off Vera Cruz. The British, who according to the American Consul in Mexico City were the only ones with legitimate claims, showed they had no intention of becoming involved in any military enterprise by sending no more than a token force of eight hundred marines and leaving the diplomatic negotiations in the experienced hands of Sir Charles Wyke, who, having broken off diplomatic relations with Juarez, now returned in the role of Commissioner to settle what, for England, was no more than a debt-collecting expedition.

Meanwhile, at Miramar, the Archduke Maximilian was falling more and more under the spell of Gutierrez's siren songs. At first, his keen sense of the ridiculous recoiled before all the flattery and 'incense' but gradually he acquired a taste for it. An Empire in the New World, which he had coveted ever since his visit to Brazil, was now being offered on a shining platter, and he saw himself once more as a man of destiny, born to regenerate a country. One of the saddest aspects of the whole Mexican affair is that the two leading protagonists, Napolean and Maximilian, were fundamentally good at heart and inspired by what they believed to be the highest motives. The one considered it his duty as a Bonaparte to trace new paths of glory for his country, the other felt himself called upon to revive the dying splendour of the Hapsburgs. Credulous and vain, pathetically vulnerable, they were both at the mercy of every ambitious adventurer. Once he had allowed himself to become involved in the Mexican gamble and to involve Maximilian as well, Napoleon had no alternative, when faced with failure, but to behave like any other political gambler who, having failed, must cut his losses and disclaim his associates.

But there were other cool, hard-headed men who should have warned Maximilian in time. There was his father-in-law, King Leopold, famous for his astuteness and political judgement. As a young widower living in England, he had been offered the Mexican throne and turned it down, but now he made no effort to dissuade the young couple from embarking on an enterprise even more hazardous than before. There was Franz Josef, usually so prudent and reserved, who had the power to exercise a veto on the actions of every member of his family, but who did nothing beyond impressing on his brother the need for caution in his dealings with Gutierrez, and the vital necessity of England's guarantee. Metternich and Rechberg did their best, faithfully bringing to his notice every unfavourable report. The Austrian Minister to Washington reported that when the newspaper first mentioned the Archduke's name as a candidate to the Mexican throne he had refused to take the matter seriously, for he was 'convinced that the three naval powers would meet with the greatest difficulties in Mexico, and it would be in every way regrettable if the name and person of the Austrian Emperor's brother were to become involved in this affair and exposed to failure'. The Ambassador to Spain was even more pessimistic, fearing that 'the whole business was fraught with danger and it would be easier to go to Mexico, than to return with honour and profit'. All those with any knowledge of Mexico and the Mexicans were of the same opinion, saying that Europe would achieve nothing in a country where 'foreigners were hated, and where any constitutional form of government would be a mockery'.

The most explicit of all was Miguel Miramon, whose arrival in Paris caused consternation among the Mexican exiles. Hidalgo and his friends were determined that the ex-President, who stated freely that there was 'no monarchist party in Mexico', should at all costs be kept away from the Tuileries, and they succeeded in slandering him so effectively that Metternich reported from Paris: 'The Empress hates Miramon, and says the Emperor will not see him.' It was impossible, however, to keep Miramon away from the opposition politicians and the press, who were beginning to devote long articles to Mexico, articles which were not always favourable to the Mexican émigrés.

But nothing could shake Eugénie's belief in Hidalgo, who in the whole course of his life had not spent more than three or four years in his country. Her confidence in Hidalgo was as misplaced as Maximilian's belief in Sebastian Schertzenlechner, whom he now sent on a confidential mission to Paris to get in touch with Gutierrez. It is doubtful whether Schertzenlechner could have found Mexico's position on the map, but he was shrewd enough to realize that Gutierrez was nothing but an empty windbag and practically told him so to his face. Knowing, however, that this was the last thing his master wanted to hear, he described him as 'the most ardent of patriots, with noble and elevated principles, who is heart and soul for the Monarchy'. And Gutierrez, who was jealous of Hidalgo's position in Paris and rightly suspected him of keeping him away from the Court, now pressed for an invitation to Miramar. Here, the ground had been carefully prepared for him by his mother-in-law, that delightful old lady who, all unwittingly, had blazed the trail which was to lead to a firing squad at Querétaro.

Maximilian was sufficiently ingenuous to believe that Countess Lutzoff did not know of his having accepted the Mexican proposals. Neither he nor Charlotte had taken her into their confidence and they would have been amazed to hear that for months she had been corresponding with her son-in-law, giving him every detail of the Archduke's character, his tastes and habits, so that when Gutierrez arrived in Miramar on Christmas Eve, 1861, he knew exactly with what words to blandish and with what sentiments to appeal to the vain, idealistic young Archduke. Rechberg's warnings were forgotten, caution was thrown to the winds. By the time their visitor left Miramar, Charlotte and Maximilian were irrevocably committed, dazzled by visions of a country which Gutierrez had not visited for over thirty years.

13

On the brink

In the New Year of 1862, it seemed as if it would be only a matter of months before Maximilian was crowned Emperor of Mexico. 'You can rest assured,' said the French Emperor to Prince Metternich, 'that it will not be my fault if we do not succeed.' But Vice-Admiral Jurien de la Gravière, commander-in-chief of the French naval squadron which landed at Vera Cruz in the first weeks of January 1862, did not share his sovereign's optimism. An honest and able sailor, more at home on the bridge of a battleship than seated at a conference table, he now found himself caught in a spider's web of diplomatic intrigue, armed with three different sets of instructions. One from the Ministry of Marine gave orders for the occupation of the strategic ports on the Gulf of Mexico, in conjunction with Spain and England. Another from the Ministry of Foreign Affairs stated: 'In case a prompt and satisfactory settlement of the claims made on the Mexican government was not forthcoming, then further action involving an advance on Mexico City would have to be considered.' Last and most devious of all were the instructions from the Emperor. Deluded in the belief that a strong monarchist party would rise in support of the allied landings, he instructed the Admiral to put himself in touch with the Conservative leaders in Mexico City with a view to forming an assembly of notables, gathered from the various states, to secure the eventual election of the Archduke Ferdinand Maximilian to the throne. These last instructions, which were contrary to the principle of political non-intervention agreed upon at the Convention of London, were to be kept strictly secret, and the Admiral's task was rendered still more difficult by the aggressive attitude adopted by his diplomatic colleague, the Count de Saligny, who was determined to sabotage all attempts at negotiation and to march on to Mexico City.

The French and English had arrived at Vera Cruz to find a Spanish flag flying above the fortress of San Juan d'Ulúa and six thousand Spanish troops encamped on the sand dunes outside the town. The English accepted the official explanation that the troops had sailed from Cuba before receiving the order to await the arrival of the allies. But Saligny immediately protested. Tempers ran high in the hot and steamy atmosphere of a port where every form of transport, every horse and cart had been moved away by order of Juarez, and where there was no sign of the joyful welcome Hidalgo and his friends had led the allies to expect. Such faces as they saw were hostile and afraid, for Juarez had issued a decree that any form of help, whether military or economic, offered to the allies would be punishable by death. Vera Cruz was closed to commerce and the custom-houses were empty of goods. But even Juarez was not prepared to defy the combined might of the naval powers, preferring to temporize and profit by the differences which were already threatening to break up the alliance.

England was merely interested in collecting her debts, while France was bent on conquest. Spanish intentions were devious, for the aims of General Prim appear to have been different to those of his government. The ambitious General and his Mexican wife saw themselves in the role of another Cortés and Marina,* while Queen Isabella was searching among her Bourbon relatives for a suitable occupant for the Mexican throne. But it was not long before both the General and the Queen's ministers realized that Mexico would never accept the rule either of a Spanish viceroy or a Bourbon prince. By the time of the allied landings, Spanish troops had already been three weeks in Mexico, long enough for General Prim to have come to the conclusion that Spain had little hope of recovering her former colony, where she was still as bitterly hated as in the days of the Inquisition. When the French, and in particular Saligny, made it clear that Napoleon was determined to establish a monarchy in Mexico and had already chosen a candidate, Spain began to lose interest in the expedition, and renouncing her own ambitions, joined with England in obstructing those of France.

All this had been foreseen by Juarez, who in reply to the allied manifesto assuring the Mexicans that they came 'not as enemies, but only to give a helping hand in the regeneration of your country', assured them with the utmost courtesy that the Mexicans were in no need of outside help, but that he was nevertheless prepared to appoint a delegate to negotiate a just settlement of their claims. Here the allies were in open disagreement, for Saligny, who was determined there should be no

* Marina, or Malinche, the Indian girl who became Cortés's mistress and assisted him in his dealings with her countrymen.

settlement with Juarez, presented a bill for damages to the property of French nationals amounting to the fantastic sum of sixty million francs, added to which he demanded the full repayment of the Jecker bonds to the tune of seventy-five million francs (fifteen million Mexican dollars), a sum which both Sir Charles Wyke and General Prim declared to be 'utterly unreasonable and unjustified'. Even his own colleague, the unfortunate Admiral Jurien, felt that Saligny was placing the French in an impossible position, for the more he saw of Mexico, the more he was convinced that the Emperor had been completely misinformed and that any action on a grand scale would involve his country in the expenses and casualties of a major war.

Meanwhile, his main concern was to remove his men as quickly as possible from the fever-ridden coastal area before the rainy season set in. The English, under the command of Rear-Admiral Dunlop, had landed only two hundred Marines, but both the French and Spanish had already suffered heavy casualties from the dreaded *Vomito Negro* and morale was correspondingly low. An ironic situation arose when the allies, devoid of transport, had to solicit the help of Juarez to evacuate their troops from Vera Cruz to the healthier hill country. It was absurd to expect the Mexicans to take an interest in the health of a foreign army which had come uninvited to their country, but here again Juarez was ready to compromise, and he sent a delegate to negotiate with General Prim, who in view of the language problem acted as the allied spokesman.

The meeting took place at La Soledad, a village a short distance from Vera Cruz, where a convention was signed on 9 February 1862. Later ratified by the British and Spanish governments, but publicly disavowed by the French Emperor, it laid down the preliminaries for negotiations to take place two months later, at Orizaba, thereby giving the commissioners the time to consult their respective governments. Pending these negotiations, the allied troops were to be quartered in the neighbourhood of Orizaba, a charming little hill town on the highway between Vera Cruz and Mexico City. Surrounded by coffee plantations and tropical gardens, enjoying a climate of perpetual spring, Orizaba lies under the shadow of the volcano which gives it is name. It must have seemed like Paradise to the soldiers coming up from the coast, and Saligny was the only one to object to the allied and Mexican flags flying side by side over the encampment.

The allies' recognition of his government was a victory for Juarez, and General Prim's 'reasonable' attitude showed that the Spanish government was choosing the path of prudence rather than glory. Sir Charles Wyke, who had never been interested in any other question beyond the settling of British claims, had already secretly come to terms with Juarez, thanks to the co-operation of the United States Consul in Mexico City, who was negotiating a loan of eleven million dollars to enable Mexico to pay her debts. But the agreement, which Sir Charles prided himself on having kept a secret from his French colleague, was later turned down by his government, partly because of Lord Palmerston's friendship for Napoleon, partly because the English mistrusted any agreement with Mexico which had the backing of the United States.

Juarez knew it was only a question of time before the Spanish and English disassociated themselves from the French. The idyllic surroundings of Orizaba did nothing to improve the tempers of the rival commissioners, who before long were all at loggerheads. The Spanish resented the high-handed manner adopted by the English, who when ex-President Miramon attempted to land at Vera Cruz, had him promptly placed under arrest and sent back to Havana on board an English destroyer. But both Spanish and English joined in protesting against the French when General Lorencez, commanding two thousand troops, arrived at the beginning of March, with Juan Almonte on board his ship. The presence of Almonte, who publicly proclaimed that he had come as Napoleon's emissary to help in establishing a monarchy, put an end to any hope of peaceful negotiation. He had barely landed before Juarez presented a request to the allies to hand over 'this traitor to his country', and both the British and Spanish were inclined to comply with this request. But already news of his arrival and of powerful French reinforcements had spread to the interior, giving fresh courage to the Conservative partisans, who till now had placed little hope in the support of the allied powers. Guerrilla troops began to offer their allegiance, but the ragged, hungry men who struggled into the French camp were not calculated to inspire confidence in the strength of a monarchist party. The clergy and the wealthy *haciendados* were still too frightened to show themselves and were waiting the turn of events.

On 9 April a stormy meeting took place at Orizaba, at which the English and Spanish delegates openly accused the French of having broken the terms of the Convention of London by extending special protection to an individual who had returned to his country for no other purpose than to destroy the existing government, and was speaking openly of establishing a foreign monarch assisted by French arms. Sir Charles Wyke, who had come down from Mexico City having successfully concluded his negotiations with Juarez, declared that the majority of the country was in his favour and that it would be hard to find any partisans for a monarchy. General Prim was of the same opinion, saying that the idea of establishing a monarchy under an Austrian Archduke on a continent full of republics was 'utterly absurd', only to be interrupted by Count Saligny, who in his most unpleasant manner remarked: 'The General only considered it absurd because he would have liked to have been the Emperor himself' – at which their colleagues had to intervene to prevent the enraged general from challenging Saligny to a duel.

Admiral Jurien, who for the past month had been the victim of Saligny's constant intrigues, and owing to the slowness of communications did not yet know that the Convention of La Soledad had been disavowed by the Emperor and that he himself was in disgrace, did his best to exercise a moderating influence. He declared that his government had decided that armed intervention was the only way of putting an end to anarchy and strife, but 'it was to be left to the Mexicans themselves to choose what form of government they wanted'. Saligny broke in to say that 'petitions were pouring in from all over the country begging the French to march on Mexico City' – a statement flatly contradicted by Sir Charles, who maintained that on his recent visit to the capital he had received the very opposite impression, and that even the French residents seemed 'to view with the utmost displeasure the prospect of a French advance on the city'.

This conference spelled the end to joint intervention and dissipated all hope of obtaining guarantees for Maximilian's future Empire. The English, who had already embarked their Marines, set sail from Vera Cruz the following evening, leaving the Commissioner, Sir Charles Wyke, to stay on in Mexico City as a private citizen, waiting for the resumption of diplomatic relations. By the middle of April, the six thousand soldiers sent by Spain to reclaim a former colony had all returned to Havana and a letter from General Prim, written before leaving the country, warned the French Emperor of the dangers of armed intervention. The General insisted that there was no monarchist feeling in Mexico, where the influence of the United States on a Liberal majority, and the dislike of all republicans for monarchist institutions, had combined to create a real feeling of hatred against the Conservative Party, a feeling heightened by the tactless behaviour of men like Almonte, who from the moment he landed at Vera Cruz had given himself the airs of a dictator. 'It will be easy,' wrote Prim 'for Your Majesty to get the Archduke Maximilian crowned as Emperor. But once you recall your troops, he will not have a chance to survive.' These warnings fell on deaf ears. For Saligny had led the Emperor to believe that Prim was in league with Juarez and had been responsible for the allies not having taken a firmer line. In the last days of April 1862, a French army of little more than six thousand men set out to occupy a country three times the size of France, and to carry out what Napoleon's ministers referred to as *la grande pensée du règne*.

Meanwhile, at Miramar, Charlotte and Maximilian had been entertaining a succession of Mexican émigrés, all of whom gave different advice. First it was Gutierrez, then Almonte, who came to pay his respects to his future sovereign before embarking for Mexico. Almonte brought with him a personal letter from Napoleon, who until then had communicated with the Archduke only through Prince Metternich. Urged by Eugénie to get into direct contact, he now wrote in his most effusive vein of how much he desired to see Maximilian 'at the head of a great and noble enterprise, which would shed further glory upon his illustrious house. Never would any achievement have finer results, for what could be more rewarding than to rescue a continent from anarchy and to set an example of good government to the whole of America?'

No words could have been more calculated to please the susceptible Maximilian, but with Napoleon it was not only a matter of fine sentiments. The financial aspect had also to be discussed, and Prince Metternich had already been sounded on three important points. First, there was the question of raising a Mexican loan to be guaranteed by the Great Powers. Then he was asked whether the Austrian Emperor would provide a battleship to take the Archduke to Mexico. Third and perhaps most important was the question of an armed force to support the new monarchy. Napoleon hinted that an Austrian corps would be the best, but this was immediately vetoed by the Ambassador, for Austria was not a naval power and it was impossible for her to involve herself in commitments overseas. Napoleon ended in agreeing with Metternich that 'it was up to those who had offered Maximilian a throne to defend him once he was there'. The Emperor had not yet received the first dispatches from Mexico and was still under the illusion that the Conservative generals would come forward with a *pronunciamento* as soon as the allies landed.

These points were fully discussed when Franz Josef and Maximilian met in Venice early in 1862. The project of a Mexican Empire was still in its first nebulous phase, but neither of the two brothers appears to have had any doubt of its success. Though both asserted that acceptance was subject to the guarantee of the naval powers, they were already interesting themselves in the smallest details such as the composition of the Imperial Household, and the decorations and titles to be given to Conservative leaders. We hear of them solemnly discussing whether ex-President Santa Anna, who from his Caribbean exile had declared for a monarchy, should be made 'Duke of Tampico' or 'Marquis of Vera Cruz'. Maximilian was still in a state of euphoria following the visit of Gutierrez, who had painted the situation in the rosiest colours. But it is incredible that Franz Josef, who usually had his feet so firmly on the ground, should have treated as an accomplished fact what was still only a chimerical idea. Not only was he agreeable to the floating of a loan of twenty-five million Mexican dollars to be effected through the banking house of Rothschild on the understanding that both French and English financiers participated, but himself offered to advance his brother two hundred thousand Austrian gulden out of the family funds to meet the preliminary expenses. Once the Mexican crown was accepted, the Archduke's annual apanage of one hundred thousand gulden was to be used in repaying the same sum back into the family funds, and in settling the still-outstanding debts on the building of Miramar. The Archduke was to be granted leave of absence from the command of the Austrian navy and provided with a battleship to take him to Mexico. The biggest concession of all was made by the Emperor in permitting recruiting for a volunteer corps to serve directly under Maximilian, independently of the French army. Officers were to be allowed to volunteer and if any wished later to return to Austria, they would be taken back into the army with the same rank they held on leaving. The only stipulation on which Franz Josef insisted was that there should be no recruiting in either Venetia or the Trientino – a condition which must have been inspired by his innate distrust of his brother's Italian sympathies. Later, this appears to have been hotly contested by Maximilian, and the Emperor's adjutant, Count Grenneville, once overheard Franz Josef saying in a rage, 'Let him go and take all his damned Italians with him!' The Venice meeting, however, was friendly and affectionate and the Emperor went out of his way to comply with Maximilian's requests. The most irrelevant details were gone into, and political problems were discussed over which they had neither knowledge nor control, such as the eventual recognition by Europe of the Southern states of America, which they decided would be given only on the understanding that the new independent states recognized the integrity of the Mexican Empire.

The one vital issue, which was later to be the cause of so much heart-searching and bitterness, was never even mentioned. Franz Josef never made his brother understand that, in accepting the Mexican crown, he would have to forfeit his rights as an Austrian Archduke. It was an issue he can hardly have ignored and, if he deliberately avoided the subject, it was because he wanted to encourage Maximilian to accept an offer which, if it succeeded, would not only give back to the Hapsburgs an Empire in the New World, but would rid him of a brother who had become a political liability. General Count Grenneville, who like most of the Emperor's entourage was opposed to any dealings with Napoleon, voiced his master's sentiments in writing: 'Whatever there may be against the Mexican project, it nevertheless provides a good opportunity of getting rid of a gentleman who will otherwise cause our poor Emperor a great deal of worry and displeasure.'

The female members of the Imperial Household were united in their disapproval, and for once the Empress was in agreement with her mother-in-law. Elisabeth could not understand why Max should want to exchange a free and happy life for the boring complications of a throne, and she blamed Charlotte for not leaving him in peace to enjoy the beauty of Miramar. But his mother, the Archduchess Sophia, who fore-saw the difficulties ahead far more clearly than either of her sons, knew that Max's restless spirit was just as dangerous as Charlotte's ambition. One of her closest friends, the German authoress Ida von Hahn-Hahn, commiserated with her in a letter: 'It is sad but only natural that some-one so alive and enterprising as the Archduke Max should seek a suit-able outlet for his talents. He is one of those fascinating, outstanding personalities whom one adores but for whom one is always afraid.'

Maximilian had forgotten his initial doubts and hesitations, and was so completely under the influence of Gutierrez that he was already nam-ing the members of a Regency for a government which did not exist and advocating the return of the exiled Mexican bishops, none of whom had any intention of returning until their country had been fully pacified by the French. Both Metternich and Rechberg were too cautious for his liking and he was contemplating appointing Gutierrez to be his official representative at the French Court. But neither Napoleon nor Eugénie could stomach the pompous, garrulous old Mexican with his antedeluvian ideas. An interview at which Gutierrez was sufficiently unwise to try to poison Napoleon's mind against Almonte was sufficient for the Emperor to realize that it was impossible to have dealings with a man whose 'narrow-minded bigotry would endanger the whole enterprise'. Eugénie remarked to Hidalgo that the views expressed by Gutierrez made her feel that she was 'back in the days of Philip II and the Holy Inquisition', a comment Hidalgo lost no time in repeating to Gutierrez, who complained in a letter to the Archduke that there appeared to be 'a regular conspiracy' against him.

By now Maximilian was ready to regard a rebuff to Gutierrez as a personal affront to himself. But both Metternich and Rechberg considered that these personal communications between the Archduke and Gutierrez were liable to misinterpretation at a time when the Mexican situation called for the utmost reserve, and Franz Josef informed his brother that all matters referring to the Mexican candidature had to pass through the official channels of the Austrian Embassy.

The news of the convention signed at La Soledad, and of the allied powers having to negotiate with Juarez, confirmed Prince Metternich's suspicions that Napoleon had been completely misinformed by his Mexican advisers. The Emperor might rage against the weakness of Admiral Jurien in allowing himself to be hoodwinked by General Prim, Eugénie might 'spit fire and brimstone' against her Spanish compatriots, but the fact remained that so far no Mexican of any importance inside the country had raised the monarchist flag. As a result Metternich thought it would be wiser for the Archduke to withdraw his candidature, and his London colleague was of the same opinion. Feeling in England was hardening against the Mexican project. The recent victories of the Union forces in the American Civil War and a statement by President Lincoln that America would not stand for any infringement of the Monroe Doctrine and that any European Power who intervened in Mexican affairs would sooner or later encounter the hostility of the United States, combined to make English ministers even more prudent. Lord Russell told Count Apponyi that he was 'amazed an Austrian Archduke should be attracted by an undertaking so bristling with difficulties', and King Leopold, who was doing his best to enlist English support for a guarantee, had to admit to his daughter that the government was dead against any kind of involvement and there was little to be expected beyond moral support. He had hoped to gain the co-operation of Victoria, but his niece was now a heartbroken and inconsolable widow who kept repeating that 'dearest Albert had always been very much against the idea'. Leopold was an old, sick man, who before he died would have liked to have established another Coburg throne, but he had little concrete advice to offer the Archducal couple when they visited Brussels in May. Their visit coincided with the news of the breaking-off of the negotiations at Orizaba and the evacuation of the British and Spanish troops. Even Maximilian realized that, for the moment, it was better not to commit himself too far, and he reluctantly postponed a projected journey to Paris. The matter of his candidature was now public knowledge and unpleasant articles had been appearing in the Vienna press on an Austrian Archduke's willingness to become a vassal of France.

Meanwhile, General Lorencez had informed the French Emperor that, without allies, France was gaining adherents every day and it was 'only a question of weeks' before he hoped to be in Mexico City. He was now marching on Puebla, a stronghold of the Church, where he was assured he would be met 'with nothing but flowers'. Lorencez did not write of the long forced marches, the difficulties of supplies, the terrible effects of the yellow fever which was decimating the troops within a few hours of their landings, so that out of seven thousand men, less than six thousand were fit to take part in the march on Puebla. Misled by this report, Napoleon wrote to Maximilian, 'The news from Mexico is very good, now that we have at last emerged from the fumbling and ridiculous advances that General Prim was making to the Mexican government; the next post will however bring decisive news, for if the great city of Puebla pronounces for us, the odds are that the rest will follow. . . . I am most anxious to know what has been going on in the last month. General Lorencez wrote that he reckoned on being in Mexico City on 25 May at the latest.'

This letter was dated 7 June, but the dispatch which arrived a few days later shattered all Napoleon's facile optimism. Puebla de los Angeles had met the invading army with gunshot instead of flowers. Each baroque church with its tiled dome had been turned into a fort, and four thousand Mexicans in shabby uniforms, fighting with obsolete British weapons left over from Waterloo and sold to them years ago by the British government, had succeeded in defeating the finest soldiers in Europe, the veterans of Sebastopol and Magenta, and had added the glorious 'Cinco di Mayo' to the annals of Mexican history.

'Withdraw while there's still time,' was the advice which reached Maximilian from all responsible quarters: from diplomats and businessmen who had lived in Mexico, to those who like Prince Metternich were witness to Napoleon's black depression and Eugénie's hysterical tears following the defeat of Puebla, and who saw how public opinion in Paris was turning against the Mexican war. But the honour of France was now at stake, and the Legislative Assembly voted unanimously to send further reinforcements which would bring the expeditionary force up to a total of thirty thousand men. Even King Leopold, who had not yet given up the hope of seeing his daughter as an Empress, had to admit, 'Everyone who knew the Mexicans had unfortunately the worst opinion of them', and experienced diplomats like Sir Charles Wyke went out of their way to warn the Archduke 'not to venture into such a hornets' nest'.

But Maximilian was only willing to listen to the flattery of Gutierrez and the optimistic letters of Hidalgo, who was determined not to leave his older colleague in sole control at Miramar. It was he, after all, who had been mainly responsible for what the Empress proudly referred to as 'her war'. But, at present, 'her war' was hardly the victorious campaign Hidalgo had led her to expect and bitter letters were arriving from soldiers and officers on the Mexican front, complaining that the whole ghastly misadventure had been 'born of a woman's whim'. The popular young Mexican found himself for the first time *persona non grata* in the Parisian drawing rooms. Relatives of men who had died in Mexico turned their backs and unpleasant remarks were made in his presence, but he still found grounds for optimism. The weeks that followed the defeat of Puebla saw the first successes of Mexican guerrillas fighting together with the French – successes which were exaggerated a hundredfold in the letters which Almonte from Mexico and Hidalgo from Paris addressed to the credulous Archduke. When Metternich advised Maximilian that this was 'the favourable moment which might not return again' to withdraw from the whole hazardous enterprise, he replied that he adhered to his original intention with regard to the throne of Mexico as 'I do not want to let down Napoleon. On the other hand, I do not want to cause him any embarrassment, should recent developments have forced him to modify his projects.'

Metternich suspected that for the present Napoleon would have welcomed the news of the Archduke's withdrawal, for the Emperor was beginning to realize that there was little hope of producing even the semblance of a plebiscite in his favour. The whole business had been grossly mishandled and Almonte had complicated the issue by publicly announcing that he had been sent by the French Emperor to set up a monarchy, whereas it should have been done in such a way as to look as if it emanated from the wish of the Mexican people themselves. Quarrels and rivalries added to the confusion. General Lorencez, who had been so sanguine of victory, now blamed his defeat on false information supplied by Saligny and Almonte. They, for their part, blamed the General for not acting on their advice. Admiral Jurien, who had arrived in Paris to defend his conduct against the accusations of Saligny, supported Lorencez in stating that the position of the military command in Mexico was rendered untenable by the intrigues of the French Minister, and that Almonte was acting entirely in his own interests. But Saligny had a powerful protector in the Duke de Morny, whose financial interests he had defended to the extent of making the repayment of the Jecker bonds a major issue in the allied ultimatum to Juarez, and Napoleon was sufficiently unwise or sufficiently weak to allow himself to be influenced by Morny and the Empress, both of whom insisted that Saligny had done more than any other Frenchman to uphold his country's prestige in Mexico.

The small expeditionary force had grown into a large army with the infantry commanded by a brilliant officer, General François-Achille Bazaine, while General Forey was in supreme command of both civilian and military affairs. Forey was 'a man of great military reputation and high sense of honour'. But to succeed in Mexico and at the same time to please the Emperor Napoleon required tact and guile, duplicity and cunning, qualities which are not usually associated with military integrity. Once again, Napoleon supplied a complete set of instructions so complicated and so contradictory that they were almost impossible to carry out.

The General was to curb the powers of Almonte while keeping on friendly terms both with him and with any other Mexican leaders who came over to his side. He was to co-operate with Saligny, but the diplomat was to be under his orders. These instructions alone would have been sufficient to tax the ingenuity of a Machievelli, for Saligny was not a man to take kindly to a subordinate position, nor would Almonte enjoy having to renounce the self-styled title of 'Head of the Nation' he had assumed on landing at Vera Cruz.

The Emperor's instructions on policy were even more involved. The

General was to show respect for religion, but at the same time assure the owners of Church property acquired under the Juarez régime that they would not have it taken away from them. He was to empower Almonte to summon an assembly of notables representing all shades of political opinion but choosing only those who had given their adherence to the French. This in itself was a fallacy, for so far not a single Liberal had supported the intervention.

Should the assembly vote for a monarchy, and it was made abundantly clear that this was the French Emperor's wish, then the name of the Archduke Ferdinand Maximilian would be brought forward as a favoured candidate. Here Napoleon inserted a sentence which showed that his intentions were not quite so altruistic as he had led people to believe. His general was told quite plainly that 'whatever prince was elected to the Mexican throne would be inevitably committed *to act in the interests of France*'.

This was a statement very different to the high-flown letters addressed to Miramar, and would not have been well received by a prince who already saw himself appointed by divine right to rule over the Mexican people. But Napoleon had larger issues in mind than the election of a Hapsburg Archduke or the repayment of the Jecker bonds. At heart, he was still the dreamer of the Fortress of Ham, envisaging the civilizing influence of France triumphant in the New World and ships flying the French flag putting in at every Central and South American port.

In March 1862, when the allies were anchored off Vera Cruz, Abraham Lincoln had dictated a note of warning to the three naval powers. The President's note declared: 'A foreign monarchy set up on Mexican soil in the presence of European naval and military forces would be an insult to the republican form of government which is the most widely spread on the American continent, and would mean the beginning rather than the end of revolution in Mexico. The sympathies of the United States would be on the side of her sister republic, for the liberation of the continent from European control has been a leading feature of American history in the past century.'

According to King Leopold, this note was largely responsible for England's 'timid' attitude in regard to Mexico. But Napoleon was still hoping for a Confederate victory. In the late summer, the Southern forces had rallied under the brilliant leadership of General Lee, and the French Emperor reverted to his original plan of securing recognition for the Southern states. King Leopold, who still persisted in regarding himself as 'the Nestor of Europe', was also convinced that recognition of the South would be in the best interests of Europe, and particularly of England, and tried to influence his niece in that direction. But the Queen's Foreign Secretary, Lord Russell, had as little intention of recognizing the Southern rebels as of supporting a monarchy in Mexico.

The months that followed the defeat of Puebla were months of nervous uncertainty for Maximilian and Charlotte. Embarrassed by the over-sanguine letters he had written in the spring, Napoleon did little beyond assuring Prince Metternich that he would 'never fail the Archduke'. There was nothing to report from Mexico, where Lorencez had been ordered to await the arrival of General Forey, due to land at Vera Cruz at the end of September 1862. The new commander-in-chief had taken the Emperor's instructions to heart and was determined not to repeat the mistakes of his predecessor and not rush into action unprepared. Over a month was spent in organizing transport and supplies. But all his caution could not prevent the terrible yellow fever from attacking troops unused to the tropics and the crowded graveyard on the island of Los Sacrificios, the very place where Cortés and his men first saw the remains of human sacrifice, was known to the French troops as 'Le Jardin d'Acclimatation'. Those who were spared the yellow fever were attacked by malaria on the long march inland to Orizaba. One regiment alone suffered nine hundred casualties, close on fifty per cent of its striking power, and Prince Metternich reported from Paris that the Emperor was 'very depressed by the heavy losses suffered by the French army. People in Paris are beginning to talk of a second Beresina, and confidence will only be restored with the capture of Mexico City.' But the rate of sickness was so high that General Forey kept his troops for three months at Orizaba before considering them sufficiently fit to undertake the ascent of the formidable Cumbres which guard the approaches to Mexico City.

Meanwhile, Juarez was profiting by the delay to add to the fortifications of Puebla. His best troops and his best officers were detailed to defend the town, and anyone who gave assistance to the enemy was summarily shot. The French reached the outskirts of the city on 19 March, and a day later went over to the attack. But it was not until two months later, three weeks after the civilian population had been evacuated, and at the end of a siege of sixty days, that the garrison was finally starved into surrender. The admiration of the world went out to the heroic defenders of Puebla. Napoleon's bitterest enemy, Victor Hugo, addressed a letter to his Mexican brothers-in-arms 'defending their liberties against the tyranny of a Bonaparte'. And when the French troops marched into the city, they found a copy of the letter posted on every wall. But Forey's prudence and caution had won the day, and the capture of Puebla with twelve thousand prisoners – including one thousand officers and some of Juarez's most experienced generals – spelt an end to all organized resistance. Left with the remnants of an army scattered all over the country, Juarez abandoned the defence of Mexico City and moved his seat of government five hundred kilometres north to the small provincial town of San Luis Potosi. But he still proclaimed his faith in an ultimate victory, and in Washington he was still referred to as the President of Mexico.

There was jubilation at the Tuileries, where Metternich reported that 'Eugénie was radiant while Napoleon wept from joy'. But the General who had conquered Puebla was denied the fruits of his success. A whispering campaign of defamation originating in letters from Mexico was assiduously spread by Hidalgo: 'Forey was a bungling fool whose dilatory tactics made a laughing stock of the French army. ... In by-passing Puebla, he might have spared hundreds of lives and reached Mexico City three months earlier. ... The situation had only been saved by Achille Bazaine, who in a brilliant action foiled an attempt to cut off the French army in the rear.'

Forey's detractors even went so far as to say that the capture of Puebla had been preceded by quite unnecessary street fighting and that the prisoners taken had been so carelessly guarded that three of Juarez's best generals had been allowed to escape. Writing to Hidalgo, Saligny described Bazaine as 'a real general, clear-sighted and energetic – a man who understands the Mexicans and speaks their language'. And Hidalgo made sure that the contents of this letter reached not only the Tuileries but also Miramar. With an incredible effrontery he boasted to the Archduke's secretary, Baron du Pont, of the nefarious intrigues by which a small group of men, including 'a certain exalted personage working in His Majesty's entourage' [who must have been the Duke de Morny], were doing their best to undermine the reputation of the commander-in-chief. 'If Forey is created a marshal, things will be much better for us, for then he will return to Paris, and we may succeed in having Bazaine at the head of the army. He is the man whom everybody wants. He is as much beloved by the French as by the Mexicans and his abilities are praised both as a soldier and a statesman.'

It was Forey who, all unconsciously, added to the growing legend of Bazaine by putting him in command of the advance columns which entered Mexico City on 7 June 1863. The population, which since the departure of the government had been living in constant fear of the bandits who ravaged the countryside and made incursions into the suburbs, welcomed the French troops with a wild enthusiasm, and Bazaine rode through the streets under a shower of flowers. Four weeks later, Prince Metternich was reporting to Count Rechberg that 'influential quarters in Paris' intended to replace Forey and entrust the direction of Mexican affairs to Bazaine.

At Miramar, the news of these victories brought not so much jubilation as relief. The long silence had told on Maximilian's health and nerves, and he was becoming increasingly uneasy over 'the incomprehensible lethargy' of England, which made his whole future dependent on the goodwill of France. Napoleon had only to change his mind and the fabric of imperial dreams would come tumbling about his ears, leaving him an unemployed Archduke, writing poetry at Miramar. The hard-won victory of Puebla had shown him that there was no organized monarchist party in Mexico. Almonte was constantly writing to him for money to feed and clothe the poor Mexicans who looked so miserable beside the well-fed French soldiers. But there were plenty of wealthy *hacendados* in Puebla and elsewhere who could have provided the money to feed the troops, and he was averse to sending funds as if he were trying to buy votes. It was only on Napoleon's insistence that he grudgingly consented to advance the sum of fifty thousand francs.

Maximilian was beginning to realize that neither Gutierrez nor Hidalgo, nor any of the other émigrés with whom he had been in touch, had any idea of the situation inside the country. The bishops living in luxurious exile in Rome may have had some inkling of the truth, for not one of them had returned to his diocese. There were times when he might have faltered before the immense difficulties and risks; times when he might have tired of all the rivalries and back-biting. But behind him was Charlotte, bored and dissatisfied at Miramar, burning with ambition to be an Empress, interpreting that ambition in the light of a sacred mission, mixing metaphysics with ordinary human vanity, recognizing the divine hand of Providence in events which the more cynical Maximilian recognized to be the very reverse of divine.

Nevertheless it was Charlotte who had the good sense to prevent her husband from sending Sebastian Schertzenlechner on a fact-finding journey to Mexico, and who insisted on the mission being entrusted to someone who had no connection with the Mexican émigrés. In a letter to her father, she explained that both she and Max wanted to hear 'an impartial account of the state of affairs in Mexico', for so far they had not heard a single report which had not passed through the hands of the Mexicans in Paris, whose numbers were too small to represent the opinion of a nation of eight million people. But the man whom she proposed to send on this mission, and from whom she hoped to receive a completely unbiased account, was an ex-correspondent of the London *Times* whom Juarez had expelled from Mexico because of his Conservative views.

Bourdillon, a naturalized Englishman of French origin, was more interested in business than in journalism, and the vast and largely unexploited mineral wealth of Mexico offered fascinating prospects to someone of his knowledge and experience. The English Minister, Sir Charles Wyke, had disapproved of some of his business dealings and had refused to give him the diplomatic protection he had asked for at the time of his expulsion. In Europe, however, he was hailed as an authority on Mexican affairs – not only in Miramar, where Charlotte and Maximilian listened to him entranced, but also at the Tuileries, where the Emperor Napoleon took particular interest in his account of mining prospects in Sonora, the great northern state which was still virtually '*terra incognita*'. King Leopold too was impressed by Bourdillon's honesty and knowledge, going so far as to say that he 'probably knew more about the country than the Mexican politicians themselves'. Even Count Rechberg gave him a friendly welcome at the Ball-platz, though he was usually inclined to suspect anyone coming with a letter of introduction from Miramar. Like Leopold, he found him likeable and honest but somewhat over-sanguine in his views, particularly when he spoke of the mineral wealth of the country and its enormous capacity for future development.

Bourdillon took on a different tone when speaking of the Mexican people, for whom he had an undisguised contempt. One sympathizes with Juarez in expelling a journalist who described the Mexicans as 'rotten to the core and good for nothing but thieving'. The rival parties, he said, were merely rival factions, led by military leaders most of whom had risen from the dregs and who, when they came to power, all behaved identically. The majority of the population was so poor that money had the greater power to corrupt and even those who made the finest protests of patriotism could be bribed. The soldiers were mostly brave, but the officers with a few exceptions were cowards. Education was non-existent, and the Indians were so ignorant and downtrodden that most of them were unaware of what government they were living under – a fact which rendered a plebiscite almost impossible. In Bourdillon's opinion, the French would have to stay a long time to pacify the country and if the Archduke wanted to reign with any hope of success, he would have to bring with him some Europeans of talent and probity, for there were few to be found in Mexico. Also, two or three thousand Swiss Guards might come in useful to protect his person.

The picture drawn by Mr Bourdillon was not very encouraging. In his eyes, 'the Archducal couple were far too good for Mexico', but if the country were properly colonized, and immigration encouraged, then it could easily become one of the richest areas in the world. And for all their lofty ideals, both Napoleon and Maximilian were as irresistibly attracted by the glittering prospect of the gold and silver mines of Mexico as were the first of the *Conquistadores*.

Bourdillon had landed in Europe in the early spring of 1863 at a time when the news from Mexico was scanty and unsatisfactory. But only a few weeks later, the myth of his infallibility had faded: the heroic defence of Puebla had proved him wrong in his judgment of the Mexican people. Half starved, and with their salaries in arrears, the soldiers of Juarez had fought with a grim tenacity – 'Something we had never been led to expect,' wrote King Leopold to his daughter in a letter from Laeken dated 11 July 1863. 'Who would have thought that such a rotten government would have found such stalwart champions? One expected it to fall at the first blow, but unfortunately, this has not been the case and such a vast country will be difficult to occupy if they keep on attacking in the rear.' Even King Leopold was beginning to lose his enthusiasm, and in the spring of 1863 we find him actively seconding the attempts of the British government to persuade Maximilian to accept the vacant throne of Greece.

Lord Palmerston and his Foreign Secretary, Lord Russell, had always had a liking for the liberal-minded Archduke, and on more than one occasion had unsuccessfully intervened with the Austrian Emperor to get him appointed either as King of Hungary or Governor-General of Venetia. Like Bourdillon, they considered him 'far too good for Mexico' and hoped to prevent him from venturing any further by offering him the throne from which his cousin Otto had been deposed a few months earlier. But they had not reckoned with Hapsburg pride and Maximilian's exaggerated sense of chivalry. Both he and Franz Josef considered it to be 'the height of bad taste' on the part of the English government to offer him the throne of a country from which their cousin Otto had had to flee on an English battleship, but to which he had never renounced his natural right. Maximilian had the tenderest memories of the beautiful and courageous Queen Amalia, and he had nothing but contempt for a people who had failed to appreciate her qualities. But what outraged him most of all was that the throne of Greece had already been offered to and declined by half a dozen princes. Yet here was King Leopold, at the instigation of Queen Victoria, urging him to accept a throne 'which was of incomparably greater importance than that of Mexico'.

With a biting sarcasm, Maximilian wrote to Count Rechberg, complaining of the lack of tact on the part of the British Cabinet in making such an offensive proposal. 'Even if it had been lawfully vacated by my cousin King Otto, I should be the last to feel inclined to accept a throne which had been hawked around unsuccessfully to half a dozen princes. I am too well acquainted with modern Hellas and its present corrupt condition not to be convinced that it would be impossible to build the firm foundations of an independent state with a people as crafty and as morally degenerate as the modern Greek'. His language to his father-in-law was more moderate in tone. He refused the offer but asked him to thank Lord Palmerston on his behalf. And as the British Prime Minister appeared to be so well disposed towards him, perhaps he could get him to support him in the Mexican candidature – 'for there lies a brilliant future – a country of immense natural riches, while Greece is poor in men and money'.

The Greek crown was not the only one Maximilian was offered in the spring of 1863. Poland, the breeding-ground of revolution, was again on the brink of revolt and a considerable body of European statesmen was in favour of restoring it as an independent monarchy. Several names were mentioned as possible Kings of Poland, including that of the Archduke Ferdinand Maximilian. Nothing came of the idea and the rebellion of 1863, put down by Russia with a sanguinary ferocity, ended all Poland's hopes of independence. The offer of two crowns within the year boosted Maximilian's morale and appealed to his somewhat childish conceit, making him less willing than ever to be dictated to by

Vienna. But in his brother's eyes, he was still an Austrian Admiral who had to obey his orders, and we find Maximilian complaining in his diary, 'Here I am refusing thrones, while in Vienna they continue to bore me with their petty details.'

14

The Mexicans
accept an Empire

On 8 August 1863, a telegram from the Emperor Napoleon arrived at Miramar, giving great happiness and joy. It announced that a national assembly convoked in Mexico City had proclaimed Ferdinand Maximilian of Hapsburg as their Emperor. In congratulating the Archduke, Napoleon professed to be very pleased at this first result, 'for what the capital proclaimed today, the country will proclaim tomorrow', and he prognosticated that before long, Maximilian would be 'summoned by the whole nation to assist in its regeneration'.

They were fine words, but in his heart Napoleon must have known that this so-called national assembly had been elected at the point of French bayonets and in no way represented the country. There was not a single Liberal among the two hundred and fifteen members chosen by a junta of ultra-Conservatives, all friends and supporters of Almonte. Forey's attempts to curb Almonte's powers had come to nothing, for the assembly had nominated him to be one of the three regents at the head of the provisional government. The other two were an elderly general, whose appointment gave neither pleasure nor offence, and the formidable Antonio Pelagio Labastida, Bishop of Puebla and Archbishop-elect of Mexico City – a man whose ultramontane views and uncompromising character were later to cause trouble for the French and disaster for Maximilian. But in June 1863, Labastida was still in Rome, prudently waiting on the turn of events, and for the time being Almonte was virtually in control.

General Forey had done his best to carry out the Emperor's instructions, but how could he be 'master of a country without giving any outward signs of it'? And how could he form a provisional government with Almonte at the head and still hope for the adherence of the Liberals, all of whom hated Almonte? The Emperor wanted the world to think that he had no intention of forcing an alien domination on the Mexican people. He attached the greatest importance to giving the Mexicans the illusion of freedom, but the French army, which was still only in control of the towns and villages on the main highway between Vera Cruz and Mexico City, could not afford to give the Mexicans even the illusion of freedom. Juarez, the little Indian lawyer who operated from a northern provincial town, was still recognized as President by the greater part of the population and issued draconian laws against all those who gave assistance to the enemy. It was up to the French in Mexico to make themselves more feared and respected than Juarez in a country which could only be ruled successfully through fear.

General Forey had ridden in triumph into Mexico City, with Saligny and Almonte on either side, men whom he knew to be his enemies but whom, according to the wishes of his Emperor, he treated as his friends. Conservatives of every class and kind now offered to collaborate – venerable politicians who had served in the cabinets of former Presidents like Bustamente and Santa Anna; veterans who had won their laurels in the Texan wars; Creole aristocrats who had supported Miramon and who now, for the first time in months, opened out their palaces. The church bells rang all over the city and nuns and friars and priests were everywhere in evidence, chanting hosannas of joy at the coming of the French, for the clergy were counting on the Emperor Napoleon and a docile Hapsburg prince to restore their privileges and give them back their confiscated lands. But the 'hosannas' soon died down when General Forey issued his first proclamation, based on Napoleon's liberal instructions decreeing that religious liberty was to be protected, and that all former Church property lawfully acquired was to remain in the hands of the purchasers and their heirs.

The problem of the confiscated Church lands was the most difficult of all the many problems to resolve, and one over which neither the French command, nor later Maximilian, could expect any support from the Conservative Party. The Church had been the predominant influence in the Mexican political scene ever since the days of the Spanish conquest, when the bishops of Spain supplanted the priests of the Aztec gods, and the flaming stakes of the Inquisition replaced the human sacrifices of Huitzilocpochtli, and the Indians found a new goddess in the miraculous Virgin of Guadaloupe. So great was the power of the Church that few Mexicans dared to buy their confiscated lands, most of which had passed into the hands of foreigners, many of them Frenchmen, and Forey's decree was inevitably looked upon as favouring his own countrymen. Napoleon had advised the General to keep on good terms with the clergy, but from his Roman exile the Bishop of Puebla had already made it clear that the Church would support foreign intervention only on one condition – the restitution of all their property. As one of the largest landowners in the country, it was a problem the bishop had very much at heart.

Maximilian had already raised the thorny subject when Labastida visited him at Miramar in the spring of 1862. This visit, arranged by Gutierrez, had not inspired confidence on either side. The Archduke found the bishop too bigoted and dictatorial, while the bishop was suspicious of a liberal-minded Hapsburg who, before he was even elected Emperor, was already writing to the Pope asking permission to raise a mortgage of one hundred million francs on property still belonging to the Church, and insisting on the reform of the clergy, 'which in many cases was utterly corrupt'. On his visit to Brazil, the Archduke had formed the poorest opinion of the Latin-American clergy and he had heard they were even more demoralized in Mexico. But it was not very tactful of him to criticize the clergy when he was counting on their support, and it was somewhat naïve of him to ask Labastida to convey his letter to Pope Pius and to expect him to champion his demand for reforms. The prudent bishop had refused to commit himself in any way, preferring to leave all onerous decisions to the Pope, who, knowing nothing of Mexican affairs, would act entirely on his advice. The Pope's reply to Maximilian's letter was polite and non-committal. He invited the Archduke and Archduchess to visit him in Rome on their way to Mexico, but he made no mention of the reform of the clergy, and specified that permission for a mortgage was only possible, providing there was 'adequate compensation for the Church of Mexico'. Labastida had already made it abundantly clear to His Holiness that 'adequate compensation' for the Church meant nothing less than the restitution of all former privileges.

None of Napoleon's Mexican advisers warned him that, in making Labastida Regent, he was committing the country to a clerical dictatorship, and that the other members of the assembly would prefer to defy the French rather than go against the wishes of the all-powerful bishop who, from the moment he landed in Mexico and took his seat on the Council of Regency, showed that he had no intention of compromising

185

and was out to fight General Forey's decrees by all the means at his command.

The bishop landed at Vera Cruz on 17 September 1863, and only a few days later General Forey was writing to the Emperor, 'I confess that I would rather undergo a second siege of Puebla than be placed in a position where I am supposed to be a restraining influence on people who do not want to be restrained. General Almonte, who has been put at the head of the Regency, is, if not a reactionary, at least a man of such extreme weakness of character that he allows himself to be talked into adopting the most deplorable measures, which I cannot sanction as I do not want the French flag to be associated with actions which are contrary to our policy. It is none the less painful for me to see that, every day, I am obliged to witness the way in which the government is abusing its power and to keep a watch over them as if they were our worst enemies.'

But by the time this letter had arrived at the Tuileries, Napoleon had already decided to recall Forey. Almonte and Saligny were jubilant at the news, and Hidalgo prided himself on the success of his intrigues. But there was general dismay among them when they heard that not only Forey but also Saligny was to be recalled. For this time Napoleon had not acted on the hints and insinuations of Hidalgo or the advice of the Empress and Morny, but had reverted to his old conspiratorial habit of consulting underground sources and giving more weight to their reports than to those of his official representatives.

The complaints of certain officers serving on the Mexican front had served to open the Emperor's eyes. They wrote that the clerical parties supported by France were 'paving the way to the blackest reaction', and suggested as the only way of getting out of the difficulties the dismissal of both Forey and Saligny, an ultra-reactionary who was universally detested, and the appointment of Bazaine, the one man who was capable of saving the situation. The bitter attacks in the Legislative Assembly, accusing him of establishing a foreign tyranny in Mexico, were making Napoleon particularly sensitive to his reputation as a liberal Emperor, and this time not even the patronage of the Duke de Morny could save his protégé. Count Saligny was peremptorily recalled and replaced by the Marquis de Montholon, son of the man who had accompanied the first Napoleon to St Helena and himself one of the most loyal of Bonapartists. But Morny no longer had any need of Saligny, for the claims on the Jecker bonds were now incorporated in

Mexico's growing debt to France – a debt for which Maximilian was later to be held responsible.

Forey's recall was softened by the offer of a marshal's baton, and Achille Bazaine stepped into the precarious position of commander-in-chief of the French expeditionary force. Three experienced officers had already failed and he was now called upon not only to pacify a country three times the size of France, but also to create an Empire, all in the course of a few months, and then to hand it over to a completely inexperienced prince who would arrive from Europe full of preconceived notions and ideas. It was a Herculean labour, but Bazaine was full of confidence. He possessed many of the requisite qualities – he was ruthless, energetic and courageous – but he lacked both character and integrity, and instead of regenerating the country he ended in succumbing to the Mexican way of life.

His first task was to conduct a vigorous military campaign in the unsubdued states, and in each conquered town to stage a plebiscite in favour of a monarchy. For neither Napoleon nor Maximilian was satisfied with the votes of the 'National Assembly', which only represented Mexico City and the towns and villages on the highway leading from the coast – villages which Sir Charles Wyke dismissed contemptuously as 'inhabited by three Indians and a donkey'. Napoleon's enthusiasm was on the wane and he had only one wish – to get Maximilian to Mexico as soon as possible, so that he could take his share of the burden. Every day, the Mexican expedition was becoming more unpopular in France, and every day it was costing him more. 'I am in a very tight place,' he confessed to Sir Charles Wyke, who had just returned from Mexico and been sent officially by the British government to enlighten him on some of the true facts. Sir Charles succeeded in destroying the Emperor's last illusions. He maintained that the intervention had been completely mishandled from the beginning and, when asked whether the Archduke Maximilian could expect a favourable reception in Mexico, he replied in the negative, saying that there was not the slightest hope of his succeeding if he continued to identify himself with the clerical party and the ridiculous Council of Regency. The only advice he could give was to dissolve the so-called 'provisional government' as quickly as possible, and to leave the country to vote according to its own laws on whether or not it wanted a monarchy.

Napoleon replied that by dissolving the government he would be admitting a mistake, 'and in France it was no longer permissible to be mistaken'. Almonte and his party had to remain in power to save his face. But in his first confidential letter to Bazaine he openly criticized the triumvirate for being too reactionary, and repeated that the rights of the present owners of Church property must on all accounts be protected. These letters to Bazaine are indicative of the French Emperor's change of heart. There is very little left of the lofty idealism of earlier days. He is already envisaging the end to French commitments overseas, and expresses the wish to limit as much as possible the extent and duration of his troops' presence in Mexico. He refers to French commercial interests and talks of sending special financial agents to control the Mexican administration. He even goes so far as to say that a part of the French claims might be settled by establishing a protectorate over the largely unexplored state of Sonora. With the appointment of Bazaine, the Mexican expedition entered into a new phase. There was less talk of regeneration and more of self-interest.

At Miramar, the Archduke too was beginning to talk of material and financial guarantees. The delight with which he received the news of his election in Mexico City had been tempered by the scepticism expressed both by Count Rechberg and his own secretary, Baron du Pont, whom we find writing to Hidalgo, 'It reads well on paper, but in all that has so far happened in Mexico, there is very little sign of the will of the whole nation. The greater majority of the states at least must declare in favour of a monarchy, for a sham vote would produce nothing but a phantom reign.'

News that a Mexican deputation was on its way to Miramar brought Maximilian an urgent summons to Vienna, where Franz Josef, acting on Rechberg's advice, warned his brother that a deputation coming from an assembly which had not yet been recognized by the Imperial government had no official position and could only be privately received. Once again he underlined the fact that it would be folly to go to Mexico without the guarantees of both the naval powers, for an Austrian Archduke could not put himself in the position of becoming a puppet of France. But still Franz Josef could not bring himself to speak openly against a project to which his Foreign Minister was becoming more and more opposed. There had been criticism in the Frankfurt 'Diet of Princes' and questions were being raised in the Reichsrat regarding the succession, but Franz Josef seems to have deliberately abstained from referring to these matters, discussion of which might have prevented Maximilian from accepting the Mexican crown.

Count Rechberg's warnings had already acted as a cold douche on the Archduke's vacillating enthusiasm. The continued victories of the Union forces in America threatened the future of the Mexican Empire, and Maximilian was haunted by the thought of a hostile and unemployed army ranging over a thousand-mile frontier. The question of guarantees was more vital than ever, and in the autumn of 1863 his letters to Napoleon became more demanding. The material support of the two naval powers was no longer sufficient. In order to be effective, it should take the form of a treaty of alliance, with the two Powers pledging themselves to defend Mexico from all armed attack during a period of fifteen to twenty years.

A visit from the American Consul in Trieste confirmed his suspicions. In a well-meant attempt to dissuade him from what he termed 'this mad adventure', the Consul warned him that if Napoleon did not withdraw his troops of his own accord, 'an American army of experienced veterans would be landed in Mexico, strong enough to enable the Mexicans to throw out the intruders. The Gulf of Mexico would be blocked and the lifeline with Europe cut.' He added that anyone aspiring to the throne of Mexico, if he really attained it, would be extraordinarily lucky if he escaped with his life. The American did not mince his words and, though the Archduke refused to be intimidated, the visit nevertheless made an impression. Hence his demand for an alliance lasting for many years – a demand Napoleon was not in a position to accede to and which he therefore preferred to ignore.

Charlotte had accompanied her husband to Vienna, fearing he might weaken when faced by his mother's opposition. The Archduchess Sophia had been against the Mexican project from the very beginning, and she was even more against it now that her nephew King Otto had been kicked off the throne of Greece. Otto's kingdom had been guaranteed by the Powers, but all they had provided was an English destroyer to carry him off to safety. In Mexico there would not even be an English battleship to rescue an unwanted Emperor from his rebellious subjects, and the Archduchess saw all too clearly that the only way of descending the Mexican throne would be by a scaffold or a firing squad. Throughout the visit, Charlotte never left Max a moment alone with his mother. She even took it upon herself to reply to a letter of warning addressed to Max, in which she begged her mother-in-law not to make them both miserable by holding an opinion contrary to their own, 'though, in any case, that would not alter Max's decision once he had made up his mind' – words which can hardly have ingratiated her with the Archduchess, who was beginning to find 'dear, sensible little Charlotte' almost as tiresome as Elisabeth. What emerges clearly from this letter is that it was Charlotte who had made up her mind and who refused to envisage the difficulties which lay ahead. Married to a descendant of Charles v, she talks of 'Austria's historic right to Mexico' and declares, 'There can be no question of foreign influence or foreign conquest as Mexico is part of Austria's dynastic possessions.' She asserts, 'The first duty of the new sovereign will be to render foreign support superfluous as soon as possible' – brave words coming from a young woman who knew nothing of Mexico except what she had read in textbooks, and whose husband's crown had been offered by courtesy of Napoleon.

The Archduchess Sophia was not the only person who needed convincing that the Mexican crown was an act of Divine Providence. Charlotte's own grandmother, the ex-Queen Marie Amélie of France, appears to have shared the Archduchess's fears and to have warned her granddaughter not to be blinded by her ambition. Charlotte's letter of reply is curiously revealing. 'I am the last person,' she wrote, 'to want a throne. As you remember, I could have had one [the throne of Portugal] when I was seventeen, which I refused because I set more store on other things, but there is a lot of difference between going in search of a throne, or of taking upon oneself the immense responsibility of refusing one, particularly when one feels in oneself both the ability and possibility to accomplish a task which is really worth while. To do so would be denying one's conscience and failing in one's duty towards God. For when one feels one is called upon to reign, then it becomes a vocation, like any other religious vocation. ... You say, my darling grandmother, that you hoped I would have a better future, but apart from the fact that it is so far away, Mexico is a very beautiful country, and there are very few thrones that are not precarious. . . . Even suppose we fail, Max still remains next but one in succession to the Austrian throne. In spite of all the rumours to the contrary, he has not relinquished by a hair's breadth any of his hereditary rights. The only thing is that he has given himself an occupation. . . . the Austrian constitution being what it is, he could have lived for ninety years with nothing better to do than to build yet another house, design yet another garden and occasionally go off on some long journey. This being the case, are you surprised if a young and active man of thirty-one is tempted to accept a job which affords such immense possibilities? For my part, I admit that, without putting too much store on the trappings of power, I have up to now known too little of life not to desire to have something to love and to strive for outside my own domestic circle. A great many people accuse me of being ambitious, but they judge others by their own standards which are certainly not mine. All I want is to accomplish some good in the world, and I need a wider horizon than I have at present.'

Charlotte was hurt to hear that her devoted Countess d'Hulst was among those who accused her of ambition, and we find her father defending her in a letter to the Countess: 'Philippe tells me that you regard our dear Charlotte as being a little bit too ambitious. But you cannot really call it ambition on her part. All she wants is to lead an active, useful life and have a greater outlet for her talents. Life at Miramar is really very boring. Max, being the second in the line of succession, has all the disadvantages of his position without the financial means to improve it. Charlotte has not been carried away by the Mexican offer. On the contrary, she is very much aware of the dangers. The really enthusiastic one is Max.'

So wrote King Leopold, who was so much to blame for encouraging the young couple in their Imperial ambitions. Charlotte had gone on to Brussels from Vienna to visit her father before he left for England, for she still believed he had sufficient influence with the British Cabinet to secure the guarantees which Franz Josef regarded as indispensable. King Leopold's vanity was such that he would not admit even to his daughter that his influence in England was not as great as it was credited to be. 'A guarantee might be difficult, for England was chary about giving guarantees, but there was still hope of securing her moral support and perhaps the offer of a frigate to accompany them to Mexico.' He promised he would do all in his power to help, instead of telling Charlotte quite plainly that it was useless to count on England's help in any shape or form. Lord Palmerston's government had no intention of becoming involved, and in August 1863, the British Prime Minister was writing to Queen Victoria, 'The last accounts from Mexico state that the government set up by the French has decided for the Archduke Maximilian as king or emperor. Viscount Palmerston apprehends that Your Majesty need feel no uneasiness or jealousy of this proceeding. She will be of the opinion that, if the Archduke should decide to go and should succeed with the help and protection of France, it would be of great advantage to all European nations having commercial intercourse with Mexico.' In short, England was willing to leave all the honour and glory, and also the expense, to France, and once Mexico was pacified to take her full share of whatever commercial benefits were going.

In Brussels, father and daughter discussed the Mexican project as if it was already a *fait accompli*. They even went so far as to amend the draft of the constitution drawn up by Max, and to plan the composition of the Imperial Household, which the King prudently advised should not be too large. Leopold appears to have reassured his daughter from every point of view, for she telegraphed to her husband: 'Enchanted, everything is for the best.'

The optimism was not shared at Miramar, where Maximilian was composing his reply to the Mexican deputation which had already arrived in Paris. It must have been humiliating to have to submit the draft for approval both to Napoleon and Franz Josef. And the latter was the more critical of the two, for he was determined not to involve his country in what he regarded purely as a family affair. The furthest he was prepared to go was in permitting the enrolment of volunteers, but there could be no question of an Austrian guarantee of the Mexican loan which was being floated in Paris – a proposal put forward by Napoleon, actively supported by Almonte and tentatively referred to by Maximilian. The Austrian Emperor's reply on this matter was completely negative: under no circumstances could Austria ever be a party to any such guarantee. He even objected to Maximilian beginning his address to the deputation with the words, 'My brother the Emperor and I are deeply moved.' Franz Josef was anything but moved, and insisted on the sentence being deleted, thereby offending the susceptible Archduke.

There was a touch of irony about Napoleon's objections. The Emperor, who prided himself on having been elected by popular vote, objected to Maximilian's references to 'parliamentary liberty' and 'constitutional rule' – noble words which would no doubt make an excellent impression in Europe, but which could hardly apply to a state which was sunk in anarchy. 'What is wanted in Mexico,' he wrote, 'is a liberal dictatorship. As regards a constitution, that must be the work of time. It cannot be applied till the country is completely pacified and the government in good working order.' The address, which Maximilian had written really from the heart, inspired by the best of motives, ended by pleasing no one but King Leopold, who telegraphed his congratulations. The Mexican delegation, many of whom had travelled over three thousand miles, were disappointed at having their offer of a crown accepted only on condition of certain guarantees. They had expected to be welcomed at Miramar with Hapsburg pomp and ceremony and were offended by the simplicity of their reception. By order of Franz Josef, Maximilian had to receive them privately, with no Archduke or minister in attendance. Apart from Gutierrez and Hidalgo, none of the deputation had ever seen him before and, though they were struck by his imposing presence and the graciousness of his manner, his address was not sufficiently effusive or grandiloquent to appeal to politicians nurtured on the fiery *pronunciamentos* of Mexican generalissimos.

The fact that Maximilian had referred to the indispensability of the guarantees without specifying who were to be the guarantors was unfavourably commented on by Franz Josef, and the Archduke had to excuse himself by saying that he thought it wiser not to mention either Spain or England by name, as they seemed to be so sensitive on the subject of guarantees. The greatest blow to the Archduke's pride was when he found that his speech had been censored in the French newspapers. Napoleon's Foreign Minister had taken upon himself to change the phrase, '*il faut que j'exige*' (I must insist) to '*il faut que je demande*' (I must ask). The Emperor did not consider that the Archduke, whom he now regarded as his protégé, had any right to 'insist' on guarantees when thirty thousand French troops were carving him an empire out of chaos. Maximilian noted and resented these corrections, which he regarded as 'an incredible impertinence' on the part of Napoleon's minister, but he would have to submit to greater impertinences and more bitter humiliations before he set sail for Mexico.

15

The price of Empire

In Paris, they were selling Mexican flags in the streets. The chefs of the Tuileries were concentrating their creative talents on 'Bombe Mexicaine' and enormous sugar confections of Mexico's national emblem, an eagle devouring a serpent on a cactus plant. Every Mexican émigré in Paris was ordering a new uniform in which to present himself to the Emperor-elect. For it was March 1864, and the long-postponed visit of the Archduke Ferdinand Maximilian of Austria and his wife, the Archduchess Charlotte, had at last materialized.

Maximilian had wanted the visit to be private, but Napoleon, who was determined to leave him no loophole of escape, had insisted on receiving him with Imperial honours. Opposition in the Legislative Assembly was assuming alarming proportions. Speaking to the applause of his party, Monsieur Thiers suggested: 'The wisest course would be for the Emperor to pocket his pride and admit frankly to the Archduke Maximilian that public opinion in France is against the enterprise and that it would be impossible to support him as energetically as he had hoped, in which case the Prince, who appears to be a man of intelligence, would probably refuse and one could then go back to Juarez who, however unprepossessing he might be, at least has the merit of representing the strongest party.'

But Napoleon had given too many hostages to fortune to retreat. The blond young Hapsburg, with his eager and enthusiastic wife, was his only hope of retrieving some of the millions he had already spent in Mexico. Hence the Mexican flag flying above the Tuileries; the reception usually reserved for crowned heads with the Emperor descending the first steps of the great staircase of honour to receive his guests; the gala performances at the Opera and Theatre, including a world premiere of 'L'Ami des Femmes', the latest play by Dumas Fils; the banquets and soirées attended by the leaders of politics and fashion,

194

prominent among them the Duke de Morny, radiating charm and bon-homie at the prospect of collecting his thirty per cent of Jecker bonds. The whole of the diplomatic corps was present, with the exception of the American Minister, Mr Dayton, who had declined the invitation on the instructions of his government, for Washington wanted to make it quite clear that they still recognized Benito Juarez as the lawful President of Mexico and would never accept a foreign Emperor.

Both Maximilian and Napoleon were well aware of the missing guest, and 'their nervous, apprehensive looks were in marked contrast to the radiant self-confidence of their wives'. Charlotte's cousin, the reigning Duke Ernest of Saxe-Coburg, who happened to be in Paris at the time, was surprised to find 'the two Empresses conversing with each other at table only in Spanish, as if they wished to dispel the apprehension of their husbands by the beautiful cadences of the Castillian tongue'. But the beautiful cadences were hardly likely to have been appreciated by their French guests, and the Duke remarked that opinion in Paris was very much divided on the Mexican war, and that much of the optimism was forced. The greater part of the population appeared to class the latest action of Napoleon as yet another of his dynastic whims. Nevertheless, there was a small, influential circle of enthusiastic politicians, both male and female, who appeared to be quite delirious with joy at the prospect of a glorious end to the Franco-Mexican war. At the head of these enthusiasts was the Empress, with whom Napoleon, however, in this as in many other cases, was not entirely in agreement. Eugénie was determined to take all the credit for herself for being the founder of the Mexican Empire and in conversation with Duke Ernest went so far as to declare that in a few years the Archduke would be 'one of the most influential rulers in the world'. 'No one,' wrote the Duke, 'shared this view more strongly than my unfortunate cousin Charlotte, who had never appeared in better looks or spirits, whereas Max looked much older than when I had seen him last and did not give the impression of having ventured on this dangerous enterprise with any of the enthusiasm of youth, but rather as one who had given his word too hastily and had now to abide by his promises.'

It was after a dinner party at which Charlotte's 'blissful self-confidence' had been particularly in evidence, that the Emperor Napoleon drew Duke Ernest aside and, in a half-apologetic fashion confessed, 'It is a bad business. In their place, I would never have accepted.' This, coming from a man who had done all in his power to blackmail Maximilian into acceptance, would surely have been repeated by Duke Ernest to his Uncle Leopold. But by now the King of the Belgians was as committed as his daughter. The young couple had stopped in Brussels on their way and had come to Paris with his blessing, together with a great deal of sound advice to pin Napoleon down to the written word and not merely to count on his promises. The King, who had an innate distrust of Napoleon, kept warning Maximilian to take no steps without first obtaining safeguards for the future: 'It is you who are helping the Emperor to pull his chestnuts out of the fire, and in return you must get him to put into writing the exact period for which the French troops are to remain in Mexico. The longer the better, as they constitute your chief support.'

Though Leopold himself had never been an ardent churchman, he was convinced that it was in Maximilian's best interests to rely for support on the Church and the Catholic party which had everything to gain by being loyal to the Crown. He advised his son-in-law to approach the Pope with a view to his 'sending out an intelligent man as Nuncio at the earliest possible date, someone who would be able to influence the Mexican clergy in the right direction'. Things might have gone easier for him in Mexico had Maximilian acted on King Leopold's advice. But his own quixotic idealism attracted him to his enemies rather than his supporters, and it was often said that Benito Juarez had no greater admirer than the Emperor Maximilian.

Meanwhile in Mexico, a general who was hampered neither by liberal ideas nor religious scruples had succeeded in a lightning campaign of less than ten weeks in occupying a vast area to the north and north-west of Mexico City. By March, all the most important of the Spanish colonial towns, Morelia, Guanajuato, Queretaro and Guadalajara, had fallen into his hands, the Peninsula of Yucatan had voluntarily declared for the Empire and Juarez had been forced to flee from San Luis Potosi northwards to Monterrey. In every conquered city, an imposing list of signatures giving their adherence to the Empire was collected and dispatched to Paris, to convince the Archduke on his arrival that the Mexican people had voted almost unanimously in his favour.

'Three-quarters of the total territory of Mexico and four-fifths of her whole population have declared for a monarchy,' wrote Almonte to the Archduke. 'Your arrival is awaited with eagerness and impatience and I hope to hear that Your Majesty will hasten your departure as much as possible so as to start upon the work of regeneration and reorganization which will raise us once more to the position of a great country.'

The rosy picture painted by Almonte was far from being the truth. Barely one-seventh of the territory of Mexico was in French hands. Of the three million people living in that area, one in twenty was an Imperialist at heart. Bazaine's brilliant campaign rested on frail foundations, for an army of thirty-eight thousand Frenchmen and one thousand eight hundred Mexican auxiliaries was too weak in numbers to garrison every town and village. No sooner had they moved on than the Juaristi appeared. But the list of signatures was impressive and Maximilian allowed himself to believe that one of the main conditions had been realized and that the great majority of the Mexican people would welcome him as Emperor.

Almonte had his own reasons for wanting Maximilian to hurry his departure. His position as Regent was becoming uncomfortable. Bazaine, who was in open conflict with Labastida, had forced the Archbishop to resign from the Council of Regency and Almonte, who owed his entire position to Napoleon, had either to accept the resignation or forfeit Bazaine's friendship. The situation became even more embarrassing when the Archbishop retaliated against the French by threatening to excommunicate the troops and close the churches on Sunday, whereupon Bazaine sent word that if the churches were closed on the following Sunday and his men were prevented from going to Mass, he would have the doors blown in by his guns. The Archbishop capitulated, but at the next meeting with the General he warned him that he would require another twenty-five thousand men in Mexico for he could no longer count on the support of the Church.

Such was the situation when Maximilian finally decided to accept the crown. The flattery of Gutierrez, the lies of Almonte, the subtle blackmail of Napoleon, who went so far as to hint that there was a Bourbon prince waiting to take Maximilian's place if he hesitated any longer — a prince, moreover, who would be more acceptable to Spain than an Austrian Archduke — all these factors combined to influence his decision. The question of an English guarantee, which he had hitherto regarded as a *sine-qua-non* of his acceptance, was completely dropped. With his persuasive tongue, Gutierrez had succeeded in convincing him that, once he was Emperor of Mexico, England would be the first to seek his alliance in the hope of securing commercial concessions, while King Leopold, who had been completely won over by

Charlotte on her last visit to Brussels, indulged in wishful thinking and predicted a favourable change in England's policy.

The only person who continued to give the Archduke honest and often unpalatable advice was his brother's Foreign Minister, Count Rechberg, who shared Prince Metternich's view that 'nothing good could come out of the Mexican adventure'. It was a colossal undertaking and the prospects of success were very dubious. The Ambassador reported that even that arch-optimist the Empress Eugénie was in 'a state of feverish excitement, brought on by the heavy responsibility which rests on her shoulders'. But it was difficult for Rechberg to persuade the Archduke because of the ambiguous attitude adopted by his Imperial master. The minister knew how easily the Emperor could have vetoed the whole project. He had expected him to do so when the Archduke dropped the question of the English guarantee and threw himself into the arms of France. But Franz Josef appeared to be disassociating himself from the whole affair, saying that he had done all in his power to point out the difficulties and dangers to his brother and, since he persisted in his course, he would place no further obstacles in his way.

This was a very erroneous statement, for the most important matter of all and, from Maximilian's point of view, the chief obstacle to his acceptance, was never even brought up in conversation till the end of January 1864, when he was in Vienna to discuss some outstanding questions which had to be settled in Paris. Everything appeared to have been amicably arranged when, at the eleventh hour, the Emperor instructed Count Rechberg to inform his brother that acceptance of the crown of Mexico would entail giving up all his hereditary rights in Austria. This was a matter which should have been brought up in the very beginning, when Franz Josef and Maximilian had their first meeting in Venice to discuss the Mexican project, and it should have been decided long before the Archduke received the Mexican deputation at Miramar. The fact that Franz Josef deliberately avoided the subject till it was too late for Maximilian to go back on his word leads one to suspect that, in spite of his objections, his continued insistence on the English guarantee, the Emperor was at heart just as anxious as Napoleon to see his brother on the way to Mexico. He had never seriously attempted to dissuade him. On the contrary, he had been the first to encourage him in Venice by pledging financial help for his preliminary expenses and opening recruiting offices for the enrolment of volunteers for Mexico. High-ranking officers and members of the Court had been given permission to accompany the Archduke overseas. The *Novara*, one of the finest frigates in the Austrian navy, was being re-fitted for the Atlantic crossing. These were all gestures which could have been attributed to fraternal affection but were more likely inspired by an overwhelming desire to get the Archduke out of the country.

As for Maximilian, he had never for a moment envisaged the possibility of having to give up his inheritance. In one of Charlotte's letters to her grandmother we read, 'Whatever should happen, Max will always be next but one in succession to the Austrian throne.' And the Archduke's reaction to Count Rechberg was one of incredulous indignation. He protested that neither his brother nor anyone else on earth could deprive him of what he had inherited by divine right from his ancestors, the heirs to the Holy Roman Empire. Hapsburg Archdukes had ruled in all parts of the world. No law had prevented Leopold of Tuscany from succeeding to the Imperial throne, so why should he, the newly-elected Emperor of Mexico, founded and ruled by their great ancestor, Charles v, be called upon to forfeit his legitimate rights and those of his as yet non-existent heirs? Maximilian's indignation makes it clear that all his ambitions were centred in Austria and that the Mexican crown was but a poor substitute for what he still coveted in Europe. Notes in his journal show that he was already half-regretting his decision. 'As I am about to leave for many years to engage in a dangerous task, for the throne of Mexico is certainly a dangerous one,' are not the words of a man confident in the future.

Count Rechberg faithfully reported the Archduke's reaction and no more was said for the moment. The two brothers met on several occasions, but the Emperor appears to have deliberately avoided a subject which would have caused unpleasant scenes and recriminations. And it was only on the eve of Maximilian's departure for Paris that Count Rechberg presented him with a document, compiled by the Court historian, Ritter von Arneth, and autographed by the Emperor. Drawing on historical analogies and parallels, the memorandum set out in lengthy detail the whys and wherefores for the Act of Renunciation. The case of Leopold of Tuscany was dismissed, for Tuscany had always been part of the Imperial inheritance, whereas Mexico's geographical position precluded such a possibility. What would happen in the event of Franz Josef dying while the Crown Prince was still a child? Would the Emperor of Mexico be able to perform the duties of a Regent when he was ruling over a country at the other side of the world, having in the intervening years become completely out of touch? At this point the historian, or more likely Franz Josef himself, deliberately appealed to Maximilian's sense of honour, exhorting him 'out of love for Mexico and its inhabitants' to devote himself to his new country and, by way of proving his devotion, to renounce his Austrian rights.

With his usual evasiveness, Maximilian gave the memorandum no more than a cursory glance before he left for Paris, dismissing it as 'vague and wordy and singularly unfelicitous in language'. Nevertheless, it cast a cloud on his spirits, and the Austrian Ambassador to Belgium, who met the Archducal couple on their arrival in Brussels, was struck by the difference in their attitudes. Glowing with happiness, the Archduchess told him that everything was settled and there were no further obstacles to their acceptance of the crown of Mexico, upon which the Archduke contradicted her flatly by saying that nothing was settled and he had not yet come to any definite decision. Hearing this, the Archduchess looked 'cross and mortified'. But for all Maximilian's doubts and hesitations, the combination of wife and father-in-law was too strong for him to withstand, and he had little chance of refusing a rôle for which Charlotte kept assuring him he was 'supremely fitted'. In a moment of depression at Miramar, Maximilian once confessed to a friend, 'If I heard that the whole Mexican project had come to nothing, I assure you I should jump for joy – but what about Charlotte?'

He might assert that nothing was 'definitely settled' but one of the reasons he stopped off in Brussels was in order to discuss with his father-in-law the question of raising a legion of Belgian volunteers for Mexico – a plan enthusiastically seconded by Leopold and his Minister of War, who thought that service overseas would be an excellent experience for the younger officers, but less enthusiastically received in the Belgian Parliament, where there was little interest in Maximilian or in Mexico.

The brilliant reception given him in Paris robbed the Archduke of his last chance of escape. But his reception was not entirely confined to banquets and to balls, for the mornings were reserved for work. And it was not long before Maximilian discovered that Napoleon's Jewish Finance Minister, Achille Fould, was determined to make the Mexican government pay the greater part of the cost of the French expeditionary force. The preposterous sum of two hundred and sixty million francs was demanded from a country whose finances were in chaos after years of civil war. This sum included the expenses of the French army only up to 1 July 1864, after which date the Mexican government was to pay one thousand francs a year for every French soldier in the country. Nor did the two hundred and sixty million francs include the repayment of the Jecker bonds or the claims of French nationals for damages suffered during the war. To settle these claims, a special committee was to be set up in Paris, composed of Mexicans, Englishmen and Frenchmen.

Napoleon interested himself personally in the floating of a two hundred million franc Mexican loan, of which sixty-six million were already earmarked for payment of the first instalment of the French claims. In spite of their country's attitude, English bankers were prepared to co-operate with their French colleagues in negotiating this loan. They had nothing to lose, for the unfortunate shareholders, misled by Napoleon's propaganda, were almost entirely French. Maximilian, whose presence was required for the sanction of the loan, was at first somewhat hesitant over borrowing in the name of a country of which he was not yet the Emperor. But Napoleon talked him out of his doubts, and he also was in need of funds, due to the heavy expenses involved in the acceptance of the crown. It was arranged that eighty million francs were to be paid to him direct, which later led his enemies to assert that part of the Mexican loan went to pay the Archduke's debts in Europe.

The financial clauses of what was later to be known as the 'Convention of Miramar' condemned the new Mexican Empire to bankruptcy from the very beginning. Maximilian had no understanding of figures or finance, and he had never been able to keep his own accounts in order. Yet neither his brother, the Emperor Franz Josef, nor his father-in-law, King Leopold, thought of providing him with a financial adviser who might have prevented him from putting his signature to documents of which he did not understand the meaning and which were to prove disastrous for Mexico. 'The burdens involved are enormous,' wrote Prince Metternich, 'and the finances will have to be very well regulated to survive such monstrous demands.' But though the Ambassador regarded the terms of the loan as very unfavourable, he admired the way in which the young Archduke had dealt with the capitalists, for his personal intervention had gone a long way towards facilitating the arrangements.

Altogether, the Ambassador was full of admiration for Maximilian, who with his tact and charm had persuaded Napoleon to promise far more than he had intended. What King Leopold considered to be the most important thing of all had been achieved. The French troops were to remain in Mexico for at least three years and were only to be gradually withdrawn. Of the thirty-eight thousand troops in Mexico, twenty thousand were to remain till 1867, while the Foreign Legion of about eight thousand men was to be placed at the disposal of the Emperor of Mexico for another six years. In a secret clause of the Convention of Miramar, Napoleon pledged himself 'that whatever should happen in Europe, France would never fail the new Mexican Empire'. They were words which at the time may have been sincerely meant, motivated by a generous impulse, but they were regretted all too soon. Metternich looked upon this clause as yet another proof of his pet theory that everything could be accomplished with Napoleon by personal contact. And he considered that the Archduke had accomplished a great deal during his Paris visit. He and his wife had made themselves extremely popular with all classes of the population and received ovations whenever they appeared in public. Charlotte in particular received many tributes of personal sympathy from former Orléanists, who saw in her the granddaughter of their beloved King. There were those who cheered but there were also those who pitied the brave, high-spirited young couple embarking on a hazardous adventure, while the Parisian wits made a cruel pun, calling the Archduke the 'Archdupe'.

Nevertheless, the 'Archdupe' managed to hold his own in bargaining with Napoleon, and he refused to consider a plan for the colonization of the state of Sonora, which the French Emperor had very much at heart. Napoleon had been attracted to Sonora ever since the London Times correspondent, Bourdillon, had fired his imagination by descriptions of the enormous potential wealth of a largely-unexploited state. In the past year, a Senator Gwyn, a Southerner who had represented California in Congress before the Civil War, had approached the French Emperor with a plan to colonize Sonora and turn it into a kind of French protectorate. It was in Gwyn's interest to get France irretrievably involved in Mexico, for a French colony on the border of the United States would sooner or later bring her into conflict with the North and make her the ally of the still-struggling South.

If Maximilian had been a realistic politician instead of an idealistic dreamer, he would have realized that it was also in the interest of the Mexican Empire to have France so deeply committed in the country that she could never afford to withdraw her help. But he was too high-minded and too essentially honest to inaugurate his reign by selling a part of Mexico to a foreign power. And he was indignant on hearing that the new French Minister to Mexico, the Marquis de Montholon, had already concluded an agreement with the Council of Regency by which Sonora was to be placed for fifteen years under the direct and sovereign protection of France, which was also to be granted all prospecting rights in return for a ten per cent royalty to be paid to the Mexican Treasury. Maximilian, whose enthusiasm for France was already on the wane, refused to be bound by this agreement and informed the Emperor that he would never consent to the cession of any territory, even to a friendly power. However much Napoleon would have liked to remind the Archduke that his whole position depended on France, he had none the less to bow to his decision, for he was far too anxious to get him off to Mexico to indulge in quarrels at the eleventh hour. There would be time enough to think about Sonora when Maximilian was installed as Emperor and had to find the money for the next instalment of the French debt.

The crowded, brilliant days in Paris were coming to an end, days when there had been little time to spare for the Mexican deputation who had been sitting in Paris all winter waiting for Maximilian to make up his mind. While her husband was in conference with Napoleon's ministers, Charlotte was being subjugated to the spell of her fascinating hostess. Even her enemies give Eugénie the credit for having been a woman of enormous charm and talent, a delightful conversationalist with a superficial knowledge on the most varied subjects. Charlotte, who had apologized to her grandmother for having come to Paris on the invitation of a man who had usurped her grandfather's throne – a visit which she assured her was only dictated by political necessity – now found herself becoming the closest friend of the usurper's wife. Together they discussed the future of Imperial Mexico and Charlotte found the impulsive, warm-hearted Spanish woman so much more sympathetic than her sister-in-law, Elisabeth, who hardly bothered to speak to her, even when she was staying in her house. The ovation given to her in Paris filled Charlotte with pride and joy. When she drove through the streets to the cheers and shouts of 'Bonne chance, Madame l'Archiduchesse d'Autriche', she felt that at last she had come into her own.

There were affectionate farewells from both the Emperor and Empress, for Napoleon and Eugénie had become genuinely fond of their young guests. They may also have felt a certain remorse at the thought that they were sending them off into the unknown, but Bazaine's glowing reports from Mexico told of continual victories, both military and diplomatic. Even the Archbishop appeared to have capitulated to the extent of celebrating a *Te Deum* in Mexico Cathedral, and the general assured the Emperor that the whole country would be pacified by the time of Maximilian's arrival and that even the United States would have to recognize the new empire which had risen on its borders. Eugénie, who refused to believe that the Southern states had practically lost the war, foresaw a glorious future for the young couple and a triumphant sequel to what she still referred to as '*ma guerre*'.

The Imperial yacht *Hortense* brought Charlotte and Maximilian to England, and Admiral Jurien de la Gravière, now reinstated in Napoleon's favour, acted as escort. It must have been hard for this honest sailor, with his first-hand experience of conditions in Mexico, to refrain from warning Maximilian of the appalling difficulties which lay ahead, but he was too loyal a servant of the Emperor to go against his wishes.

After Paris London was an anti-climax. Queen Victoria gave the young couple an affectionate welcome, but she welcomed them as members of her family, not as Emperor and Empress of Mexico. Not even the presence of King Leopold, who in spite of illness had crossed the Channel in a last attempt to 'help the children' could induce the British government to depart from its attitude of polite reserve. In view of the immense vitality and growth of modern Mexico, it is interesting to note that in Lord Palmerston's opinion, 'Mexico was destined to be devoured by the Anglo-Saxon race before it disappeared altogether, as the Redskins did before the white man.'

Formal congratulations were all that Maximilian received at Downing Street. But in family circles at Twickenham and Claremont, there was loud and outspoken criticism. The Orléans princes in exile could not understand that a Hapsburg should consent to become the vassal of a Bonaparte, and with tears the widowed Queen Marie Amélie tried to persuade her beloved granddaughter to relinquish her ambitions. But the cheers of the Paris streets still rang in Charlotte's ears, and she was only sad that her grandmother did not share her joy.

There was a touching scene when, on saying goodbye, the old Queen collapsed in grief. She appeared to have a sudden, terrible premonition, and cried out to Maximilian, 'They will end by assassinating you!' Charlotte's little cousin, the six-year-old daughter of the Duc de Nemours, saw the tears pouring down Maximilian's face, while Charlotte remained outwardly calm. Turning to her mother, the little girl said in surprise, 'It is usually the women who cry. This time, it is a man.'

The Emperor of Austria had given orders to receive his brother with Imperial honours, and the reception at the Hofburg outvied in magnificence that of the Tuileries. All the princes and high-ranking officials of the Empire were present to do homage to the future Emperor and Empress of Mexico. But while Charlotte, resplendent in her diamond and emerald tiara, and glowing with happiness, was feeling herself for the first time the equal of the Empress Elisabeth, Max was only conscious of the sad look on his mother's face and his father's trembling voice when he wished him good luck. All the older members of the Imperial family were against the Mexican project. Even his godfather, the ex-Emperor Ferdinand, and his wife, the Empress Maria Anna, had telegraphed from Prague begging him not to go.

Only the young and adventurous were on his side, for the aristocracy as a whole were bitterly opposed to the idea of an Austrian Archduke accepting a throne from a Bonaparte. Those who were most against it were diplomats, like Count Hübner, who had been accredited to Paris and knew how little Napoleon's word could be relied on. We find Hübner writing to his son, one of the many young men who wanted to volunteer for Mexico, 'There is no reason why you should risk your life for a lot of Mexican monkeys, in a country where you have nothing to expect but ingratitude, intrigues and yellow fever – so let us hear no more of this idea.' But no open criticism was voiced now that His Imperial Majesty appeared to have given his consent, and assiduous courtiers surrounded the Archducal couple with compliments and congratulations. Only the Imperial Cabinet knew the price Maximilian would be made to pay. On the morning after the state banquet, Count Rechberg had the unpleasant task of calling on the Archduke and presenting him with a copy of the 'Family Pact' – a solemn Act of Renunciation Franz Josef now required him to sign.

The document which Maximilian had already in his possession only dealt with the historical arguments which made such a pact necessary. But here, set out in black and white, were clauses which deprived him and his eventual heirs of their hereditary rights in Austria, so long as any male member of the Hapsburg family, however distantly related, was still alive. Even most of the financial benefits he had hitherto enjoyed, and which had been assured him for the future, were now to be denied him. And for the first time, Maximilian realized the full consequences of his actions. The indignation Rechberg had encountered when he first brought up the subject before his departure for Paris was as nothing compared to the violence of his present reaction. He refused to discuss, still less to sign, such an ignoble document, whereupon the Ministers informed him that in such a case the Emperor would refuse his consent.

The following day, Franz Josef, who hated scenes and preferred always to rely on the written word, addressed a letter to his brother which said, 'I can give my consent to your accepting the crown of Mexico only on condition that you solemnly confirm the deed, of which I enclose a copy, renouncing for you and your heirs the rights of succession and inheritance in Austria. If you are unable to consent to this and prefer to refuse the crown of Mexico, I will take it upon myself to notify the foreign countries of your refusal, and in particular the Imperial crown of France.'

The last thing Franz Josef wished was to hear of his brother's refusal, but he would never admit to himself that he was personally involved. He could say, in all fairness, that he had acted on the advice of his ministers and in the best interests of his country. But the scene he tried to avoid was inevitable, for Maximilian had asked their mother to intervene, and the Archduchess Sophia, who had done all in her power to prevent her son from leaving, now begged the Emperor not to take away his birthright. She had little faith in the future of the Mexican Empire and she foresaw her beloved Max returning to Europe a penniless outcast, deprived of his inheritance. But all her prayers were to no avail, and only succeeded in irritating the Emperor. Hurt and angered by his attitude, she left the Hofburg and retired to Laxenburg.

Many years later, the Empress Elisabeth recalled the terrible scene between the two brothers, when Maximilian, white with rage, accused Franz Josef of having 'deliberately misled him by withholding his conditions till now, when he had pledged his word to a population of nine million people, signed the convention and contracted a loan in all good faith, believing he was free to do so'. These arguments were repeated in a letter addressed to the Emperor from Laxenburg, where Charlotte and Maximilian had joined the Archduchess Sophia. The Archduke wrote, 'In the circumstances, I find myself forced to announce my withdrawal to a people who have placed their trust in me.' Two days later, he and Charlotte boarded the Trieste Express at Baden to return to Miramar.

The day they left, the Mexican envoys arrived in Vienna from Paris, expecting to find a royal welcome, but all that awaited them was a laconic message from the Archduke, telling them to join him in Trieste, while the Emperor was too busy to receive them. The members of the deputation, who had left Mexico in the late summer of 1863, had been led by Gutierrez and Hidalgo to believe that the Archduke was only awaiting their arrival to pack his bags and leave for Mexico. They had already been disillusioned by their reception in October. For five months they had been sitting in Paris, listening to stories they no longer believed in, only rarely received at Court, where Hidalgo allowed few Mexicans to appear other than himself. Then Maximilian had finally arrived, dispelling by the graciousness of his manner the chilling effects of the past months. They had seen very little of him, but that little had been enough to raise their morale. Now they found themselves summoned to Trieste in an ominous atmosphere of crisis.

There was consternation among the Archduke's household at Miramar. With Tegetthoff away at sea, Maximilian had not a friend or member of his entourage on whom he could rely. His secretary, Baron du Pont, was a worthy mediocrity, his aide-de-camp, Stefan Herzfeld, was a loyal young naval officer with no knowledge of politics. Neither Charles Bombelles, who was eager for the adventure, nor Sebastian Schertzenlechner, who in the past months appeared to have acquired an even greater influence and who now saw himself as the power behind the Mexican throne, were in a position to advise him. His two gentlemen-in-waiting, the Marquis Coria and Count Zichy (the latter had remained behind in Paris to see the Mexican loan through its final stages), were courtiers rather than diplomats. The only person in Maximilian's entourage with a clear, incisive brain was his young wife.

If Maximilian was outraged, Charlotte was in despair at the foundering of her ambitions, but she refused to give way to lamentations or recriminations, doing her best to support her husband and to keep his emotions under control. One moment, he was talking of defying his brother, publicizing his grievances to the world, and embarking on a French boat for Mexico; another moment, in a mood which Charlotte regarded as far more dangerous, he was talking of retiring to the peace and obscurity of Lacroma. In letters and telegrams, she besought her father's help, but before he could reply, Franz Josef had sent their cousin, the Archduke Leopold, to Miramar to force Maximilian into signing the Act of Renunciation. It was not a happy choice, for Leopold was the son of the Archduke Rainier, whose behaviour as Italian Viceroy had been openly criticized by Maximilian. The two cousins had never been on friendly terms, and Maximilian saw in Leopold one of the many Archdukes who stood to gain by his renunciation. Not only did he refuse to sign, but he told his cousin that he would now receive the Mexican deputation, who could not be kept waiting any longer, and give them the true reasons for his withdrawal. He and his wife would then leave in their yacht for Civitavecchia, as he was anxious to go to Rome and explain the situation to His Holiness in person.

This time there was consternation in the Hofburg. Franz Josef was appalled at the prospect of Maximilian airing his grievances at large, discussing what he considered to be purely a family affair with the Pope and Cardinal Antonelli. Envisaging a public scandal, the Emperor resorted to what, for him, must have been a desperate measure. He evoked the aid of his ex-enemy, Napoleon, and requested him to intercede with the Archduke.

The scene of action moves to the Tuileries, to the evening of 27 March 1864, when Napoleon received two telegrams, one from his Ambassador in Vienna, the Duke of Grammont, the other from Hidalgo in Trieste. Though still in ignorance of what had actually happened, he realized with an incredulous horror that the Archduke was about to refuse the throne provided for him by French arms and French credit. For some paltry reasons of his own, Maximilian was leaving France to shoulder the whole burden of the Mexican debt at the very moment when he had just announced to his Finance Minister, Achille Fould, that the budget commission could now count on receiving the first instalment on the debt. Napoleon rarely lost his temper and one of his greatest assets was the imperturbable calm which he maintained in moments of political stress. But it was another matter with Eugénie, who was quick-tempered and impulsive and already overwrought by the sense of her own responsibility in the Mexican affair. At two o'clock in the morning, the Austrian Ambassador was woken by an Imperial messenger with a letter from Eugénie – the letter of an angry, frightened woman rather than of an Empress.

'My dear Prince,' it ran, 'I have just received Hidalgo's telegram. The Archduke has decided to decline with thanks the offer of the Mexican deputation, and will immediately afterwards set out for Rome and leave Austria, abandoning his dreams. I say nothing of the appalling scandal which this will cause to the House of Austria, but for ourselves you must admit that there can be no excuse, whatever may be the obstacles which have arisen in various quarters. You had plenty of time to consider everything and to go into every detail, and you cannot at the very moment when the arrangements for the loan have been concluded and the convention signed, put forward a family matter of no importance, compared with the confusion into which you are throwing the whole world. Let us have your last word, for this is a very serious business. Will you please notify your government immediately. Believe me, yours in a most justifiable bad temper, Eugénie.'

It was not a pleasant letter to receive, particularly for Metternich, who was sick and tired of the whole business and had been against it from the beginning. Time and again, he had urged the necessity for discretion and caution, and neither he nor Rechberg had ever had any faith in the reports of the Mexican émigrés. He was now 'furious at being dragged into a controversy before a tribunal so ill-suited to give judgment on matters of right and wrong', and we find him writing to Rechberg, 'This business must be settled. The scandal of the Archduke leaving the country and the *brouille mortelle* between the two brothers would be too great. The whole affair seems to me to be so undignified that it makes me blush with shame.'

On the early morning of the twenty-eighth, he was already at the Tuileries, received by Napoleon in his private study. The Emperor, who showed signs of having spent a sleepless night, accused Austria of having 'deliberately prevaricated, so as to place France in an impossible situation'. Public opinion would see in the Archduke's decision nothing but an obstacle placed in his way by the Vienna Cabinet, and the Emperor feared there would be hostile demonstrations which would lead to 'a regrettable tension between the two countries'. Metternich did his best to reassure him that his government was 'animated by the most friendly feelings towards France'. He said the letter of his Imperial master was a proof of his affection and the fact that he desired nothing better than to find a solution to what was essentially a family problem, the laws of the House of Hapsburg forbidding the acceptance of a foreign throne without a previous renunciation of the rights of succession. Here Napoleon interrupted, 'But the Archduke must have known this from the beginning. The matter should have been settled three years ago.' And for a moment, he lost control, saying with bitterness,

'It really seems as if I have no luck with Austria. It looks as if I am being deliberately left in the lurch at the last moment.' To which there was little the Ambassador could say.

Napoleon was not content to leave matters in the hands of a diplomat who he knew had been against the Mexican project from the very beginning. Always believing in the personal approach, he dispatched an urgent telegram to Miramar, begging the Archduke 'not to arrive at any decision contrary to our engagements' before receiving his letter. This letter was entrusted to his aide-de-camp, General Frossard, who was sent to Austria on a double mission, first to seek an audience with Franz Josef and then to proceed to Trieste.

At Miramara, Maximilian's old friend and physician Dr Jilek, who had been with him since his early boyhood, had been viewing the situation with growing concern, wondering how long the Archduke's delicate, highly-strung nature would stand up to the strain. He was being harried on every side: by Charlotte, who refused to accept defeat, confident that she could still persuade her brother-in-law to go back on his decision; by the Archduke Leopold, who had stayed on in Trieste in the hope that he might still sign the Act of Renunciation; by the Mexican deputation, desperate at the prospect of failure, begging him not to desert them and doing their best to convince him that the crown of Montezuma was worth the price of his rights as an Austrian Archduke. Even a stronger nature than Maximilian's might have cracked under the ordeal, and now there arrived Napoleon's letter, attacking him on what he held most dear – his honour. Writing under what he described as 'the influence of strong emotions', the French Emperor reminded him: 'Whatever might be the nature of the family questions between you and your august brother, by the treaty concluded between us and mutually binding; by the assurances given to Mexico; by the pledges exchanged with the subscribers of the loan, Your Imperial Highness has entered into engagements which you are no longer free to break. What indeed would you think of me if, once Your Imperial Majesty had arrived in Mexico, I were to say that I can no longer fulfil the conditions to which I have set my signature? No. It is impossible that you should give up going to Mexico, and say to all the world that you are obliged by family interests to disappoint all the hopes that France and Mexico have placed in you.' The letter ended, 'It is absolutely necessary in your own interests and those of your family that matters should be settled, for the honour of the House of Hapsburg is at stake. Forgive me for this somewhat severe language, but the circumstances are so grave that I cannot refrain from telling you the whole truth.'

This letter incriminates Napoleon in the eyes of history. Only a few weeks earlier he had openly admitted to Duke Ernest of Saxe-Coburg that the Mexican affair was 'a bad business' and that in Maximilian's place he would never have accepted to go. His correspondence with Bazaine shows that he was already envisaging cutting down on his commitments. And within two years, he would be openly repudiating his promises, refusing to fulfil the conditions to which he had put his signature. When he received this letter, Maximilian had not yet signed the Convention of Miramar, nor given his irrevocable acceptance to the Mexican deputation. He was still in a position to retreat. But, by appealing to his honour, Napoleon struck at what he knew to be the most vulnerable part of his defences. And both in Vienna and Miramar, General Frossard was instructed to talk of Hapsburg honour to the proudest family in Europe.

Franz Josef not only received Napoleon's envoy, but went so far as to admit that he was partly to blame in not having insisted on the Archduke's renunciation before the Paris visit. He refused however to commit himself when Frossard, still acting on instructions, hinted that some proof of brotherly love, some assurances for the future, would help to relieve the situation. Condescension had already gone too far and the Austrian Emperor was not going to have his line of conduct dictated by a Bonaparte. Nevertheless, it was after General Frossard's visit, following urgent representations from Trieste, that he wrote to his brother, offering him what he had already offered him two years before in Venice, but of which there had hitherto been no mention in the 'Family Pact'. He was prepared to continue his apanage of one hundred and fifty thousand gulden a year, of which one hundred thousand were to be paid out annually in Vienna, while fifty thousand would go towards the payment of his personal debts and the expenditure of his preliminary expenses in accepting the Mexican crown. When these expenses had been defrayed, the payment of the fifty thousand would cease.

A direct appeal from Maximilian, asking for assurances that if things went wrong in Mexico he would be reinstated in all his rights as an Austrian Archduke, resulted in a further letter which Count Rechberg considered 'the utmost limits of concession', but which in no way satisfied either the Archduke or his wife. This time, Franz Josef declared that in the eventuality of his brother being deprived of the throne of Mexico and being forced to return to Austria, he would take 'the necessary measures to safeguard your position in the Empire as far as is compatible with the interests of the country'.

On reading this letter, Charlotte took the momentous decision to go herself to Vienna and to plead directly with her brother-in-law. In the past days, she had hardly dared to leave her husband's side, fearing he might carry out his threat and renounce all his ambitions. When General Frossard reminded Maximilian that his pledges to France and Mexico counted for more than his personal dignity as an Austrian Archduke, it was Charlotte who replied, with all the pride of her Bourbon forebears, that both she and her husband were fully aware of the service they were rendering to Napoleon. But Charlotte could now leave for Vienna without any fear of Maximilian going back on his promises. Napoleon's letter had won her the coveted crown, and her husband would now see the Mexican enterprise through to the bitter end.

However much Franz Josef may have dreaded his sister-in-law's arrival, he nevertheless went out of his way to receive her in the most flattering manner, meeting her himself at the station, lodging her in the finest apartments of the Hofburg, listening to her interminable arguments with patience and understanding. She herself admits that she harangued him for three hours on end, forcing him to abandon all his arguments. But Franz Josef was not of a nature to argue, once he had made up his mind, and all she achieved was a promise to continue Max's yearly allowance of one hundred and fifty thousand gulden, and to come himself to Miramar to induce his brother to submit to the demands he was forced to make, not only as Emperor of Austria but as head of the House of Hapsburg. Charlotte was quick to see that Franz Josef was far more involved than he admitted, and that he was just as anxious as Napoleon to see his brother on the way to Mexico. He insisted that the matter called for a prompt solution, that any further delay would be 'detrimental to the country's external policy and to the Archduke's particular position with regard to the Emperor of the French'. The offer to come himself to Miramar – an offer of which his ministers disapproved – was sufficient proof of his 'fraternal love' and Charlotte had no other choice than to accept it in this spirit.

The Emperor was relieved to have been spared her tears and recriminations. On the contrary, she had argued with him as clearly as any man. But there must have been moments when even her heroic courage failed her at this alien Court, where the Empress treated her with a thinly-veiled hostility, and even her mother-in-law avoided her. For the Archduchess Sophia looked upon this second visit as a deliberate attempt on Charlotte's part to force Maximilian's hand. Even her father's advice had failed her. For King Leopold was with his niece at Windsor and so little in the picture that he kept sending letters and telegrams: 'Give up nothing, consent to nothing which would deprive you of your birthright, but on no account give up the Mexican business for what would cause endless difficulties' – advice which only served to confuse his already distracted daughter. At long last, Charlotte was beginning to realize how little her father's influence in England had achieved. Victoria's government had even refused the loan of an English frigate to accompany them to Mexico, and where England had refused, Spain had followed suit.

Left on his own at Miramar, Maximilian had relapsed into a state of melancholy. The beauty of the gardens in the first burst of spring, with the magnolias and the Judas trees in flower, only added to his despair, reminding him that he was leaving, perhaps for ever, the place he loved best in the world. Below the terraces, anchored in the bay, the *Novara* and her escort, the French frigate *Themis*, were already waiting to escort him across the ocean. The nostalgia of his mood inspired a poem which can be interpreted either as an accusation against Charlotte or against his other self, that part of him which from his earliest youth felt called upon to rule, driven by ambition, haunted by Imperial dreams.

'Must I leave for ever, my beloved country,
The scenes of my earliest joys?
You want me to abandon my gilded cradle
And break the links which tie me to my home.

The land where I spent the happy days of childhood,
Where I fell in love for the first time,
Must I leave all this for an uncertain fate,
Inspired by the ambition you rouse in my heart?

You speak to me of sceptres, of palaces and power.
You open before me limitless horizons.
Must I follow you to those distant shores,
Across the ocean waves?

You wish to weave with gold and diamonds
The frail thread of my life.
But can you give me the peace of mind
Which is worth more than all the riches of the world?

Oh, leave me in peace to follow my quiet path
Hidden away among the myrtles.
Believe me, the study of sciences and the cult of the Muses
Is worth more than the glitter of diamonds and of gold.'

They are the verses of a dreamer and of a poet who would have been only too happy to renounce the throne. But in those very days, Maximilian was writing to Napoleon, that he had kept his word and 'out of personal loyalty would make every sacrifice compatible with my honour'. When his faithful old doctor tried to remonstrate for the last time against his going to Mexico, he replied: 'Though the enterprise might end in failure, it is nevertheless well worth trying for.'

At eight o'clock on the morning of Saturday, 9 April, the Imperial train with Franz Josef on board drew up at the private station at Miramar, where Maximilian was waiting to receive him. The Emperor was accompanied by an impressive retinue: seven Archdukes, including his two brothers, Karl Ludwig and Ludwig Viktor; three ministers, one of them Count Rechberg; the Chancellors of Hungary, Croatia and Transylvania; the Chief of the General Staff and the civil and military governors of Venetia and of Istria, accompanied by a bevy of secretaries and aides-de-camp. But not even Count Rechberg was witness to the private conversation between the two brothers, which lasted for nearly two hours. Officers of the *Themis* and the *Novara*, anchored off Miramar, assert that at one time during the interview they saw the Archduke come out onto the terrace and pace up and down in an obvious state of agitation, till he was recalled by one of the Emperor's aides-de-camp. It was past eleven when the two brothers returned to the state apartments to put the final signature to the 'Family Pact', witnessed by the highest dignitaries of the Empire. And though Maximilian was later to declare that he had been forced to sign under duress, it was noted at the time that not only the Archduke but also the Emperor had reddened eyes, as if he regretted what he had been forced to do.

The 'pact' was signed. The naval band playing outside the castle struck up *Gott Erhalte Unser Kaiser* and Charlotte, her radiant composure in striking contrast to that of her husband and brother-in-law, came forward to take the Emperor's arm and lead him into the state banqueting hall. At half past one, Franz Josef was already at the station. The farewells had been formal and correct. But at the moment of boarding the train, he appears to have felt a twinge of tenderness and regret. All the dissensions of the past years, all the bitterness and suspicions were forgotten. He knew only that he was parting, perhaps for ever, from a once-beloved brother. In a voice broken with emotion, he called out, 'Max!', holding out his arms to embrace him for the last time. Ministers and generals looked away, for both the brothers were in tears.

On the following morning of 10 April, the Mexican deputation, headed by Gutierrez and Hidalgo, were driven in the Archduke's state carriages from Trieste to Miramar. It was a Sunday when the gardens were open to the public, and they had never been more crowded than on this day. The Mexicans were welcomed with cheers and flowers, a happy change after those winter months of uncertainty and gloom, waiting in a Paris hotel for Maximilian to make up his mind. Count Zichy, the newly-appointed master of ceremonies, conducted them to the state apartments, where Maximilian and Charlotte, the latter spectacularly beautiful in a rose-coloured dress and diamond crown, stood surrounded by their household. Maximilian, who as usual was wearing naval uniform, looked so white and strained that his doctor feared that he was going to faint. Beside him on a small table was a parchment roll containing a list of all the Mexican towns which had given their adhesion to the Empire and he kept nervously fingering this roll as if it were the only justification for acceptance. It was again Gutierrez who acted as spokesman, speaking in the name of a country he had not visited for a quarter of a century, rolling off rhetorical phrases in French, which came more naturally than his mother tongue. Maximilian took care to reply in Spanish, which he and Charlotte had learnt and mastered in the past two years. Thanks to the decision of the notables of Mexico, he said, he could now justly regard himself as the elect of the Mexican people. This was the first condition he had made when, in October, they had honoured him with the offer of the throne. Thanks to the magnanimity of the Emperor of the French, the guarantees he had mentioned at the time of his first visit had also been provided, and he was therefore able to accept the crown and would endeavour, once he was on the throne, to devote himself 'heart and soul to work for the freedom, prosperity and greatness of Mexico'.

His speech aroused the greatest enthusiasm. The Mexicans, who had waited so long in suspense, broke into loud cheers, 'Long live the Emperor and Empress of Mexico!' And Charlotte, who was now the 'Empress Carlota', raised her proud little head still higher as she acknowledged their homage. Maximilian swore by the Holy Gospels to 'assure by all the means in my power the prosperity and well-being of the nation and to defend the independence and integrity of its territory'. As he spoke, the Mexican Imperial Standard was hoisted on the flagstaff and twenty-one cannon shots were fired in salute from the warships anchored in the bay. The Mexican Empire was born.

But there had been no mention in Maximilian's speech of England or of Spain, whose guarantees had once been the *sine-qua-non* of his acceptance. He had openly admitted that it was only the guarantees of France which had made his acceptance possible, and standing behind him in the place of honour was Napoleon's envoy, General Frossard, entrusted by his master with the power to put the final signature to the Convention of Miramar, which condemned the ill-fated Mexican Empire to insolvency from the very beginning.

16

From Miramar to Mexico

The Mexican standard fluttered over the turrets of Miramar and the Italians saw this strange, outlandish symbol of an eagle devouring a serpent as a sign of ill-omen. There was general regret at the departure of their beloved Archduke, and most of the household were in tears. The friends and relatives of those who were sufficiently adventurous to accompany their master overseas filled the hotels and lodging-houses of Trieste. A hundred dockers and porters had been mobilized to load the trunks and strong-boxes on to the boats which kept plying between the landing-stage and the *Novara*, at anchor in the bay.

The castle telegraph office was working overtime, dealing with messages of congratulation from all over the world. But it was Charlotte, not Maximilian, who read the telegrams, received the deputations and presided alone at the gala dinner which inaugurated their reign. The departure was to have taken place the following day, Monday, 11 April. But on the evening of the tenth, Doctor Jilek had gone into the library and found the Archduke in a state of complete collapse. The strain of the past days, the mental anguish caused by the decisions he had been forced to make, had overtaxed an already-delicate constitution and he was on the verge of a nervous breakdown. Even now, the doctor had the greatest difficulty in dissuading him from attending the state banquet, for he was obsessed by the fear of failing his new subjects and of showing his weakness in front of Napoleon's envoy. It was only when Jilek promised to issue a bulletin describing his illness as 'a feverish chill' that he consented to retire with him to the seclusion of the garden pavilion, where he had lived with Charlotte during the building of Miramar.

The departure had to be postponed for three days until Maximilian was fit to travel. Meanwhile, he saw no one but his doctor and his valet. A walk in the grounds and a chance encounter with a gardener was sufficient to upset his equilibrium. Doctor Jilek recounts that they were having breakfast on the morning of the eleventh when Charlotte appeared bringing a telegram of congratulation from Napoleon, whereupon Maximilian, in a sudden excess of rage, flung his knife and fork down upon the table, shouting, 'Leave me in peace! I do not want to hear of Mexico at present.' And Charlotte, without saying a word or appearing at all disconcerted, quietly left the room. The discipline instilled in her from childhood, her own pride and strength of will, helped her to carry off a situation which would have tried many an older and more experienced woman. Behind her were those harrowing days in Vienna, spent in arguing with the obdurate Emperor, those terrible hours of battling against Max's indecision. A letter written but never posted to the Empress Eugénie in an hour of despair when Max was on the point of renouncing the crown of Mexico shows that, for all her loyalty to her husband, she was against his decision, 'the consequences of which are, in my opinion, incalculable'. At last she had triumphed. The crown she had always coveted for Max was won. She was still convinced that he had all the qualities necessary for success. 'Even if the task is a difficult one,' she wrote, 'it is not impossible, and certainly not for Max. It would have been madness for anyone else to try.'

What he was suffering from now was only a passing weakness, natural for someone so sensitive and finely-tuned. It was up to her, the stronger and more practical of the two, to carry out his duties as well as her own, and she did not hesitate to correct a letter he had written to Napoleon, of which she did not consider the language to be sufficiently diplomatic. She felt herself very much her father's daughter, nurtured in statecraft. But she forgot that she was also as vulnerable and highly-strung as her mother who, unknown to her, had suffered from religious mania in the last years of her life. The tremendous self-discipline, the pride which would never allow her to confide, was later to prove her undoing. Too many violent emotions, too many disappointments and disillusions were dissimulated and ignored, till the brilliant young Empress broke under the appalling mental strain.

But now, on the eve of departure, when everyone else was in tears and Miramar was in a state of confusion, Charlotte alone remained smiling and calm. She had a kind word for everyone, in particular for poor old Countess Lutzoff, who was so overcome by the consequences of her own actions that she spent most of her days in prayer. Everyone was impressed by the young Empress's composure, but it was noted that she never expressed one word of regret at leaving Miramar, 'the enchanted castle' of which Max once told her she was to be 'the fairy queen'. She had been too lonely and unhappy in the past years to express a regret she was far from feeling. Mexico promised a full and glorious life which she could share with Max just as she had shared his labours and his triumphs in the days of the Italian Viceroyalty.

The Mexican delegates were one and all in love with their beautiful Empress, who presided with so much elegance and grace at the state banquet, served with all the luxury and taste for which Miramar was famous. Seated between the Cardinal Patriarch of Venice and General Frossard, speaking Italian to the one and French to the other, addressing her new subjects in an almost faultless Spanish, Charlotte appeared to be in radiant spirits and in no way concerned over her husband's indisposition. There were those who disapproved of these radiant spirits and regarded her as hard and unfeeling. One of them was her young brother-in-law, Ludwig Viktor, who at his mother's request had stayed behind at Miramar to accompany Max to Rome on the first stage of his journey. Ludwig Viktor was the effeminate younger brother whom Max had once envisaged as a future Emperor of Brazil. He was even later to consider making him his heir to the Mexican throne. But the young Archduke had never any intention of following in the wake of 'poor old Montezuma' (Max), whom he assured his mother 'would never have gone on with the Mexican business, had it not been for Charlotte's nagging'. But who could have foreseen in that month of April 1864 that the lovely young Empress, who appeared to be so supremely sure of herself, would in less than three years be back at Miramar, a pathetic wreck of a woman with terror-haunted eyes?

On the morning of the fourteenth, the day of his departure, Maximilian came out of his seclusion to find the gardens and the four kilometres of sea road between Trieste and Miramar one solid mass of people, all wanting to pay a last tribute and have a last glimpse of their 'Sailor Prince'. They were the Italian people he had grown to love and understand, more than he had ever loved the Austrians, more than he would ever understand the Mexicans. The day before, he had written to the Mayor of Trieste, bidding a last farewell to the 'dear and beautiful city which has become my home', and that morning the municipal councillors of Trieste and the members of the Chamber of Commerce had arrived in six steamers of the Austrian Lloyd to present him with an ivory-bound volume containing views of the city, and an address signed by no less than six thousand citizens. Had it not been for the doctor's insistence, Maximilian would never have brought himself to face the ordeal of receiving the deputation, and by the end of the mayor's speech he was again reduced to tears. But tears were the order of the day, for there was hardly a dry eye among the hard-headed businessmen and city councillors of Trieste.

There were scenes which were even more poignant and even harder for Maximilian to endure: saying goodbye to his household; walking for the last time in the gardens he had created; receiving a heart-broken telegram from his mother, 'Our blessings, Papa's and mine, on leaving a country where we may never see you again' – the pathetic message of two old people to the son they were both destined to survive. By now it was two o'clock, the *Novara* was already under steam, the crowds were becoming impatient and calling out his name. Pride of race asserted itself. Pale and erect, with Charlotte on his arm, Maximilian came slowly down the marble steps leading to the landing-stage, where a launch covered by a red and gold embroidered canopy was waiting to take them on board. As soon as they appeared, every man in the enormous crowd took off his hat and burst into spontaneous cheers, while the women pelted them with blossom. Musicians from Trieste struck up the Mexican Imperial Anthem, composed not in Mexico but in Paris and quite unrecognizable to the new Emperor, still accustomed to the strains of '*Gott Erhalte Unser Kaiser*'. Old retainers, overcome with grief, pressed forward to kiss their hands, their feet, even the hems of their garments. Doctor Jilek, who had been so bitterly opposed to the whole Mexican enterprise, was now himself on the verge of collapse, and Maximilian, who was too moved to speak, could only acknowledge the acclamations with a gesture of the hand. But Charlotte's face was wreathed in smiles – the happy, spontaneous smiles of a child who had at last achieved her heart's desire.

As they boarded the *Novara* the Mexican flag was hoisted to the mast and a salute of a hundred guns roared from the forts and ramparts of Trieste. The two accompanying frigates, the Austrian *Bellona* and the French *Themis*, fired a volley in reply, and the crowds on shore could hear the cheers of the crew welcoming their former commander-in-chief on board. Preceded by the yacht *Fantaisie*, escorted by the two frigates and followed by the flag-bedecked steamers of the Austrian Lloyd and a whole fleet of fishing boats, saluted in passing by every boat at anchor in the harbour, the *Novara* sailed out into the bay on a sea as calm as a lake. '*Arrivederci*,' '*Auf Wiedersehen*,' 'God keep you safe,' shouted the people from the shore – but Maximilian had already gone below. After one long, last look at Miramar, he had retired to his cabin to nurse his grief in private.

The news that Maximilian was at last on his way to Mexico caused immense relief at the Hofburg and the Tuileries, though both Emperors were concerned over the Roman visit. Franz Josef was afraid that his impetuous brother might complain to the Pope of having been forced to sign the Act of Renunciation – a matter which was entirely a family affair and had nothing to do with the Vatican. Napoleon, for his part, was nervous that the Pope and Cardinal Antonelli might bring up the thorny subject of the sequestered Church properties and intimidate Maximilian into making concessions which were contrary to French policy in Mexico. In his recent letters, General Bazaine was becoming increasingly critical of the enormous expenses incurred by the Council of Regency and of the reactionary attitude and pretensions of Almonte, whom Maximilian had appointed 'Lieutenant-General of the Realm'. Bazaine wrote: The Regency has made itself a Court, when there is as yet no Emperor; it has surrounded itself with the expenses of a government when, as yet, there is nothing to govern. ... Of what use are ministers without ministeries? For instance, the Minister of War, when there is no army, other than a few guerrilla troops, which ever since our arrival have been commanded, fed and paid by us?' The Finance Minister, Achille Fould, reminded the Emperor that everything so far had been paid by France and the only hope of retrieving the money was to get control of the ports and the mines. The loan which had been raised in London had not been fully subscribed. And a leader in *The Times* complacently asserting, 'The less our government interferes in Mexico, the better the public will be pleased,' was certainly not calculated to encourage English investors to place their money in such a hazardous enterprise – an enterprise rendered still more hazardous by the uncompromising attitude in Washington.

With their armies united under the leadership of General Grant, and the South in the last throes of an unequal stuggle, the American House of Representatives could now afford to administer a rebuff to the European powers who in the past years had to a greater or lesser degree favoured the rebels. In a unanimous resolution, they declared themselves 'utterly opposed to the recognition of a monarchy, set up on the ruins of a republican government, under the auspices of any and what-

221

soever European power'. The time had now come for Washington to tell the world that it would not tolerate the slightest infringement of the Monroe Doctrine, which in the words of the Austrian Minister had become their 'holy gospel', and the unfortunate Archduke who was on his way to Mexico was to be the first victim of American wrath.

But no Emperor and Empress were ever given a more magnificent reception than Maximilian and Charlotte on their arrival in Papal Rome on 18 April. There were flowers and cheers and flag-waving from the moment they landed at Civitavecchia, where they found the Duke of Montebello, commander of the French forces of occupation, and the Ambassadors of Austria, France and Belgium waiting to receive them. Protected by French troops, Pope Pius ix was enjoying the last years of temporal power, and the Church still had hopes of having all its ancient privileges in Mexico restored under the rule of a Hapsburg prince. Papal *Zouaves* and French *Chasseurs* formed the guard-of-honour when Their Imperial Majesties boarded a special train for Rome. Here no less a person than Cardinal Antonelli, the all-powerful Secretary of State, met them at the station. Large, sympathetic crowds, attracted by the combination of the young, the beautiful and the exotic, acclaimed them all the way to the Palazzo Marescotti, the magnificent residence in the Via dei Cesari, where the wealth derived from the hennequen plantations of Yucatan enabled Gutierrez d'Estrada to live in luxurious exile.

After forty years, all Gutierrez's ambitions were now being realized. The Emperor and Empress of Mexico were lodged under his roof. But in spite of his vaunted patriotism, he had declined the offer of representing his country in Vienna. Was it because he had hoped for a more brilliant reward, and resented the appointment of his rival, Almonte, to the post of Lieutenant-General of the Realm? Or was it because he had spent so many years in Rome that he was frightened of finding himself an unwanted stranger in his own country? In public, he asserted that he wanted no greater honour than to have been 'the architect of the Empire'. If Maximilian offered what appeared to be an inadequate reward, one must remember that Gutierrez had always been *persona non grata* with the French, and the young Emperor may well have feared the reactionary influence of this loyal friend of Santa Anna in a country where he hoped to conciliate the liberal elements.

The most important member of the Mexican deputation, an elderly Conservative politician called Velasquez de Leon, had been entrusted with the formation of the new government, but he had no experience of

European diplomacy and in Rome was more of a hindrance than a help to the new Emperor in dealing with the astute and able Papal diplomats. Outstanding differences, the grave divergencies between Church and State in Mexico, the vital necessity for a *concordat* and the appointment of a Nuncio, all matters which should have been fully settled before the Emperor's departure, were given the most superficial attention.

Maximilian, who from all accounts had completely recovered his spirits, appeared to be as gratified as Charlotte by the splendour of their reception, and in characteristic fashion evaded unpleasant issues which might spoil his visit. After Mass held by the Pope in the Sistine Chapel, Charlotte wrote ecstatically to her grandmother of her emotion at 'receiving the Sacraments from the hands of the Holy Father, who gave us a touching and appropriate sermon'. But the sermon which Charlotte described as touching could also have been interpreted as a warning for the future, for His Holiness made a point of reminding Maximilian: 'Though the rights of the people are great and must be respected, those of the Church are greater and more sacred,' an intimation that neither the Vatican nor Archbishop Labastida had any intention of renouncing any of their claims. But the admonishment was easily forgotten in the friendly atmosphere of the Papal breakfast table, where His Holiness treated Maximilian with the same paternal kindness he had shown in the old days at Pesaro. That same afternoon, the Pope paid a visit on the Emperor and Empress of Mexico. It was a proud moment for old Gutierrez when the gala coaches, preceded by the *Guardia Nobile*, clattered down the Via dei Cesari. It was also a proud moment for Maximilian, for the Papal embrace, an embrace described as 'unusually effusive', made him feel that he was now Emperor by divine right, and not only by the will of his people. When His Holiness left the Palace, the crowds waiting outside saw the tall young Emperor kneel down in the street to receive a last blessing.

The previous evening there had been a large reception at the Palazzo Marescotti, to which over three hundred guests were invited. One of these guests, a young German traveller, has left his impressions of 'that adventurous young couple who are expatriating themselves and seeking their fortunes overseas'. He describes Maximilian as 'slim and well-built, without much hair on his head but with a luxuriant blond beard. His chief defect is his ugly teeth, which he shows too much when he speaks. His voice is rather high and loud, like most of the Austrian aristocracy. While the Emperor is very blond with blue eyes, the Empress is very dark. Also she has a superb figure and very graceful movements.' The Italians were less critical. They found the Emperor romantically handsome and his wife exceedingly pretty, but the general opinion was that they had been duped by Napoleon. Noting the French guard-of-honour outside the Palazzo Marescotti, a cynic commented, 'No wonder they guard Maximilian so well. They would have difficulty in finding anyone else to take his place,' and the same view was reflected in the 'Pasquinade', which circulated in the town.

> Massimiliano, non ti fidare.
> Torna al Castello di Miramare.
> Quel trono facile di Montezuma
> E un nappo gallico colmo di spuma.
> Del timeo Danaos, del ti ricorda.
> Sotto il porpora trova la corda.
>
> [Maximilian, do not be misled.
> Go back to the Castle of Miramar.
> That beguiling throne of Montezuma
> Is nothing but a cup of Gallic froth.
> Remember Danaos and his dangerous gifts.
> Under the purple you may find the hangman's rope.]

Charlotte and Maximilian were probably the only people in Rome who did not hear the rhyme, and the former wrote to her grandmother in England, 'Everyone is impressed by Max's spirit of abnegation and self-sacrifice in undertaking such a difficult task.' She did not realize that they inspired pity rather than admiration. In those two crowded, dazzling days, there was so much to do, so much to see. There were family duties to carry out, such as a visit to their relatives, the ex-King and Queen of Naples, now living in exile in the Farnese Palace; a hurried tour of the principal sights, a drive to the Pincio and the Borghese Gardens and an expedition to the Colosseum by moonlight. By the evening of the twentieth they were back on board the Novara. The guns blared, the flags waved, the Ambassadors of France and Austria paid their last respects, hurrying home to write to their Imperial masters that everything had gone smoothly without any diplomatic complications. Nothing had been settled, nothing had been divulged. Maximilian had made no promises to the Pope, but neither had he received any assurances in return. Contrary to his angry threats, the matter of the 'Family Pact' had never once been mentioned. It was only later, under Charlotte's influence, that the Archduke was to expose his grievances in public.

A pleasant surprise awaited them in Gibraltar, where the *Novara* put in for four days to take on supplies. Queen Victoria had ordered the garrison to salute the Mexican standard with Imperial honours. Though the British government was still sitting on the fence before officially recognizing the new Emperor, King Leopold had been able to secure this small compensation from his niece. It was little enough reward for his efforts. But for Charlotte and Maximilian, it was of inestimable value, holding out a prospect of recognition and guarantees for the future. Spain and Portugal followed suit, and the salute of guns echoed from Gibraltar to Cadiz, from Cadiz to Lisbon, as the *Novara*, escorted by the French *Themis*, sailed into the Atlantic. 'We are in official relations with all the Powers', wrote a proud and happy Charlotte from Madeira, the last port of call.

During the long six-weeks' voyage, Charlotte and Maximilian spent most of the time working in their cabins. But from all accounts the Emperor's work consisted largely in drafting the rules and regulations for a Court which was to be modelled as closely as possible on the Hofburg. It would seem a somewhat trivial occupation in view of the enormous problems which confronted him, and his critics interpreted it as proof of his essential frivolity. The Abbé Domenech, Chaplain to the French Forces, who later served in Maximilian's press department, wrote in his '*Histoire de Mexique*': 'One understands some of the appalling administrative and political blunders of the reign when one considers the total lack of preparedness, the puerile matters which absorbed the attention of the passengers on board the *Novara*. Elaborate rules were laid down on matters of *placement* and etiquette; new medals and decorations were distributed; a Palatine Guard was created; an extravagant Court was organized – all this in a country crippled with debts and commercially, economically and politically in ruins.'

But we must remember that Maximilian was still smarting under the injustice of the 'Family Pact', still bitterly regretting all he had given up in Austria, and that he had only one desire – to make the Court of Mexico as brilliant and as civilized as the Hofburg. His upbringing had convinced him that the pomp and ceremony of a court were necessary to preserve imperial prestige. And there is something rather pathetic at the thought of this young man, whose natural element was the sea and who would have been far happier on the bridge instead of shut up in a stuffy cabin, drawing plans and diagrams of Court ceremonies, listing the duties of chamberlains and high stewards, all of which were later to be compiled into a volume running to no less than six hundred printed pages. What is even more pathetic is the fact that among the hundred-odd passengers aboard the *Novara* there was not one who was capable of giving him good advice.

Those who were the closest to him were the most dangerous. There was that equivocal figure Sebastian Schertzenlechner, whose position in Maximilian's household is so difficult to understand, and who had now been elevated to the position of private secretary. Detested by the other members of the entourage, and particularly by the Emperor's personal friends, such as the two Zichys and Charles Bombelles, Schertzenlechner was soon to find his influence challenged by a newcomer, Felix Eloin, who had been recommended to Maximilian by his father-in-law as a man whose versatile talents and knowledge of the New World would be useful to him in Mexico. Cleverer and far more educated than Schertzenlechner, Eloin was destined to have a disastrous effect on Maximilian's policy, for he was both anti-French and anti-clerical – an unfortunate combination in an adviser to a monarch who had been brought into power by the French and was supported by the Conservatives.

How this mining engineer from Namur succeeded in gaining the confidence of King Leopold has never been fully explained. The King appears to have been impressed by a report he had made on mining prospects in Australia and the Fiji Islands, which leads us to suspect that Napoleon was not the only monarch to interest himself in the mineral wealth of Mexico, where a Belgian engineer in a key position at Maximilian's Court would be able to advise his King on profitable investments for Belgian capital.

These two adventurers, Schertzenlechner and Eloin, were witnesses to a compromising document which the Emperor and Empress were sufficiently misguided to compose and sign on board the *Novara*. It was nothing less than a repudiation of the 'Family Pact', which they declared to have been forced to sign under duress. Written and inspired by Charlotte, it was addressed 'to the various peoples united under the Imperial Crown of Hapsburg Lorraine, whose provincial Diets alone had the right to effect changes in the fundamental laws of the pragmatic sanction'. In this document, both Maximilian and Charlotte swore under oath that they had 'never heard or read the text of the Act of Renunciation' until the Archduke had been 'forced to sign at the eleventh hour, under tremendous moral pressure, in which full advantage was taken of the complicated situation between France and Austria'.

This protest, addressed to Franz Josef's subjects, was not only equivalent to treason, but it also deviated from the truth, for Maximilian knew of the sacrifices his acceptance of the crown of Mexico would entail before he left for Paris. All might have been well if this document had been allowed to remain sealed and locked in the Mexican archives, a panacea for wounded pride, only to be used in the eventuality of a dynastic crisis. But with men like Schertzenlechner and Eloin in the young Emperor's confidence, it was not long before the secret leaked to the Imperial Cabinet in Vienna, forcing Franz Josef to make a public statement in the Reichsrat, and straining the relations between the Hapsburg brothers almost to breaking-point. Charlotte, that loving and devoted wife, never rendered a worse service to her husband than in encouraging him to sign this document. But one is inclined to blame King Leopold more than his twenty-three-year-old daughter, for Charlotte had been brought up to think of her father as an oracle of wisdom, and in his last letters and telegrams to Miramar, the old King still kept insisting, 'Max must give up nothing of what is his by right.'

Countess Paola Kollonitz, one of the two ladies-in-waiting who accompanied Charlotte to Mexico, writes that her young mistress was 'so completely absorbed in her new vocation that she seemed completely unmoved by anything not immediately connected with it. Even in the evening, when the rest of us watched the sunset, she showed little interest and continued to study by the light of the ship's lanterns.' Unlike her mistress, Paola Kollonitz, an unmarried woman in her early thirties who had accepted the post of temporary lady-in-waiting from a love of travel and adventure, was interested in everything and everyone. She has left us a vivid account of life on board the *Novara* and during the first months in Mexico, describing the vicissitudes of the hundred ill-assorted Europeans who had followed Maximilian overseas. There were those who had followed him out of loyalty and affection, faithful retainers and childhood friends, like the Zichys, husband and wife, Charles de Bombelles and the Italian Marchese Coria, who had been attached to his Court at Monza; there was the little group of

Mexicans, 'shy, silent men, gentle and courteous in manner, lost and bewildered among all those loud-voiced foreigners'; but the majority of the passengers on board were opportunists and adventurers, deluded by the popular belief that life in Mexico would 'be a bed of roses in a field of gold'.

The Countess wrote, 'At first, everyone was in the best of spirits. When we entered the area of the Trade Winds, the weather became delightfully cool and fresh, tempting even the Empress out on deck. But then the *Novara* ran short of coal and had to be taken in tow by the French frigate *Themis* which had larger supplies on board. This was very humiliating for the Austrian captain and crew, and there were certain sarcastic comments on the Emperor going to Mexico in tow of the French.'

Martinique gave the passengers their first view of the tropics, and Charlotte discarded her habitual reserve and enthused over the 'poetical beauty of the landscape, the richness and variety of the vegetation'. The French authorities on the island provided Maximilian with the opportunity of playing the role of a magnanimous Emperor by releasing the Mexican prisoners who had been captured at Puebla and had now given their adherence to the Empire. Each one was provided with money to buy himself a passage home, and eight of them were taken on board the already overcrowded *Novara*, much to the resentment of the Mexican Conservatives. At Jamaica, the Emperor and Empress received a royal welcome, both from the British Governor and the Admiral in command of the North Atlantic station. But after Jamaica the weather changed. The *Novara* was not a passenger ship, and violent gales and rainstorms soon made life intolerable on board. Conditions in the cramped saloon were so appalling that Countess Kollonitz preferred remaining out on deck, wrapped in a tarpaulin with the rain pouring down on her. At one time, water flooded most of the cabins, including the Empress's. But no mention of these discomforts transpire in Charlotte's letters home: 'I am already in love with the tropics. I only dream of butterflies and humming-birds. I would never have thought that this part of the world would have such an appeal for me. . . . I also pictured the ocean as being far larger. . . . altogether the New World is far more accessible than I had imagined.' They were brave words to write after days of seasickness and squalor, at the end of a six-week crossing, but they were characteristic of all Charlotte's letters from

Mexico. To the very end she persisted in deluding her correspondents even after she had lost all illusions herself.

The storm died down. In calm, cool weather, the *Novara* sailed by coral reefs and palm-fringed islands into the Gulf of Mexico. At dawn on 28 May, the first outline of the coast appeared on the horizon. Maximilian was out on deck, 'gazing quietly and serenely into the distance', so absorbed in his thoughts that he may not have noticed the American frigate going the other way. On the orders of Washington, the United States Consul was leaving Mexico before the Emperor's arrival.

17

Emperor of Mexico

The Spaniards called it *Villa Rica di Vera Cruz*, the Rich Town of the True Cross, but Vera Cruz in the 1860s bore little relation to the town founded by Cortés nearly three hundred and fifty years before. It was a dismal, tumbledown port with peeling customhouses and desecrated churches, where *zopilotes* (buzzards) fattened on the filth and garbage in the streets, and the surrounding morasses were the breeding-ground for flies and the terrible *vomito negro* which raged for eight months in the year.

Both inhabitants and *zopilotes* were still asleep when the guns of the *Themis*, sent on ahead to announce the *Novara*'s arrival, thundered across the water. Nothing was ready, for the Emperor was not expected until the end of the month; the local authorities and the French command were taken completely by surprise. General Almonte, the Lieutenant-General of the Realm, had not even arrived. Fearful of exposing himself and his family to the perils of a prolonged stay in a town which had the reputation of being one of the most unhealthy in the world, he was waiting at Orizaba to hear definite news before proceeding to the coast. He had also had to mobilize a military guard to ensure that Their Imperial Majesties would not be exposed to guerrilla attacks on their journey to Mexico City, for when writing to Europe of the 'impatience of the Mexicans to welcome their *Emperador*' he had omitted to mention that it was dangerous to venture even a few miles from the capital without an armed escort. It was unfortunate that the Emperor had to arrive at Vera Cruz, a town of republican sympathies which had long been a stronghold of Juarez and where natives and Europeans alike had flourished on contraband and the general state of disorder and corruption prevailing in the customs. No one in Vera Cruz wanted either a foreign Emperor or an ordered government, and it was left to the authorities to mobilize a few Indians to put up some triumphal arches and prepare a semblance of a welcome.

Shortly after midday, the *Novara* cast anchor in the roads off Vera Cruz. The French fleet was assembled off Sacrificios Island. But Maximilian did not want to give the impression that he was coming to Mexico under the protection of the French, and deliberately gave orders to anchor to the south of the old Spanish fortress of San Juan de Ulúa. An atmosphere of excitement and expectancy prevailed on board, but the first impressions were not encouraging. Countess Kollonitz wrote that the first sight which greeted them on approaching was the wreck of a French ship, stranded on a coral reef, and the cemetery for the French soldiers of the first expeditionary force who had fallen victim to an epidemic of yellow fever. The *Themis* had gone on ahead, but all was silent. No one had come to receive the Emperor, who was quietly sarcastic at his own expense. After some time, the commander of the French fleet, Admiral Bosse, and his aide-de-camp arrived on board in a very bad humour, because the Emperor had not anchored in the midst of the French fleet. 'He had the impertinence,' wrote the Countess, 'to show his anger in front of the Emperor, telling him that he had chosen the most contagious spot and that it would be dangerous to spend the night there. He also spoke of the perils to which they would be exposed on the journey to Mexico City, for some notorious bandits had threatened to capture Their Imperial Majesties and General Bazaine had not sufficient time at his disposal to look after their safety.'

It cannot have been very pleasant for Maximilian to hear that the French Commander-in-Chief was too busy to 'ensure their safety' and to have the Admiral address him in a tone that the highest official in the Austrian Empire would never have dared to use in his presence. But Charlotte persisted in seeing everything through rose-coloured spectacles, and found the first view of Vera Cruz 'infinitely pleasing, a more oriental version of Cadiz'. The situation improved towards evening with the arrival of Almonte, whose 'handsome face and charming manners' made an excellent impression on the Austrian suite, though courtiers used to formality of the Hofburg were amazed to see Madame Almonte greeting the Empress with the Mexican *abrazo* and all the notables who came on board with Almonte shaking the Emperor familiarly by the hand. Charlotte never got used to the *abrazo*, and her instinctive recoil from this spontaneous embrace wounded the feelings of the susceptible Mexican ladies.

Vera Cruz woke up at night. The streets were illuminated in the Emperor's honour, and the French fleet hung lanterns from their masts and let off a trail of rockets. On the walls of the cafés appeared Maximilian's first manifesto to the Mexican people, in which he vowed to consecrate himself heart and soul to their welfare, to work with them for prosperity and peace, so that, 'having won their glorious independence, they could now enjoy the benefits of civilization'. The young Emperor was sincere in his intentions, but for the people of Vera Cruz it was just another *pronunciamento*. Iturbide, Santa Anna, Juarez and Miramon had all promised the same things. The French generals had also been lavish with their promises, but the only difference was that under their supervision it had become more difficult to cheat the customs.

Later that night, the *Norte* blew in force, extinguishing the Bengal lights and scattering the decorations so that by six o'clock in the morning, when the Emperor and Empress landed, saluted by the cannon of San Juan de Ulúa and the guns of the French warships, they found the streets practically deserted and the triumphal arches lying in the dust. It was too early in the morning and the inhabitants were too indifferent to come out of their houses and cheer. Owing to the fear of contagion, no arrangements had been made to prolong their stay in Vera Cruz, and the authorities hurried them through the empty streets to the central plaza, where a single-track railway, constructed by the French, was to take them on the first stage of their journey. This chilling reception left Maximilian outwardly calm, but now, for the first time, Charlotte's proud spirit broke and she could hardly restrain her tears. If the Empress was upset, her retinue were appalled by their first view of Mexico. There was no proper station, no signalmen along the line which ran through marsh and desert. Even the excellent breakfast provided by the French authorities at Soledad in no way allayed their fears, for a few miles from Soledad the railway came to a sudden end in a little Indian village. The sight of the lumbering, old-fashioned stagecoaches, each drawn by eight mules, which were to convey them for the rest of their four-hundred-kilometre journey to Mexico City, was not calculated to reassure them. As none of the stopping places on the way had sufficient accommodation to house eighty-five people with over four hundred pieces of luggage between them, the party was divided: the Emperor and Empress, accompanied by Almonte and Velasquez de Leon, travelled by shorter stages with longer stops on the way.

Charlotte's spirits were revived by the attentions of the French officers, the smart turn-out of the Mexican guard, and the enthusiasm of the inhabitants of the Indian villages, in contrast to the apathy of the townspeople. Both she and Maximilian were full of optimism when they mounted the elegant English travelling-carriage they had brought with them from Europe. But it was not long before they discovered that European springs and axles were not made for Mexican roads, which in many instances were no more than dried-up riverbeds with great rocks in the middle. In describing her experience to the Empress Eugénie, Charlotte wrote: 'The road leading across ill-cultivated plains to the Chiquihuite Mountains is abominable. The only civilized spots are the French guard-houses, with the canteens beside them. . . . The Mexicans kept apologizing for the road, and we kept assuring them that we did not mind in the least bit. As a matter of fact, they were ghastly beyond all words, and we needed all our youth and good humour to get off without cramp or a broken rib.'

But for Maximilian the discomforts of the journey were compensated by the fantastic beauty of the almost uninhabited countryside. The sand dunes and marshes of the coast had given way to a tropical jungle, to groves of mangoes and bananas and giant coconut palms. Huge pink and yellow bushes of bigonia, orchids of every colour and variety, flaming bombax and colorines lighted the forest with bursts of vivid colour, while mysterious little rivers glided through moss and fern to end in lily-covered pools. Here and there rose a solitary hut built of wattle and bamboo, where brown, half-naked children played ball with coconuts and women in brightly-coloured rags same out to offer them bananas and *papaya*. But there was no hut so poor that it was not planted round with flowers, for Maximilian was to find in his Indian subjects a love of flowers akin to his own. Twenty-five years before, in the gardens of Schönbrunn, he had played at being king of the jungle and today his dream had come true. This country was a part of his realm, these poor, downtrodden Indians were the people he had come to free from centuries of serfdom. No one could have been more genuine in his intentions or more ready to help his subjects than the Hapsburg Prince whom the Emperor Napoleon's ambition had brought to rule in Mexico.

Commanding the escort was a tall, handsome young man whose smart appearance attracted the Emperor's attention. This was Miguel Lopez, who after three years of Imperial favour was to sell him to his enemies. But no thought of future treachery disturbed Maximilian's dreams as his carriage lurched and bumped along the horrible road which climbed ever-higher into the mountains. He accepted gaily the hazards of the journey, remaining quite unmoved when, towards the evening, in the middle of a dense forest, the wheel of their carriage broke and they had to proceed in one of the ordinary stagecoaches, from which no one had even troubled to remove the sign *'Deligencia della Republica'*. They had arrived in Mexico at the beginning of the rainy season, and now there was suddenly a cloudburst which transformed the road into a river of mud. The coach in front of them, with Velasquez de Leon on board, crashed at the edge of a ravine and the six occupants barely escaped with their lives, Maximilian's Minister of State just managing to save himself by climbing out of the window. By now, night was falling and even Charlotte's courage began to fail her. Remembering the warnings of the French Admiral at Vera Cruz, she pictured bandits waiting to ambush them behind every rock and tree. 'Things looked so odd,' she wrote, 'that I should not have been surprised if Juarez himself had appeared with some hundreds of *guerrilleros.'*

It was two o'clock in the morning by the time they reached Cordoba, tired, aching and hungry, without having dined or supped. But the little town in the mountain valley was still brilliantly illuminated under a starlit sky, the rains having stopped as suddenly as they had begun. The entire population was out in the decorated streets to welcome the *Emperadors*: hundreds of white-clad Indians waving branches of fern and garlands of flowers; the local authorities in uniforms stiff with gold embroidery; an impressive array of French officers wearing their ribbons and medals. There was an elaborate banquet followed by endless toasts and speeches, so it was nearly five in the morning before they got to bed. But the warmth of the reception was such a happy contrast to the hostility of Vera Cruz that Charlotte wrote, 'We did not feel in the least bit tired'.

Her suite felt otherwise. Owing to mismanagement, the two parties which had divided at Vera Cruz met again at Cordoba. Here a rich *haciendado* had placed his comfortable house at Their Majesties' disposal, but no accommodation had been provided for eighty other tired people, and it needed someone as healthy and adventurous as Paola Kollonitz to make light of the vicissitudes of Mexican travel, and to appreciate the miracles performed by the coach service: 'Large stables, connected with taprooms, appeared at regular intervals in what at times appeared to be inaccessible places.' She was also full of praise for the muleteers, who ran the most appalling risks with the utmost sang-froid, contending not only with the abominable roads but the constant risk of being attacked by bandits. Yet they always remained courteous and polite, addressing one another as '*Señor*'.

The enthusiasm grew as the Imperial cortège penetrated even further into the interior. Even the poorest village had made the effort of erecting a triumphal arch of flowers. At Orizaba, which had always been reputed for its Republican sympathies, they were delighted to find themselves welcomed by no fewer than ten thousand Indians, who came crowding round their coach, clinging to the wheels, gazing at them with wide-eyed admiration. Did these poor primitive people see in the blond young Emperor the reincarnation of the gentle bird-god Quetzalcoatl who, driven out by his enemies, had sailed away towards the sun in a boat of snakeskin and, according to legend, would one day return in the shape of a big, white man with a golden beard? Pagan and Christian legends were closely interwoven in their simple, childish faith, which had helped them to support their privations during centuries of oppression.

The Imperial couple stayed two days at Orizaba. 'As pretty a place as you can find,' wrote Charlotte, 'reminding one of Italy and the Southern Tyrol. The air is delicious and extremely light.' Today Orizaba is still a charming little town, though progress in the form of cheap stores, cinemas and a plethora of hideous advertisements has done much to destroy its beauty. Surrounded by orange groves and banana and coffee plantations, it lies in a narrow valley, shadowed by the volcano which gives it its name. There is still the painted Municipal Palace, with delicate wrought-iron balconies, where Maximilian received the deputations which came to pay him homage, and the Cathedral where a *Te Deum* was sung in his honour. Waiting to receive Their Imperial Majesties at Orizaba was the nucleus of their Court, the lords and ladies-in-waiting who had not dared to risk the journey to Vera Cruz. All of them owed their appointments to Almonte and belonged exclusively to the old Creole aristocracy who prided themselves on being descended from the first Spanish settlers. But both Charlotte and Maximilian were far more thrilled by the deputation of Narvanjal Indians, one of the oldest and most powerful of the Indian tribes, who had come down from the mountains dressed in their traditional costumes of silver-embroidered jerkins and short, white calico trousers, with machetes at their belts and heavy gold rings in their ears. Charlotte was enchanted when the chief of the tribe presented her with a ring set with large diamonds – a relic from the family of Montezuma, whom he claimed as an ancestor. Maximilian invited the heads of the various deputations to dine at his table, a tactful gesture which won their hearts, but which was in no way appreciated by the descendants of the *Conquistadores*.

At Orizaba began the ascent of the formidable Cumbres, and the delicately-nurtured Mexican ladies, who rarely ventured out of doors except in carriages or litters, were amazed to see their Empress appear in riding habit and sombrero, prepared to ride across the mountains on horseback. The experience was not as pleasurable as Charlotte had anticipated, for they ran into a torrential rainstorm and arrived at the country house of the Bishop of Puebla cold and soaked to the skin.

But the next day the sun was shining, the tiled domes of Puebla glittered under a brilliant sky, and the bells of its hundred churches pealed in welcome when the Imperial cortège drove into the town. The cheering was such that the French could hardly believe that this was the town which, little more than a year ago, had offered such a desperate resistance and had fought so heroically in defence of the Republic. The wealthy clergy, who in those days had not dared to show their faces, were again in control and they were ready to support both a foreign army and a foreign Emperor, so long as they upheld their privileges.

Charlotte celebrated her twenty-fourth birthday in Puebla and the French garrison gave a splendid ball in her honour, including a superb display of fireworks, where Latin ingenuity went to the length of showing the Castle of Miramar in a blaze of golden stars. The Emperor and Empress and the population of Puebla were equally entranced, and that night there was not a man or woman in the town who would not have called themselves *Emperialisti*. Delighted by the warm welcome they had received in Puebla, 'a welcome which, on my birthday, makes me feel that I am among my own people, in my own country, surrounded by loving friends', Charlotte sent a letter to the Prefect, enclosing a sum of seven thousand piastres (thirty-five thousand francs) to be spent on restoring a hospital and almshouse she had noticed in ruins.

Puebla was one of the most prosperous towns in Mexico but both she and Maximilian were horrified by the primitive conditions, the terrible contrasts between rich and poor. 'Everything in this country has got to be begun all over again,' Charlotte wrote to Eugénie. 'One finds nothing but nature, whether in the physical or in the moral sense; the people's education has to be undertaken down to the smallest detail. Outside the towns, you do not find a single white person, but no sooner do you arrive in a place of importance, than as if by the wave of a magician's wand, there appear Prefects in embroidered uniforms and Tricolor sashes, almost like in France, except that the embroideries are of gold. It is such an incredible contrast to the rest of the country. Most of the Indians can read and write. They are in the highest degree intelligent and, if the clergy instructed them properly, they would be a very enlightened race. But the priests do not even teach the Catechism in the schools – and this in Puebla, the clerical town par excellence. . . . The ephemeral governments which have succeeded one another for the past forty years have never been more than minorities supplanted by other minorities. They have never had any root in the Indian population which is the only one which works and which enables the State to live.'

One marvels at the authority with which Charlotte gave her judgment after only a few days in Mexico, and in certain things her judgment was correct, though she overestimated the education and intelligence of the Indians, who in most parts of the country were still primitive and illiterate. Apart from the Indians, who had no voice in the running of their country, Maximilian's supporters were drawn almost entirely from the upper classes – the great landowners and the so-called 'silver barons', the mine-owners who had accumulated vast fortunes in the days when Mexico supplied one-third of the world's silver. They were people who lived for pomp and show, and the last thing they wanted was a liberal-minded Emperor who travelled round the country dressed in plain, civilian clothes, treating the Indians as their equals and talking of constitutional rule and the rights of man. Maximilian had already shown that he had no intention of forming a government of reactionaries. After enjoying for a few weeks the proud title of Lieutenant-General of the Realm, Juan Almonte had handed over his powers at Vera Cruz, where he had been profusely thanked and decorated by his Emperor. But the only position he had been offered was the purely titular dignity of 'High Marshal of the Court and Grand Master of the Imperial Household'.

From Puebla, the Imperial party proceeded to Cholula, once the greatest of all Aztec cities, now a small town of less than twelve thousand inhabitants – but those twelve thousand had been the first to give their allegiance to the Empire, and the Emperor had come in person to thank them. On the thirteenth day, they climbed the last ascent to the pinewoods of Rio Frio, and below them, over seven thousand feet above the sea, stretched the great fertile vale of Mexico, studded by white-walled towns with baroque spires, intersected by gleaming lakes, surrounded by snow-capped volcanoes – a view which has thrilled every traveller since the days of Cortés and must have reconciled Maximilian for all he had given up in Europe.

On 12 June, the anniversary of the French march into the capital, Maximilian and Charlotte made their state entry amid scenes of an almost delirious enthusiasm, with Indians, *Mestizos* and Creoles joining in welcome. 'We have witnessed five or six triumphal marches into the city,' wrote the veteran editor of the local French newspaper, *L'Estafette*. 'We have seen the strident, vainglorious manifestations of victors drunk with power; celebrations in which the insolence of the conquerors was given free rein and the passion for revenge was unleashed and where the illuminations often ended in flames. Today, there was neither clamour, nor boasting, nor a single cry of revenge. All the *"Vivas"* seemed to come from the heart, inspired by a genuine emotion at the sight of these young sovereigns so confident and trusting in their love. And the most touching thing of all was the way in which everyone has made an effort to give them a worthy reception. Even in the most isolated streets in outlying districts, far from the centre, there was hardly a house which had not made some attempt at decoration – a wreath of leaves, a branch of palm, or a few brightly coloured rags. And these humble efforts were as heart-warming as the opulent decorations of the great palaces.'

French taste and Mexican fantasy had combined to stage a brilliant fiesta against the background of the old Spanish colonial city. The Emperor and Empress drove in a state coach ordered in Trieste so many months ago, when the future of the Mexican Empire was still in the balance. Maximilian wore, for the first time, the full dress uniform of a Mexican general, the newly-created Order of the Grand Cross of Guadaloupe and the jewelled collar of the Golden Fleece, while Charlotte, in a diamond crown and a mantilla of the finest Brussels lace, paraded in front of her admiring Mexican subjects a wealth of Hapsburg and Bourbon heirlooms. The enthusiasm grew to a frenzy as they approached the centre of the town. Women threw flowers from the balconies, fire-crackers rent the air and men stood in doorways waving their sombreros, shouting 'Viva el Emperadors!'. Time after time, hysterical crowds broke into the procession as it crossed the tree-shaded Alameda, along the crowded commercial thoroughfare of Plateros and into the Zócalo, the great central square in front of the Cathedral, flanked on one side by the Palaçio Naçional which to European eyes looked more like a barracks than a palace.

Not even Santa Anna, in the days of his glory, could have mustered such a magnificent cortège. First came the Mexican Imperial Guard, under the command of the handsome Captain Lopez, followed by detachments of *Zouaves* and *Chasseurs d'Afrique*. Then came the Imperial coach, with General Bazaine and General Neigre, Commander of Mexico City, riding on either side, holding aloft their bared swords. To the French went the honours of the day, for the various commanders of the expeditionary force with their flags and military bands took pride of place over members of the government, whose carriages followed in the rear. As a young French officer commented, 'It was France who surrounded and presented to the Mexican people the Emperor chosen for them by Napoleon III'. And the French thought that this was only right, 'considering we had paid for it all'. But the young sovereign, who acknowledged the cheers of his subjects with the effortless grace of those who are born to rule, already saw himself as the elect of God, rather than of Napoleon III. He was intoxicated by this atmosphere of optimism and goodwill, and dazzled by the brilliant sunshine and the vivid colours. It was a day when everything seemed possible, and even the formidable Archbishop, waiting to receive him at the portals of the Cathedral, looked gentle and conciliatory. Kneeling at the gilded *reya* of the high altar as a thousand voices sang in chorus, '*Domine Salvum Fac Imperatorum*', Maximilian believed it might still be possible to found a dynasty on the throne of Montezuma.

That night, it seemed as if the Mexicans would never allow their new sovereigns to go to bed. Time. after time, they called them out on to the balcony in a frenzy of cheering. It was only towards dawn, when the last of the fireworks had died and the last of the torches were extinguished, that the exhausted young couple were allowed to retire to their cold, comfortless rooms, which had seen so many Presidents come and go in the past forty years, where so many had camped but no one had really lived. Everything had been prepared for them at the last minute. Precious carpets had been laid on dusty floors, velvets and brocades hung on lice-infested walls. The ladies of Mexico had contributed a dressing-table of solid silver, but none of them had thought of sending in cleaning women with adequate supplies of disinfectant. Legend has it that, on their first night in Mexico City, the Emperor and Empress were driven from their beds by vermin and that Maximilian ended the night in sleeping on a billiard table.

18

Maximilian meets his subjects

Far to the north, in the state of Nuevo Leon, Benito Juarez was waiting on the turn of events. Every day brought more defections, more ministers and Generals declaring for the Empire. With the exception of Porfirio Diaz and the troops under his command, who were still holding out in the south at Oaxaca, the Republican army was reduced to scattered guerrilla bands, most of whom were ordinary bandits rather than *Juaristi*. But still he waited with all the stoic patience of his race for the last guns to stop firing across the border, pinning his hopes on Washington, where Congress had made it clear that they would never recognize the Empire, and where their letters were still addressed 'President Juarez'. Once the Confederates had surrendered, there would be a surplus of army material waiting to be smuggled across the Rio Grande and numberless volunteers from the North wanting to fight for the Mexican Republic in defence of the Monroe Doctrine. But for the time being, he had no troops left to defend his last strongholds when Bazaine turned northwards in one of his lightning campaigns.

Even their enemies paid tribute to the brilliance of French tactics and the efficiency of an administration which brought order out of chaos in the most backward villages. The Empress Charlotte was not the only one to pay tribute to 'the civilizing influence of the French', for we find one of Juarez's ministers writing to his chief: 'One cannot help but be impressed when one sees what the enemy has been able to achieve in the past year. How have they managed to establish their lines of communication, to carry out works which are usually only carried out in peace time, to put the telegraphic line between Queretaro and Vera Cruz into working order, to build a railway line along the coast and organize a regular postal service? . . . In view of their extraordinary progress, there are times when one fears that they will end by realizing the impossible.'

This is an eloquent tribute to General Bazaine and the efficiency of his corps commanders, but with the coming of Maximilian, Bazaine was no longer in sole control. The civilian administration was now in the hands of the Emperor and, though Bazaine remained in sole command of the French expeditionary force, it had never been definitely stipulated at the Convention of Miramar who was to be supreme commander of all the armed forces in Mexico, including the native troops and the foreign volunteers who were being recruited in Belgium and in Austria. This was later to lead to endless friction and impair the efficiency of the fighting forces. But for the time being, Bazaine was doing his best to carry out the instructions of Napoleon, who kept stressing the necessity for tact and discretion in dealing both with Maximilian and the Mexican generals. In his orders to his officers in the field, Bazaine repeatedly warned them to avoid 'at all cost' becoming involved in civilian affairs, but to inform him if any suspected treachery or political abuse came to their notice. He in turn would pass on the information to the Emperor Maximilian.

With his fluent Spanish, his jovial, friendly personality, Bazaine himself was on excellent terms with the Mexicans, and though a recent widower of over fifty, was already successfully courting a beautiful sixteen-year-old señorita. Coming from a somewhat obscure background, for though his father was an army officer, he himself was supposed to be illegitimate and had made his career from the ranks, Achille Bazaine now found himself fêted and adulated in a town where everything could be obtained through influence and graft, and where power had an even more corrupting influence than in Europe. He was in the position of mentor and adviser to a Hapsburg prince who, having been placed on the throne by Napoleon, could reasonably be expected to act in the interests of France. But from the first day, it was apparent that the young Emperor had arrived full of preconceived notions of the divine right of kings, combined with a quixotic brand of liberalism, wanting to rule with clemency a country which could only be ruled by force, trying to reconcile elements which did not want to be reconciled, and choosing as his ministers politicians who had openly expressed themselves against the French intervention.

The docile, accommodating Secretary for Foreign Affairs who, under the Regency, had been persuaded by the French Minister into signing an agreement which would have made Sonora into a French protectorate, was summarily dismissed in favour of an eminent liberal lawyer,

Don Hernando Ramirez, who a year before had refused to become a member of the junta appointed by Forez, and whose house had remained conspicuously barred and closed when the French entered the city. This was hardly calculated to improve Franco-Mexican relations, or to endear Maximilian to the Marquis de Montholon, who had hoped to obtain a French foothold in Sonora. One suspects Maximilian of having been influenced by King Leopold, for whom his admiration had grown with the years and who kept exhorting him 'not to rely too much on the French and to be careful about employing foreigners, so as not to excite the jealousy of the Mexicans'. Both Leopold and Maximilian were fundamentally anti-French, a sentiment which was in no way shared by Charlotte, who prided herself on her Bourbon blood and was invariably treated by Bazaine's staff officers with a chivalry due to a French princess.

King Leopold's advice was diametrically opposed to that of Napoleon, who kept warning Maximilian 'not to allow himself to be influenced by Mexicans, who are naturally jealous of foreigners'. He wrote that he had already received reports of the waste and apathy prevailing in the country whenever the French forces relaxed their control. This was not very pleasant reading for Maximilian, but he was soon to learn through bitter experience that the French Emperor was right: no Mexican was capable of administering the finances of his country.

Both Charlotte and Maximilian gave proof of enormous courage and perseverance in face of the difficulties and discomforts which confronted them during their first weeks in Mexico. Countess Kollonitz writes: 'The Imperial couple seem exceeding pleased with the country, the people and their reception. The Empress in particular finds everything delightful, and displays an enthusiasm of which I would not have thought such a quiet person capable.' Was Charlotte's happiness due only to her becoming an Empress, or was there a secret and more intimate reason? Had the dangers and hardships they shared on the journey, their mutual experiences and mutual delight in the physical beauty of Mexico, led her and Maximilian to resume a relationship broken for so many years? We know that Maximilian was always attracted by the novel and the exotic, and Charlotte, seen against a tropical background, surrounded by butterflies and humming-birds, may have been invested with a poetical quality she had never possessed for him at Miramar. Certain statements made by the Emperor during his first months in Mexico, his references to 'his future heirs', his bitter resentment of the Family Pact and the misguided steps he took to publish his grievances to the world, lead us to believe that he was still hoping for a child.

Small wonder that Charlotte was enthusiastic over Mexico, which had provided her with a throne and given her back her husband. But the Empress's enthusiasm was in no way shared by her entourage, who in many cases were reduced to a state of despair. Devoted servants who had carried out their duties admirably at Milan and Miramar and had shown great self-sacrifice in enduring the hardships of the journey, now wandered like lost souls through the vast rabbit-warren of a palace, unable to make themselves understood and at their wits' end as to how to procure even the barest necessities of life. Countess Kollonitz relates that the Empress's personal maid asked her for the loan of insect powder, as there was none left for Her Majesty. The Mexican ladies, who had spared neither time nor expense in furnishing the Empress's rooms in what they considered to be the best European taste, had been too proud to seek the advice of the French officers' wives, and the result was that her drawing-rooms were as tasteless and impersonal as any hotel sitting-room in London or Madrid. There was no efficient manager or housekeeper in charge of the hordes of untrained Mexican servants, who regarded their European counterparts with suspicion and dislike, and did not hesitate to rob and defraud them at every opportunity.

Many of the Emperor's retainers had come across the ocean with their wives and children, and their salaries were quite inadequate to the high cost of living in a town where European goods were in short supply. Jacob von Kuhacsevich, who had been Maximilian's Treasurer at Miramar, had no knowledge of Mexican currency and was as helpless as any of the servants. Nor were any of the gentlemen and officers of the household capable of sorting out the chaos. Courtiers used to the luxury of Miramar grumbled at having to do without their daily comforts and found it difficult to adapt themselves to the somewhat spartan existence led by their young sovereigns who, immersed in their own problems, were totally unaware of the complaints of their attendants, and the fact that over half of them were planning to return to Europe as soon as possible.

To add to the confusion, there were continual festivities and Charlotte's exquisitely embroidered crinolines from Paris had to be unpacked in rooms still impregnated with the stench of unwashed *guerrilleros*. But the festivities themselves were magnificent, beginning with a *corrida* in which the leading gentlemen of Mexico took part, cheered by over ten thousand spectators. There were gala performances both at the Opera and the Theatre, which the Austrians were amazed to find as elegant and as spacious as those in Vienna. But the Mexicans had no idea of punctuality and at the first performance the Emperor and Empress, trained to the punctuality of the Hofburg, arrived in a completely empty theatre, to the amusement of Maximilian and the horror of the Austrian suite. The Mexicans themselves were genuinely mortified by their unintentional bad manners and on the next occasion made superhuman efforts to appear on time. Nevertheless General Almonte, the new Grand Marshal, had the greatest difficulty in training his undisciplined countrymen in the niceties of Hapsburg etiquette. Charlotte found herself encumbered with no less than fourteen ladies-in-waiting, for however much they might aspire to the honour, none of them could face being on duty more than once a fortnight. Altogether, it was a thankless task for a politician who had dreamt of being a king-maker, and even the Order of the Legion of Honour, which according to Charlotte he wore 'with visible pride', could not compensate Almonte for his thwarted ambitions.

The week of festivities culminated in a great ball given by General Bazaine at the French headquarters. From all accounts it was a brilliant spectacle, for which the Emperor Napoleon defrayed half the expenses out of his Privy Purse. Mexico had never seen a ball on such a scale. The decorations were superb. The ballroom, a converted patio hung with tapestries and flags and banners, was lit by forty-eight crystal chandeliers. The supper was a triumph of French gastronomic art; the fireworks, in which Mexicans delight, provided a fantastic display of French pyrotechnic skill; there was unlimited champagne for all. The Imperial couple, who had driven from the palace escorted by a detachment of French cavalry, arrived at nine o'clock, the Emperor opening the ball with the daughter of the municipal Prefect and the Empress with General Bazaine, and did not leave until one in the morning.

But the evening, which was meant to cement goodwill between the Mexicans and Europeans, gave a lot of unnecessary offence chiefly on account of the tactless behaviour of Bazaine's adjutants, who issued invitations to all the young and pretty women and very often omitted the elderly and the most important. Wives were invited without their husbands and sisters without their brothers, with the result that many did not come at all while others only accepted out of respect for the sovereigns. Countess Kollonitz, who has little good to say for the French, deplored the conduct of their officers towards the Mexicans, 'of whom they speak with the most profound contempt, being completely without sympathy for the people or the country'. 'They cannot understand,' she writes, 'how we find so much to admire and appreciate and are so willing to return their civilities, and do not, with the customary intolerance of Europeans, denounce all Mexican failings.'

There appears to have been a certain amount of truth in the Countess's assertions. Reading an account of the ball in the unpublished diary of a Madame de Courcy, the wife of a high-ranking officer on Bazaine's staff, one notes an unconscious superiority when writing of the Mexicans. Watching her dance a quadrille with General Almonte, who was of mixed blood, her husband remarked that 'he never thought he would see me partnered by a nigger'. Madame de Courcy quite rightly replied that 'Almonte is no more of a nigger than I am, and that anyway I have no choice'. Chosen by Bazaine to act as hostess at the ball, she had not only to dance with Almonte, but to spend the rest of the evening in attendance on Their Majesties, standing behind their thrones, waiting for one or the other to address her a word. 'It was more of an honour than a pleasure,' was her rueful comment. But she made up for it later by remaining at the ball till five in the morning, by which time all pretence of decorum had been laid aside and even the Countesses Zichy and Kollonitz, the latter a respectable Canoness of the Order of Savoy,* forgot their dislike of the French under the mellowing influence of the champagne and went so far as to join in the chorus of the 'Marseillaise' and in applauding a can-can.

One of the young French staff captains wrote in his diary that he had the impression that Empress Carlota would have loved to have joined in the fun. Earlier in the evening, he saw her gazing rather wistfully at the dancing couples and she looked on like a fascinated child when the Mexicans danced their national *habanera*.

Most of the officers on Bazaine's staff were young and impressionable, and Charlotte seems to have known how to use her powers, both as an Empress and a pretty woman, with the result that their memoirs and diaries are full of her praise. Even Bazaine appears to have been of the opinion that it would have been easier to govern Mexico with

* A lay order for unmarried daughters of the nobility dating from the times of the Holy Roman Empire.

Charlotte than with her husband. Her clear, well-ordered mind, her practical common sense, the political intuition she had inherited from her father, were qualities the French could appreciate and understand, whereas they were completely at sea with the volatile Maximilian – poet and philosopher in turn, charming and affable, so ready to agree but never willing to commit himself to any definite policy. Charlotte did not share Maximilian's resentment at being dependent on France and her letters to Eugénie, extolling the efficiency and courage of the French army, are completely genuine, whereas Maximilian's flattery of Napoleon sounds false and stilted.

Countess Kollonitz, who gives an accurate and sympathetic account of the young sovereigns, says that the Emperor's position with regard to the French was beset with difficulties and unpleasantness. It was ill-defined and unnatural, and very few of the French authorities had sufficient tact and delicacy to mitigate this feeling of dependence, which the Countess maintains was probably harder for Maximilian to bear than all his other difficulties. Napoleon's letters, courteous and amiable at first, then gradually hardening in tone, with suggestions turning to orders, robbed him of the illusion of freedom. He was tied by the heels to the millstone of the French debt, which absorbed the greater part of the custom-house receipts of Vera Cruz. Port and excise duties were an important part of the Mexican revenues, but the French had not yet cleared the *Juaristi* out of Matamoros or Tampico, the Gulf ports through which passed the greater part of the North American trade, and their naval squadrons in the Pacific had made no attempt to capture any of the western ports, whose custom receipts might have offset the ruinous cost of military operations.

The Emperor had only to look at the map of Mexico to realize how little of the country he could call his own. Vast areas of the north and west were unpacified. The southern stronghold of Oaxaca was still in the hands of guerrillas led by Porfirio Diaz. Even round Mexico City one could not venture further than the suburbs without running the risk of being attacked by bandits, and the only efficient local security forces were those financed and equipped by the English-owned mining companies to escort the silver trains to the coast.

There is already a note of discouragement in Maximilian's letter to Napoleon, written only six weeks after his arrival. 'The disorder is so great that everything remains to be done,' he writes. 'Commissions have already been appointed and are at work charged with drawing up

1 The Archduchess Sophia

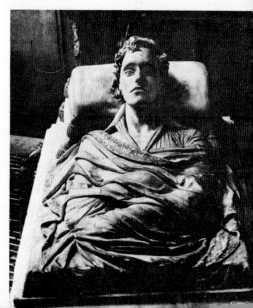

The effigy of the Duc de Reichstadt

3 The three young Archdukes. Franz Joseph in the centre with Karl Ludwig on his right and Maximilian on his left

4 The Palace of Schönbrunn

5 Maximilian as a naval lieutenant

6 Maximilian's first fiancée, Maria Amalia with her mother, the ex-Empress of Brazil

7 Charlotte as a child, by Winterhalter

8 King Leopold I of the Belgians

9 The castle of Laeken outside Brussels

10 Maximilian and Charlot
just after their engagem

11 Charlotte in Lombard
national costume

12 The palace of Monza
outside Milan

Maximilian as Admiral
of the Fleet

14 Maximilian's castle of Miramar

15 and 16 Emperor Napoleon III and Empress
Eugénie

17 Gutierrez d'Estrada presenting the Mexican deputation to Maximilian at Miramar

18 Maximilian and Charlotte embark for Mexico

19 Vera Cruz on the Gulf
of Mexico where
Maximilian and
Charlotte landed in
Mexico

20 Benito Juarez,
Maximilian's
republican opponent

21 The castle of
Chapultepec

he Palacio Nacional

23 and 24 Maximilian and Charlotte as Emp and Empress of Mexico

25 The Foreign Volun-
teers in Mexico

26 Colonel Alfred
van der Smissen

27 Generals Mejía and
Miramon, who shared the
Emperor's fate

28 'Last Moments of Maximilian of Mexico' by Laurens
29 The *Novara* returning to Trieste with Maximilian's body

30 The castle of Bouchout, Charlotte's last home

31 Charlotte on her deathbed in 1927

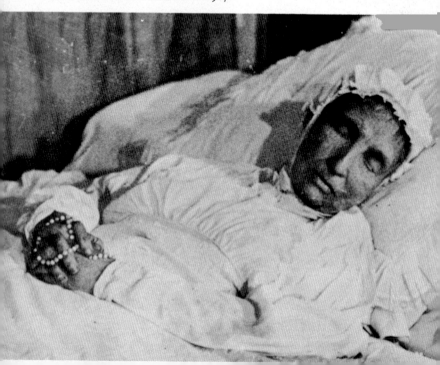

projects, relative to the army, finance and the law. But I am bound to recognize that capable men are almost impossible to find amongst the Mexicans.' It was a sad admission for a sovereign who a few weeks before had been determined to employ only Mexicans in his government, and it was even sadder to have to add, 'I therefore look to the French element in particular for intelligent and practical schemes, which will enable me to turn my hand to the work of general reorganization, indispensable to the development of the wealth of this beautiful country.' Maximilian might talk in practical terms, but what attracted him most in Mexico was the fantastic beauty of the country, the glorious climate where it had only to rain for an hour for every plant and tree to burgeon into a richer and more vivid life, and where the light, rarefied air had a luminous quality which made the snow-capped volcanoes look as floating and unsubstantial as the 'Fata-Morganas' he had seen on the Hungarian plains on breathless summer days.

Mexico City as we know it today, with its smog and sky-scrapers and its aggressive, flaunting vitality, has as little in common with the Mexico of the 1860s as Maximilian's capital had in common with the fabled Aztec city of Tenochtlitan, rising from the glistening waters of Lake Texcoco, and which, according to the chronicles of Cortés, was 'richer and more beautiful than Venice'. The pagan city was destroyed, and on its ruins the *Conquistadores* built a Spanish colonial town with broad streets and spacious squares, and low, flat-roofed houses. Churrigueresque churches rose on the foundations of Aztec temples; aqueducts bringing good mountain water to the town took the place of the flower-bordered canals, which were drained and irrigated so that Mexico City was no longer an island city.

What the Spaniards built, the so-called 'liberators' allowed to fall into decay. The Presidents of the Mexican Republic, who in the past forty years had followed one another in such rapid succession, lavished money on themselves rather than on the town. Monasteries lay in ruins, the stone and plaster carvings on the baroque churches were crumbling, water trickled from the broken arches of the aqueducts and overflowed the fountains. In the cathedral which was once the glory of New Spain, the gilded *reya* on the high altar was chipped and broken, the delicate glazing of the Puebla tiles cracked and faded. The beggars, the so-called *leperos*, had multiplied with the wars, and exposed their sores and mutilations at every street corner, while rubbish was left piled high even in front of the Royal Palace.

Maximilian was appalled by the dirt and squalor of his capital, and the Wittelsbach blood, which in him was so much stronger than the Hapsburg, urged him to start at once on building projects. His enormous barrack of a palace, with its eleven hundred windows, might serve as an official residence, but it could never be his home. On the western outskirts of the city rose a wooded hill surrounded by a vast park, known to the Aztecs as Chapultepec, 'the Hill of the Grasshoppers'. Here Montezuma had built his summer palace, and on its ruins one of the more enterprising of the Spanish Viceroys had erected a fortified castle which Maximilian immediately envisaged as another Miramar. He had brought his own architect from Europe, a man who fortunately had some knowledge of Spanish. And by employing European engineers and recruiting hundreds of Indian workmen, a neglected fortress which had served as a military academy at the time of the Mexican-American War was rendered sufficiently habitable for him and Charlotte to move into one wing within eight days of their arrival.

At Chapultepec, their attendants suffered even greater discomfort than in the palace, and Paola Kollonitz has little good to say of it as a royal residence: 'The principal building is low and narrow. The shape is unpleasing and its arrangement uncomfortable. It is surrounded by fortifications and one ascends to a terrace by a small walled garden through which no European of moderate size can pass without having to bend. Another small flower garden has been made on the right of the terrace, from where a few steps lead directly down to Their Majesties' reception room, which they also use as a dining room. This, together with the bedchambers, forms the only private part of the Imperial residence. . . . The narrow steps in the fortifications lead further down to the rooms allotted to the lady and gentleman-in-waiting on duty, who are always obliged to mount to the small garden in order to reach Their Majesties' rooms, which does not add to their comfort especially in the rainy season. As the garden lies higher than these rooms, they are often flooded by the rain, which streams through the leaking glass doors, and there are continual draughts.'

It was a far cry from the luxury of Monza and Miramar. But the inadequacy of the accommodation was more than compensated by the wonderful view from the terrace and the beauty of the park, which was the remains of a primaeval forest, overgrown with every form of parasitic life. The fabled gardens of Montezuma, the grottoes and follies of eighteenth-century Viceroys, were lost in an enchanted wilderness inhabited by brilliant-plumaged birds and enormous butterflies.

From the terraces of Chapultepec, one looked out over the whole vale of Mexico, beyond the city's spires and domes, the villas and gardens of the surrounding villages, beyond the orchards and the fields of maize and of *maquey*, to the distant lakes and the snow-covered volcanoes Popocatapetl and Iztaccihuatl, which dominated the plateau. It was impossible for Maximilian, as a poet or a gardener, to resist the appeal of Chapultepec, and his first letters to his brother Karl Ludwig are almost entirely confined to lyrical descriptions of his new residence, which is described as 'the Schönbrunn of Mexico, built on a basalt crag, surrounded by Montezuma's giant trees, offering a prospect of a beauty, the like of which I have never seen, except perhaps at Sorrento'.

These are the letters of an enthusiastic traveller, a prince on the Grand Tour, rather than of a sovereign faced by almost insurmountable problems. His unfortunate Treasurer, who was only too familiar with Maximilian's building mania, and who saw the eight million francs allotted to the Emperor for his personal expenses out of the Mexican loan gradually dwindling away, wrote home to the wife of the Prefect of Miramar, 'The building operations in Mexico and Chapultepec quite frighten me. The Emperor's passion is well known. I should at least have waited until the honeymoon was over. For who can say how this marriage is going to turn out?'

It was not long before the honeymoon was over, before the clergy and the Conservatives, the Emperor Napoleon and the foreign bankers were all putting in their claims. The only ones content to wait were the Indians, those gentle, long-suffering people who were still ready to believe that the white-skinned stranger from across the ocean was the harbinger of a golden age. No one else was under such illusion. The crucial question of Church property had still to be resolved, and as yet there was no sign of the 'capable Nuncio with reasonable views' whom Maximilian had asked for from Rome. Instead, he had to deal with an Archbishop who had no intention of being reasonable.

Antonio Pelago Labastida had left the Council of Regency rather than come to terms with the French. He had defied them with threats of excommunication, and had been persuaded to open the churches only at the point of their guns. All over the country, the bishops and the higher clergy were following his lead, even going so far as to refuse the Sacraments to dying men who had in all good faith acquired estates taken from the Church. Rumours that Maximilian was preparing the text of a *concordat* by which the State was to pay the clergy salaries in return for their properties were not likely to appeal to the Archbishop, who was one of the richest landowners of Mexico and who on returning from his Roman exile is said to have asked after the condition of his crops before enquiring after the souls of his flock.

But in the first weeks, the 'handsome and distinguished-looking' Labastida was frequently to be seen at the Imperial dinner table, where Countess Kollonitz noted his curious habit of helping himself from every dish and eating nothing. 'He would sit with his head on one side, continually smiling,' answering her eager questions on the country and the people with polite monosyllables in broken French. But invitations to dinner became less frequent when Maximilian discovered that the Archbishop was obstructing all his efforts at reform and that it was largely due to his machinations that the Nuncio had not yet arrived.

Critical and fastidious by nature, brought up in the most elegant Court of Europe, Maximilian can have found little to admire in the Court created by the Regency, a Court in which there was neither dignity nor tradition, where none of the courtiers knew how to behave, and where the richest families always expected to have the best places regardless of the rules of protocol. The previous occupants had robbed the palace of any objects of value, and in a country which had once produced one-third of the silver in the world, there was barely sufficient silver cutlery for the Imperial dinner table. The service ordered by Maximilian from the Parisian silversmith Christophe had not yet arrived, and the deficiences in silver and glass had to be camouflaged by the exquisite floral arrangements of the Indian gardeners. Even the cooks the Emperor had brought with him from Europe were so demoralized by the general disorder that they produced very indifferent food, and Countess Kollonitz writes that Maximilian turned to her in the middle of one dinner, and said in German, 'Have you ever eaten so badly as in my house?'

The Countess had the feeling that the Emperor's keen sense of the ridiculous made him particularly sensitive to the inadequacies of his Court. The first time he put on Mexican uniform at Miramar, she remembered him whispering to her, 'Can anything be more absurd than to find oneself wearing such a uniform?' And again in Mexico, when he went out riding for the first time, dressed in the national *charro* costume, he confessed to her with a laugh that 'he had slipped out of the palace as inconspicuously as possible and only lost the feeling of being in fancy dress once he had mounted his horse'. Remarks of this kind suggest that underlying the serious, well-intentioned Emperor, there was still the supercilious young Austrian Archduke, ready to be witty at his own expense and that of his *'rastaquere'* Court. Even Paola Kollonitz admits: 'Though the Emperor could charm by his attractive kindliness, there were times when he offended by his cold wit and his innate love of raillery, whereas the Empress's behaviour was always the same, her expressions about people were always in accordance with her way of treating them.' But Charlotte, like her father King Leopold, had very little sense of humour and took herself and the Mexicans equally seriously. Simple in her daily life, she delighted in representation and took every opportunity of appearing before her admiring subjects in gala dress with velvet embroidered train.

On these occasions, the Emperor usually absented himself for one reason or other. He was rarely present at the weekly *soirées* held by Charlotte at the palace. After supervising every detail, in which he religiously tried to copy his mother's *Kammerbälle* at Schönbrunn, at the eleventh hour he would seize on some pretext and retire to the peace and quiet of Chapultepec, leaving Charlotte to receive her guests without him.

Yet in his letters to Karl Ludwig he was always referring to 'the rich and elegant society of Mexico, the brilliance and animation of Charlotte's balls'. He wanted the world, and in particular his own family, to think of Mexico as a great civilized country which had cast off some of the antiquated shibboleths of Europe. He assured his brother: 'The country is very advanced politically, far more than many countries in Europe that have a high opinion of themselves. . . . All the stiffness and humbug with which we hamper ourselves in Europe and will still continue to do so for many years, have long been forgotten over here.' Another time we read: 'The so-called 'entertainments' of Europe, the dreary receptions, the gossip of tea-parties, all of hideous memory, are quite unknown here. The Mexican's chief enjoyment is to ride about his beautiful country on a fine horse and to go frequently to the Theatre. I naturally follow this example, particularly as there is excellent Italian Opera at the principal theatre, which is one of the finest in the world.'

But while writing in this vein, he was wasting precious hours in finishing the lengthy manual on etiquette he had started on board the *Novara*. For all his vaunted freedom, he continued to be obsessed by the mystique of royalty, and it was not until the following year that large and formal receptions were held at the palace, by which time the Mexican aristocracy had learnt the rudiments of Hofburg etiquette and his cooks had settled down to conditions in the New World and were producing the same exquisite dinners they had served at Miramar.

'Maximilian should have brought with him the qualities of a squatter: hard-working, energetic, self-denying. Instead of which, he was a spend-thrift, a man of pleasure, thinking he had come on a mission of civiliza-tion and full of the foolish liberalism which never stands the test of sacrifice.' Such was the somewhat uncharitable judgment of the formid-able Queen of Holland after the Mexican experiment had ended in tragedy. But in 1864 there were many people in Europe, and even in England, who thought the Mexican Empire had a good chance of sur-vival. Maximilian had been on the throne for only a couple of months before Queen Victoria accredited a minister to his Court. To describe the young Emperor as a man of pleasure was palpably unjust, for no one worked harder than Maximilian during this first year in Mexico. Un-fortunately, he brought with him too many preconceived ideas from Europe, trying to model Mexico on Austria, which boasted the most efficient bureaucratic system in Europe; trying to treat his enemies with tolerance and reason as if they were sophisticated and highly civilized Italians. Many of the decrees, the so-called 'statutes', emanat-ing from his pen were excellent in themselves, but they became so much waste-paper in the hands of the provincial Prefects, who continued to interpret or rather misinterpret his orders according to their own ad-vantage.

It was discouraging for both the Emperor and Empress to discover that the Mexicans were unwilling or incapable of helping themselves. During the civil war, the ordinary citizen had preferred concealment to resistance. Many of them were so apathetic that they allowed them-selves to be pillaged and robbed without attempting to defend them-selves. 'Rien n'est organisé dans mon pays excepté le vol,' was the cynical comment of a veteran Mexican diplomat, and robbery to a lesser or greater degree permeated all branches of the civil service. Uncertain as to their future, the members of each party tried to feather their nests while they remained in office. Charlotte had not been a month in Mexico before she was writing to the French Empress: 'The Mexicans, in spite of all my affection for them, do not know how to govern themselves. Now their quarrels are in abeyance. Everyone is looking for redemption. But I do not know if they will do anything to help, for people here prefer to rely on miracles.' A year later Charlotte had lost all her affection for the Mexicans. 'The masses,' who in the first weeks she described as 'docile and intelligent', by 1865 were being stigmatized as 'excessively stupid and illiberal, which explains the stranglehold the clergy have managed to obtain on them'. After a year in Mexico, Charlotte was writing, 'We see nothing to respect in this country, and shall act in such a way as to change it.' She uses the plural, but her views were in no way shared by her husband; during that first year in Mexico, Maximilian had learnt to love both the people and the country.

After months of waiting for a Nuncio who did not arrive, pressed by Napoleon to settle the question of Church property regardless of Rome, but still hoping that Pope Pius would agree to a *concordat*, Maximilian postponed the issue by starting out on a tour of some of the outlying states, leaving Charlotte behind to act as Regent.

This tribute to her sagacity and judgment was not misplaced, once the Mexican politicians had got used to the idea of a European woman of twenty-four presiding at their meetings and giving her opinion on the most varied subjects in a clear confident manner which left no room for argument. As for the French, they made no secret of the fact that they found the practical and intelligent young Empress, with her quick, perceptive mind, far easier to deal with than the dreamy, indecisive Emperor who was always inclined to see the other point of view.

Throughout the year 1864 to 1865, Charlotte dominated most of her husband's decisions. In many ways her influence was beneficial, and the general opinion was that, left on her own, she would have accomplished even more. But the fact remains that the two major decisions taken by Maximilian during the year – both of which were to have disastrous results, leading to strained relations both with Vienna and with Rome – were directly inspired by Charlotte.

Judging by their letters, there can be little doubt that in the first months, Charlotte and Maximilian were, if not in love, at least so close that it could easily be interpreted as love. Those who assert that Charlotte never forgave her husband for some infidelity in their early years of marriage, or hint at some contagious illness contracted by Maximilian on his journey to Brazil and transmitted to his wife, have only to read her letters to her grandmother, written in the late summer and autumn of 1864. Charlotte's love and admiration for her husband permeate every page, and they are certainly not written by a woman with a physical or moral grievance. On the contrary, they are full of a feminine pride in his achievements: 'Max is wonderful! ... Max has achieved miracles. ... The whole country has confidence in Max. ... He was respected from the first day but now he is adored. ... The Republicans say that even if they are not *Emperialisti*, they are all "Massimilianisti".' One panegyric follows another and, however much she may have delighted in her position as Regent, she writes like any other woman in love: 'I hope to have Max back before long, for I would so much rather have him near me, than have to govern in his absence.'

But Max was gone for over two months. His journey was prolonged owing to an attack of laryngitis which developed into severe bronchitis and kept him in bed for over a fortnight in the little town of Irapuato, where there was fortunately a French garrison with an excellent military doctor. The Emperor was so ill that for several days he was unable to write, and a note dated 10 September, when he got up for the first time, makes pathetic reading: 'For three days I could not speak at all ... but the worst of all was to be so far away from you, my darling – so utterly lost and alone. I was terribly homesick, longing to be back with you at Chapultepec. The nights were ghastly because I coughed and choked the whole time and could hardly breathe and was unable to sleep.' Charlotte must have longed to rush to his sickbed and only her strong sense of duty kept her at her post. She unburdened herself to Eugénie, 'Not being with him you can imagine how worried I am. Tomorrow, we shall have been separated for a month.'

The Emperor's illness was to have lasting consequences. Instead of returning to convalesce in Mexico he proceeded on his journey, with the result that he never really recovered his strength and afterwards was subject to chest complaints and intermittent fever, which sapped both his energy and his morale.

The journey which took him to the principal towns in central and north-west Mexico would even today entail long hours of motoring across precipitous mountain passes with hairpin bends, continually changing altitude and climate, ranging from intense cold to tropical heat. One is astounded at Maximilian's endurance and the organization of the French, who had established sufficient control over a perimeter of approximately two hundred and fifty miles to the north and north-west of the capital, to enable him to travel with a comparatively small escort. It was largely terror which kept the country at peace, for General Forey's draconian laws were still in force, by which any attempt at sedition was summarily tried by a French court-martial. Maximilian, however, was encouraged to believe that the welcome he received was the spontaneous expression of the people. There were everywhere crowds of Indians, waving their coloured flags and branches of fern, and pretty women throwing flowers from the balconies. 'I have not seen such lovely women since I was in Andalusia,' he wrote to his brother, and even his letters to Charlotte are full of references to the beauty and elegance of the women of the interior who were 'so much better bred and better dressed than our Court ladies in the capital'. Wherever he stayed, the local *hacendados* offered him feudal hospitality, and he felt completely at home in their white, rambling houses, the patios gay with birdcages and the stables full of the finest horses.

Maximilian saw and noted with an acute and sensitive eye, but he judged by the standards of Europe. He was too ready to welcome recalcitrant Republicans and to believe in their professions of loyalty, when in nine cases out of ten they were merely reverting to the Mexican habit of coming in on the winning side. He was too ready to give expression to his liberal sentiments, thereby offending worthy Conservatives who genuinely supported the Empire. Above all, he was too ready to listen to the advice of Sebastian Schertzenlechner, the ex-lackey from Schönbrunn, who had seized on the opportunity of accompanying his master in order to insinuate himself still further into his confidence and to score against his rival, Felix Eloin, who had remained behind with the Empress.

The pampered palace servant was not prepared for the rigours of Mexican travel, when for over a week they had to spend 'twelve to fourteen hours a day in the saddle, travelling over mountains which were solid blocks of stone, crossing desert wastes where nothing grew but thorny cactus bushes, or wading through marshes where the mud and slime came up to the horses' bellies'. But the aches and pains he suffered were a small price to pay for his ambition, which was nothing less than to become a titled 'Excellency'. Schertzenlechner's ambition was soon to overreach itself, but not before he had made serious trouble for his master both in Vienna and Mexico. He was a deplorable influence on this journey, encouraging Maximilian in the belief that he could rule Mexico independently of the clergy and the French, whose armies should be subservient to his orders. But every day it was becoming more obvious that there were very few elements which could be relied on among the governing classes of Mexico. Scandal upon scandal came to light on this journey. In the old Spanish city of Queretaro, where there is a church or convent in every street, the Emperor summoned the bishop, only to find he had been absent from his diocese for months, enjoying the amenities of the capital with the excuse that his house in Queretaro was uninhabitable. Not many miles away, hidden among the hills, was an Indian village which no priest had visited for twenty-five years and where a whole new generation was waiting to be baptized. Maximilian made a point of visiting this abandoned village, where he attended a mass baptism at which the priest used what looked suspiciously like a fireman's hose. Before the ceremony, the Emperor was presented with the embarrassing present of a little Indian boy whose parents, too poor to have him baptized, had disappeared into the mountains. Maximilian provided money for the child and put him in the care of nuns, with instructions to send him later to Mexico City.

If the clergies neglected their duties in Queretaro, they were overzealous in other parts of the country in defending their material rights and in browbeating the people into submission. Writing to the Emperor Napoleon, Maximilian complained that the clergy 'while warmly protesting their boundless loyalty, are secretly getting ready their weapons to try to fight and obstruct my ideas of progress'. But the clergy were not the only ones to obstruct his projects or to extort money from the people. A large part of the revenues gathered by the tax-collectors went into their own pockets. Public funds were misappropriated, while hospitals and almshouses were left to fall into ruin. The Emperor was so indignant at what he saw that there was a purge of government officials — and as most of them belonged to the Conservative Party, it was hardly calculated to improve his position in the country.

Nevertheless, Maximilian accomplished a great deal through the personal magnetism which was one of his greatest assets. The anniversary of Mexican Independence, 16 September, found him in the little town of Dolores Hidalgo, where in 1810 the heroic priest Don José Hidalgo rang the bell of his parish church and called on his countrymen to rise against the Spaniards with the cry of 'Mexicans, long live Mexico!' The rebellion came too soon and was crushed with a ferocity and cruelty which set the standard for all the civil wars to come. Hidalgo and his fellow revolutionaries were captured and executed and their heads exposed on the walls of Guanajuato. But the humble parish priest has come down in history as the father of Mexican inde-

257

pendence and every year, at eleven o'clock at night on 15 September, the cannons roar and the bells ring out in every town in Mexico, and the President or Prefect unfurls the flag, repeating the famous *grito* of Hidalgo: 'Mexicans, long live Mexico!'

It was somewhat of an anomaly for a descendant of Charles v to shout these words from the windows of Hidalgo's house. Maximilian appears to have felt a certain embarrassment at the prospect, confessing in letters both to Charlotte and his brother that he feared it might have 'a somewhat comical effect'. But his ability to throw himself into the rôle of the moment and his own poetical fantasy resulted in a personal triumph. Even the French were impressed by his eloquence when in a strong, firm voice (he was just recovering from laryngitis) he evoked, 'The glorious word of "independence", which flashed like a meteor across the dark night sky and woke a nation from the sleep of centuries, lighting the way to liberty and emancipation'. He referred to 'the years of internecine strife, of brother fighting brother, which had threatened to destroy all that the heroes of revolution had tried to create'. And in an impassioned plea for unity, he declared: 'A country can only lay the foundations of liberty and justice when independence is associated with union. Then, secure in the protection of the Almighty, it can rise invincible in the world.'

He writes that by the end of the speech, 'everyone was shouting their heads off – the people, the troops and the local authorities.' After a torchlight procession had escorted him back to his lodgings, they were still cheering under his windows. 'But this time, the cheers were for me, not Hidalgo.' That night there was not a man in Dolores who would not have died for his Emperor. Enthusiasm rose to a crescendo the following day, during a banquet at which the Hapsburg Prince drank a toast to 'the heroes of revolution'.

Dolores, Guanajuato, Leon, each town surpassed the other in its welcome, and generals who only a few weeks before had been fighting for the Republicans, now swore allegiance to the Empire. In optimistic mood, Maximilian wrote to his wife, 'It really looks as if Juarez is finished.' But the guerrillas still continued to harry the countryside, and from Guanajuato he issued an edict reinforcing General Forey's original law by which guerrillas and highway robbers were subject to the death penalty. It went against his nature to be so severe, but it was the only way of safeguarding 'the interests of innocent, peace-loving people'. Here, in the richest states of Mexico, he was more than ever struck by the incredible contrast between the wild, desolate country-side beset by bandits, where the highways were little more than mule-tracks, and the sophisticated opulence of the towns, where churches and public buildings had floors of porphyry and onyx, and the Jesuit fathers had harnessed the artistic genius of the Indians into the carving and gilding of *reyas* which were among the wonders of the New World. Nowhere was this opulence so evident as in Guanajuato, the wealthiest and most civilized of all the cities he had visited so far – 'Much cleaner and better kept than the capital'. Here a Creole aristocracy, grown rich on the profits of the silver mines, had built palaces which rivalled in splendour those of Paris and Madrid. And the young Emperor was offered hospitality on a scale which would not have disgraced the Hofburg. His host, who owned one of the loveliest of the palaces, gave a dinner for one hundred and fifty guests, representing every shade of political opinion from the blackest of reactionaries to the reddest of radicals – men who a few months before would not have sat in the same room. 'We were very gay,' wrote Maximilian, 'for the further north one goes, the gayer, the better-looking and the freer are the people. ... Afterwards, I spoke in four languages to each of the guests, for apart from the Mexicans there were English, French and Germans among them.'

The majority of the European businessmen whose jobs and interests had brought them to Mexico had at first been somewhat sceptical over the prospect of a monarchy. But Bazaine's continued successes in the field and the enthusiasm with which the Mexicans were welcoming their Emperor was gradually bringing them around to the idea, and Maximilian's charm succeeded in winning them over completely. Those whom he singled out the most were the English, whose alliance and co-operation he was so anxious to enlist. British investors were already reported to be taking an interest in the future of Mexican railways, and communications were the most pressing of Mexico's priorities. The Emperor was made painfully aware of this urgency when travelling from Guanajuato to Leon, a distance of barely thirty miles which entailed two days of riding over mule-tracks, often obliterated by the rains. But no sooner had he reached the outskirts of Leon than he returned to civilization. Leon was like a commercial Spanish town, painted in more vivid colours. He was not yet used to the ease with which Mexicans changed their loyalties and was surprised to find himself the guest of General Uraga, who only a month ago had been campaigning for Juarez. He was even more surprised to find this ardent liberal living in the greatest luxury, in a superb *hacienda* where he gave a brilliant fiesta beginning with a dinner of such gastronomic variety that Maximilian took the trouble of enclosing a menu in one of his letters to Charlotte. Though written in a somewhat faulty French, its '*hors d'oeuvre*' and '*entrées*', its '*relevés*' and its '*entremets*', are almost entirely European, interwoven with Mexican specialities, and one's heart goes out to the abstemious Maximilian having to do justice to these elaborate banquets, so unsuited to the high altitude of the Sierras, which must have contributed to the liver complaint which developed within a few months of his arrival.

He enjoyed himself in Leon and even more so in Morelia, which he reached after an eight-day journey in almost continual rain over appalling roads, spending the nights in wretched little villages on the way, finally breaking down in his English travelling-carriage and having to proceed by mule. But a heart-warming welcome awaited Maximilian in Morelia, the capital of Michoacan, noted for its republican fervour and said to be one of the most politically troublesome spots in the Empire. To the surprise of the Emperor, the French garrison and the local authorities themselves, the enthusiasm was tremendous. The crowds were such that it was impossible to proceed on horseback. When Maximilian dismounted, the people wanted to carry him on their shoulders. 'The heat was terrific,' he writes, 'and we were all sweating as in a Turkish bath.' Five hundred ladies, 'some of them very beautiful', mobbed him at a ball, all wanting to give him the *abrazo*, 'which I politely got out of'. But he was far from being indifferent to these feminine charms, and in letters to Charlotte there was less talk of loneliness and homesickness, and rather too many references to 'the warmth and friendliness, the elegance and beauty of the women of the Interior'.

Reading Maximilian's letters to his wife and brother, it is difficult to refute the accusation of frivolity so often raised by his critics. He is sensitive and appreciative of the beauty of the landscape, the architectural splendours of the cities and the fascination of the women. But he appears to have had no real understanding of the enormity of the task he had undertaken, or of the problems which he had to tackle. Back in Mexico City, in the gloom of the Royal Palace, his young wife, who in his absence was presiding over ministerial councils, struggling with financial reports, trying to make order out of choas, had a far greater understanding of the difficulties which lay ahead, and the more she understood, the more depressed she became. All her youthful optimism had gone, and in its place was a grim determination to succeed. With a supreme self-confidence she maintained: 'The Mexicans will have to be helped in spite of themselves.'

19

Intrigues round the Throne

On 30 October the Emperor was back in his capital, welcomed with the same enthusiasm as on his first arrival. Charlotte, accompanied by Bazaine, who was now a Marshal of France, had driven out to meet him at Toluca, a little town forty miles west of Mexico City. They had broken the journey at a French camp situated in a beautiful mountain valley, and Bazaine's staff captain had made such elaborate preparations for the Empress's comfort that she felt far more at home 'in this small corner of France' than in her own gloomy palace. A large, airy tent, hung with brocades and carpeted with Oriental rugs, was placed near a mountain stream and planted round with trees to ensure her privacy. A dinner served in the Marshal's tent included all her favourite dishes, and the whole encampment was a mass of flowers. For once Charlotte forgot to be royal, enjoying the admiration of the young officers, happy to get away from the work and worries of the city, and happiest of all at the thought of seeing Max.

Their reunion, which was witnessed by the entire population of Toluca, was so warm and loving as to disarm the most cynical onlooker. In her eagerness to embrace her husband, Charlotte jumped so quickly out of the carriage that she exposed a pretty leg to the delighted view of Captain Blanchot, who was already one of her most fervent admirers. Bazaine was paternally benevolent in his attitude to the young sovereigns, and Maximilian paid a graceful tribute to his recent victories and his elevation to the rank of Marshal. But in spite of all the appearance of friendship, there was already a rift in their relations. Bazaine's first loyalties were to his own Emperor, and it had long been Napoleon's wish to settle the Mexican affair as speedily and as satisfactorily as possible. In the past months, he had been urging Bazaine to hurry on with the organization of Maximilian's native troops and of the foreign volunteers, so that their own men could return to France.

And without consulting either Maximilian or Charlotte, who was acting as Regent at the time, and in face of the criticism of the greater part of the general staff, Bazaine complied with his master's wishes by repatriating the brigade commanded by General Douay, who was among the most outspoken of his critics.

This action was hasty and ill-timed, for the first detachments of Austrian and Belgian troops had barely arrived at Vera Cruz, and several weeks would have to elapse before they were acclimatized to fighting in the High Sierras. The three outstanding Imperialist Generals, Leonardo Marquez, Miguel di Miramon and Tomas Mejía, were all ardent conservatives and therefore distrusted by the liberals whom Maximilian had brought into his government. Nor was the situation in the country as satisfactory as Bazaine made out in his reports to Paris, which were almost as inaccurate as Maximilian's letters to Vienna. His successes had been prodigious. The capture of Matamoros and of Monterez had forced Juarez to seek refuge in the deserts of Chihuahua, while a successful assault on Tampico had brought another Gulf port into French hands and assured a second lifeline to Europe. But in the south, Porfirio Diaz was still holding out at Oaxaca and the Pacific ports were still open to the *Juaristi*. In one of his well-intentioned decrees, designed to encourage trade, Maximilian had ordered the lifting of the blockade enforced by the French Pacific squadron – a measure of clemency not calculated to endear him to the Admiral in command.

General Douay was of the opinion that the French expeditionary force should have been reinforced instead of reduced. He maintained that it was impossible to subjugate a country three times the size of France with an army of under fifty thousand men, which included untrained volunteers and eighteen hundred Mexican auxiliaries. Time after time, towns were captured by the French and handed over to the Imperialist forces, too weak or too apathetic to defend them from the *Juaristi*, who reappeared within a few weeks, inflicting the most horrible reprisals on the helpless population. Charlotte, who was naturally on the side of Douay, echoed his opinions in a letter to the Empress Eugénie, whom she looked upon in the light of an older sister to whom she could pour out all her troubles.

'Although they are well disposed, the people here are so apathetic, partly by nature, partly as a result of their misfortunes, that if the effective strength of the French army were suddenly reduced, it would cause the greatest discouragement to those who look forward to a future for this country, as well as the greatest insecurity for the inhabitants. The Indians in the villages are coming in daily to the French headquarters, asking for just one company of French soldiers to guard them. I was told recently that, in one place in the Sierras where the French garrison was moving out, the Colonel was asked to have just one sub-lieutenant left behind. This will give Your Majesty some idea of the need which these poor people feel for the French army ... not to mention the fact that, though Juarez has been driven out of Monterry, he still occupies the three richest states in the north.' Charlotte knew how to present her case, for the north and Sonora in particular, was the part of the country in which Napoleon was the most interested. He was still pressing for the mineral rights, in spite of Maximilian's refusal to discuss the matter. But for the time being, neither Emperor could claim control of a state which was unpacified.

Charlotte's letters to Eugénie give a far truer picture of the situation than those of Bazaine or Maximilian. But it would have been wiser for her to have refrained from becoming involved in the intrigues of the high command. General Douay was trying to oust Bazaine from his position as commander-in-chief, and in sending him back to France, the Marshal was hoping to be rid of a dangerous rival. But Douay had good friends at the War Ministry and succeeded in being posted back to Mexico within the year. His return, which had nothing to do with either Charlotte or Maximilian, was nevertheless considered by Bazaine to have been engineered by the Empress. One can understand his suspicion, for Charlotte's letters to Eugénie, while expressing her appreciation of 'the excellent Marshal, so full of heart, so loyal and devoted to his country', at the same time accuse him of being 'too easily influenced, too ready to trust those who are not worthy of his trust'. She singles out for attack Bazaine's military secretary, a certain Colonel Boyer, whom she holds responsible for the backbiting and dissension prevailing at French headquarters, where no other officer was ever allowed to share in the Marshal's limelight. She even goes so far as to say that General Brincourt was on the point of attacking Oaxaca when he was deliberately recalled and sent on an expedition to the north, so that Bazaine should have the glory of capturing the city, with a spectacular and expensive campaign, and she quotes Monsieur Corta, the French financial expert, who in her hearing had called Bazaine 'the biggest spender in the French army'.

Charlotte did not realize how much the situation in Europe had changed in the past months. Eugénie was no longer the understanding elder sister, ready to acclaim and sympathize. Subjected to a growing barrage of criticism at home, she was in no mood to listen to the complaints of the young Empress she had helped to place upon a throne. It was more pleasant to be lulled into security by Bazaine's optimistic dispatches and Hidalgo's glowing reports of life in Mexico, which Charlotte was beginning to feel were doing them more harm than good. Writing to Maximilian of the recall of the French brigade, which gave her such a shock when she first heard of it that she 'nearly fell under the table', she adds with a certain bitterness: 'We might have been spared all of this, but for that silly Hidalgo.'

Charlotte had developed and matured during her husband's absence. She had dropped her rose-coloured spectacles and looked on Mexico and the Mexicans with a clear, dissecting eye, telling the Emperor: 'You might as well know that your ministers have done nothing of what you told them to do. I am only asked about things which should already have been done.' But love still blinded her in her judgment of Maximilian. 'You are not as other mortals,' she writes. 'When I hear accounts of your journey, and of all you had to endure, I am so lost in admiration that I see you as an angel rather than as a human being. . . . I am jealous of all the good you do without me, jealous of your very thoughts, those noble, genial and at the same time practical ideas. . . . Bazaine has sent Napoleon an account of your journey, and I am sure he is as full of admiration as I am.'

But Napoleon was not so lost in admiration as Charlotte seemed to think. In their confidential reports, both his minister Montholon and Bazaine referred to the anti-French bias of Maximilian's entourage. They criticized his extravagance, reporting the enormous sums being spent on embellishing the National Palace and Chapultepec, and the Emperor's plan for a two-mile avenue from his castle to the city, which was to be wider and finer than the Champs-Elysées – all at a time when French engineers were working day and night on the fortifications and arsenal blown up during the Civil War.

Everything turned on the question of finance. Maximilian had come back to his capital amidst the '*vivas*' and flag-waving of the population to find the French Minister waiting on his doorstep to present him with the accounts of his creditors. It was only now that the Emperor began to grasp the extent of his obligations and the enormity of the debt for which he had made himself responsible in signing the Convention of Miramar. The information he had gleaned from the journalists and economists he had seen in Europe had led him to believe that the fabled wealth of Mexico would provide him with an unending flow of gold. He had never faced up to the fact that the loan issued in London and Paris had been a failure, and that out of the two hundred million francs, Mexico had received no more than thirty-four million, while all that the Imperial government was able to squeeze out of an impoverished country was almost entirely devoted to the payment of the French troops he had agreed to support at the rate of one thousand francs per annum for every soldier on Mexican soil. Meanwhile, there remained an initial debit of two hundred and seventy million francs, the calculated cost of the French expeditionary force up to June 1864 – a sum for which Maximilian should never have allowed himself to be held responsible. And now the Marquis de Montholon, whom the Emperor described as 'a cantankerous, disagreeable character, who, with his petty intrigues, showed that he had never shaken off the habits of a former consul', was pressing him to come to a reasonable and amicable agreement for the repayment of the notorious Jecker bonds.

In the early summer of 1864, the French Finance Minister, Achille Fould, had sent a special envoy to Mexico to study the economic situation and to see how the burden of the Imperial Treasury could be lightened. Monsieur Corta, a Deputy of the Legislative Assembly, had succeeded in gaining the confidence of the young Mexican sovereigns, who did everything in their power to induce him to stay on in Mexico, Charlotte going so far as to say that Monsieur Corta had become 'as necessary to us as our daily bread'. Like so many financiers before and after him, Corta appears to have been dazzled by the potential wealth of Mexico, but he had no intention of giving up his career in France in order to act as tutor to the young Emperor. He left with his reputation as a financial genius unimpaired, both Emperor and Empress still convinced that all would have gone well in Mexico 'if he had not left us in the lurch'. But Corta remained a true and faithful friend and it was largely due to an optimistic speech he made in the Assembly, giving a glowing picture of the future of Mexico 'under the wise and prudent government of the Emperor Maximilian', that a second Mexican loan was floated in Paris, and a National Bank of Mexico founded under the guarantee of French and English banks.

Figures and accounts were anathema to Maximilian. He had expected to find a country established on a peaceful footing, the mines and factories working, the lines of communication established – instead of which everywhere was chaos. Writing to Napoleon on 27 December, he gives voice to his disillusion: 'On arriving in Mexico, I hoped that the Regency and the French administration, which had had the entire authority, would not only have cleared the way but taken such preparatory measures as would have enabled me to get down to the great questions of reform and reorganization of the country. I can only repeat to Your Majesty what Monsieur Corta must also have admitted, that everything remains to be done. Before I arrived in the country, it was possible for me to believe that the capital placed at my disposal by the Mexican Loan would be sufficient to enable me to wait till the finances of the Empire were reorganized. From the moment of my arrival, this illusion vanished, and as soon as I had ascertained that there were no Mexican experts capable, I appealed to the devotion of Monsieur Corta, who has retired, I hope only temporarily, just as his presence was becoming more and more necessary.'

The Mexican émigrés, who had fed him with so much false information, were beginning to be viewed with a suspect eye. In Paris, Hidalgo appeared so anxious to keep on good terms with Eugénie that he deliberately refrained from handing on unpleasant news. Maximilian was also beginning to be suspicious of Gutierrez and his friendship with Archbishop Labastida, and he appears to have taken a certain pleasure in telling him how, on his journey, he had been 'forced to make some severe examples of the clergy'. When describing conditions in the provinces, he writes, 'There are three classes which are the worst I have found in this country so far – they are the judges, the army officers and the greater part of the clergy. None of them knows their duties, and they live for money alone. The judges are corrupt, the officers have no sense of honour and the clergy are lacking in Christian charity and morality. But all this does not make me lose hope for the future. ... The most necessary thing of all is a *concordat*, and a Nuncio with a good Christian heart and an iron will. It is only then that the clergy will be reorganized and made Catholic, which they are not at present. We are impatiently awaiting the arrival of the Nuncio, which was promised us months ago.'

This letter was written on 30 October, the day of his return to his capital. By the time it reached Gutierrez, the Nuncio was already on his way to Mexico. But his arrival only made the situation worse, for

Monsignor Meglia was a rigid, narrow-minded ultramontane who had come to dictate and not to compromise.

Maximilian had come back from his journey mentally and physically exhausted, longing to relax in the peace and beauty of Chapultepec, to lead just for a few weeks the kind of life he had led at Miramar. The rainy season had ended. In the abandoned gardens of the Spanish Viceroys, violets and roses, peach blossom and tuberoses were all bursting into flower with a glorious disregard for the seasons, bringing to autumn the gay expectancy of spring, the ripe fulfilment of summer. Old friends were returning to Europe: the two Zichys, who had been the companions of his childhood, the devoted Coria and Paola Kollonitz, whose wit and good humour had enlivened the palace dinner parties. He was sad to see them go, though a letter from Melanie Zichy, preserved among the Eloin papers, suggests that neither Charlotte nor Maximilian gave much thought to the comfort of their Austrian retinue, once they had handed over their official duties to their Mexican counterparts. In a stiff, offended note, Melanie Zichy complained of being left short of funds and of not receiving the treatment that was due to their position and rank. The situation appears to have righted itself, for by the time she had got to Europe, the Countess had forgotten her grievances. Distance lent enchantment to the view, and Eugénie reported, 'The Countess Zichy has passed through Paris and told Prince Metternich that she was delighted with her stay in Mexico. She was enthusiastic about everything – the climate, the richness of the soil, and all that she saw there. She does not even seem to dislike the *guerrilleros* – she says they add to the picturesque. The way she spoke did a great deal of good here.'

The one who was really sad to leave was Paola Kollonitz, who was returning to the dreary existence of a well-born spinster of limited means. In Mexico she had formed a romantic attachment for the Belgian Felix Eloin, who in spite of his somewhat unprepossessing appearance, seems to have been a man of considerable wit and charm. Years later, after the Mexican adventure had ended in disaster, these two middle-aged people, coming from totally different backgrounds, ventured into a brief and unsuccessful marriage. Paola relates that, on saying goodbye, the Emperor's last words to her were, 'Tell my mother I do not underrate the difficulty of my task, but I have not for one moment regretted my decision.'

Meanwhile, the first of the Belgian and Austrian volunteers had arrived in Mexico — gay, reckless spirits, bored with the slowness of promotion at home, the restricted life in small garrison towns, all hoping to find fame and adventure in the New World. Travelling on the same packet were the first diplomats accredited to the Imperial Court of Mexico: the Austrian Minister, Count Guido Thun; Queen Victoria's envoy, Sir Peter Campbell-Scarlett, whose arrival was particularly welcome to Maximilian; and the long-awaited Nuncio, who from the moment he landed at Vera Cruz behaved as if he were 'the Syllabus in person', welcomed in every town and village by adoring crowds of Indians organized by the clergy with the deliberate intention of showing the Emperor who was the real master of the country.

'The Nuncio arrived in Mexico City yesterday evening, without demonstrations of any kind. Arrangements had been made to prevent them, if any had been attempted,' wrote Charlotte to Eugénie in a letter dated 8 December, thereby showing that trouble had been anticipated. The following day, Monsignor Meglia presented his credentials and handed over the Pope's letter, which made it clear that there were to be no concessions of any kind. His Holiness categorically demanded the annulment of the reform laws and the reinstatement of the bishops in all their ancient privileges, the right of the clergy to control all private and public instruction, and the establishment of the Catholic Church to the exclusion of all other creeds.

The counter-proposals, in a draft for the *concordat* drawn up by the Emperor with the help of his wife and his ministers, claimed that the question could be settled in an entirely Catholic but also perfectly liberal sense. This of itself was an illusion when dealing with the Latin-American clergy backed by the Roman Curia, and only someone as idealistic as Maximilian could have expected the Vatican to renounce its claims to the nationalized property or consent to the clergy becoming state employees. Above all, it could never tolerate liberty of worship in a country where, in recent years, a growing American influence had made many Protestant converts. After a short, outspoken interview with the Emperor, Monsignor Meglia retired into conference with the bishops. No more was heard for two days, at the end of which Maximilian sent a confidential messenger to the Nuncio's house. He returned with the news that the Monsignor had no other instructions but to deliver the Pope's letter, stating his demands, and as these demands had not been complied with there was nothing left for him to say.

This message enraged Maximilian to a point that he allowed himself to be influenced to take drastic and precipitate action. How much he was influenced by his anti-clerical advisers, and how much by his wife, is open to question. The problems which confronted him were too much for him to cope with in his debilitated state of health. The high altitude was beginning to tell on his nerves. Where in Italy he would have been conciliatory, in Mexico he lost his temper, and at a ministerial council at which Charlotte was present, he announced that, should Rome persist in its refusal to sign a *concordat*, he would have 'no other choice than to ratify the Reform Laws of 1859'. An ultimatum to this effect would be presented to the Nuncio.

The Empress was even more indignant than her husband, and she complained to Eugénie of being 'in the greatest tribulation with the Nuncio. I should not have thought it possible, where the interests of religion are so obviously bound up with the *concordat*, that we would have the slightest difficulty. But he is like a madman, and I made the Marshal laugh on Sunday by saying irreverently that the best thing he could do would be to throw the Nuncio out of the window. . . . There is a blindness, an obstinacy about this man, against which it is impossible to contend. He actually ventures to maintain that this country, which loathes bureaucracy, desires the property of the clergy to be restored. It is just as if someone were to come and tell one in broad daylight that it was night, but unfortunately, and it is a humiliation for us Catholics to have to admit it, the Roman Curia is made that way.'

From the heated tone of this letter, one feels that it would have been wiser of Maximilian to have kept Charlotte out of the discussion. An angry and impulsive young woman was not likely to make much headway with a cool, hard-headed Roman prelate 'from whom all arguments fell off as if from polished marble'. But with her superb self-confidence, Charlotte was convinced that she could still coax the Nuncio into submission, and acting on her own initiative, she offered to present him with the ultimatum. 'I talked to him for two hours,' she wrote, 'and I may tell Your Majesty that nothing has given me a truer idea of hell than our conversation, for hell is nothing but a hopeless impasse. To want to convince somebody, and to feel that it is time wasted, that one might as well be talking Greek because he sees things black and you white, is a task worthy of the damned. . . . Finally, he ended by telling me that it was the clergy who had made the Empire. This I ventured to contradict, by saying it was not the clergy, it was the Emperor on the day of his arrival. I put forward every argument, I was serious, playful, grave and almost prophetic in turn, for the issues seemed bound to lead to complications, perhaps even to a rupture with the Holy See. But nothing was of any use. He brushed aside my arguments like so much dust, and put nothing in their place. In fact, he seemed to take pleasure in the nothingness he created around him. I then presented him with the ultimatum of the Emperor's letter and said to him, on rising, "Monsignor, whatever may happen, I shall take the liberty of reminding you of this conversation. We are not responsible for the consequences; we have done all we can to prevent what is going to happen, but if the Church will not help us, we will serve her in spite of herself".'

Infuriated by the ultimatum, the Nuncio threw off all pretence at civility and composed a letter so insolent in tone that the minister to whom it was presented refused to submit it to the Emperor. In it, he protested against 'measures which would reduce the Ministers of God to the slaves of a temporal power, and would offend the religious sentiments of the Catholic Mexican people'. The breach was complete. On 7 January 1865, the Emperor not only ratified the nationalization of Church property but issued a further decree by which Papal Bulls and Briefs would not be carried into effect without the Imperial sanction. These two decrees aroused the wrath and indignation of the entire religious hierarchy and the most powerful section of the Conservative upper classes, while the Liberals jubilated in public over the ratification of the '*Ley Teyado*' and secretly despised an Emperor who wanted to be friends with all men. All parties now joined in criticizing Maximilian for allowing himself to be dominated by his wife, and clandestine rumours gradually began to undermine Charlotte's influence.

Only a few months after the break with the Nuncio, a certain Abbé Alleau was arrested for circulating a seditious pamphlet, calculated to ferment further unrest among the clergy. Alleau was said to be a secret agent of the Vatican, sent to Mexico to report on the situation, and among his papers was found a confidential letter from Gutierrez d'Estrada, wishing him good luck for his mission. Maximilian may no longer have listened to Gutierrez's advice, but he had hitherto regarded him as a loyal friend, and it was a bitter blow to find him hand-in-glove with his enemies. Apart from the seditious pamphlet, the French Abbé was also found to have in his possession a confidential memorandum dealing with Maximilian's private life, which asserted that the Empress Carlota was 'wearing out her health and nerves in ceaseless activity, in order to compensate her for the disappointment of not having a child', and that the Emperor put up with her continual interference because he knew himself to be responsible for her unhappiness, 'having as a young man caught a disease off a Brazilian prostitute, which, though cured, precluded the possibility of his ever having an heir'. This was the first of a series of slanders in a whispering, defamatory campaign deliberately instigated by the Church and encouraged by the *Juaristi*. The accusations were equally humiliating to Charlotte and to Maximilian, and they came at a time when the excitement and enthusiasm of the first months had given way to frustration and to disillusion, when the Mexican climate was already beginning to have its effect on Maximilian's health and he was no longer either willing or capable of satisfying a passionate and demanding wife.

'It is a most thankless business to reduce a corrupt clergy to submission, and for my part I could have wished that previous governments had undertaken the task,' wrote Charlotte in a letter to Eugénie. For the first time, she expressed her fears and anxieties for the future. Advice from her father, urging his 'dearest children to go gently with the clergy' had arrived too late. The bishops were mortally offended by the publication of the Emperor's ultimatum and were using all the means in their power to thwart his intentions, spreading the grossest libels and stirring up resistance in every class. Even the Empress's ladies-in-waiting were addressing petitions of 'filial remonstrance' while some of the richest *hacendados* in the country were posing as champions of a religion which they seemed to think consisted of 'tithes and the power to hold property'. 'We have some bishops,' wrote Charlotte, 'who would willingly abandon their palaces and crosses, but not their revenues. A state salary would never bring them in so much, and their ideal would be to live in Europe on their money, while we are struggling here to establish the position of the Church.'

Behind all the steps taken by the Nuncio, the Empress detected the guiding hand of the Archbishop Labastida, 'whose bad Italian I know so well that I recognize it in every line of the Nuncio's letters'. Meanwhile, the Liberals were aggravating the situation by maliciously exulting over their opponents and claiming that Juarez's policy had triumphed. But also they began to grumble on hearing that the Emperor was reinforcing General Forey's decree by which all sales of Church property made in the past ten years were to be re-examined, and whatever had not been legally acquired was to return to the State. In fact no one was pleased, and Charlotte complained with a certain amount of bitterness: 'For the first six months, everyone finds the government charming; but only touch something, set your hand to any task and you are execrated.' The twenty-four-year-old Empress had not yet realized that Eugénie's enthusiasm for Mexico was on the wane and that as a fervent Spanish Catholic she would be the first to criticize her for having been too sharp in her language with the Nuncio. The general opinion in Paris, in Vienna and in Rome, even among Charlotte's own relatives and friends, was that Maximilian would never have been so intransigent with the clergy had it not been for the influence of his wife.

But those who were closest to Maximilian, like Charles de Bombelles and the Treasurer, Jacob Kuhacsevich, put all the blame on Sebastian Schertzenlechner, whom they held responsible for having encouraged the Emperor in the dangerous policy of antagonizing the Church. Schertzenlechner, who had been snubbed by Cardinal Antonelli on his first mission to the Vatican, was bitterly anti-clerical, and he used his influence with the Emperor to excite him against the clergy. His compatriots, who detested this lowborn upstart, referred to him contemptuously as 'the Great Moo', a variation on the Great Chu, the highest of the temples in the ancient Aztec city of Cholula. 'The Great Moo governs, and says that everything is going splendidly, when nobody is sure of his life. His Majesty is always running to him for advice as to what he ought to do,' wrote Frau von Kuhacsevich to the wife of the Prefect of Miramar. This middle-aged, comfort-loving Viennese, who had accompanied her husband overseas out of loyalty to their beloved Archduke, does not give a very happy picture of life in Imperial Mexico. Writing from the Castle of Chapultepec, in what was obviously a moment of panic, she says, 'The disorder is very great, the clergy are rabid at the Emperor's decree, and are conspiring against him. A rebel general has escaped from prison in Mexico, and is six leagues from here with a thousand men. The sentinels are doubled. Nobody rides into the city from here without carrying a revolver . . . They say a couple of bishops will have to be hanged. I am more afraid of them than of the *guerrilleros*, especially as regards poison.' Then, in a gallant attempt to reassure her friend, she adds, 'But in spite of all this, our health is good, and whenever possible, we forgather in the evening and are quite merry.'

Both the Emperor and Empress set an example of courage. Mexico

City was short of troops and at Chapultepec they lived in continual fear of raids by robber bands. Bazaine had left with a large army for the long-deferred attack on Oaxaca, five hundred kilometres to the south, and the scanty French forces were scattered all over the vast country, from the deserts of Chihuahua to the jungles of Chiapas. The Austrians and Belgians had only just arrived in the capital, while the best of the Mexican Imperialist generals were strong supporters of the Church. Schertzenlechner led Maximilian to believe that it was dangerous to employ men like Marquez and Miramon, who might at any moment go over to the enemy. At a time when he could ill afford to lose them, Maximilian sent two of his most capable Generals abroad on useless and expensive missions – Miramon to study Prussian military strategy in Berlin and Marquez on an embassy to the Sublime Porte, and a pilgrimage to the Holy Places of Jerusalem – a singularly unsuitable mission for a general notorious for his cruelty, even by Mexican standards.

Maximilian might assert that in Mexico 'the blacks were bad and weak and the enormous majority were white and liberal', and desired progress in the fullest sense of the word. But neither his Liberal ministers, nor his Liberal generals, were making any serious attempt to bring order into the country. All hope of peace had vanished with the arrival of the Nuncio. Constructive projects like the building of a Mexico-Vera Cruz railway and the foundation of a Franco-Mexican Bank were forgotten in the bitter struggle for political power. Conservative newspapers, one of which boasted the name *La Monarquia*, were temporarily suspended by the Emperor for their violent attacks on his government. Maximilian, so trusting by nature, was beginning to find that no one could be trusted. The army and the police were corrupt – guerrilla leaders captured in battle were mysteriously released – and the local inhabitants protected the bandits.

Already in the autumn, Charlotte was writing to her husband, 'We will soon be eaten up by thieves, there are robberies every night in the town and the mountains are beset by bandits.' The situation does not appear to have improved. At Christmas, she was complaining to Eugénie, 'I am sorry to tell Your Majesty that, whether owing to the recall of the troops, necessary though I realize it to be, or through some ill-luck or other, the pacification of the country is again much hampered. Yesterday, for instance, the bandit Romero attacked Toluca, which is only a few hours from here, and I would not be surprised if he suddenly took a walk in our direction.'

But no mention of these vicissitudes appear in Maximilian's letters to his friends and relatives in Austria. There are lyrical descriptions of riding out with Charlotte to 'enjoy the glorious morning air, wearing a Mexican riding costume and using the excellent Mexican saddle'; giving dinner at Chapultepec to a deputation of real heathen Indians from the far northern frontier, 'genuine Fennimore Cooper characters' whom he entertained in Montezuma's cypress grove on the very spot where the Aztec Emperor used to hold his great banquets. He tells his brother, Karl Ludwig, of the successful balls given by Charlotte, 'where one sees the most ravishing women, wearing enormous ropes of pearls from the Pacific', and of the efforts he had made to improve the cuisine and the Imperial cellars, which were now among the best in the country, with the result that 'the diplomats who come to dinner gorge and swill to such an extent that, by the end of the evening, they are quite incoherent'. He is lighthearted, superficial, even ironical at times, but the only political information he gives is to send his brother a detailed account of his dealings with the Nuncio, 'who has gone hopelessly wrong with his insincere and out-of-date diplomacy. But as I expect, the proceedings of my government will be calumniated in ultramontane Europe, and these slanders will probably be repeated to Mama and make her anxious. I would like you to tell her the truth.'

Even then, there is no word to suggest an atmosphere of crisis, no hint that in that month of January 1865 the situation was so desperate that there were times when both Charlotte and Maximilian seriously considered throwing in their hands and returning to Europe. If Maximilian really had had faith in the future of a Mexican Empire, he would not have been so angry on reading in the French press of the Emperor Franz Josef's having informed the Austrian Reichsrat of the terms of the Family Pact concluded at Miramar. The news reached Mexico when Maximilian was in the throes of his problems with the Nuncio, and was low both in health and morale. His indignation at having been neither consulted nor forewarned vented itself in a series of foolish and ill-considered actions, damaging to his reputation both at home and abroad. A wise or experienced councillor would have advised him to ignore what was already an established fact, but his advisers were the impulsive and tactless Eloin, the arrogant Schertzenlechner, and the young wife who had never forgiven her brother-in-law her abortive visit to Vienna, or become reconciled to her husband's loss of his Austrian inheritance.

One must remember it was Charlotte who dictated the secret document drawn up on board the *Novara*. The wording of the bitter attack which appeared in the Mexican French-language newspaper *L'Estafette*, and the phrasing of the official protest which was dispatched to the various European Courts, are so similar in tone as to make one suspect that Charlotte inspired both the article and the note. There are the same accusations, the same deviations from the truth. Both assert that it would have been better for the Austrian government to have drawn a veil over a pact which constitutionally was both invalid and illegal. Both declare that the throne of Mexico was offered to Maximilian on the initiative of the Emperor Franz Josef and that it was only at the eleventh hour, after Maximilian's formal acceptance, that the Austrian Emperor, accompanied by his ministers, came to Miramar and forced his brother to sign away his inheritance.

This unfortunate document, inspired by wounded vanity and outraged pride, was received with considerable embarrassment in London, Paris and Brussels. The British government did the kindest thing by ignoring it. The Emperor Napoleon would have liked to follow suit and when asked by Prince Metternich to make a public disclaimer, replied that he had ordered his government to behave 'as if the note had not arrived'. At the same time, he asked as a personal favour that 'the Emperor Franz Josef might be sufficiently generous to forgive his brother and do nothing which might render his delicate position still more difficult'.

In Belgium, the prudent old King was appalled at his children's foolishness and put all his diplomatic talents into play to prevent an open breach between Austria and Mexico. He is even said to have recommended the attitude taken by Maximilian's Minister in Vienna, a Mexican of Irish origin by the name of Murphy, who had the good sense to depart on holiday without presenting the note, which he warned his master might have the gravest consequences and lead to the breaking-off of relations between him and his family. If His Majesty did not approve of his action, he said, he would have no alternative but to send in his resignation. But by the time his letter arrived in Mexico, Maximilian was in possession of certain facts which turned his indignation into other directions and made him aware of his mistake in having published his grievances to the world. In those days, all telegrams between Mexico and Europe still went by way of New Orleans, where Juarez's agents were active in intercepting messages and in spreading reports of 'the Emperor Maximilian's concern over his Austrian inheritance, which shows how little faith he has in the future of his Mexican Empire'.

Maximilian also heard that his Imperial brother had only announced the terms of the Family Pact under pressure from his ministers after reports had appeared in the public press giving the text of the secret protest drawn up on board the *Novara*. These leakages meant that there were spies in his own secretariat, and the two most likely suspects were Eloin and Schertzenlechner, both witnesses to the signing of the protest. The two men hated one another: Schertzenlechner, who coveted Eloin's position in the Imperial Chancery, was always intriguing with the Mexicans who worked under the Belgian and who disliked him for his bad manners, his candour and his incorruptibility; Eloin, for his part, despised and distrusted Schertzenlechner, and delighted in pointing out to the Emperor the mistakes and weaknesses of a man who had neither culture nor education. His chance to destroy his rival came sooner than he had hoped. Schertzenlechner was sufficiently unwise to accuse him in front of the Emperor of having sold the text of the 'secret protest' to the Austrian press. The Belgian did not even trouble to defend himself. He merely produced certain documents proving Schertzenlechner to be still on the payroll of the Austrian Court, drawing the allowances of a palace servant. And what was even more damaging was that the sums received were considerably in excess of a valet's salary.

'There was a shocking scene,' writes Karl Schaffer, one of the two naval officers who had accompanied Maximilian to Mexico. 'Both abused each other like pickpockets in front of the Emperor.' In a fit of hysterical rage, Schertzenlechner threatened his resignation, which to his surprise was promptly accepted by Maximilian, who was not only disgusted by the scene but thoroughly disillusioned by his vulgarity and treachery. Thwarted in his ambitions, the ex-lackey reverted to type, insulting and blackmailing the master to whom he owed his whole existence, spreading alarmist rumours and threatening to publish letters and documents which Maximilian had been sufficiently unwise to entrust to his keeping. Both the French and Austrians wanted to have him locked up, but for some strange and unaccountable reason the Emperor not only forgave him, but gave him permission to return to Europe with the title and salary of a Counsellor of State.

His disgrace caused general rejoicing at the Palace. 'The Great Moo has gone, and Bombelles is reviving, as he was always spying on him,' wrote Frau von Kuhacsevich to her friend at Miramar. 'It is the greatest luck for the Emperor to have got rid of him. He says so himself, but one does not know whether things can still be put right in the government.' These few words show what power a man like Schertzenlechner was able to wield at the Mexican Court, where he was in a position to spy on the Emperor's closest friend. The whole episode was discreditable to Maximilian for it showed him to be vulnerable to outside influences and all too easily swayed. His clemency was interpreted as weakness and his gentleness as fear. 'The tragedy of Maximilian,' wrote Madame de Courcy, 'is that it is easy to adore him, but impossible to fear him and, in Mexico, one can only inspire respect through fear.'

Charlotte, on the contrary, realized that 'one could only rule the Mexicans with an iron hand, as the Spaniards did before us', and she knew this could only be achieved with the help of the French. She kept urging her husband to take a strong line with the French and, at the same time, to make use of them, 'for you are the sovereign, and no one else. The French are paid by us, and they reach out a brotherly hand for our money.' She told him to remember that the French never did anything by halves. 'They either do everything or nothing. In my opinion, one must have them wholly on one's side, otherwise there is no point in their being here.' She encouraged Maximilian always to have French financial advisers, 'for it is better to let them be responsible for unpopular measures. The Mexicans do what they tell them while, if left to themselves, they only start intriguing, which is what they have been doing for the past forty years. In front of foreigners, they are ashamed of behaving in this way, and make an effort to use their intelligence for the good of the State.'

Charlotte never forgot that her grandfather had been King of France. She remembered standing as a child at a window of the Tuileries when the guards presented arms, and she confided once to General Douay that her heart beat faster whenever she saw French soldiers on parade, carrying their tattered banners, 'the trophies of so many glorious victories'.

It was Charlotte rather than Maximilian who established friendly relations with the French officers, inviting them to her dinners and balls, 'for even the paymasters had a great longing to dance'. She was at her best in their company, gay and at ease, using her wiles as a pretty woman to win the French generals to her side, and one would often see the Empress riding out on the Paseo or on the tree-shaded Alameda, wearing a grey habit and a white sombrero, accompanied by a bevy of French officers.

But Maximilian was an Austrian and a Hapsburg, and fundamentally anti-French. He might be personally attracted to certain French officers, like Colonel Loysel, who, with Napoleon's permission, had been seconded to his military cabinet. He might admire what he called the 'genius' of his Imperial ally, but he chafed under the tutelage of the plebeian Bazaine and was all too ready to listen to the insinuations and complaints of those elegant, soft-voiced Creoles to whose charm he was beginning to succumb, as in the past he had succumbed to the charm of the Italians. He made the same mistakes as he had made in Italy in believing that his personal magnetism was sufficient to win over the Liberals to his side, and make them forgo their Republican aspirations and national ideals. Charlotte warned him not to count too much on their loyalty, 'for though you may fascinate the hardiest Republican, through your personality, opposite convictions do not mix well. Juarez and his kind will always remain stronger democrats than you are, and besides, they were born here.' But the Emperor was beginning to tire of the advice of a clever wife whose judgments were not always as infallible as she thought.

By now, he was aware of having been too drastic with the clergy, and unconsciously he put the blame on Charlotte's injudicious language to the Nuncio. She was also responsible for the strained relations with his family. Without her, he would never have drawn up and signed a document denouncing the Family Pact or allowed anti-Austrian articles to appear in the Mexican press. But Charlotte had been so vehement and passionate in his defence that he had allowed his natural indignation to get the upper hand. There had been a moment when it seemed as if Count Thun might be recalled, and Franz Josef might stop the flow of Austrian volunteers to Mexico. Fortunately, King Leopold's diplomatic tact and his mother's prayers had saved the situation from developing into an open quarrel. But Maximilian knew that he had burnt his boats, and that he could return to Austria only as an exile. However homesick he might feel for 'the breezes of Lacroma, the oleanders of Miramar and the blue waters of the Adriatic', he had now to accept the fact that there was no longer any future for him in Europe and that he must adapt himself to life in the New World.

279

It was a life of infinite variety and contrast, of the utmost sophistication alternating with a primitive simplicity — where travelling across the country he might spend one night with an Indian chieftain, sharing his meal by a campfire, and the following night be entertained in the greatest luxury by a wealthy *hacendado*, in a vast house furnished entirely in the English style. From one of these *haciendas*, we find him writing to his wife, 'My vassals offer me hospitality on a scale which only English lords can allow themselves in Europe.' In Mexico City, alarums and incursions, robbery and violence formed the background to the Carnival festivities of fancy dress balls, Italian Opera and elaborate religious processions at which the bishops made a point of parading the pomp and pageantry of the Church, while the sovereigns were careful to respect the customs and superstitions of the people.

Writing from Chapultepec at the beginning of February 1865, Charlotte describes their life as being almost like the Middle Ages. 'We are gay, contented and calm, yet there is nothing to prevent a band of *guerrilleros* from falling upon us at any moment. Up here we have cannon and a system of signals for communication with the city. But that does not prevent us from always being on the lookout. The night before last, I got up on hearing cannon fire. It was a tumultuous celebration in honour of the Virgin of Tacubaya, as if the presentation had taken place at four in the morning. I suppose it was to allow for the difference of time between here and Jerusalem. All religious festivals take place here at night, amidst the explosion of firecrackers. In the daytime, festivals go off more quietly. There is no denying that this country has a character all of its own.'

But Charlotte was beginning to find nothing to like or to admire in the character of the country or of the people, whereas Maximilian was beginning to fall under the spell of Mexico and the Mexicans. And this fundamental difference in their attitude towards the country of their adoption contributed to their growing estrangement.

20

Threatening clouds on the Rio Grande

'Knowing Your Majesty's benevolent intentions, and relying upon your judgment, I cannot understand by what fatality it always happens that the most essential measures are adjourned and opposed. Mexico owes her independence and her present régime to France, but it looks as if some mysterious influence is always stepping in to prevent the French agents from devoting themselves to the good of the country, and even our just claims do not always meet with a hearing.'

Napoleon's language to Maximilian, in the spring of 1865, was very different to the blandishments of 1863. The kid gloves were off and the Mexican Emperor was being told quite frankly that the day of reckoning was at hand. French claims must have priority in the new loan which was being floated in Paris, for French nationals were complaining that the commission established to settle the Mexican debt always gave preferential treatment to the English. The efforts of French agents to watch over the receipts of the customhouses were being constantly sabotaged by local officials. Even the question of the revision of Church property had been mishandled, and while congratulating Maximilian on the energy he had displayed, Napoleon regretted that he had not regarded the matter as settled by the French provisional government, and thereby avoided jeopardizing his own popularity. A delicate matter, which should have been promptly settled, had been allowed to drag on *ad infinitum*, while the properties under interdiction were not adding a penny to the revenues of the State.

This letter was a solemn warning that the French government was not prepared to go on footing the bill. Napoleon's Finance Minister, Achille Fould, was urging his master to obtain a tighter control over Mexican revenues, while the ex-correspondent of *The Times*, Bourdillon, who appears to have been continually travelling between Mexico and Paris, was prompting the French Emperor to persist in his efforts to secure the mineral rights in the rich northern states. The Duke de Morny, one of the principal instigators of the whole Mexican enterprise, was dying and the banker Jecker, faced with the loss of his powerful patron, was pressing his claims with the assistance of the French minister, Montholon, who from the very first had been inimical to Maximilian. Meanwhile, in the French Legislative Assembly, the Opposition were redoubling their attacks on a profitless and costly expedition in which thousands of French lives were being lost, to impose a foreign prince on a country Republican in sentiment and tradition. Nor were the reports received by the Quai d'Orsay in any way favourable to Maximilian's rule. Both Bazaine and Montholon wrote of his frivolity and instability, his obsession with detail and evasion of serious issues. Above all, they drew attention to the untrustworthiness of the Imperial entourage, all of whom encouraged the young Emperor to assert his independence of France.

These reports were leading Napoleon to wonder whether he had made a mistake in the choice of his candidate, and there is a marked change in the tone of the letter of 16 April, in which he admonishes Maximilian 'to exercise the greatest economy in the administration of the hundred and ten million francs which will come to Mexico out of the new loan, for it will not be possible to raise any more loans for Mexico in Europe for a very long time.' The French Emperor mentioned the sum of one hundred and ten million francs, but no more than a small percentage of the two hundred and fifty million loan ever found its way to Mexico, and most of that was swallowed up in the expenses of the army.

This letter reached Maximilian at a time when he was not in a mood to suffer criticism and admonitions. Marshal Bazaine had returned to the capital after a resounding victory at Oaxaca, culminating in the surrender of Porfirio Diaz, but the cost of 'this military promenade', entailing the construction of a four-hundred kilometre road and a force of five thousand men, had run into millions of pesos and the general opinion in the army was that General Brincourt could have taken Oaxaca the previous summer with only a thousand men. Bonnefonds, the French financial expert who had taken the place of Corta, had proved himself a man of straw, unable to adapt himself to the climate or the people. This excellent 'inspecteur de finances' on his own territory was an utter failure in Mexico, with neither the health nor the energy to carry out his task. Maximilian, who was kept waiting indefinitely for the budget he had asked him to prepare, complained bitterly of his laziness and inefficiency.

Bonnefonds was not the only subject of his complaints. In his reply to Napoleon's letter of 16 April, the Mexican Emperor referred to Bazaine's extravagance, which was eating up the resources of the country, leaving nothing over for the economic reforms and commercial enterprises he had planned. Some of the grievances against Bazaine were justified. A commission under his presidency had been entrusted with the reorganization of the Mexican army, but the Marshal appears to have deliberately procrastinated, thwarting everything the Emperor had attempted to do. When Maximilian suggested that either General Brincourt or General d'Herrillier should be put in charge, two generals whose names are constantly cropping up in Charlotte's letters to Eugénie, and always referred to with the highest praise, the request was bluntly refused, for both these officers supported General Douay in his efforts to supplant the Marshal in the supreme command.

Meanwhile, chaos reigned in what remained of the Mexican army. Units were broken up and generals deprived of their commands; hurriedly-formed detachments were sent into battle before they had time to complete their organization – all of which added to the general confusion and ended by swelling the ranks of the *Juaristi*. Finally, Maximilian had no other choice than to entrust General Count Thun with the reorganization of the Mexican army and the formation of an Austro-Belgian brigade, which was to serve as a model for the other brigades. We find him writing to Bazaine: 'I am placing General Count Thun in charge of the army reorganization, for lack of a Mexican or a French general who either cares to, or can assume the task' – a phrase deliberately calculated to wound the Marshal's self-esteem.

Dissensions grew with the arrival of the Austrian and Belgian volunteers. The Convention of Miramar had stipulated that in all Franco-Mexican regiments the commanding officer should be a Frenchman, but there had been no mention of the volunteers, and the pretensions and rivalries of European commanders disrupted the unity of the high command. General Thun lost no time in writing to Bazaine that he hoped their mutual relations would be 'placed on such a footing as is usual between the armies of two allied powers', implying that he expected to be in sole command of his troops. Bazaine was naturally opposed to a divided command, and the Emperor had to intervene by sending the Austrians to garrison Puebla and the surrounding district. The Belgian commander, Lieutenant-Colonel Baron Van der Smissen, with a force of only sixteen hundred men, could not aspire to an independent command. A brilliant and daring officer of great personal bravery, Alfred Van der Smissen's choleric disposition and reckless behaviour caused endless friction both with the Mexicans and the French, who resented the small Belgian force calling themselves '*Les Gardes de l'Imperatrice*' and suspected the young sovereigns of giving them favoured treatment. With Marquez and Miramon in gilded banishment, the Indian general Méjia and Colonel Raoul Mendez were the two outstanding officers of the Mexican Imperialist forces. Both remained loyal to Maximilian to the end, and submitted albeit unwillingly to the orders of Bazaine, who displayed considerable tact and skill in managing the heterogenous army at his disposal.

Nevertheless, Bazaine's rôle remained an ambiguous one, and to this day the historians of the French intervention in Mexico are divided among his supporters and his detractors. There are those who assert that Bazaine was disloyal both to Maximilian and Napoleon, and had only his own interests at heart. Others are passionate in his defence, saying that from first to last he only carried out the orders of his master, Napoleon, and thereby placed himself in an invidious position with regard to Maximilian. One can hardly blame Bazaine, who till now had always been in a subordinate position, if his almost unlimited powers went slightly to his head, affecting both his policy and judgment. To have placed an efficient, well-organized native army at Maximilian's disposal would only have added to his difficulties, making the Emperor still more intractable and the Mexicans even less ready to submit to French control. Nevertheless, his failure to establish an efficient native army lost the Mexican Empire its last chance of survival.

Bazaine also appears to have been considerably influenced by his entourage. Infatuated by his seventeen-year-old fiancée, surrounded and flattered by her Mexican relatives, there may have been a moment when he indulged, as General Prim indulged before him, in the ambition to make Mexico into a French Protectorate, with himself in the rôle of Viceroy. It was not impossible. The era of *pronunciamentos* was not dead, and successful generals in gold-braided uniforms with clanking swords were far more a part of the Mexican tradition than a poetical, humanitarian prince, whose favourite recreation consisted in chasing butterflies.

In April 1865, Maximilian left Mexico City on a tour of the eastern states, glad to escape from the incessant worries of the capital, where one crisis succeeded the other, and hoping to recover his health, which had suffered from the high altitude. Charlotte again became Regent in his absence, an overwhelming task for a young woman who refused to delegate and who, trusting no one, interfered in every branch of the administration. Her self-confidence was unimpaired. Like Napoleon I, she maintained that 'the word "impossible" does not exist in the French language'. In writing to her husband, she begged him not to get worried over rumours. 'I will look after them, and if necessary take very energetic measures. Your journey is politically important, so you can rely on me to keep the fort at home. I have told Bazaine to count on me if circumstances require his presence in the field. Give me some good *Zouaves* and one or two capable officers and I can deal with whatever situation may arise.' In a letter to an old friend in Belgium, we read: 'If necessary, I can lead an army. Do not laugh at me. I have gained some experience of warfare, just from being in continual contact with guerrilla skirmishes, which are a part of our life here.'

The letters are very different in tone from those written in the previous autumn. One senses the nerves strained to the utmost, and a hint of the abnormal in the almost megalomaniac self-confidence. But above all, one senses the utter disillusion, the growing irritation with Maximilian's vacillation, and with the Austrian bureaucratic methods he was trying to introduce in a country where bureaucracy spelt chaos. Mexico was being divided into fifty different departments, under prefects and sub-prefects; admirable decrees were being promulgated and commissions appointed to see that the decrees were carried into effect, all of which might have been successful had the country been at peace and the Treasury full. Neither being the case, the commissions lapsed into futility. Charlotte was too quick and too impatient in character to approve of such measures. On one occasion, when a minister suggested putting off a certain decision until the Emperor's return, she replied, 'I do not believe in affairs which are allowed to drag on. They are either feasible or they are not. If you await the Emperor's return for him then to speak to Bazaine, he will put off speaking to the Marshal, and the Marshal will put off coming to a decision, and the whole matter will be put off until doomsday.'

The ministers found that business was handled far more quickly in the Emperor's absence. The Empress Carlota would preside over a council, saying, 'Gentlemen, I have come to a decision. What is your opinion – yes or no?' She would listen to their arguments, but her own were usually the most conclusive. More liberal at heart than Maximilian, who, with his gentle irony, would say, 'I am a Liberal but the Empress is a Radical,' she nevertheless realized the dangers of relying on an almost exclusively Liberal government. With the exception of the Foreign Minister, Ramirez, and the Minister of Justice, Escudero, very few of the government could be trusted. Information on French troop movements was passed on to the enemy. State secrets appeared in the public press. Cortez d'Esparzo, a minister who had served under Juarez and whom Maximilian prided himself on having taken into his government, had to be summarily dismissed and Charlotte warned her husband not to replace him by a Liberal or a lawyer, for there are already far too many in your government. It is better to take on a man of no definite party. A capable businessman would be better. . . . Your ministers are beginning to look like a group of conspirators rather than advisers. If you give in too much, you will not be able to free yourself, and the alternative will be to get rid of a lot of people, which is not easy to do. They are already not allowing you to appoint as a minister any but the most fervent Liberal. If I were you, I would show them who is the master, by choosing the first good Prefect you can find, so long as he pleases you, regardless of what colour of the rainbow his political opinions are.'

Her position as Regent was far more difficult than in the previous summer. Then everyone was ready to collaborate in the first flush of enthusiasm for the Empire – now the majority were either hostile or apathetic. She would drive through the streets past silent and indifferent crowds. On one occasion, when she stepped out of her carriage and a group of men stood by without even troubling to take off their hats, the Empress did not hesitate to call out in her clear, young voice. '*Señores! Abaso los sombreros!*' Since then, she always made a point of driving out in a carriage drawn by eight mules with silver bells, preceded by outriders and postillions. But no display of pomp and pageantry could win her the spontaneous cheers of the first months, and she wrote in a letter to Eugénie, 'People here are used to a change every six months, if not in the men at the head of the government, for they adapt themselves to different systems, at any rate in the form of government. So some people are already tired of us, and there is a certain apathy in the capital. In the country districts, this is fortunately not the case, but it is this so-called white minority – the black-coated class – that is the first to criticize and has always been the source of social convulsions in the country.' What the Empress called 'the white minority' included the foreign nationals, all of whom were complaining for one reason or another, some on account of the taxes, others on account of the revision of the sale of Church land. Criticism in the French-language newspaper *L'Estafette* was so outspoken that the paper was temporarily suspended by order of the Empress, which caused considerable excitement in the French colony.

Meanwhile, the clergy were systematically undermining the situation, while outwardly appearing to be supporting the monarchy. The Nuncio had condescended to celebrate High Mass in the Cathedral on Easter Sunday before leaving for Guatemala, where he had been ordered to await the turn of events, and the Archbishop had called on the Emperor to receive the Grand Cross of Guadalupe presented by Maximilian to all those who had contributed to the making of the Empire. In an attempt to settle his differences with Rome, the Emperor had sent a mission to the Vatican headed by the Conservative Velasquez de Leon. But a Papal Encyclical condemning the Imperial policy of Mexico, and the publication of Maximilian's decree on religious toleration, combined to destroy all hope of a *concordat*. Charlotte does not appear to have been entirely in favour of her husband's decree, though she was scandalized on hearing one of her husband's more conservative ministers opposing it on the grounds that 'foreigners coming to Mexico do not want to worship in their own fashion. They are only interested in making money, and get on perfectly well without any religion.'

There is no doubt that this decree was primarily intended to win over public opinion in the United States, where Maximilian was doing all in his power to secure some form of recognition. But all his efforts in this direction were doomed to failure, for across the border events were moving inexorably in favour of Benito Juarez, and the growing certainty of a northern victory was giving fresh courage to the Mexican dissidents. Maximilian's well-intended decree ended by pleasing no one but the English, with whom the Emperor was at present on the best of terms, Lord Palmerston giving his paternal blessing and the British envoy and his family being entertained by the Empress to musical *soirées* and country picnics. 'Scarlett tells me how pleased the English are over your religious decrees, and what a friendly interest Lord Russell takes in your régime,' wrote Charlotte to her husband after what she describes as 'a very enjoyable evening in the company of the British Minister'. To which Maximilian replied, 'I am delighted to hear that your evening with Scarlett was such a success. It is very important to keep on good terms with the British. Though they may not help us, they can do us a lot of harm, so it is always better to have them on our side. I knew I would please Lord Russell in advocating religious freedom. That has always been his Achilles' heel.'

But it was more important for Maximilian to be on good terms with the Pope, rather than with Lord Russell, who had never had any intention of letting his country become involved in the Mexican imbroglio, least of all now when Europe would have to take into account a United States in the full flush of victory. Maximilian had already left the capital when the news reached Mexico of the fall of Richmond and of General Lee's surrender at Appomattox courthouse. After losing nearly a million men in dead and wounded, the remnants of the Confederate forces had succumbed to the vast bull-dozing forces of the north. A proud, united nation was now ready to dictate its terms both to a vanquished enemy and to all those who in Europe had secretly hoped for and abetted a Southern victory – in particular to France who, profiting by America's difficulties, had sought to impose a monarchy on Republican Mexico. The US Secretary of State had already refused to receive Maximilian's Consul-designate, stating that it was not the habit of the United States 'to have official or private dealings with the revolutionary agents of a country with whose legal President [Benito Juarez] the United States is in diplomatic and friendly relations'.

This must have been the first time in history that a Hapsburg heard himself referred to as a revolutionary. But not even this insult deterred Maximilian from spending large sums on propaganda in the States, nominating agents and subsidizing journalists to write glowing accounts of life in Imperial Mexico. It was money thrown down the drain. Republican clubs supporting Benito Juarez were springing up in all the larger cities of America, and the tenacious Indian, whom the French army had chased to the northern confines of his country, was more confident than ever in his victory, now that supplies of arms and ammunition could again be smuggled freely across the Rio Grande.

The news of the Confederate defeat reached Maximilian at Orizaba, where a wealthy *hacendado*, Don Luis Bringas, had placed his house at his disposal, and where his health and spirits had already begun to revive 'in the balmy air of the tropics'. The enthusiasm with which he had been greeted throughout the journey had revived his facile optimism. 'One could do something with the ordinary people,' he writes, 'and also with the Indians. It is only the people on top who have no sense of patriotism.' But patriotism could hardly flourish in the atmosphere of insecurity which prevailed throughout the country, to which was now added the fear of an American invasion. Maximilian was still day-dreaming of a vast Central American Empire, extending as far as Panama, when the news from Washington awoke him to the dangers of the present. But neither he nor Charlotte appear to have grasped the full extent of this danger, nor the gravity of the news contained in the telegram which followed shortly afterwards, announcing President Lincoln's assassination. So bad were the communications in those days that the telegram reporting the tragic events of the night of 17 April did not reach Mexico for ten days, and it was only very much later that Maximilian read the full text of Lincoln's last speech, in which the American President pleaded for generosity towards the vanquished and an end to all wars.

But the new President, Andrew Johnson, was a man of a very different calibre, lacking all Lincoln's humanity and moderation. Maximilian's letter of condolence remained unanswered and his suggestion of a meeting to discuss the problem of Southern refugees crossing over into Mexico was completely ignored. One of the first consequences of peace was the influx of disbanded Confederate soldiers, and though both Maximilian and Bazaine would have welcomed an addition of experienced soldiers in the Foreign Legion, it was more likely that hungry and desperate men would make common cause with the first guerrilla band they encountered on the Rio Grande. Maximilian was alive to the danger of this long, unprotected frontier which neither he nor the French had sufficient troops to garrison, and he considered it was time to remind Napoleon of the secret clause appended to the Convention of Miramar, in which the French Emperor had promised that 'whatever eventuality might arise, the Mexican Empire could always count on France'.

Felix Eloin, who was accompanying the Emperor on his tour and was 'already half-dead from fatigue' from the long days spent in the saddle, was now sent at a few hours' notice to Europe, bearing confidential letters to the Emperor Napoleon, Lord Palmerston and King Leopold. The French high command, who disliked Eloin as cordially as the Mexicans, prided themselves on having persuaded the Emperor to get rid of him by sending him off to Europe. But this was far from being the case. Maximilian chose Eloin for his envoy because he was the only one he trusted sufficiently to undertake such a difficult and a delicate task. 'I think his journey will be useful and important,' he confided to Charlotte, 'but it is a great sacrifice to let him go at this moment.'

Eloin's task proved to be a thankless one, for in his absence his enemies succeeded in working on the Emperor's impressionable mind. They decried his arrogance and his ambition, and insinuated that he was trying to transform the secretariat into a central government in which the Emperor was to function only as a figurehead. Maximilian, as usual, was only too ready to listen. He was jealous of his personal prerogatives and had been brought up by his mother to believe that 'a servant should be useful but never indispensable'. 'Eloin's journey will make a good impression on the Mexicans,' he wrote, 'and show them that the government continues to function smoothly, even in the absence of one of its leading members. It will also be a good opportunity for the Belgian to prove what he is worth.'

But even the greatest genius could not have made a success of his mission. Eloin arrived in Paris to find public opinion almost unanimously against further intervention in Mexico. The Emperor Napoleon was in Algeria and the Empress, who was acting as Regent in his absence, received him at the Tuileries. Eugénie was at her most charming. Her questions on Mexico were intelligent and well-informed, and her personal sentiments towards the young sovereigns appeared to be as affectionate as ever. But her attitude changed on reading Maximilian's letter and, with a certain show of anger, she told Eloin that his Emperor had really too many pretensions. He was always asking for the impossible. France had already made enormous sacrifices. Before leaving for Algeria, her husband had given orders to maintain the effective strength of the army of occupation. But in the present circumstances, there could be no question of increasing it. To occupy the whole of Mexico would be a physical impossibility, and there were already sufficient troops to garrison the vital areas and to protect the interests of the French nationals, and to guard the honour of the French flag. These words showed all too clearly that France was now more concerned with the protection of her commercial interests than with the future of Maximilian's Empire.

21

The Imperial ménage

In spite of the critical situation, Maximilian continued on his journey. His health was not yet restored and both Charlotte and his doctor dissuaded him from returning to the capital. He was always at his happiest when travelling, exploring the beauties of the Mexican countryside. Writing from Molina de Flores, sitting beside a waterfall in a tropical garden, he assured his wife: 'This place would be Heaven, if only you were with me, my darling.' But one senses that at heart he was glad to get away from Charlotte's continual admonitions and advice. He appears still to have placed his trust in Napoleon, relying on him to deal with the new threat of invasion from the north. It was up to the French to strengthen their garrisons along the Rio Grande, and for the French Emperor and the Belgian King to obtain the necessary guarantees from the various European Powers, who now more than ever would be opposed to any further American expansion. Having entrusted Eloin with his mission, Maximilian reverted to daydreams. In his letters to his wife there are no more than passing references to the events which threatened to disrupt his Empire.

His pleasure in sightseeing was as intense as ever. At Teotihuacan the stout and plethoric Ramirez was dragged out at sunset to climb the great pyramids of the sun and the moon and the Emperor was shocked to find that his foreign minister had never visited them before. He was always amazed at the lack of interest of most of his subjects in their own native art. Neglected archaeologists and impoverished artists found him a generous and enthusiastic patron. Visitors to Mexico who now come in their thousands to admire the treasures of pre-Columbian art displayed in the superb archaeological museum, can be grateful to Maximilian for having rescued these relics from rotting in jungles or lying forgotten in dusty warehouses. We have only to read the journals of Madame Calderon de la Barca dating from 1841 in which she describes the disorder produced by years of civil war and unsettled government, to understand and sympathize with Maximilian if he preferred putting his museums in order and financing work on the archaeological sites, to discussing army estimates with Marshal Bazaine. At Tlaxcala, he was met by General Thun with a detachment of Austrian hussars, who accompanied him through the whole of the Puebla district. Maximilian was delighted at being again in the company of his compatriots – gay, high-spirited young men who had enrolled under his flag, some of them for profit, mostly for the sake of the adventure, and a few for the sake of an ideal. The majority of the officers were aristocratic by birth, the younger sons of the great families; others were mercenaries ready to fight in any and every war. There were Italians, Poles and Hungarians among them, even an Englishman and an Irishman. No one could doubt their bravery, but their discipline left a lot to be desired, and one and all resented being under Bazaine's supreme command. 'Recently, it required all the tact of the Prefect here to prevent the French and Austrians from coming to blows,' wrote Maximilian from Puebla, and that his sympathies were doubtless on the side of those who gave him their undivided loyalty, and who shared his typically Austrian point of view that 'a situation might be desperate, but it is never serious'. A terrible wave of homesickness came over him one evening at a regimental concert which included songs from the Wienerwald and from the Venetian lagoons – songs which harked back to another life. 'Luckily it was dark,' he wrote, 'so they could not see my tears.'

The Emperor was on his way to Puebla when he met the celebrated Spanish poet José Zorilla, who was living in Mexico at the time. Zorilla was noted for his Republican sympathies, and Maximilian had never invited him to Court for fear of a rebuff. But while he was staying in a *hacienda* belonging to one of Charlotte's ladies-in-waiting, his hostess introduced him to the poet, who during the evening was prevailed upon to recite some of his verses. After expressing his admiration for his genius, the Emperor told Zorilla that he was leaving early the following day and would like to have his company on the drive, as he knew the country so well. The offer was accepted and Zorilla describes how they set out from the *hacienda* on a wonderfully clear morning before their hosts, who had not reckoned with the Emperor's matutinal habits, were awake. Maximilian was travelling by carriage, Zorilla on horseback. When the Emperor had finished reciting his morning prayers, he opened his window and invited the poet to ride beside him so that they could talk undisturbed, his secretary and military escort all being Austrians who did not understand Spanish. Every possible subject was discussed during the drive, from Shakespeare to Aztec art, from the cultivation of the *maguey* plant to the poetry of Heine – everything except politics. The poet was fascinated and charmed by the wide range of the Emperor's mind, and by the end of the day he had agreed to become the director of a new national theatre, which was to be entirely free from politics. From that day, Maximilian could count on Zorilla's friendship and his death in the following year was a severe personal loss.

Plans were made for a national theatre, with prizes for the best native playwright; an Academy of Science, a Council of Public Instruction, presided over by his private physician, Dr Semeleder; new curriculums for the schools, which were to include 'the much-neglected study of philosophy' – all this in a country where nearly fifty per cent of the people were illiterate. Such were the subjects with which the Emperor was concerned, at a time when the end of the American war was causing fresh outbreaks of Juarism throughout the country, and the anniversary of the 'Glorious *Cinco di Mayo*' was being openly celebrated in both Puebla and the capital. Three of Juarez's best generals were again operating in Michoachan, less than a hundred miles from Mexico City, though Bazaine in his light-hearted fashion persisted in referring to the fighting as 'mere guerrilla skirmishes'.

Charlotte did her best to cope with the rising difficulties, and there must have been times when even the most devoted of wives was exasperated by Maximilian's poetical meanderings. While loyally asserting that his journey was politically important, and encouraging him to pursue it, she must secretly have felt that he should have been back in his capital spurring on his ministers to action. Her political acumen told her that the whole system of government was at fault. Theoretically, Maximilian ruled through a Cabinet of nine ministers and an Imperial Chancellery divided into civil and military cabinets. Added to which there was a series of personal advisers whose influence waxed or waned according to the Emperor's mood. It was Napoleon who first suggested this form of benevolent dictatorship as preferable for Mexico to the constitutional rule Maximilian had advocated in his first speeches at Miramar. But the benevolent dictatorship was too 'benevolent', and not one of his ministers took upon himself the responsibility of government. Charlotte accepted the fact that this form of government had failed. 'One must gradually establish a new system,' she writes, 'some form of constitutional rule based on the Italian and Belgian model.' But

Maximilian had lost his taste for constitutional rule. Later, when Napoleon, swayed by events in the United States, suggested he should convoke a Congress, which 'however ineffectual in the past' had always been part of the Mexican tradition, he replied: 'Having been elected by the unanimous wish of the Mexican people, I see no reason to model my government on that of the United States.' Who else but Napoleon had given him the advice that constitutional rule could only be gradually applied in a country which had been plunged in anarchy for years?

Charlotte, being her father's daughter, saw in a constitution a safeguard against anarchy. The De Redo family in Mexico City have still in their possession the rough draft for a constitution written out in the Empress's hand. There must have been many such drafts sent to Maximilian for approval, only to be buried under piles of papers and forgotten. Undeterred, the Empress struggled on, winning respect even from her enemies. Her charities were boundless. A maternity hospital in Mexico City was financed entirely out of her private funds. Almshouses and communal kitchens were opened on her initiative to feed the beggars who swarmed all over the town. We hear of her riding out with Bazaine to visit the new fortifications, and in a rare moment of relaxation, going to the theatre to hear Concha Mendez, 'the Cuban Nightingale', whose interpretation of *La Paloma* had taken Mexico by storm. Charlotte lived and dressed in the Mexican way, and although she was always chaperoned by Madame Almonte or one or other of her fourteen ladies-in-waiting, she somehow gave the impression of being completely self-sufficient. No one appears to have been taken into her confidence, or could boast of her intimacy. But there were times when she struck some of the more romantically-minded young officers as being pathetically alone, and her maids noted a growing nervousness and a curious habit of putting her handkerchief in her mouth and tearing at the corners with her teeth, so that by the end of the day the lace was torn in shreds.

Maximilian had only been gone a week when Charlotte received the news of the 'disaster of Tacambaro', in which a small force of Belgians, two hundred and fifty in all, had been caught in a trap and surrounded by three thousand Republicans. It was the Belgian Legion's first major engagement and ended in a miserable defeat with eight young officers killed and over two hundred survivors being led into captivity. It was particularly humiliating for the commander of the legion, Alfred Van der Smissen, who was in Morelia at the time and who, after hoping for an independent command, had been forced to take orders from a Frenchman. Colonel de Potiers had been campaigning in Michoacan for the past months and, knowing the terrain, should never have sent a young and inexperienced force into such a dangerous and exposed position. Van der Smissen was not a man to mince his words, and he openly accused the Colonel of criminal negligence and gross incompetence, so that it needed all Marshal Bazaine's tact and skill to prevent the two men from challenging one another to a duel.

The Marshal's position was particularly delicate, for the Belgian was known to have the Empress on his side. Charlotte took the defeat of her 'guards' as a personal tragedy. 'It haunts me day and night,' she wrote. 'It is a catastrophe – like an earthquake.' Again one senses a rising note of hysteria, for Tacambaro was not a major battle to be regarded as a catastrophe. It was unfortunate in so far as it had enormous repercussions in Belgium, where public opinion had never been in favour of a Mexican expedition. But one can understand the jealousy of the French, who had many of their own men in Republican hands, when the Empress sent a gift of ten thousand francs to alleviate the sufferings of the Belgian prisoners. So much has been written of Mexican cruelty in battle that it speaks for the honour and chivalry of the Republican commanders that, in spite of the poverty and hardship suffered by their own soldiers, the money was safely delivered. But it caused bad blood at French headquarters, where it was openly said that the handsome, dashing Van der Smissen, to whose grievances Charlotte was only too ready to lend a sympathetic ear, had become the Empress's favourite.

So started the legend connecting Charlotte's name with that of her compatriot, a man who was in every sense the antithesis of Maximilian – hard and aggressive, vainglorious and dominating, ready to give an eye for an eye and a tooth for a tooth in the savagery of guerrilla warfare, but as ready to respect a chivalrous opponent as a chivalorus ally – a man more loved by his soldiers than his officers, a man who, when the last act of the Mexican tragedy was ending, paid out of his own pocket the arrears of salary due to his men. He was never personally sympathetic to the Emperor, who disliked his arrogance and contempt for the Mexicans and was embarrassed by his wife's exaggerated championship of an officer who was constantly causing trouble by his pretensions. But there is no reason to suspect Maximilian of jealousy. Charlotte, in his eyes, always remained on a pedestal, 'the loyal and faithful companion, who shares my toils and dangers', a woman whom he loved but with whom he was no longer in love, whom he respected and admired but by whom he was no longer fascinated, whose superior intellect he relied on but at the same time resented.

On his journeys he wrote to her every day – loving, affectionate letters, yet how different in tone from the ones dated from the first year of their marriage, when on returning to Monza, he would write, 'I am longing to be at home in my warm nest, alone with my little dove.' Now he had reverted to his bachelor habits, happiest in the company of his male companions with whom he could relax after dinner over a cigar, exchanging a few of the ribald stories in which the Mexicans delighted and which he appears to have thoroughly enjoyed. He was a witty, amusing companion, and like many men who are not particularly highly sexed, he liked giving the impression of being a womanizer and was not above making innuendos or personal remarks on the morals and habits of the ladies of his Court. He was a charming guest and, though some of his hosts might disapprove of his liberal principles, rich land-owners like the Barrons, the Bestiguis and Escandons were by now too compromised with the Empire to withdraw their support. Their hospitality was on a princely scale, and their handsome wives and pretty daughters vied with one another in their attentions, which Maximilian found so agreeable that there were times when he felt impelled to re-assure his wife that he was not neglecting his duties. He wrote telling her that all the Prefects from the surrounding districts had been sum-moned to Orizaba to discuss military depositions with General Thun, and that in the enchanting town of Jalapa he had come across a young man in the local municipality who was said to be a financial genius, 'not what one would expect to find in the so-called "City of Flowers".'

'As always, I remain immersed in these wretched financial problems.' But it was hard to concentrate on figures and statistics in the gentle, enervating air of the tropics, working in the cool of a veranda, looking out at the snow-covered peak of Orizaba, rising above the dense green of tropical forests. His attention was too easily distracted by the sudden passage of a humming-bird, the raucous cry of a parrot, or an iguana softly slithering through the grass. His secretary relates that the Em-peror was in the habit of dictating when travelling by carriage. But Maximilian was so impressionable to the beauties of nature that one doubts whether any serious work was accomplished on these journeys.

José-Luis Blasio, a twenty-two-year-old interpreter in the Imperial

Chancellory who arrived one day at Orizaba with some important papers for the Emperor to sign, never imagined that within a week he would be travelling in Maximilian's private carriage, sharing a picnic of cold turkey and a bottle of hock. He had barely arrived in Orizaba when the Austrian secretary, Captain Poliakowitz, fractured an arm in a riding accident and the young Mexican, who was known to be a good linguist, was called in to take his place. He was pleasant, modest and good-mannered and the Emperor took an instant liking to him, with the result that within a week he was installed as his private secretary. For once, Maximilian appears to have been right in his judgment, for Blasio was to prove the most loyal and faithful of servants, to whom historians of the Mexican Empire can be grateful for his sympathetic, entertaining and, on the whole, unbiased account of Maximilian's Court. He takes us behind the scenes to Maximilian's dressing room, where the Emperor, wearing a blue flannel dressing gown and chamois slippers, would summon him to work at five in the morning. A few hours later, Maximilian would go riding, wearing the grey *charro* costume 'which became him so well'. Otherwise he always wore white in the tropics, fine merino suits like the ones he had worn in Brazil, and he wore a sombrero whenever possible, for at thirty-three he was already going bald and complained of feeling cold in the head. He was very sensitive to the cold, and even when travelling through the tropics, always had a thick plaid over his knees. Blasio regarded the Emperor as extremely elegant and handsome, but those who had known him all his life, like Charles de Bombelles, were horrified to see how much he had changed in the past year. Intermittent bouts of fever had made him so thin and nervous that even the sun-tanned face could not hide the strained look and the tired eyes.

The Imperial couple were united in Puebla, where elaborate preparations were made to celebrate the anniversary of their arrival and of Charlotte's twenty-fifth birthday. But some sea-food eaten at a party held by the directors of the English company working on the Vera Cruz–Mexico railway had given Maximilian another bout of dysentery, and he had to prolong his stay in Puebla for a fortnight. It was on this occasion that Blasio noted a curious incident which at the time he found difficult to understand. When taken by his host to inspect the magnificent apartments prepared for the Empress's reception, complete with a huge double bed hung with lace and ribbons, Maximilian expressed the greatest satisfaction with the arrangements. But no sooner had his host gone away than he ordered his valet to find a room in another part of the house in which to install his camp bed. The order was given in a cross, peremptory manner, completely at variance with his usual affability, and it was only later that Blasio discovered that the Imperial couple never slept together.

But no one witnessing their affectionate reunion in Puebla would ever have questioned their relationship, and they gave the impression of a happy, devoted couple as they drove through the sunlit streets under a rain of flowers. 'Every balcony and roof was crowded and the enthusiasm was indescribable', reports Major von Kodolitsch of the Austrian volunteer corps. It was curious to find such enthusiasm in a town which only a few weeks previously had celebrated, in defiance of the government, the anniversary of the *Cinco di Mayo*. But the Mexican population were as impressionable and as volatile as their Emperor, and the Empress Carlota's birthday was an occasion for a fiesta in which all the town took part, with the exploding of firecrackers and the ringing of church bells, with the waving of French, Belgian, Austrian and Mexican flags, and military bands blaring in every square. The day concluded with the inevitable fireworks, and a great ball held by the Emperor and Empress, where Maximilian, who had high fever at the time, had to lead the quadrille with the local Prefect's wife who was in the last stages of pregnancy.

More festivities awaited them in Mexico City, festivities for which Maximilian had little taste or interest but which in the past months had provided the principal subject of conversation in every French officers' mess. On 26 June, the fifty-four-year-old Marshal Bazaine was marrying a seventeen-year-old Mexican girl, Dona Josefa de la Pena, whom Charlotte described to Eugénie as 'a very pretty girl, with great grace and simplicity, beautiful blue-black hair and an expressive Spanish type of face'. She added that she spoke excellent French and was still 'completely unspoilt by all the adulation'. Both she and the Marshal gave the impression of being 'very much in love'.

Maximilian, who had very little sympathy for Bazaine, was more inclined to be cynical, complaining to his brother Karl Ludwig: 'We have, alas, on Monday another great entertainment in the palace, the wedding between Marshal Bazaine and a charming seventeen-year-old Mexican, who will do us great credit in Europe with her beauty and amiability. The elderly Marshal is as much in love as a young subaltern. I only hope that his precarious conjugal bliss agrees with him.'

The Marshal's infatuation was such that he could not tear himself away from the capital, and his long-planned expedition to the north was now entrusted to General Douay, who to Bazaine's anger and Charlotte's delight had returned to Mexico. 'The Marshal is in a *humeur de chien* on account of Douay's return', wrote the Empress on a note of triumph. 'It is no little thing to cross the ocean twice in two months, when one has not been home for three years, and few friends would have done so much for one.' But Bazaine was sufficiently astute to cope with the situation. Douay was welcomed as a valued friend, invited to be sponsor at his wedding, and appointed to the important northern command, which would take him to San Luis Potosi, five hundred kilometres distant from the capital and the palace.

The French Marshal's wedding to a Mexican, whose uncle was a former President of the Republic, was a popular event among all classes of the population. The whole town was *en fête* for the occasion, with the usual crowd of Indians, hawkers and beggars conglomerating round the palace. Archbishop Labastida had consented to celebrate the Nuptial Mass in the palace chapel, both he and the bridegroom having conveniently forgotten that, little over a year ago, the one had threatened excommunication and the other had threatened to blow in the doors of the Cathedral with his guns. The wedding breakfast was given by the Emperor, and he and the Empress, following a Mexican tradition, acted as godparents to the bride. The dirty and neglected Palaçio Naçional had been transformed by Maximilian into the semblance of an Imperial palace. A series of small, squalid rooms overlooking the Zócalo had become a vast throneroom, known as the '*Salon des Ambassadeurs*', hung with Italian brocade and illuminated by Venetian chandeliers. The original cedar beams, which had been clumsily painted and re-stuccoed, were now stripped and gilded, and large Sèvres vases, recently arrived from Paris as a gift from the Emperor Napoleon, were prominently displayed. Maximilian's old Austrian major-domo from Miramar presided over a banquet which would have done justice to the Tuileries, while the red and white uniforms and silver-embossed helmets of the Palatine Guard would not have disgraced the Hofburg. But some of the guests were critical of this splendour – in particular the European businessmen whose claims against the Mexican government were still unsettled. With characteristic generosity, the Emperor had given the bride, as a wedding gift, the beautiful palace of Buenavista on the understanding that when she left Mexico, the property would revert to the State, which in return would present her with a dowry of one hundred thousand pesos. Needless to say, the Republican government never paid her one peso and years later, long after her husband's disgrace and death, Madame Bazaine returned to Mexico to die, poor and forgotten, in an asylum.

But on 26 June 1865, the future looked very bright for the seventeen-year-old Madame la Maréchale. Half the families in Mexico City claimed some kind of relationship and the Zócalo was crowded with carriages full of pretty young women, wearing their finest dresses and mantillas. Some even boasted hats from a new French milliner who had opened up a shop on Plateros, and was said to get her merchandise easily through customs owing to her friendship with certain high-ranking French officers. The varied uniforms vied in brilliance with the dresses of the women, and the *Zouaves*, as usual, stole the show. Even the Archbishop was smiling and conciliatory, for however much he might disapprove of Maximilian's liberal policy, fear of an American invasion and the resurgence of Juarism forced him into reluctant support of the Empire.

Maximilian himself was at his most charming and most affable, honouring Bazaine not as a man but as Napoleon's military representative, paying a graceful tribute in his speech, 'to our great and enlightened ally', while Charlotte condescended to the length of embracing the bride in public. The whole of the diplomatic corps was present, including the new French Minister, Monsieur Dano. The Marquis de Montholon, before leaving, had bullied the Mexican government into paying an instalment of over twelve thousand francs on the notorious Jecker bonds. It was the last money Jecker and his family succeeded in extorting from the impoverished Mexican Treasury. His powerful patron, the Duke de Morny, was dead and the opposition party in France was openly criticizing the Emperor's association with a notorious banking house, whose claims were given precedence over the French Treasury. Montholon had been posted to Washington and his dispatches to the Quai d'Orsay, reporting the growing tension and animosity in the United States with regard to the presence of foreign troops in Mexico, had a considerable influence on Napoleon's decision to get out of Mexico at the earliest possible moment.

Of all this, Maximilian must have been fully aware when he toasted his friend and ally at Bazaine's wedding banquet. He had seen Douay on his return from France, and the latter had not hesitated to tell him: 'Everyone in Paris wants the expedition to come to an end.' Eloin had written back in the same strain, but the Emperor persisted in believing that Napoleon's sense of honour would never allow him to desert him. His tragedy was that he measured other people's standards of honour by his own. Only two days after accepting for his wife the gift of one of the most beautiful palaces in Mexico, Bazaine was writing home to his master, 'The military situation continues to be satisfactory, but as always the weakness lies in the government of the Emperor Maximilian.'

The military situation was far from being as satisfactory as Bazaine depicted in his reports to Napoleon. Exhausted by their continual marches across mountains and deserts, debilitated by disease, with very little prospect of the riches and glory its members had hoped for, the French expeditionary force was growing demoralized and disillusioned. Letters from home spoke of the strong possibility of a European war, with militant Prussia threatening French possessions on the Rhine. Surely the soldiers' place was there and not in some miserable Indian village, fighting for an Emperor whose cause no one believed in, with allies who were liable to desert overnight and go over to the other side. The native population, which in the beginning had welcomed them with flowers as the harbingers of peace, had become either indifferent or actively hostile. Villages over which the tide of war had ebbed and flowed in the past years now lived in dread of the bloodthirsty reprisals enacted by the *Juaristi* as soon as the French moved on. Victories became purposeless when there were not sufficient troops to consolidate the gains.

In Michoacan, Imperialist forces commanded by the Belgian Alfred van der Smissen and the Mexican Raoul Mendez had avenged the defeat of Tacambaro by a resounding victory. In the north, General Brincourt had chased the enemy out of his positions in Chihuahua and forced Juarez to take refuge in the little frontier town of Paso del Norte. But these so-called victories did nothing to alleviate the underlying situation. Desertions from the Imperialist forces were growing at an appalling rate, while many members of the municipalities handed in their resignations in fear of Republican reprisals. Juarez's language on the Rio Grande was just as defiant as ever, and his belief in victory continued to inspire those who without leadership would have given up long ago. This was the moment chosen by Santa Anna to repudiate the Empire and issue a manifesto calling on the Mexicans to unite under his banner. No one wanted him back, but he had the advantage of being immensely rich and of having powerful connections in the United States. And Juarez was cynical enough to make use of an enemy so long as he provided him with arms and ammunition.

Meanwhile, Santa Anna's old friend Gutierrez was writing to the Emperor Maximilian, blaming him for his policy, reminding him that he had come to Mexico to restore Catholicism, that the country was by tradition both Catholic and monarchist, and that he should disown his Liberal friends and 'hold fast to the Conservative Catholic party, which alone had the strength to resist a Protestant, Anglo-Saxon invasion from the north.' These letters were in no way appreciated by the Emperor, who resented Gutierrez referring to himself as 'the founder of the Empire.' In replying, Maximilian drew attention to the fact that Gutierrez had been absent from his country for twenty-five years and had no idea of present conditions in Mexico. There had never been a real monarchy in the country, for it was absurd to compare the despotic rule of the Spanish Viceroys, who during their tenure of office thought only of enriching themselves, with a hereditary monarchy loved and respected by the people. As for religion, good Catholics were in the minority and the majority were utterly indifferent, as was the case in almost the whole of the American continent. Even the majority of the clergy did not know what good Catholicism meant, and their moral record made sad reading. The Emperor was infuriated by 'the childish insolence' with which the Papal Court had treated the commission he had sent to Rome. Their audience with the Pope was being constantly postponed and he looked upon Gutierrez and his ultramontane friends as being largely responsible for this treatment.

Maximilian's first impressions of the Latin-American clergy in Brazil had been confirmed in Mexico. In Brazil he had been shocked by their tacit acceptance of slavery; in Mexico, both the bishops and the Conservative *hacendados* flourished on a system of peonage which was but little removed from slavery. The Indian peon was paid, for a fourteen-hour day, at the rate of one or two *réals* a day – barely sufficient to keep him and his ever-growing family in food. He was allowed to buy other necessities on credit from the *hacienda* store, which supplied him with clothes, tobacco and the inevitable *pulque*, an alcoholic beverage distilled from the *maguey* plant which was the Indian's only solace. This system of buying on credit, of making debts he could never hope to repay, tied the Indian to the *hacienda* as effectively as any form of slavery, and in many cases the peon was still paying off the debts contracted by his father. Inspired partly by King Leopold, who without knowing the country was always advocating the rights of the Indian majority, and partly by his own humanitarianism, Maximilian introduced a law to benefit the *classes menestrosas*, by which the peon was to be given a living wage and all forms of corporal punishment were abolished. No man was to be held responsible for the debts of his father, and the credit given in a *hacienda* shop was to be limited to a certain sum. It was an admirable decree which, if properly carried out, would have ranked as one of the outstanding achievements of the Empire. But it was no sooner promulgated than it encountered opposition even from members of the government. The new Minister of the Interior went so far as to say that the education of the Indian would only lead to insurrection: 'He is quiet and submissive so long as he is kept under. Place him on a level with the whites, and there will be an outbreak of revolution.'

This advice, cynical but true, was hardly of a nature to appeal to the idealistic young sovereigns. Maximilian might have ended by giving way to the opposition, but the Empress Carlota was made of sterner stuff, and the decree became law during one of the Emperor's temporary absences from the capital. With justifiable pride she informed her husband, 'I can report success all along the line. My projects have been approved by the ministers, and the decree concerning the Indians went far better than I had hoped. At first they shuddered at the idea, but when it came to voting, there was general enthusiasm, with only one dissenting voice. I really feel today as if I have made history.'

It was the month of August, in the middle of the rainy season. The ministers were tired and bored, and confronted by their dynamic young Empress, lecturing to them on the social injustices under which the country had been labouring for hundreds of years, they may have found it easier to acquiesce than to resist. They knew the law could never become effective till the peon became a peasant-proprietor, and for all Maximilian's good intentions, he would never have the power to break up the big *haciendas*. The *hacendados* reacted to the decree by dismissing peons who insisted on their rights. The *hacienda* stores were closed and within a few months the starving Indians, bitterly disillusioned in their 'Emperador', were begging to return to their former masters. Nothing was changed, except that it made Maximilian unpopular both with the Indians and the ruling classes.

Another matter which aroused all the latent xenophobia of the Mexicans was colonization. In her letters to Eugénie, Charlotte made no secret of the fact that their hopes for the future rested entirely on immigration. As early as the spring of 1865, she was writing, 'It is our mission gently but none the less surely to attract to Mexico a constant stream of population which shall absorb the old one. For there is nothing to be done with the existing elements. I would say this quite openly, if I were not afraid that it would be repeated here. . . . If we were not convinced that immigration would be considerable, I would be bound to admit to Your Majesty that all we are doing here would be to no purpose.'

The summer of 1865 brought to Mexico City an American commodore who, by a curious coincidence, had already been in correspondence with Maximilian when the Archduke was still in command of the Austrian Imperial Navy. Commodore Maury was one of America's greatest experts on navigation and oceanography, and before the war had been director of the naval observatory in Washington. His scientific studies had won him an Austrian decoration, given by Franz Josef on Maximilian's instigation. Coming from a Virginian family of French extraction, he had sided with the South in the Civil War, and was now one of a group of Confederates who had crossed the Rio Grande to put their services and experience at the disposal of the Empire and to help in recruiting honest and hard-working colonists from the devastated Southern states. They were men who had been rich and influential in their own country, and included former generals, judges and planters, Southern patriots too proud to submit to the indignity of living under Yankee rule. They arrived in Mexico at a propitious moment, when the Emperor had just returned from a visit to the silver mines of Real del Monte, which for the past twenty years had been owned and run by an English company. Maximilian had been enormously impressed by the efficiency and order which the English managed to maintain in the territory under their jurisdiction. Their roads were superb, and the *Gardes Rurales*, paid and trained by the company, disciplined and honest. With its English church, well-kept gardens and neat houses where the mine manager and staff lived in comfort and luxury, Real del Monte was a monument to Anglo-Saxon initiative, and in striking contrast to the chaos which prevailed in the neighbouring town of Pachuca, where the administration was so corrupt that the Emperor had to make a clean sweep of all the officials, beginning with the Prefect. Today, one still finds living in the neighbourhood of Pachuca, the descendants of the two hundred Cornish miners who came out to Mexico in the 1850s. They are red-haired, blue-eyed Mexicans who, together with the native *frijoles* and *tamales*, will serve you a *pastete*, highly spiced with chillies, but still recognizable as the original Cornish pasty.

As unwilling as the Emperor had been to listen to Senator Gwyn's French-sponsored proposals for the mining rights of Sonora, as ready was he to welcome the idea of Anglo-Saxon colonization in the south. Commodore Maury and his associates were invited to Chapultepec and beguiled by generous promises. The government was in possession of vast areas of uncultivated land in the neighbourhood of Cordoba, lying on the direct Mexico–Vera Cruz highway and within fifty kilometres of the railway, which was due to arrive at Cordoba by the end of the year. These lands, which were exceedingly fertile and particularly suited to the cultivation of tobacco, were now open to colonization at the nominal rate of one dollar an acre. Preferential treatment was to be given to married men with large families, who would be allowed to acquire up to six hundred and fifty acres, while bachelors would be restricted to three hundred and fifty. The Mexican government pledged itself to provide free transport for those who were unable to pay for their own fares and to exempt all immigrants from taxation for the first ten years. The new colony was to be called the 'Carlota Colony' in honour of the Empress, and Maury was appointed to be the first Immigration Commissioner. For a few months, Maximilian and the prospective colonists were equally enthusiastic about the scheme, though the latter began to have doubts when the Emperor offered them an armed guard to escort them to their new homes, but made no mention of who was to guard them once they had arrived. These doubts became confirmed when they heard that the Indian squatters on the untenanted lands refused to be dislodged, and that the government was powerless to take action.

Meanwhile, opposition broke out on every side: opposition from the Indians, opposition from the *hacendados*, opposition from the Church and press, who spread the story that the Emperor was allowing Mexican territory to be exploited by foreigners. But the strongest opposition of all came from the other side of the border – not only from Washington, where the State Department viewed with a jaundiced eye a powerful nucleus of Confederate leaders settling in Mexico, but also from the Southern states, where there was bitter criticism of prominent citizens who left the country at the very time when they were most needed to help in the slow and painful work of reconstruction. Before long, the deteriorating military and financial situation had made it impossible for the Emperor to fulfil his promises, and gradually the disillusioned

Confederates drifted away, either to Europe or back to their own country. All that survives today of the ill-fated Carlota Colony are the flourishing groves of *cinchonas*, the quinine-producing tree which Maury, at Charlotte's instigation, first introduced into the country.

Maury himself remained in Mexico as yet another of the Emperor's foreign advisers who by their contempt for the Mexicans only multiplied his difficulties. Unfortunately, Maximilian had the habit of always listening to the latest comer, who was looked upon as a genius for the first few months and then dismissed as a mediocrity. Even the faithful Eloin, who had been doing all he could do to further his cause in Europe, was temporarily out of favour, with the Emperor complaining: 'The Belgian is now more than ever the arrogant European, criticizing everything that has been done in his absence, trying to mix himself up in everything, and always talking of how one rules in Belgium, etc. – completely forgetting that we are in a New World and in Mexico.'

The constant worries and disappointments, the constant complaints on every side, with the Mexicans complaining of the French and the French complaining of the Austrians, were reacting not only on the Emperor's health but on his temperament, making him intolerant and impatient, unable to suffer the proximity even of his closest advisers. Eloin, on his return from Europe, found to his pained surprise that almost all the officials in the civil cabinet had been dismissed, and the door leading from this office to the Emperor's private apartment deliberately walled up. The French colonel, Loysel, who as head of the military cabinet had intrigued against the Belgian in his absence, was astonished to find himself treated in the same fashion, the Emperor excusing himself on the grounds that owing to his 'unfortunate character', there were times when he had to be left completely alone and could not stand the slightest interference. He explained that the Empress had always respected this weakness and never disturbed him in his work without being expressly invited, which was one of the many factors which contributed to their harmonious relationship.

But were their relations so harmonious? Rumours to the contrary were too persistent to be ignored. Neither the climate nor the political situation could account for the tragic change in the young Empress's appearance. At twenty-five, she already looked a mature and disappointed woman. She herself was conscious of this change, and in a letter to her grandmother wrote: 'Now that my years add up to a quarter of a century, I no longer enjoy those official ceremonies which

I revelled in when I was in Italy at the age of eighteen. Then, nothing gave me so much satisfaction as to hear the cheers and acclamations of the crowd. Now I feel I am growing old. Others may not see it, but I can assure you that my sentiments and feelings are very different from what they appear in public.' Sarah Yorke, a young American living in Mexico, where she frequented the Empress Carlota's 'Monday evenings' (which incidentally she says were 'deadly dull'), has left us a description of the Imperial couple which gives a clear insight into their characters. Maximilian she recalls as 'tall, slight and handsome, with a certain weakness and indecision in his expression, but very attractive in his manner, always saying the right thing, with a natural kindliness and affability and a dignity without *hauteur*. He had a gift of putting people at their ease, and was possessed of a far greater personal magnetism than the Empress, whose strong, intelligent face was somewhat hard at times, though her determined expression impressed one with a feeling that she was the better equipped of the two to cope intelligently with the difficulties of practical life. Unfortunately, her haughtiness of manner, a dignity too conscious of itself, was inclined to put off many who felt kindly disposed towards her.' Miss Yorke adds, 'It is more than likely that under her proud mien, she concealed a suffering spirit, or at least a consciousness of a superiority which had to efface itself.'

Sarah Yorke confirms that the general opinion among the French, beginning with Bazaine, was that left on her own the Empress Carlota would have been a far better ruler than her husband. Commodore Maury was of the same opinion, and the Empress was the only one to whom he gave unstinted praise in the highly critical report on conditions in Mexico which he submitted to the Emperor. Maximilian was warned of 'the greed and untrustworthiness of his ministers, who were paralyzing his goodwill, and of the laziness and corruption which prevailed in every department, where nobody worked for the Empire, but only for themselves'. He himself was called upon to show more energy and strength and to give his orders 'loudly and firmly, so that they would have to be obeyed'. But the Empress Carlota's enemies, and there were many, knew how to turn the praise into a weapon against her by playing on the Emperor's susceptibilities and unavowed jealousy of his wife's superior intellect. They insinuated that a ruler who allowed himself to be dominated by a barren wife forfeited his prestige in a country where a woman's rôle was confined to childbearing and to serving her husband's bodily needs. Derogatory reports of the Empress's extravagant habit and ostentation began to appear in both the Mexican and American press. Certain European papers picked up these reports, which presented Charlotte as a ruthless virago, driven by a lust for power. We find her defending herself against these accusations in her letters to her grandmother, in which she stresses her loyalty to Max and refers for the first time to what has been preying on her mind for the past years, and what has now developed into an obsession – the humiliation of being unable to produce an heir. The Republicans, and even some of the Conservatives, exploited her vulnerability by encouraging pamphleteers and street-singers to compose lewd and obscene verses on the theme of 'Mama Carlota', which were sung quite openly in the capital within the hearing of the Imperial Guards.

There is something very pathetic about Charlotte's letters home. So many things are unnecessarily stressed, and so many things left deliberately unsaid. She writes, 'It is said that I have influence over Max, that I am responsible for this or that decree. But Max is so far my superior in every way that I cannot really see how I could ever hope to inspire him. I have never wanted to impose myself. What Max does not choose to tell me, I would never attempt to ask. I am very particular about this, more so than ever now that he is a reigning monarch, and one has to guard his dignity. I help Max in whichever way I can. All I can do is to alleviate some of his burdens and to save him some extra work. For we are the only ones who really work in the government. I do not even pride myself at being very good at it. But it seems to me only natural in a position like ours, that the wife who is not the mother of a family should try to help her husband. I help because Max wants me to help, and because I crave for some useful occupation – not just out of ambition. With the peasants, the wife often helps the husband to till the fields. This country is a vast field in need of cultivation. And there are only the two of us, with no children or anything else to do but to till that field.'

A decision taken by Maximilian, without even consulting her, was a crushing blow to Charlotte's pride both as a woman and as a wife. On Mexican Independence Day, 16 September 1865, the Emperor publicly announced that the two grandsons of the late Emperor Iturbide, whose reign had barely lasted a year, were to be given princely rank, and that one of them, the two-year-old Agustín, descended from Iturbide's second son, was to be placed under the joint guardianship of himself and the child's unmarried aunt, who was also to be given the title of

Princess and lodged in the palace. The fact that the other child, the fourteen-year-old Salvator, descended from Iturbide's third son, was to be sent to study in Paris, where Hidalgo was instructed to see that he did not develop into 'a disturbing element', shows that the Emperor had the intention of adopting the little Agustín as his official heir.

This measure, which was no doubt intended to consolidate the Imperial dynasty, ended by having exactly the opposite effect and only added to the troubles already converging on the throne. The Iturbide family, who up to the time of the French intervention had been living in impoverished exile in the United States, saw a heaven-sent opportunity of improving their financial and social position. Though none of the late Emperor's three sons was included in the honours accorded to their children, they were nevertheless ready to forfeit their rights for a considerable financial settlement which the Mexican government could ill afford. By a secret agreement between the Emperor and the family, only Agustín and his aunt were to reside in Mexico, the others pledging themselves not to enter the country without the Emperor's permission. The only member of the family to rebel against this agreement was Dona Alicia, Agustín's mother, an American by birth who was devoted to her child and begged the Emperor to leave him in her care for at least another few years. But the kind and gentle Maximilian, who was always so ready to forgive his enemies, appears on this occasion to have acted with a curious lack of humanity and feeling, dismissing the plea of 'an hysterical, half-crazy woman' whose influence could only be damaging to a child. Forced into submission by the family, Dona Alicia was packed off to Europe, where her first visit was to the American Legation in Paris to pour her sad story into the sympathetic ear of the Minister, Mr Bigelow.

By bringing the little Agustín Iturbide to live in the palace, Maximilian publicly proclaimed the fact that he had given up all hope of his wife's giving him an heir. And we find Charlotte, hurt and resentful, but still loyal to her husband, defending his action to her family: 'It was a simple act of justice for the Emperor to take under his protection the descendants of a former Emperor who was not of the blood royal.' To those who might question why the grandsons, and not the sons, had been raised to Imperial rank, she explains: 'This would have been quite impossible in view of the gambling and drinking habits to which they had become addicted during their exile in the United States.' What she refused to admit was that this alien child and still more alien aunt had come to live permanently in the palace. 'They are only staying here at present,' she says, 'waiting for a house to be prepared for them.' Of Agustín Iturbide, she writes with a certain coldness, 'The child is fresh and rosy, but not too well-behaved at present,' thereby making it quite clear that none of her frustrated maternal feelings was going to be lavished on this grandchild of a Creole officer.

The pyschological effect of Agustín Iturbide's arrival at the palace reflected on Charlotte's character and behaviour. She became morose and detached, withdrawing into herself, leading her own life independently of her husband, whom she rarely saw except at meals. Blasio relates that when they were residing at Chapultepec, both Emperor and Empress drove every day into the capital, but never at the same time, and that Charlotte, who until recently had taken such an active part in politics, now confined her activities to the administration of her various charitable foundations. She rarely attended the ministerial councils, and even then was sometimes forced to leave the room on a sign from her husband, who no longer seemed to wish her to participate in his confidential discussions with his ministers.

While Maximilian was forever extolling their 'harmonious relationship', and Charlotte kept writing to her family that she and Max were 'so united in politics and in everything else that there was never any fear of anyone coming between us', rumours of their growing estrangement circulated in Mexico and beyond the borders. There was talk of the Emperor's infidelities, of Court ladies being introduced into the palace at night through a little door which gave out not on the Zócalo but on a side street. From Paris, Mr Bigelow reported: 'The Archduke Maximilian's entourage is of a kind to disgust a virtuous wife'. But Maximilian's fickleness, his fundamental lack of interest in women, prevented any of these affairs from developing into a romance. Some of them were started out of curiosity, others in self-justification, in a country where so much store is set on sexual prowess. There was never an official favourite in the palace, and apart from her wounded pride, Charlotte had nothing to fear from these transient enthusiasms. A far more dangerous influence was on the horizon, in the shape of a Jesuit priest of German extraction who, within a few months, had obtained such an ascendancy over the Emperor that we can trace this influence in two decisions, completely alien to Maximilian's character – the formal recognition of Agustín Iturbide's hereditary rights, and the signing of the fatal October Decree.

22

Charlotte in Yucatan

Of all the foreign adventurers who found their way to Mexico in the early 1860s, one of the cleverest and the most unscrupulous was Father Augustin Fischer. A German and a Protestant by birth, he had emigrated to Texas in the 'forties and worked for some years as an agricultural labourer before joining in the Gold Rush to California. In San Francisco, which was rapidly growing from a village into a flourishing town, Fischer became converted to Catholicism and was admitted into the Society of Jesus.

How and why this man of dissolute morals and strong sexual appetites ever entered the priesthood remains as much a mystery as his early beginnings in Germany. From all accounts, Fischer appears to have been highly educated, with the affable and polished manners of a man of the world. The Jesuits recognized his talents and sent him to Mexico, where he became secretary to the Bishop of Durango. He did not hold the job for long, for in a few months the scandals of his private life had resulted in his dismissal. He was, however, too clever and useful to be dropped. There were not many German-speaking priests in Mexico, and with the coming of Maximilian, Fischer was sent on a trumped-up mission to the capital, where he lived under the protection of Don Carlos Sanchez di Navarro, a Creole aristocrat and one of the few courtiers to enjoy the Emperor's favour.

There can be little doubt that this equivocal priest of obscure background and unsavoury reputation was deliberately introduced into Maximilian's entourage because he was the kind of flamboyant adventurer most likely to attract the volatile and romantic Emperor. Before long, Fischer had insinuated himself into Maximilian's inner councils. Sanchez Navarro was an old friend of the Iturbide family, and one recognizes the hand of his protégé in the agreement made between the Emperor and the ex-Imperial family.

Fischer's first important contribution to the Conservative cause was in persuading Maximilian to put his signature to a decree which was to cost the lives of many brave and honest Republicans, and in the end to contribute to the Emperor's own death sentence. What later became known as the 'October Decree' was no more than a severer version of the measures introduced by General Forey and confirmed by the Emperor in the spring of 1865. But formerly, all sentences had to be reviewed and passed by the Emperor, who with his natural kindliness and love of popularity was constantly revoking the death penalty and granting amnesties to men whose first action on regaining their liberty was to take up arms against him.

Now, for the first time, he allowed himself to be persuaded that further clemency would be misplaced. Juarez, he was told, had taken refuge in the United States. Whether his informants knew this rumour to be false is open to question, but it was a rumour Maximilian was only too ready to believe. He was acting in all good faith when he declared: 'Every form of organized resistance being at an end, it is no longer a question of fighting a gallant enemy, but of suppressing a lawless horde of bandits who pillage and murder peaceful citizens, and rape defenceless women.' It was characteristic of Maximilian to start the first paragraph of his decree by a tribute to Benito Juarez, who had showed 'such constancy and courage in defending a lost cause'. But this chivalrous gesture was completely misunderstood by friends and enemies alike, who merely interpreted it as a gesture of weakness or of naivety.

The decree, which pronounced the death sentence on anyone found with arms in their hands, or convicted of belonging to a guerrilla band, gave no right of appeal to the accused, who were summarily executed within twenty-four hours. In the event of an enemy being captured in battle, the functions of the court-martial devolved upon the officer in command, who was thus given the power of life and death over his prisoners. Unfortunately, one of the first results of a decree so open to abuse was to encourage personal vendettas, as in the case of Arteaga and Salazar, two Republican generals who fell into the hands of the cruel and vindictive Raoul Mendez. In revenge for the murder of an old friend Mendez had them both tried and shot. Neither of these Republicans, who had been leading the anti-Imperialist forces in Michoacan, could be classed as bandits, and their execution only served to intensify the hatred against the government, providing fuel for anti-imperialist propaganda in the United States, where the Republican leaders were represented as martyrs to the cause of liberty.

To this day, historians are divided as to whether Bazaine or Maximilian is to be blamed for the decree. General Gaulot, whose history of the Mexican Empire is based on papers entrusted to him by Bazaine's executors, categorically denies Bazaine's responsibility, but admits to his having followed up the October Decree by an unofficial order to his officers calling for reprisals against the savagery of lawless bandits who were not worthy of mercy. 'One has either to kill or be killed. There is no other alternative.' This ruthless order sickened many of the officers and men who had to enforce it. Desertions in the French army became more frequent; acts of chivalry, which on both sides had hitherto illumined the horrors of civil war, became rarer as the hopes of peace receded ever further.

In condemning the October Decree, one must take into account that both Bazaine and Maximilian were acting under pressure from Napoleon, who kept urging the one to finish off the war, and the other to show more energy and firmness. Whatever action Bazaine had taken against his better judgment, such as reducing the army, evacuating strategic areas, sending a large and expensive expedition into the wilds of Sonora when the troops were badly needed elsewhere – all had been done on the orders of Napoleon, and to the detriment of his relations with Maximilian, who, while distrusting and disliking Bazaine, could not yet bring himself to suspect his Imperial ally of disloyalty. By the autumn of 1865, Maximilian's letters to the French Emperor are full of grievances against Bazaine, whom he accuses of being dominated by the desire to please public opinion, and thinking only of the immediate future. He holds him responsible for having disbanded the original army and thereby increasing the number of *guerrilleros* to a dangerous extent; he blames him for preventing the organization of an efficient native army on the excuse that he needed the material for his own troops. 'The Marshal may say whatever he likes,' wrote Maximilian, 'but the situation is far worse than a year ago, which can only be attributed to two factors – too many troops having been sent home and too much money having been spent on the war.' Reading this letter, one finds it hard to believe that Maximilian would have acted on Bazaine's advice in signing what he himself referred to as a draconian decree. In contradiction to Gaulot, who denies Bazaine's responsibility, can be quoted a letter from the Marshal to Napoleon, in which he claims to have 'advised the Emperor Maximilian to take strong measures against the *guerrilleros*, who with the departure of Juarez have no longer the backing of a political principle', and he hoped that the Emperor's decree would make a good impression on the Conservatives.

Bazaine had to reassure his master that the situation in Mexico was still entirely under his control. It was not in his interest to admit that the influence of a German Jesuit had succeeded in making Maximilian display an energy the French had so often advocated with such little success. In Paris, Napoleon's Mexican mail brought complaints from both Maximilian and Bazaine, to whom the French Emperor complained in turn: 'The Emperor Maximilian must understand that we cannot stay in Mexico for ever. He should build fewer palaces and theatres, and introduce more order into the finances and public security. It is time for him to realize that a Government that has done nothing to enable it to live on its own resources will be all the more easily abandoned.'

The arrival of a new French financial adviser in October introduced a ray of light into the chaos of Mexican finances. Langlais was one of the best financial brains in France, and fully deserved the glowing tribute paid him by Napoleon in his letter of introduction to the Mexican Court. But these flattering remarks were in sharp contrast to the remarks – one might almost say admonitions – addressed to Maximilian, who was bluntly told that he must pay more attention to the finances of the country and introduce honest men into the administration. Most important of all, he must only take into his confidence 'men who were devoted to the policy of French intervention, since the original motive of the war had been to settle the rights of French nationals'. There was no longer any idealistic talk of working together for the regeneration of Mexico, and for the first time Napoleon betrayed his anxiety for the future: 'I hope that America will not trouble the new Empire of Mexico. Whatever may happen, I shall firmly uphold the rights of intervention, but in this respect, it is necessary that Your Majesty's government should cause no embarrassment to France, who is making so many sacrifices for Mexico.' This letter was written at the end of August 1865 by which time in Paris the American Minister was already presenting letters at the Quai d'Orsay, asking when the French government contemplated withdrawing its troops from Mexico, 'where their continued presence may end in undermining the cordial relations between our two countries'.

Thanks to Hidalgo's deliberate misrepresentations, Maximilian had no clear picture of the situation in Paris till Eloin on his return from Europe warned him that there would be no more money and no more troops coming to him from France. This report was both too honest and too depressing for the Emperor's taste; he preferred to listen to the plausible and persuasive Father Fischer, who painted a rosy picture of the future of Mexico, once Maximilian had effected a reconciliation with the Church. The Jesuit, who appears to have been all things to all men, produced a new version of the *concordat*, which he offered to take to Rome, and by now the Emperor had fallen so completely under his spell and was so convinced of his 'superior talents' that he appointed him honorary Court Chaplain, and in a letter to Pope Pius described him as 'one of the most distinguished members of the Mexican clergy'. This must have caused a certain ironic amusement in the Vatican, which had in its possession a full dossier of Father Fischer's activities and probably knew just how and why he had come to Mexico.

It is interesting to note that the Pope, who had kept the eminent members of the Mexican mission waiting for months for an audience, received Father Fischer immediately on arrival and spoke to him confidentially and at length of the Emperor Maximilian's 'well-meant but misguided intentions'. According to Fischer, His Holiness went so far as to admit the necessity of reforms in Mexico, but insisted that those of an ecclesiastical nature had to come from the Holy See and not from the Emperor. In describing his audience, Father Fischer expatiated on His Holiness's 'affability and goodwill'. The German was a witty raconteur and his pithy anecdotes of life in Papal Rome entertained Maximilian immensely. But as regards a *concordat*, he achieved no more than his predecessors.

Nevertheless, he was the first to warn Maximilian of the danger of the American threat. On his way to Rome he had stopped off in New York, where he noted such strong resentment of the Mexican Empire that he was of the opinion that a war between Mexico and the United States 'could hardly be avoided'. The Emperor appears already to have envisaged this possibility, and to have become resigned to the loss of his frontier provinces. Hence his growing interest in the semi-independent peninsula of Yucatan, situated to the south-east of his Empire, where the population of ancient Mayan stock had never given their adherence to Juarez, and had been the first to pronounce for the Empire. Yucatan's main towns, Merida and Campeche, were among the oldest cities in the New World and the descendants of the original Spanish settlers had stronger links with Europe than with America.

With the enemy practically on his doorstep and the highways of his country infested with bandits, Maximilian still clung to the idea of a vast Central American Empire. 'The day will come', he wrote, 'when a few frontier provinces may have to be ceded to the United States. I would willingly part with them in exchange for solid gains in Central America, for our true orientation consists in regarding the Empire as the Central position in the new continent, conceding the dominion in the north to the United States and that in the south to the Brazilian Empire.' This shows he had not given up hope of establishing a Hapsburg hegemony in the New World. His ambitions may have been a form of escapism from the grim reality of the present, the ever-lasting complaints, the ever-mounting bills and the continually-growing deficit.

Monsieur Langlais' economy measures — the ruthless cutting-down of government expenses and an insistence on the dismissal of certain officials in the Treasury, including the 'young financial genius' whom the Emperor had prided himself on finding in Jalapa — had antagonized the Mexican ministers to an extent that many of them threatened resignation, and Maximilian had to forgo a long-cherished visit to Yucatan in order to avoid a government crisis. Charlotte was to take his place, and for fear that her journey might be misinterpreted in Europe, he wrote to his brother Karl Ludwig, 'The reason why I am not leaving Mexico at present is, thank God, a very satisfying one. Lately there has been such an improvement in the administration, and the organization of the country is making such a vigorous progress, that it would be most harmful to let the central control out of my hands, just when things are beginning to be accomplished.' His pride would not allow him to refer to the critical situation or admit that the Mexican Treasury was virtually bankrupt, and that he was pinning all his hopes on a foreigner, and a Frenchman at that, to put the country on its feet.

Charlotte set out for Yucatan on 4 November 1865. She had agreed unquestioningly to undertake a journey which was both uncomfortable and dangerous, much of it through territory unknown even to her entourage. Perhaps she was glad to absent herself from the palace, where the presence of the Princess Iturbide and the little Agustín was a source of constant irritation; perhaps she was glad to have again the opportunity of proving herself indispensable to her husband. For the importance of the journey was stressed in the secret instructions given her by Maximilian, in which he spoke of Yucatan as 'the central point of gravity for the other states of Central America'. She travelled with the escort of a ruling sovereign, accompanied by the Foreign Minister Ramirez,

General Uraga, and a bevy of ambassadors, including the representatives of England and Belgium, who had probably volunteered for the journey with a view to exploring the terrain for future investment, rather than out of devotion to the Empress. Felix Eloin, who had only recently returned from Europe, was to act as her personal adviser, though Maximilian advised her to beware of Uraga and Eloin, 'who always want to be so aristocratic, which will get you nowhere in Yucatan where the people are very democratic and have no use for pomposity and etiquette'. His instructions prove him to have been aware that people criticized his wife for her ostentation and haughty manner, and he advised her to 'dress simply, which in any case is always more becoming to you', and when inviting the local landlords always to include the village headman and leaders of the Indian deputations, 'for the more these people are invited, the more they will be won over, and the more the foreign ambassadors will be impressed'. And he reminded her: 'Above all, never keep these people waiting.'

Neither Maximilian nor Charlotte appears to have taken into account the hazards and dangers of a journey undertaken at the end of the rainy season, when the roads were partly washed away and the rivers had swollen into torrents. In her letters, Charlotte makes light of the vicissitudes of the journey: 'the terrible mud' when a detachment of French *cuirassiers* had the greatest difficulty in preparing the ground on which to pitch their tents; the appalling state of the roads between Orizaba and Cordoba, which drove both her and the ambassadors to ride through the mountains rather than to go by carriage – which was just as well, because the royal coach stuck in the mud and another carriage carrying her chaplain overturned. The military escort were in a hurry to get through to Cordoba by daylight because a strong guerrilla force, led by French deserters, was said to be roaming the neighbourhood. Charlotte was not frightened either of bandits nor of broken bones. What haunted her was the sense of her growing unpopularity, the cold reception she received both in Puebla and Orizaba, towns which only a few months ago had welcomed the *Emperadores* with a frenzied enthusiasm. She made no mention of this in her letters to Maximilian, in which she dwelt on the 'beautiful torchlight procession' arranged by the Austrian garrison of Puebla and the magnificent banquet given by the municipality at Orizaba. 'It was all very tiring,' she wrote, but she said nothing of the unfriendliness of the population, the veiled insults, the lewd remarks in Spanish which neither the

French nor the Austrians understood and which her Mexican escort preferred to ignore. The growing fear of an American invasion, and of blood-thirsty reprisals on the part of the *Juaristi*, seemed to paralyse every gesture of goodwill.

In Mexico, Maximilian waited eagerly for news. He might criticize Charlotte for her arrogance and be exasperated by her nagging, but she was still his only ballast and support in a country where he felt the ground to be slipping from under his feet. 'The further you go, the more I miss you and the more melancholy I feel,' he wrote. 'I wander like a lost soul through the empty rooms and to add to the depression, the weather is freezing. One needs more furs than in Milan in winter.' In contrast to his wife, who always kept her troubles to herself, Maximilian unburdened himself in his letters. He had not felt so low and so depressed for years and the iron and quinine prescribed by the doctor was not doing him any good. He envied her the warmth of the '*tierra caliente*' and the sea journey to Yucatan. He resented staying behind and having to cope with financial matters which were little to his liking ('*y medio gustado*'). The French expected him to account for every penny and to make drastic cuts in his Civil List, while Bazaine and his young wife continued to live on a princely scale under the cloak of 'military expenditure'.

Meanwhile, the situation was growing steadily worse. American freebooters were operating on the Rio Grande, and in spite of Washington's professions of neutrality, General Sheridan of the U.S. forces was turning a blind eye on the arms and ammunition being smuggled across the river. Maximilian complained that the French were doing nothing 'and when they do give battle, they are defeated'. Monterrey and Chihuahua had both been captured by the dissidents, and even 'the brave Mejiá who, invincible as a rock, was keeping guard on the frontier, could not achieve miracles when there was no help to be had from his allies'.

But at last came good news from Charlotte. Contrary to expectations, Republican Vera Cruz had given her a royal welcome,. The last part of the journey had been made by train, and hundreds of people had travelled out to meet her at Paso del Macho, the last place on the line, while a deputation of ladies, all wearing Paris hats, had braved the torrid heat to welcome her at the station. Accompanied by these ladies, she had driven through the streets of Vera Cruz in a triumphal chariot constructed by the local artisans, and she wrote in a glow of pride, 'Everyone agrees they have never seen such enthusiasm. Blondeel [the

Belgian Minister] says that my presence is worth more than an army.' But she was sufficiently tactful to add, 'The cheers are not for me, but because I am your wife.'

The most Republican of towns was the one which had prospered most under the Empire. Trade with Europe had trebled. In spite of French supervision in the customs, contraband continued to flourish, and from the stevedore to the merchant, not excluding the French customs officials, everyone had a share in the profits.

'They were against us at first,' wrote Charlotte, 'but now they want to show us their respect and gratitude. Everyone here seems to have money and they are all very well dressed. They are not in the least like the Mexicans, much more European in their outlook. There is no dislike of foreigners, and some of the schools, which are very good, are directed by Spaniards. Many of the natives are of Spanish descent, with the remains of the old Spanish *grandezza* in their blood. They are very proud and independent. Everyone works. ... There is no deficit in the municipality, which has just paid one hundred and fifty thousand pesos out of its profits on restoring the local hospital. They are so rich that they can afford to give fiestas and receptions like nowhere else.'

But even the balls and fiestas must have been more of an ordeal than a pleasure in the terrible clammy heat, with the *Norte* blowing a gale, bringing heavy tropical rain, and the nights made hideous by a plague of mosquitos. After being held up for two days by storms, the Empress embarked for Yucatan in rough seas under a lowering sky. To the ambassadors' surprise, she insisted on taking a wretched Mexican packet steamer in preference to the Austrian corvette which was lying in the roads off Vera Cruz. 'The Empress of Mexico,' she declared, 'can travel only by Mexican transport.' And while the ambassadors and most of her suite voyaged in comparative comfort on board the *Dandalo*, Charlotte had a nightmare journey in a heavily-listing ship, emerging from her cabin on arrival looking and feeling, as she described, 'like a poor sick bird'.

Merida, known to the Spaniards as the '*cuidad blanca*' (white city), welcomed its foreign Empress to the pealing of church bells, amidst the flutter of doves and a deluge of flowers. To Charlotte, only gradually recovering from the horrors of the journey, the clean white town, the clear, sparkling light of Yucatan and the gentle, smiling Mayan faces belonged to another world. 'It seems so beautiful, so peaceful, in comparison to Mexico. One begins to believe in human beings again. For these Indians strike one as being so good and sweet and unspoilt. The reception has been wonderful. Thousands of people filling the roofs, the doorways and the balconies. All your prognostications were right. Yours in a happy mood, Charlotte.'

Today Merida is still a charming, friendly town which enjoys a reputation for being one of the cleanest cities in the Americas. The local aristocracy, who are all inter-related, claim direct descent from the first of the *Conquistadores*, and are as cultured as any aristocracy in Europe. But beyond Merida, only a few miles from the well-worn tourist routes leading to the Mayan ruins, Yucatan is still a remote, rather sinister land of scrub and jungle and vast hennequen plantations, stretching for miles under a merciless sun. Even now, only the most enterprising of tourists would venture to stay in the primitive villages in the Campeche district, which the Empress visited on her tour and where she stayed in the houses of the village headmen or the local priests, when no better accommodation was available.

She must have been one of the first European women to visit the Mayan ruins of Uxmal, riding the best part of the fifty-eight miles from Merida 'accompanied by half the youth of the town, most of whom had never ridden so far before'. Today, visitors to the luxurious air-conditioned hotel of Uxmal are shown the signature of 'the unfortunate Empress Carlota', whose visit is incorporated in the local legends. We can picture her, still elegant and neat in spite of the oppressive heat, wearing a light travelling cloak, large sombrero and heavy boots to protect her from the snakes, climbing the pyramids and exploring the ruins, all the time making extensive notes in her precise, rather pedantic fashion, which were then incorporated in her letters home. In these letters, she complained of the unhealthy atmosphere, the terrible food, 'the local dishes, which were like the black brews of the Spartans'. This must refer to one of the favourite Yucatan desserts, in which the black fruit of the *zapote* tree is mixed with brandy and the juice of limes. She felt sick and faint from exhaustion and overcome with depression, unnerved by the brooding silence of the jungle, the cruel stone faces of the Mayan gods, and the vast empty spaces which made her more conscious of her own loneliness and desolation. It was an exhausting journey by any standards, and Charlotte was nearing the end of her endurance. For the first time, one gets the feeling that she was afraid. 'We will see how my visit goes in Campeche, and whether it is wise for me to stay there. I am not in the least bit nervous,' she insists, 'only one must not tempt Providence too much. It is strange enough for me to be here at all.'

She, who was usually cold and reserved, was touchingly pleased when one of her palace ladies, a niece of Gutierrez and a native of Campeche, travelled out to meet her at the little village of Calkini, where Charlotte cried with emotion on seeing some Indian peons carrying a banner on which was written, *'Viva el Grande Leopoldo!'* Unknown to Charlotte, who did not hear the news until her return to Mexico, King Leopold had died on that very day, 10 December, 1865. He had been suffering for many weeks, but he only admitted to being mortally ill on hearing of the death of his old enemy, Lord Palmerston, whom he said he would 'soon be following to the grave'. Two survivors of the eighteenth century, they had played the game of power politics to the end. Leopold had placed his relatives on almost every thone in Europe, but he died a lonely and embittered man, estranged from his sons, separated from the daughter he adored, and aware that the Mexican adventure, over which he had allowed Coburg ambition to override his better judgment, had failed. His last letters to Max from Laeken show his mind to have been as lucid as ever. He advised his son-in-law not to spend large sums on propaganda in the United States for 'the only thing that counts in America is success. The rest is poetry and a waste of money.'

23

Death of King Leopold

King Leopold's death was as great a loss to his son-in-law as it was to his daughter. The King had always acted as Maximilian's advocate in Europe, representing the interests of Mexico in discussions with the Emperor Napoleon and at times making suggestions which would have been unwelcome coming directly from Maximilian. He had given the benefit of his diplomatic experience to the Mexican envoys in London and Vienna, and it was largely due to his efforts that Queen Victoria had accredited an envoy to Mexico.

The new King, Leopold II, who as Duke of Brabant had been the first to congratulate Maximilian on undertaking 'such a great and noble adventure', was far too cynical and intelligent not to recognize that the adventure had been a failure. Family sentiment in no way obscured his judgment, for he and Charlotte had never been very close. As a delicate, sensitive boy, he had always resented the clever, precocious little sister for whom their father showed such an obvious preference. From the moment he came to the throne, Belgian-Mexican relations became as formal as with any other state. There was no further recruiting for volunteers and the King confined his attentions to sending his sister and brother-in-law a military mission to announce his succession. Even Charlotte's favourite brother, the gentle and scholarly Philippe, Count of Flanders, appears to have been out of sympathy with her imperial ambitions, writing to one of his Orleans uncles that 'Charlotte was always determined to have a throne at any cost'. Her father's death forced Charlotte to realize that the Belgian Court had become as indifferent as the Hofburg to the future of the Mexican Empire.

A cryptic telegram received at Vera Cruz on her return from Yucatan gave Charlotte the first intimation that her father was dying. He had been ill for many years but he never wrote of the gravity of his malady and the news came as a shock for which she was completely unprepared. Maximilian, who met her at Puebla, found her in a tearful and highly emotional state, spending her nights in prayer and refusing to speak of her triumphs in Yucatan, triumphs that had taken place on the very days when her father was dying. At Cuernavaca, on the feast of the Epiphany, the arrival of mail from an American packet-steamer brought them the confirmation of the King's death. 'I heard Max sobbing in the room next door and that told me all,' wrote Charlotte to her old friend, the Countess de Grünne. 'We wept together but we were not alone in our grief. The whole placed shared in our sorrow. With the intuitive tact of certain primitive people, the Indians, in the space of a few hours, had replaced the triumphal arches by signs of mourning. In Mexico City everyone of their own accord put bands of crepe in the doors and windows.' In her misery, Charlotte was grateful for these tokens of sympathy which proved that the Mexicans, whatever they might think of the regime, had nevertheless a certain affection for their sovereigns, and she mentioned with pride: 'Everything has taken place just like in the old monarchies of Europe, only here it is more spontaneous than in certain places, where the sovereigns are not loved.'

It is now that we hear for the first time of Cuernavaca, which more than any other place in Mexico is associated with the memory of Maximilian. In his wife's absence, the Emperor had become bored and restless in the capital. Chapultepec was damp and cold, and he chafed at the restrictions which made it impossible for him to carry out any of the journeys he had planned. A trip to Acapulco on the Pacific coast had been vetoed by Bazaine because it entailed passing through the wild state of Guerrero, which the French had never been able to pacify. When he suggested meeting his wife at Jalapa, General Thun advised against it, on the grounds that the troops required to ensure his safety were badly needed elsewhere. Maximilian complained that he was 'beginning to feel as atrophied as a tortoise or an oyster, or what is worse, like one of the former presidents of Mexico who never dared to venture out of the capital'. Even his rides and excursions into the country, which were his favourite form of relaxation, were frowned on by the high command, for he insisted on travelling without a military escort and there was always the danger of his being kidnapped or assassinated.

On one of these excursions he discovered Cuernavaca, the place where Hernando Cortes once had his summer palace, and where the Emperor came across a deserted *quintas* (country house) surrounded by a beautiful overgrown garden which, in the eighteenth century, had belonged to José La Borda, whom the silver mines of Taxco had made into one of the wealthiest men of his age. He is reputed to have spent a million pesos on the gardens of Cuernavaca which, when Maximilian visited them in the 1860s, had already fallen into ruin. But the crumbling verandas, the statues and fountains overgrown with roses, the lily pools choked with weeds, and the tangled groves of oranges and mangoes, were ruins of a nature to appeal to a man who was so much more of a poet than an emperor. Gardeners and architects were summoned from Mexico City, and La Borda Quintas, only sixty miles from the capital, became the Emperor's favourite retreat.

Writing to his friends and relatives in Austria, Maximilian expatiated on the charms of Cuernavaca. There was no word of his country's bankruptcy, his own rapidly deteriorating health, or the treachery and dangers by which he was surrounded. Escaping into the realms of fancy, he wrote in the somewhat poetical style which was then the fashion: 'Picture to yourself a broad, level valley, blessed by Heaven, stretching out before you like a golden bowl, surrounded by range upon range of mountains, coloured in all the various shades of the rainbow . . . and beyond them the giant volcanoes lifting their snow-covered crests to the deep blue heavens. . . . Imagine this golden bowl filled all the year round for there are no seasons here, with a wealth of tropical vegetation of intoxicating fragrance and luscious fruits – and to crown all, a climate as lovely as an Italian May.'

To his mother's old friend, Baroness Binder, he describes, 'our pleasant, unpretentious *quinta*, where a terrace runs the length of our rooms and our hammocks hang in the shade of a veranda, while innumerable fountains cool the air and the dark green foliage of the oranges soothes the eye'. His descriptions are so lyrical, his life is made to sound so romantic, that his correspondents must have found it hard to reconcile them with the reports that appeared in the Austrian press. Even Charles de Bombelles, who had been sent to Vienna to seek some alleviation of the Family Pact and to obtain further volunteers for Mexico, had been secretly instructed to give only the most favourable accounts and to contradict 'the nonsense which had been appearing in the newspapers'. The Emperor was particularly sensitive on this point and in a letter to a former aide-de-camp we read: 'Both the country and the people are far better than their reputation, and you would be surprised to see how the Empress and I have become regular Mexicans and live quite at our ease among them. I suppose it is natural that the

European press cannot understand this for they have no standards to judge us by. They are eaten up by envy because we, on our continent, are more healthy and virile than in decadent old Europe.' Maximilian, whose health at the time was causing the doctors considerable concern, describes himself as 'stronger and more able-bodied than before, working ten to twelve hours a day . . . dashing off on wild horses like a proper *ranchero*, and sporting a moustache which would do justice to a Hungarian' – though he confesses that his bald patch is assuming 'formidable proportions'. This letter, which was written at a time when Charlotte was suffering from the deepest depression, talked of her as being 'fresh and gay', while the descriptions of his worn and harassed servants were even further from the truth.

Poor old Kuhacsevich, who was wondering where to get the money to pay the household bills, would have found difficulty in recognizing himself as the glamorous figure 'exciting the amazement of the natives as he rushed to and fro on his fiery steed', bearing important documents between Chapultepec and the Palaçio Naçional, while his fat, middle-aged wife, constantly battling with a horde of inefficient and thieving servants, would have been astonished to hear the Emperor describe her as 'blooming and overflowing with health and well-being, doing nothing all day but swinging in a hammock in the shade of a mango tree, waving mute orders with her fan to deferential and admiring Indians'. This was a very different picture to the one given by the Kuhacseviches themselves in their letters to their friends in Trieste, and one wonders how many of Maximilian's friends and relatives were taken in by his lyrical descriptions. Count Thun's reports from Mexico of the strained relations between Maximilian and Bazaine, and Prince Metternich's dispatches from Paris, warning the Vienna Court that the anti-Mexican party in Paris was gaining the upper hand and that it would not be long before it triumphed over Napoleon's 'last scruples', must have opened Franz Josef's eyes to the truth. If he continued to believe in his brother's optimism, it was because he wanted to believe him.

Austria was going through a period of crisis. The threat of a war with Prussia was looming on the horizon; Venetia was in a state of ferment; and in the Hungarian Diet, the Nationalist Party was questioning the validity of a Family Pact which had been signed under duress. In these circumstances, there was nothing that Franz Josef and his advisers wanted less than Maximilian's return to Europe. One has only to read the memoirs of Franz Josef's adjutant, General Count

Grenneville, to see with what distrust and dislike Maximilian was regarded by his brother's entourage, in contrast to his popularity with the general public. No one saw the situation more clearly than the Archduchess Sophia, who was not for a moment taken in by her 'Maxl's' flights of fantasy, but at the same time realized that his situation would be untenable in Europe. 'She is far more frightened for her beloved son than she will admit,' was the comment of a devoted lady-in-waiting. And Bombelles found his defences breaking down before a mother's anxious questions. The Count's mission was only partially successful. Franz Josef consented to a limited recruiting for volunteers for Mexico, which was somewhat surprising considering Austria's own critical situation and the imminence of war. But with regard to the Family Pact, all that Bombelles obtained was the reassurance that, in the remote eventuality of Maximilian ever having to return to Europe, his brother the Emperor would do all in his power to secure him a position worthy of his rank. He also entrusted the Count with a friendly letter to Maximilian acceding to his request for some of the Mexican treasures of the Imperial collections, something he would hardly have done had he realized the precarious nature of his brother's throne. Bombelles returned with Montezuma's shield and the original manuscript of Cortés's first report to the Emperor Charles v on the conquest of Mexico. The most precious of the Mexican treasures, a manuscript in Aztec hieroglyphs, was justifiably refused.

Count Grenneville's comment was that 'His Imperial Majesty was being far too magnanimous in his treatment of a gentleman who had caused him nothing but trouble'. But Maximilian himself was bitterly disappointed in the results of Bombelles' mission. 'My family have never understood me,' he complained in a letter to Karl Ludwig, 'and are therefore unable to sympathize with my work or my views. They will not do so at any rate until the distant future, when it will perhaps be too late ... but I will try to return good for evil, for though I had such bitter experiences on leaving home, I still cling to my own people.' The tragedy was that neither Franz Josef nor Maximilian had any idea of the difficulties with which the other was contending. The former was determined not to become involved with either France or America over Mexico, and the Austrian Minister in Washington was under orders to maintain the strictest neutrality on Mexican affairs – orders which sometimes entailed having to submit to the grossest insults.

At a public dinner held in memory of President Lincoln and attended both by the Government and the diplomatic corps, a member of the United States Senate, reviewing recent developments abroad, referred to the Emperor Maximilian as 'that Austrian adventurer'. Count Wydenbruck's first reaction was to protest and leave the room. But he remembered his instructions and, red with embarrassment and anger, remained in his seat. Later he complained to Secretary Seward and was bluntly told he had no right to complain, since his country had so often asserted her neutrality in Mexican affairs. When Maximilian heard this story, he fumed in rage against the unfortunate Wydenbruck, who had allowed a Hapsburg to be insulted in his presence.

But given his mercurial spirits, Maximilian still allowed himself to be deceived about the future. According to the constitution of Republican Mexico, Juarez's legal term of office had terminated at the end of November 1865. If no fresh election were possible, the terms of the constitution decreed that the supreme power was to be provisionally transferred to the President of the Supreme Court, who in the Republican government had been Gonzalez Ortega. But profiting by the fact that Ortega had sought refuge in the United States, Juarez, who was then still operating from Paso del Norte, took advantage of the situation to prolong his own presidency. Some of his followers resented his highhanded action and in one or two instances went over to the Empire. These isolated cases, which Maximilian's sanguine spirits interpreted as the beginning of the break-up of the Republican Party, coincided with a letter from his former secretary, Baron Du Pont, telling of a visit he had received from Juan Teran, now acting as Juarez's agent in Europe.

It was Teran who, before the acceptance of the Mexican crown, had come to Miramar to warn Maximilian against embarking on such a mad adventure. He appears to have had a genuine liking and respect for the idealistic young Emperor, and to have visited du Pont for no other reason than to tell him of the enormous risks that Maximilian would be incurring by remaining in Mexico, where there was not a single party he could rely on and where sooner or later the United States would come out openly on the side of Juarez. Teran declared that Maximilian's only course was to abdicate by telling the Mexican people that he had come 'to bring them happiness and not to sacrifice them for the maintenance of his throne. In this way he would leave his honour unimpaired, conscious of having done his duty.' Du Pont, who was impressed by Teran's honesty, handed on his message to the Emperor. But Maximilian chose to interpret it as a tentative approach from Juarez who, finding his leadership questioned by his own party, was prepared to collaborate with the Empire. Maximilian had always wanted a *rapprochement* with Juarez, whom he sincerely and openly admired: 'If, as I believe, Juarez really wants the peace and prosperity of his country, he should come forward and help me with his undeniable intelligence and iron will in carrying out the heavy task I have undertaken.' The little knowledge Maximilian had, either of Juarez or of the Indian character, is pathetically evident when he writes, 'Surely he must see that no Mexican has such warm feelings for his country as I have. So let him come and help me faithfully and sincerely and I will receive him as I would receive any good Mexican.' He did not realize that Juarez could now afford to ignore critics, even in his own party. Public feeling in the United States was solidly behind him, and it was only a question of time before Washington discarded the last pretences of neutrality. Nor did the Emperor realize that the one thing which was anathema to Juarez and the United States was a monarchy established on the other side of the Rio Grande.

In Maximilian's entourage, all the faults and setbacks were attributed to Bazaine. Even the French Minister, Monsieur Dano, was beginning to be suspicious of the Marshal. Why was he so unwilling to organize an efficient native army or to delegate some of his powers to other and more energetic generals? Maximilian had complained to Dano that the Marshal was always saying 'Yes' and acting 'No'. And the minister was beginning to suspect that Bazaine, under the influence of his ambitious young wife and her still more ambitious family, was planning to rise to power on the ruins of the Empire. These suspicions were not without foundation, for as early as May 1865, Bazaine was writing to the French Minister of War, 'Rather than submit to the American yoke, I know that the Conservative Party would prefer to have as their leader the man who has defended their interests and on whom they place all their hopes', who was none other than himself. Since then, the Marshal's attitude had become more and more equivocal. French officers and administrators attached to Maximilian's staff like Loysel, Langlais and young Captain Pierron, whose personal devotion to the Emperor had made him the object of the Marshal's particular dislike, all found themselves being spied on by his secret police. The marriage which made Bazaine so popular in Mexican society was losing him the allegiance of some of his own officers. General Brincourt even went so far as to offer his resignation, rather than see the honour of France degraded by successive evacuations from places where the people who had given his troops their trust were then exposed to horrible reprisals from the *Juaristi*.

The dissensions between the Emperor and the Marshal came into the open over the case of Colonel Dupin. As commander of the so-called 'counter-guerrillas', Dupin committed acts of such sadistic cruelty that his name was execrated even by his own countrymen, and Maximilian asked and obtained his withdrawal. Back in France, Dupin had an interview with the Emperor Napoleon and managed to convince him that, given a force of a few thousand men and the powers to carry out the necessary measures of severity, he could wipe out in the space of a few months the sixteen thousand *guerrilleros* who were terrorizing the country. His return to Mexico on Napoleon's orders had nothing to do with Bazaine, but Maximilian chose to interpret it as a deliberate attempt on the part of the Marshal to flout his authority. At a New Year's reception at the palace, the Emperor complained to the French Minister in the hearing of the other diplomats that he had been 'deliberately disobeyed'. Maximilian's voice was naturally loud and the whole room heard him saying in an angry tone, 'Will you please notify the Marshal that I intend to be obeyed and will see that I am in the future.' By pure chance, the Emperor made the statement on the very day when Bazaine was writing to him a letter of apology explaining the situation. Maximilian's reprimand was too public to be ignored and Bazaine took it as an insult to his position as a Marshal of France. In a cold, discourteous note, he reminded the Emperor of Mexico that, by the terms of the Convention of Miramar, he had no authority over the French armed forces and that a French Marshal was responsible to no one but his own Emperor. The letter ended with a threat that he would complain to Napoleon of his treatment.

This was only one example of the accusations and counter-accusations contained in the Emperor Napoleon's Mexican mail. There was always a discrepancy between the reports of Dano, the French Minister and Bazaine, while the unofficial sources to which Napoleon was so prone to listen painted a far gloomier picture than either the minister or the Marshal would have cared to present. In the general confusion, all that emerged was that the French nation as a whole was not prepared to make any fresh sacrifices for Mexico. '*Il faut en finir,*' was the general refrain. The Empress Eugénie, who at the beginning had looked upon herself as the guardian angel of the Mexican expedition, was now the first to press for the withdrawal of the troops, picking on the mistakes committed by the unfortunate Maximilian to justify this volte-face. She accused him of having quarrelled with the Church (forgetting that he had only been carrying out the liberal policy advocated by Napoleon), of being in arrears with the payment of his debts (forgetting that only a fraction of the loans had ever found their way to Mexico). An unfortunate remark by the Empress Carlota in one of her letters that 'the money was there to be spent' gave Eugénie an excellent opportunity of castigating their extravagance.

But her husband was reluctant to renounce the enterprise which had cost so many millions and so many lives. In a desperate attempt to disengage himself from his commitments, he wrote to Maximilian as early as September 1865 of 'the advantage it would be to everybody if Your Majesty were to use your Austrian troops for the organization of a proper army. In this way I would be able to withdraw the greater part of my troops which would remove all pretext for America's complaints.' No explanation was given as to why America should object less to Austrian than to French troops, or why Franz Josef should suddenly consent to doubling or even tripling the number of Austrian volunteers, when Bombelles had with difficulty persuaded him to allow further recruitment to make up the losses in the original force of a little over six thousand men. It is difficult to grasp Napoleon's meaning when he wrote that 'a predominantly Austrian army would give the Mexican government an appearance of stability and contribute to establishing confidence both at home and abroad'. It was a letter written by a tired, sick man, snatching at any straw to get out of an impossible situation. In the last year, a constant nagging pain, caused partly by his gall bladder, partly, some said, as a result of his sexual excesses, had robbed him of his energy and made him prematurely old.

There is no doubt that the deteriorating health of the two leading protagonists in the Mexican drama had a considerable effect on the course of events. Just as Napoleon was no longer the man of destiny of the coup d'etat of 1852, so Maximilian was no longer the brilliant liberal-minded Prince whose energy and initiative in Italy had earned him the grudging admiration of Cavour. The Mexican climate, the high altitude and sudden changes in temperature, the heavily-spiced, indigestible food, and tropical fruits, were making ravages on an already delicate constitution. His liver also suffered from the fact that he had taken to drinking large quantities of champagne and sherry to give him energy, and it was only later that a French doctor forbade him all forms of alcohol other than red wine. Observers noted that, though naturally elegant, he was becoming increasingly careless in his dress, preferring loose, comfortable clothes, wearing embroidered native slippers in the house. The strict training of his youth had taught him to control his quick impulsive temperament, and Blasio recounts that only a frown or pained look of disapproval showed when he was angry. But now his moods were becoming more and more unpredictable, alternating from the deepest melancholy to the wildest optimism. His tongue, which had always been sarcastic, became even sharper and his natural kindliness was tempered by irritation. His dislike of Bazaine, which had become almost an obsession, vented itself in supercilious and sarcastic remarks at his expense, and his reply to Napoleon's letter of September 14, which only reached him at the end of December, was a long and bitter tirade against the Marshal.

After flattering the French Emperor to the extent of referring to his totally irrational plan regarding Austrian troops as being 'as happy an idea as all those which emanate from Your Majesty's lofty intelligence', he proceeded to reiterate his accusations against Bazaine. The Marshal was accused of 'carrying out a policy so sinister that people are beginning to say that the object is to prove the incapacity of the Mexican government and to draw Your Majesty into adopting measures of extreme severity on the pretext that the Mexican government is incapable of governing itself'. Maximilian went on to refer to the rumour, already believed by Dano, that the Marshal was planning to make Mexico into a French protectorate under his command. 'It is only a rumour,' he wrote – but he nevertheless passed it on for Napoleon's information.

The letter was in part an accusation against 'those by whom Your Majesty has not always been served as well as he ought to have been' and partly an attempt to justify his own mistakes, but above all it was a desperate plea to an ally whom he still refused to believe would ever desert him: 'For some time past, the European press has been hinting that Your Majesty is contemplating a public announcement to the effect that, in a short time, you will be withdrawing your troops from Mexico. . . . I feel bound to tell Your Majesty that such a declaration would undo in a day all the work painfully accomplished in the past few years, and that the announcement of such a measure, combined with the refusal of the United States to recognize my government, would be enough to cause the collapse of all respectable peoples' hopes and destroy all public confidence in the future.'

This highly confidential letter was entrusted to Colonel Loysel, of his military cabinet, who was going on a short leave to France. The boat which took Colonel Loysel to Europe crossed in mid-Atlantic with the French packet-steamer *L'Imperatrice Eugénie*, having on board a certain Baron Saillard bound on a special mission to Mexico, with two autographed letters from his sovereign – one for the Emperor Maximilian, the other for Marshal Bazaine.

24

The Idyll of Cuernavaca

In the winter of 1865–6, so full of political disappointments and disillusions, Maximilian spent a few of the happiest months of his life in the seclusion of the Borda Gardens of Cuernavaca. 'Here we lead a really tropical life, surrounded by handsome, friendly and loyal natives.' This one sentence and a few poems written in the romantic vein are the only clue the Emperor gives of the romance which links his name with that of a beautiful Indian girl, the wife of one of his gardeners. Most of the novelists and historians writing of the Mexican Empire, with the exception of the correct and circumspect Count Corti, give credence to the legend. Colonel Blanchot, who, as a young captain on Bazaine's staff was always ready to tilt his lance in favour of the Empress, writes in his memoirs. 'Cuernavaca was poisoned for the Empress by the knowledge that, in those enchanted bowers dwelt an Armida who had cast a spell over her husband's volatile affections.' Others repeated the gossip in less poetic language and the Emperor's Hungarian valet confided to Blasio that there was a small door in the garden wall, giving directly into the Emperor's apartments, through which a nocturnal visitor could pass unseen by the guards on duty.

That Maximilian indulged in a passing liaison with a beautiful Indian girl is in all probability true. He had always been fascinated by the strange and exotic, and a gentle, sensitive creature, living among the birds and flowers of a tropical garden in blissful ignorance of politics or the outside world, would have been a welcome contrast to a forceful and energetic wife. But the legend goes further and says that Concepción Sedano gave birth to a son in August 1866, and died from grief a year later on hearing of the Emperor's execution. The child is said to have been taken to France under the protection of the Bringas family, the wealthy *hacendados* in whose house the Emperor always stayed on his visits to Orizaba. Nearly fifty years later, during the First World War, a man claiming to be the son of Concepción Sedano by the Emperor Maximilian turned up in Paris, where he was accused of spying for the

Germans and sentenced to death. The story provides an ironic and bitter sequel to a tragedy already so full of rumours and suppositions. Was Maximilian Reichstadt's son and was the man who met his death before a firing squad at Vincennes the greatgrandson of Napoleon Bonaparte? The former is the easier to believe, even though all proofs are lacking. The latter is no more than a rumour which was fostered by the late Emperor's enemies without any foundation of truth. We hear that the man who claimed to be Maximilian's son wore his hair and beard in the style of the late Emperor and affected a regal manner, but in the reports of his trial there is no mention of his having been of mixed blood, a fact not likely to have been ignored either by the journalists or the police. Maximilian visited Cuernavaca for the last time in September 1866, and stayed for no more than a few days. Surely he would have prolonged his stay if Concepción Sedano had been the mother of his new-born son. Nor is there any hint of his ever having confided in the few faithful friends who were with him till the end. Neither Blasio nor Prince Salm have anything to say on the subject, though the former is not always discreet in discussing the Emperor's numerous love affairs. The more conscious Maximilian became of his declining virility, the more anxious he became to assert his masculinity, flaunting his admiration for beautiful women, indulging in open and often blatant liaisons, which caused pain and unhappiness to his wife.

During the first months in Mexico, he appears to have cherished the hope that the invigorating air of the High Sierras would strengthen his constitution, and in the brief period of their second honeymoon, both he and Charlotte still discussed their hopes of having an heir. The Empress once confided to Madame de Courcy that she could sympathize with and understand the Indian women who visited the shrine of the Madonna of Guadalupe, who, in their eyes, possessed the powers of the ancient Goddess of Fertility. 'To have a child, after all, is the natural and legitimate desire of every woman,' – but Charlotte's own pilgrimages to the Madonna of Guadalupe were of no avail, and Maximilian's adoption of the little Agustín Iturbide publicized her failure to the world. The affection with which her husband treated the child, who now shared all his holidays at Cuernavaca, added to her unhappiness. It is curious that she should have put the blame on herself rather than on Max. The acute depression from which she suffered ever since her return from Yucatan bred strange delusions in her mind, among them the idea which later grew into an obsession, that Maximilian was only waiting to rid himself of a barren wife. Charlotte, who was the one person who should have known the rumour to be untrue, believed her husband to be responsible for the pregnancy of the gardener's wife, and the belief acted as a poison on her nervous system. She grew silent and brooding, and it became an effort for her to smile.

Yet Max had never been more loving and considerate with her than now, grateful for all she had accomplished in Yucatan, sympathizing in her grief over her father's death. Visitors to Cuernavaca describe what sounds like an idyllic relationship. The atmosphere was friendly and relaxed, with a total absence of court etiquette, the Emperor receiving his guests in the rôle of a country gentleman, the hostess looking young and charming in a white crinoline with black mourning ribbons and a bunch of fresh flowers at the waist. Both Emperor and Empress enjoyed bathing in the pool and boating on the lake, and Charlotte and her ladies spent many hours searching for rare butterflies under the supervision of the Court naturalist, Maximilian's beloved old Dr Billimek, who had accompanied him from Miramar. José Blasio has left a description of La Borda *Quinta* as it was in the days of Maximilian – a series of pavilions giving out on patios and colonnaded galleries, of which the walls were covered in vines and orchids, while large tubs of flowering plants, tanks full of ornamental fish and cages of many-coloured birds filled both patios and verandahs – the perfect retreat for a nature lover and a poet, but not for a nervous and suspicious woman, tormented by the fear that both her marriage and her crown were in danger.

La Borda was not Maximilian's only retreat at Cuernavaca. On the outskirts of the town, in the little village of Acapazingo, the Emperor had acquired a small coffee plantation, where he was building what he called an 'Indian chalet', with a water garden surrounded by olive and orange groves. He made no secret of his plans to Charlotte, but he also made it clear that this was a place where he wanted to be alone and, by now, Charlotte had learnt to resign herself to his caprices. We hear of her visiting Acapazingo in his absence, but she was not present when he celebrated the laying of the first foundations by holding a party for his neighbours, 'those gentle, simple people who give me an unquestioning affection which is dear to me'. Did Charlotte suspect Acapazingo to be an abode of love? According to the gossip of her ladies-in-waiting, she took an almost morbid interest in the progress of the building and always kept up the pretence of sharing in her husband's interests.

Judging by their correspondence, Charlotte and Maximilian were rarely in Cuernavaca at the same time. Her success in Yucatan had restored the Emperor's confidence in his wife's diplomatic talents, and Charlotte spent many weeks alone in the capital, trying to grapple with a situation which was rapidly getting out of hand. The *guerrilleros* who terrorized the countryside had doubled in strength and the sixty-kilo-metre road between Cuernavaca and the capital had to be constantly patrolled by police. A tragic incident in the early spring, in which the Belgian deputation sent by King Leopold II to announce his accession was attacked by bandits on the heights of Rio Frio, barely twenty miles from the capital, made a bad impression in Europe among those who still believed in the future of the Mexican Empire. It had particularly unfavourable repercussions in Belgium, for the one fatal casualty was young Baron Huart, ordnance officer of the Count of Flanders and a personal friend of the Prince. Maximilian did all in his power to help by hurrying in person to the scene of the incident, taking with him his own physician to look after the wounded. But the reports of the Belgian Minister spoke of 'criminal negligence' on the part of the Mexi-can authorities, who had not taken adequate precautions to ensure the protection of their foreign guests.

The tragedy of Rio Frio, followed by the announcement that the Belgian Ministry of Defence had closed the recruiting lists for Mexico, led to a growing estrangement between Charlotte and her family, thereby adding to her loneliness and misery. Yet, in a letter to her old governess, she still insisted that life in Mexico, for all its difficulties and disappointments, was preferable to the '*dolce far niente*' of Miramar. The task they had undertaken was difficult but not impossible. 'I am not of a nature,' she writes, 'to turn back because there are a few dark clouds in the sky and a few rocks ahead. Anything is better than to sit contemplating the sea at Miramar, with nothing to do but watch the years go by.'

It is only in her letters to Max that one perceives the growing signs of a mental derangement. She writes from Chapultepec on a cold, rainy day in March, 'feeling melancholy and depressed, as if there was nothing left in life which could give me either comfort or solace'. Her loathing of Mexico City and its inhabitants had assumed abnormal proportions. 'The capital is a forum for the lowest passions which, added to xeno-phobia and wounded national pride, and the filth and corruption of centuries, makes life in the town really dangerous both for the govern-ment and inhabitants.' One senses an underlying bitterness in reply to one of Max's letters from Cuernavaca: 'I am glad you are happy in your earthly paradise, but, for me, there is no longer any paradise on earth.'

Maximilian had a gift, in common with many poets, of being able to shut out the world and its problems and give himself entirely up to the contemplation of nature. He would spend hours bird-watching with Dr Billimek, in planning a water garden and in writing to Europe for rare plants and seeds. The worse the political situation, the more necessary it became for him to escape into a dream world, and it is characteristic that one of the last orders received at Miramar was for two thousand nightingales, which were already on their way to Mexico when he was captured at Querétaro.

But one is at a loss to understand Maximilian's attitude to his wife. For all his apparent devotion, he appears to have been singularly unperceptive to the moods and symptoms which had already been noted by her attendants. He dismissed her melancholia as no more than nervous indigestion and told her that the best cure was to 'go for long walks and to work very hard, for all these complaints come from the liver or the stomach'. Was he being deliberately obtuse? Had Charlotte had mental breakdowns in the past, and was this casual attitude dictated by the doctors? A letter written to him in the middle of March must have warned him that she was on the verge of a breakdown. It begins quite rationally in discussing the appointment of a new minister, then tails off into a series of incoherent and inconsequential sentences. 'I have sent Alexandra [the Princess of Wales] some photographs of Chapultepec. I think you should send Victoria a decoration, so that you can get the Garter. God have mercy on our souls in Purgatory. I think it is going to snow. If only it's cool for you there [presumably Purgatory]. The Princess Josefa has had a cold and has been here yesterday. Also she does not find it very gay.' This can hardly be described as the letter of a normal woman, but for the time being such letters were rare. Those written in the following weeks were all perfectly clear and rational, with only here and there a sentence which denoted a troubled mind. We know that Charlotte had always been prone to melancholia. Even at Miramar, she complained of 'black moods' when she had nothing worth while to do. Throughout her life, periods of an almost hysterical religious fervour contrasted with what was normally a somewhat critical disapproval of the shibboleths and superstitions of the Church. Even at her wedding, the Prince of Saxe-Weimar had observed that 'the young Princess had a queer look in her eyes'.

337

The 'queer look' is painfully evident in a portrait which hangs today in a house in St Angel on the outskirts of Mexico City. It was painted at the time when the Empress Charlotte was in mourning for her father and the black clothes accentuate the bitterness in the pale, rather heavy face with the dark, haunted eyes – a face so sad that the owners have relegated it to a corridor rather than hang it in a living room, where it cast an atmosphere of gloom. Only Maximilian seems to have ignored what Colonel Blanchot referred to as the 'farouche and brooding silences with which the Empress isolated herself from the world'. But one must remember that Maximilian had grown up in a family where eccentric behaviour and nervous breakdowns were so prevalent that they were usually quietly and tactfully ignored, nor would he ever have thought of blaming himself for what the Colonel openly said was at the root of Charlotte's troubles. She was an ardent, full-blooded young woman of twenty-six, humiliated at being a deserted and neglected wife, unconsciously rebelling against an unnatural life. With their derisive songs to the theme of 'Mama Carlota', the *Juaristi* had found a way of wounding her as effectively as if they had used the bows and arrows of the Indians, and the rumour of the pregnancy of the gardener's wife at Cuernavaca added poison to their barbs.

Charlotte's mental delusion, the gradual clouding of her mind, has at times been attributed to a dose of poisoned mushrooms (*totoache*) having been administered to her in Yucatan – a poison said to be fatal when taken in large doses and in a smaller quantity apt to cause hallucinations and madness. But Charlotte was already in a state of mind when there was no need of poisoned mushrooms to turn her mad. Fears for the future of the Empire, the crushing burden of her own responsibility in having forced her husband to accept the crown, added to her yearnings and her failure as a woman, were sufficient to upset her mental equilibrium, making her believe a rumour which in ordinary circumstances she would have ignored, and maybe influencing her to act out of character.

In her loneliness and misery, it was natural she should turn to a compatriot with whom she could talk of Belgium and of her father. Alfred Van der Smissen, who was stationed at Toluca, in the neighbourhood of Mexico City, had come to condole with her over King Leopold's death. For all his arrogance and truculence, Van der Smissen must have been an attractive personality, brave and dashing, uncompromising and loyal and, what to Charlotte must have been the most attractive quality of all, passionately devoted to the memory of her father. Both Bazaine and Maximilian found his quarrelsome disposition more of a liability than a help, while his contempt of the Mexicans was too outspoken to be tolerated. His opinion of his military colleagues is summed up in a letter: 'None of you in Belgium can have any idea of what the Mexican army consists – five or six thousand bandits, ex-muleteers or baker boys who have become colonels overnight. Even Mendez, who is one of the best, was twelve years ago a draper's assistant in Mexico City, had up for stealing handkerchiefs. Recruits are forcibly conscripted and led into barracks between two rows of bayonets, so it is not surprising if the poor devils desert *en masse* the minute they find themselves in a field of sugar cane where they are able to hide. There is no doubt that the Mexican Empire will disintegrate the day the French army embarks.' Charlotte shared his opinion and never for a moment deluded herself that the Empire could survive without the French. Van der Smissen's hard and inflexible character, his realistic outlook which reminded her of her father, must have been a welcome contrast to Max's impractical daydreams.

Colonel Blanchot writes in his memoirs of the neglected young Empress spending solitary evenings on Lake Chalco, being rowed in a canoe among the *chinampas*, those rafts sewn with vegetables and flowers on which the Indians market their produce in the capital. But there are rumours which suggested that the Empress was not always as solitary as Colonel Blanchot believed, and that on more than one occasion Alfred Van der Smissen acted as the military escort without whom she would not have dared to venture out at night. Two months later, the Belgian Legion commanded by Van der Smissen was ordered north to San Luis Potosi and this time it was said that the order came from Maximilian rather than from Bazaine.

The Empress was in Mexico City, the Emperor in Cuernavaca, when Napoleon's letter dropped like a bombshell out of a clear sky. It had taken many weeks of heart-searchings and hesitations before the French Emperor could bring himself to renounce an enterprise on which he had staked so much and from which he still hoped to salvage some lasting benefit for France, to compensate for the appalling waste of money and incalculable loss of prestige. He could not afford a failure for the whole fragile papier-mâché edifice of the Second Empire rested on success. It was difficult to admit even to himself that the evacuation of Mexico was dictated by a fear of America as much as by the situation at home. Washington had now turned the tables on him and was playing the game he had played in 1862, profiting by the political difficulties in Europe to put pressure on his government. His offer to withdraw his troops in return for American recognition of the Mexican Empire had been scornfully refused. With the mounting tension in Europe, and the imminence of an Austro-Prussian war, Mr Bigelow's visits to the Quai d'Orsay were becoming more frequent and his language more peremptory, while on the Rio Grande the United States army no longer even tried to keep up a pretence of neutrality, and the sacking of the port of Bagdad by a horde of drunken negro soldiers who terrorized the population and murdered most of the Imperialist garrison, went practically unpunished by the authorities. A strongly-worded protest from the French captain in command of the unit stationed at the mouth of the river met with an insolent reply. Many years later, General Sheridan admitted in his memoirs: 'Juarez would never have been victorious without the help of the United States.'

The French officers, brave veterans of the Crimea, resented the loss of face, the humiliating withdrawal before the American threat and put the blame on Bazaine, not knowing that he was merely carrying out the policy of his Imperial master. Only someone as supple and as accommodating as the Marshal could have succeeded in coping with Napoleon's vacillating policy. One moment he was ordering him to strengthen the Foreign Legion (which according to the Treaty of Miramar was to remain in Mexico for the next three years) by incorporating the Austrian and Belgian volunteers in its ranks, all of whom would be paid by France. The next moment, he was urging him to hurry on with the formation of an efficient native army, which Bazaine had neglected to do for the past two years and for which there was now neither money nor equipment. At one time, he was ordering him to do all in his power to consolidate Maximilian's position before the departure of the army. Another time, he was advising him to come to an agreement with any of the more reputable Republican leaders, other than Juarez, so as to safeguard French interests in the event of a debacle.

Bazaine's behaviour was as devious as that of his master. He knew that the Mexican Empire was doomed, but he persisted in assuring Napoleon that the military situation was 'as favourable as possible, so long as the United States remains neutral' and that 'the forces at Maximilian's disposal after the departure of the French will be amply sufficient'. The efficiency of his spies had given him access to all the Mexican

Emperor's private correspondence with Napoleon and he recommended his master 'to act independently of the Mexican government, whose ill-will arising out of unjustified complaints, is not far removed from ingratitude'.

Bazaine in Mexico, Fould and Drouyn de Lhuys in Paris, even his own wife were pressing Napoleon to desert the Emperor Maximilian, but still he hesitated before taking the final step and the letter brought to Maximilian by Baron Saillard at the end of 1865 was a half-hearted attempt to justify his action. 'It is not without pain', he wrote, 'that I find myself forced to come to a decision and put a definite term to the French occupation. The difficulties caused me by the Mexican question, the impossibility of getting any further subsidies from the Legislative Assembly for the upkeep of an expeditionary force, and Your Majesty's own statement that you are unable to contribute to its maintenance, leave me with no other choice than to withdraw my army. The evacuation, which will begin as soon as possible, will be done gradually and in such a way as not to upset public opinion or endanger the interests we both have at heart. . . . The departure of the French troops may cause Your Majesty a temporary embarrassment but it will have the advantage of removing all pretexts of interference from the United States.'

The idyllic life at Cuernavaca had lulled Maximilian into a false sense of security. The progress made by Langlais in tackling the financial problems had encouraged a certain optimism. He had always believed in the French Emperor's personal loyalty, and however much he may have resented the tutelage of France, he was still under the spell of Napoleon's personality. All the mistakes committed by the French were laid at the door of Bazaine and he had hoped that his last 'frank and open note' would result in the Marshal's dismissal. But Napoleon's letter made no secret of the fact that he was preparing to go back on his word, however impossible it might be for Maximilian to believe that 'the wisest monarch of the century and the most powerful nation of the world would give in to the Yankees in this undignified fashion'. Disillusion and wounded pride dictated the reply which Prince Metternich defined as 'in every way worthy of a Hapsburg'. While reproaching Napoleon for breaking the solemn treaties he had signed only two years before, Maximilian assured him with a scathing politeness that he was too much his friend to wish to cause him embarrassment. 'I propose, therefore,' he wrote, 'that you withdraw your troops immediately from the Mexican continent, while I, for my part, guided by my honour, will try to defend my Empire with the help of my new countrymen.'

Felix Eloin, who appears to have been still in his master's confidence, took once more the road to Europe and on arrival in Paris was received at once at the Tuileries, but the audience lacked the cordiality of the previous year. The French Emperor, who had visibly aged, looked nervous and ill at ease. He had already read the letter which, in Hidalgo's absence, had been presented by Metternich. It could not have been pleasant reading for him, though he assured Eloin that he took 'no offence at the tone, for it was only natural that the Emperor was annoyed. But there were certain circumstances over which one had no control.' Napoleon sought refuge from his own embarrassment by blaming Maximilian for not having carried out his financial commitments and he quoted the adverse reports received from Mexico. When Eloin tried to exonerate his Emperor by referring to the strained relations between him and the commander-in-chief, which may have influenced these reports, Napoleon dismissed his arguments with a frown. The interview was cut short by the arrival of the Empress Eugénie who, after making some perfunctory enquiries after the health of Their Mexican Majesties, said that the weather was so beautiful that she had come to take her husband for a walk. Eloin was dismissed without Napoleon either offering his hand or giving him his 'habitual smile'.

The same glacial atmosphere prevailed in all political circles. No one wanted to hear anything more of Mexico. The eyes of France were on the Rhine and many blamed the Mexican fiasco for the present weakness of French policy in not coming out openly on the side of Austria. The atmosphere in Belgium was as frigid as in Paris, and Eloin found the new King too busy to receive him, while in military circles there was already talk of recalling the volunteers. Eloin blamed Maximilian's envoys in Europe, and in particular Hidalgo, who had been so anxious to ingratiate himself at the Tuileries that he had forgotten his duties to his own country. The vain little *boulevardier* who had played at politics for his own personal ambition cut a sorry figure when he was forced to return to Mexico after an absence of nearly twenty years. Terrified of bandits, he appeared before his Emperor armed to the teeth and, when invited to go out riding, was horrified to find that Maximilian was only accompanied by a groom. The Emperor might laugh at his cowardice but he was also disgusted. The two self-styled 'creators of the Mexican Empire', Hidalgo and Gutierrez, were now showing themselves in their true colours. The latter, who had always been such a great 'aristocrat', never asking anything for himself but only for his sons, was now pressing his claims for compensation on *haciendas* alleged to have been looted during the Civil War and, while continuing to write to the Emperor hundred-page letters of admonition and advice, was intriguing against him with the Mexican clergy and showing his private correspondence both to Napoleon and to Cardinal Antonelli.

Wherever Maximilian turned, there seemed to be someone ready to betray him. His new friends, whether French or Mexican, were either recalled to France or, as in the case of his favourite minister Ramirez, dismissed on the insistency of Bazaine. The Mexican climate had also taken its toll of victims – the most regretted of all being the devoted and efficient Langlais, who died suddenly of a heart attack on the eve of preparing his budget.

Meanwhile, the military situation was deteriorating daily. Bazaine was beginning to carry out the systematic evacuation of the northern states. On the Pacific coast, Mazatlan, the only port still held by the Imperialists, was rendered useless as all the surrounding country was in the hands of insurgents. Tomás Mejía was beleaguered in the Gulf port of Matamoros, already lost and regained half a dozen times, and was sending frantic telegrams for money with which to pay his troops. The whole of the country between Matamoros and Tampico was virtually controlled by the rebels, and merchandise sent under military convoy was being continually attacked and plundered. Maximilian's Empire was visibly shrinking and even the towns on the highways to Vera Cruz were attacked, but the hardest blow of all was when Austria, in response to pressure from the United States, suspended the recruitment of volunteers. Of the four thousand due to leave in 1866, two thousand were on the point of embarking at Trieste when the order came for them to return to barracks. From the other side of the ocean, with letters taking more than a month to arrive from Europe, Maximilian can have had no conception of Austria's perilous situation in the spring of 1866. Not even the most generous of brothers would have been ready to embroil his country in a conflict with America on the eve of a European war, and Franz Josef was far from being the most generous of brothers. If he had consented to increase the number of volunteers, it was because he was interested in keeping Maximilian in Mexico for as long as possible. But whatever his motives, he did not deserve his brother's bitter reproaches. 'If Austria had been loyal,' wrote Maximilian to Karl Ludwig, 'she would at once have embarked the troops,

343

but such a cowardly and faithless government could not be expected to behave otherwise.'

Austria's desertion shattered his last hopes. The happiness he had experienced during the winter months at Cuernavaca, the brief moment of euphoria in the early spring, gave way to a deep depression accentuating the stomach pains and dysentery from which he now suffered almost continually. Abandoned on every side, he felt he had no longer the health or stamina to cope with this labour of Sysiphus too heavy to be borne and, for the first time, he began to listen to the few loyal friends who counselled abdication. But at the first hint of abdication, Charlotte came out of her retirement, geared for battle, straining every nerve, throwing the full force of her powerful personality into the struggle to preserve their crown.

25

Charlotte prevents abdication

The spring of 1866 brought the Empress nothing but sorrow. Her beloved grandmother, the ex-Queen Marie Amélie of France, died in England at the end of March, barely three months after her father, and a flood of childhood memories served to confuse the present issues in her unhappy and distracted mind. All her life she had been haunted by the fear of abdication, ever since that dreadful morning at Laeken, when gathered round the breakfast table, the Belgian Royal Family had heard the news of her grandmother's flight from Paris. Her mother's slow decline dated from that day, and King Leopold had always been bitter rather than sympathetic when talking of his father-in-law's abdication. Charlotte had been brought up to believe that Louis Philippe had compromised both himself and his dynasty by giving up his throne, thereby discrediting his government after a prosperous reign of over eighteen years. She refused to contemplate either for herself or for Max the life that was led by the Orléans princes in England, condemned either to an idle, purposeless existence, or to service under a foreign flag. It would be a thousand times preferable to die amidst the débris of the Empire, rather than to return to Europe as ridiculous failures to endure the pity or the mockery of the Austrian Court.

Her reaction to Napoleon's letter of 15 January had been far more violent than that of her husband, for unlike him, she had no illusions that the Empire could survive without the help of the French. In her anger she had refused to receive Baron Saillard, thereby adding to the grievances of the Empress Eugénie, who seized on every opportunity to complain of alleged acts of discourtesy against the French. The correspondence between the two Empresses had degenerated into a series of mutual recriminations, and superficial forms of politeness barely masked growing irritation and annoyance. By the end of May, the correspondence which had begun with so much enthusiasm had died a natural death.

Where Charlotte deluded herself was in the belief that Napoleon could not afford to give up the Mexican expedition. King Leopold had always led her to believe that they had done the French Emperor an immense service by accepting the Mexican crown. Already at Miramar, one heard her proudly reminding General Frossard that it was they who were 'helping Napoleon out of his difficulties', and the same note of presumption is apparent throughout her correspondence: 'We must make use of the French, otherwise what is the use of them being here?' And one recognizes her hand in the extraordinary instructions given to poor Juan Almonte, who was to succeed Hidalgo in Paris.

Only someone as compromised as Almonte, whom the Liberals had never forgiven for the rôle he had played during the Regency, would have undertaken a mission which he must have known would fail. But it was a chance of getting himself and his family out of Mexico and, on arrival in Paris, he was openly congratulated by his friends on having got away in time, which was hardly the usual way of congratulating an envoy from an allied power. Meanwhile, Hidalgo had found life in Mexico so little to his liking that he secretly decamped one night, without taking leave of the Emperor, and returned to Europe to live as a private citizen with a grievance, maintaining that Maximilian, whom he had systematically betrayed, still owed him a living.

Eugénie was always saying that 'the Mexican sovereigns demanded the impossible', but the memorandum entrusted to Almonte exceeded the bounds of reality and common sense. It enclosed the draft of a convention which went far beyond the terms of the Treaty of Miramar, demanding nothing less than the retention of French troops for an indefinite period, until Mexico was completely pacified, and a French fleet to be put at the Mexican government's disposal to protect both the Pacific and the Atlantic coastlines. A reduction in the size of the expeditionary force was allowed for, on the understanding that Marshal Bazaine, whose rank would then be too important for the post, should be recalled to France and a general of lesser standing appointed in his place who would take his orders directly from the Emperor of Mexico. Maximilian went so far as to pledge himself to continue honouring his financial obligations, but for the time being the French Treasury was asked to continue to advance sums for military expenditure till the

346

country was sufficiently organized to permit the collection of regular revenues.

It is not surprising that this document evoked incredulity, hilarity and anger, or that Napoleon's reply was as short and as discourteous as a letter to a fellow sovereign would permit. He wrote: 'General Almonte has acquainted me with Your Majesty's ideas, and I was already aware from the memorandum of the considerable discrepancy between my judgment and yours. In order to clear up the outstanding issues once and for all, I have caused a note to be drawn up, which I recommend to Your Majesty's serious consideration. I beg you to be assured of the sentiment of my highest esteem and sincere friendship and I remain Your Majesty's good brother, Napoleon.' There may have been some excuse for a letter written in a moment of exasperation, but there was no excuse for the memorandum, dictated and compiled by a group of hard-headed politicians, of whom Achille Fould was the leading spirit, and which was so cruel and so unfair that it destroyed Napoleon's future reputation as effectively as it destroyed the last hope of survival of the Mexican Empire.

All the mistakes committed in the past years were laid at Maximilian's door. France could only consent to a new convention if she were assured of certain guarantees, such as full control over the custom houses and one half of their revenues in payment of outstanding claims. If the Mexican government were prepared to accept these terms, then France, on her side, would abide by her engagements, the Foreign Legion would remain at the disposal of the Emperor Maximilian for the next three years and Marshal Bazaine would be authorized to advance half a million francs a month out of the army Treasury towards the equipment of the new Mexican army. The evacuation of the French troops would be carried out gradually and in such a way as to preserve law and order in the country. Should, however, the Mexican government refuse, then France would consider herself free from all her obligations. All troops, including the Foreign Legion, would be immediately embarked and all payments immediately suspended.

Even Dano and Bazaine were surprised at the harshness of the terms, which deprived the Mexican government of three-quarters of its principal source of revenue, twenty-four per cent of the customs receipts being already earmarked in settlement of the English debt. Without these revenues, it would be impossible for the Empire to survive, its last lifeline would be cut and the Emperor reduced to the position of a pensioner of France. Instructions given by Maximilian to Almonte may have been unreal and absurd, the desperate gesture of a gambler staking his all on a last throw, encouraged by a wife whose judgment was distorted by a growing megalomania. But however foolish, however unreasonable, it did not deserve the brutality and the finality of the French reply, which at last opened Maximilian's eyes to the fact that Napoleon was no longer interested either in him or in Mexico but only in how much money he could recoup before the last of his soldiers embarked at Vera Cruz. In the cold light of disillusion, abdication seemed to be the only possible and the only honourable solution; but Maximilian was reckoning without Charlotte.

The news of Queen Marie Amélie's death, which reached Mexico at the beginning of April, had reduced Charlotte again to a state of nervous collapse, with a recurrence of the terrible headaches from which she had been suffering for the past year. The doctors forbade her all mental activity and sent her to recuperate at Cuernavaca, where the state of her mind may be judged by her letters to Max, pathetic little notes so different from her usual forceful style, while his letters in return carefully avoided mentioning any political news which might excite or disturb her. One finds her writing of simple everyday things: of a humming-bird alighting on a branch of datura that grows outside her window; of the rare butterflies she has caught for Dr Billimek's collection; of how her favourite lady-in-waiting, a daughter of old Gutierrez, is trying to teach her to play a *habanera* on the mandolin. She attends a Mass for her grandmother in the cathedral of Cuernavaca, where the congregation are mostly Indians 'who may lack crinolines but who have more religion in their hearts than other people, and at least know how to pray. ... If one sees the Mexican people in places where they are still unspoilt, then there still appears to be some hope for them.' She is lost and lonely in a place which her husband loves so much. When she wanders through his rooms, she finds there 'the spirit of the old poet', and she askes him in a plaintive way, 'Are you not coming here at all? All nature is waiting for you to conjure it to a new and more vivid form.'

But Max was kept busy in the capital, desperately trying to organize the Mexican army with the half-hearted co-operation of Bazaine; his task made all the more difficult by the unwillingness of the Austrian and Belgian volunteers to be merged into the Foreign Legion under the orders of a French general. General Thun and his staff were threatening resignation, Van der Smissen, who had joined his regiment in the north to man the new defence line around San Luis Potosi, warned him that the Belgians were on the verge of mutiny. The Emperor himself was ill and overworked, trying to revive his flagging spirits by drinking excessive quantities of champagne and sherry. 'It is not very cheerful here,' he writes, 'but everything is in working order.' He still found time to superintend the building of the new National Theatre, to collect the archeological treasures of Mexico under one roof in the old Palacio de la Minerias, to lay out a wider and more spacious Alameda and to plant the Zócalo with shady trees. The road from Chapultepec into the city, known as the Calzado del Emperador, was completed, and, in the evenings, already crowded with carriages. However precarious might be his throne, however bankrupt his finances, his Wittelsbach blood still urged him to continue to embellish his capital.

By the end of May, the Empress was sufficiently recovered to return to Mexico City, where she made her first public appearance on the feast of Corpus Christi, deliberately wearing a white crinoline covered in diamonds, to give the lie to a rumour that she had sent her jewels for safe custody in England. This was only one of the many rumours circulating round the capital, where every second person was a spy and no story was too fantastic to be believed. The native population lived in fear and uncertainty of the future, while panic spread among the European colony following the news that the town of Hermosillo in the state of Sonora had been captured by the dissidents and every one of the thirty-seven French inhabitants brutally murdered. The reaction against Marshal Bazaine was on this occasion so violent that for several days he did not dare to venture out into the streets and he was openly accused of being more concerned over the health of his wife who was expecting a child than over the safety of his own nationals, whose interests the French army had ostensibly come to Mexico to protect.

Napoleon's ultimatum arrived in Mexico on 28 June, at a time when Maximilian's spirits were at their lowest ebb, and abdication appeared to be the only way out of a hopeless impasse. But the word was barely whispered before Charlotte intervened, all her energy and vitality revived at this new threat to her future, roused out of her depression to make a last superhuman effort which, in the end, was to cost her her sanity. At first, her arguments made little headway with the Emperor who, acting on the advice of Captain Detroyat and Captain Pierron, two well-intentioned and devoted young Frenchmen attached to his secretariat, was already planning to announce his abdication in a public proclamation. But her husband's momentary weakness in making a decision taken on the advice of two young Frenchmen, probably acting on the orders of Bazaine, was not going to deprive Charlotte of the crown for which they had already sacrificed so much. She herself would go to Paris and confront Napoleon with his broken promises, reminding him that an Emperor cannot afford to break his word. She would go to Rome and throw herself at the feet of the Holy Father and convince him that they were better Christians and more loyal champions of the Church than the bishops whose privileges he upheld – and that, without an Empire, Mexico would again relapse into anarchy and atheism. She would open the eyes of European statesmen to the growing menace of the United States and force the bankers to open their coffers in defence of a free and independent Mexico.

Maximilian listened and wavered. Common sense fought with pride. He dreaded the ridicule of failure, of returning to Europe like a battered Don Quixote, with mud-bespattered armour and a broken lance, which was how the French radical Jules Favre had described him in one of his most scathing speeches. Charlotte brought every possible pressure to bear. When her passionate pleading failed, she resorted to the written word, presenting her arguments in a long, disjointed memorandum, full of empty rhetorical phrases and far-fetched historical analogues. 'Abdication,' she wrote, 'is only excusable in old men and idiots. It is not permissible in a young man of thirty-four, full of life and hope for the future, for sovereignty is the most precious of all possessions.' From the moment one assumed responsibility for the destiny of a nation, one did so at one's own risk, she argued. One did not abandon a post before the enemy, so why should one abandon a crown? Both Charles x of France and her own grandfather had ruined themselves by abdication, which amounted to pronouncing sentence on oneself, labelling oneself as incompetent. With her own strange logic, she wrote: 'Emperors do not give themselves up. So long as there is an Emperor, there is still an Empire, even if he has no more than six feet of earth belonging to him, for the Empire is nothing without the Emperor.' All unconsciously she spoke the truth, for the Empire of Mexico was nothing but the Emperor – an Empire created out of Maximilian's illusions and ambitions. Unfortunately, he had still sufficient illusions to listen to a woman whose judgment he knew to be at fault, with whose irrational moods he was already familiar but who, in appealing to his honour, had made him feel that any danger was preferable to ridicule. 'For what could be more ridiculous,' she asked him, 'than to come forward as an apostle of civilization to save and regenerate a country and then to return to Europe on the plea that there was nothing to civilize or to save?'

With these words, Charlotte won her unhappy victory. He allowed himself to be influenced against his better judgment, and with a heavy heart gave orders for the journey, drawing on the last cash reserves kept to cover the paper currency, to provide his wife with a suite worthy of an Empress. Martin Castillo, the new Foreign Minister, represented the Mexican government; Bombelles, the faithful friend, was to watch over Charlotte's health and safety. The suite was chosen from among the most devoted and loyal members of the court: the Empress's Grand Chamberlain, the Count del Valle, who had been one of the original members of the first Mexican deputation to Miramar; the del Barrios, husband and wife, he belonging to the old Creole aristocracy and she a daughter of old Gutierrez and a granddaughter of Countess Lutzoff, who had died two years before and therefore was fortunately spared being witness to a tragedy of which, all unwittingly, she had written the prologue. Last but not least were the Kuhacseviches, husband and wife, both delighted to be returning to Europe but miserable at leaving their beloved Emperor behind.

'Charlotte's voyage is the heaviest sacrifice I have yet made to my new country,' wrote Maximilian to his brother Karl Ludwig. 'It is all the harder since she has to travel through the deadly yellow fever zone during the worst season. But duty demands this sacrifice and, God willing, it will not be in vain. With her sure tact, Charlotte will ascertain how far we can still rely upon the help of sluggish old Europe.' In another letter, to an old friend, we read: 'Who is in a better position to act for us than the coldly calculating Empress who, alone besides myself, is familiar with the ins and outs of our policy?'

For all his reputed infidelities, his romantic philanderings in the gardens of Cuernavaca, Maximilian was so touched and impressed by the heroic gesture of his wife that it inspired him with a tenderness and affection such as he had not felt for years. 'It is terribly hard,' he wrote to his mother, 'to have our loving and faithful companion, the shining star of one's existence, so far away from us and that at a time when perhaps the whole of Europe is in flames.' Both of them were so beset by pride, so pathetically anxious to do their duty as sovereigns by

351

divine right, that they ended in hurting themselves and alienating their families. It was hard for Maximilian to have to tell his mother that it would be impossible for Charlotte to visit Vienna on account of Austria's behaviour over the volunteers, and still harder for Charlotte to forgo a pilgrimage to her father's grave because of her brother having given orders to close the recruiting lists for Mexico.

To facilitate her mission, Maximilian capitulated to the French, accepting the onerous terms of the ultimatum, making friendly overtures to Bazaine who, only a few days before, he had refused to receive before his departure for a tour of inspection in the north. But, however much the Marshal may have been flattered at the Emperor and Empress offering to act as god-parents to his newborn child, whatever concern he may have felt for the future of Mexico and in particular for members of his wife's family, who would be among the first to be spoliated by the *Juaristi*, he nevertheless had no other choice than to carry out his master's orders, to suspend the monthly payments till the custom house revenues were handed over, and to proceed with the systematic withdrawal of his troops. Monterrey, the capital of Nuevo Leon, a rich commercial centre in the north which had changed hands no less than six times in the past four years, was the latest place to be evacuated on the excuse that it was wiser to set back the frontier, thereby making the country easier to defend and requiring a smaller deployment of troops. Bazaine omitted to mention that the loss of Monterrey, with its rich mercantile population, would mean a drop of seven million pesos in Mexico's already depleted finances.

Although Maximilian's civil list was now cut down to half, the Imperial Court continued to function, with its Palatine Guards in silver-embossed helmets and its elegant aides-de-camp in gold-embroidered uniforms. On 6 July there was still a Te Deum held in the cathedral to celebrate the Emperor's birthday, at which Archbishop Labastida agreed to officiate in the presence of the French general staff and the whole of the diplomatic corps. The cathedral was crowded, for although the official announcement of the Empress's journey was not given out until the following day, it was already common property in a town so rife with rumours. It was generally noted that the Empress Carlota, who appeared without the Emperor, remained longer on her knees and prayed more fervently than was usual at an official ceremony. Maximilian was laid low with fever at Chapultepec. To add to his personal anxiety, his birthday had brought him the news that his own country was at war with Prussia. The telegram had taken nearly three weeks to reach him and it was to be another three weeks before he learned of the disaster of Sadowa and of Austria's humiliating defeat. All he knew of politics was from the French-controlled newspapers and he envisaged Napoleon as the arbiter of Europe, dictating the peace terms to Austria and to Prussia. He little knew that, by the time Charlotte had arrived in France, Bismarck would have given the French Emperor his first rebuff and Napoleon would be no more than a tired aging man who had lost all taste for adventure.

Their last night together was spent at Chapultepec, with Charlotte memorizing the instructions she redrafted in her own words. They were in principle the same as those already given to Almonte, perhaps slightly more defiant, more arrogant in their assumption that Bazaine would have to be recalled, with abdication used as the ultimate threat – neither Maximilian nor Charlotte yet realizing that Napoleon had become indifferent whether the Emperor remained or went, so long as France could disentangle herself from the Mexico fiasco without too great a loss of prestige. At four o'clock on the morning of 9 July, the wagons laden with trunks, the cortège of mule-drawn carriages and coaches, escorted by a detachment of Imperial cavalry, moved slowly down the hill. 'I will be back in three months,' the Empress had assured her ladies-in-waiting on the previous evening, when one of the most devoted of them, a certain Señora Pacheco, asked permission to embrace her because she felt she might never see her again, upon which all the ladies burst into tears and even the Empress had the greatest difficulty in maintaining her self-control.

Maximilian had got up from his sick-bed to accompany his wife on the first stage of her journey. The sun was rising behind Popocatepetl as the procession fanned out on to the great plateau. It was one of those clear, bright Mexican dawns, when the cactus hedges washed by the recent rains glittered like silver knives and the maize fields turned to waving sheets of gold. But neither Charlotte nor Maximilian saw the beauty of the countryside, for their eyes were blinded with tears. When they parted at Ajotla, a little village some twenty miles from the capital, the Emperor, still weak from fever, broke down completely and had to be supported back to his carriage. Later that night, Charlotte wrote to him from Rio Frio that the sight of his tears made her 'so miserable that I became half-unconscious and wept quite openly in front of the muleteers'. But she was still obsessed by the fear that those in favour of abdication might profit by his weakness and she warned him: 'Beware of the Fran [the French]. Even the nicest of them, Pierron, is supposed to have said that I will never come back. Do not listen to him. It would break my heart, wherever I should be, if I ever heard that you had been talked into giving up the throne for which we have sacrificed so much and which can still have such a glorious future. . . . There are many here who are loyal and who would never betray you, and they do not deserve to be betrayed through the betrayal of others.'

Her spirits were indomitable. All those who saw her in her primitive quarters in Rio Frio or, on the following evening presiding at a banquet at Puebla, later recalled that they had never seen her more natural and more affable. General Thun's aide-de-camp, a young Baron Malorte, escorted her with a detachment of Polish lancers through the whole of the Austrian zone and has left us one of those romantic descriptions which the Empress Carlota inspired in chivalrous young officers of every nationality. 'There was something strange, almost uncanny,' he writes, 'in the spectacle of all those vehicles and horsemen suddenly appearing out of nowhere on a lonely moonlit road, where the aloes cast gigantic shadows on the ground. The Empress was riding ahead on a splendid thoroughbred – a truly glorious vision in her white dust-mantle over a dark, well-fitting habit and a large sombrero with a long, floating veil which made her appear like the Queen of the Elves racing through the night.' (Like all good German romantics, Malorte had been nurtured on Goethe's 'Earl King'.) One is inclined to cast a doubt on his truthfulness for the Empress's entourage, and in particular Bombelles, would never have allowed her to expose herself on horseback to the cold night air, nor can she have arrived so late in Puebla, for Malorte himself describes her attending a dinner where she 'sparkled with witty repartee, which was completely lost on the Mexican guests'.

How can one reconcile these accounts of her high spirits with an incident which took place later that night? Charlotte, who had already gone to bed, suddenly got up, rang her servants and told them to order a carriage to take her to the house of the ex-Prefect, Senor Esteva, where she and Maximilian had dined on a previous visit. The house was empty. Señor Esteva was in Vera Cruz but Charlotte refused to listen to prayers or persuasion. The caretaker was woken up, the candles were lit, and without giving a word of explanation the Empress wandered through the empty rooms as if she were searching for something or someone she could not find. The following morning, she was her usual self and she did not make the slightest reference to this strange nocturnal visit. But what was even stranger was that neither Bombelles nor the Empress's doctor reported this incident to Maximilian; nor did the doctor attempt to warn his master that the hazards of the voyage might prove too great a strain on the Empress's nervous system.

The dangerous part of the journey began with the ascent of the Cumbrés, where the roads in the rainy season were gullies of mud and landslides brought boulders of rock crashing down the mountains. To add to the risks, the population of some of the villages they passed were actively hostile, living in terror of the *guerrilleros* who roamed the mountains and made continual raids on their farms. Afterwards, Charlotte admitted that they would never have got through to Vera Cruz without the strong escort of French *Chasseurs* who took over from the Austrians at the foothills of the Cumbrés. The weather got worse as they descended into the Tierra Caliente. Torrential rain and thunderstorms impeded their progress, mules floundered in the mud, carriages overturned. Late in the evening, in the neighbourhood of Cordoba, a wheel of the Empress's carriage broke and she had to take shelter in a wayside inn where a noisy party of travellers had just arrived by stagecoach and were singing and drinking in the room next door. Colonel Rolland of the *Chasseurs* deemed it wiser not to reveal the Empress's identity and Charlotte and her ladies had to listen to the refrains of bawdy songs, accompanied by loud laughter and obscenities – among them the latest version of '*Mama Carlota*' sung to the tune of '*La Paloma*':

Adios, Mama Carlota,	Farewell, Mama Carlota,
Adios, mi tierno amor,	Farewell, my tender love,
Se fueron los Franceses,	If the French go,
Se va el Emperado.	The Emperor goes too.

The insulting words re-echoed throughout the room. Her ladies pretended not to hear. The French officers had enough on their hands without picking a quarrel with some harmless travellers. But it was more than Charlotte's jangled nerves could stand. Suddenly, it seemed as if there were enemies all around her. It was all part of a plot. The wheel had been deliberately broken to prevent her from reaching Vera Cruz in time to catch the boat. She refused to await the arrival of another carriage and ordered the horses to be saddled immediately. She would ride through the night to Paso del Macho, from where she could take the train to Vera Cruz. Fortunately, a carriage arrived from Cordoba before she could carry out her threat.

Paso del Macho was reached at one in the morning, and at two o'clock the following afternoon, on the inauspicious date of Friday, 13 July, the royal party arrived at Vera Cruz where, only eight months before, the Empress Carlota had received such a rapturous welcome. This time there were no flowers or flag-waving, no deputations of welcome or triumphal chariots, only the *zopilotes*, those birds of ill-omen, flapping their black wings in the sultry air, and indifferent to resentful faces in the streets. The rumour had gone round that the Empress was going to Europe and not coming back and that the Emperor was following her shortly.

The crowning insult for Charlotte was when, arriving at the port, she found that there was no royal standard flying from the French packet-steamer anchored in the roads and no Mexican flag on the launch which was to take her on board. White with anger, she summoned the port authority to inform the French commander of the naval station that she refused to board the ship until the captain had hoisted the French flag with the Mexican flag. There was general consternation and embarrassment. The officials of the Compagnie Transatlantique had only been told of the Empress's journey a few days before. French nationals returning to Europe had had their passages cancelled at the last minute to make room for the royal party, and now Her Imperial Majesty had the presumption to demand that the French flag on one of their own ships should be replaced by the Mexican. Commander Cloué was justifiably irritated but the boat was due to sail and there was no point in arguing with an Empress who appeared to be on the verge of hysteria. The Mexican standard was hoisted on the launch and he himself conducted Her Majesty on board. She had regained her self-control and thanked him for his courtesy. But as soon as the ship weighed anchor, Charlotte retired alone to her cabin where, in spite of the intense heat, she remained for the greater part of the journey to Havana. The passage was rough and she suffered not only from seasickness but also from a terrible headache, aggravated by the vibration of the engines, while drumming in her ears was the constant refrain, '*Se fueron los Franceses, se va el Emperador*'.

26

Charlotte pleads with Napoleon

On the morning of 8 August, the Mayor of St Nazaire was in a state of panic. The packet-steamer *L'Impératrice Eugénie*, with the Empress of Mexico on board, was due to arrive in an hour's time. He had been given the news only the day before, and neither the Prefect nor the Vice-Prefect had arrived, nor was there a Mexican flag to be found in the whole town. In the end, they had to make do with a Peruvian one, produced by one of the town councillors who had lived in Peru for several years, and it was generally assumed that no one would know the difference. There seems to have been considerable confusion over the Empress's movements. Maximilian had given no previous notice to Bazaine of his wife's impending journey, and the Marshal, who was in San Luis Potosi at the time, only read the official announcement in the newspapers. He immediately sent a telegram to Napoleon, warning him of the Empress's arrival in Europe, but this news was later officially contradicted in *Le Moniteur*, with the result that only the Almontes, husband and wife, had taken the trouble of travelling to St Nazaire to meet the boat from Mexico, on the assumption that the Empress Carlota would be on board.

It must have been a nightmare journey for Charlotte, worried over her husband's health, haunted for the first time of the possibility of failure and the nagging sense of her own responsibility. Fear of infection from the *Vomito Negro* had prevented her from landing either at Havana or St Thomas, and she spent most of the day in her airless cabin trying to forget her seasickness and distract her thoughts by re-reading the novels of Dumas. The weather became fine on leaving the Caribbean and they had a smooth crossing, but Charlotte, who was rarely seasick, suffered almost continuously from nausea, which was commented on at the time and later contributed to the legend of her pregnancy. When she made her rare appearances on deck, the other passengers found her silent and preoccupied, joining very little in the conversation and sitting alone staring into space with a curious fixed look, while her attendants noted that all her lace handkerchiefs were being torn to shreds, which was always the sign of a nervous crisis.

On arrival at St Nazaire, the Empress waited impatiently for an emissary from Napoleon or a committee of welcome to come on board. But there was no one except the Almontes, the General looking apprehensive and his wife carrying a bouquet of rather wilted roses. There were no officers in uniform on the quayside, no bemedalled Prefect, only a stout mayor and a few town councillors in frock coats which had grown too tight, and, to compensate for the lack of protocol, the spontaneous cheers of a warm and friendly population. But the Empress was too humiliated to appreciate the cheers. Fulminating with rage, she cut in on the mayor's well-meant but inept address, asking him where were the Prefect and guard of honour? If St Nazaire, which the Mexican expedition had raised from a small fishing port to a prosperous town, could not give the Empress of Mexico a more fitting reception, then there was no point in her prolonging her stay. She demanded to be taken immediately to the railway station, where, after sending a few telegrams and eating a hurried meal, both she and her suite boarded the train for Nantes.

In the meantime, Almonte informed Charlotte about the situation in Europe. She learnt for the first time of the disaster of Sadowa, a defeat which was almost as catastrophic for France as it was for Austria. She heard that the Emperor Napoleon was suffering severely from his gallbladder and had only just returned from Vichy, which had not done him so much good as in the previous years. The illness which sapped his vitality made him nervous and indecisive, while the Empress, who was generally blamed for the failure of the Mexican expedition, had completely lost her influence. It was not an encouraging picture, but it did not deter Charlotte from sending Napoleon a telegram in which she announced her arrival in Europe, saying she had been entrusted by her husband with a mission to discuss with him 'certain matters concerning Mexico'.

This telegram was as much of a bombshell for Napoleon as the French ultimatum had been to Maximilian. To be faced with a righteously indignant woman, reminding him of all the promises made and broken, was more than he could stand up to in his present state of health. He retired to bed at St Cloud and was ready to stay there indefinitely, providing it gave him the excuse of postponing this dreaded interview. In answer to Charlotte's telegram, he wrote, 'I have just returned from Vichy and I am forced to stay in bed, so that I am not in a position to come to see Your Majesty. If, as I suppose, Your Majesty is going first to Belgium, this will give me time to recover.' Napoleon was playing for time. He did not know of the telegram which Charlotte, at the cost of her own personal feelings, had sent her brother in Brussels, telling him that the attitude of the Belgian government over Mexico unfortunately prevented her from visiting her country. A telegram to the same effect was sent to Vienna to the Archduchess Sophia, and in both cases only served to alienate members of the famly who would otherwise have been well disposed. We find the Count of Flanders writing to his uncle, the Prince of Joinville, 'I am afraid I am unable to give you any information as to Charlotte's plans. Her movements seem to be very erratic and are dictated by a touchiness which verges on the ridiculous. I presume she will come here later, but I do not know when, and I doubt if she will be going back to Mexico. It is more likely that her husband will shortly be returning to Europe.'

Charlotte's telegram created a bad effect in Vienna, for though Franz Josef and Elisabeth were thankful to be spared a visit from their tiresome sister-in-law, Max's attitude was regarded as being ungrateful and unreasonable. And the Archduchess Sophia, who was longing for first-hand news of her beloved son, and had not yet received the letter explaining the situation, put all the blame on Charlotte, little realizing how lonely she felt in Europe without any family to go to for comfort or advice.

She fully realized that the Emperor Napoleon was attempting to put off, or at least postpone, an unwanted visit, but she refused to take the hint and telegraphed that evening from Nantes that she would be arriving in Paris the following day. Here again, there was nothing but muddle and confusion. The Court carriages sent to meet her at the station had inadvertently gone to the Gare d'Orléans instead of Montparnasse, and Charlotte found no one at the station but a handful of Mexicans, hurriedly alerted by Almonte, among them old Gutierrez, one of his sons and young Salvador Iturbide. Their presence could hardly compensate for the fact that there was no red carpet on the platform, no gala carriages or invitation to stay at the Tuileries. Fighting back her tears, she accepted the offer of Gutierrez' carriage to drive her to the Grand Hotel, where Almonte had providentially booked the whole first floor to give some semblence of grandeur. She was barely installed when Napoleon's emissaries, General Waubert de Genlis and Count Cossé-Brissac, appeared, flustered and apologetic, to explain the mistake and present a message from the Empress Eugénie asking when it would be convenient for her to call, and how long Her Imperial Majesty intended to remain in Paris. It was a harmless question but it was interpreted as an insult by a woman grown morbidly sensitive from the fear of impending failure. Charlotte replied in her haughtiest manner that she would be delighted to receive the Empress at whatever time she chose. As for her plans, she intended to stay on in Paris until she had accomplished her mission, for she had 'no family or interests in Europe which were not bound up with Mexico', upon which the Emperor's messengers bowed and withdrew. No sooner had they gone than she broke down completely, shutting herself up alone in her room and refusing admittance even to her maids who, waiting outside, could hear her heart-rending sobs. Later in the evening, she joined her ladies, outwardly calm and collected but looking, as Madame del Barrio remarked 'like a walking ghost'.

The atmosphere at St Cloud was almost as gloomy as at the Grand Hotel. The Empress Charlotte's arrival coincided with that of the French Ambassador to Berlin, who brought with him the news of Bismarck's refusal to consider French claims to the Saar and the Bavarian Palatinate in compensation for France's neutrality in the Austro-Prussian War. Backed by a victorious army, still fully mobilized, Bismarck had gone so far as to threaten war if France persisted in her claims. And war in support of Austria was what the Foreign Minister, Drouyn de Lhuys, had been urging on Napoleon for the past weeks. But now it was too late. Austria was on her knees, France was not fully mobilized and over thirty thousand of her crack troops were bogged down in the sierras and deserts of Mexico. When Eugénie tried to rally her sick and lethargic husband to adopt a more vigorous policy, she was asked whose fault was it if the best generals and the best men were still on the other side of the ocean? Whose fault was it that the Empress of Mexico had appeared in Paris at a moment when all that the Emperor asked for was peace and quiet?

Eugénie was conscious of her responsibility for the Mexican fiasco and was genuinely concerned for the future of the two young sovereigns. But now her first duty was to spare her husband unpleasant scenes for which he did not have the health to cope, and it must have been with a heavy heart and a sense of dread that she set out for the Grand Hotel in the early afternoon of 10 August.

Charlotte had been at work all morning, coaching her ladies in European etiquette, for she wrote somewhat pathetically to Maximilian that she wanted to give 'a good impression of the elegance and good breeding of the court of Mexico'. Fortunately, she never heard the malicious comments of the sophisticated Parisians and particularly those of the author Prosper Merimée, one of the intimates of St Cloud, who in writing to his friend Sir Anthony Panizzi in London, commented on Charlotte's ladies, 'We had been hoping to see some *houris* of Mahomet – instead of which we saw ladies with flashing eyes, complexions like gingerbread and a certain similarity to orang-outangs.'

Meanwhile, a constant stream of carriages drove up to the Grand Hotel, with ministers and diplomats, generals and bankers, all of whom at some time or other had had some connection with Mexico, and now came to pay their respects to the Empress Carlota. Among the first to arrive was Napoleon's aide-de-camp General Frossard, whom Charlotte had not seen since those fateful days at Miramar, and whom she now presented with the memorandum she had brought with her from Mexico, containing both an answer to the French ultimatum of 31 May, and an indictment of Marshal Bazaine, repeating all the old accusations already raised in Maximilian's letters. It was a savage indictment and particularly embarrassing for Frossard, who knew how closely Bazaine had been keeping to the instructions of his sovereign. In reproaching the Marshal, the Empress was in reality reproaching the Emperor, which was not going to facilitate her mission.

At two o'clock Empress Eugénie drove up to the Grand Hotel, accompanied by the beautiful Countess of Montebello and her life-long friend Madame Carette, and escorted by the Chamberlain and aide-de-camp who had gone to meet Charlotte at the station on the previous day. The Count del Vallé welcomed the Empress at the door while the young Foreign Minister, Martin Castillo, stood with Charlotte at the top of the staircase. When the Empress of Mexico came down the stairs to greet the Empress of the French with 'a sisterly kiss', everyone present was struck by the contrast between the two women: the beautiful forty-year-old Eugénie, dressed in summery muslins, a flowered bonnet on her burnished hair – a little stouter, a little older than when Charlotte had seen her last, but still the unchallenged queen of elegance; and Charlotte, fifteen years her junior, her face already lined with worry, her eyes infinitely sad, wearing a plain black frock in mourning for her grandmother, but for all her simplicity, immensely royal, proclaiming in every gesture generations of Bourbon blood.

It was a painful interview. Charlotte was in no mood for trivialities, and lost no time in getting to the point. The situation in Mexico was deteriorating every day and she was enlisting Eugénie's support for a country and a people who, without the help of France, would founder in anarchy. Her husband had sacrificed his health and youth for his new country. He had tried to rule according to the liberal principles of his enlightened ally, the Emperor Napoleon, but, as her father wrote in one of his last letters, 'all that counted in the Americas was success'. If France stood by them now Mexico would become a great country and the United States would have no choice but to accept the Empire and applaud. Charlotte was eloquent and emotional, and the impressionable Eugénie was nearly moved to tears. Desperately she tried to steer the conversation into lighter and more mundane channels: Madame de Courcy had told her of the charming parties given by the Empress at the Palaçio Naçional, and of how the Mexican ladies were taking to French fashion; so many of the young officers seemed to have lost their hearts to the Creole beauties; everyone in Paris was singing *La Paloma*. Bravely she battled on, trying at all costs to evade the serious issues and prevent the Mexican Empress from asking questions to which she had not the courage to reply.

But in Charlotte's resentful eyes, this beautiful woman, dressed in the height of fashion, chattering away on trivialities, seemed an insult to her grief. Abruptly she broke in to ask when she might return her visit, and Eugénie, slightly taken aback, replied, 'The day after tomorrow, if Your Majesty wishes.' But now Charlotte became more insistent: 'And what about the Emperor, will I see him then?' Eugénie looked embarrassed and hesitated before replying, 'Alas, that will be impossible. The Emperor is far from well and is still confined to his bed.' But she already knew that lies and excuses were of no avail against this forceful and determined woman. Charlotte had heard that the Emperor was leaving for the Camp of Châlons and everything depended on seeing him before he went. Leaving Eugénie no loophole of escape, she announced that she would be coming to St Cloud on the following day, adding with a show of playfulness which deceived no one, 'If the Emperor refuses to see me, I shall break in on him.' And Eugénie had no doubt that she was ready to carry out her threat. The French Empress returned to St Cloud, her heart full of pity for the unfortunate young woman who in such a short time had lost all her youthful bloom, and at the same time nervous and apprehensive as to what tomorrow held in store.

The reaction of Napoleon's entourage to the Mexican visit was summed up by Prosper Merimée, who wrote, 'The Emperor was hoping to profit by the fine weather, to enjoy a few peaceful days at St Cloud, instead of which he has Her Mexican Majesty on hand. ... She is a masterful-looking woman, the very spit of her grandfather, Louis Philippe. ... They will give her a dinner but I very much doubt if she gets any money or troops. Maximilian, I imagine, will have to abdicate, after which there will be a republic, or rather anarchy, followed by the Yankees, lynch-law and an Anglo-Saxon colonization.' Reading these comments, it is not surprising to find Charlotte complaining to her husband, 'I know more about China than these people know about Mexico, where they have embarked on one of the most ambitious enterprises in which France has ever been involved.'

At midday on 11 August, the Empress of Mexico arrived in state at St Cloud, driving in an open victoria belonging to the Imperial stables, accompanied by Madame Almonte and followed by a second carriage occupied by Madame del Barrio and the Count de Vallé. It was a lovely summer's day and cheering crowds lined the road all the way to St Cloud, for however unpopular the Mexican expedition might be in political and military circles, the courageous young Empress had captured the imagination of the public. In ordinary times, Charlotte would have been delighted by her reception, but now she was too nervous and agitated to care. Her colour came and went and she kept clutching at Madame Almonte's hand for reassurance. Throughout a sleepless night, she had kept rehearsing what she had to tell Napoleon but now, at the eleventh hour, she was beginning to feel addled and confused. She was trembling so violently that Madame Almonte thought she was going to faint, but she regained her self-control on arriving at St Cloud, where she found the guard of honour lined up at the entrance to the castle and the whole of the Imperial Household assembled at the foot of the staircase leading to the private apartments. The little Prince Imperial, a handsome child of ten, wearing the Order of the Mexican Eagle and a smart new uniform, ran forward to help her out of her carriage and, taking her by the hand, led her up the stairs where Eugénie was waiting to welcome her with her most charming and reassuring smile.

In this brilliant, flamboyant Court, the Empress of Mexico and her ladies, 'two plain little women with neither elegance nor grace' must have seemed very dowdy and provincial. Sharp eyes noticed that the Empress was 'very red in the face', either on account of the long drive or because of suppressed excitement. It was also observed that the black dress she was wearing was still creased from the folds of the packing, and that she kept nervously fingering her mantilla. Charlotte had made an attempt to be fashionable by sending Madame del Barrio to buy her a hat at one of the leading milliners. And the young Mexican woman had wanted to do honour to her mistress by choosing the most expensive and elaborate one she could find. But the dressy, white creation was totally unsuited to the Empress's somewhat severe features and the general verdict was that 'she was wearing a very unbecoming hat'. But Charlotte was concerned with more important matters than her appearance and she had difficulty in restraining her emotions, when Eugénie conducted her to Napoleon's study, and she found herself face to face with the man on whom their whole future depended. He was looking twenty years older than when she had seen him last, and she noted that he was obviously in pain and that his illness was genuine. He was as courteous and as friendly as ever, but she could see that he was nervous and on his guard.

So many people claim to have been present at this interview and to have overheard Charlotte's hysterical reproaches. Romanticized biographies and memoirs have, over the years, repeated and distorted these accounts. But the interview, at which only Charlotte and the Imperial couple were present, took place behind closed doors. Madame del Barrio, from whom Malortie in particular claims to have received an eye-witness account, spent the whole of the two hours sitting with Madame Almonte in an ante-chamber, making stilted conversation with the French ladies-in-waiting, who, when at a loss for topics, kept plying them with refreshments. The only authentic account comes from Charlotte herself, who in a letter to Maximilian wrote: 'I did everything that was humanly possible.' She pleaded, cajoled and menaced, presenting Napoleon with every kind of document and memorandum on the military and financial situation; bringing up again the three points of Maximilian's ultimatum – the recall of Bazaine, the continuation of the monthly subsidies to pay the native troops, and the retention of the expeditionary force in Mexico for another three years. She painted a pathetic picture of what would happen to Mexico and the people who still believed in French promises if the troops withdrew before their work was accomplished. 'Surely a nation of forty million people, disposing of enormous capital and credit, could not give up an enterprise which had world-wide interests at stake, just because of a few American threats.' But, for all her efforts, she had the impression that 'though the Emperor spoke a lot about Mexico, he had already forgotten all about it.'

It must have been a harrowing experience for someone as kind-hearted and chivalrous as Napoleon, to be faced by this distraught and unhappy woman who, only a few years ago, he had seen so young and radiant and full of hope. Charlotte herself admitted that he 'appeared to be utterly helpless, with tears pouring down his cheeks, continually turning to his wife for support'. The unexpected appearance of a Court lackey, carrying a silver salver with a jug of orangeade, interrupted her impassioned appeal. Madame del Barrio had confided in Madame Carette, one of Eugénie's ladies-in-waiting, that in summer her mistress always had a cooling drink at this time of the day, and the orangeade had been ordered in a well-intentioned attempt to please the royal guest.

This harmless incident was later to be completely distorted by Charlotte's mental aberrations. Eugénie, who was as surprised as her guest at the inopportune interruption, was later accused of having tried to poison her. Charlotte's initial reluctance to partake of any refreshment, which she was only prevailed upon to do when Eugénie herself offered her a glass, was dramatized by Malortie and his successors into a poignant scene in which she is said to have recoiled in horror from the drink, screaming that they were trying to poison her and falling in a dead faint from which she was brought back to consciousness by the French Empress. Her reluctance to accept the drink was probably due to no more than a natural irritation at being interrupted at such a solemn moment.

The interview ended with Napoleon promising to consult again with his ministers before giving his final reply. He assured her that it no longer depended on him but on his government – a sorry admission from the great Imperatore who had asked neither opinion nor advice before embarking on 'la plus grande pensée du règne'. After refusing an invitation to remain for lunch, the Empress called for her carriage.

There was an unfortunate delay and Charlotte, unable to control her impatience, kept pacing up and down the rooms, too agitated to keep up the pretence of polite conversation. She was so visibly distressed that even the most cynical of courtiers commiserated with her grief. Staring ahead with blank, unseeing eyes, she walked unassisted to her carriage, refusing the arm of an aide-de-camp when he tried to help her into her seat, and, on the way home, collapsing completely and weeping like a child in the arms of Madame Almonte.

Yet still she refused to admit defeat. She had failed to convince Napoleon but she might still succeed in convincing his government. On the following day, Drouyn de Lhuys, Randon and Fould were all bidden in turn to the Grand Hotel. Each in turn was polite and evasive before her impassioned arguments. Each in turn promised to examine her proposals. No one wanted to be the first to utter the final 'non possamus' to this loyal and courageous Princess, who according to Felix Eloin commanded 'universal admiration'. Eloin, who had just returned to Paris after a short visit to Vienna, had spent too much time in the French capital to entertain any hopes of the outcome of the Empress's visit, but he judged it wiser to let her preserve her illusions, 'for it is her shining faith and ardour which give her that lucidity of spirit which makes her so strong. If anyone can succeed in making the government change its mind, it would be Her Majesty. Everyone is impressed by the force and clarity with which she presents her case.'

Prince Metternich, who admired the young Empress's tenacity of purpose, tried to assist her in every way, warning her not to place too much faith in the polite phrases of Latin politicians. Fould might appear to be dazzled by her descriptions of the potential wealth of Mexico, but he was a hard-headed businessman who only measured success by the credit entries in his account books, and he would be the first to advise his Imperial master to get out of Mexico as quickly as possible. It was easy for Drouyn de Lhuys to agree with her arguments, for he had already handed in his resignation, not on account of Mexico but because he disapproved of Napoleon's weak-kneed policy in Germany. Metternich told her that the principal factor to take into consideration was that 'the French Emperor had been degenerating both physically and mentally for the past two years, and was no longer capable of making a decision', and that Eugénie, in attempting to direct affairs, had done 'more harm than good'.

But Charlotte still thought she could shame Napoleon into accepting her proposals. He had barely recovered from the shock of her first visit when she appeared again at St Cloud. This time, she came on what she called 'a working visit', accompanied by the Foreign Minister, Castillo, whom she assured the Emperor 'knew the finances of Mexico by heart'. But the last thing that Napoleon wanted to hear about were the finances of Mexico. He was nervous and irritable and in danger of losing his temper with a woman whom a succession of sleepless nights had rendered more desperate and more demanding than on her previous visit. This time, she appeared before him not as a suppliant but as an avenging fury, reminding him of promises made to Maximilian in the spring of 1864, placing in front of him the fatal letter of 28 March, in which he had written: 'What would you think of me if, when Your Royal Highness was once in Mexico, I were suddenly to say to you that I cannot fulfil the conditions to which I have set my signature?' It was not very pleasant reading for a man who was already bitterly ashamed of himself, and Charlotte noted with contempt that the Emperor 'wept even more than before'.

Meanwhile, Eugénie was doing all she could to put an end to this painful interview, finally succeeding in getting Charlotte out of the Emperor's study and into her own private apartments, where the Ministers of War and Finance, summoned at the Empress of Mexico's express request, were waiting for further talks. But Charlotte had worked herself into such a state of agitation that she was incapable of reasoning. Discarding etiquette, forgetting her manners and completely ignoring Eugénie, she stormed and raved against the ministers, accusing the French bankers and financiers of having misappropriated part of the Mexican loans. She vituperated against Bazaine and brought up again the sordid matter of the Jecker bonds. 'Who are the persons,' she cried, 'whose pockets are filled with gold at Mexico's expense?' The Minister of War was too horrified and shocked at her outburst to reply, but Achille Fould was not going to be accused of fraud in front of his own sovereign, and he contested every one of her assertions with counter-accusations, in which he did not hesitate to call the Mexicans 'dishonest, distrustful and ungrateful'. There was a limit to the sacrifices a country could be called upon to make and, in his opinion, France had already gone beyond that limit.

By now, Eugénie had come to the end of her endurance and, bursting into tears, flung herself on to a sofa and pretended to faint. The meeting ended in confusion, with the ministers making half-hearted apologies and Castillo leading away a hysterical and raging Empress. If she had been in a normal state of mind, Charlotte would never have insulted the ministers on the eve of a cabinet council which was to decide the future of Mexico. Her heart-rending descriptions of the country's financial plight, of the shortage of native troops and the growing strength of the *guerrilleros*, only served to convince the ministers that, throughout the four years of occupation, the Mexicans had done nothing to help themselves. When the council met on the next day, 14 August, the Empress's proposals were deemed to be unacceptable. A unanimous vote decided in favour of the immediate evacuation of the expeditionary force and instructions were sent to Bazaine confirming the orders which Charlotte had hoped to cancel by her intervention.

These decisions were given to Almonte who in turn was to acquaint the Mexican Foreign Minister, Castillo, but Charlotte refused to accept the reply from anyone except the Emperor who, in order to avoid further visitations to St Cloud, had left for the Camp of Châlons, hoping to find Her Mexican Majesty gone by his return. Charlotte, who was determined to see him again, stayed on for another miserable week, exhausting herself in interviews with bankers and economists, juggling with figures and statistics which her tired brain could no longer grasp, tormented with worry over Max and dreading having to admit that her mission had been a failure. She was hurt that neither of her brothers had come to see her in Paris, forgetting that she and Max were primarily responsible for this seeming indifference. The offer of a gala dinner before the Emperor's departure was politely refused, but the Court carriages waited every day outside the Grand Hotel and baskets of flowers and fruit continued to arrive from the Imperial greenhouses. By now, Charlotte was animated by such a fierce hatred of Napoleon that she could barely taste of the fruit or look at the flowers, and to add to all her other troubles, the American Alicia Iturbide was in Paris agitating for the return of her little Agustín.

Bombelles had advised the Empress to see Madame Iturbide, whose claims were being backed by the United States Minister in Paris, but Charlotte saw it as a deliberate attempt to add to her humiliations. She had always resented Max's having adopted the Iturbide child and would willingly have passed him back to his lawful mother. But loyalty to her husband forced her to take his side. Alicia Iturbide had antagonized the Emperor by enlisting the help of Bazaine, who had handed on her complaints to his government. The Empress, who was already suffering from the first signs of persecution mania, interpreted Alicia's presence in Paris as having been deliberately engineered by the Marshal to undermine her position. She consented to see her, but was at her haughtiest and most unsympathetic with a woman who wanted nothing more than the return of her son. She reminded her of the financial benefits she and her family had received from the Emperor who of his own free will had conferred Imperial titles on her son and nephew, to which Alicia replied that the money was owed to her family by the Mexican nation and that they all had 'the right to call themselves princes, titles they had discarded when living in America'.

It was on this occasion that Charlotte made the remark which has been so often quoted: 'Why should we want your child? What advantage is he to us? We are both young and may still have children of our own.' Was it a remark thrown out at random, spoken in anger and dictated by pride to silence this insolent American who dared to sit uninvited in her presence and to address her as an equal, or did she still cherish the hope of having a child? Was there some secret knowledge which she shared only with a doctor and a maid? Alicia Iturbide was summarily dismissed and told to write again to the Emperor but to be sure to write properly. Her visit was a trivial incident in comparison with the enormous problems confronting Charlotte, but the memory of it continued to rankle, conjuring images she was trying to forget.

On 19 August, Napoleon was back in Paris, bracing himself for the courtesy visit which Charlotte regarded as her due. He was genuinely distressed by his inability to help and, after their last meeting, had confided to a friend that he would never forget 'the look of anguish on her face'.

The following morning, 20 August, the Emperor arrived at the Grand Hotel, where Charlotte was waiting for him with some new proposals even more fantastic than the last. She suggested, in all seriousness, that he should summon the Legislative Assembly and ask them to vote a ninety million franc loan for Mexico, to be paid in monthly instalments. If the loan were refused, he should dissolve the Assembly and appeal to the country. She was sure that the people of France would rally to support a sovereign who had the courage and the vision to carry out a great enterprise to the end. 'France,' she declared, 'requires a balance of power in the New World, and the prosperity of Mexico means the prosperity of France.' The Emperor tried on more than one occasion to interrupt these flights of fancy and to bring her back to earth, but each

369

time she tried to stop him from speaking, for she knew already what he was going to say. Finally, he cut in, telling her quite bluntly that neither the Legislative Assembly nor the people of France were prepared to make any further sacrifices for Mexico and that it was useless to indulge in any further illusions. These few words robbed Charlotte of the last vestiges of sanity. Turning on him with burning cheeks and blazing eyes, she cried, 'Your Majesty is as much concerned in this affair as we are, so it would be better if you did not indulge in any illusions either.' Upon which, Napoleon got up from his chair, bowed to her coldly and left without saying another word.

On 21 August, the eve of her departure from Paris, the Empress of Mexico received the formal notification that the Emperor Napoleon regretted he was unable to comply with her request, and a few days later he wrote to Maximilian what must have been the hardest letter he had ever had to write: 'We had the great pleasure in receiving the Empress Charlotte, yet it was very painful for me to be unable to accede to her requests. We are in fact approaching a decisive moment for Mexico, and it is necessary for Your Majesty to come to a heroic resolution; the time for half-measures has gone by. I must begin by stating to Your Majesty that it is henceforward impossible for me to give Mexico another écu [crown] or another soldier.' And on the same day, a demented and defeated woman sent her husband a telegram in Spanish: '*Todos es inutil*' (All is useless).

27

A losing battle

In Mexico, Maximilian was waiting anxiously for news. The days following Charlotte's departure had been among the saddest in his life. He had never loved her so tenderly and so deeply as now, and he had never felt more lost without her. He wrote, 'Since you left, I have not known a quiet hour or a happy moment.' Yet it was now, when his Empire was falling apart, when his allies were deserting him, that he felt himself for the first time really in touch with the people, 'who at last begin to understand the sacrifice we have brought. I went yesterday evening out on the Paseo, and I have never had a warmer welcome. The people waved to me out of their carriage windows and from their balconies, and I was deeply moved, for it is a long time since I have been greeted in this way. A nun who visited me last night told me that all the nuns in the convent were praying for you twice a day, and supposedly unknown to me, your ladies are having daily Masses to ensure your safe return.'

Gestures of affection came to him not only from Mexico, but also from abroad. Stefan Herzfeld, the young naval officer who served as his aide-de-camp at Miramar, had thrown up his post as Consul-General in Vienna to join him in Mexico. The lonely and homesick Emperor welcomed his old friend with delight: 'Stefan Herzfeld has arrived to cheer me up with news of home and his natural *joie de vivre*. He will be of enormous help to me, especially in matters of finance in which he is an expert.' Where Herzfeld was chiefly valuable to his Emperor was in giving him honest and disinterested advice, and he had not been many weeks in Mexico before he realized that Maximilian's position was untenable, and that he must at all costs be persuaded to abdicate. But the simple sailor was no match for the wily Jesuit, who was now on his way back from Rome after months of good living at the Emperor's expense. Father Fischer had achieved little more than the other members of the commission. The Pope had handed over his responsibilities to the Mexican bishops, who were to examine the drafts of the *concordat* drawn up by Fischer and decide for or against it. Knowing the Mexican bishops, Maximilian had very little faith in the outcome. But the Jesuit's persuasive tongue at last convinced him that he had scored a personal triumph and that Mexico would have a *concordat* with Rome in a couple of months.

Meanwhile, the internal administration of the Empire was showing some signs of improvement, thanks to the energetic measures taken by two capable French generals, Osmont and Friant, whom Maximilian had brought into his government as Ministers for War and Finance. These appointments were made as part of a plan to involve France still further in Mexican affairs so that it would be impossible for Napoleon to extricate himself from his commitments. Two years before, the French Emperor had assured his ally that he would always be ready to lend the services of French officers to help in the administration. Now Maximilian had taken Napoleon at his word, but Bazaine gave no more than his provisional consent when he was asked to confirm the appointments.

Both General Osmont and Commissary-General Friant, who was a paymaster in the French forces, were among the sternest critics of the Marshal's extravagant campaigns, and the commander-in-chief saw with a jealous eye the favour they enjoyed at the Mexican Court. 'Osmont has achieved in three weeks what Bazaine was either unwilling or unable to do in three years', wrote the Emperor in praise of his new Minister for War. The Marshal did nothing to prevent the two officers from entering the Emperor's cabinet because he knew it was only a question of time before Washington formally objected to the presence of French serving officers in Maximilian's government, and Paris would have to cancel the appointments. Bazaine had not long to wait. By September, Secretary Seward's letter of protest was on its way to the Quai d'Orsay, and an official notice was inserted in *Le Moniteur* stating that 'neither General Osmont nor Commissary-General Friant have been authorized to accept posts in the Mexican government, which is incompatible with their position as serving officers in the French forces.' The two generals, who were genuinely devoted to Maximilian, were forced to resign, and Friant complained bitterly to Pierron, 'What do they really want to do? If they are trying to destroy Maximilian, why don't they say so openly?'

Meanwhile, place after place was being evacuated without a single shot being fired. The whole of the north was now in the hands of the *Juaristi*. Mazatalan and Guymas, the last of the Pacific ports, had gone, and the first week of August brought the news of the fall of the important Gulf port of Tampico, where the French garrison had been ordered to hand over the town and fortifications intact to the enemy, before they were evacuated by sea. Two days later, the Imperialist Prefect, one of the few Prefects known for his honesty and probity, was publicly hanged in the central square. On hearing this news, Maximilian gave vent to his indignation: 'Bazaine covers himself with shame. It is not only the honour of France, but my own honour which is at stake.'

The Emperor's relations with Bazaine were somewhat similar to those he had endured in Italy with General Gyulai. Both were looked upon as personal enemies, whereas they were no more than jealous subordinates carrying out the orders of Paris and Vienna. Bazaine's own position was not an enviable one. He himself was ashamed of a role, which was losing him the respect of the army of whom he had formerly been the idol. There was even a moment when he contemplated asking for his recall and leaving his rival General Douay to carry out the humiliating withdrawal. But financial and family ties kept him in Mexico. The eighteen-year-old Madame la Maréchale, who on the Empress's departure had become the most important woman in the country, enjoyed her new position far too much to relinquish it without a struggle. She and her family had too many vested interests in the Empire to consent to her husband leaving the country before he had received his marching orders.

The Emperor and the Marshal might dislike and distrust one another and indulge in mutual recriminations in their letters to the Tuileries, but their own correspondence continued to be amicable – on Maximilian's side almost affectionate, which lays him open to a charge of duplicity. One must remember that he was in a desperate situation, not daring to offend a man who was still in supreme control both of the French expeditionary force and of the Foreign Legion. Nor did Bazaine dare to speak frankly to an Emperor whom, in view of Napoleon's vacillating policy, he might still be called upon to defend. He kept assuring Maximilian that though the present situation forced him to evacuate strategic points in the northern and western states, 'those places could easily be retaken, once the enemy had been tired out and weakened'. There were several letters on this theme written between

August and October 1866, when Bazaine was already fully aware that by the following spring the bulk of the expeditionary force would already have embarked for France.

Meanwhile, Lopez de Santa Anna, like an old carrion crow hoping to feed on the debris of the Empire, had arrived in New York where he launched yet another proclamation, calling on the people of Mexico to rally round their old leader, who would deliver them from foreign tyranny. But all this bravado and sword-clanking was outdated and the group of prominent American businessmen who had given their financial backing in the hope of obtaining future concessions in Mexico, were heavily out of pocket. The only result of the proclamation was to gain Juarez fresh adherents from among the more moderate Liberals who had hitherto shunned his revolutionary policies.

The week of the fall of Tampico brought the news of the fall of Königsgratz and the defeat of Sadowa, news which by the time it reached Mexico was already a month old, but which made as great an impact on the unhappy young Emperor as if it had happened the day before. Maximilian forgot that he was Emperor of Mexico and only remembered that he was a Hapsburg, that Vienna was his capital and that perhaps at this very hour Prussian troops were tramping down the Graben. Both his former secretary, Baron du Pont, and the Mexican envoy in Vienna reported the panic in the Austrian capital, the utter demoralization of the people, and the carriages and carts, laden with valuables, leaving the city. Eloin, who was in Vienna in the days following Sadowa, wrote of the intense bitterness against the high command, and of the repetition of scenes which had followed Solferino. He personally had seen the Emperor Franz Josef drive through the streets in a chilling silence, suddenly broken by cries of 'Long live the Archduke Max!' and the Belgian added that, in this time of crisis, everyone was regretting that 'our Max was so far away'. These were dangerous words to repeat to a young man for whom the Mexican Empire had never been more than a substitute for secret, unrealizable ambitions. 'I had foreseen a catastrophe of this kind,' wrote Maximilian, 'but I never imagined it would come so suddenly. I was not surprised by the result, as I knew the causes, but I had hoped for more dignity and a little more ability.' The Prussian Minister, Baron Magnus, was surprised at the objectivity with which the Emperor discussed the Austrian defeat, which he attributed to the unfortunate system of giving commands to princes and counts, irrespective of their capacity.

Unfortunately, some of these criticisms found their way back to Vienna, where they were exaggerated a hundred-fold, strengthening Franz Josef in his determination not to give way over the Family Pact, hardening his feelings against Max. By the autumn, relations became still more strained through the unfortunate publication of what was meant to be a highly confidential report sent by Eloin to the Emperor Maximilian and dated 17 September. Eloin, who had returned to Brussels after visiting the Empress Charlotte at Miramar, wrote how, in passing through Austria, he had noted the general feeling of discontent which prevailed in all classes of the population: 'Nothing is being done; the Emperor is utterly discouraged and the people are becoming impatient and publicly demanding his abdication. In contrast, Your Majesty's reputation has never been so high. You are loved in all parts of the Empire and in particular in Venetia, where a large section of the population would like to see the return of their former Governor.' This letter, marked 'Secret and Confidential', was sent for greater safety via the Mexican Consul-General in New York, Eloin either having forgotten or being ignorant of the fact that there were two Mexican Consuls in New York, and that the one accredited to Juarez was generally recognized to be the official representative of the Mexican government. Inadvertently, this letter provided superb material for Republican propaganda, and Juarez lost no time in publishing it in American and European newspapers, where it had enormous repercussions, particularly in Austria. The Emperor Max's enemies spoke openly of treason, for Eloin was known to be one of his most trusted agents, and the publication of this letter may well have been one of the deciding factors which led members of the Imperial family to write to Maximilian warning him not to return to Austria, where his position would be untenable.

One piece of news from home gave Maximilian 'the truest and most heartfelt joy'. Wilhelm von Tegetthoff had vindicated his country's honour by winning the great naval battle of Lissa against the Italians, who had come into the war as Prussia's allies. The Imperial Austrian Navy, re-equipped and modernized by Maximilian, had won its first laurels, and Tegetthoff's flagship, the *Erz-Herzog Ferdinand Max*, had led the fleet to victory. The Emperor of Mexico, whose heart was still with his sailors in the Adriatic, wrote home, 'I can hardly control my grief that I was not there on the flagship that bears my name, among my splendid officers and my beloved Dalmatian and Istrian sailors. But all that belongs to the past. Nothing remains except the gratification of having done my duty.'

In Mexico, the news of Königsgratz had a disturbing effect on the already demoralized Austrian corps who, in the past months, had had to bear the brunt of the fighting in mountainous districts where they were often short of food and surrounded by 'an undependable and treacherous population'. Disagreements with the French who from the very first had resented the higher pay of the foreign mercenaries and their pretensions to an independent command, had reached a point where General Thun openly disobeyed the Marshal's orders, and both he and his general staff now took the opportunity of handing in their resignations, saying it was their duty to return to Austria.

But many of the young officers remained loyal to 'Kaiser Max', even though they knew his cause was doomed. Colonels Pollak and Alfons von Kodolitsch took over the command of what remained of the infantry and cavalry regiments. The twenty-five-year-old Count Khevenhüller offered to raise and equip at his own expense a regiment of hussars. Count Wykenburg and Lieutenant-Colonel Baron von Hammerstein were still defending the Imperial standard in Mexico City when Maximilian was already a prisoner in Queretaro. The Belgians, on the whole, were less heroic than the Austrians. They had enlisted as volunteers for the Empress's private guard, and had not reckoned with long months of arduous campaigning in a vast, uncivilized country and for the hard months of captivity which followed on Tacambaro. Released after an exchange of prisoners, they had returned to their regiment, many of them converted to the Republican cause and practically on the verge of mutiny. But some of the officers, including Van der Smissen, remained loyal to the Emperor for many months after Charlotte had left for Europe.

Maximilian may have been lacking in many of the qualities of leadership, but he possessed to the highest degree that personal magnetism which inspired devotion in the most disparate elements. What was it that won the devotion of a man like Tomas Mejía, an Indian chieftain from the wilds of the Sierra Corda? 'Mejía came to me yesterday. He is more intelligent, more devoted and more honest than ever, and he has not lost his spirit. On the contrary, he is a tower of strength,' wrote Maximilian to his wife after the fall of Tampico. What did eminent Mexican lawyers like Ramirez and Escudero, both of them bitterly opposed to the French intervention, see in this blond young Hapsburg to make them serve in his government, and after their dismissals, continue to be his friends?

A last desperate attempt to win the favour of Napoleon had forced Maximilian to get rid of the anti-French elements in his government, and the even more grievous necessity of coming to terms with the bishops was now forcing him to take Conservatives into his cabinet. But he loathed them at heart: 'Some of them, I know, are very worthy, but it is a great sacrifice for me to govern with them and to be continually in their company, for most of them are deadly dull and utterly *borné*, and I need my liberal friends to stimulate me mentally. . . . Both Ramirez and Escudero continually come to see me, and Herzfeld is struck by their wit and good humour.' The Emperor needed his friends to distract him from giving way to the blackest melancholia. To add to his depression, the weather was bad and Chapultepec, with the Princess Josefa Iturbide acting as hostess, was painfully reminiscent of the last months in the Reggio of Milan, when old Countess Lützoff deputized for Charlotte. But Dona Pepa, or *'La Primas'*, as he called her on account of her royal airs, had none of the Countess's charm and sweetness. She was a narrow-minded, bigoted old spinster, glorying in this interlude of power and forever gossiping and intriguing. 'You might ask Almonte whether he really visited Santa Anna at St Thomas, and let me know what he replies,' Maximilian wrote. 'Dona Pepa assures me it is true because she read the letters herself.' And again: 'You can tell that vain old Gutierrez that it is very painful for me to hear that he shows my most intimate letters to all his circle in Rome. He even sent the Pope a copy of my last one with comments attached. One would not do this to an ordinary friend, still less to a sovereign. That is the result of a Jesuit education and of Jesuit principles.'

It was unfortunate that Maximilian, in common with Napoleon, had the habit of listening to the gossip of whoever was near him at the time. Gutierrez was just as ready to criticize him to his face as behind his back for he had never forgiven him for betraying the interests of the Church, and did not hesitate to say so in the voluminous epistles in which he continued to give his unsought and often unpalatable advice. Gutierrez' friendship with Santa Anna rendered him particularly suspect at a moment when some of the leading citizens in Mexico City had been arrested for their part in a conspiracy against the Emperor's life, said to have been financed by the old Generalissimo. Twenty of the ringleaders were deported to Yucatan and all Santa Anna's properties confiscated. 'I now rule with an iron hand,' wrote Maximilian. 'They have had their two years of clemency and strangely enough, they seem to be more friendly towards me now than when I was granting amnesties.' How could anyone so gentle and humane begin to understand a people who only respected whom they feared? 'The other day I visited a town where they had recently killed two of my Prefects, and in spite of this they gave me a great ovation.' All this hatred and bloodshed, of which he sometimes felt himself to be the cause, filled him with horror, but everyone in his entourage, from old Dona Pepa to young Captain Pierron, now head of his Secretariat, kept urging him to adopt severer measures.

Only Cuernavaca, with its happy, unsophisticated inhabitants, remained an oasis of peace, where his health and spirits revived in a climate of perpetual spring, and where on every visit the gardens of El Olvido grew in beauty. Here he could relax in the company of Stefan Herzfeld and Dr Billimek, and entertain some of his favourite young officers, Don Miguel Lopez of the Imperial Guard and Colonel Lamadrid of the *Cazadores*, who often escorted him to and from the capital. Writing to Charlotte, Maximilian expatiates on the beauty of Cuernavaca: the constantly changing colour of the mountains; the moonlight gleaming on the twin volcanoes; the daily rains which always bring some new, exotic flower to life, so that Billimek is in his seventh heaven. 'But nothing,' he assures her, 'gives me pleasure when you are not there to share it.' Surely Maximilian would not have written in this vein if Conçepcion Sedano had just given birth to his son. He would not have been so cruel as to describe 'his few happy days at Cuernavaca' if he had spent them in the arms of an Indian mistress. He was suffering from severe pains of the gallbladder and almost continuous dysentery, a complaint far too debilitating for amorous dalliance. He was too ill and too worried to embark on or to revive a transient love affair, for everything now depended on the success of Charlotte's mission.

Father Fischer had returned from Rome without a *concordat*, but still convinced that the bishops, if properly handled, would end by accepting the Emperor's draft, and Blasio was now sent to Europe with fresh instructions for Charlotte's forthcoming visit to the Vatican. 'You must tell the Pope everything, and clear the atmosphere. Both he and Napoleon must know that I am their best friend.' Maximilian continued to delude himself on the situation, for this letter to Charlotte was written before he had received her first report from Paris, or the desperate telegram she sent him on her departure, by way of the newly-opened transatlantic cable which brought news to Vera Cruz in under three days. Still unsuspecting of the terrible malady which was gradually clouding her mind, the symptoms of which he had always attributed to nervous fatigue, he wrote to her, 'Do not let yourself be talked over in Paris. To come back to Mexico without results would be deplorable to the country and equally deplorable for you,' words which may well have precipitated a crisis in a woman tortured by the sense of her responsibility and the nature of her failure.

Charlotte left Paris on 23 August in such a state of nervous agitation that she was no longer able to act or reason normally. Her hatred for Napoleon had become pathological. Childhood memories of some Dürer engravings of the Revelations of St John now haunted her with apocalyptic visions in which Napoleon featured as the Devil, 'the Anti-Christ'. An incoherent, hysterical letter to her husband gives us some idea of what her unfortunate attendants had to contend with: 'I have achieved nothing, but at least I have the satisfaction of having upset all their arguments and shown up their falsehoods. He refuses categorically all help and no power can aid us, for he has Hell on his side. He is the Devil in person and at our last interview, he had an expression which made my hair stand on end – he was so hideous – it was the expression of his soul. ... He never loved you from the beginning for he is not capable of loving anything. He fascinated you like a serpent and I feel you must escape from his claws as soon as possible. Perhaps you will think I am exaggerating, but it reminds me so much of the Apocalypse and this place is Babylon. He is the Devil and Bazaine and Fould are his attendant satellites and they in turn have others.' There was more in the same vein – mad, turgid ravings interspersed with germs of common sense and sound political advice, but always harking back to that terrifying persecution mania which by now had become an obsession. 'You cannot exist in the same hemisphere as him, for he will burn you to ashes. You must get rid even of the financial agents, or else master them, and separate your army from the French, otherwise you are lost – there is not one of them you can trust.'

Yet, two days later, she was capable of writing a perfectly rational and affectionate letter to her old governess. Even the wise and astute Prince Metternich attributed her nervous excitability to no more than a natural disappointment and advised her to visit the Imperial family in Vienna, where her presence would serve to clear up so many misunderstandings. But Charlotte's pride would not allow her to visit the Hapsburgs who had been so cruel to Max, and she preferred instead to go directly to Miramar, where she could await his further instructions.

Having refused all practical help, Napoleon was now prodigal in his attentions. An Imperial train took the Empress across France. At Mâcon, where she spent the night, she was given a civic welcome and cheered by large crowds, all of which would have encouraged her in ordinary times but which she now dismissed as 'contemptible'. Her spirits improved after crossing Mont Cenis and arriving at the Italian frontier. 'It is such a relief to be leaving a country where he [Napoleon] poisons the air with his villainy.' But the jolting of the long carriage ride over the mountains gave her a terrible nausea and after two days of public receptions in Turin and Milan, where all classes of the population gave her a warm and friendly welcome, she arrived at her father's old villa on Lake Como in a state of utter exhaustion. Her doctor, who without her knowledge had been administering daily doses of bromide in her coffee, advised several weeks of rest, and for a few days she gave the impression of having regained her peace in the beautiful surroundings of the Villa d'Este, of which she had such happy memories. If only she could have prolonged her stay and forgotten her mad dreams of Imperial grandeur. If only she could have brought herself to persuade her husband to abdicate, convincing him that honour was satisfied, that it was useless to go on sacrificing their health and youth for a country where they would always remain foreigners. But that fatal combination of Coburg ambition and Bourbon pride would not let her rest, and there is no word of abdication in the loving, nostalgic letter which Charlotte wrote to Max from the place where they had spent some of the happiest months of their lives: 'I never cease thinking of you, my darling. Everything here speaks of you. Your Lake of Como of which you were so fond, lies before my eyes, so calm and blue. All is the same, only you are over there – so far, far away, and nearly ten years have gone by, yet I remember it all as if it were yesterday. Nature here speaks to me of nothing but untarnished happiness, not of difficulties and disappointments. . . . I live once more in our Lombardy as if I had never left it. . . . Here in my bedroom, I have found your youthful portrait, probably put there on purpose with the inscription "*Governatore Generale del Regno Lombardo-Veneto*". The moon is shining now and they are singing outside. It is all beautiful beyond words.' Yet she was still working incessantly for 'the task you have set me to do.' What she had accomplished in Paris was little enough but it was always something. She had managed to prevent the conversion of the two Mexican loans and to persuade the Franco-Mexican commission to pay the arrears of the salaries due to the various legations in Europe, and she hoped her 'dear Treasure' would be satisfied with what she had done.

After only a few days at Lake Como, her nerves got calmer and her spirits settled down. Her doctor and attendants begged her to prolong her stay but she insisted on leaving for Miramar, where she hoped to find news from Mexico. Her journey through Lombardy and Venetia was a personal triumph, for even the most fervent of nationalists remembered with affection the liberal young Archduke and his pretty bride. 'All sovereign honours were shown to me by both Austria and Italy, King Victor Emmanuel travelled from Rovigo to Padua especially to meet me. It is right that the powers of Europe should bow towards an American sovereign.' Again one finds her possessed by that megalomania which was driving her to disaster. At Desenzano, on Lake Garda, a detachment of Garibaldian volunteers in their red shirts formed a guard of honour round a Mexican flag embroidered by the ladies of Bari. At Peschiera, one of the last fortresses of the Quadrilateral remaining in Austrian hands, cannon fired a royal salute for the Emperor Franz Josef's sister-in-law, and at Padua station, in the suite of the King of Italy, Charlotte found an old friend, Count Cittadella, who had introduced her to the works of Tasso in the first months of her married life at Monza. 'King Victor Emmanuel was immensely cordial and full of affection for you', wrote Charlotte to her husband, enclosing a treatise she had compiled on the new Kingdom of Italy. It was typical of her feverish activity to produce a long, political dissertation on a country which was no longer any concern of theirs.

But the proudest moment of her journey came after crossing by boat from Venice to Trieste. There, lying at anchor, was the squadron which Admiral von Tegetthoff had led to victory at Lissa. All the crews were out on deck to cheer her as she sailed into the harbour and in spite of the rough sea and the pouring rain, she insisted on boarding the flagship to congratulate Tegetthoff in person.

It was a victory which had helped Austria very little, for though the Italians had been beaten by land and sea, the peace of Zurich and the mediation of Napoleon had given them Venice. In these days, Trieste was expecting a visit from the Emperor Franz Josef, who was to inspect the victorious fleet before it left for the new naval base at Pola, but he deliberately postponed his visit on hearing that his sister-in-law was expected at Miramar and he wrote to his wife, 'I cannot go to Trieste at present, for Her Mexican Majesty, having failed to accomplish anything in Paris, is due to appear there at any moment, so I prefer to stay here at present.' From the tone of this note, it would seem as if the Imperial family were not so affectionately disposed towards Charlotte as Prince Metternich would have had her believe. The only member of the family to visit Charlotte at Miramar was the Archduke Ludwig Viktor, sent by his mother not out of affection for Charlotte but in order to get news of Max.

There were many devoted old friends and retainers waiting to welcome the Empress at the castle. There was Radonetz and his wife and old Dr Jilek, who had been against the Mexican enterprise from the beginning, and in the dining room, above the Imperial arms, had placed a wreath of thorns. There were the same gardeners, proudly showing the progress of every bush and tree planted by their beloved Archduke. 'Your ivy bower by the summerhouse has become one of the wonders of the world', wrote Charlotte. 'The fan palms, pines and weeping willows have grown to a tremendous size, and you may be pleased to hear that the Mexicans are enraptured by Miramar, and that I too appreciate it fully for the first time.' But even at Miramar she remained obsessed with her illusions of grandeur. 'Everybody is amazed by those two works of the absent Prince, the Battle of Lissa and the Castle of Miramar. These ideas are associated in everybody's speeches, and even before their eyes, for today the victorious squadron will pass in front of Miramar, in the same order of battle as at Lissa, with Tegetthoff leading on the *Erz-Herzog Ferdinand Max*. It is leaving Trieste and perhaps disappearing from history. It cast the first ray upon your coming power, upon your dearly-bought independence; it saved the coast which was so dear to you . . . its mission is accomplished. So is yours. The honour of the House of Hapsburg crossed the Atlantic with the name of one of the last Austrian victories, Novara.* It is sinking here with the sun, to rise again over there . . . Charles v showed the way. You have followed him. Do not regret it. God was with him.'

Till now, these delusions had appeared only in her letters to Max. There was nothing abnormal in her behaviour in those days at Miramar,

---

* The battleship in which Maximilian crossed the Atlantic was named after an Austrian victory against the Italians in 1849.

where she appeared to be delighted with everything and visitors and deputations were graciously received. Elaborate preparations were being made to celebrate Mexican Independence Day with fireworks and a garden fiesta, but those who had not seen the Empress for two years were shocked by her appearance – the hectic flush on the haggard cheeks, the hard look in the unnaturally brilliant eyes – and it was noted that in spite of the intense heat she always wore a mantilla and a shawl. Dr Jilek looked worried and spent hours in anxious conference with Dr Bohuslavek, and over Madame Radonetz's tea table, the ladies gossiped among themselves. Only her devoted Austrian maid, Martha Doblinger, kept her own council and confided in no one.

The news of the fall of Tampico was a fresh shock to her already unbalanced mind. Maximilian's telegram, which had been sent to Paris by way of New York, only arrived in Europe on the last day of August and reached Miramar after a few days' further delay. The telegram told her that the customs convention demanded by France had been signed, and complained that in violation of his written promises, Bazaine was evacuating one place after the other and that the *Juaristi* were already fighting near Vera Cruz and Jalapa. At the same time, Maximilian informed her that Blasio was on his way to Europe with fresh instructions. No sooner had she received this news than the Empress worked herself into a fever of agitation, shutting herself up alone in her room, composing letter after letter to Napoleon which were no sooner written than they were destroyed, for her pride would not allow her to humiliate herself again in front of a man whom she considered to be the Devil Incarnate. Impatiently, she awaited Blasio, who finally arrived on the eve of Mexican Independence Day. He had travelled almost continuously, by rail and coach, ever since his arrival at St Nazaire, but in place of the welcome he expected and deserved, he found himself treated by the Empress with the utmost suspicion. She received him immediately. Dressed in the deepest mourning, looking ill and drawn, she greeted him without a smile, asking crossly why he had delayed so long, why he had broken the journey in Paris, when he knew how anxiously he was being awaited, and was he sure that no one had tampered with his dispatches on his journey through France. Embarrassed and disconcerted, the young man protested that he had come as soon as he could, but that having arrived in Paris on a Sunday, he had to wait till the following day to cash a letter of credit. His Emperor's dispatches had been in his keeping both day and night, and Her Majesty could see for herself that the seals were intact. To which the Empress somewhat grudgingly conceded that she did not question his loyalty, but he was young and ingenuous and did not realize the depths of iniquity of which their enemies were capable.

Blasio was mystified by the Empress's strange behaviour until both her doctors and Kuhacsevich confided in him their growing fears for her sanity, and the terrible persecution mania which made her distrust her oldest and most faithful servants. But the following evening, no one could have appeared more normal or more charming than the Empress Carlota when she received her guests on the terraces of Miramar, toasting the future of the Mexican Empire while the words '*Independencia*' and '*Evviva Messico*' glittered in fireworks over the Adriatic. Felix Eloin, who was leaving for Brussels the following day, was so carried away by the beauty of the scene that he wrote to the Emperor in all sincerity, 'I left the Empress Carlota radiant with youth and health, surrounded by flowers in the enchanted gardens of Miramar.'

28

'Todos es inutil'

Late at night on 25 September 1866, a special train with the Empress of Mexico on board drew up in front of an illuminated, flower-decked platform of Rome's Termini Station, where a galaxy of Cardinals, Papal Chamberlains, Roman aristocrats and representatives of the diplomatic corps were waiting to receive her. It was a brilliant climax to an exhausting journey which had lasted for over a week. Cholera having broken out in Trieste, the Italians had imposed a fortnight's quarantine on all boats arriving from Austria, and rather than submit to the delay, Charlotte had chosen to take the long overland route via Marbourg and Bozen, travelling by train and carriage and crossing the Italian frontier at Mantua. Blasio and Kuhacsevich had been sent on in advance to make the necessary arrangements, while the Empress, accompanied by Castillo, del Vallé and the two del Barrios, travelled by easier stages.

She had not yet recovered from the exertions of the previous journey and her doctors had implored her to postpone her Roman visit, but she had refused to listen either to them or to Bombelles, whose opposition to her plans enraged her to the point of her suspecting him of being in the pay of Napoleon, and she refused to let him accompany her to Rome. Her attendants lived in continual apprehension of her moods, and they had not got as far as Bozen before it became apparent that she was in no fit state to travel. Wherever they stopped overnight, some harmless maid or waiter became the object of her suspicions. Driving through a village of the Dolomites, she caught sight of a peasant walking home from a local fair proudly carrying a gun covered with trophies won at the shooting range. Clutching hold of Señora del Barrio's arm, trembling with agitation, the Empress ordered the coachman to drive on as quickly as possible, for she was convinced the peasant was Almonte in disguise, come to assassinate her on the orders of Napoleon. An organ-grinder in the streets of Bozen was taken for Colonel Lamadrid of the

Mexican *Cazadores* regiment, who she imagined had followed her to Europe to spy on her actions. When her devoted lady-in-waiting tried to calm her fears, a furtive look would come into her eyes which made Señora del Barrio feel that if she protested too much she would end by being suspected herself.

In Bozen, the Empress had such a violent attack of nausea and nervous palpitations that Castillo was told to cancel all arrangements because she was returning to Miramar, but a few hours later she decided to continue her journey and the order was countermanded.

It must have been a terrible ordeal for the small party of Mexicans with no previous experience of Europe to find themselves travelling across Italy in the wake of a mistress who could no longer be treated as a rational human being. In the absence of Bombelles, there was no European among them with sufficient authority to take control. Dr Bohuslavek was young and timid and incapable of dealing with a psychiatric patient. None of the Mexicans, whether it was the Foreign Minister Castillo, who had been sent on this mission after only a few months in office, or the gentle, soft-voiced Creole aristocrat, del Vallé, or the devoted del Barrios, were able to stand up to their capricious Empress. The tragic irony of this journey was that it outwardly gave the appearance of a triumphal progress. Austria and Italy vied with each other in paying homage to the Empress Carlota, and large crowds assembled in every place she passed. In Mantua, where there was still an Austrian garrison, a salute of one hundred and one guns was fired in her honour and she was given a state welcome. Reggio and Bologna followed suit with salvos of artillery and military bands which she would willingly have dispensed with. Banquets and civic receptions followed one another, and at each one the Empress appeared with a radiant smile and a gracious manner, but each time it became more of an effort, and on returning to the hotel or palace where she was staying, she would retire into her rooms, lock herself in and relapse into a brooding silence.

At Reggio she had an unexpected visitor in Leonardo Marquez, one of the two Conservative generals Maximilian, on the advice of his Liberal ministers, had sent on expensive and useless missions which were a form of gilded exile. Now that the Conservatives were regaining their influence Marquez and Miramon were returning to Mexico to place their swords at the service of the Empire. Formerly, Charlotte would have had sufficient political insight to know that the return of the two generals would only intensify an already sanguinary civil war. Marquez, who was notorious for his sadistic cruelty, was loathed by all but the most fanatical of Conservatives, while Miramon in his brief tenure of power had dared to lay hands on the property of foreign nationals and was anathema to the whole European community. By placing himself in the hands of these two ruthless and ambitious men, Maximilian would be alienating the sympathies of all the more moderate elements in the country. But in her present state of mind, the Empress was ready to delude herself in the belief that the return of the generals heralded a victory for the Empire.

At Foligno, she was met by Velasquez de Leon and the other members of the Mexican commission in Rome, but she felt too ill to attend the banquet in her honour and dined alone in her room with Señora del Barrio, who afterwards recalled that the entire conversation turned on the subject of poison and poisoners. According to the Empress, there was hardly a crowned head who had died a natural death. Her father, her mother and the Prince Consort of England had all been poisoned.

Blasio describes the Empress Carlota's arrival in Rome, 'dressed in the deepest mourning and looking as pale as a ghost'. Outside the station, it was pouring with rain, and the crowds huddling under their black umbrellas added to the funereal effect of the torchlight procession which escorted the Empress from the station to the Hotel Roma on the Corso, where Velasquez de Leon had reserved her the royal suite. The next morning, the sun was shining and Charlotte awoke refreshed and in an optimistic mood. She was delighted at finding herself back in Rome and was pleased with the magnificence of her reception. Tributes of flowers kept arriving at her door; Papal troops in resplendent uniforms formed a guard of honour outside the hotel, and she took as a good omen the fact that her rooms looked out on the church of her patron saint, San Carlo Borromeo. Ignoring her doctor's advice to rest in preparation for the strenuous days ahead, she insisted on going sightseeing, returning shortly after midday worn out by the terrible heat and bathed in perspiration. She had barely time to change before Cardinal Antonelli was announced.

The all-powerful Secretary of State was calling on the Empress of Mexico to prevent her from embarrassing the Pope with impossible demands and to spare her the humiliation of the historic 'non possuamus' of a Papal rebuff. Wearing scarlet and purple robes and preceded by a powdered lackey, the Cardinal, who had risen from comparatively humble origins to be the virtual ruler of Rome, presented the appearance of a suave and polished man of the world, rather than a man of God. He was determined not to commit himself in word or deed and to forestall any attempt on the Empress's part to seek Papal intervention with Napoleon, for the Vatican was hardly in a position to interfere with French policy in Mexico at a time when the Papal States only continued to exist by virtue of French bayonets. Charlotte had to listen to a long and elaborate dissertation on the errors and mistakes committed by the Emperor Maximilian: his encouragement of heresy in a country which for over three hundred years had been a bulwark of Catholicism, his having allowed his Liberal ministers to defraud the Church of the greater part of its revenues. She listened not with humility but with resentment, writing to Max after her visitor had left: 'Cardinal Antonelli has just been to see me. Like Fould, he spoke of nothing but money.'

After voicing his disapproval of Imperial policy in the past, the Pope's emissary gave her the assurance that a *concordat* would be concluded 'as soon as the Emperor makes his peace with the bishops'. His Holiness had been happy to hear that Maximilian had already summoned them to a council, Antonelli added that in spite of all that had happened, the Holy Father took a benevolent interest in Mexico and its sovereigns, and as a proof of his goodwill, would be pleased to receive her the following day. Upon which His Eminence took his leave, bestowing benedictions on his way. The Cardinal's assurances amounted to very little, but Charlotte was ready to seize on any straw which would justify her in her husband's eyes. She could not forget his having told her that 'to return to Mexico without results would be deplorable for the country and deplorable for you'. Hence the false optimism of the letter where she tells him: 'Things are beginning to look up. No one has anything against us here and our relations with Rome are good. With the fall of the Papal power, one can ask of them what one likes.' In her own despair, she still felt the need to boost Maximilian's morale and to make every effort to conceal from him the truth, whereas it was she who was in the greater need of reassurance. She was still sufficiently lucid to realize that the Cardinal had come to prepare her for failure – but Antonelli was not the Pope. She remembered Pope Pius's gentle face, his soft voice when he said Mass for them in his private chapel before their departure for Mexico, and she placed her last hopes on that wise, kindly old man, who even if he had wanted to help, was powerless to do so.

Unfortunately, there was no one to advise her, no elderly woman friend to whom she could confess her fears. Perhaps it was the fault of her own introverted character, the result of a lonely, unhappy childhood, which made it so difficult for her to confide. But there is little doubt that this proud reserve, this iron self-discipline, contributed to her final mental breakdown. A few days later, when the Empress's insanity had become the talk of Rome, the Belgian envoy reported to his Foreign Minister in Brussels, 'One can trace these nervous disorders to the many anxieties and disillusions which Her Majesty has been at such pains to hide. It appears that since her arrival in Europe she had confided in no one, not even in her Foreign Minister, Castillo, who was never told of what took place at her private audiences, either with Napoleon or the Pope, and was never shown the telegrams she sent to or received from the Emperor Maximilian. I feel it would have been an enormous help to the Empress Charlotte, had she been able to share her troubles with some sympathetic woman friend. Who knows if it might not have averted the final tragedy?'

The King and Queen of Naples, who were living in exile in the Farnese Palace, were among the Empress's first visitors, and Maria Sofia wrote to her sister Elisabeth in Vienna that they found Charlotte 'in a state of nervous agitation, talking incessantly of poison'. But there was no sign of madness in the elegant, dignified young Empress who on the morning of 27 September drove through the streets of Rome in a state coach drawn by four horses, escorted by members of the Guardia Nobile and followed by a cortège of carriages containing the members of her suite. At the Vatican she was received with all the honours due to a reigning sovereign. Swiss Guards, wearing the uniforms designed by Michelangelo, flanked the great staircase. Papal Chamberlains, in black velvet and lace ruffs, accompanied her through the long, frescoed galleries to the magnificent throneroom where, seated on a golden throne under a crimson canopy, surrounded by the highest dignitaries of the Church, Pope Pius IX was waiting to receive her.

Blasio writes: 'At the Empress's approach, the seventy-four-year-old Pope rose from his throne – a tall, majestic figure, somewhat stout, of affable expression with lively eyes and a soft, harmonious voice. The Empress Carlota knelt to kiss the Papal slipper, but he stopped her and, extending his right hand, permitted her only to press her lips to the

Papal ring. Then he invited her to take a seat on his right and all of us who had accompanied Her Majesty filed before His Holiness and knelt to kiss his slipper. He then blessed us all and everyone retired while the Pope took the Empress into an adjoining room.' The audience lasted for the unusually long time of one hour and a quarter but what took place during that time, what was asked for and what was refused, has never been divulged. It is known that the Empress presented Pope Pius with a draft *concordat*, and there is no doubt that the evasive nature of his reply, his indeterminate promises, his apparent inability or unwillingness to help, ended in convincing the unhappy Charlotte that she had come to the end of the road and that in front of her rose the stone wall of utter failure. The shock of this final disappointment destroyed the last remnants of her sanity.

Meanwhile, her attendants had been taken on a tour of the Vatican's art treasures, but anxiety over the outcome of the visit and their concern for their mistress prevented them from concentrating on the beauties of the frescoes of Raphael and Michelangelo. On rejoining the Empress, they saw from her distraught expression and gloomy silence that their worst forebodings had been realized. Cardinals and bishops accompanied Charlotte to her carriage. As in Paris, so now in Rome, honours and attentions were being lavished on her to cloak the brutality of her rebuff. Blasio writes that on their return to their hotel, 'the Empress was silent and taciturn. Her suite, who had been waiting to hear something to quell their anxiety, were left in suspense, and after ordering some food to be served in her rooms, Charlotte shut herself up without allowing anyone to speak to her.' Later in the afternoon, she ordered the Grand Chamberlain, the Count del Vallé, to ask the authorities to withdraw the Papal troops and the military bands posted outside the hotel, for from now on she declined to accept any form of official honours. To everyone's surprise, the Empress appeared at a dinner to which she had invited the members of the Mexican commission, but she was so obviously in a bad mood that no one dared to speak for fear of giving offence. When the coffee and sherbet were handed round, she refused to be served before the others, and on seeing that the silver coffee-pot was slightly dented, had it immediately removed. Looking round at her guests with a hard, suspicious look, she said, 'It is obvious that someone is intent on poisoning me.'

The following day she ate alone in her room with Señora del Barrio, one of the few people she still appeared to trust. The lady-in-waiting noted that she ate nothing but oranges and nuts, carefully examining every shell and peel to see that it was not broken. There was an unpleasant altercation when Velasquez de Leon, who was suffering from a slight indisposition, excused himself from attendance. The Empress, who immediately suspected that he had been poisoned the previous evening, insisted on seeing him, threatening to appear in his rooms to verify his symptoms. In the end, he preferred to get up from his sick-bed rather than cast suspicion on one of his colleagues. All of them lived in dread of how the Empress would behave when the Pope returned her visit on the afternoon of 29 September. The guards she had asked to be dismissed were now doubled in number and the people who loitered all day outside the hotel in the hopes of seeing the Empress and her colourful retinue of Mexican servants, dressed in *charro* costume, now swelled to a large crowd to view the Papal visit. His Holiness who must have already noted the Empress's mental aberrations, had curtailed his visit to a minimum, and came accompanied by Cardinal Antonelli to support him in case of need. But Charlotte remained outwardly calm and all that was noticed was her growing distrust of her retinue and an obsession that Napoleon's agents were spying on her in Rome.

The chief victims of her mistrust were those who were the most devoted: the gentle and kindly del Vallé, who as her Chamberlain had often to countermand absurd and illogical orders; the Kuhacseviches, husband and wife, who presuming on their long years of devoted service with the Archduke, gave her well-meant and commonsense advice, which only served to infuriate her. The one she suspected most of all was the unfortunate Dr Bohuslavek, whom she had seen putting sedatives in her coffee and who was now banished from her presence.

Her retinue was in despair. All were agreed that she was in need of medical care but no one dared to introduce a stranger, and it was decided to await the arrival of Dr Jilek, who together with Count Bombelles had been urgently summoned from Miramar. But owing to the quarantine still enforced on the frontier, they would take several days to arrive. The Empress's suite were later accused of having completely lost their heads and Felix Eloin, who was always ready to criticize the Mexicans, complained to Stefan Herzfeld, 'Little can be said in favour of the Mexicans, judging from what went on in Rome during those first difficult moments. No one took any initiative, precious time was wasted when a firm decision should have been taken at once.

Instead of which, indecision and misplaced susceptibilities all served to complicate the situation.' But it is doubtful whether Eloin would have succeeded in doing any better himself. One's heart goes out to those well-meaning, devoted and totally inexperienced Mexicans having to deal with an impossible situation and trying to prevent the news of the Empress's insanity from becoming the talk of Rome.

The story of Charlotte's tragic calvary, which was to enclose her in the terror-haunted world of the insane for over sixty years, began on the morning of 30 September, when Señora del Barrio was bidden to the Empress's room to find her at eight o'clock already fully dressed in black bonnet and cloak, telling her to order a carriage to drive them to the Fontana dei Trevi. All those who saw Charlotte leaving the hotel were struck by her feverish, unnatural appearance, the dark, sunken eyes contrasting with the red, flushed cheeks. On arriving at the fountain, she got down from her carriage and to her lady-in-waiting's astonishment knelt by the water, cupping it in her hands and drinking avid gulps. saying, 'Here, at least, it will not be poisoned. I was so thirsty.' Astonishment turned to consternation when Señora del Barrio heard the Empress direct the coachman to drive to the Vatican. Here, she asked to see the Pope, and when the horrified lady-in-waiting protested, 'But Your Majesty is not dressed for a Papal audience!' she replied in her haughtiest manner, 'You forget, Manuelita, it is the Emperors who make the rules of etiquette. They themselves are above them.' There was something so tragic and so desperate about her that neither the guards nor the chamberlains dared to turn her away. The Pope received her immediately. He had just returned from Mass and was quietly enjoying his breakfast when Charlotte, with the tears pouring down her face, entered, or rather erupted, into his room, throwing herself at his feet, and implored him to protect her 'from the assassins who are planning to kill me'. Napoleon's spies were everywhere, she cried. Her servants, even her ministers, were in his pay. She begged to be allowed to stay in the Vatican, which was the only place in which she felt safe. Clinging to the Pope's knees, she refused to move until he promised her protection.

He treated her as gently as if she were a frightened child. He realized he was dealing with a madwoman when Charlotte, seeing on the breakfast table a steaming cup of hot chocolate, dipped her fingers in it, sucking them with relish and crying out, 'I'm starving! Everything they give me is poisoned.' Even now the Pope maintained his calm, merely ringing for another cup of chocolate for his guest, but Charlotte wailed that the cup was sure to be poisoned and begged to be allowed to share his own. The Holy Father, who was beginning to be slightly exasperated, gave in to her wishes and whereupon she became quite calm and rational, talking of Mexico and the political situation there, but every now and then interrupting the conversation to ask him what he considered to be the most effective antidote to poison – to which he answered, 'The rosary and prayer'.

The hours passed and still she showed no signs of leaving, till finally the Pope had to make it quite plain that he had other things to do than to spend all day discussing Mexico. Meanwhile, he succeeded in sending an urgent message to Cardinal Antonelli, telling him to procure two doctors and to disguise them as Papal Chamberlains, for the Empress appeared to have a particular fear of doctors. At the same time, he was to warn Velasquez de Leon of the Empress's condition and of her suspicions of some of her attendants, who had better be moved to another hotel before her return.

From now on, the Cardinal took matters into his hands. After conferring with Castillo and Velasquez de Leon, it was decided to telegraph the King of the Belgians, telling him what had happened. Señora del Barrio was then consulted as to her mistress's tastes and predelictions. They finally succeeded in luring Charlotte away from the Pope's room by offering to show her some of the treasures of the Vatican library. Even then she insisted on being accompanied by the Pope, who managed to make his escape at a moment when she was engrossed in looking at an illuminated missal. She spent the rest of the morning quite happily in visiting the Vatican gardens in the company of her lady-in-waiting and the head of the Papal gendarmerie, stopping every now and then at some fresh spring to quench her still-parching thirst. Midday came and she showed no sign of leaving, so Cardinal Antonelli invited her and Señora del Barrio to luncheon, where she behaved quite normally, apart from insisting on eating from the same plate as her lady-in-waiting. Later in the afternoon she consented to see Velasquez de Leon, who persuaded her to return to her hotel on the understanding that all those she suspected had already been arrested. Accompanied by what the Empress believed to be a Papal Chamberlain (in reality a doctor in disguise), she arrived at her apartment to find that the keys were missing: they had been taken away with the intention of locking her up in her room at night.

The sight of the empty lock was sufficient to bring on a fit of hysterics. Screaming that the assassins were inside, waiting to murder her, she insisted on going back to the Vatican. She was ready to sleep on the floor, in the corridor, anywhere, so long as she could remain under the protection of the Holy Father. No prayers or persuasion could calm her, and the doctor, who feared a sudden attack of violence, ended in giving way.

It was already ten o'clock at night when, to the horror and consternation of the Papal entourage, a weeping, dishevelled woman sought readmittance to the Vatican. Even Antonelli was at a loss how to deal with a problem which had never arisen in nearly eighteen hundred years of Papal history. There was no alternative but to arouse the Pope who, exhausted by the days' events, had already retired for the night. With patience and resignation, Pope Pius accepted the situation and ordered the Vatican library to be transformed into a bedchamber for the Empress and her lady-in-waiting, adding with a characteristic flash of humour, 'Nothing is spared me in this life – now a woman has to go mad in the Vatican.' But the woman in question was still a reigning Empress, sister-in-law of his Catholic and Apostolic Majesty, the Emperor of Austria, sister of the King of the Belgians and first cousin to the Queen of England. Two bronze bedsteads with coverlets of the finest lace and linen, a pair of golden candelabras, a dressing table set of vermeil, transformed the library into a sumptuous bedchamber. Charlotte was at last at peace and fell asleep at once, after drinking hot milk containing a sedative prepared for her by the doctor she still believed to be a Papal Chamberlain. Only the unfortunate lady-in-waiting remained sleepless not daring to close an eye for fear of her mistress waking.

The following morning found her quiet and serene, but the mood changed as soon as the Pope refused her demand to hear Mass in his private chapel. His nerves were too shaken to face her again and he suggested her hearing Mass in St Peter's, where the royal pew would be put at her disposal. The very suggestion of her going to a church where assassins might be lying in wait filled her with horror, and she refused to leave her room or to touch any food other than which had been prepared for His Holiness. Her obsession with death was pitiable, for she was convinced she had only a few more days to live, and in this mood she wrote a farewell message to her husband: 'God is calling me to Him, but before I go, I want to thank you, my dearest treasure, for the happiness you have always given me' – a note which must have filled Maximilian with remorse when it reached him a month later in Mexico. But she was no more lucid when she wrote it than later at Miramar when her condition became worse and she pictured her once-beloved husband as a murderer who, ever since her journey to Yucatan, had been trying to get rid of a wife who was unable to produce an heir.

By noon on 1 October, the news was all over Rome. The sensation of a woman having spent the night in the Vatican outweighed the tragic fact of the young Empress having become insane. Throughout the morning the Pope crept about his palace as stealthily as a thief, for fear of running into the Empress in one of the corridors. On returning home from his morning drive, he inquired anxiously whether she had gone. By the afternoon, everyone was becoming desperate. Charlotte categorically refused either to go out for a drive or to be taken sight-seeing, and it was only when Cardinal Antonelli resorted to guile that she was persuaded to leave. The Mother Superior from a neighbouring convent was instructed to invite the Empress to visit their orphanage, telling her how proud and happy the children would be. Charlotte agreed and for the first part of the visit was kind and gracious, sweet to the children, offering a donation for the chapel and generally showing such interest that the Mother Superior took her on a tour of inspection of the building. All went well till they reached the kitchens, where Charlotte, who had not eaten since early morning, commented on the appetizing smell of the ragoût being cooked for the evening meal. Hoping to please her, the sister in charge offered her some to taste. Unfortunately, there was a speck of dirt on the knife, and Charlotte no sooner saw this than she became hysterical, recoiling in horror from what she took to be a poisoned knife, and screaming, 'Can't you see those marks? It's poison! Only God has saved me.' And kneeling down in front of the terrified nuns, she gave thanks for her deliverance. But her gnawing hunger would no longer be denied, and seeing some large pieces of beef simmering in a cauldron, she plunged her hand in to snatch a bit of meat. In doing so, she scalded her fingers so badly that while they were treating the burns, she fainted from the pain. Her suite took the opportunity to bring her back to the hotel, but she recovered consciousness on the way, and it required two strong men of the Guardia Nobile to carry her, still struggling, into the hall. According to one report, 'she had to be put into a strait-jacket,' but Blasio and other reliable witnesses write that she regained some measure of self-control on entering the hotel and was seen to walk quietly up the stairs, supported by Señora del Barrio and her faithful Viennese maid, Martha Doblinger.

For the next week, this simple peasant woman was her constant and almost sole companion. On the orders of the Roman doctor, all members of her entourage, with the exception of Señora del Barrio, were to keep away unless they were specially summoned. Frau Kuhacsevich, who would have been only too ready to serve her, was looked upon with hatred, and when bidden to Charlotte's room a few hours after her arrival, was bitterly upbraided for her ingratitude and accused of having sold her to Napoleon's agents. The poor woman threw herself at Charlotte's feet and protested her innocence, but in a cold fury the Empress refused to listen, telling her: 'Warn your accomplices that their plots are discovered and they had better flee for their lives.' This sudden loathing of the harmless Kuhacseviches must have had its origin in some latent grievance, some incident which may have occurred in Mexico. From her letters we know Frau Kuhacsevich to have been a gossip and she may have taken upon herself to enlighten her mistress on the Emperor's love affair at Cuernavaca, of which Charlotte would have preferred to remain in ignorance. She may even have spied on those evening excursions on Lake Chalco, of which so little is known.

All these conjectures are as difficult to answer as a far more vital question – whether Charlotte was pregnant when she undertook the journey to Europe. Certain indications give substance to a rumour too persistent to be ignored: the nausea and sickness she suffered throughout the journey, though the Atlantic crossing was smooth; nausea again on the carriage drives through the Alps and Dolomites, when she had never been known to complain of sickness on the appalling mountain roads of Mexico. The fashion of the day, the crinoline and shawl, made it comparatively easy for a woman to hide her pregnancy in the first months, and it was noted in Paris that, in spite of the heat, the Empress always wore a cloak or a shawl. Doctor Bohuslavek was not her regular physician and was travelling with her for the first time, and it is doubtful whether he was ever allowed to make a thorough examination. The only person ever admitted into her intimacy was the maid, Martha Doblinger. What gives the rumour credibility was the callous treatment Charlotte was to receive from the Hapsburgs during the winter of her isolation at Miramar. Her failure to produce an heir, the unsatisfactory nature of her marital relations with the husband she adored, had prayed on her mind from the earliest days of her married life, added to which were the stories of Max's infidelities; the Mexican contempt for a barren woman; the physical impact of a sinister, beautiful country she had grown to hate. All these factors may have combined to undermine a passionate and possessive nature and Charlotte may well have allowed herself to be loved by Van der Smissen on some moonlit evening on Lake Chalco. Later would have come the fears and torments of her religious scruples, the misery of expecting a child she could never acknowledge, the child she longed to have had by Max, and this anxiety and fear added to all her other worries may have brought about the terrible mental collapse which ended in insanity.

Meanwhile, a telegram had arrived from Brussels to say that the Count of Flanders was on his way to Rome, where he would be arriving on 7 October. The Emperor of Austria had been notified of the Empress's illness and was sending Dr Riedel, director of the Vienna Lunatic Asylum, to consult with Dr Jilek on her return to Miramar. But it was not until 5 October that Martin Castillo and Velasquez de Leon found the courage to compose a telegram to the Emperor Maximilian telling him that his wife was suffering from 'a severe congestion of the brain' and was being taken to Miramar. Dr Bohuslavek was embarking for Mexico at the earliest possible date so as to give the Emperor a detailed account of his wife's illness.

What is even more inexplicable is that for almost a week, from the evening of 1 October, when Charlotte returned to her hotel, up to the arrival of Dr Jilek on 6 October, she was free to come and go as she liked and received all her medical treatment from her maid, a young woman quite inexperienced in maladies of this nature. By order of the Papal doctors, the hotel was cleared of guests. Even the servants remained hidden when the Empress went out for her daily drive, accompanied by either Martha Doblinger or Manuelita del Barrio. She would order the coachman to take her to one or the other of the Roman fountains, where she collected fresh water in a crystal jug which she always carried herself, and which she drank from a glass taken from the Pope's room. Sometimes she would order one of the Papal guards, who were still in attendance, to buy her some roasted chestnuts, which she would peel and eat during her drive. The rest of the day would be spent brooding in her room, or in composing some imaginary decree, forgotten as soon as it had been written. The only food she would touch had to be prepared and cooked in front of her. Live chickens were procured by

Martha in the market and killed and trussed in the royal suite. Night was turned into day, for the Empress rarely slept, and the wakeful maid would hear her pacing up and down the room, talking incoherently to herself in various languages and only towards morning crying herself to sleep. Sometimes her malady took a turn for the worse and she appeared haggard and unkempt, because she imagined a comb to be a poisoned weapon. But in her better moods, she dressed with all her habitual elegance, and she was perfectly calm and rational when Charles de Bombelles arrived from Miramar on the evening of the sixth. She spent two hours with him in discussing her inheritance from her father in a completely lucid manner, but Dr Jilek took a grave view of her condition and thought that the road to recovery, even if possible, would be long and slow.

Blasio, who was summoned to her room on the morning of 7 October, found her as dignified and elegant as ever, addressing him in a sad but pleasant manner, but so tragically changed that he had difficulty in recognizing her. 'The face was haggard, the eyes wild in their expression, either fixed and staring or roaming vaguely round the room as if searching for some absent figure.' She ordered him to write out a number of decrees, all of them accusing one or other of her attendants of treason, then only a few moments later asking him what happened to Castillo or to del Vallé, the very men she had indicted. Not daring to contradict her, the young man wrote out her orders, now and then giving a surreptitious glance around the room, where two live chickens were tied to the leg of a gilded table, and a basket of eggs and a spirit stove were placed on an inlaid writing desk. The brocade hangings were permeated with the smell of cooking and the guttering candles told of wakeful nights. Blasio was so moved by this interview that he was close to tears when he kissed her hand on saying goodbye.

Yet we hear of her going with Bombelles in the evening to meet her brother at the station. She was delighted to see her 'bon Phillipe' and to hear all the family news. But on the way back to the hotel, she warned him not to touch anything at the *table d'hote*, as it was all poisoned. The following day, brother and sister were seen arm in arm touring the sights of Rome and Phillipe was amazed at Charlotte's knowledge of the churches. But the effort was too much for her tired brain, and after her farewell visit to the King and Queen of Naples, the Queen noted, 'Poor Charlotte's condition has sadly deteriorated.' That night, the Count of Flanders sent the maid to bed and remained in his sister's room. But neither he nor Charlotte slept, for she talked all night, rambling on about Max and the palaces he had built in Mexico; the wealth of the Empire, which commanded two oceans; Napoleon's jealousy of Max and his determination to destroy him. Hour after hour she talked, till her brother, who was a man of a few words and already afflicted by deafness, was so exhausted that he dozed off in his chair.

The next day they boarded a special train for Ancona, where they were to take the boat for Trieste. Velasquez de Leon was the only Mexican allowed to see them off at the station – the others had been ordered to keep away. 'Where are my ministers and where are my servants?' Charlotte asked in her old imperious manner, but a vague reply appeared to satisfy her. The Belgian Minister, the Austrian Chargé d'affaires, the Papal representatives, were all there to pay their last respects to a woman they knew to be insane. Pope Pius had sent her a kind and affectionate letter of farewell, telling her he was praying daily for the recovery of her peace of mind, and ending his letter, 'I bless you with all my heart.' But enclosed in the envelope was the draft of the *concordat* on which she had pinned her last hopes. The journey passed without incident, and Charlotte seemed happy to be returning to Miramar. Maximilian's old retainer Radonetz was waiting on the threshold, the servants had filled the rooms with flowers. But behind Radonetz was Dr Riedel, one of Europe's leading authorities on nervous diseases. To him Charlotte was not the Empress of Mexico, but merely another patient, a poor demented creature, in need of special care.

29

Maximilian's despair

'Who is Dr Riedel?' asked Maximilian of the young Jewish doctor he had recently appointed as his personal physician, and without thinking Dr Basch replied, 'Director of the Vienna Lunatic Asylum.' The Emperor's face turned ashen. That one short phrase confirmed all he had suspected, feared and evaded in the past eighteen days. Blow upon blow had come in swift succession. Charlotte's telegram from Paris, '*Todos es inutil*', had given him the first intimation of failure. Over a month later, on 1 October, had arrived two fateful letters – the one from his wife, telling him she had achieved nothing with Napoleon, the other from the Emperor himself, informing him bluntly that France could not afford to give Mexico 'another ecu or another soldier'. If he thought he could maintain himself by his own strength, the French troops would abide by the convention and remain until 1867. If he felt called upon to abdicate, other measures would have to be taken and Napoleon suggested his issuing a manifesto to the country, stating the insuperable obstacles which had forced him to take this step. The latter part of the letter made it plain that the French Emperor had already planned with Maximilian's abdication in view. A national assembly would be convoked while the French army was still in the country, and this assembly would be invited to elect a government, which would offer some guarantee of stability. Stability in this case could be interpreted as an agreement to safeguard the interests of France. There was no word in the letter of future compensation in Europe for the thirty-four-year-old Emperor, who had renounced his hereditary rights and sacrificed his health and fortune in attempting to realize Napoleon's dream. He was merely told the dream was over and that they could 'no longer afford to have illusions'. This must have been the same language Charlotte had heard in Paris and the shock of failure had sent her out of her mind.

Her hysterical letter full of wild accusations against Napoleon must have prepared Maximilian for the news contained in two telegrams which arrived on 18 October – the one from Castillo dated 6 October, telling him of the Empress's 'grave and sudden illness', the other sent nearly a week later from Miramar, in which Bombelles informed him of Charlotte's safe arrival and of Professor Riedel having been called in for consultation. The faithful friend had tried to soften the blow by adding, 'The Professor has not yet given up hope of a cure.' But Dr Basch had now all unwittingly exposed the truth. 'Director of a lunatic asylum' conjured up dreadful visions of padded cells and barred windows, and Maximilian, who was suffering from a bad attack of malaria, broke down completely and had only one thought in mind – to announce his abdication and take the first boat to Europe. Abdication had been in his mind for weeks. Napoleon's brutal letter had already inclined him to listen to Stefan Herzfeld's disinterested advice that the situation was too complicated and the prospects too uncertain to make the risks of staying worth while.

Yet only a month before, on Mexican Independence Day, the Emperor had addressed a cheering crowd from the balcony of the Palaçio Naçional and in a stirring speech declared: 'No true Hapsburg would ever leave his post in time of danger.' The festivities, which the foreign diplomats had feared might be the scene of Republican demonstrations, turned out to their surprise to be a personal triumph for the Emperor, with deputations of his loyal subjects calling all day at the palace. Occasions such as these encouraged a dangerous optimism in Maximilian's mercurial temperament, and throughout the month of September he continued to delude himself in the belief that he could still preserve the throne. His two French cabinet ministers had made considerable progress in organizing the native troops; a few scattered Imperialist successes had put fresh heart into the Mexican army; and the Emperor was assured that even after the departure of the French he would have an efficient fighting force of over forty thousand men at his command. False information from his agents in New York led him to believe that there was still hope of coming to terms with the Americans. And as late as 20 September he was writing to Bombelles, in reply to a letter in which the Count had given him an accurate picture of the situation in Paris and of Napoleon's failing morale: 'I refuse to believe that illness and the Prussian needle-gun have so far crushed the Emperor Napoleon that he is tottering helpless towards an abyss. He will recover his accustomed fortitude, and the cool judgment of the Empress [Charlotte], who stands before him like our living conscience, will succeed in reviving in his sick mind, the sacred duty or abiding by his plighted word.' And he added, 'But whatever may happen, I shall continue steadily on the way which my high duties and personal dignity make incumbent on me.'

In this month, he was still sufficiently optimistic to lend an ear to a daring plan put forward by Colonel Van der Smissen, who, chafing at the inglorious rôle he and his Belgians were being made to play, had evolved a plan by which the Emperor should lead his army in the field. The Belgian described how, in evacuating most of the north, Bazaine had opened the way for the Republican General Escobedo who, with eight thousand bandits supported by a large number of American filibusters, had already penetrated as far south as San Luis Potosi. 'It needs only one division, led by the Emperor, to halt this advance,' Van der Smissen explained. 'It could be composed of a Mexican brigade under Colonel Lopez, a brave soldier on whom Your Majesty can rely, two battalions of the French Foreign Legion, Mejía as Chief of the General Staff, and myself in command of the Austro-Belgian brigade. ... I would beg Your Majesty to allow me to lead the main attack against the enemy, and I pledge my word as a man of honour that we shall gain a brilliant victory, and take at least three thousand prisoners. A shout of triumph will arise from the whole Empire, and thousands will rally round the throne.'

The whole idea was characteristic of the man – brave, reckless, foolhardy. But the thought of leading his soldiers into battle appealed to Maximilian's incorrigible romanticism. It was not long before Van der Smissen himself had destroyed the illusion. Acting contrary to the orders of Bazaine, he bullied his already mutinous troops into attacking a heavily-fortified *Juaristi* stronghold in the neighbourhood of Tula. The Mexicans, and also some of the Belgians fighting under his command, went over to the enemy, and though Van der Smissen and his young officers performed miracles of valour – the Colonel had three horses killed under him – the whole affair ended in a miserable debacle, costing the lives of eleven officers and inflicting yet another blow to Imperialist prestige.

All Maximilian's enthusiasm had vanished by the end of September. The Emperor Napoleon's letter reached him when he was lying in bed in the depths of gloom. He spent hours in discussing it with his 'two wise friends', Stefan Herzfeld and Father Fischer, who since his return from Rome had succeeded in ingratiating himself still further into his confidence and was living at Chapultepec, acting as both his private secretary and Court librarian. With his honest common sense, Herzfeld put the correct interpretation on the letter, which was a clear intimation to abdicate. But the Jesuit, who represented the vested interests of both the Church and the Conservative Party, among whom were some of his earliest patrons, put a far more flexible interpretation on the letter and presented what to Maximilian was a far more attractive solution. Father Fischer was in favour of a national congress, but it should be convoked by the Emperor, not by the French. No attempt should be made to prevent Bazaine and his troops from leaving the country. In the past year, they had been more of a hindrance than a help. But it was imperative to restore good relations with the Marshal, so as to ensure that all military supplies were handed over before he left. Only the Belgians and Austrians should be encouraged to remain, by being offered higher grades in the Mexican army.

Father Fischer seems to have been endowed with superb health and a limitless vitality. All those who met him were charmed by his genial manner and endless fund of good humour. To someone as moody and impressionable as Maximilian, his outstanding quality was his sanguine optimism. But for all his optimism, the intelligent Jesuit could not seriously have believed that the United States President would ever consent to 'act as intermediary between Maximilian and Juarez in persuading the latter to lay down arms, pending the decision of a National Congress'. Washington had already made it clear that it would never recognize any other than a Republican government in Mexico. Too much money had been spent in supplying Benito Juarez with arms and ammunition to repudiate him on the eve of victory.

Father Fischer was playing for time. Once the French had gone, Maximilian would be no more than a chattel in the hands of the Conservatives. He would have lost his last lifeline of retreat, and such as he got from Europe would be employed in the interests of the Church. A predominantly Conservative government was already forcing the Emperor to adopt measures of which he disapproved and to dismiss the last of his Liberal friends and advisers. General Uraga, one of his favourite aides-de-camp, had been accused of conspiring with the enemy and rather than expose him to the vengeance of his ministers, Maximilian had sent him on a mission to the Empress in Europe. Uraga, his family and a retinue of servants arrived at Miramar, to find Charlotte insane and in the charge of doctors who forbade her to see anyone or hear anything which might remind her of Mexico. It was not long before these Mexican expatriates were bored with the scenic beauties of Miramar and moved to a hotel in Trieste, where Bombelles complained of their running up enormous bills which he was expected to pay although the Emperor had given him no instructions.

Maximilian was profoundly unhappy with his reactionary government. Little progress had been made either in the army or in the administration since the departure of the two French generals at the end of September. He had so little hope in the future that most of his personal valuables were being transported to Vera Cruz and transferred on board the Austrian corvette *Dandolo*. But he bitterly resented the idea of leaving in the wake of the French army, and he seized on the idea of a national congress to provide him with a dignified way of retreat. Meanwhile, he planned to stay at Orizaba, from where he would proceed to Vera Cruz to meet the Empress, who according to her letters from Como and Miramar was due to arrive at the beginning of November. Still unsuspecting of the terrible events of Rome, Maximilian was writing to his wife as late as 5 October: 'I shall be meeting you at Vera Cruz. If the nation proclaims in favour of the Empire, we shall be returning to the capital, stronger and more powerful than before and prepared to devote the rest of our lives to the service of our country. If the nation desires another form of government, then we shall retire with dignity, conscious of having done our duty.' There is always that pathetic obsession with honour and duty, which in the end was to cost him his life.

As usual, he consulted too many people. Among those whose opinion he valued the most was the British envoy, Peter Campbell-Scarlett, who allowed his dislike of the French and his concern for the ratification of certain trade agreements between England and Mexico to outweigh more humane considerations. He proved a valuable ally for Father Fischer in advising Maximilian against an abdication, which would enable the French to come to terms with his opponents through the mediation of the United States.

But the telegrams which reached the Emperor on 18 October banished all thoughts of congresses and proclamations. In those initial moments of despair, nothing counted and nothing mattered but to go to Charlotte by the first boat. In his misery, he turned to the loyal and devoted Herzfeld who, believing that he was about to abdicate, notified the commander of the *Dandolo* to stand by in readiness for the Emperor's arrival at Vera Cruz. Unfortunately, Herzfeld was sufficiently ingenuous to confide in Father Fischer, who heard the news with horror and consternation. Maximilian's abdication would spell the ruin of the Conservative Party, the end of his own career. But Fischer was not a man prepared to accept defeat without a struggle. He knew Maximilian sufficiently well to realize that his decisions were never irrevocable. The Conservatives might panic, the government might threaten to resign, but the Jesuit kept his head. Simulating sympathy and respect for the Emperor's grief, concern for his health and still more concern for his honour, he begged him not to impair his future reputation by leaving the country without making an attempt to protect those who put their trust in him and who stood to lose all by his departure. Should it be said that a Hapsburg had deserted the Austrian compatriots who had left their homes to fight in his defence, that he had handed over his imperial crown to Bazaine, for the Marshal either to place it on his own head or to mortgage it to any Republican general ready to protect the interests of France? Father Fischer was eloquent. According to his own account, he was 'frank and unequivocal in his disapproval', but though Maximilian was moved by the priest's reproaches, he was morally too shattered to think of anything else but of his poor, unhappy wife left in the care of strangers.

Fortunately he was spared the knowledge of her madness having entered on a new phase in which she suspected him of having tried to kill her ever since her journey to Yucatan. Deep in her subconscious was the obsession that he had always wanted to be rid of a barren wife. If only she could have known how little his transient love affairs counted in her husband's life. The orange groves of El Olvida, the Indian chalet in which he had only lived for a few weeks; Concepçion Sedano and the baby who had no claim on his affections – all were merely characters and scenery in an act on which the curtain had already rung down. Even little Agustín Iturbide, whose arrival at the palace had given her so much heartache in the past, had now been handed back to his mother, yet another prop to be removed from a stage already cleared for the tragedy of the final act.

While Herzfeld tried to persuade his master to adopt Napoleon's advice and issue a manifesto handing over his powers to a Regency before taking the boat to Europe, Fischer still played for time. Enlisting the help of young Dr Basch, he suggested the Emperor should travel to Orizaba by easy stages so as not to endanger his health. At Orizaba, where Maximilian counted many friends, the Jesuit hoped to prepare him a royal welcome which would banish all thoughts of abdication. But for the time being, the Emperor was too physically broken to be able to come to any definite decision. Forty-eight hours after receiving the telegrams from Rome and Miramar, he was already on the way to Orizaba, handing over to Bazaine the task of maintaining law and order in the capital. He wrote to the Marshal, whose dismissal he had been trying to bring about for the past year: 'I count more than ever on the friendship and loyalty which you have always shown me.' The wording is so Jesuitical in tone that one suspects the hand of Father Fischer, for on the eve of his departure, Maximilian was in no fit state to write or to think coherently.

The official Court circular, *Diario del Impero*, gave out that the Emperor was going to Orizaba to convalesce from his recent illness and to be nearer Vera Cruz, as he was awaiting further news from Miramar. But his hurried, almost furtive, departure from Chapultepec in the early hours of the morning of 21 October, choosing a route which avoided the town, was more in the nature of a flight, and the rumour which circulated in the capital, arousing panic among the Conservatives, was that the Emperor was on his way to Europe. It required all Father Fischer's powers of persuasion, and the threats of Bazaine, to prevent the Government from resigning *en masse*. Writing from a *hacienda* only a few leagues from the city, where a recurrence of fever had forced him to take to his bed, Maximilian addressed a letter to Bazaine over which Father Fischer was clearly not consulted, and which leaves no doubt that at that moment he had every intention of abdicating: 'Tomorrow I propose to place in your hands the necessary documents to put an end to a situation which is as intolerable for Mexico as it is for me.' His last orders on leaving the capital were in keeping with his true character. All court-martials were to be suspended, the notorious October Decree was to be annulled and there was to be an end to all political persecution, for his conscience had never become reconciled to the methods he had been forced to adopt.

Meanwhile, in Paris, the Emperor Napoleon was also suffering from pangs of conscience. The Empress Charlotte's visit, followed by the distressing news from Rome, had made a painful impression on him.

He knew that many of his subjects held him responsible for the tragic collapse of the gifted young Empress. The romantic appeal of the Mexican sovereigns had captured the public imagination, and the general reaction in Paris was to pity Maximilian and to blame the politicians at home. But what was even more painful to Napoleon was the nature of the news from Mexico and the growing distrust of Marshal Bazaine among all ranks of the expeditionary force. That he was merely carrying out his orders did not make the situation any better, and the storm of protest roused by the surrender of Tampico forced him to revise his plans and to put a halt to the evacuation of further troops. The growing strength of the enemy made it dangerous to continue embarking the troops in echelons as had been originally planned, and it was decided to evacuate the whole expeditionary force together in the first months of 1867.

The recriminations of high-ranking officers against the discreditable rôle they were being made to play in deserting those whom they had come to defend, and the dishonour which reflected on the French flag, were particularly humiliating to a Bonaparte nurtured on the legend of his country's invincibility. There was something definitely wrong at French headquarters, when an experienced general like Brincourt threatened resignation and an honourable officer like Douay was in open opposition to his commander-in-chief. In his dispatches to the Quai d'Orsay, the minister, Monsieur Dano, never failed to make veiled allegations against the Marshal's probity, and in view of these recriminations and allegations, Napoleon decided to send General Castelnau, one of his most trusted aides-de-camp, on a special mission to Mexico to report on the situation and make Maximilian understand that there would be no going back on the decisions contained in the letter of 29 August, and that both for his own and for his country's sake, abdication presented the only logical solution.

But would Maximilian be logical? In his last letter, Bazaine had intimated the fear that a man of the Emperor's character, finding himself with his back to the wall and full of bitterness at what he regarded as the betrayal of France, might try to come to terms with the enemy before the French had left the country. The Marshal, who was far more cynical and ruthless than his master, believed it to be more in the interests of France to continue to co-operate with Maximilian and to maintain him in power until the embarkation of the French troops. If chaos followed, that would no longer be the concern of France. This was tough, cynical advice, but Napoleon was not sufficiently cynical to accept it. He had a genuine liking for Maximilian, and felt an obligation to save him, if not his crown. Bazaine's enemies, and there were many of them, hinted that part of the new-found anxiety to keep Maximilian on the throne was to make sure of the hundred thousand pesos which the Emperor, with his habitual munificence, had promised to hand over to the young *Maréchale* when the wedding-gift Palace of Buenavista was given back to the state. The Marshal had been greatly criticized for lending himself to a transaction by which the city of Mexico paid his wife a large rent while the palace was being used as the French headquarters.

All this shiftiness and double-dealing was anathema to Castelnau, the correct and straightforward brigade general whom Napoleon had sent to report on the ethics and conduct of a Marshal of France. He had even entrusted him with the power to replace Bazaine by Douay should the circumstances warrant such a drastic decision. It was an impossible situation and if Bazaine had been a prouder and more independent character, he would not have tolerated it for a moment. But at heart he had remained a subordinate, more used to taking orders than to giving them. Years of service in Africa had taught him to adapt himself to '*le systeme arabe*' – to be subtle, accommodating and devious – which enabled him to understand the mystifications of Napoleon's politics far better than any of his predecessors. Whatever may be held against Bazaine, he could never be reproached for disloyalty towards his master, and one can hardly blame him if he felt a certain animosity towards the proud and confident young General, who was empowered to dictate French policy in a country of which he was completely ignorant and where he did not speak a word of the language. It is not surprising if, in these circumstances, Bazaine made no attempt to facilitate his task, or if he later took a certain pleasure in his inevitable failure.

From the moment of landing at Vera Cruz, Castelnau found himself caught up in a web of rumours and intrigue. He was met by Captain Pierron, who was still occupying the ambiguous position of Maximilian's military secretary. Genuinely devoted to the Emperor and therefore distrusted by Bazaine, who had done his best to ruin his career, Pierron was one of those French officers with divided loyalties, of whom Castelnau was to meet many in the next few weeks. Pierron had nothing but good to say of Maximilian as a man, extolling his nobility of character, although he deplored his inertia and inability to rule with severity and firmness. In contrast to Pierron's affectionate criticism was the undisguised contempt with which Colonel Dupin of the counter-guerrillas spoke of the Emperor. The Colonel, whose troops escorted Castelnau to the capital, described the Emperor as 'a superficial weakling, swayed by every adventurer who comes his way and good for nothing but botanizing'. By the time he had crossed the Cumbres, Castelnau had collected so many different opinions and heard so many versions of the situation that it was becoming hard to disentangle the truth. But one point of agreement emerged: the Emperor Maximilian was incapable of ruling. Those who loved him attributed his vacillations and lack of initiative to the state of his health, others blamed them on his 'dissipations and incurable frivolity'.

An incident at Ajotla, where the General crossed with the royal party and put up at the same inn as the Emperor, made him inclined to doubt the gravity of his malady. When Castelnau requested the honour of an audience, Colonel Kodolitsch, who was acting as aide-de-camp, replied that he was too ill to be disturbed. But half an hour later, on looking out of the window, the General saw Maximilian looking quite strong and active, jumping lightly into his carriage to continue his journey, which gave him to understand that the Emperor was in no mood to receive further communications from Napoleon.

Maximilian continued on his journey. But even a strong escort of Austrian cavalry could not protect him from unpleasant incidents on the way. In Aculingo, the six white mules of the Imperial carriage were stolen during the night, bawdy Republican songs including 'Mama Carlota', every word of which was a stab at his heart, were sung in the village streets. His companions noted that he looked and behaved like a man in a trance. At first the weather fitted his mood, for the narrow defiles of the Cumbres were shrouded in fog, which suddenly lifted as the road began to descend into the Tierra Caliente. The Emperor stopped the carriage to proceed on foot down the zig-zag road, which at every turn revealed a more spectacular view of range upon range of mountains, falling into tiered terraces and luxuriant valleys, while every moment the vegetation took on a brighter sheen or exploded into bursts of more brilliant colour. He walked rapidly, talking to Dr Basch, who had difficulty in keeping up with him. Sometimes, he paused to linger at some favourite view, as if he were looking at it for the last time, and the young doctor saw the tiredness in the sad, white face under the blond beard, the thin shoulder blades sticking out from under his long grey cloak, and wondered how long he could stand the nervous strain.

But a happy surprise awaited Maximilian at Orizaba, where Father Fischer and the local Conservatives had prepared him a royal welcome. Everything had gone to plan and the Emperor found himself greeted by thousands of Indians pressing round his carriage and waving their branches of palm and amid the ear-splitting noise of firecrackers and the joyful pealing of church bells. '*Evviva Massimiliano! Evviva el gran Emperador!*' The cheering sounded spontaneous, the jubilation sincere. But it needed more than a few thousand cheering Indians to turn him from his thoughts of abdication. The cases of valuables continued to be loaded on board the *Dandolo*, farewell letters and telegrams were sent off to his friends and relatives. Kodolitsch was instructed to sell the Austrian artillery, which was the Emperor's private property, and distribute the money among the disabled officers and men of the volunteer corps. In the event of an abdication, Bazaine was requested to embark the Belgian and Austrian corps at the same time as the French; to secure a pension for old Princess Iturbide; to guarantee two months' payment and fresh employment for the staff of his secretariat; and to settle the outstanding debts of his civil list. Meanwhile, assisted by Herzfeld, Maximilian sat down to compose the draft of the manifesto in which he was to announce his departure.

Father Fischer's chief concern was to get rid of Herzfeld. In order to undermine his influence with the Emperor, the Jesuit never referred to the journey to Orizaba except as a 'flight'. He kept telling the Emperor of the consternation and panic in the capital, the bitter disillusionment of the people in the man they had regarded as a god. He kept telling the Emperor that he could not forgive those who had advised such a course: 'If Herzfeld were not such a good friend of Your Majesty, I would suspect him of being in the pay of Napoleon.' Maximilian, who according to his doctor was on the verge of a complete mental collapse, had become increasingly suspicious and distrustful. After a week at Orizaba, Stefan Herzfeld was ordered to proceed to Europe on the pretext of preparing for the Emperor's journey. Father Fischer intrigued so successfully that he managed to prevent Maximilian from taking leave of his friend, for the Jesuit did not dare to run the risk of Herzfeld making a last impassioned appeal to abdicate.

Herzfeld himself appears to have been completely unaware of Father

Fischer's Machiavellian intrigues, and to have blamed Captain Pierron for his disgrace. We find him addressing a pathetic letter to Fischer from Havana in which he begs him to continue with him in their joint efforts to get their beloved Emperor out of Mexico: 'Every hour's delay increases the danger, for in a few weeks, this country will be the scene of the bloodiest of civil wars. The storm is gathering on all sides. The Yankees are about to invade the country from the north. Miramon has landed at Campeche and has launched a *pronunciamento*. You must urge the Emperor to leave at all costs. . . . Do not allow yourself to be influenced from Mexico. Fulfil your duties as a priest. Save not only the Emperor but the man.' It is strange that this letter should have survived. One would have thought Fischer himself would have destroyed it rather than risk its falling into the Emperor's hands. Herzfeld's departure cleared his path, and support now came to him from unexpected quarters.

The indiscretions contained in Felix Eloin's letter from Brussels, which had come into possession of Juarez's agent in New York, had now been published in the European press, arousing resentment both in Austria and in France. Eloin had written of the Emperor Napoleon with the greatest contempt, reviling his personal character and accusing him of treachery: 'I am convinced Your Majesty does not care to provide him with the satisfaction of contributing to a policy which sooner or later will have to answer for the fatal consequences of its odious acts. Once freed from the pressure of foreign intervention, Your Majesty should issue a call to the people of Mexico, asking for the material and financial support which is indispensable to the continued existence of the Empire. If this call is not answered, then Your Majesty will have carried out your noble mission to the end, and can return to Europe with all the prestige which attended your departure. In the midst of important events which will not fail to arise, you will be able to assume the rôle which is yours by right.' Eloin knew how to flatter his master as adroitly as Father Fischer. But though his advice was more often than not disastrous, there is no denying that he was genuinely devoted to the Emperor, never sparing himself in his service, one moment in Paris, the next in Miramar, and in November making his preparations for returning to Mexico at a time when anyone thinking of preserving his own skin would have stayed in Europe. He remained faithful to Maximilian to the end, suffering the hardships of prison and finally returning to Europe no richer than when he had left.

The publication of Eloin's letter, with its references to Maximilian's growing popularity in Austria and the general discontent with his brother's regime, was too near the truth to savour of anything but treason. Franz Josef was incensed and for the moment could not bear to hear his brother's name mentioned in his presence. When General Thun, on his return from Mexico, spoke in admiration of Maximilian's courage, he was heard in icy silence. Even the Archduchess Sophia did not dare confide in the Emperor her fears for Max's safety. Now came the telegram announcing Maximilian's plan to abdicate and return to Europe – a telegram which, according to historians as eminent as Emile Ollivier, led the Archduchess Sophia to write Maximilian a letter warning him against returning to Austria, 'where he would be badly received and his position would be made ridiculous and untenable'. This letter was said to have influenced his fatal decision to remain in Mexico, but no one, not even Count Corti in his meticulous researches among the Vienna archives, has ever seen a copy of this letter. Nor is it likely that an adoring mother, whom we know to have been in constant fear for the safety of her son, would ever have taken upon herself the responsibility of writing such a letter. Later, when Maximilian had already made his decision, both the Archduchess and Karl Ludwig wrote applauding his courage, but by then they had no other alternative but to applaud what they no longer had the power to prevent.

A note in the diary of the Archduchess's lady-in-waiting, the Landgrävine Fürstenberg, mentions the joyful relief with which Sophia heard of her son's intention to return. 'The swindle has at last been exposed. The poor Archduke is coming home to live as a philosopher at Lacroma. How long he stands it there is another matter, and where will his unquiet spirit take him next? My mistress was in a great state of anxiety and thought they might murder him, and so is delighted that he is coming back.' These few words exonerate the Archduchess from the accusation of having tried to put pressure on her son to remain in Mexico.

But though the Archduchess never wrote, and the Austrian Foreign Minister sent no instructions to the Legation in Mexico, Baron Lago, who had replaced Count Thun as Franz Josef's envoy at the Mexican Court, took it upon himself to inform his colleagues that the Emperor Maximilian was *persona non grata* in Austria.

The choice of Baron Lago, a secondary diplomat of no outstanding ability, to act as Franz Josef's representative was resented by Maximilian as a personal slight. The Baron was kept at a distance while the British envoy, Peter Campbell-Scarlett, was loaded with attentions – and he revenged himself by sending home unfavourable dispatches describing the Emperor as 'surrounded by arrant adventurers and physically and morally incapable of arriving at any decisions. In spite of the critical times, his principal occupation appears to be chasing butterflies.' Lago was not the only one who failed to sympathize with the Emperor's interest in bird-watching and butterfly hunting. But his expeditions in the forests with old Dr Billimek, were what helped to preserve his sanity at a time when all else seemed to be slipping away from under his feet.

Captain Pierron, who kept him posted on every rumour in the capital, informed him that the Austrian Minister had been instructed to state in an official note that his government 'would not allow the Emperor of Mexico to go to Miramar or any other place in Austria'. The following day the Captain corrected his report by adding that 'he would not be allowed to land so long as he persisted in calling himself Emperor of Mexico or claimed a contingent right of succession to the Austrian throne. If he wished to return to his country, he would have to go as a simple Archduke. Whatever Lago may have said, and he later denied having received such instructions, Maximilian was ready to believe the story, and he appealed to the British Minister to place him under the protection of the British flag in the event of his leaving the country and an official note from Austria making it impossible for him to embark on the *Dandolo*. In the circumstances he refused to avail himself of French transport.

Campbell-Scarlett, who was going on leave to England, stopped off in Orizaba to say goodbye to the Emperor, whom he found in a state of the deepest depression, terribly affected by the news of the Empress's illness and living in dread of what the next letter might bring. He told him: 'If the Empress dies, I would not have the courage or desire to stay on in Mexico. I came here more on her account than on my own, and I have no ambition to continue alone after her death, especially as I have no children or successors.'

Scarlett pressed the Emperor to return to the capital, whatever his future decision might be. His precipitate departure was looked upon as an ignominious flight, and he owed it both to himself and his country

413

to return. Though the British government had given him clear instructions not to interfere in Mexico's internal affairs, Scarlett took it upon himself to entreat the Emperor 'to carry out Napoleon's original wish, to summon a congress or national assembly, for it was by no means certain that the Mexican people might not in the end prefer an Empire to the anarchy of civil war'.

Scarlett, no more than Fischer, can have believed in the possibility of convoking a congress in the prevailing chaos. Oaxaca, the last remaining stronghold in the south, had surrendered to Porfirio Diaz, without the French making any attempt to hold it. Six hundred Austrians who had tried to halt the enemy advance had been cut to pieces, and by the end of November only Mexico City, Queretaro, San Luis Potosi, Puebla and Vera Cruz were still in Imperialist hands. It was being openly said that Bazaine was already seeking the mediation of the United States, to ensure the safety and interests of French nationals following his departure. Washington was taking Maximilian's abdication so much for granted that a mission was already on its way to Vera Cruz to enter into negotiations with Juarez and prevent the French from espousing a rival claimant.

Meanwhile Marquez and Miramon had arrived at Orizaba to place themselves at the Emperor's service. The two generals, who had a great reputation in Conservative circles, rallied the flagging spirits of the Emperor's ministers and the President, Theodosio Lares, made an impassioned appeal to Maximilian reminding him of a speech he had made on Independence Day in which he had promised never to desert his post in time of danger. From the safety of his Roman exile Gutierrez sent one of his long, bombastic letters harping on the same theme, calling on him to uphold the honour of the Hapsburgs. But when Scarlett left for Vera Cruz on 18 November Maximilian was still talking of abdication: 'His Majesty gave me to understand that his resolution to leave Mexico was now quite determined. A personal reason for taking this step was his repugnance to attempt governing the country in any other way than by the liberal principles to which he had always been attached, but in which he had not succeeded in gaining the support of the Liberal Party. He believed it to be true that a strong and iron hand was the only way of governing Mexico as it was at present constituted, but he could not divest himself of those maxims of liberty which he felt to be right, in order to govern by the reactionary or Church party and by violent measures rather than in a mild, paternal way.'

Yet only three days later Maximilian convoked the council of state to meet at Orizaba to decide for or against his application. Of the eighteen members, three were moderate non-party men. The remaining fifteen, who included four ministers, were all fanatical Conservatives, which rendered their decision a foregone conclusion. What decided Maximilian to place his future in the hands of men whom he personally disliked and who he knew were only using him for their own ends? What decided him to make himself responsible for the bloodthirsty acts of Marquez, the financial extortions of Miramon? The loyal and faithful Blasio, who returned to Mexico at the end of November, is the only one who provides us with a clue by telling us that a few days earlier, Dr Bohuslavek had arrived by way of New York and given the Emperor 'a detailed account of the Empress's illness' and that Father Fischer had told him that Maximilian had been deeply affected by the details of his wife's madness and warned him not to refer to it unless he was questioned. Blasio found the Emperor physically broken: 'There were none of the jokes and good humour of former days, and his head which before had been so proud and erect was bowed as though by the weight of worries and sufferings. . . . He asked me a multitude of questions about my journey, without saying a word about the Empress.'

The wounds were too painful to be reopened. In his pedantic, conscientious fashion, Dr Bohuslavek had spared Maximilian none of the terrible details of his wife's insanity – her growing paranoia, the hysterical scenes at the Vatican, the sudden attacks of violence, the furtiveness and cunning of the mad. He left him with no illusions and held out no hope of the future. The thought of returning to Europe, to the gardens of Miramar, haunted by the screams of his mad wife, was more unbearable than the thought of a violent end in Mexico. When there was so little to live for, it was easy to be heroic. So the Mexicans were astonished to see the Emperor go off into the forests with Dr Billimek while the council deliberated on his future. In spite of the composition of the assembly, eight members voted for his abdication, but the ministers, each of whom had two votes, won the day. The Emperor was to return to the capital, and Maximilian, professing himself 'deeply moved by the evidences of love and loyalty I have met with from the ministers and councillors of state', declared himself ready for every sacrifice.

On the following day, 29 November, the United States frigate *Susquehanna* cast anchor in the roads off Vera Cruz. General Sherman and Colonel Campbell, prospective minister to Juarez were on board.

They found Vera Cruz brilliantly illuminated in celebration of the Emperor's decision to remain. In the circumstances no diplomatic mission could have been a greater blunder and they had no alternative but to return to New Orleans.

30

The fatal decision

The scene moves back to Mexico City, where panic and confusion caused by a mass of conflicting rumours was paralyzing business and fanning a growing xenophobia among all classes of the population. Now that the French were clearing out, no one any longer bothered to be polite to them. In a play at one of the principal theatres, in which Napoleon, Maximilian, Juarez and their partisans all figured on the stage, the *Juaristi* were applauded, while Maximilian and more particularly Napoleon were insulted and booed. Bazaine had still sufficient power to order the Minister of Justice to close the theatre and dismiss the head of police, but this only served to exasperate the government as an act of unwarranted interference on his part. Nowhere was the prevailing confusion and dissension more evident than at French headquarters, where the arrival of General Castelnau brought to a head a longstanding enmity between the Marshal and the French Minister, Dano, who took a very pessimistic view of the situation and saw no other way of safeguarding the interests of French subjects than by seeking the help of the United States and coming to some agreement with Juarez. Bazaine, who had spent four years campaigning against the implacable Indian, was ready if necessary to come to terms with any Republican leader other than Juarez. But so long as there was some kind of established government in Mexico, and so long as French troops from the outlying districts were still marching across the Sierras, he deemed it wiser and more expedient to encourage Maximilian on the one hand while on the other opening negotiations with the Republicans to prevent them attacking the French army in the rear.

A significant incident is related by Campbell-Scarlett, who on his way to Orizaba in a convoy escorted by French troops, ran into a large band of *guerrilleros* led by a notorious bandit, Rodriguez. No attempt was made to hold up the convoy or rob the stagecoach – for Rodriguez told

Scarlett that he was under orders not to attack the French. Towns and villages evacuated by Bazaine were immediately occupied by the *Juaristi*. The only skirmishes occurred when some over-eager Republicans tried to occupy a place before the French had pulled out. Bazaine explains his devious policy in two dispatches addressed to the French Minister of War and dated 28 and 29 November, just after receiving the news of Maximilian's decision to return to the capital: 'Only those who have shared my anxiety and concern over getting the troops who are scattered all over the country safely back to base, can understand the expediencies to which I had to resort in keeping in with all parties, so as to ensure that the men are not unduly fatigued, and the prestige of our army is unimpaired in a country where every day the guerrilla forces grow in audacity and strength; where the Liberals are chafing to see the last of the Empire and the Conservatives are fighting with their backs to the wall. The latter have now succeeded in inspiring the Emperor Maximilian with sufficient confidence to go back on his original intention of abdicating and after an abortive attempt to rule with the help of the other parties, to throw himself in the arms of the Conservatives. The experiment is about to begin, and it would reflect badly on us if we went against the man we had helped to place upon the throne. The Emperor declares that he can maintain himself by his own resources. So be it. Our rôle is at an end. There is nothing for us to do but to retire. Let us get out of Mexico as soon as possible. I will have the army ready to embark by the beginning of February. The Empire will then last as long as it can. But when it falls, no one will be able to reproach us for having contributed to its collapse. We will have carried out our commitments and on leaving will have assured our rights, our claims, the interests of our nationals, all things which any government other than that of Maximilian would systematically refuse.' In his second dispatch the Marshal commented on Dano's suggestion to come to an agreement with the United States: 'Is it not to be feared that such an agreement would cause so much bitterness in the country as to unite all parties against us and thereby impede our retreat? . . . Because of this I have considered and I still consider it to be in our interests to uphold the Empire as long as it can maintain itself on its own resources.'

Bazaine spoke as a realist, responsible for the safety and well-being of twenty-six thousand men. Unfortunately, he abstained from taking Castelnau into his confidence and the young brigade general, still imbued with the high standard of honour of St Cyr, had promised his master to persuade or if necessary coerce the Emperor Maximilian to abdicate, so that no future tragedy or act of violence could be laid at Napoleon's door. Castelnau attributed his failure to the machinations of Bazaine, but neither Bazaine, nor Dano, nor even Castelnau were prepared for the brutality of the cablegram which reached them on 13 December: Napoleon, furious over Maximilian's refusal to abdicate, ordered the immediate evacuation of all troops, including the Foreign Legion, which by the Treaty of Miramar was supposed to remain in Mexico for another six years. All Frenchmen attached to Maximilian or serving in a Mexican regiment were to be given the opportunity to leave. The same facilities were to be offered to members of the Austrian and Belgian regiments. In short Maximilian was to be deprived of his last resources in direct violation of all previous treaties. On receiving this cablegram Dano and Castelnau decided to make a last effort to speak to Maximilian, so as to try to convince him of the hopelessness of his cause.

Maximilian left Orizaba on 12 December. Blasio writes that it was a sad departure, 'for the Emperor, sensitive to impressions, seemed to divine that he would never return to the charming little town which had so many pleasant memories for him'. The people in the villages he passed greeted him with astonishment; most of them believed him to be already on his way to Europe and those who were devoted to him saw with concern a return which would only intensify the bitterness of the war. Sharing his carriage, surrounded by an escort of troops, Blasio saw him in the light of a prisoner – 'another Louis XVI being brought back from Varennes'. But Maximilian had made his own choice, pronounced his own death wish, and a letter from Eloin, giving him fresh details of Charlotte's illness, only served to strengthen his resolve to accept his fate in Mexico. He was perpetually haunted by thoughts of Charlotte, and Eloin's letter told him what he dreaded to hear – of his wife living under rigid supervision in the *Gartenhaus* of Miramar, 'where closed shutters permit a constant watch without Her Majesty seeing or being aware'. The doctors had prescribed a healthy, moderate diet calculated to give the patient an appetite, so that she no longer refused food for fear of it being poisoned. The principal treatment was to empty her mind, to keep her from thinking of her *ideé fixe* of poison. The entourage was still suspect. Bombelles for the moment could not show himself, while Frau Kuhacsevich had to be kept away. The Empress occupied herself with music and drawing or an occasional game of cards, and when it was fine she went walking or rowing with the doctor. The wish to write, which was so natural to her, had gone; a letter from the Empress Elisabeth, written with the intention of pleasing, had remained unanswered, her Majesty saying she was 'still too tired to write'.

It was impossible for Maximilian to envisage Charlotte with an empty mind, too tired to write a letter, spied on day and night, ordered about like a child. She must resent the supervision, for Eloin wrote: 'At first she tried to run away and was found wandering in the park without bonnet or shawl. Now she admits she is ill and has to have special treatment.' The Belgian spared his master the tragic account of the Empress's wild, impotent rages when she smashed the mirrors and attacked the doctors. But one laconic passage, 'when the weather is wet and she is unable to go out, the august invalid becomes still more difficult', conjured up a pathetic picture of resentful misery which haunted Maximilian throughout that sad and gloomy journey back to his capital. An underlying reluctance to return and another bout of fever kept him for a fortnight in Puebla, where he stayed in the bishop's *hacienda* outside the town. Here he wrote one of his last letters to Charlotte – a letter such as one might write to a child who had left for school: 'I was miserable at going into the room where we had so often stayed together.'

Dano and Castelnau arrived in Puebla on 18 December to make a last attempt to persuade Maximilian to abdicate. They had got Bazaine to sign a joint declaration protesting against his decision to remain, which would only serve to rekindle the flames of civil war. Maximilian was as charming and courteous as ever, but he replied to their protests by taking out of his pocket a recent telegram from Bazaine in which the Marshal told him he would make every effort to uphold his throne. What Maximilian claimed to be a message from Bazaine may have been merely a telegram from Pierron, who kept him informed of all the Marshal's devious manœuvres and of all the quarrels and dissensions at French headquarters. But it succeeded in completely confusing the two honest Frenchmen, infuriated by what they believed to be the treachery of Bazaine. Castelnau observed; 'The Emperor seemed to enjoy our confusion, saying in his gentle, ironic way, "I see you are not used to our Marshal's ways. I have seen through him for a long time. I deplore his lack of frankness, of which I more than anyone else have been the victim. But though I no longer count on him, I am ready to make use of him if it suits me. He has ended in betraying everybody and thinking that everybody is his dupe, whereas everyone's eyes are opened to his duplicity. Does he think I do not know that on 2 December he entertained Porfirio Diaz and does he think the Liberals do not know that on the same day he made all kinds of promises to Miramon?" '

Under Father Fischer's influence, Maximilian had become as subtle and as devious as Bazaine. His bitterness against the French was such that he felt justified to make use of any ruse or deceit which might spread confusion in their ranks. He clung to the idea of a congress and – what was even more chimerical – the hope of coming to an understanding with Juarez, a hope he had secretly entertained from the time of his arrival in Mexico and which had been responsible for so many of his mistakes. 'My position,' he remarked, 'is that of a sentinel remaining at his post, true to his orders until he is discharged.' He said he fully expected that the Mexican nation, which was entirely opposed to monarchy, would opt for Juarez and the Republican form of government. He would accept this decision and would be the first to congratulate the elect of the nation, after which he would leave the country without a stain on his honour. Castelnau returned to Mexico City bitterly disappointed at the failure of his mission, angry and at the same time pitying the brave, misguided young Prince, who in deciding to stay had signed his own death warrant. For even Bazaine, after receiving Napoleon's orders to evacuate immediately down to the last Frenchman, had been heard to say that if Maximilian insisted on remaining, 'they would hang him in the end'.

Meanwhile Maximilian had circulated a letter to the various foreign embassies, announcing his decision to maintain his throne, and accusing the French of having broken the terms of their agreement. Dano protested to Lares at the tone of the letter, but got little satisfaction from the ultra-conservative minister, whose illusory promises boosted the Emperor's failing morale.

The last days of the French occupation were embittered by petty recriminations and sordid financial transactions. In an attempt to coerce Maximilian into abdicating, Dano and Castelnau empowered the French authorities to enforce the customs convention which the Emperor had signed but never ratified. When the Mexicans refused to obey their orders, the French levied duties on their own account, whereupon the Mexicans levied others, with the result that merchants and foreign firms had to carry a double burden. Contrary to the intentions of Bazaine, Castelnau insisted that all arms and ammunition which the French could not take with them should be destroyed instead of being handed over to the Imperialists, while the horses were to be sold off at public auction. Many of the French cavalry officers were so ashamed of this shabby behaviour that they gave away their horses as presents to their Imperialist friends. Nor were the French the only ones who seemed determined to deprive Maximilian of his last resources. The Austrian Minister and the Belgian Chargé-d'affaires considered it their duty to prevent the formation of an Austro-Belgian brigade by encouraging their nationals to break their agreements with the Emperor and to avail themselves of the offer of French transport, pointing out the dangers to which they would be exposed by remaining in Mexico. They had little difficulty in persuading the rank and file who were already thoroughly disillusioned: Kodolitsch's Austrian army corps was reduced to one hundred and seventy-three officers and six hundred and fifty men, while Khevenhüller had to fill the ranks of the hussar regiment he had raised at his own expense either with Mexicans or with French deserters.

Alfred van der Smissen, who was neither an adventurer nor an idealist and who had always recognized that the Empire had no future once the French had gone, met Maximilian on the road between Puebla and Mexico City and implored him to reconsider his decision, 'for it was useless to continue a struggle which could only end in a catastrophe'. There had never been any sympathy between these two men, diametrically opposed. Maximilian may have been unconsciously jealous of his wife's admiration for a brave compatriot, while the Belgian may have considered the Emperor to be unworthy of his wife. But in begging him to abdicate, Van der Smissen spoke from the heart. He was more intelligent and more experienced than Kodolitsch, the romantic adventurer who had encouraged Maximilian to remain, and as always the Emperor's sympathies were on the side of a romantic. He received Van der Smissen with a cold indifference, speaking to him in Spanish, for his dislike of the French had reached the point when he was even averse to speaking their language.

On 6 January the firing of rockets and the pealing of church bells announced the Emperor's return to the capital. General Marquez, at the head of a thousand men, had ridden out to meet him at Rio Frio. A group of wealthy Conservatives had collected two million pesos for military expenses. But there was no note of triumph in his return.

Maximilian avoided driving through the streets of his capital and refused to live in the palace, where 'he felt that at any moment he might have to leave by one door, while the next President came in at the other'. Chapultepec was unhabitable, having been dismantled of his personal belongings and pillaged by his servants in his absence, and he lived instead in a modest *hacienda* barely a mile away, which belonged to a Swiss merchant. It was a far cry from the luxury of Monza and Miramar, the powdered footmen with *boutonnières* of rosebuds, the orchestras playing in the gallery. Even his entourage was embarrassed at seeing him living in a place so unsuitable for a royal residence. But there had been difficulty in finding him accommodation: none of the wealthy *hacendados* in the neighbourhood wanted to incriminate themselves to the extent of having the Emperor living under their roof.

The partisans of Marquez and Miramon were gathering round their leaders and the British Chargé-d'affaires, a Mr Middleton, noted: 'In the capital no one takes any longer an interest in Maximilian. All attention is centred on the two generals, whom the Conservative upper classes have welcomed with a great enthusiasm in no way shared by the foreign colony or by the ordinary people, who are subjected to extra taxes and the unpopular *leva* (enforced conscription). Even those who still profess to uphold the Empire never use it as a rallying point. The two parties, whose endless animosities have spread desolation throughout the country for so many years, stand as it were face to face again, just as they did previous to the French intervention, and one sees how little the Imperial system ever took root.' Baron Lago reported to his government with a certain gloomy satisfaction: 'The Emperor was greeted in his capital with a cold indifference, at times with an irony not unmixed with bitterness.'

Maximilian appears to have been aware of his equivocal position and rarely went into the town. He had barely returned when he received the news of the capture and plundering of Cuernavaca, where the small Imperialist garrison had been overwhelmed by a strong Liberal force. La Borda and its contents had been ransacked and not even the garden had escaped the savage zest for destruction. Maximilian was heartbroken, for Cuernavaca with its simple, friendly inhabitants represented all he loved best in Mexico. Colonel Lamadrid of the *Cazadores*, one of the bravest and most devoted of his officers, asked leave to march his regiment to Cuernavaca to dislodge the *Juaristi*. The operation was successful and the enemy was put to flight, but on his return the Colonel was ambushed and killed.

The death of one of his favourite officers was a personal grief for the Emperor, but the news that came in from all over the country was so appalling that personal tragedies counted for little in the general collapse. Place after place had been lost to the Republicans. General Escobedo was victorious throughout the north, Porfirio Diaz was in command of the south and the south-east and was now preparing to move against Puebla. Corona, Regulés and Riva Palacio were advancing from the west, and Juarez, as patient and as inexorable as ever, had moved his headquarters from Chihuahua to Zacatecas. Even Maximilian realized that a congress was no longer practicable and that the victorious Liberals would never consent to an armistice. Unable or unwilling to make his own decisions, he now summoned a junta consisting of his ministers, various Conservative notables and, surprisingly enough, Marshal Bazaine, who was still officially the military commander of the capital. The Marshal was in an unenviable position, for wherever his personal sympathies might lie he had now no choice but to obey the orders of Napoleon, who in his last telegram had told him, 'not to force Maximilian to abdicate but on no account to delay the embarkation of the troops as the ships had already left'. This telegram was largely the result of renewed pressure from Washington, where Secretary Seward kept insisting on a speedy evacuation of all foreign troops from Mexico.

Whatever may have been their differences in the past, Bazaine felt nothing but pity for the young sovereign, whose misguided sense of honour compelled him to remain. Speaking to a largely hostile audience, he expressed his views with clarity and feeling. The survival of the Empire had become impossible. The Imperialist troops would desert or be deserted, in which case Maximilian would sink to the level of a mere party leader. It was necessary for his honour and his safety that he should hand over his powers to the nation. But only two of the thirty-three men present had the courage to cast their vote with Bazaine. Of the rest, twenty-five voted in favour of the Emperor remaining and taking the offensive against the enemy, while five abstained.

The Marshal paid a visit to the *hacienda* of La Teya in a last attempt to persuade Maximilian to leave. From all accounts the meeting between the two men, whose relations had been marred by so much bitterness and misunderstanding, was friendly, almost affectionate. The Emperor took the Marshal by the arm and walked with him for an hour in the garden, while Bazaine tried to make him understand the hopelessness of the situation. Maximilian declared that he had 'no longer any illusions'. He believed the Conservatives to have deceived him, but he refused to give the impression that he was abandoning his post by running away. It was the last time Bazaine was allowed to see the Emperor. From now on Father Fischer and Lares did all in their power to prevent Maximilian from seeing foreigners. The European envoys had their audiences cancelled or postponed and the Emperor was led to believe that he would increase his popularity if he were escorted by Mexican rather than Austrian troops. Pierron, the devoted young Frenchman who till now had kept him informed of what was going on at French headquarters, had been ordered to rejoin his regiment of *Zouaves*, but Blasio still managed to carry messages between him and the Emperor by visiting him at the Hotel Iturbide, which had become rather like a barracks full of young officers preparing for their departure. Pierron's last advice to the Emperor, now that he had decided to stay, was to place himself at the head of the army and to lead it against the enemy rather than to stay in Mexico at the mercy of every faction and intrigue.

At nine o'clock in the morning of 5 February 1867, the French army evacuated Mexico City. Bazaine rode at the head of his men, followed by a brilliant galaxy of staff officers. Discipline had been maintained to the end and the troops marched proudly through the streets, with the bands playing, the flags fluttering in the breeze. Reclining in a litter, guarded by a strong escort, was young Madame Bazaine, already in an advanced state of pregnancy and weeping bitterly at having to leave her family and her home. It was a bright, sunny day and the whole population was out in the streets or crowding the balconies. But there were no cheers and few smiles for the departing French. Only here and there a pretty woman threw one of them a flower from a balcony or called out, '*Bon voyage!*' The majority saw them pass with a sullen indifference and the silence was only broken by the explosion of ammunition being blown up at the arsenal. The troops marched through the Alameda, down the Calle de San Francisco, along Plateros and across the Zócalo, past the Imperial Palace where the doors and windows were all barred and closed. But behind the shutters of a window giving out on the Calle de Moneda stood a tall figure wrapped in a grey cloak. When the last of the soldiers had gone, Maximilian turned to an aide-de-camp, saying: 'At last we are free.'

It was a phrase, like so many others he had used in the past weeks, which he himself was the last to believe in. But today he was heartened by news from the interior, where Miramon with four thousand men had carried out a bold and brilliant attack against Zacatecas, the seat of Juarez's government. The garrison had fled and Juarez only escaped by a miracle. The news was hailed with jubilation by the Conservatives and Maximilian was sufficiently optimistic to address a letter to Miramon in which he ordered: 'In the event of Juarez or one of his associates being captured, they are to be tried, but the sentences are not to be carried out without the Imperial sanction.' Unfortunately this letter fell into the hands of the *Juaristi*. The news of victory was premature. General Escobedo, commanding a vastly superior force, succeeded in outflanking Miramon and his exhausted soldiers, who were cut to pieces at what became known as the massacre of San Jacinto. It was a battle of unparalleled ferocity with all the worst elements of a civil war. Juarez had ordered that no mercy be shown to the Imperialists and in particular to the foreigners. Over a hundred prisoners, most of them French legionnaires who had volunteered to stay on in Mexico, were summarily executed. Miramon's dashing and brave action had cost the Imperialists their war chest of twenty-five thousand pesos and over three thousand men killed, wounded and captured.

By a cruel irony, the news of this disaster reached Maximilian on the same day as he received New Year wishes from his mother, in a letter which reopened all the old wounds and revived the heartache. Though the Archduchess may never have written her son the letter which she is supposed to have addressed to Orizaba and of which no one has seen the text, her letter of 1 January is sufficiently incriminating, for it left him with no other choice than to stay in Mexico. That the Archduchess, who adored her son, could have written him such a letter can only be explained by the fact that she realized he had no future in Europe. The latest news from Charlotte had been good. She had long lucid intervals in which she resumed her old habits, writing normal, intelligent letters to her old friends in Belgium, reading books on history and philosophy and even attending to her accounts. At one moment the doctors hoped for a complete cure and Eloin in his well-meaning but blundering way sent Maximilian a telegram saying that the Empress was 'on the way to recovery'. The telegram arrived in a garbled form and Maximilian read with joy that his wife was completely cured. The subsequent contradiction was all the more painful to bear.

The Archduchess's letter appears to have been written during one of Charlotte's lucid periods, for she writes of the 'pretty, loving and quite rational letter in which Charlotte thanked me for the presents which Papa [the Archduke Franz Karl] and I arranged in her room on Christmas Eve.' The affection with which the Archduchess wrote of Charlotte to her son was not entirely sincere, for apart from an occasional letter and present, the unfortunate young Empress was utterly abandoned by her husband's family. Not one of them came to visit her at Miramar, where she lived completely isolated, without even a lady-in-waiting for company. Old friends and former governesses were discouraged from visiting her, and six months later when her sister-in-law, the Queen of the Belgians, came to take her away from Miramar and back to her own country, Marie Henriette was horrified by the cruelty and harshness with which she had been treated by the Hapsburgs. But there must be some explanation as to why the Archduchess Sophia should have neglected the wife of her favourite son and been so unsympathetic of her affliction. Involuntarily one turns back to the rumour of Charlotte's pregnancy. It would explain the atmosphere of secrecy, the seclusion in which she was kept that winter at Miramar; above all it would explain the tone of the Archduchess's letter to her son, applauding his decision to stay on in Mexico 'in spite of your natural desire to hasten back to Charlotte'. She knew him so well, knew he could never face up to the horror of a mad wife, and the even greater humiliation of a wife who had given birth to the son he had never been able to give her. It was better to remain in Mexico 'so long as the rich people of the country make your remaining possible'. It was a terrible and at the same time a pathetic letter, appealing to his vanity, telling him how much everyone admired him for his decision to maintain his throne, then finally breaking down, showing herself to be an ordinary loving mother, longing for her Max: 'When the whole family was gathered round the Christmas Tree, Papa and I and our four grand-children with their parents, suddenly the big clock struck, the one with *your* works from Olmütz, and it seemed to me like a greeting from you, chiming in the family circle from afar. Tears came into my eyes. The Emperor noticed them, I think, and guessed the cause, for he turned hastily away. And yet I am *bound* to want you to stay so long as it is possible and can be done with honour.' When her son received this letter he knew that he had no other choice but to remain, even if the situation was no longer 'possible'. All he could allow himself was a last heroic gesture, to leave his capital and ride into the interior at the head of his army, putting an end to the dissensions of the rival generals by taking on himself the supreme command. What Van der Smissen had suggested to him in the autumn, what Pierron had urged him to do before he had left for France, represented the only means of escape from the ministers who had become his jailers.

Bazaine was on his way to Orizaba when he heard of the disaster of San Jacinto. Hoping this might induce Maximilian to change his mind, he sent a special courier to tell Dano that there was still time to save the Emperor and that he would wait a week for him at Orizaba. But Bazaine's messenger passed another on the road – a courier dispatched by Dano to the Marshal, telling him that on 13 February Maximilian had left his capital for Queretaro.

31

The last stand

The Emperor's last letter to his ministers before he left for Queretaro was utterly disillusioned. None of the promises had been kept, there was no sign of peace and the civil war was increasing in savagery every day. Neither the monarchy nor the Church had any longer any hold on the people, while the Liberals were strong in the conviction that they were fighting for the independence of their country. Of the two million pesos promised by wealthy Conservatives, barely a hundred thousand had materialized and many of those who had promised to contribute were already on their way to Europe. The departure of the French expeditionary force had been followed by an exodus of Europeans and of the rich upper classes, both Liberal and Conservative, who had collaborated with the Empire. Among the first to avail himself of the offer of French transport had been Archbishop Labastida, who had left the city secretly on the same day as Bazaine. 'As if he had been appointed Chaplain to the French army,' was Maximilian's sarcastic comment. Yet Marquez and Miramon were still ready to fight for the Church. The humbler members of the clergy were still prepared to be martyrs for their faith and the Imperialist forces converging on Queretaro, a hundred miles north of Mexico City, had chosen it as their citadel, not on account of its strategic position on the highway to the north, but because Queretaro had always been a Conservative and clerical stronghold, where the inhabitants were loyal to the Empire and every friar and nun inside the city was ready to collaborate in its defence.

His ministers had applauded Maximilian's decision to put himself at the head of his army. It was vital for them to get him away from the influence of the foreign envoys who might still induce him to change his mind. They had little love or respect for their Emperor, who was no more to them than a useful pawn in securing the interests of their party. Juarez might still be persuaded to negotiate favourable terms, so long as Maximilian and his loyal generals stood at the head of a strong organized army. Without the Emperor, the generals would degenerate into mere guerrilla leaders and the Liberals would sweep to victory in every state from Sonora to Guerrero.

The Emperor joined his army outside the city gates. They were supposed to have been ten thousand, they were only sixteen hundred. Seven thousand had been left behind to defend the capital, including the two Austrian regiments of Hammerstein and Khevenhüller who had stayed on in Mexico for no other reason than to fight for Kaiser Max, and now found themselves left to defend a government they despised and a population whose growing xenophobia was venting itself against all foreigners. They had implored the Emperor to take them with him and not to put his trust in Marquez, who was deliberately trying to separate him from his countrymen. But Maximilian had replied that the time had come when he must show his subjects that he was heart and soul a Mexican, no longer dependent on foreign support. He promised he would send for them as soon as he got to Queretaro. The promise was kept but Marquez and his henchmen in the capital took care that the order should be intercepted.

The General had his way. With the exception of his Austrian doctor and Hungarian cook and valet, the Emperor's suite was entirely Mexican. There were his two aides-de-camp, Pradillo and Ormacheo, the faithful Blasio who had insisted on sharing his master's fate, and among the subordinate officers, the handsome Colonel Lopez who had first attracted Maximilian's attention when he commanded the escort which brought him from Vera Cruz to Mexico City. Lopez had prospered under the Empire; the captain was now a colonel, his uniform covered in decorations, including the Cross of the Legion of Honour, presented to him by Bazaine, not so much on account of his valour, but because he was related to the Marshal's wife. Lopez knew how to get on with foreigners. Even the critical Van der Smissen had recommended him to the Emperor 'as a loyal officer on whom Your Majesty can rely.' With his polished manners and agreeable ways, Lopez had been among the favoured few admitted to the intimacy of La Borda. No-one knew better how to organize a *tertulia* or to play a *habanera* on the guitar. Maximilian had honoured him by acting as godfather to his child, and, because he was poor, had given him a house in his native city of Puebla. But Lopez' popularity with the Emperor and with foreigners did not extend to his own countrymen. The older officers who had fought with

Santa Anna avoided his company. There was said to be something discreditable in his past which, in spite of the Emperor's favour, would prevent him from ever becoming a general. But he cut a gallant figure in his red gold-trimmed jacket as he rode beside the Emperor and General Marquez at the head of sixteen hundred men to join up with the bulk of the Imperial forces converging on Queretaro. All in all, there were not more than nine thousand, including the debris of the army Miramon had been able to save from the slaughter of San Jacinto; the Indian troops which Mejía had recruited in the Sierra Corda and the élite brigade commanded by Mendez, of whom a large percentage were French. Marquez might talk of a national army, but nearly a third were foreigners; men of every race and creed, fought under the standard of a prince many of them had never seen, but whom in Queretaro they learnt to love, almost to idolize, inspired by his cool courage and selfless heroism. There were Mexicans and Spaniards, French and Germans, Austrians, Russians, Poles; ex-legionnaries, deserters from Bazaine's army and failed adventurers who had drifted across the Rio Grande in search of the fabled gold of Mexico. Among these adventurers were a few for whom war was a natural element and who had come, not in search of gold, but in order to practise the only trade they knew, the trade of soldiering. Prince Felix Zu Salm-Salm, the Emperor's last and truest friend, belonged to this category and of all the adventurers who in the past three years had gathered around Maximilian's throne, he was by far the most sympathetic.

The younger son of one of the great princely families of Germany, Salm had served with distinction as a cavalry officer in his own country, until his mounting debts forced him to leave his regiment and take service in Austria. But before long his creditors in Vienna were as pressing as his creditors at home. His family paid his passage to America where the outbreak of the Civil War gave him the chance of distinguishing himself in the Federal forces, where his Prussian military training won him the rank of Brigadier-General. In America, Salm met the twenty-two year old girl, who later became his wife and of whose origin little is known, except that she was of French extraction and at some time in her life had been a circus rider. These two people of completely different backgrounds appear to have been ideally suited to one another, a couple who belonged to the new frontier society of the West rather than to the aristocratic European world in which he was born. Of the two, she was the more intelligent, knowing how to use her feminine charms, which were considerable, in furthering her husband's career and in protecting him from the consequences of his reckless impulses and fiery temper. In her own words, he was 'just like a cocked pistol always ready to go off,' and it was her job to 'keep a restraining hand on the trigger.' Her courage matched his own. She followed him to the front, working in field hospitals throughout the Civil War. But the end of the war found the Prince again unemployed and unable to adapt himself to life in a small garrison town, when there was a full-scale war going on across the border with a romantic Hapsburg Emperor in desperate need of trained and efficient officers. Armed with introductions from the Prussian and Austrian ministers in Washington, the Salms arrived in Mexico City in the late summer of 1866, expecting to be welcomed with open arms, both at Court and in Mexican society.

They were disappointed in their hopes. A Prussian officer was *persona non grata* in Maximilian's predominantly Austrian entourage. Many looked upon him as an imposter, while his handsome wife with her free and easy ways, found little favour among the European and Creole ladies of the capital. Agnes Salm never had a chance of meeting the Emperor till she visited him in his prison cell, and it was only through the friendship of the Prussian minister, Baron Magnus, that the Prince finally succeeded in obtaining an audience. His first months in Mexico were spent fighting with the Belgian division under Van der Smissen, and these two men, so similar in temperament, appeared to have been on the best of terms. But then came the disbanding of the volunteers, Van der Smissen's departure for Europe and the Emperor's decision to take over the command of his army. Prince Salm was among the first to request a post on his staff, and was refused for the same reason Hammerstein and Khevenhüller had been refused. But he was not a man to take 'no' for an answer. 'It did not seem natural to me to be left behind, when there was fighting to be done,' he wrote, and only a few hours after the Emperor's departure, he also was on the road to Queretaro, having managed at the last moment, and again through the mediation of Baron Magnus, to get himself attached to General Vidaurri's company. The General was a former Liberal who had given his adherence to the Empire soon after Maximilian's arrival in Mexico. He was known for his honesty and generosity towards his enemies, and was as popular with his men as he was disliked by the Conservative generals. Maximilian, who appreciated his talents, had appointed him Paymaster of the Forces. But his distrust of Marquez, whom he had once beaten in battle, was such that he never moved without his own bodyguard of tough *Rancheros* from his native state of Nueva Leon.

On reviewing his troops on the second day of the march, Maximilian was astonished to find the debonair Prince Salm, with his shining buttons and waxed moustaches, standing at the head of Vidaurri's brawny and hirsute bodyguard. 'Good God, Salm, how on earth did you get here?' he asked, to which the Prince replied: 'Your Majesty would not take me with you, so General Vidaurri brought me instead.' 'You know the reason,' said the Emperor, adding with a smile, 'but now that you are here, I'm delighted to see you.' So started a friendship which was to brighten the last tragic months of Maximilian's life. The Emperor who had no future, and the soldier of fortune with no thought of tomorrow, were inevitably drawn together by their mutual ties to a Europe they had turned their backs on, a way of life they had discarded but could not disown. On the second day of the march Maximilian was already inviting Colonel Salm to keep him company, discussing with him in his frank and open way subjects he would never have broached with his Mexican generals. Salm was at his side when they were attacked by a reconnoitring enemy force, and the Emperor, throwing himself into the thick of the fighting, gave his first military commands, finding in the exhilaration of battle, the smell of gun powder, the wild war cries of his troops, a strange, savage exaltation. By the time he reached Queretaro, Maximilian realised that he was happier than he had been in months, that this was the only life in which he could forget his haunting memories of a mad wife, shut up at Miramar.

Queretaro, which Mejía had conquered from the Liberals only a few years before and where he was still regarded as a demi-god by his Indian tribesmen and the Creole aristocracy, welcomed the Emperor and his generals with enthusiasm. Everyone was out in the streets to cheer those whom they called the 'Five Magic M's' – Maximilian, Mejía, Marquez, Miramon and Mendez. There were other generals in Queretaro, as brave and often more experienced. But these were the five who had captured the imagination of the people. And it was the rivalry between Marquez and Miramon, and Mendez's hatred for Miramon, which caused such bitter dissensions in the councils of war and such lack of cohesion in the plan of campaign. Marquez, the Chief of Staff, had no knowledge of strategy and sabotaged every plan proposed by Miramon who, in turn, was far too reckless to be in command of the infantry which Mendez rightly thought should have been given to him.

But no-one questioned Mejía's rights to command the cavalry. The ugly yellow-faced little Indian, who had managed to extricate his troops from San Luis Potosi after the French had handed over the town, and fighting off continual enemy attacks, had brought them safely to Queretaro, was loved and respected by everyone. But for all the festivities and speeches, the flag-waving and the flowers, the lack of money and the lack of troops hampered operations from the first day, and at a council of war it was decided to send to Mexico City for the Austrian regiments and the urgently needed funds.

Queretaro, situated in a fertile valley, surrounded by low hills, and to the north-east by the mountain range of the Sierra Corda, is a charming colonial city, which owes much to one of its Spanish governors who in the eighteenth century embellished it with churches and monuments by Tresquerras, exquisite iron-work, and fountains supplied with fresh mountain water from the splendid aquaduct built outside the town. The dominating building, constructed on a rock to the south-east of the city, is the so-called Collegio de la Cruz, dating from the time of the Spanish conquest, part convent, part fortress, with massive stone walls, extensive patios, a chapel and a pantheon. This building and the isolated rocky hill known as the 'Cerro de las Campañas' (The Hill of the Bells), which arises about fifteen hundred metres to the west of the town, were the two key points in the defence of Queretaro.

In the first days, Maximilian had his headquarters on the *Cerro de las Campañas*, which commanded a view over the town and the surrounding valley, with its orange groves and maize fields and white-washed *haciendas*, rich in produce to feed a hungry army. But Marquez, his Chief of Staff, never took the ordinary precaution of occupying these *haciendas*. 'Anyone experienced in strategy,' wrote Prince Salm 'had only to stand on the Cerro to realise that Queretaro was the worst place in the world to defend, as every house could be reached by gun fire from the surrounding hills, and could only be protected if there were sufficient troops to occupy those hills.'

But the government's reply to the Emperor's request for troops had been as negative as their reply to a request for funds. They were too frightened for themselves and too concerned in keeping open the last escape route to Vera Cruz, to come to the rescue of their beleaguered Emperor. Before leaving, the French had handed back the custom houses of Vera Cruz, and General Osmont, who had been put in control there since resigning from Maximilian's government, had placed a considerable sum in the hands of the Imperialist authorities. But there was no way of getting this money from Vera Cruz to Queretaro, and Puebla, the only town on the direct route between the port and the capital, which was still in Imperialist hands, was already invested by Porfirio Diaz. Father Fischer, who had been ordered by Maximilian to collect the arrears of payment from his civil list and the money resulting from the sale of his personal effects, his silver plate and carriages, sent only one consignment of fifty thousand pesos. And within a week of their arrival the Imperialists had to resort to raising a forced loan from the wealthier citizens of Queretaro. Precious time was wasted in waiting for the reply from Mexico City, while Escobedo, with an army of sixteen thousand, was advancing on Queretaro from the north, and Corona and Regulés, with another ten thousand troops, were approaching from the west. Miramon was in favour of launching a full-scale attack against Escobedo's forces, before the two armies had time to join up. But Marquez insisted that they must first consolidate their own troops, and then 'annihilate the enemy at a single blow'. The General always spoke of the Liberals with the utmost contempt, as if they were a worthless rabble in comparison with his own army.

This was the time for Maximilian to assert his authority, and to come out with a definite plan of campaign. But, while willing to share all the hardships of his troops, bivouacing in the open, sleeping wrapped up in a blanket on the hard ground, from which the cactus had just been removed, his vacillating character made it impossible for him to come to a definite decision. As usual, he consulted too many people and listened to too much advice. At heart he still clung to the idea of coming to some honourable agreement with Juarez, who had now moved his government to San Luis Potosi. He is even said to have sent messages to Juarez, none of which received a reply. Failing to come to an agreement, he saw no other alternative than to die bravely on the battlefield and he seized every opportunity of exposing himself to danger. On 14 March, when the enemy launched a full-scale attack against the town, the Emperor's example was an inspiration to his troops.

The story of the siege of Queretaro is a story of unquestioning heroism and of fantastic courage, in which Emperor and soldiers fought with the same reckless bravery, and where even the ordinary citizens, down to the nuns in the convents, helped in the defence. The Imperialists emerged victorious from this first attack. Prince Salm, who had been put in command of the Cazadores, performed miracles of valour, arousing the admiration even of the enemy. By the end of the day, Escobedo's forces had retreated in confusion all along the line, having lost thousands of men. Had Salm's advice been taken, the Imperialists might have gone over to the attack and swept the demoralized Liberals from their fortified positions on the hills. Conscripted troops were always ready to change sides at the first sign of defeat and with sufficient reinforcements they might have advanced against San Luis Potosi. One victory would have been sufficient to win back the northern provinces, where Viddurri, who was a former governor of Nueva Leon, was still a name to conjure with. It was hazardous advice, but it was preferable to remaining in a town where the trap was gradually closing. Salm, however, was a foreigner, already distrusted as 'the Emperor's latest advisor', envied by men like Lopez when Maximilian raised him to the rank of Brigadier and made him his principal aide-de-camp.

The enemy was given time to recover, and to bring up its reinforcements. By the end of March they were nearly forty thousand, stretched in a thin screen across the hills. Yet their attacks continued to be repulsed and the garrison made a number of successful sorties. In the first weeks Maximilian was filled with a strange euphoria, which is reflected in a letter addressed to Herr Radonetz at Miramar. 'My old comrades in the navy will be astonished to hear that their former Commander-in-Chief has put himself at the head of his army. The Admiral has for the moment given place to the Generalissimo, complete with highboots, spurs and a huge sombrero. I have taken to my new role with enthusiasm. Army life agrees with me and I find it immensely stimulating, especially when one commands such young and courageous troops. I work on the same principles as when I was in the navy, carrying out day and night inspections and paying surprise visits to the outposts. The enemy seems to have become familiar with my habits, for when I go out on horseback or on foot to visit the fortifications, I and my suite are always greeted with a hail of bullets. The other day a hand grenade exploded almost at my feet. I'm sending you a small piece as a souvenir to put in our museum at Miramar.' To the end of his life, Maximilian remained the dilettante whether in peace or war. One day, 13 March, repaid him for all the hardships and fatigue. It was the day when he distributed medals for valour to his officers and men – the soldiers receiving medals of gold and silver and the officers of bronze. At the end of the ceremony, General Miramon stepped forward and, in the name of the army, pinned a bronze medal on the Emperor's uniform, saying 'Your Majesty has deserved this more than any of us.' This gesture from an ex-Republican President of Mexico, who had never been a Monarchist till now, touched Maximilian to the heart. At this moment, he felt perhaps for the first time that he really belonged to Mexico.

This was the week after Marquez had left for the capital. The situation had become so serious, the shortage of food and ammunition was so acute, that the General who was dissatisfied with his position as Chief-of-Staff and wanted to get out of Queretaro, where there were too many rivals for his liking, succeeded in prevailing upon the Emperor to send him on a special mission to Mexico City. Given a thousand horsemen, he volunteered to break through the enemy lines. Having arrived in the capital, he would dismiss what he called 'this government of old women' and establish a firm military rule. Having collected money and reinforcements, he would then return to Queretaro and attack the enemy from the rear. Full of gratitude and admiration for his courage and devotion, the Emperor fell in with his wishes, and appointed him Lieutenant-General of the Empire, armed with supreme power and entrusted with a document that, in the event of the Emperor's being either killed or captured at Queretaro, Marquez was to act as Regent, pending the convocation of a congress where the people should be allowed to decide on what form of government they wanted. Only someone as idealistic as Maximilian would have entrusted such a document to the cruellest and most rapacious of his generals. On the night of 22 March, Marquez set out from Queretaro where he was never seen again. All that concerned him was his own future. He was a political gambler about to risk his last stand on a desperate chance.

On 27 March, the news spread through Mexico City that Marquez with a thousand men had arrived from Queretaro, bringing news of splendid victories won by the Imperialists. All Mexico was in a flutter of excitement and Marquez was the hero of the hour. But it was not long before Don Leopardo, as he was called, showed himself in his true colours, levying enormous taxes on the inhabitants and resorting to the dreaded *leva* (enforced conscription). Instead of sending the Austrian regiments straight to Queretaro, they were ordered to march with him to the relief of Puebla, where he already saw himself triumphant with the customs receipts of Vera Cruz safely in his hands.

Agnes Salm, who was staying with friends outside the city, at Tacubaya, anxiously awaiting news of her husband, visited General Marquez

437

on his arrival, and with her shrewd feminine eye noted his almost megalomaniac conceit. 'He behaved and spoke as if the Emperor were only his pupil and he himself the most important personage in all Mexico. While speaking of my husband in the highest terms as one of the bravest officers of Queretaro, he declared that it was *he* who had decorated him, and *he* who had made him a General.' But Marquez was to present a very different figure before the week was out. Porfirio Diaz forestalled him at Puebla and the city fell when he and his army were still en route. News of the defeat spread like wildfire through his troops. The paid conscripts deserted en masse, throwing down their arms and running off to hide among the sugar cane and maize fields. On 10 April, the Liberal advance guard caught up with the retreating columns and panic spread on all sides. The infantry went over to the enemy, the artillery men cut their horses traces, mounted the teams and took flight. The retreat became a rout, with Marquez abandoning his army and fleeing for safety. Only the foreign troops stood firm, and through the bravery of Colonel Kodolitsch and his Hussars, succeeded in bringing the remnants of the column back to Mexico City. This was the last act of useless heroism performed by the Austrian Brigade, for a few days later the troops of Porfirio Diaz were already in the suburbs of the capital.

Meanwhile at Queretaro, the garrison which was now reduced to barely seven thousand, waited anxiously for news. Marquez had promised the Emperor to be back within a fortnight, but the day he was to have returned went by without bringing any news. Indians and priests continued to pass in and out of the city, the former bringing messages across the enemy lines, rolled up in their *cigaritos*, while the priests, who most of the Republican soldiers were too superstitious to search, carried news from one village to another. Marquez would have had no difficulty in getting a message through to the besieged city but by the middle of April there was still no sign of him and Mejía and Miramon spoke openly of treason. Only the Emperor continued to say it was not possible, till on 22 April, prisoners brought in for interrogation told him of the fall of Puebla and of Marquez's ignominious defeat at the hands of Porfirio Diaz. Pathetic attempts were made to prevent this demoralizing news from spreading through the garrison. But by the end of the month, there was not a person in Queretaro who still believed in victory. In the first two months, there had hardly been one deserter, now there were as many as fifty a day.

Maximilian's brief period of euphoria was now succeeded by the deepest depression. His health, which had improved in the first weeks, could no longer stand the strain and his doctor insisted on him moving his headquarters from the Cerro to more comfortable quarters in the Convent of La Cruz. But he still insisted in carrying out his military duties and Prince Salm relates how, one night, when he had fallen asleep in the trenches, he suddenly awoke to see the Emperor standing beside him, 'with that kind, benevolent smile, which warmed the heart.' The Prince writes how 'without any aide or orderly, armed only with his inseparable little eyeglass, Maximilian would visit the trenches during the night, and as he knew that some of the Mexican officers were apt to maltreat their soldiers and deprive them of part of their allowances and pay, he would stop and ask them as to whether they had received the rations that were due to them. This show of interest was so unusual and so flattering to these poor, simple men that they adored the Emperor, who treated them not as cannon fodder but as human beings and who was ready to share with them all their dangers and privations.'

It was not so much the dangers as the privations which were beginning to sap the vitality and loyalty of the garrisons. The Liberals were in occupation of all the outlying *haciendas*. There was hardly any food for the troops or fodder for the horses, which were now being killed to feed the men. At the Hotel Deligencias, where most of the officers messed, roast mule and tortillas was the daily *table d'hôte*. The nuns in the convent baked every day a small loaf of bread for the Emperor out of supplies reserved for the Host, and it was characteristic of Maximilian to divide the loaf with the members of his entourage. The town people suffered almost as much as the garrison and the voices in favour of capitulation were growing louder every day. At the councils of war, Mendez and Miramon were always at each other's throats, mutually and wrongfully accusing one another of treachery. But treachery was in the air. When Prince Salm volunteered to go unescorted to Mexico City to bring a personal message from the Emperor to the officers of the Austrian Regiments, he found that his plan had been betrayed to the enemy. A strong enemy barrage met him wherever he tried to pass, and guns had been placed in positions which were usually unoccupied. Furious and humiliated, he had to withdraw, but he was far from suspecting a traitor in the Emperor's entourage.

The story of the betrayal of Queretaro has been told so often. Miguel

Lopez, who opened the defences of La Cruz to the enemy has himself published his defence, and no less a person than the eminent historian, Emile Ollivier, has supported his claims. Lopez insisted that he acted on the instructions of the Emperor Maximilian who, in order to put an end to all the senseless bloodshed, ordered him secretly to enter into negotiations with the enemy. This would have been so completely alien to Maximilian's character and so contrary to his high principles of honour that it cannot seriously be taken into consideration. The evidence against Lopez is too strong to be denied. His betrayal is in keeping with what we know of the man, weak and mean, irresolute and spiteful, a nature compounded of vanity and pride, warped by jealousy which a succession of events combined to bring to a head. He might never have betrayed his Emperor had not Miramon prevented Maximilian from making him into a General by producing evidence proving him to be unfit for the position. As a young ensign serving in Santa Anna's army, Lopez had incited the President's bodyguard to revolt and had been dismissed from the army for disgraceful conduct.

Maximilian abided by Miramon's decision but he nevertheless felt sorry for the man who had never been allowed to expiate his youthful errors, and he continued to give Lopez his confidence to the extent of putting his regiment in charge of the defences of La Cruz. But Lopez, who was inordinately vain and sensitive, felt that he had lost the Emperior's affection and had been supplanted by Prince Salm who was now the inseparable companion with whom Maximilian would remain closeted for hours, discussing the plan of campaign, while Lopez was not even admitted to the councils of war.

By 10 May the situation had become untenable. The enemy had cut the water supply, the people were starving and it was only a question of days before an epidemic broke out in the town. Even Miramon now realized that Queretaro could no longer be defended. For once, the generals agreed and it was unanimously decided to attempt to break through with the whole of the garrison in the hopes of reaching the Sierra Corda and the coast. Midnight of 14 May was the time and date fixed for the sortie, and to prevent any possible treachery the place for the attack was not to be divulged till the eleventh hour. Three thousand of Mejía's tribesmen, living in the city, were to occupy the positions evacuated by the garrison and distract the enemy's attention by musketry and gunfire. At daybreak, they would throw away their arms

440

and return to their homes. It was a wild, reckless plan but it might have succeeded. Everything was ready by the evening of the fourteenth, when Mejía asked for another twenty-four hours to organize his men and the Emperor approved of the delay.

That night and the previous evening, Lopez crossed over into the enemy lines. At first, he may not have intended to play the role of Judas in betraying the Emperor he professed to love. He had so often heard Maximilian expressing the hope of coming to some honourable agreement with the enemy, that he may well have seen himself in the rôle of mediator. Some of the Liberal spies, and there were plenty in the town, may have encouraged him in this belief. But on his first visit to Escobedo's camp, his cowardice and avarice got the upper hand. The General demanded unconditional surrender. If Lopez handed over the defences of La Cruz, he was promised his liberty, his life and a handsome remuneration, and Lopez, we must remember, was poor.

Prince Salm has left a factual account of the events of the night and morning of 14–15 May. He had retired to his quarters in a bad temper, angered by what he considered to be a dangerous delay. It was still dark when he woke in the morning to hear a tremendous noise going on outside. A few minutes later, Lopez came rushing into his room, 'shouting in a very queer and excited voice, "Quick! Save the Emperor, the enemy is in La Cruz!"' The Prince had barely time to buckle on his sword and put his revolver into his belt, when the Emperor's valet came in looking utterly distraught and telling him to go to his master. Grill was followed by Doctor Basch who had been up half the night looking after the wounded and had no idea as to what had happened. Salm went to the Emperor whom he found already fully dressed, looking white and ill but outwardly calm. In a low voice, very different from his usual tone, he said, 'We are betrayed. Go down and order the hussars and bodyguard to come out. We will try to get to the Cerro. I will follow you directly.'

Salm went out on to the plaza and to his amazement found it completely empty. In the place of the noise he had heard an hour before, there was now an almost uncanny silence,. There was nowhere a soldier to be seen. Even the guard before the Emperor's room had disappeared. The company whose duty it was to guard the entrance to La Cruz had vanished, and there was no sign of the 'Empress's Regiment'. On reaching the gates, he saw in the first light of dawn that one of the guns of the fortifications had been deliberately overturned, while some soldiers were creeping cautiously through an embrasure of the wall. On looking closer, he saw they were wearing the grey uniform of one of Escobedo's crack regiments. He turned and ran back to the Emperor, whom he met coming down the staircase wearing a greatcoat over his uniform and carrying two revolvers in his hand. Behind him was old General Castillo and his secretary, Blasio. Salm ran up to Maximilian, took the pistols out of his hand and in his excitement seized him by the arm, crying, 'Hurry, Your Majesty, there is no time to lose.' They had barely got out of the door, before they ran into a group of Republican soldiers. To their surprise, Lopez was among them, talking to a young colonel. The colonel belonged to a family who had collaborated with the Empire and his sister had been maid-of-honour to the Empress. He knew the Emperor well, but when the soldiers tried to stop them from going through, he called out in a loud voice, 'Let them pass, they are peaceful citizens,' and the Emperor with Salm and Castillo, both in full uniform, went unmolested on their way.

Was it Lopez who, in spite of his betrayal, had bargained to save the Emperor? Or was it, as Maximilian seemed to think, because the young colonel was grateful for some favour shown to his sister in the past. A little later they ran again into Lopez who, this time, came up to the Emperor and beseeched him to take refuge in the house of the banker, Don Carlos Rubio, but Maximilian looked at him coldly saying, 'I do not hide myself.' And suddenly beside them, they saw one of the Emperor's horses fully saddled, with a groom holding the reins. Lopez had meant the Emperor to escape, only he had misjudged his character.

In the general confusion, Maximilian and his companions passed unhindered through the western suburbs. The sun had risen by the time they reached the Cerro and they could see the enemy troops pouring into the city, their own men throwing down their arms and surrendering en masse. Only one battalion was left guarding the Cerro, the rest had fled. Mejía, with a few of his bodyguard and a small detachment of cavalry, had been able to follow them, but Miramon had been badly wounded and had been brought to a doctor's house. All in all, there were not more than a couple of hundred men desperately defending the cactus-covered rock which was the last Imperialist citadel, while all the batteries from the surrounding hills opened fire against them and a serried mass of infantry, followed by cavalry, was gradually surrounding the hill. Three times, the Emperor turned to Mejía to ask him whether there was a chance of breaking through, and three times the brave little Indian had to answer that it was useless to attempt it as they would only be mown down by enemy guns. Maximilian then turned to Salm and said: 'Let us hope for a lucky bullet.'

32

The Hill of the Bells

Queretaro had fallen after a heroic defence of seventy-two days, and Maximilian was a prisoner, but the news took several days to reach the outside world. Communications with Europe were disrupted: telegraph wires had broken down, Mexico City was in a state of siege and even diplomatic couriers between the capital and Vera Cruz were prevented from going through. In Austria there had been no news of Maximilian since his departure for Queretaro, and both at Court and among the general public there was growing anxiety for his welfare. As early as 5 March, Prince Metternich was instructed to obtain personal assurances from Napoleon, 'that the Emperor Maximilian was in no kind of danger from possible reprisals'. The Ambassador was received at the Tuileries in what must have been a painful interview for Napoleon, all the more painful because he and the Empress were on intimate terms with Prince Metternich, who from the very beginning had doubted the success of the Mexican adventure. Now he had to admit that following the embarkation of the French troops, there was nothing more he could do for the young Emperor who against his advice, and that of the whole French general staff, had insisted in staying behind and placing himself at the head of his guerrilla troops. It was a gesture which may have been heroic but which involved dangers for which France could not be held responsible.

The Austrian Ambassador was not the only one to whom Napoleon had to make his explanations and excuses. In a speech held at the opening of the spring session of the Legislative Assembly, he had referred to 'the unfortunate train of events, which had prevented France from carrying out to the end the task of regenerating an ancient Empire and opening out new markets for her expanding commerce'. Napoleon added: 'On the day when the sacrifices seemed to me to exceed the interests which had called us across the ocean, I resolved on my own initiative to evacuate the troops.' In his speech there was no mention of the Emperor Maximilian, nor of the pressure exercised by Washington, which more than anything else had contributed to the failure of the enterprise.

Seeing that there was nothing more to be hoped for from Paris, the Austrian Government referred to Washington, in the hope that those who had been largely responsible in bringing Senor Juarez back to power would be able to persuade him to show clemency towards the vanquished. The Austrian Minister, Baron Wydenbruck, who was more in touch with events than his superiors, had already acted on his own account and had succeeded in getting Secretary Seward to instruct Colonel Campbell, the accredited Minister to Juarez, to request the Mexican 'President' that in the event of the fall of Queretaro and the capture of the Emperor Maximilian, the latter would be treated 'as civilized nations treat prisoners of war'. This was an oblique reference to the massacre which had occurred after the battle of San Jacinto, when the Republicans murdered in cold blood over one hundred European officers. American public opinion, till then favourable to Juarez, had been profoundly shocked by this event and Seward's decision to intervene was generally approved.

But the reference to 'civilized nations' was not likely to be appreciated by Juarez, who refused to be dictated to by the Americans however much they might have helped him in the past. To appear as the tool of Washington would be fatal to his own position in a country where the people still remembered the Texan war and lived in dread of another invasion. Juarez sent a polite but firm refusal to Seward's note. In the event of the fall of Queretaro the Archduke Ferdinand Maximilian of Hapsburg had no right to be treated as a prisoner of war, he said. He had usurped the throne with the help of foreign arms and 'incited the Mexicans to revolt against the lawful government of the country and with his own hand had signed the notorious October Decree by which hundreds of innocent people had been put to death.' Juarez might not have dared to be quite so arrogant if the United States had had a worthier representative than Campbell, who since his one abortive journey to Vera Cruz had been sitting comfortably in New Orleans with no intention of crossing the border. Seward's note was sent on by courier and only arrived at Juarez's headquarters after considerable delay. By the time the Mexican President's reply was received in Washington, Queretaro had fallen, Maximilian was a prisoner and all the

European Courts were calling on the American President to intervene. Campbell was instructed to go to San Luis Potosi and intercede directly for the Emperor and the other prisoners, and it was now that Campbell proved himself utterly contemptible. Whatever his political beliefs, ordinary humanity should have prompted him to go, instead of which he dallied and prevaricated, wasting precious time sending telegrams asking whether he should proceed by sea or land. On 11 June President Johnson, reacting to the growing indignation of the American press, ordered him to appeal personally on his behalf and to ask President Juarez to commute the death sentence. Campbell's reply was to send in his resignation.

There was one American subject who did not wait on orders from her government and had sufficient courage to brave President Juarez on her own. Agnes Salm was still in Tacubaya on 20 April, when Porfirio Diaz established his headquarters in what had been the Archbishop's summer residence. A young American-born princess who kept bringing food and money to the Austrian prisoners captured at Puebla and now quartered at Chapultepec was suspect enough. But when that Princess, whose husband was fighting with Maximilian at Queretaro, was constantly inviting his own young officers to her house, General Diaz began to think that it was time for her to leave the country. The Princess had other ideas. She was determined to get to Queretaro and she found a complaisant general who succeeded in persuading Diaz to let her proceed to Escobedo's headquarters. She records with indignation that the General refused to provide her with a military escort. But there were others ready to be more gallant. Within twenty-four hours an English superintendent on the new railroad had provided her with mules and a driver and a Mexican businessman travelling with an armed servant had offered himself as escort. She had bought a superannuated, bright-yellow fiacre, and accompanied by her maid and her terrier Jimmy, she set out for Queretaro.

Her arrival at Escobedo's headquarters on the last day of April caused a sensation. A beautiful, elegantly-dressed young woman who had travelled a hundred miles on the brigand-infested road in an absurd little fiacre, asking as if it were the most natural thing in the world for permission to visit her wounded husband in the besieged city, was sufficient to stagger the most hardened of *guerrilleros*. The fact that her husband was not wounded and had done more damage to the Republican army than any single officer fighting in the Imperialist garrison only made her demand the more preposterous, and it speaks for Mexican chivalry that the Princess was not put under lock and key. On the contrary, she was treated with the greatest consideration and lodged in the most comfortable *hacienda* in the neighbourhood. But General Escobedo seems to have been as anxious to get rid of her as General Diaz. The following day she was told that a diligence was leaving for San Luis Potosi, and that the General would provide her with an escort and a letter for President Juarez.

Juarez was polite but evasive and the Princess, who was far from sharing her husband's dislike for 'that blood-thirsty Indian', had the impression of a man 'who reflected a great deal and deliberated long and carefully before acting'. But for all his politeness he refused her request to return to Queretaro and advised her to remain in San Luis until the fighting was over. The advice was an order and Agnes Salm was still in San Luis when on 15 May the ringing of bells and the firing of guns told her that the Imperial citadel had fallen. On the following days, one of the group of young officers by whom she seems always to have been surrounded called on her to tell her that 'Queretaro had been sold to the Liberals for three thousand ounces of gold, by a certain Colonel Lopez, that the Emperor was a prisoner and her husband wounded'. Without waiting for Juarez's permission, she left that night for Queretaro, and on 19 May was back in Escobedo's headquarters, asking him to allow her to visit the Emperor and her husband who now really was wounded. She found the victorious General in the best of humours and ready to comply with her wishes.

Four days had gone by since the white flag of surrender had been hoisted on the *Cerro de las Campañas*, and Maximilian of Hapsburg had handed over his sword to Escobedo, the ex-mule-contractor from Morelia. But the Republican generals knew how to be chivalrous in victory and General Riva Palacio, who conducted the prisoners back to La Cruz, deliberately avoided passing through the centre of the town where the troops were celebrating their triumph in libations of *pulque* and singing the most scurrilous verses of '*Mama Carlota*'. When the Emperor dismounted, he presented his horse to the General in thanks for his courtesy. But it was now that Maximilian's proud spirit broke: on returning to his rooms he found them ransacked. All that remained were a table and his camp bed, on which the mattress had been slashed in search of money. Weak from exhaustion and lack of food he turned to Doctor Basch, who had joined him at La Cruz, and embracing him burst into tears. But this was the only time in the whole month of his imprisonment that he showed any signs of giving way. His conduct throughout was so admirable that even his enemies paid tribute to his courage.

Prince Salm relates that some of the articles stolen from the Emperor's rooms, including a silver toilet set and wash basin, were later found in Colonel Lopez's room. Two valises containing books and clothes were returned to the Emperor, only the friend who had betrayed him kept his share of the spoils. But the kindness which was shown to the fallen Emperor by the people of Queretaro helped to restore his faith in human nature. Men and women who had suffered privations during the siege and had contributed to the forced loans levied by the army, continued to help the prisoners now that their own lives had returned to normal. Rubio, the wealthy banker whose *hacienda* had become Escobedo's headquarters, supplied the Emperor's meals throughout his captivity, and many others followed his example in looking after individual prisoners. A German merchant provided Maximilian with money, without demanding any form of security or guarantee, while the ladies of the city, hearing that he was short of linen, provided it in such abundance that he laughingly said, 'I have never had so much underlinen in my life.' In adversity he still kept his humour. Visitors were amazed not only by his resignation but by his good spirits. Jailers were given nicknames: a certain squint-eyed Indian with a particularly ferocious expression was known as 'the Hyena', Felix Salm, who was nervous and irritable in prison and from the first day was already making plans for them to escape, was referred to as 'the lion in his cage', while the gentle little Blasio was teased for his attempts to keep up Court protocol in prison.

The Emperor and his generals were comparatively well treated during the first days of their confinement. The doctor and servants were left at liberty and allowed to attend to their master's needs. The guard was lax and the prisoners were allowed to visit one another at all hours of the day. What Maximilian suffered from most was the continual noise, the terrible lack of privacy, the constant coming and going of Republican officers who visited either to gloat or merely out of curiosity.

Escobedo's army counted even more adventurers and filibusters than there were among the Imperialists, and ranged from the cultured Liberal to the Red revolutionary. There were those who like Riva Palacio were generally revolted by the atrocities committed by their subordinates and who secretly hoped that the Emperor would be spared. But the majority were thirsting for his blood. Escobedo himself was at a loss how to behave. If he maltreated his prisoners, he would incur the odium of the European and American press. On the other hand if he showed too great a leniency he might end by losing his popularity in the army. Like most successful Mexican generals he had political ambitions, so now he waited for his orders from San Luis Potosi.

On her visits to the *Juaristi* headquarters Agnes Salm had learnt that clemency was not to be expected either from Juarez or from Lerdo Tejada, the one minister who had never deserted him when they were fleeing before the French troops. Neither of them could forgive Maximilian the months they had spent as fugitives escaping from one frontier town to another. They could not forgive him the defection of their former colleagues and above all they could not forgive him for having called himself a Liberal. Of the two, Tejada was the more ruthless and Juarez the more implacable, upholding what he believed to be his right. When in April 1862 the three maritime powers had landed at Vera Cruz, Juarez had issued a decree by which all followers captured with arms in their hands trying to invade the country, and all Mexicans who aided and abetted them in any way, were liable to the death penalty. It did not matter whether the foreigner was a French soldier or an Austrian Archduke.

As an American, Agnes Salm came nearer to understanding his mentality than any of the European envoys who pleaded for Maximilian's life. Imbued with the mystique of royalty, they did not see that all the guarantees and promises, the blandishments and veiled threats, made on behalf of the Emperors and Kings of Europe only served to strengthen Juarez in his resolution to assert the independence of Mexico before the world. So long as Maximilian lived, there was still an Empire, *guerrilleros* would continue to raise his standard in the Sierras, a Court of discontented Mexican exiles would gather at Miramar, and the day would come when, like the Emperor Iturbide, he would try to stage a comeback. The reasoning was logical, but what Juarez failed to take into account was that Maximilian, escorted as a prisoner to Vera Cruz and put on a boat for Europe, would be a pitiable, ridiculous figure whom no Mexican general would ever follow again, and from whom there was nothing to fear for the future – whereas in condemning him to death he would be making him into a legend.

On 17 May the prisoners were transferred from La Cruz to the Carmelite convent of La Teresita. By now Maximilian was suffering severely from dysentery and spent most of the day in bed. No attempt had been made to furnish his new quarters until after his arrival, though Prince Salm grudgingly admitted that the nuns had left the place very clean. However, the princess who visited the Emperor here for the first time, was horrified at the appalling conditions in which he was living: the dirty staircase, the bedraggled guards playing cards and smoking their evil-smelling *cigaritos* in the corridors, and the wretchedly furnished rooms in which Maximilian received her. He was lying in bed looking very ill and sad for that morning Raoul Mendez, who had been hiding in the city, had been discovered and executed without any form of trial. The Republicans had never forgiven him the killing of Arteaga and Salazar, and he was shot like a dog in the prison yard. Before dying he had been allowed to visit the Emperor – an interview which shattered Maximilian not only because he was fond of the brave little Indian who fought for him so well, but also because it reminded him of the fatal October Decree which Father Fischer and the Conservatives had forced him to sign, and for which Bazaine had been largely responsible.

Agnes Salm was warned by her husband not to mention Mendez's name, and the presence of a handsome, vital young woman bringing him news of the outside world distracted the Emperor from his gloomy thoughts. But she brought him bad news from both Mexico City and San Luis. Marquez, who had returned to the capital as a fugitive, was now terrorizing the city. The enemy was closing in and the people were starving, but as Lieutenant-General of the Empire he continued to issue decrees in Maximilian's name, disseminating false information of victories won at Queretaro and of the Emperor marching to the relief of the city. Any traveller coming through the enemy lines who dared to tell the truth was instantly put in prison, for Marquez knew that the foreign troops, the only ones he could still rely on, would lay down their arms the moment they heard of the Emperor's surrender. Porfirio Diaz had already offered them a safe conduct to the coast, an offer which till now they had refused to consider.

The betrayal by Lopez and now the treachery of Marquez – of the two Maximilian found the latter the harder to bear, for the General was using his name to bring the Empire into disrepute and endanger the future of the foreign troops, for whose safety Maximilian was more concerned than for his own. Escobedo had promised to treat him and his generals as prisoners of war. Maximilian believed in his word and still

450

hoped that in the end he would be allowed to abdicate with honour, for there were moments when the natural wish to survive was stronger than all the heroics, and the thirty-five-year-old Emperor still dreamed of freedom, of returning to Europe and of sailing again on his beloved Adriatic, picnicking in the myrtle-scented woods of Lacroma, writing his memoirs at Miramar. Part of this dream was that Charlotte had recovered and they would be leading a happy, peaceful life, never wanting to return to Mexico. He would talk to Blasio and to Felix Salm of the places they would visit together – a few weeks in London, a winter in Naples, a cruise on his yacht in the eastern Mediterranean. It was significant that neither Paris nor Vienna was ever mentioned among the places they would visit.

But Agnes Salm brought depressing news from San Luis Potosi. There was talk of the Emperor and his generals being brought before a court-martial, where the death penalty would be inevitable. Some regarded even a trial as unnecessary. Now for the first time Maximilian became aware of the full horror of his situation: he and his generals were to be treated as common felons, not as prisoners of war. On Prince Salm's advice he sent a message asking the Prussian Minister, Baron Magnus, to come to his aid and to enlist the services of the best lawyers in the capital. Prussia was a neutral power which had always had friendly relations with the Mexican Republic, and Magnus was accredited as minister, whereas Austria, Belgium and England, since Campbell-Scarlett's departure, were only represented by Chargé-d'affaires. The Emperor already had good reason to believe that there was little help to be expected from Austria's Baron Lago, and it was only when the trial by court-martial was publicly announced that he sent for Lago and his Belgian colleague Monsieur Hooricks to come to Queretaro to settle his family affairs and witness the signing of his will.

The Salms continued to work unceasingly on his behalf. While the Prince thought only in terms of escape, his wife, who had completely fallen under the spell of Maximilian's 'melancholy blue eyes', kept beseeching Escobedo to move him to better quarters where he could have some privacy and peace. According to her the General would have granted her request if orders had not come through from San Luis to treat the prisoners with the utmost severity. Unfortunately the Princess was too ready to believe in Mexican promises and too inclined to over-estimate her powers of fascination. She was flattered when Escobedo appointed one of his adjutants to act as her interpreter and both she and her husband were sufficiently credulous to believe that the charming young Colonel, who had been educated in Germany, secretly sympathized with the Emperor. The 'well-furnished private house', Agnes Salm had hoped to secure for the prisoners turned out to be another convent, belonging to the Capucine monks, to which they were removed at the end of the month. It was a place of ill omen for Maximilian, for in the crypt of the Capucine church in Vienna was the Hapsburg family vault. By a macabre coincidence his new guard, a former bandit who was filled with animosity towards him, arranged for him to spend the first night in the crypt and when he ventured to remonstrate, replied: 'You must stay here for the night, so that you realize that your end is near'. The ignorant Indian did not know the full measure of the torture he was inflicting. But Maximilian remained composed, spending the night calmly reading Cesare Cantu's '*Storia degli Italiani*'. Even Escobedo was shocked by the jailer's act of unnecessary brutality and the following morning the Emperor and General Mejía were moved to two adjoining cells on the upper floor of the convent, where they were joined by Miguel Miramon, still with a bandaged head from the wound received on the last day of the siege.

Their cells gave out on an open gallery which overlooked the cloister and a small garden, planted with lemon and orange trees, where the prisoners took their exercise. Doctor Basch, who occupied a cell on the same floor, was still at liberty to attend to his master, who was now suffering from continual stomach pains and spent most of the day in bed. Felix Salm relates how he found him one day reading the life of King Charles I of England. It is curious that Maximilian should have included a life of the unfortunate Stuart King among the small collection of books he took with him to Queretaro, but he had been fascinated by him in his youth. When touring the galleries of Florence he singled out the Van Dyck portrait of Charles as one of his favourite pictures in the Uffizzi. It was almost as if he had a presentiment of a similar fate and he wrote in his diary what might later have served as his own obituary: 'He failed through weakness, but he had the opportunity if not to live well, at least to die well.'

Felix Salm tried to convince him that he still had a chance to live. The Prince had friends in the town and among the Liberal officers, who promised to help them to escape. Once they had reached the Sierra Corda they would be in Mejía's territory, from where they could make their way to the coast and be picked up by one of the two Austrian battleships still cruising in the Gulf. But the Emperor refused to consider escaping without Miramon, who was not yet fully recovered from his wounds. Maximilian was frightened that his own health would not be able to stand up to the long and dangerous journey and he continued to hesitate, torn between a natural wish for self-preservation and the fear of being ignominiously caught in flight.

Meanwhile Salm completed preparations for the escape, which was to be attempted on the night of 2 June. Money and horses had been procured, guards had been bribed, the officer on duty won over, when that morning a telegram arrived from Mexico City, saying that the Prussian minister and the two lawyers were on their way. Maximilian decided to await their arrival. The Prince heard with horror and consternation that all his plans were ruined, because the Emperor deemed it incompatible with his dignity for the minister and the lawyers to arrive and find that he had fled. Riva Palaccio, the father of the general, and Martinez de la Torre were two of the most respected jurists in the capital, and as members of the Liberal Party might yet succeed in convincing Juarez to commute the death penalty to banishment. One suspects that Maximilian used Baron Magnus's arrival as an excuse to back out of a plan in which he had very little confidence. He distrusted the co-operation of the Liberal officers whom Salm believed to be his friends and feared they might be luring him into a trap, which would give Juarez the chance of getting them all killed and then publishing to the world that Maximilian of Hapsburg and his Generals had been accidentally shot while trying to break out of prison. But none of the Emperor's arguments convinced Prince Salm, who on his knees beseeched him to avail himself of what might well be their last chance to escape. But Maximilian was a sick man who however tempted by the prospect of freedom had only the courage left to die.

The efforts of Felix and Agnes Salm on behalf of a man who did so little to co-operate were heroic but unwise, and in the end only served to aggravate an already hopeless situation. The Princess had her moment of triumph when she returned to San Luis and succeeded in persuading Juarez to grant a postponement of the trial, so as to give the lawyers the time to prepare their defence. In her youthful optimism she was convinced that during these ten days' respite the American President would exert pressure on the Mexican government to prevent Maximilian's death. News of the abortive escape plan had meanwhile come to the ears of the authorities and Felix Salm was moved back to La

453

Teresita and prevented from communicating with the Emperor except in the presence of one of Escobedo's adjutants. It was hard for Maximilian to be deprived of the company of the man whom in the past weeks he had grown to love as a brother, and he told Baron Magnus when he arrived: 'If I ever regain my freedom the Salms will become part of my household.' And in the event of his death, he wanted his family to provide adequate pensions for both husband and wife.

The Prussian Minister arrived in Queretaro on the morning of 5 June. He had had the greatest difficulty in getting out of the capital, where Marquez had put every obstacle in the way of allowing him to go to the help of the Emperor, whereas Porfirio Diaz had behaved with the greatest courtesy. Lago and Hooricks, who had wanted to come with him, were still waiting for their visas. By the time the Baron reached Queretaro, the prisoners were so closely guarded that any attempt at escape would have been impossible. He had no difficulty in getting permission to visit the Emperor but he had to pass through a barrier of sentries before entering the gates, while the main entrance was practically blocked by a horde of dirty, ragged soldiers and by their even dirtier wives and children sprawling all over the place, so that he had to step over their bodies to get up the stairs. In these circumstances Magnus was amazed to find the Emperor composed and even cheerful, though he appeared to be under no illusions as to his ultimate fate. His cell was clean but bare. The only furniture other than the bed was an ordinary washing stand, two small tables, an armchair and a couple of stools. But at least the bed looked comfortable and had fresh linen. The only luxury was a couple of silver candlesticks and an ivory crucifix.

When Magnus expressed his admiration at the equanimity with which the Emperor bore his trials, Maximilian replied half-laughing: 'When one has no longer the power to give orders one has perforce to accept them. I am not the first sovereign to have been taken prisoner. My grandfather the Emperor Franz was also for a time a prisoner and I consider I have a duty towards my fellow monarchs, and to history in general, to show that I am worthy of my breeding.' He told the minister that he had always believed Juarez to be a man of high ideals dedicated to working for the good of his country. But now he realized that he was 'as bloodthirsty as the rest of them, even worse than some of my own followers, which is saying a great deal'. This was a reference to Marquez, of whom the Emperor spoke with the greatest bitterness.

'If Juarez were to give me the chance of hanging either Marquez or Lopez, the man who betrayed me, I would choose the former'.

On the following day Baron Lago and his Belgian and Italian colleagues arrived in Queretaro. Whatever may have been the Austrian diplomat's personal feeling for Maximilian, he was now in duty bound to do all in his power to help him. The whole of Austria was concerned for his safety, and a message transmitted from Washington to one of the Austrian warships anchored off Vera Cruz and relayed through the good offices of Porfirio Diaz brought the news that the Emperor Franz Josef had reinstated his brother 'the ex-Emperor of Mexico' in all his hereditary rights and prerogatives as a Prince of Hapsburg-Lorraine and second in succession to the Austrian throne. Did Franz Josef really believe that his belated recognition of Maximilian's rights would make any impression on the Indian Juarez? On the contrary, it only strengthened him in his resolve to assert his independence and as a descendent of the Aztecs to take his revenge for the long centuries of oppression by publicly humiliating a descendent of Charles v. At Juarez's headquarters the lawyers pleaded eloquently, but in vain. The American press called on the Mexican President 'not to stain with unnecessary cruelty the young republic, so gloriously reborn'. Garibaldi sent him a telegram congratulating him on his victory and asking him to spare Maximilian's life. On the advice of the lawyers Baron Magnus journeyed to San Luis, to offer guarantees in the name of the king of Prussia that in the event of Maximilian's banishment he would never be allowed to interfere again in Mexican politics. But both Juarez and Tejada always gave him the same reply: It was not the government but the people of Mexico who demanded 'the blood of the two traitor generals and of the foreign usurper who after the departure of the French had merely prolonged the civil war.' Maximilian's death, they said, was necessary '*por la utilidad y la convienença publica*'.

The trial began on 12 June and was mounted as a public spectacle in the Iturbide Theatre, the stage being the court and the stalls and the boxes reserved for the public. It speaks for the courage of the ladies of Queretaro that not one of them accepted the invitation to attend, and the only women present were the wives of the Liberal officers. Juarez may have ordered this public show to humiliate the fallen Emperor, but it only served to accentuate the farcical nature of a 'justice' by which the accused were condemned prior to their trial and where the judges

455

were six young subordinate officers, presided over by an equally youthful lieutenant-colonel in an elegant new uniform.

When Maximilian heard he was to be made an object of public exhibition, he declared they would never get him to the theatre as long as there was a breath of life in his body. And it was now, when escape had become impossible, that he seriously envisaged it for the first time. Prince Salm was in prison and closely guarded, but his wife was at liberty to come and go as she pleased and still resolved to do all in her power to help him. She still believed that given sufficient money even the senior officers in charge of the prisoner coud be bribed. In believing this and relying too much on her own personal charms she played unconsciously into Escobedo's hand. There can be little doubt that the handsome Colonel Villanueva, in whom she had such unbounded confidence, acted in connivance with his chief. Escobedo appears to have been more sensitive to foreign opinion than either Juarez or Tejada and he wanted to get rid of the foreign envoys before the opening of the court-martial.

The bribes required were enormous and Maximilian had very little ready money. To alleviate his difficulties, Colonel Villanueva suggested to Princess Salm that he and a brother officer would be ready to accept bills of change signed by the ex-Emperor, providing they were countersigned by the European diplomats. That Maximilian should ever have entertained such a proposal proves the extent of his despair. He went to the lengths of asking Baron Lago to countersign two bills for one hundred thousand pesos each and to get the signatures of his Belgian and Italian colleagues. The Baron, who was timid by nature and always frightened for his own skin, begged him not to endanger his position still further by attempting a flight which had no chance of success and was in all probability a trap. But Maximilian persisted in his demands and Lago had orders to assist him in every way. Reluctantly he complied with his wishes and the other diplomats followed suit. But they all took fright, when Princess Salm informed them that the Mexican colonels required them to add their official titles to their signatures. In this way they would be compromising not only themselves but their governments. Lago, who had already affixed his signature to one of the bills, was in a panic; the Italian, Curtopassi, who appears to have been the most resourceful of the three, seized a pair of scissors and cut off his signature from the bill. On hearing of the diplomats' sensible but cowardly behaviour Maximilian felt himself abandoned by the very people who should have helped him. Only Baron Magnus, still pleading for his life in San Luis, had shown himself to be a true friend.

Colonel Villanueva's brother officer, an Indian by the name of Palacio (in no way related to the Creole General), appears to have become involved in the escape plan against his will. And it was only Villanueva who seems to have played a double game. The Princess was determined to win over Palacio. She not only bribed him with money, but went so far as to entice him to her room, locking the door and beginning to undress, when the terrified colonel, crying out that his honour was now doubly at stake, threatened to jump out of the window unless he was immediately released. That night Palacio went to Escobedo's camp and revealed the whole plan. The following morning Agnes Salm was placed under arrest, and without being able to take leave of either her husband or the Emperor, was made to leave the city in the charge of an armed guard. Even now she refused to be intimidated, meeting Escobedo's cold sarcasm with an angry defiance, saying she had done nothing of which she was ashamed and nothing which he would not have done in her place. So well did she defend herself that Escobedo is reported to have said that he would 'rather face a whole Imperialist battalion than an angry Princess Salm'. Before leaving Queretaro the Princess saw Mejía and Miramon being led to trial. The former, who had never properly recovered from an attack of typhus earlier in the year, looked ill and dejected, passing through a town of which he had formerly been the hero. But Miramon, in spite of his bandaged head, 'looked as bright as if he were going to a ball'. Colonel Villanueva had done one good action in persuading Escobedo that the ex-Emperor was too weak to stand up to public trial and Maximilian was tried *in absentia*.

Meanwhile the foreign envoys were given notice to leave Queretaro. For all their caution they now found themselves incriminated in the Emperor's attempted escape, and they were glad to get away with their skins. Lago for one was in such a hurry to leave that he went off with the codicil of the Emperor's will unsigned. The trial was a travesty of justice but Juarez may have argued it was not more of a travesty than the Assembly of Notables which met under the shadow of French guns to elect Maximilian to the throne. Thirteen grounds of accusation were levelled against the ex-Emperor: he had been the chief instrument of foreign intervention; he had threatened the freedom and independence of Mexico, and had usurped her sovereignty; he had been responsible for the barbarous October Decree of 1865, by which hundreds of innocent people had been done to death. His lawyers defended him with ability but all their rhetoric was so much wasted breath. To give the trial a semblance of legality, three of the six young captains who served as judges opted in favour of banishment for life. The other three voted for the death penalty and the casting vote was given by the President, an elegant young colonel in kid gloves who condemned the Emperor and his generals to die as casually as if he had been assisting at a bullfight.

No visitors other than the two generals' wives, the lawyers and the Emperor's doctor were admitted to the convent during the trial. Miramon, who kept a diary, recounts that during one of the last visits of his wife, he was kissing her hand in a very tender fashion and was embarrassed to see the Emperor looking very upset. He begged pardon for his weakness and began to talk of the Empress Carlota when Maximilian interrupted, saying: 'I am only weeping because you do not deserve to endure these sufferings on my account, when otherwise you could be so happy.' Whereupon Miramon took again his wife's hand and with a rather bitter smile said: 'I am here because I would not listen to this woman's advice,' and the Emperor cut in: 'Do not feel remorse – I am here because I did listen to my wife.'

It was now that Maximilian was told of Charlotte's 'death'. Mejía's wife had heard a rumour in the town and the General repeated it to the Emperor, knowing how much he suffered at the thought of leaving behind him a mad and helpless wife. Maximilian was saddened by the news and at the same time comforted. In a letter to Baron Lago, in which he asked him to make every effort to save the Austrian officers and soldiers who were still in Mexico and get them back to Europe, he added in a postscript: 'I have just heard that my poor wife is released from her sufferings. The news, however heartbreaking, is at the same time an unspeakable consolation to me. I have now only one wish on earth, that my body should be laid beside that of my wife. With this mission I entrust you my dear Baron, as the representative of Austria.'

The trial was over and at ten o'clock on the morning of 16 June the death sentence was read aloud to the three condemned men, who were to be executed on the Hill of the Bells at three o'clock that afternoon. While Mejía and Miramon spent their last hours with their wives, Maximilian finished his letters, addressed to friends and relatives who from his prison cell already seemed to belong to another world, in which the inhabitants still believed in the divine right of kings. Dr Basch, who was with him night and day, was almost awed by the unnatural composure with which he made his preparations for the end, recording his last wishes, dividing his few remaining possessions among his friends and – what was strangely macabre – discussing the arrangements for the embalming of his body.

All day they waited to be summoned to the execution. They had confessed and taken communion and now sat listening for the convent clock to strike the given hour. But the hours passed and no one came till four o'clock, when Colonel Palacio appeared with a telegram from San Luis. For a moment a ray of hope lighted the gloomy cell. Had Juarez relented before the pressure of the United States, the approbrium of the whole civilized world? Had his heart been touched by the tears of young Madame Miramon when she went with her children to San Luis to plead for her husband's life, or by the petitions signed by the two hundred ladies of Queretaro, begging him to show mercy? But the telegram contained merely a postponement of three days, a concession made to Baron Magnus to give him time to return to Queretaro to attend to the Emperor's last wishes. The indomitable Princess Salm had returned to San Luis and forced her way into the President's room, falling on her knees before him and beseeching him to spare the Emperor. But he only replied, 'I am grieved, Madame, to see you on your knees before me, but if all the kings and queens of Europe were at your side I could not spare his life. It is not I who take it away, it is my people, and if I did not do their will the people would take his life and mine as well.' At the same time he solemnly promised he would save her husband.

Maximilian described to Baron Magnus the ordeal of that long summer's day when they waited in their cells for their death summons. From their windows they could see the cloudless blue sky outside, the sunlight glittering on the leaves of the orange trees in the cloister garden. They had made their peace with the world and were prepared to die, but it was hard to have to endure it all a second time. The Baron begged forgiveness for the delay for which inadvertently he had been responsible. But the Emperor answered that he was glad to see him again, so as to be able to thank him and the King of Prussia for all the help they had given him. He sent messages to the Crown Princess who was Charlotte's cousin and one of her closest friends, and told Magnus of the consolation it had given him to hear of her death: 'I have not long to wait before we will meet again.' Magnus, who knew the rumour to be false, had not the heart to contradict it. The Emperor's last words to him were, 'It is strange that from my earliest youth I have always had the feeling I would not die a natural death, and for a long time I have known that I would never leave this country alive'.

Apart from Tudos, the Emperor's Hungarian cook, Magnus and two German businessmen were the only Europeans to witness the execution on the Hill of the Bells. The minister had forced himself to attend in order to record the last tragic moments for the Emperor's family.

On 18 June, the eve of his execution, Maximilian put out his light at ten o'clock. Earlier in the day he had addressed a last message to President Juarez. 'I give my life willingly,' he wrote, 'if the sacrifice will promote the welfare of my new country. But nothing good can grow on soil saturated in blood, therefore I entreat you to let mine be the last blood you shed.' By midnight the Emperor was already asleep when he was awoken by a visit from General Escobedo, who had come to bid farewell and perhaps also to make his peace with the prisoner to whom he had broken his word. From the Emperor's cell Escobedo went on to Mejía, of whom he had once been a prisoner, and who on that occasion had allowed him to escape. Now it was his turn to repay his debt by offering him his liberty and a chance of reaching his home in the Sierra Corda. But Mejía repeated he would only avail himself of the offer if it included the Emperor and Miramon. Escobedo regretted this was beyond his power, whereupon the noble Indian, who had just seen his wife and newborn baby for the last time, said: 'Then let me be shot with my Emperor.'

Morning dawned on 19 June and platoons of soldiers were already moving out of the city in the direction of the Hill of the Bells. In the convent of the Capucines the guards were searching in every nook and cranny for some chance intruder. The Emperor was known to have many secret sympathizers in the town, who might yet attempt a rescue. Maximilian slept peacefully till three o'clock, when he got up, dressed and went in to his companions, calling out in a loud, clear voice: 'Are you ready gentlemen? I am prepared.' Father Soria, who had been his confessor in prison, celebrated Mass but at certain moments was so overcome with emotion that he was near to breaking down, and even some of the guards were in tears. Poor Dr Basch was so prostrated by grief that he had not the strength to accompany his master on his last journey. In their cells at Teresita, José Blasio and Felix Salm and all the other officers imprisoned in the convent prayed silently for the

Emperor, to whom they had not even been allowed to say goodbye.

Dr Basch was entrusted with the messages for Maximilian's family and given his wedding ring and rosary to take back to his mother. At the last moment the Emperor took from his neck a gold medal which the Empress Eugénie had once given him for luck. He had bequeathed it to the widowed Empress of Brazil, the mother of the girl he had wooed long ago in his early youth, before he met the proud Coburg Princess whose ambition had proved so fatal to them both.

By now the sun had risen. It was six o'clock when Maximilian, wearing black civilian clothes, came down the staircase followed by the two generals, also wearing black. After weeks of confinement, they breathed in the fresh morning air and the Emperor turned to his companions, saying, 'What a wonderful day! I have always wanted to die on a morning like this.' Three carriages were waiting, and each in turn, accompanied by his confessor, stepped into his own carriage. Escorted by strong detachments of cavalry and infantry, followed by the firing squad with the pathetic little figure of Tudos bringing up the rear, the gloomy cortège passed through silent streets where most of the doors and windows remained shuttered and the only people about wore mourning out of respect for the condemned men. Women wept when they saw Mejía's young wife with her baby at her breast, run sobbing after her husband's carriage and only being prevented by the soldiers' bayonets from clinging to the wheels. The cortège stopped at the foot of the hill, which was entirely surrounded by soldiers. And the three men, each carrying a crucifix and accompanied by a priest, walked slowly up the hill. The Emperor went first, walking with a firm step, his head held high, his face perhaps a little paler than usual, but with such a wonderfully spiritual expression, that Magnus, who was hidden in the crowd, wrote: 'He already seemed to belong to another world! Beside him trotted his little Hungarian cook like a faithful dog hanging on his last words. The Emperor turned to him with a smile, laying a hand on his shoulder, saying, "You refused to believe it would ever come to this. You see you were wrong. But to die is not so difficult as you think." '

The troops on the top of the hill were drawn up in three sides of a square, the fourth being formed by a low adobe wall. The prisoners were led into the square and placed with their faces turned towards the town. For the last time Maximilian looked out over the tiled domes and baroque steeples, the orange groves and gardens of Queretaro, where he had found so much loyalty and devotion. An order was given and the seven men of the firing squad moved into line. Father Soria said a short prayer and the Emperor embraced his two companions. Miramon was as proud and composed as always but Mejía, who could still hear the heart-rending cries of his young wife, could hardly stand upright. The officer in charge of the firing squad appears to have been so moved by the Emperor's behaviour that he attempted a few words of apology, but Maximilian answered, 'You are a soldier and it is your duty to obey.' Then he handed a gold ounce to each of his seven executioners, asking them to take good aim and not to deface him, so that his mother could look upon him again. The young officer was about to raise his sword when Maximilian stepped forward and called out in Spanish: 'I forgive everybody. I pray that everybody may also forgive me, and I hope that my blood which is about to be shed will bring peace to Mexico. *Viva Mexico! Viva Independencia!*' The last words had hardly been spoken when a sword flashed in the air and seven shots rang out simultaneously. The Emperor fell backwards, his body still twitching convulsively on the ground, though later it was ascertained that he had died instantaneously. The young officer stepped forward and pointing to the heart, ordered a soldier to give the *coup de grâce*. Now came the turn of Miramon and Mejía, both of whom died as heroes crying, 'God bless the Emperor.'

The three dead men lay on the cactus-covered ground, their clothes still smoking from the shots. The *zopilotes* were already hovering overhead, and there was a sudden hush and stillness in the air. Even the soldiers were silenced before a death which had attained the sublime.

Epilogue

Never had Paris been so gay as in the spring of 1867. People from all over the world had flocked to the banks of the Seine to visit L'exhibition Universelle held in the Champs de Mars. Never had the gilding on the Napoleonic Bees seemed brighter, or the eagles more triumphant. Never had the Parisian public appeared to be more devoted to the reigning dynasty. Foreign sovereigns, who, a few years ago, had labelled Napoleon and Eugénie as adventurers and upstarts, now accepted their hospitality with pleasure. The King of Prussia with whose country France had been on the brink of war, was both pleasant and conciliatory; the Czar of Russia had visited for the first time a city where the names of some of the Squares and Bridges evoked painful memories of the Crimea.

1 July, the day of the prize-giving in the Palais d'Industrie, was to be the highlight of the Parisian season. The exhibition had been a financial and political success. Huge contracts had been signed in every branch of industry and commerce, and the Emperor and Empress were to present the prizes, accompanied by their guests who included the Sultan of Turkey, the Prince of Wales, Prince Humbert of Italy and the Count and Countess of Flanders. With all these Royal visitors and their suites to look after, the secretaries at the Quai d'Orsay were working overtime. Only one young man, the Count of Gontaut-Biron, was on duty in the Minister's office, when a telegram in cypher arrived from Washington which, decoded, gave the news that, according to information transmitted from Captain Groeller of the S.S. *Elisabeth* stationed off Vera Cruz, the Emperor Maximilian had been executed on the nineteenth of June. Gontaut-Biron was young and zealous and he lost no time in bringing the message to the Tuileries, where the Emperor was so shattered by the news that he burst into tears in front of the embarrassed young secretary; but, on regaining his self-control, Napo-

leon said, 'You and I are the only ones who have heard the news. To-morrow is the prize-giving of the exhibition. No one must be told anything till the end of the ceremony. So keep it to yourself.' He then went to break the painful news to his wife who, for the past months had been filled with uneasy premonition and, according to Prince Metternich, was haunted by the sense of her own responsibility. Now she broke down completely and for a while it seemed as if she would not have sufficient strength to carry on with the ceremony the follow-ing day.

At eight o'clock on the morning of 1 July, the Empress, dressed in mourning and accompanied by one of her ladies, was seen entering by a side door into the Church of St Roch, where she remained for over an hour in prayer. Later in the day, she appeared as a radiant figure dressed in white, a diamond coronet in her hair, driving with the Em-peror in a gala coach up the Champs-Elysées. But no sooner had the Imperial couple and their distinguished guests taken their places on the platform, when an aide-de-camp arrived with another telegram, confirming the news that the Captain of an Austrian frigate had cabled from New Orleans to his legation in Washington, 'that the Emperor of Mexico had been executed and that Juarez refused to deliver up the body.' Looking round, Napoleon noted that the places reserved for the Count and Countess of Flanders were vacant. The news he had heard the night before had already appeared in the morning edition of 'L'Inde-pendence Belge'. Prince and Princess Metternich, who were present, were immediately notified and left quietly and unobtrusively, followed by various Austrian and Hungarian officers. The ceremony went on, but with every presentation the Empress's smile became more forced and, on her return to the Tuileries, she collapsed completely and had to be carried half-fainting to her bed.

Meanwhile, the rumour spread like wildfire throughout the town, from the Bourse to the Legislative Assembly, from the Jockey Club to the cafés of the Boulevards. The tragedy of Queretaro brought back to the minds of every Frenchman the failure of the Mexican gamble, which the Emperor had been at such pains to make them forget by dazzling them with fêtes and fireworks and gala processions and surfeiting them with all the outward signs of the material prosperity and progress attained in his reign. But those who had lost their husbands and sons in Mexico, and those who had been ruined in buying Mexican bonds, did not find it easy to forget, and even the most fickle of Parisians remembered with affection the fair young Archduke and his pretty bride who, only three years ago, had been given just as magnificent a welcome as the sovereigns of today. Now Maximilian was shot and Charlotte mad, and in the Legislative Assembly and in the Senate, Napoleon's opponents branded him as the criminal responsible for the tragedy. All gaiety was extinguished. The foreign sovereigns left and Paris was suddenly plunged into mourning.

In England, the news made almost as great an impression as in France. Questions were asked in Parliament as to why the British Minister in Mexico was on leave in these crucial months. In the safe, complacent world of Victorian England, it was generally believed that, if the country had been properly represented, Juarez would never have dared to shoot a cousin of the Queen of England. Victoria was at Windsor when she received the first report, which she could not bring herself to believe was true. But a day later, it was confirmed and she noted in her Journal: 'The dreadful news is true. Poor, dear Charlotte, bereft of reason, and her husband killed. What a shocking end to their luckless undertaking, which I did all I could to prevent, and which dearest Albert was so much against.'

Franz Josef was in Bavaria spending one of his rare holidays with his wife and children when, on 30 June, the terrible news burst like a thunderbolt over his head. He had never thought it would come to this in the end. Only a fortnight ago, Mr Seward had assured Baron Wydenbruck that 'the Archduke's life was as safe as his own.' But the great American republic had been powerless to prevent the man whose cause they had supported and financed for the past two years from carrying out his bloodthirsty revenge. Without waiting for confirmation, the Emperor hurried back to Vienna to be the first to tell his parents. Now that Max was dead, all their quarrels and differences were forgotten. What remained was an overwhelming remorse that he should ever have allowed him to go to that barbarous country. Karl Ludwig and Ludwig Viktor joined the Emperor in Vienna, but none of them knew how to comfort the mother who had lost her favourite son, and who, on hearing the news, collapsed into her husband's arms sobbing: 'Those brutes, those savages! They have murdered him, my darling, my beautiful lighthearted Max! They have shot him down like a common criminal!'

From that day, the proud, erect Archduchess turned into a pathetic little old woman, shutting herself up in her grief, refusing to read Napoleon's letter of condolence and only consenting to see the officers who returned from Mexico with stories or messages from her son. In these days, she is said to have added the codicil to her will in which she asked to be buried between the Duke of Reichstadt and her beloved Max, should his body ever be brought back from Mexico. For Juarez was refusing to deliver up the body until the Emperor of Austria had officially recognized his brother's murderer as President of the Mexican Republic.

All Trieste was in mourning. The flags were at half-mast and the churches were full. Masses were being said on every ship in the Adriatic. There was mourning not only in Trieste but throughout the whole of the former 'Regno di Lombardo-Veneto'. In Venice and in Milan, Maximilian's portrait was on view in every shop window. Representatives of every class and of every shade of political opinion attended a Requiem Mass in the Duomo of Milan, in memory of the Prince whose kindness and humanity had led the Italians to forget that he was born a Hapsburg.

Only at Miramar there was no sign of mourning. The servants were forbidden to wear black and Maximilian's oldest friends, like Bombelles and Radonetz, were forced to dissimulate their grief in front of the Empress who, on Doctor Jilek's orders, was not to be told of her husband's death. The doctor had succeeded in curing Charlotte of the obsession of her husband wanting to poison her. When she spoke of him now, it was only with affection. 'He would be joining her soon,' she told them, 'but there is still so much to do over there, so many evil forces to destroy.' At other times she would appear at dinner and ask why the Emperor was late. But a moment later she could forget that she had ever asked. She spoke very little but, often at night, her attendants could hear her holding long, animated conversations in French and Spanish, arguing, pleading or shouting in anger and, only towards morning, falling exhausted to sleep.

Late in July, a royal train drew up at the private station of Miramar. The Queen of the Belgians, accompanied by one of the leading neurologists of Brussels, and her private secretary, the Baron Goffinet, had arrived to fetch her sister-in-law, the ex-Empress of Mexico, and to bring her back to Belgium. Rumours had reached King Leopold of the Hapsburgs' cruel and neglectful treatment of his sister. Certain events that winter may have confirmed his suspicions and no sooner had he received the confirmation of Maximilian's death, than he demanded custody of the widow. Weeks of hard bargaining followed. The Hapsburgs did not renounce their rights so easily, for Charlotte, by her father's will, was now a rich woman. But Leopold was determined the Hapsburgs were not going to administer a Coburg fortune. He offered in his sister's name to relinquish her claims on her husband's estate and to give Lacroma, which was her own private property, in free gift to the Austrian Crown, providing she was allowed to return to her own country. Franz Josef gave in and, once the bargaining was concluded, entertained the Queen, born an Austrian Archduchess, as his guest at Schönbrunn. From there, she proceeded to Miramar accompanied by the Archduke Karl Ludwig, come to take leave of his brother's widow, whom not one member of the family had bothered to visit since her tragic return from Mexico.

Charlotte welcomed her sister-in-law with joy. 'She seemed pathetically pleased to see me,' wrote Marie-Henriette, who was horrified by her appearance, 'all skin and bone and terrified of everyone and everything.' She showed no regret at leaving Miramar, and the gardens blooming in all their summer glory. But, on the morning of her departure, she went out on the terrace where Max always kept his telescope and, looking out over the blue Gulf and the lovely Istrian coast, was heard to murmur, 'I shall wait for him sixty years.'

At the end of November, 1867, the mortal remains of the ex-Emperor of Mexico were transported on board the *Novara*, where Admiral Tegetthoff was waiting to receive them. The *Novara* had been six weeks anchored off Vera Cruz before Juarez had consented to deliver up the body of the man whom, even in death, he could not bring himself to forgive. He could not forgive him the silent crowds in the streets of Queretaro when he entered in triumph, or the general condemnation expressed in the American press. The *New York Tribune* did not hesitate to write, 'Mexico owes her liberty to America more than to anyone else, and against the wishes of the American nation, Maximilian has been shot.' But now at last Juarez had had the satisfaction of inflicting the final humiliation, by forcing the proud Emperor of Austria to humble himself by asking him, as the President of the Mexican Republic, to hand over the body, not of the ex-Emperor of Mexico but of the Archduke Ferdinand-Maximilian. And the coffin which had been brought in secret to the capital and for the past month had been hidden away in the Chapel of St Andrees, was finally released. Six weeks later, the *Novara* sailed into the Adriatic, past the wooded island of Lacroma, under the white towers of Miramar and into the harbour of Trieste, from where three and a half years before a handsome young couple had set out, full of ambitious plans for the future.

Maximilian's two younger brothers accompanied the funeral train to Vienna where Franz Josef and the representatives from all parts of the Empire were waiting to receive at the station. Those who had denied him his rights in his life time had now prepared for him an Imperial funeral. Among the princes, diplomats and statesmen who followed the hearse were a few faithful, heartbroken friends like Radonetz and Bombelles, Eloin and Blasio, the last of which who had just been released from a Mexican prison. But not one of those who claimed to be the architects of the Mexican Empire, neither Gutierrez nor Hidalgo nor Almonte, all of whom were in Europe at the time, had taken the trouble to come to Vienna to pay him their last respects. It was snowing when they carried his coffin from the Hofburg to the Church of the Capucines, but in spite of the bitter wind and icy cold, his mother insisted on accompanying him to the family vault, where according to her wishes, he was buried beside the Duke of Reichstadt.

Sixty years later, an old lady of eighty-six, whom her attendants still addressed as 'Imperial Majesty', died peacefully in a moated castle in Belgium. For over half a century she had lived in a dream world, peopled by shadows, ignoring the happenings in the world outside her castle gates, the fall of dynasties – Bonaparte, Hapsburg and Hohenzollern – the march of armies, the flames of war, the passing of generations. Only every year, as the spring came round and the buds burst into blossom, she would go down to the little boat which was anchored in the moat and, stepping into it, turn to her attendants saying in the voice which had remained so young, 'Today we leave for Mexico.'

Appendix

The rumour of Charlotte having been pregnant when she left for Europe in July, 1866, and that she gave birth to a child during the months in which she was kept in seclusion at Miramar, are too persistent to be ignored. It would explain the harsh and unfeeling treatment of her husband's family, the fact that none of her former friends, such as the Countess de Grünne or the Countess d'Hulst or Paola Kollonitz, all of whom offered to come to look after her, were ever allowed to visit her, and she was left entirely in the charge of Radonetz and Bombelles, both of whom were quite unfitted for the task but who were entirely devoted to the Hapsburgs. Writing in 1924, when the Empress was still alive, Count Corti ignores the rumour. Since then, various biographers, and more particularly novelists, have enlarged on the story, some going to the lengths of saying that the child Charlotte gave birth to at Miramar was the son of Maximilian. If this had been the case, Maximilian would never have allowed his wife to undertake the hazardous journey to Europe. If Charlotte was pregnant at the time, it was entirely unknown to Maximilian and the necessity for secrecy may have contributed to the tension and nervous strain under which she was suffering at the time.

The rumour of Charlotte's pregnancy is inevitably linked with what is known as 'the Weygand legend'. In his excellent book on his father, Jacques Weygand, referring to the mystery of the General's antecedents in a chapter entitled 'La legende', writes that 'when the Empress Charlotte died in 1927, Weygand, who was then at the peak of his career, got several letters always saying the same thing, 'Your mother has just died. Further information is available'. But he never pursued the matter, nor was he present at the Empress's funeral, as has frequently been stated.

It was in Mexico that I first heard of Charlotte's relationship with

Colonel Alfred Van der Smissen, and was shown a portrait where I was immediately struck by the extraordinary resemblance between him and General Weygand. A few months later, I was in Brussels visiting Monsieur Sabbé, the late curator of the Royal Archives of the Galerie Ravenstein. He admitted to me that he had not the slightest doubt of Colonel, later General, Van der Smissen having been the father of General Weygand. As the Royal Archivist, he contented himself by saying that the mother was one of the Empress Charlotte's ladies-in-waiting.

It is known that Weygand who, throughout his early youth went by the name of Maxime de Nimal, had his education and the fees for his board and lodging regularly paid by a Count Duchatel, a member of the Royal Household. Why should the King of the Belgians pay for the education of the child of one of his sister's ladies-in-waiting? There are those who maintain that Weygand was in reality King Leopold's son, but the King made no mystery of his bastards, most of whom were openly acknowledged and provided for. So again we come back to Charlotte and those months of seclusion at Miramar, of which so little is known, but where she may well have given birth to a child, who was secretly brought back to Belgium, where he is officially stated to have been born in January in the Boulevard Waterloo in Brussels.

As for Van der Smissen, he never married, rose to the heights of his profession and finally died by his own hand.

Genealogical Tables

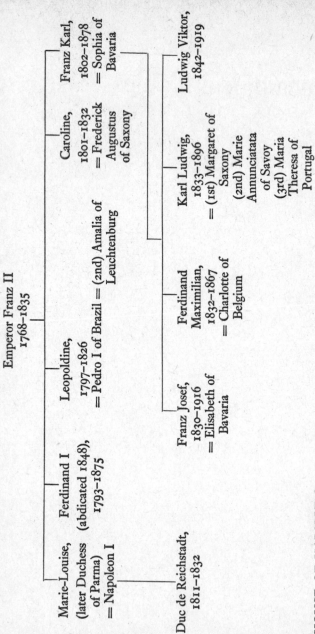

Emperor Franz II
1768–1835

Marie-Louise, (later Duchess of Parma) = Napoleon I

Ferdinand I (abdicated 1848), 1793–1875

Leopoldine, 1797–1826 = Pedro I of Brazil

= (2nd) Amalia of Leuchtenburg

Caroline, 1801–1832 = Frederick Augustus of Saxony

Franz Karl, 1802–1878 = Sophia of Bavaria

Duc de Reichstadt, 1811–1832

Franz Josef, 1830–1916 = Elisabeth of Bavaria

Ferdinand Maximilian, 1832–1867 = Charlotte of Belgium

Karl Ludwig, 1833–1896 = (1st) Margaret of Saxony (2nd) Marie Annunciatata of Savoy (3rd) Maria Theresa of Portugal

Ludwig Viktor, 1842–1919

HOUSE OF HAPSBURG

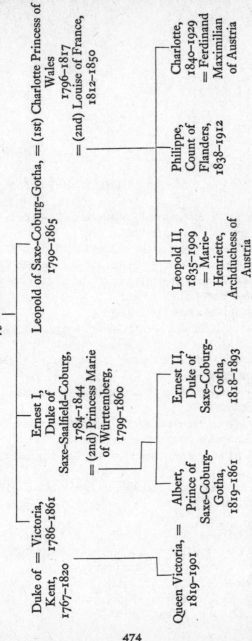

Francis Frederick of Saxe-Saalfield-Coburg,
1750–1806

Leopold of Saxe-Coburg-Gotha, = (1st) Charlotte Princess of
1790–1865   Wales
                                        1796–1817
                               = (2nd) Louise of France,
                                        1812–1850

Ernest I, Duke of
Saxe-Saalfield-Coburg,
1784–1844
= (2nd) Princess Marie
of Württemberg,
1799–1860

Duke of = Victoria,
Kent,   1786–1861
1767–1820

Leopold II,   Philippe,   Charlotte,
1835–1909   Count of   1840–1929
= Marie-   Flanders,   = Ferdinand
Henriette,   1838–1912   Maximilian
Archduchess of   of Austria
Austria

Ernest II,
Duke of
Saxe-Coburg-
Gotha,
1818–1893

Albert,
Prince of
Saxe-Coburg-
Gotha,
1819–1861

Queen Victoria, =
1819–1901

HOUSE OF COBURG

474

Bibliography

Unpublished Sources

Archives de Mexique, January–April 1866. Ministry of Foreign Affairs, Paris.

Breve Notizie del Recevimento y Permanencia de S.I.M. en la Ciudad de Puebla, privately printed (Puebla, 1864).

Catalogue of Exhibition of the reign of King Leopold I, 1968.

Da Miramar a Mexico. Viaje del Emperador Massimiliano y de la Emperatrize Carlota, printed privately (Orizaba, 1864).

The Eloin Papers, Rice Institute, Texas.

Hof Haus und Stadt Archivs, Vienna, 1861–3.

Hof Haus und Stadt Archivs, Nos 501–600, Congress Library, Washington.

Letters of Mademoiselle Bassompierre, Lady-in-Waiting to the Empress Charlotte, 1867–8.

Papers relating to Mexico in the Archives of the Ministry of Foreign Affairs, Brussels.

Public Record Office, London, Fo. 367, 377, 388, 397, 406, Despatches from British Ministers and Consuls in Mexico.

Unpublished private correspondence of the Emperor and Empress of Mexico.

US State Department Papers relating to Foreign Affairs, 1865–6, US Embassy, Paris.

Published Sources

Acton, Lord: *Historical Essays and Studies* (London, 1919).

Aubry, Octave: *L'Impératrice Eugénie* (Paris, 1931).

Aubry, Octave: *Napoléon II* (Paris, 1933).

Aubry, Octave: *Le Second Empire* (Paris, 1938).

Avenir National, 15 March 1865 (Paris).

Bancroft, Hubert: *History of North American Pacific States*, vol. 9 (San Francisco, 1886).

Barail, General: *Mes Souvenirs* (Paris, 1895).

Basch, Samuel: *Erringerungen aus Mexico* (Leipzig, 1883).

Beust, Count: *Aus Drei Viertel-Jahr Hunderten* (Stuttgart, 1887).

Bigelow, John: *Retrospections of an Active Life*, Vols 1 and 2 (New York, 1909).

Blanchot, Charles: *L'Intervention Française au Mexique*, 3 vols (Paris, 1911).

Blasio, José: *Maximilian, Emperor of Mexico* (Translation Yale University Press, 1934).

Buffin, Camille: *La Tragédie Mexicaine* (Brussels, 1925).

Cantu, Cesare: *Cronistorio del Independenza Italiano*, vols 2, 3 and 4, Appendix *L'Archiduca Massimiliano* (Turin, 1877).

Carette, Madame: *Souvenirs Intimes de la Cour des Tuileries*, 1861–70 (Paris, 1890).

Cheetham, Sir Nicholas: *Mexico, A Short History* (London and New York, 1971).

Coffin, Robert: *L'Impératrice Fantôme* (Paris, 1938).

Cooper, Lady Diana: Memoirs, Vol 2, *The Rainbow Comes and Goes* (London, 1958).

Corti, Egon Cesar: *Leopold of Belgium* (London, 1923).

Corti, Egon Cesar: *Maximilian and Charlotte*, 2 vols (London 1928).

Corti, Egon Cesar: Franz-Josef Trilogy: *Von Kind zu Kaiser* (Vienna, 1950).

Corti, Egon Cesar: *Mensch under Herrcher* (Vienna, 1952).

Da costa, Sergio Corréa: *Every Inch a King*, English translation (New York, 1950).

Dawson, Daniel: *The Mexican Adventure* (London, 1935).

De Bourgoing, Jean: *Papiers Intimes du Journal du Duc de Reichstadt* (Paris, 1928).

De Bourgoing, Jean: *Le Fils de Napoléon* (Paris, 1932).

Decaux, Lucille: *Charlotte et Maximilien* (Paris, 1937).

Desternes, Suzanne: *Maximilien et Charlotte* (Paris, 1964).

Domenech, Emmanuel: *Voyages et Souvenirs* (Paris, 1968).

Domenech, Emmanuel: *Histoire de Mexique*, Vol 3 (Paris, 1869).

Duchesne, Albert: *L'Expédition Belge au Mexique 1864–7*, 2 vols (Brussels, 1970).

Fleury, Count Maurice: *Memoirs of the Empress Eugénie* (New York, 1920).

Gamillscheg, Felix: *Kaiser Adler über Mexico* (Graz und Koln, 1964).

Franz-Josef: *Briefe Kaiser Franz-Josefs an Kaiserin Elisabeth* (Munich, 1966); *Briefe Kaiser Franz Josefs an seinen Mutter*, edited by Franz Schnurer (Munich, 1930); *Franz Josef und seinen Briefen*, edited by Otto Ernst (Vienna, 1924).

Gasperini, Luisa: *Storia del Governatore del Lombardo-Veneto* (Rome, 1934).

Gasperini, Luisa: *Massimiliano d'Austria – Nei Suoi Ricord* (Rome, 1935).

Gasperini, Luisa: *Archiduca Massimiliano nel Venezia-Tridentina*, 1863 (Trento, 1934).

Gasperini, Luisa: *Massimiliano Nel Messico* (Rome, 1938).

Gaulot, General: *La Verité sur L'Expédition du Mexico*, 3 vols (Paris, 1890).

De La Gorce, Pierre: *Histoire du Second Empire*, vol 4, 9 vols (Paris, 1894–1905).

El Sol (Mexico City, 1867).

Gregorovious, Ferdinand: *Roman Journals, 1852–74*, English translation (London, 1907).

Guedella, Philip: *The Second Empire* (London, 1932).

Guedella, Philip: *The Two Marshals* (London, 1943).

Harding, Berlita: *Phantom Crown* (London, 1935).

Haslip, Joan: *The Lonely Empress* (London, 1965).

Hubner, Count: *Neuf Ans de Souvenirs d'un Ambassadeur d'Autriche à Paris*, edited by his son (Paris, 1904).

Huscher, Herbert: *Charles Gaulis Clairmont*, Keats, Shelley Memorial Bulletin (Rome, 1953).

Hyde, Montgomery: *The Mexican Empire* (London, 1946).

Keratry, Count Emile: *L'Empereur Maximilien, son Elevation et sa Chute* (Paris, 1868).

Keratry, Count Emile: *La Contro-Guerilla Française au Mexique* (Paris, 1873).

Kollonitz, Countess Paola: *The Court of Mexico*, English translation (London, 1868).

Kurtz, Harold: *The Empress Eugénie* (London, 1964).

Lefèvre, E.: *Documents Officiels Receuilli dans la Secretaire Privée de Maximilien* (Brussels, 1869).

Loliée, Frederick: *Frère de l'Empereur. Le Duc de Morny et la Societé du Second Empire* (Paris, 1909).

Magnus, Baron: *Das Ende das Maximilianischen Kaiser Reichs in Mexico* from *The Papers of Baron Magnus*, edited by Joachim Kuhn (Göttingen, 1968).

Malortie, Count Karl: *Old Times and New*, English translation (London, 1869).

Malortie, Count Karl: *Here, There and Everywhere*, English translation (London, 1868).

Martin Percy: *Maximilian, the Story of the French Intervention in Mexico* (London, 1914).

Marx, Adrian: *Révélations sur la Vie Intime de Maximilien* (Paris, 1868).

Masseras, E.: *Un Essai d'Empire au Mexique* (Paris, 1879).

Maximilian, Emperor of Mexico: *Recollections of my Life*, English translation (London, 1868); *On the Wing*, English translation (London, 1868); *Correspondence with the Empress Charlotte*.

Merimée, Prosper: *Lettres à Monsieur Panizzi* (Paris, 1881).

Metternich, Prince Richard: *Mémoires et Documents d'Ecrits Divers de Metternich* (Paris, 1883).

Niox, Jean: *Expédition de Mexique 1861–7* (Paris, 1874).

Ollivier, Emile: *L'Empire Libérale*, vols 6, 7, and 9 (Paris, 1895–1912).

Paléologue, Maurice: *Les Entretiens de l'Impératrice Eugénie* (Paris, 1928).

Parkes, Bamford: *History of Mexico* (London, 1862).

Phillips, Alison: *Modern Europe, 1815–1899* (London, 1917).

Préviel, Armand: *La Vie Tragique de L'Impératrice Charlotte* (Paris, 1930).

Radziwill, Princess Catherine: *The Austrian Court From Within*, English translation (London, 1910).

Reinach-Foussemagne, Countess Henriette: *Charlotte de Belgique, Impératrice de Mexique* (Brussels, 1925).

Richardson, Joanna: *Dearest Uncle* (London, 1961).

Salm-Salm, Prince Felix: *My Diary in Mexico, 1867*, 2 vols (London, 1868).

Salm-Salm, Princess Agnes: *Ten Years of My Life*, 2 vols (New York, 1868).

Shefer, Christian: *La Grande Pensée de Napoléon II* (Paris, 1939).

Sheridan, General: *Personal Memoirs*, 2 vols (New York, 1888).

Sonolet, Louis: *L'Agonie du l'Empire de Mexique d'apres les notes inédites du General Castelnau* Revue de Paris, July–August, 1927.

Sonolet and Fleury: *La Société du Second Empire*, 3 vols (Paris 1911).

Soustelle, Jacques: *The Arts of Ancient Mexico*, English translation (London, 1967).

Soustelle, Jacques: *Mexico*, English translation (London, 1969).

Stevenson, Sarah York: *Maximilian in Mexico* (New York, 1897).

Tozzi, Tomaso: *Vittime Impériale* (Pallanza, 1917).

Tyrnauer, Tyrner: *Lincoln and the Emperors* (London, 1962).

Van der Smissen, Baron Alfred: *Souvenirs du Mexique 1864–67* (Brussels, 1892).

Victoria, Queen of England: *Letters of Queen Victoria*, edited by George Buckle, 2 vols (London, 1926); *A Selection of Her Majesty's Correspondence between the Years 1837–61*, edited by Benson and Esher (London, 1907).

Venosta, Giovanni Visconti: *Memoirs of Youth. Things Seen and Known*, 1847–60 (London, 1914).

Von Battenberg, Prince Alexander: *Kampf unter Drei Zaren* (Vienna, 1920).

Von Bulow, Paola: *Aus Verklungenen Zeiten* (Leipzig, 1924).

Von Schlötzer: *Römische Briefe* (Berlin, 1913).

Von Tavera, Schmidt Ritter: *Die Mexikanishe Kaiser Tragödie* (Vienna, 1903).

Walton, Emile: *Souvenirs d'un Officier Belge au Mexique* (Brussels, 1868).

Wertheimer, Edward: *The Duke of Reichstadt*, English translation (London, 1906).

Weygand, Jacques: *Mon Père Weygand* (Paris, 1970).

Index

489

494

Van Dyck, 49, 452
Venetia, 169, 180, 214, 325, 375, 381
Venetia-Lombardy, 31, 38, 47, 66, 71, 87, 90–1, 95, 107–20 passim, 466
Venice, 87, 134; Franz Josef in, 29–30, 56; Maximilian in, 29–30, 56, 66, 67–8, 69, 109, 110, 111, 112, 118; Franz Josef and Elisabeth in 88–91, 95–6; state entry of Maximilian in, 95–6; Charlotte in 104–5, 109, 111, 112; blockade by French, 118; proposed independence for, 120; Franz Josef-Maximilian meeting in (1862), 169–70, 198; Charlotte's return to, 381; ceded to Italy, 381; and death of Maximilian, 466
Vera Cruz, 138, 150, 167, 168, 174, 176, 184, 343, 354, 404, 406, 408, 414, 444, 445, 449, 463; in civil war, 143, 144; and Spain, 151, 159; and allied intervention, 159, 160, 163–6, 175, 449; French in, 163–6, 241, 247; Labastida's arrival, 186; arrival of Maximilian, 230–2, 234; Juarists in, 230, 383; communications with, 230, 232, 241; arrival of foreign troops, 263; Charlotte in, 318–19, 322, 355–6; French embarkation at, 348, 434; held by Imperialists, 383, 414, 434; US frigate Susquehanna turns back from, 415–16
Verona, 28, 90, 110, 118, 119
Vichy, 160, 358, 359
Victor-Emmanuel, King of Italy, 70, 116, 118, 119, 381
Victoria, Princess, 86
Victoria, Queen of England, 71, 78, 80, 83, 86, 87, 96, 98, 99, 100, 102, 135, 171–2, 176, 181, 191, 204, 213, 225, 253, 269, 322, 334, 337, 465
Vidaurri, General, 432–3, 436
Vienna, 72, 132, 324, 380; arrival of Archduchess Sophia in, 13; marriage of Ferdinand, 15; climate, 16; illness and death of Franz Reichstadt, 16–18; Duchess of Parma in, 18; arts in, 22, 31–2; in 1848 Revolution, 34–6; Maximilian's romance with Paola von Linden in, 52–6; arrival of Charlotte, 101–4; popularity of Maximilian in, 121, 133, 374; Mexican deputation's visit to, 207; Charlotte's abortive visit to Franz Josef, 212–13, 218; during Austro-Prussian War, 374; Maximilian's funeral in, 468
Vienna Lunatic Asylum, 397, 400
Villa d'Este, Lake Como, 112, 380
Villafrance, 119, 120
Villa Lazarovic, 47, 48, 104, 124
Villaneuva, Colonel, 456–7
Virgin of Guadaloupe, 184
Visconti-Venosta, Giovanni, 106
Vittorio, 129
Vosges Mountains, 113

Wagner, Richard, 63
Walewski, Count, 73, 153
Walewski, Maria, 73
Wasa, Princess of, 71
Westmorland, Lady, 81
Weygand, General, 469–70
Weygand, Jacques, 469
Wildauer, Professor, 107
Wimpfen, Baron, 67, 68
Windischgrätz, Field Marshal Prince, 35, 36
Windsor Castle, 98, 213, 465
Winterhalter, 81
Wurtemberg, 52, 55
Wyke, Sir Charles, 151, 160, 165, 166, 167, 173, 179, 187
Wydenbruck, Count, 327, 445, 465
Wykenturg, Count, 376
Wympfen, General, 117–18

Yorke, Sarah, 307
Yucatan, 140, 196, 222, 315, 316–21, 322, 323, 334, 335, 336, 338, 395, 405

Zacatecas, 424, 426
Zichy, Count, 129, 207, 215, 226, 268
Zichy, Countess, 226, 227, 246, 268
Zorilla, José, 292–3
Zoute, 104
Zuloago, 144
Zurich, Peace of, 381